PISA 2009 Results: What Students Know and Can Do

STUDENT PERFORMANCE IN READING, MATHEMATICS AND SCIENCE

(VOLUME I)

OECD

This work is published on the responsibility of the Secretary-General of the OECD. The opinions expressed and arguments employed herein do not necessarily reflect the official views of the Organisation or of the governments of its member countries.

Please cite this publication as:

OECD (2010), PISA 2009 Results: What Students Know and Can Do – Student Performance in Reading, Mathematics and Science (Volume I)
http://dx.doi.org/10.1787/9789264091450-en

ISBN 978-92-64-09144-3 (print)
ISBN 978-92-64-09145-0 (PDF)

The statistical data for Israel are supplied by and under the responsibility of the relevant Israeli authorities. The use of such data by the OECD is without prejudice to the status of the Golan Heights, East Jerusalem and Israeli settlements in the West Bank under the terms of international law.

Photo credits:
Getty Images © Ariel Skelley
Getty Images © Geostock
Getty Images © Jack Hollingsworth
Stocklib Image Bank © Yuri Arcurs

Foreword

One of the ultimate goals of policy makers is to enable citizens to take advantage of a globalised world economy. This is leading them to focus on the improvement of education policies, ensuring the quality of service provision, a more equitable distribution of learning opportunities and stronger incentives for greater efficiency in schooling.

Such policies hinge on reliable information on how well education systems prepare students for life. Most countries monitor students' learning and the performance of schools. But in a global economy, the yardstick for success is no longer improvement by national standards alone, but how education systems perform internationally. The OECD has taken up that challenge by developing PISA, the Programme for International Student Assessment, which evaluates the quality, equity and efficiency of school systems in some 70 countries that, together, make up nine-tenths of the world economy. PISA represents a commitment by governments to monitor the outcomes of education systems regularly within an internationally agreed framework and it provides a basis for international collaboration in defining and implementing educational policies.

The results from the 2009 PISA assessment reveal wide differences in educational outcomes, both within and across countries. The education systems that have been able to secure strong and equitable learning outcomes, and to mobilise rapid improvements, show others what is possible to achieve. Naturally, GDP per capita influences educational success, but this only explains 6% of the differences in average student performance. The other 94% reflect the potential for public policy to make a difference. The stunning success of Shanghai-China, which tops every league table in this assessment by a clear margin, shows what can be achieved with moderate economic resources and in a diverse social context. In mathematics, more than a quarter of Shanghai-China's 15-year-olds can conceptualise, generalise, and creatively use information based on their own investigations and modelling of complex problem situations. They can apply insight and understanding and develop new approaches and strategies when addressing novel situations. In the OECD area, just 3% of students reach that level of performance.

While better educational outcomes are a strong predictor of economic growth, wealth and spending on education alone are no guarantee for better educational outcomes. Overall, PISA shows that an image of a world divided neatly into rich and well-educated countries and poor and badly-educated countries is out of date.

This finding represents both a warning and an opportunity. It is a warning to advanced economies that they cannot take for granted that they will forever have "human capital" superior to that in other parts of the world. At a time of intensified global competition, they will need to work hard to maintain a knowledge and skill base that keeps up with changing demands.

PISA underlines, in particular, the need for many advanced countries to tackle educational underperformance so that as many members of their future workforces as possible are equipped with at least the baseline competencies that enable them to participate in social and economic development. Otherwise, the high social and economic cost of poor educational performance in advanced economies risks becoming a significant drag on economic development. At the same time, the findings show that poor skills are not an inevitable consequence of low national income – an important outcome for countries that need to achieve more with less.

But PISA also shows that there is no reason for despair. Countries from a variety of starting points have shown the potential to raise the quality of educational outcomes substantially. Korea's average performance was already high in 2000, but Korean policy makers were concerned that only a narrow elite achieved levels of excellence in PISA. Within less than a decade, Korea was able to double the share of students demonstrating excellence in reading literacy. A major overhaul of Poland's school system helped to dramatically reduce performance variability among

schools, reduce the share of poorly performing students and raise overall performance by the equivalent of more than half a school year. Germany was jolted into action when PISA 2000 revealed a below-average performance and large social disparities in results, and has been able to make progress on both fronts. Israel, Italy and Portugal have moved closer to the OECD average and Brazil, Chile, Mexico and Turkey are among the countries with impressive gains from very low levels of performance.

But the greatest value of PISA lies in inspiring national efforts to help students to learn better, teachers to teach better, and school systems to become more effective.

A closer look at high-performing and rapidly improving education systems shows that these systems have many commonalities that transcend differences in their history, culture and economic evolution.

First, while most nations declare their commitment to education, the test comes when these commitments are weighed against others. How do they pay teachers compared to the way they pay other highly-skilled workers? How are education credentials weighed against other qualifications when people are being considered for jobs? Would you want your child to be a teacher? How much attention do the media pay to schools and schooling? Which matters more, a community's standing in the sports leagues or its standing in the student academic achievement league tables? Are parents more likely to encourage their children to study longer and harder or to spend more time with their friends or in sports activities?

In the most successful education systems, the political and social leaders have persuaded their citizens to make the choices needed to show that they value education more than other things. But placing a high value on education will get a country only so far if the teachers, parents and citizens of that country believe that only some subset of the nation's children can or need to achieve world class standards. This report shows clearly that education systems built around the belief that students have different pre-ordained professional destinies to be met with different expectations in different school types tend to be fraught with large social disparities. In contrast, the best-performing education systems embrace the diversity in students' capacities, interests and social background with individualised approaches to learning.

Second, high-performing education systems stand out with clear and ambitious standards that are shared across the system, focus on the acquisition of complex, higher-order thinking skills, and are aligned with high stakes gateways and instructional systems. In these education systems, everyone knows what is required to get a given qualification, in terms both of the content studied and the level of performance that has to be demonstrated to earn it. Students cannot go on to the next stage of their life – be it work or further education – unless they show that they are qualified to do so. They know what they have to do to realise their dream and they put in the work that is needed to achieve it.

Third, the quality of an education system cannot exceed the quality of its teachers and principals, since student learning is ultimately the product of what goes on in classrooms. Corporations, professional partnerships and national governments all know that they have to pay attention to how the pool from which they recruit is established; how they recruit; the kind of initial training their recruits receive before they present themselves for employment; how they mentor new recruits and induct them into their service; what kind of continuing training they get; how their compensation is structured; how they reward their best performers and how they improve the performance of those who are struggling; and how they provide opportunities for the best performers to acquire more status and responsibility. Many of the world's best-performing education systems have moved from bureaucratic "command and control" environments towards school systems in which the people at the frontline have much more control of the way resources are used, people are deployed, the work is organised and the way in which the work gets done. They provide considerable discretion to school heads and school faculties in determining how resources are allocated, a factor which the report shows to be closely related to school performance when combined with effective accountability systems. And they provide an environment in which teachers work together to frame what they believe to be good practice, conduct field-based research to confirm or disprove the approaches they develop, and then assess their colleagues by the degree to which they use practices proven effective in their classrooms.

Last but not least, the most impressive outcome of world-class education systems is perhaps that they deliver high-quality learning consistently across the entire education system, such that every student benefits from excellent learning opportunities. To achieve this, they invest educational resources where they can make the greatest difference, they attract the most talented teachers into the most challenging classrooms, and they establish effective spending choices that prioritise the quality of teachers.

These are, of course, not independently conceived and executed policies. They need to be aligned across all aspects of the system, they need to be coherent over sustained periods of time, and they need to be consistently implemented. The path of reform can be fraught with political and practical obstacles. Moving away from administrative and bureaucratic control toward professional norms of control can be counterproductive if a nation does not yet have teachers and schools with the capacity to implement these policies and practices. Pushing authority down to lower levels can be as problematic if there is not agreement on what the students need to know and should be able to do. Recruiting high-quality teachers is not of much use if those who are recruited are so frustrated by what they perceive to be a mindless system of initial teacher education that they will not participate in it and turn to another profession. Thus a country's success in making these transitions depends greatly on the degree to which it is successful in creating and executing plans that, at any given time, produce the maximum coherence in the system.

These are daunting challenges and thus devising effective education policies will become ever more difficult as schools need to prepare students to deal with more rapid change than ever before, for jobs that have not yet been created, to use technologies that have not yet been invented and to solve economic and social challenges that we do not yet know will arise. But those school systems that do well today, as well as those that have shown rapid improvement, demonstrate that it can be done. The world is indifferent to tradition and past reputations, unforgiving of frailty and complacency and ignorant of custom or practice. Success will go to those individuals and countries that are swift to adapt, slow to complain and open to change. The task of governments will be to ensure that countries rise to this challenge. The OECD will continue to support their efforts.

***

This report is the product of a collaborative effort between the countries participating in PISA, the experts and institutions working within the framework of the PISA Consortium, and the OECD Secretariat. The report was drafted by Andreas Schleicher, Francesca Borgonovi, Michael Davidson, Miyako Ikeda, Maciej Jakubowski, Guillermo Montt, Sophie Vayssettes and Pablo Zoido of the OECD Directorate for Education, with advice as well as analytical and editorial support from Marilyn Achiron, Simone Bloem, Marika Boiron, Henry Braun, Nihad Bunar, Niccolina Clements, Jude Cosgrove, John Cresswell, Aletta Grisay, Donald Hirsch, David Kaplan, Henry Levin, Juliette Mendelovitz, Christian Monseur, Soojin Park, Pasi Reinikainen, Mebrak Tareke, Elisabeth Villoutreix and Allan Wigfield. Volume II also draws on the analytic work undertaken by Jaap Scheerens and Douglas Willms in the context of PISA 2000. Administrative support was provided by Juliet Evans and Diana Morales.

The PISA assessment instruments and the data underlying the report were prepared by the PISA Consortium, under the direction of Raymond Adams at the Australian Council for Educational Research (ACER) and Henk Moelands from the Dutch National Institute for Educational Measurement (CITO). The expert group that guided the preparation of the reading assessment framework and instruments was chaired by Irwin Kirsch.

The development of the report was steered by the PISA Governing Board, which is chaired by Lorna Bertrand (United Kingdom), with Beno Csapo (Hungary), Daniel McGrath (United States) and Ryo Watanabe (Japan) as vice chairs. Annex C of the volumes lists the members of the various PISA bodies, as well as the individual experts and consultants who have contributed to this report and to PISA in general.

Angel Gurría
OECD Secretary-General

Table of Contents

This book has...

StatLinkS

A service that delivers Excel® files from the printed page!

Look for the *StatLinks* at the bottom left-hand corner of the tables or graphs in this book.
To download the matching Excel® spreadsheet, just type the link into your Internet browser, starting with the ***http://dx.doi.org*** prefix.
If you're reading the PDF e-book edition, and your PC is connected to the Internet, simply click on the link. You'll find *StatLinks* appearing in more OECD books.

BOXES

FIGURES

TABLES

Executive Summary

PISA's conception of reading literacy encompasses the range of situations in which people read, the different ways written texts are presented, and the variety of ways that readers approach and use texts, from the functional and finite, such as finding a particular piece of practical information, to the deep and far-reaching, such as understanding other ways of doing, thinking and being. Research shows that these kinds of reading literacy skills are more reliable predictors of economic and social well-being than the number of years spent in school or in post-formal education.

Korea and Finland are the highest performing OECD countries, with mean scores of 539 and 536 points, respectively. However, the partner economy Shanghai-China outperforms them by a significant margin, with a mean score of 556.
Top-performing countries or economies in reading literacy include Hong Kong-China (with a mean score of 533), Singapore (526), Canada (524), New Zealand (521), Japan (520) and Australia (515). The Netherlands (508), Belgium (506), Norway (503), Estonia (501), Switzerland (501), Poland (500), Iceland (500) and Liechtenstein (499) also perform above the OECD mean score of 494, while the United States, Sweden, Germany, Ireland, France, Denmark, the United Kingdom, Hungary, Portugal, and partner economy Chinese Taipei have scores close to the OECD mean.

The lowest performing OECD country, Mexico, has an average score of 425. This means that the gap between the highest and lowest performing OECD countries is 114 points – more than the equivalent of two school years. And the gap between the highest and lowest performing partner country or economy is even larger, with 242 score points – or more than six years of formal schooling – separating the mean performance of Shanghai-China and Kyrgyzstan (314).

Differences *between* countries represent, however, only a fraction of overall variation in student performance. Addressing the educational needs of such diverse populations and narrowing the gaps in student performance that have been observed remains a formidable challenge for all countries.

In 18 participating countries, including Mexico, Chile and Turkey, the highest reading proficiency level achieved by most students was the baseline Level 2.
Level 2 is considered a baseline level of proficiency, at which students begin to demonstrate the reading skills that will enable them to participate effectively and productively in life. Students who do not reach Level 2 have difficulties locating basic information that meets several conditions, making comparisons or contrasts around a single feature, working out what a well-defined part of a text means when the information is not prominent, or making connections between the text and outside knowledge by drawing on personal experience and attitudes. The proportion of 15-year-olds in this situation varies widely across countries, from fewer than one in 10 in four countries and economies to the majority of students in 10 countries. Even in the average OECD country, where nearly one student in five does not reach Level 2, tackling such low performance remains a major challenge.

At the other end of the proficiency spectrum, an average of 7.6% of students attain Level 5, and in Singapore, New Zealand and Shanghai-China the percentage is above twice the OECD average.
However, for some countries, developing even a small corps of high-performing students remains an aspiration: in 16 countries, fewer than 1% of students reach Level 5. Students at this level are able to retrieve information requiring the reader to locate and organise several pieces of deeply embedded information, inferring which information in the text is relevant. They can critically evaluate information and build hypotheses drawing on specialised knowledge, develop a full and detailed understanding of a text whose content or form is unfamiliar, and understand concepts that are contrary to expectations.

Results from the PISA 2009 assessment show that nurturing high performance and tackling low performance need not be mutually exclusive. The countries with the very highest overall reading performance in PISA 2009, Finland and Korea, as well as the partner economies Hong Kong-China and Shanghai-China, also have among the lowest variation in student scores. Equally importantly, Korea has been able to raise its already-high reading performance even further, by more than doubling the percentage of students reaching Level 5 or higher since 2000.

Korea, with a country mean of 546 score points, performed highest among OECD countries in the PISA 2009 mathematics assessment. The partner countries and economies Shanghai-China, Singapore and Hong Kong-China rank first, second and third, respectively.

In the PISA 2009 mathematics assessment, the OECD countries Finland, Switzerland, Japan, Canada, the Netherlands, New Zealand, Belgium, Australia, Germany, Estonia, Iceland, Denmark, Slovenia as well as the partner countries and economies Chinese Taipei, Liechtenstein and Macao-China also perform significantly above the OECD average in mathematics.

Shanghai-China, Finland, Hong Kong-China and Singapore are the four highest performers in the PISA 2009 science assessment.

In science, New Zealand, Canada, Estonia, Australia, the Netherlands, Germany, Switzerland, the United Kingdom, Slovenia, Poland, Ireland and Belgium as well as the partner countries and economies Chinese Taipei, Liechtenstein and Macao-China also perform significantly above the OECD average.

Some 14.6% of students in Shanghai-China and 12.3% of students in Singapore attain the highest levels of proficiency in all three assessment subjects.

High-level skills are critical for innovation and, as such, are key to economic growth and social development. On average, across OECD countries, 16.3% of students are top performers in at least one of the subject areas of science, mathematics or reading. However, only 4.1% of 15-year-old students are top performers in all three assessment subject areas.

Girls outperform boys in reading skills in every participating country.

Throughout much of the 20th century, concern about gender differences in education focused on girls' underachievement. More recently, however, the scrutiny has shifted to boys' underachievement in reading. In the PISA 2009 reading assessment, girls outperform boys in every participating country by an average, among OECD countries, of 39 PISA score points – equivalent to more than half a proficiency level or one year of schooling.

On average across OECD countries, boys outperform girls in mathematics by 12 score points while gender differences in science performance tend to be small, both in absolute terms and when compared with the large gender gap in reading performance and the more moderate gender gap in mathematics. The ranks of top-performing students are filled nearly equally with girls and boys. On average across OECD countries, 4.4% of girls and 3.8% of boys are top performers in all three subjects, and 15.6% of girls and 17.0% of boys are top performers in at least one subject area. While the gender gap among top-performing students is small in science (1% of girls and 1.5% of boys), it is significant in reading (2.8% of girls and 0.5% of boys) and in mathematics (3.4% of girls and 6.6% of boys).

Countries of similar prosperity can produce very different educational results.

The balance of proficiency in some of the richer countries in PISA looks very different from that of some of the poorer countries. In reading, for example, the ten countries in which the majority of students are at Level 1 or below, all in poorer parts of the world, contrast starkly in profile with the 34 OECD countries, where on average a majority attains at least Level 3. However, the fact that the best-performing country or economy in the 2009 assessment is Shanghai-China, with a GDP per capita well below the OECD average, underlines that low national income is not incompatible with strong educational performance. Korea, which is the best-performing OECD country, also has a GDP per capita below the OECD average. Indeed, while there is a correlation between GDP per capita and educational performance, this only predicts 6% of the differences in average student performance across countries. The other 94% of differences reflect the fact that two countries of similar prosperity can produce very different educational results. Results also vary when substituting spending per student, relative poverty or the share of students with an immigrant background for GDP per capita.

The following table summarises the key data of this volume. For each country, it shows the average score of 15-year-olds in reading, mathematics and science as well as on the subscales that were used to measure reading skills in greater detail. Cells shaded in light blue indicate values above the OECD average. Cells shaded in medium blue indicate values below the OECD average. Cells shaded in dark blue indicate values that are not statistically different from the OECD average.

Table I.A
COMPARING COUNTRIES' PERFORMANCE

Statistically significantly **above** the OECD average
Not statistically significantly different from the OECD average
Statistically significantly **below** the OECD average

	On the overall reading scale	On the reading subscales					On the mathematics scale	On the science scale
		Access and retrieve	Integrate and interpret	Reflect and evaluate	Continuous texts	Non-continuous texts		
Shanghai-China	556	549	558	557	564	539	600	575
Korea	539	542	541	542	538	542	546	538
Finland	536	532	538	536	535	535	541	554
Hong Kong-China	533	530	530	540	538	522	555	549
Singapore	526	526	525	529	522	539	562	542
Canada	524	517	522	535	524	527	527	529
New Zealand	521	521	517	531	518	532	519	532
Japan	520	530	520	521	520	518	529	539
Australia	515	513	513	523	513	524	514	527
Netherlands	508	519	504	510	506	514	526	522
Belgium	506	513	504	505	504	511	515	507
Norway	503	512	502	505	505	498	498	500
Estonia	501	503	500	503	497	512	512	528
Switzerland	501	505	502	497	498	505	534	517
Poland	500	500	503	498	502	496	495	508
Iceland	500	507	503	496	501	499	507	496
United States	500	492	495	512	500	503	487	502
Liechtenstein	499	508	498	498	495	506	536	520
Sweden	497	505	494	502	499	498	494	495
Germany	497	501	501	491	496	497	513	520
Ireland	496	498	494	502	497	496	487	508
France	496	492	497	495	492	498	497	498
Chinese Taipei	495	496	499	493	496	500	543	520
Denmark	495	502	492	493	496	493	503	499
United Kingdom	494	491	491	503	492	506	492	514
Hungary	494	501	496	489	497	487	490	503
Portugal	489	488	487	496	492	488	487	493
Macao-China	487	493	488	481	488	481	525	511
Italy	486	482	490	482	489	476	483	489
Latvia	484	476	484	492	484	487	482	494
Slovenia	483	489	489	470	484	476	501	512
Greece	483	468	484	489	487	472	466	470
Spain	481	480	481	483	484	473	483	488
Czech Republic	478	479	488	462	479	474	493	500
Slovak Republic	477	491	481	466	479	471	497	490
Croatia	476	492	472	471	478	472	460	486
Israel	474	463	473	483	477	467	447	455
Luxembourg	472	471	475	471	471	472	489	484
Austria	470	477	471	463	470	472	496	494
Lithuania	468	476	469	463	470	462	477	491
Turkey	464	467	459	473	466	461	445	454
Dubai (UAE)	459	458	457	466	461	460	453	466
Russian Federation	459	469	467	441	461	452	468	478
Chile	449	444	452	452	453	444	421	447
Serbia	442	449	445	430	444	438	442	443
Bulgaria	429	430	436	417	433	421	428	439
Uruguay	426	424	423	436	429	421	427	427
Mexico	425	433	418	432	426	424	419	416
Romania	424	423	425	426	423	424	427	428
Thailand	421	431	416	420	423	423	419	425
Trinidad and Tobago	416	413	419	413	418	417	414	410
Colombia	413	404	411	422	415	409	381	402
Brazil	412	407	406	424	414	408	386	405
Montenegro	408	408	420	383	411	398	403	401
Jordan	405	394	410	407	417	387	387	415
Tunisia	404	393	393	427	408	393	371	401
Indonesia	402	399	397	409	405	399	371	383
Argentina	398	394	398	402	400	391	388	401
Kazakhstan	390	397	397	373	399	371	405	400
Albania	385	380	393	376	392	366	377	391
Qatar	372	354	379	376	375	361	368	379
Panama	371	363	372	377	373	359	360	376
Peru	370	364	371	368	374	356	365	369
Azerbaijan	362	361	373	335	362	351	431	373
Kyrgyzstan	314	299	327	300	319	293	331	330

Source: OECD, *PISA 2009 Database*.
StatLink http://dx.doi.org/10.1787/888932343342

Introduction

The Programme for International Student Assessment (PISA) reviews the extent to which students near the end of compulsory education have acquired some of the knowledge and skills that are essential for full participation in modern societies, particularly reading, mathematics and science. This section offers an overview of the Programme, including which countries participate and which students are assessed, what types of skills are measured and how and to what extent PISA 2009 differs from previous PISA assessments.

PISA – AN OVERVIEW

PISA 2009: Focus on reading

Are students well prepared to meet the challenges of the future? Can they analyse, reason and communicate their ideas effectively? Have they found the kinds of interests they can pursue throughout their lives as productive members of the economy and society? The OECD Programme for International Student Assessment (PISA) seeks to answer these questions through its triennial surveys of key competencies of 15-year-old students in OECD member countries and partner countries/economies. Together, the group of countries participating in PISA represents nearly 90% of the world economy.[1]

PISA assesses the extent to which students near the end of compulsory education have acquired some of the knowledge and skills that are essential for full participation in modern societies, with a focus on reading, mathematics and science. PISA seeks to assess not merely whether students can reproduce knowledge, but also to examine how well they can extrapolate from what they have learned and apply it in unfamiliar settings, both in and outside of school.

PISA has now completed its fourth round of surveys. Following the detailed assessment of each of PISA's three main subjects – reading, mathematics and science – in 2000, 2003 and 2006, the 2009 survey marks the beginning of a new round with a return to a focus on reading, but in ways that reflect the extent to which reading has changed since 2000, including the prevalence of digital texts.

Success in reading provides the foundation for achievement in other subject areas and for full participation in adult life. The ability to convey information in written form, as well as orally, is one of humankind's greatest assets. The discovery that information can be shared across time and space, without the limits of the strength of one's voice, the size of a venue and the accuracy of memory, has been fundamental to human progress. And yet, learning how to read and write requires effort because it cannot be achieved without mastering a collection of complex skills. The brain is biologically primed to acquire language, but writing and reading are relatively recent achievements in human history. Becoming a proficient reader is a goal that requires practice and dedication.

To date, PISA 2009 offers the most comprehensive and rigorous international measurement of student reading skills. It assesses not only reading knowledge and skills, but also students' attitudes and their learning strategies in reading. PISA 2009 also updates the assessment of student performance in mathematics and science.

This report presents the results of PISA 2009. For easier access to information on specific areas examined in PISA, the report is published in six volumes. A description of the contents of each volume appears in the section "Reporting results from PISA 2009", below.

The PISA surveys

PISA focuses on young people's ability to use their knowledge and skills to meet real-life challenges. This orientation reflects a change in the goals and objectives of curricula themselves, which are increasingly concerned with what students can do with what they learn at school and not merely with whether they have mastered specific curricular content.

PISA's unique features include its:

- Policy orientation, which connects data on student learning outcomes with data on students' characteristics and on key factors shaping their learning in and out of school in order to draw attention to differences in performance patterns and to identify the characteristics of students, schools and education systems that have high performance standards.
- Innovative concept of "literacy", which refers to the capacity of students to apply knowledge and skills in key subject areas and to analyse, reason and communicate effectively as they pose, interpret and solve problems in a variety of situations.
- Relevance to lifelong learning, which does not limit PISA to assessing students' competencies in school subjects, but also asks them to report on their own motivation to learn, their beliefs about themselves and their learning strategies.
- Regularity, which enables countries to monitor their progress in meeting key learning objectives.
- Breadth of geographical coverage and collaborative nature, which, in PISA 2009, encompasses the 34 OECD member countries and 41 partner countries and economies.[2]

The relevance of the knowledge and skills measured by PISA is confirmed by studies tracking young people in the years after they have been assessed by PISA. Longitudinal studies in Australia, Canada and Switzerland display a strong relationship between performance in reading in the PISA assessment at age 15 and future educational attainment and success in the labour market (see also Chapter 2).[3]

Decisions about the scope and nature of the PISA assessments and the background information to be collected are made by leading experts in participating countries. Governments guide these decisions based on shared, policy-driven interests. Considerable efforts and resources are devoted to achieving cultural and linguistic breadth and balance in assessment materials. Stringent quality-assurance mechanisms are applied in designing the test, in translation, sampling and data collection. As a result, PISA findings have a high degree of validity and reliability. Through them, learning outcomes in the world's most economically advanced countries, as well as those in earlier stages of economic development, can be better understood and compared. Although it was OECD countries that originally created PISA, it has now become a major assessment tool in many regions around the world. Beyond OECD member countries, the survey has been completed or is currently being conducted (*i.e.* in countries marked by an asterisk) in:

- **East and Southeast Asia:** Himachal Pradesh-India*, Hong Kong-China, Indonesia, Macao-China, Malaysia*, Shanghai-China, Singapore, Chinese Taipei, Tamil Nadu-India*, Thailand and Viet Nam*.

- **Central, Mediterranean and Eastern Europe,**[4] **and Central Asia:** Albania, Azerbaijan, Bulgaria, Croatia, Georgia*, Kazakhstan, Kyrgyzstan, Latvia, Liechtenstein, Lithuania, Macedonia, Malta*, Moldova, Montenegro, Romania, the Russian Federation and Serbia.

- **The Middle East:** Jordan, Qatar and the United Arab Emirates.

- **Central and South America:** Argentina, Brazil, Colombia, Costa Rica*, Netherlands-Antilles*, Panama, Peru, Trinidad and Tobago, Uruguay and Miranda-Venezuela*.

- **Africa:** Mauritius* and Tunisia.

■ Figure I.1.1 ■
A map of PISA countries and economies

OECD countries

Australia	Japan
Austria	Korea
Belgium	Luxembourg
Canada	Mexico
Chile	Netherlands
Czech Republic	New Zealand
Denmark	Norway
Estonia	Poland
Finland	Portugal
France	Slovak Republic
Germany	Slovenia
Greece	Spain
Hungary	Sweden
Iceland	Switzerland
Ireland	Turkey
Israel	United Kingdom
Italy	United States

Partner countries and economies in PISA 2009

Albania	Mauritius
Argentina	Miranda-Venezuela*
Azerbaijan	Montenegro
Brazil	Netherlands-Antilles*
Bulgaria	Panama
Colombia	Peru
Costa Rica*	Qatar
Croatia	Romania
Georgia*	Russian Federation
Himachal Pradesh-India*	Serbia
Hong Kong-China	Shanghai-China
Indonesia	Singapore
Jordan	Tamil Nadu-India*
Kazakhstan	Chinese Taipei
Kyrgyzstan	Thailand
Latvia	Trinidad and Tobago
Liechtenstein	Tunisia
Lithuania	Uruguay
Macao-China	United Arab Emirates*
Malaysia*	Viet Nam*
Malta*	

Partners countries in previous PISA surveys

Dominican Republic
Macedonia
Moldova

* These partner countries and economies carried out the assessment in 2010 instead of 2009.

Policy makers around the world use PISA findings to gauge the knowledge and skills of students in their own country in comparison with those of other countries. PISA reveals what is possible in education by showing what students in the highest performing countries can do. PISA is also used to gauge the pace of educational progress by allowing policy makers to assess the extent to which performance changes observed nationally are in line with performance changes observed elsewhere. In a growing number of countries, PISA is also used to set policy targets against measurable goals achieved by other systems, to initiate research and peer learning designed to identify policy levers and to reform trajectories for improving education. While PISA cannot identify cause-and-effect relationships between inputs, processes and educational outcomes, it can highlight key features in which education systems are similar and different, sharing those findings with educators, policy makers and the general public.

Box I.1.1 **Key features of PISA 2009**

Content

- The main focus of PISA 2009 was reading. The survey also updated performance assessments in mathematics and science. PISA considers students' knowledge in these areas not in isolation, but in relation to their ability to reflect on their knowledge and experience, and to apply them to real-world issues. The emphasis is on mastering processes, understanding concepts and functioning in various situations within each assessment area.

- For the first time, the PISA 2009 survey also assessed 15-year-old students' ability to read, understand and apply digital texts.

Methods

- Around 470 000 students completed the assessment in 2009, representing about 26 million 15-year-olds in the schools of the 65 participating countries and economies. Some 50 000 students took part in a second round of this assessment in 2010, representing about 2 million 15 year-olds from 9 additional partner countries and economies.

- Each participating student spent two hours carrying out pencil-and-paper tasks in reading, mathematics and science. In 20 countries, students were given additional questions via computer to assess their capacity to read digital texts.

- The assessment included tasks requiring students to construct their own answers as well as multiple-choice questions. The latter were typically organised in units based on a written passage or graphic, much like the kind of texts or figures that students might encounter in real life.

- Students also answered a questionnaire that took about 30 minutes to complete. This questionnaire focused on their personal background, their learning habits, their attitudes towards reading, and their engagement and motivation.

- School principals completed a questionnaire about their school that included demographic characteristics and an assessment of the quality of the learning environment at school.

Outcomes

PISA 2009 results provide:

- A profile of knowledge and skills among 15-year-olds in 2009, consisting of a detailed profile for reading, including digital literacy, and an update for mathematics and science.

- Contextual indicators relating performance results to student and school characteristics.

- An assessment of students' engagement in reading activities, and their knowledge and use of different learning strategies.

- A knowledge base for policy research and analysis.

- Trend data on changes in student knowledge and skills in reading, mathematics and science, on change in student attitudes and in socio-economic indicators, and also on the impact of some indicators on the performance results.

Future assessments

- The PISA 2012 survey will return to mathematics as the major assessment area; PISA 2015 will focus on science. Thereafter, PISA will turn to another cycle, beginning with reading again.

- Future tests will place greater emphasis on assessing students' capacity to read and understand digital texts and solve problems given in a digital format, reflecting the importance of information and computer technologies in modern societies.

Interest in PISA is illustrated by the many reports produced in participating countries,[5] numerous references to PISA results in public debates and the intense media attention PISA attracts throughout the world. A number of countries have also begun developing and administering PISA-related assessments, either as part of or, in addition to their national assessments.

WHAT IS DIFFERENT ABOUT THE PISA 2009 SURVEY?

A new profile of how well students read

In 2009, PISA modified and enhanced the way in which reading was assessed by revising the framework used in PISA 2000 and tailoring it to address the changes in analysing how people read. PISA 2000 looked at how well students *retrieved* information; PISA 2009 also looked at how well they *accessed* it. PISA 2000 looked at how well students *interpreted* what they read; PISA 2009 also looked at how well they *integrated* it. Like PISA 2000, PISA 2009 considered how students *reflected* on and *evaluated* what they read.

An assessment of reading digital texts

PISA first ventured into computer-based assessments in the subject of science in 2006. This was followed, in 2009, by an assessment of how well students read digital texts. Twenty countries opted to undertake this assessment. Students were given a number of different types of questions that simulated how they would use digital texts to acquire information. For example, they were required to use a search engine and to make choices regarding key words and the correct pages in order to answer the question.

More detailed assessment of a wider range of student abilities

In previous PISA surveys, a number of countries scored well below the OECD mean and had large percentages of students scoring below the range of described proficiency levels. In PISA 2009, a new set of reading items, suited for more basic reading skills, was developed in order to better describe the performance of lower-performing students. Some countries opted to include these new items and were given booklets that were adapted to assess more basic reading skills. The proficiency levels were also extended to obtain more detailed descriptions of high-performing students and to identify highest-performing students.

More emphasis on educational progress

Since PISA has now been implemented for a decade, it is possible to explore not just where countries stand in terms of student performance, but also how learning outcomes or gaps between higher- and lower-performing students are changing. Every three years, PISA measures student knowledge and skills in reading, mathematics and science, covering each of these areas once as a major focus and twice as a minor area across a nine-year cycle. The basic survey design remains constant to allow for comparability from one PISA assessment to the next. In the long term, this will allow countries to relate policy changes to improvements in educational standards and to learn more about how changes in educational outcomes compare with international benchmarks.

The 2009 round marks the first time in PISA that reading has been re-assessed in detail. This provides an opportunity for countries to evaluate, in detail, changes that may have occurred in the nine years since the assessments were first administered. A number of the reading items from PISA 2000 have remained the same throughout the years, and so help to give a measure of change over time.

Introducing new background information about students

Because the data on students' engagement in reading activities, knowledge and use of different learning strategies provided favourable policy insights in 2000, an improved version of this topic reappeared in 2009:

- Students were asked about the techniques they used to learn, particularly how they understood and learned concepts or texts and what approaches they used to summarise texts, and their awareness of and ability to use a variety of strategies when processing texts.

- Given the close association between students' reading proficiency and their engagement in reading activities observed previously, students were asked whether and how their teachers provided stimulation to become engaged in reading.

- New questions asked students whether or not they used libraries for borrowing books, reading or for using the Internet.

- Modifications were made to the questionnaires to better reflect the ways in which 15-year-olds use new technologies. For example, there were new questions about how students use new technologies for the Internet and entertainment. Students in 44 countries[6] completed this optional PISA questionnaire.

WHAT PISA MEASURES AND HOW

International experts from participating countries developed a framework and conceptual underpinning for each assessment area in PISA. Following consultations, these frameworks were adopted by the governments of the participating countries (OECD, 1999; OECD, 2003; OECD, 2006; OECD, 2009). The framework starts with the concept of literacy, which includes students' capacity to extrapolate from what they have learned and apply their knowledge in real-life settings, and their capacity to analyse, reason and communicate effectively as they pose, interpret and solve problems in a variety of situations.

The concept of reading literacy used in PISA is much broader than the historical notion of the ability to read. It is measured on a continuum, not as something that an individual either has or does not have. While it may be necessary or desirable to define a point on a literacy continuum below which levels of competence are considered inadequate, PISA charts continuous gradations of performance above and below such a threshold.

The acquisition of literacy is a lifelong process that takes place not just at school or through formal learning, but also through interactions with family, peers, colleagues and wider communities. Fifteen-year-olds cannot be expected to have learned everything they will need to know as adults, but they should have a solid foundation of knowledge in areas such as reading, mathematics and science on which they can build. In order to continue learning in these areas and to apply their learning to the real world, they also need to understand fundamental processes and principles, and to use these flexibly in different situations. PISA thus measures students' ability to complete tasks relating to real life, tapping a broad understanding of key concepts, rather than limiting the assessment to subject-specific knowledge.

PISA also aims to examine students' learning strategies, their competencies in areas such as problem solving that involves multiple disciplines and their interests in different topics. This kind of broader assessment started in PISA 2000, which asked students about their motivation and other aspects of their attitudes towards learning, their familiarity with computers and, under the heading "self-regulated learning", about their strategies for managing and monitoring their own education. The assessment of students' motivations and attitudes continued in PISA 2006, with special attention given to students' attitudes towards and interest in science. Returning to reading as the major subject of assessment, PISA 2009 focused on students' engagement in reading activities and their understanding about their own reading and learning strategies. This is elaborated in detail in Volume III, *Learning to Learn*.

Performance in PISA: What is measured

PISA 2009 defines the areas of assessment within a framework that includes:

- knowledge in each subject that students need to apply;
- competencies in each subject that students need to apply;
- contexts in which students encounter problems; and
- students' attitudes and dispositions towards learning.

The frameworks for assessing reading, mathematics and science in 2009 are described in full in *PISA 2009 Assessment Framework: Key Competencies in Reading, Mathematics and Science* (OECD, 2009), and summarised in Volume I. Figure I.1.2 below also summarises the core definition of each assessment area and how the first three of the above four dimensions are developed in each case.

The PISA instruments: How skills are measured

As in earlier PISA surveys, the assessment instruments in PISA 2009 were developed around units. A unit consists of stimulus material, including texts, diagrams, tables and/or graphs, followed by questions on various aspects of the text, diagram, table or graph, with the questions constructed so that tasks students had to undertake were as close as possible to those they might come across in the real world.

The questions varied in format. Around half were multiple-choice questions in which students made either one choice from among four or five given alternatives (*simple multiple choice*) or chose one of two possible responses (*e.g.* "yes/no" or "agree/disagree") to a series of propositions or statements (*complex multiple choice*). The remaining questions required students to construct their own responses. Some required a brief answer (*short response*), others a longer response (*open-constructed response*). The latter allowed for the possibility of different individual responses and, sometimes, an assessment of students' justification of their viewpoints.

■ Figure I.1.2 ■
Summary of the assessment areas in PISA 2009

	READING	MATHEMATICS	SCIENCE
Definition and its distinctive features	The capacity of an individual to understand, use, reflect on and engage with written texts in order to achieve his/her goals, to develop his/her knowledge and potential, and to participate in society. In addition to decoding and literal comprehension, *reading literacy* also involves interpretation and reflection, and the ability to use reading to fulfil one's goals in life. PISA focuses on reading to learn rather than learning to read. Therefore, students are not assessed on the most basic reading skills.	The capacity of an individual to formulate, employ and interpret mathematics in a variety of contexts. It includes reasoning mathematically and using mathematical concepts, procedures, facts and tools to describe, explain and predict phenomena. It assists individuals in recognising the role that mathematics plays in the world and in making well-founded judgments and decisions that constructive, engaged and reflective citizens would require. *Mathematical literacy* is related to wider, functional use of mathematics; engagement includes the ability to recognise and formulate mathematical problems in various situations.	The extent to which an individual: ■ Possesses scientific knowledge and uses that knowledge to identify questions, acquire new knowledge, explain scientific phenomena and draw evidence-based conclusions about science-related issues. ■ Understands the characteristic features of science as a form of human knowledge and enquiry. ■ Shows awareness of how science and technology shape our material, intellectual and cultural environments. ■ Engages in science-related issues and with the ideas of science, as a reflective citizen. *Scientific literacy* requires an understanding of scientific concepts, as well as the ability to apply a scientific perspective and to think scientifically about evidence.
Knowledge domain	The form of reading materials: ■ *Continuous texts:* including different kinds of prose such as narration, exposition, argumentation ■ *Non-continuous texts:* including graphs, forms and lists ■ *Mixed texts:* including both continuous and non-continuous formats ■ *Multiple texts:* including independent texts (same or different formats) juxtaposed for specific purposes	Clusters of relevant mathematical areas and concepts: ■ *Quantity* ■ *Space and shape* ■ *Change and relationships* ■ *Uncertainty*	*Knowledge of science,* such as: ■ "Physical systems" ■ "Living systems" ■ "Earth and space systems" ■ "Technology systems" *Knowledge about science,* such as: ■ "Scientific enquiry" ■ "Scientific explanations"
Competencies involved	Type of reading tasks or processes: ■ *Access and retrieve* ■ *Integrate and interpret* ■ *Reflect and evaluate* ■ Complex – *e.g.* finding, evaluating and integrating information from multiple electronic texts	Competency clusters define skills needed for mathematics: ■ *Reproduction* (simple mathematical operations) ■ *Connections* (bringing together ideas to solve straightforward problems) ■ *Reflection* (wider mathematical thinking)	Type of scientific tasks or processes: ■ *Identifying scientific issues* ■ *Explaining scientific phenomena* ■ *Using scientific evidence*
Context and situation	The use for which the text is constructed: ■ *Personal* ■ *Educational* ■ *Occupational* ■ *Public*	The area of application of mathematics, focusing on uses in relation to personal, social and global settings, such as: ■ *Personal* ■ *Educational and occupational* ■ *Public* ■ *Scientific*	The area of application of science, focusing on uses in relation to personal, social and global settings, such as: ■ "Health" ■ "Natural resources" ■ "Environment" ■ "Hazard" ■ "Frontiers of science and technology"

The remaining test questions required students to construct their own responses, based on a very limited range of possible responses (*closed-constructed response*) that were scored as either correct or incorrect. The percentages of the different question formats varied across different subjects and can be found in the *PISA 2009 Technical Report* (OECD, forthcoming). Scoring the answers to PISA questions is governed by strict adherence to an internationally agreed coding guide that establishes codes that are then assigned to various responses. It is implemented by trained specialist coders. Some questions can be assigned simply a credit or no credit, while partial credit is given for partly correct or less sophisticated answers in other questions. To ensure consistency in the coding process, a proportion of the questions were coded independently by four coders. In addition, a sub-sample of student responses from each country was coded by an independent panel of centrally trained expert coders in order to verify that the coding process was conducted uniformly across countries. The results show that consistent coding was achieved across countries. For details on the coding process, see the *PISA 2009 Technical Report* (OECD, forthcoming).

The total assessment time of 390 minutes was organised in different combinations in 13 linked testing booklets, with each individual tested for 120 minutes. The total time devoted to the assessment of reading across all the booklets was 210 minutes (54% of the total), 90 minutes were devoted to mathematics (23% of the total) and 90 minutes to science (23% of the total). Each student was randomly assigned one of the 13 test booklets.

The PISA student population

In order to ensure the comparability of the results across countries, PISA devoted a great deal of attention to assessing comparable target populations. Differences between countries in the nature and extent of pre-primary education and care, in the age of entry to formal schooling, and in the structure of the education system do not allow school grade levels to be defined so that they are internationally comparable. Valid international comparisons of educational performance, therefore, need to define their populations with reference to a target age. PISA covers students who are aged between 15 years 3 months and 16 years 2 months at the time of the assessment, and who have completed at least 6 years of formal schooling, regardless of the type of institution in which they are enrolled, whether they are in full-time or part-time education, whether they attend academic or vocational programmes, and whether they attend public or private schools or foreign schools within the country. (For an operational definition of this target population, see the *PISA 2009 Technical Report* [OECD, forthcoming].) The use of this age in PISA, across countries and over time, allows the performance of students to be compared in a consistent manner before they complete compulsory education.

As a result, this report can make statements about the knowledge and skills of individuals born in the same year who are still at school at 15 years of age, despite having different educational experiences, both within and outside school. The number of school grades in which these students are found depends on a country's policies on school entry and promotion. In some countries, students in the PISA target population represent different education systems, tracks or streams.

Stringent technical standards were established to define the national target populations and to identify permissible exclusions from this definition (for more information, see the PISA website *www.pisa.oecd.org*). The overall exclusion rate within a country was required to be below 5% to ensure that, under reasonable assumptions, any distortions in national mean scores would remain within plus or minus 5 score points, *i.e.* typically within the order of magnitude of 2 standard errors of sampling (see Box I.1.2). Exclusion could take place either through the schools that participated or the students who participated within schools. There are several reasons why a school or a student could be excluded from PISA. Schools might be excluded because they are situated in remote regions and are inaccessible or because they are very small, or because of organisational or operational factors that precluded participation. Students might be excluded because of intellectual disability or limited proficiency in the language of the assessment.

In 29 out of the 65 countries participating in PISA 2009, the percentage of school-level exclusions amounted to less than 1%; it was less than 5% in all countries. When the exclusion of students who met the internationally established exclusion criteria is also taken into account, the exclusion rates increase slightly. However, the overall exclusion rate remains below 2% in 32 participating countries, below 5% in 60 participating countries, and below 7% in all countries except Luxembourg (7.2%) and Denmark (8.6%). In 15 out of 34 OECD countries, the percentage of school-level exclusions amounted to less than 1% and was less than 5% in all countries. When student exclusions within schools were also taken into account, there were 9 OECD countries below 2% and 25 countries below 5% (see Annex A2).

Restrictions on the level of exclusions in PISA 2009:

- School-level exclusions for inaccessibility, feasibility or other reasons were required not to exceed 0.5% of the total number of students in the international PISA target population. Schools on the sampling frame that had only one or two eligible students were not allowed to be excluded from the frame. However, if, based on the frame, it was clear that the percentage of students in these schools would not cause a breach of the 0.5% allowable limit, then such schools could be excluded in the field, if at that time they still had only one or two students who were eligible for PISA.

- School-level exclusions for students with intellectual or functional disabilities, or students with limited proficiency in the language of the PISA assessment, were required not to exceed 2% of students.

- Within-school exclusions for students with intellectual or functional disabilities, or students with limited language proficiency were required not to exceed 2.5% of students.

Within schools in PISA 2009, students who could be excluded were:

- Intellectually disabled students, defined as students who are considered, in the professional opinion of the school principal, or by other qualified staff members, to be intellectually disabled, or who have been assessed psychologically as such. This category includes students who are emotionally or mentally unable to follow even the general instructions of the assessment. Students were not to be excluded solely because of poor academic performance or common discipline problems.

- Students with functional disabilities, defined as students who are permanently physically disabled in such a way that they cannot perform in the PISA testing situation. Students with functional disabilities who could perform were to be included in the testing.

- Students with limited proficiency in the language of the PISA assessment, defined as students who had received less than one year of instruction in the language of the assessment.

Box I.1.2 **The population covered and the students excluded**

The PISA assessment aims to be as inclusive as possible. For the definition of national target populations, PISA excludes 15-year-olds not enrolled in any form of educational institution. In the remainder of this report, the term "15-year-olds" is used to denote the PISA student population. The percentage of the target population of 15-year-olds within education covered by PISA is very high compared with other international surveys: relatively few schools were excluded from participation. Within schools, exclusions of students remained below 2% in most and below 5% in all countries, and most of the exclusions were unavoidable. The high level of coverage contributes to the comparability of the assessment results. The effect of student exclusions on national mean scores depends on the extent of (inverse) correlation between a student's performance and his or her propensity to be excluded. Even with a relatively high correlation of 0.5, exclusion rates below 5% would suggest that national mean scores would be overestimated by less than 5 score points; with a more modest correlation of 0.3, it would be below 3 score points. For this calculation, a model was used that assumes a bivariate normal distribution for the propensity to participate and performance.

The specific sample design and size for each country aimed to maximise sampling efficiency for student-level estimates. In OECD countries, sample sizes ranged from 4 410 students in Iceland to 38 250 students in Mexico. Countries with large samples have often implemented PISA both at national and regional/state levels (*e.g.* Australia, Belgium, Canada, Italy, Mexico, Spain, Switzerland and the United Kingdom). The selection of samples was monitored internationally and adhered to rigorous standards for the participation rate, both among schools selected by the international contractor and among students within these schools, to ensure that the PISA results reflect the skills of the 15-year-old students in participating countries. Countries were also required to administer the test to students in identical ways to ensure that students receive the same information prior to and during the assessment (Box I.1.3).

> Box I.1.3 **How a PISA test is typically carried out in a school**
>
> When a school has been selected to participate in PISA, a school co-ordinator is appointed. The school co-ordinator compiles a list of all 15-year-olds in the school and sends this list to the PISA National Centre in the country, which randomly selects 35 students to participate. The school co-ordinator then contacts the students who have been selected for the sample and obtains the necessary permissions from parents. The testing session is usually conducted by a test administrator who is trained and employed by the National Centre. The test administrator contacts the school co-ordinator to schedule administration of the assessment. The school co-ordinator ensures that the students attend the testing sessions. This can sometimes be difficult because students may come from different grades and different classes. The test administrator's primary tasks are to ensure that each test booklet is distributed to the correct student and to introduce the tests to the students. After the test is over, the test administrator collects the test booklets and sends them to the National Centre for coding.
>
> In PISA 2009, 13 different test booklets were used in each country. Each booklet had a different subset of PISA questions, so that students answered overlapping groups of questions, in order to produce a wide range of test items while limiting the test time for each student. With 13 different booklets, in each group of 35 students, no more than 3 students were given the same booklet. Booklets were allocated to individual students according to a random selection process. The test administrator's introduction came from a prescribed text so that all students in different schools and countries received exactly the same instructions. Before starting the test, the students were asked to do a practice question from their booklets. The testing session was divided into two parts: the two-hour-long test to assess their knowledge and skills, and the questionnaire session to collect data on their personal background, their learning habits, their attitudes towards reading, and their engagement and motivation. The length of the questionnaire session varied across countries, depending on the options chosen for inclusion, but generally was about 30 minutes. Students were usually given a short break half-way through the test and again before they did the questionnaire.

REPORTING RESULTS FROM PISA 2009

The results of PISA 2009 are presented in six volumes:

- Volume I, *What Students Know and Can Do: Student Performance in Reading, Mathematics and Science*, summarises the performance of students in PISA 2009. It provides the results in the context of how performance is defined, measured and reported, and then examines what students are able to do in reading. After a summary of reading performance, it examines the ways in which this performance varies on subscales representing three aspects of reading. It then breaks down results by different formats of reading texts and considers gender differences in reading, both generally and for different reading aspects and text formats. Any comparison of the outcomes of education systems needs to take into consideration countries' social and economic circumstances, and the resources they devote to education. To address this, the volume also interprets the results within countries' economic and social contexts. The volume concludes with a description of student results in mathematics and science.

- Volume II, *Overcoming Social Background: Equity in Learning Opportunities and Outcomes,* starts by closely examining the performance variation shown in Volume I, particularly the extent to which the overall variation in student performance relates to differences in results achieved by different schools. The volume then looks at how factors such as socio-economic background and immigrant status affect student and school performance, and the role that education policy can play in moderating the impact of these factors.

- Volume III, *Learning to Learn: Student Engagement, Strategies and Practices*, explores the information gathered on students' levels of engagement in reading activities and attitudes towards reading and learning. It describes 15-year-olds' motivation, engagement and strategies to learn.

- Volume IV, *What Makes a School Successful? Resources, Policies and Practices*, explores the relationships between student-, school- and system-level characteristics, and educational quality and equity. It explores what schools and school policies can do to raise overall student performance and, at the same time, moderate the impact of socio-economic background on student performance, with the aim of promoting a more equitable distribution of learning opportunities.

- Volume V, *Learning Trends: Changes in Student Performance since 2000*, provides an overview of trends in student performance in reading, mathematics and science from PISA 2000 to PISA 2009. It shows educational outcomes over time and tracks changes in factors related to student and school performance, such as student background and school characteristics and practices.

- Volume VI, *Students On Line: Reading and Using Digital Information*, explains how PISA measures and reports student performance in digital reading, and analyses what students in the 20 countries participating in this assessment are able to do.

All data tables referred to in the analysis are included at the end of the respective volumes. A Reader's Guide is also provided in each volume to aid in interpreting the tables and figures accompanying the report.

Technical annexes that describe the construction of the questionnaire indices, sampling issues, quality assurance procedures and the process followed for developing the assessment instruments, as well as information about reliability of coding, are posted on the OECD PISA website (*www.pisa.oecd.org*). Many of the issues covered in the technical annexes are elaborated in greater detail in the *PISA 2009 Technical Report* (OECD, forthcoming).

Notes

1. The GDP of countries that participated in PISA 2009 represents 87% of the 2007 world GDP. Some of the entities represented in this report are referred to as partner economies. This is because they are not strictly national entities.

2. Thirty-one partner countries and economies carried out the assessment in 2009 and ten additional partner countries and economies carried out the assessment in 2010.

3. Marks, G.N (2007); Bertschy, K., M. Alejandrea Cattaneo and Stefan C. Wolter (2009); OECD (2010a).

4. This report uses the terms Macedonia, Moldova, Montenegro and Serbia to refer, respectively, to the former Yugoslav Republic of Macedonia, the Republic of Moldova, the Republic of Montenegro and the Republic of Serbia.

5. Visit *www.pisa.oecd.org* for links to countries' national PISA websites and national PISA reports.

6. Australia, Austria, Belgium, Bulgaria, Canada, Chile, Croatia, the Czech Republic, Denmark, Estonia, Finland, France, Germany, Greece, Hong Kong-China, Hungary, Iceland, Ireland, Israel, Italy, Japan, Jordan, Korea, Latvia, Lithuania, Macao-China, the Netherlands, New Zealand, Norway, Panama, Poland, Portugal, Qatar, the Russian Federation, Serbia, Singapore, the Slovak Republic, Slovenia, Spain, Sweden, Switzerland, Trinidad and Tobago, Turkey and Uruguay.

Reader's Guide

Data underlying the figures

The data referred to in this volume are presented in Annex B and, in greater detail, on the PISA website (*www.pisa.oecd.org*).

Five symbols are used to denote missing data:

a   The category does not apply in the country concerned. Data are therefore missing.

c   There are too few observations or no observation to provide reliable estimates (*i.e.* there are fewer than 30 students or less than five schools with valid data).

m   Data are not available. These data were not submitted by the country or were collected but subsequently removed from the publication for technical reasons.

w   Data have been withdrawn or have not been collected at the request of the country concerned.

x   Data are included in another category or column of the table.

Country coverage

This publication features data on 65 countries and economies, including all 34 OECD countries and 31 partner countries and economies (see Figure I.1.1). The data from another ten partner countries were collected one year later and will be published in 2011.

The statistical data for Israel are supplied by and under the responsibility of the relevant Israeli authorities. The use of such data by the OECD is without prejudice to the status of the Golan Heights, East Jerusalem and Israeli settlements in the West Bank under the terms of international law.

Calculating international averages

An OECD average was calculated for most indicators presented in this report. In the case of some indicators, a total representing the OECD area as a whole was also calculated:

- The OECD average corresponds to the arithmetic mean of the respective country estimates.

- The OECD total takes the OECD countries as a single entity, to which each country contributes in proportion to the number of 15-year-olds enrolled in its schools (see Annex B for data). It illustrates how a country compares with the OECD area as a whole.

In this publication, the OECD total is generally used when references are made to the overall situation in the OECD area. Where the focus is on comparing performance across education systems, the OECD average is used. In the case of some countries, data may not be available for specific indicators, or specific categories may not apply. Readers should, therefore, keep in mind that the terms "OECD average" and "OECD total" refer to the OECD countries included in the respective comparisons.

Rounding figures

Because of rounding, some figures in tables may not exactly add up to the totals. Totals, differences and averages are always calculated on the basis of exact numbers and are rounded only after calculation.

All standard errors in this publication have been rounded to one or two decimal places. Where the value 0.00 is shown, this does not imply that the standard error is zero, but that it is smaller than 0.005.

Reporting student data

The report uses "15-year-olds" as shorthand for the PISA target population. PISA covers students who are aged between 15 years 3 months and 16 years 2 months at the time of assessment and who have completed at least 6 years of formal schooling, regardless of the type of institution in which they are enrolled and of whether they are in full-time or part-time education, of whether they attend academic or vocational programmes, and of whether they attend public or private schools or foreign schools within the country.

Reporting school data

The principals of the schools in which students were assessed provided information on their schools' characteristics by completing a school questionnaire. Where responses from school principals are presented in this publication, they are weighted so that they are proportionate to the number of 15-year-olds enrolled in the school.

Focusing on statistically significant differences

This volume discusses only statistically significant differences or changes. These are denoted in darker colours in figures and in bold font in tables. See Annex A3 for further information.

Categorising student performance

This report uses a shorthand to describe students' levels of proficiency in the subjects assessed by PISA:

Top performers are those students proficient at Level 5 or 6 of the assessment

Strong performers are those students proficient at Level 4 of the assessment

Moderate performers are those students proficient at Level 2 or 3 of the assessment

Lowest performers are those students proficient below Level 2 of the assessment

Abbreviations used in this report

ESCS   PISA index of economic, social and cultural status

GDP   Gross domestic product

ISCED   International Standard Classification of Education

PPP   Purchasing power parity

S.D.   Standard deviation

S.E.   Standard error

Further documentation

For further information on the PISA assessment instruments and the methods used in PISA, see the *PISA 2009 Technical Report* (OECD, forthcoming) and the PISA website (*www.pisa.oecd.org*).

This report uses the OECD's StatLinks service. Below each table and chart is a url leading to a corresponding Excel workbook containing the underlying data. These urls are stable and will remain unchanged over time. In addition, readers of the e-books will be able to click directly on these links and the workbook will open in a separate window, if their Internet browser is open and running.

2

A Profile of Student Performance in Reading

What can 15-year-olds do as readers? This chapter compares student performance in reading across and within countries. It discusses the PISA definition of the term *reading literacy* and the reading tasks associated with each PISA proficiency level. The chapter then digs deep into the reading results, showing gender differences in reading skills, and detailing the levels of student proficiency in various aspects of reading, such as students' ability to *access and retrieve, integrate and interpret,* and *reflect and evaluate* the information they obtain through reading. It also discusses students' ability to read and understand *continuous* and *non-continuous texts*.

What do 15-year-olds around the world know and what can they do as readers? Can they find what they need in written texts, interpret and use the information, and reflect upon it critically in relation to their own experience and understanding? Can they read different kinds of texts for different purposes and in a variety of contexts, either for personal interest and satisfaction or for practical reasons? The assessment of reading in PISA 2009 sets out to answer these questions.

Since reading was the main focus of the PISA 2009 assessment, more detailed probing is possible than was the case in PISA 2003 and PISA 2006, when a relatively small amount of testing time was devoted to reading. In PISA 2009, three-and-a-half hours of test material were dedicated to assessing reading in each participating country. Reading is the first of the assessment areas to be revisited as a major focus of PISA. As such, a full review of the assessment framework and development of assessment instruments was undertaken.[1] A comparison of students' performance in reading over the period 2000 to 2009 is provided in Volume V, *Learning Trends*.

Box I.2.1 **Reading performance and success in adult life**

It is now well established that education is associated with enhanced life experience at many levels. Earnings increase with each level of education completed, and the advantage increases with age (OECD, 2010d). The non-economic returns from education in the form of better health and greater social cohesion, indicated by cultural and political participation, are regarded as important benefits alongside economic and labour-market returns. Education is often also considered to contribute to quality of life in its own right.[2]

Levels of *reading literacy* are more reliable predictors of economic and social well-being than is the quantity of education as measured by years at school or in post-school education. The OECD report, *The High Cost of Low Educational Performance*,[3] uses data from PISA and other international assessments to demonstrate that it is the quality of learning outcomes, not the length of schooling, that makes the difference.

The relationship between PISA reading literacy scores and subsequent life outcomes in Canada is also documented in the OECD report *Pathways to Success: How Knowledge and Skills at Age 15 Shape Future Lives in Canada*.[4] Tracking Canadian students who had taken part in the PISA 2000 reading assessment, the study found that, after adjusting for background variables such as parental, school, demographic and geographic factors, proficiency on the PISA reading literacy scale was associated with a significantly higher likelihood of continuing in education, rather than making the transition to work, or inactivity, by the age of 21.

■ Figure I.2.a ■
Likelihood of participation in tertiary education among 21-year-old Canadians, as associated with their PISA reading proficiency and school marks at age 15[1, 2]

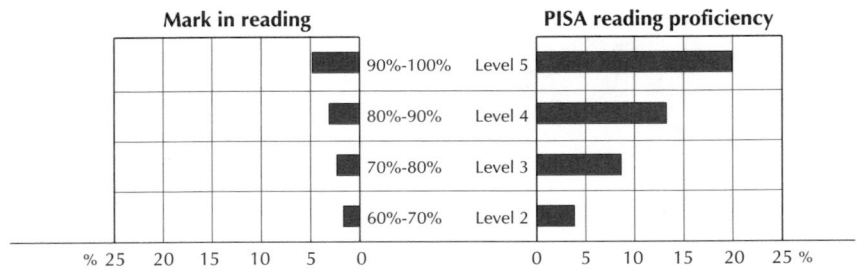

1. After accounting for school engagement, gender, mother tongue, place of residence, parental, education and family income.
2. The reference group for the PISA reading proficiency levels is Level 1, and for the marks in reading it is the group that obtained less than 60%.
Source: OECD, 2010a.

StatLink ⟨⟨⟨⟨ http://dx.doi.org/10.1787/888932343133

....

The study also found reading scores of 15-year-old students were an important predictor of earnings for both males and females.

While the Canadian study reported longitudinal data only up until the age of 21, a time when many young adults have not yet begun their careers, the benefits to human capital as measured by the PISA reading literacy scale are likely to continue into adulthood.

Data from national and international surveys of adults conducted over the past 20 years both support and extend the findings shown by Canada. Literacy and numeracy skills have become a currency in modern societies around the world. Those with below-average skills cannot hope to earn above-average wages in an increasingly global economy. According to a growing body of data, literacy and numeracy skills influence whether or not individuals will graduate from high school and, if so, whether and where they will go on to higher education. These skills also seem to influence what individuals choose to study in higher education and their persistence in earning a degree. A university degree, along with literacy and numeracy skills, is also important in influencing the type of job individuals obtain, as well as the wages and annual income they earn. Literacy and numeracy skills are not only connected with economic returns. Data show that these skills are also associated with the likelihood that individuals will participate in lifelong learning, keep abreast of social and political events, and vote in national elections. Other data suggest that literacy links education and health and may contribute to the disparities that have been observed in the quality of healthcare that many people receive.

Given the broad range of life experiences with which literacy is associated, including health, well-being, and cultural and political participation, and given that the aim of PISA is to measure how well education systems are preparing young people for life, the PISA assessment was developed to represent a wide and deep conception of reading. The PISA conception of *reading literacy* aims to encompass the range of situations in which people read, the different forms in which written text is presented, and the variety of approaches that readers bring to texts, from the functional and finite, such as finding a particular piece of practical information, to the more expansive: reading to learn and understand other ways of doing, thinking and being.

This chapter begins by explaining how PISA measures and reports student performance in reading, and then presents the results of the assessment, showing what students know and can do as readers in different countries. This section is followed by a discussion of the results in reading by gender, examining areas of relative strength and weakness for boys and girls. While the chapter mainly reports on the assessment of reading in the print medium, it also includes a brief section on the assessment of reading digital texts.

Although PISA conceives of reading both print and digital media as a single construct, the results are reported separately in order to allow countries to observe differences in their students' reading performance across the two media. This may prompt discussions about policy changes in resourcing, curriculum and pedagogy. Reading digital texts is different from reading printed texts in important respects: in the small amount of text visible to the reader at any moment, in the amount of text *available* to the reader, beyond what is immediately visible, and in its demand for using a range of unique navigation tools and features. While this volume focuses on print texts, the reading of digital texts and its relationship with print reading are presented in Volume VI, *Students On Line*. The term "reading" used throughout this report denotes the reading of texts printed on paper, unless otherwise specified as digital or electronic reading.

A CONTEXT FOR COMPARING THE PERFORMANCE OF COUNTRIES

Comparing reading performance, and educational performance more generally, poses numerous challenges. When teachers give a reading test in a classroom, they require students with varying abilities, attitudes and social backgrounds to respond to the same set of tasks. When educators compare the performance of schools, they give the same tests across schools that may differ significantly in the structure and sequencing of their curricula, their pedagogical emphases and instructional methods, as well as the demographic and social contexts of their student populations. Comparing the performance of education systems across countries adds further layers of complexity, because students are given tests in different languages and because the social, economic and cultural context of the countries that are being compared can be very different. However, while different students within a country may learn in different contexts according to their home background and the school that they have attended, they are subjected to common tests and exams because in adult life they will all face common challenges, having to compete for the same jobs. Similarly, in a global economy, the benchmarks for educational success are no longer national standards alone, but increasingly, the best performing education systems internationally. As difficult as international comparisons are, they are important for educators, and PISA has made significant efforts to ensure that such comparisons are valid and fair.

This section discusses countries' reading performance in the context of important economic, demographic and social factors that can influence assessment results, so as to provide a framework for interpreting the results that are presented later in the chapter.

As shown in Volume II, *Overcoming Social Background*, a family's wealth influences the educational performance of children, but that influence varies markedly across countries. Similarly, the relative prosperity of some countries allows them to spend more on education, while other countries find themselves constrained by a lower national income. It is therefore important to keep the national income of countries in mind when comparing the performance of education systems across countries. Figure I.2.1 displays the relationship between national income as measured by the per capita Gross Domestic Product (GDP) and students' average reading performance.[5] The figure also shows a trend line[6] that summarises the relationship between per capita GDP and mean student performance in reading among OECD countries. The scatter plot suggests that countries with higher national incomes tend to perform better in reading. The relationship suggests that 6% of the variation between the OECD countries' mean scores can be predicted on the basis of their per capita GDP. Countries with higher national incomes are thus at a relative advantage, even if the chart provides no indications about the causal nature of this relationship. This should be taken into account particularly when interpreting the performance of countries with comparatively low levels of national income, such as Mexico, Chile and Turkey. Table I.2.20 shows an "adjusted" score that would be predicted if the country had all of its present characteristics except that per capita GDP was equal to the average for OECD countries.

While per capita GDP reflects the potential resources available for education in each country, it does not directly measure the financial resources actually invested in education. Figure I.2.2 compares countries' actual spending per student, on average, from the age of 6 up to the age of 15, with average student performance in reading.[7] The results are expressed in USD using purchasing power parities. Figure I.2.2 shows a positive relationship between spending per student and mean reading performance among OECD countries. As expenditure on educational institutions per student increases, so does a country's mean performance. Expenditure per student explains 9% of the variation in mean performance between countries and relatively low spending per student needs to be taken into account when interpreting the performance of countries such as Turkey, Mexico or Chile. At the same time, deviations from the trend line suggest that moderate spending per student cannot automatically be equated with poor performance by education systems. For example, Estonia and Poland, which spend around 40 000 USD per student, perform at the same level as Norway, Switzerland and the United States, which spend over 100 000 USD per student. Similarly, New Zealand, one of the highest performing countries in reading, spends well below the average per student.

Given the close interrelationship between a student's performance and his or her parents' level of education, it is also important to bear in mind the educational attainment of adult populations when comparing the performance of OECD countries, as countries with more highly educated adults are at an advantage over countries where parents have less education. Figure I.2.3 shows the percentage of 35-44 year-olds that have attained tertiary level of education. This group roughly corresponds to the age group of parents of the 15-year-olds assessed in PISA and how this relates to reading performance.

■ Figure I.2.1 ■
Reading performance and GDP

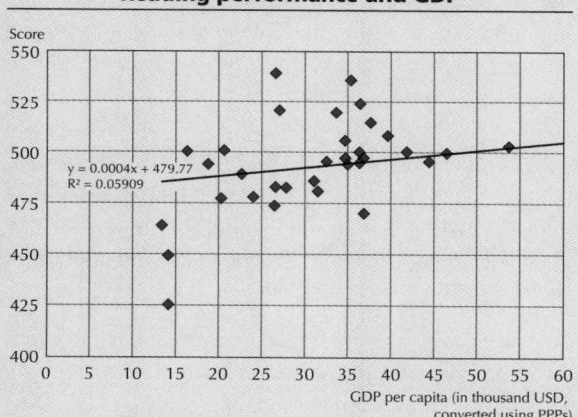

$y = 0.0004x + 479.77$
$R^2 = 0.05909$

GDP per capita (in thousand USD,
converted using PPPs)

Source: OECD, *PISA 2009 Database,* Table I.2.20.
StatLink ⬛ http://dx.doi.org/10.1787/888932343133

■ Figure I.2.2 ■
Reading performance and spending on education

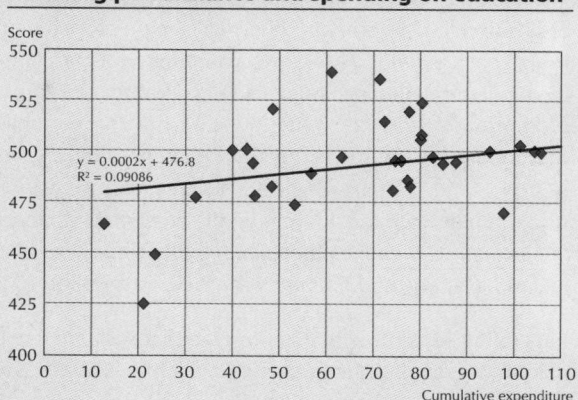

$y = 0.0002x + 476.8$
$R^2 = 0.09086$

Cumulative expenditure
(in thousand USD, converted using PPPs)

Source: OECD, *PISA 2009 Database,* Table I.2.20.
StatLink ⬛ http://dx.doi.org/10.1787/888932343133

■ Figure I.2.3 ■
Reading performance and parents' education

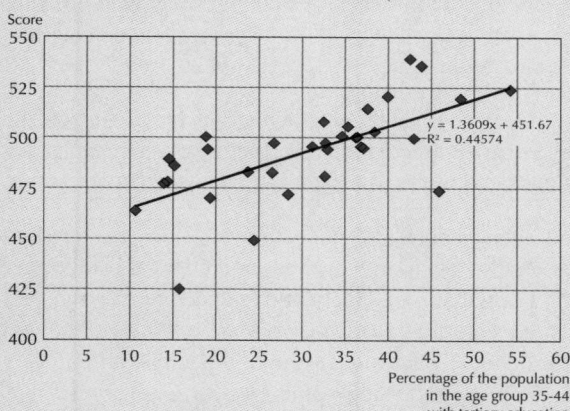

$y = 1.3609x + 451.67$
$R^2 = 0.44574$

Percentage of the population
in the age group 35-44
with tertiary education

Source: OECD, *PISA 2009 Database,* Table I.2.20.
StatLink ⬛ http://dx.doi.org/10.1787/888932343133

■ Figure I.2.4 ■
Reading performance and share of socio-economically disadvantaged students

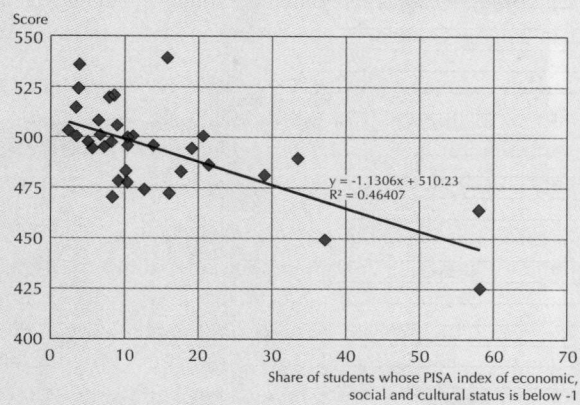

$y = -1.1306x + 510.23$
$R^2 = 0.46407$

Share of students whose PISA index of economic,
social and cultural status is below -1

Source: OECD, *PISA 2009 Database,* Table I.2.20.
StatLink ⬛ http://dx.doi.org/10.1787/888932343133

■ Figure I.2.5 ■
Reading performance and proportion of students from an immigrant background

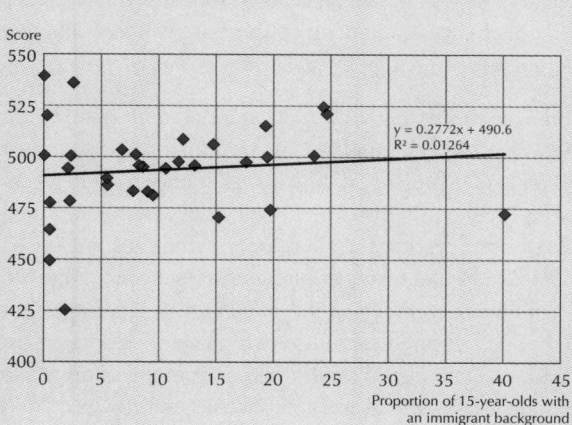

$y = 0.2772x + 490.6$
$R^2 = 0.01264$

Proportion of 15-year-olds with
an immigrant background

Source: OECD, *PISA 2009 Database,* Table I.2.20.
StatLink ⬛ http://dx.doi.org/10.1787/888932343133

■ Figure I.2.6 ■
Equivalence of the PISA test across cultures and languages

Rank on own preferred new PISA 2009 questions
and link questions from previous cycles

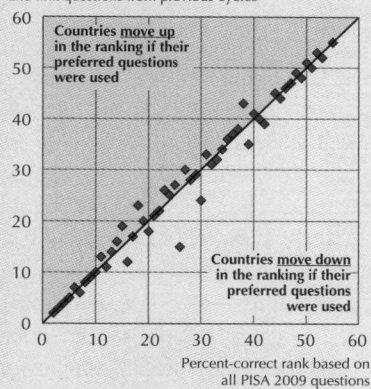

Countries move up
in the ranking if their
preferred questions
were used

Countries move down
in the ranking if their
preferred questions
were used

Percent-correct rank based on
all PISA 2009 questions

Source: OECD, *PISA 2009 Database,* Table I.2.21.
StatLink ⬛ http://dx.doi.org/10.1787/888932343133

Socio-economic heterogeneity in student populations poses another major challenge for teachers and education systems. As shown in Volume II, *Overcoming Social Background*, teachers instructing socio-economically disadvantaged children are likely to face greater challenges than teachers teaching students from more advantaged social backgrounds. Similarly, countries with larger proportions of socio-economically disadvantaged children face greater challenges than countries with smaller proportions of disadvantaged students. Figure I.2.4 shows the proportion of students at the lower end of an international scale of the economic, social and cultural background of students, which is described in detail in Volume II, and how this relates to reading performance. The relationship is strong and explains 46% of the performance variation among countries. Turkey and Mexico, where 58% of students belong to the internationally most disadvantaged group, and Chile, Portugal, Spain, Italy and Poland, where this proportion reaches more than 20%, thus face much greater challenges than, for example, Norway, Australia, Iceland, Canada and Finland, where the proportion of disadvantaged students is less than 5%.

Integrating students with an immigrant background can also be challenging, and the level of performance of students who immigrated to the country in which they were assessed can be only partially attributed to their host country's education system. Figure I.2.5 shows the proportion of 15-year-olds with an immigrant background and how this relates to student performance.

When examining the results for individual countries as shown in Table I.2.20 it is apparent that countries vary in their demographic, social and economic contexts. The last column in Table I.2.20 summarises the different factors discussed above in an index.[8] The index shows Norway, Japan, Iceland, Luxembourg, Finland and the United States with the most advantaged demographic, social and economic context and Turkey, Mexico and Chile with the most challenging context.

These differences need to be considered when interpreting PISA results. At the same time, the future economic and social prospects of both individuals and countries depend on the results they actually achieve, not on the performance they might have achieved under different social and economic conditions. That is why the results that are actually achieved by students, schools and countries are the focus of this volume.

Even after accounting for the demographic, economic and social context of education systems, the question remains: to what extent is an international test meaningful when differences in languages and cultures lead to very different ways in which subjects such as language, mathematics or science are taught and learned across countries? It is inevitable that not all tasks on the international PISA assessments are equally appropriate in different cultural contexts and equally relevant in different curricular and instructional contexts. To gauge this, PISA asked every country to identify those tasks from the PISA tests that it considered most appropriate for an international test. Countries were advised to give an on-balance rating for each task with regard to its relevance to "preparedness for life", authenticity and relevance for 15-year-olds. Tasks given a high rating by each country are referred to as that country's most preferred questions for PISA. PISA then scored every country on its own most preferred questions and compared the resulting performance with the performance on the entire set of PISA tasks (see Figure I.2.6). It is clear that generally, the proportion of questions answered correctly by students does not depend in significant ways on whether countries were only scored on their preferred questions or on the overall set of PISA tasks. This provides robust evidence that the results of the PISA assessments would not change markedly if countries had more influence in selecting texts that they thought might be "fairer" to their students.

Finally, when comparing student performance across countries, the extent to which student performance on international tests might be influenced by the effort that students in different countries invest in the assessment must be considered. In PISA 2003, students were asked to imagine an actual situation that was highly important to them, so that they could try their very best and invest as much effort as they could into doing well. They were then asked to report how much effort they had put into doing the PISA test compared to the situation they had just imagined and how much effort they would have invested if their marks from PISA had been counted in their school marks. The students generally answered realistically, saying that they would make more effort if the test results were to count towards their school marks but the analysis also established that the reported expenditure of effort by students was fairly stable across countries. This finding counters the claim that systematic cultural differences in the effort made by students invalidate international comparisons. The analysis also showed that within countries, effort was related to student achievement with an effect size similar to variables such as single-parent family structure, gender and socio-economic background.[9]

THE PISA APPROACH TO ASSESSING STUDENT PERFORMANCE IN READING

The PISA definition of *reading literacy*

Reading literacy includes a broad set of cognitive competencies, from basic decoding, to knowledge of words, grammar, and linguistic and textual structures and features, to knowledge about the world. It also includes metacognitive competencies: the awareness of and ability to use a variety of appropriate strategies when processing texts.

Historically, the term "literacy" referred to a tool used to acquire and communicate information. This is close to the notion that the term *reading literacy* is intended to express in PISA: the active, purposeful and functional application of reading in a range of situations and for various purposes.

PISA 2009 defines *reading literacy* as:

> *understanding, using, reflecting on and engaging with written texts, in order to achieve one's goals, to develop one's knowledge and potential, and to participate in society.*

The words "understanding, using, reflecting on" are readily connected with important elements of reading and cognition.

Understanding refers to the reader's task in constructing meaning, large and small, literal and implicit, from text. This can be as basic as understanding the meaning of the words, or it can be as complex as comprehending the underlying theme of a lengthy argument or narrative. *Using* refers to the kind of reading that is directed toward applying the information and ideas in a text to an immediate task or goal or to reinforce or change beliefs. Much reading is of this kind. In some cases, using a text in this way requires just minimal understanding, combining recognition of the meaning of the words with some elementary recognition of structure (many menus, for example). In others, it requires using both syntactic and more complex structural understanding to extract the information. In all cases, though, the reader approaches the text with a specific task in mind. In *reflecting on* texts readers relate what they are reading to their thoughts and experiences. They may use the text to cast new light on something in their own lives; or they may make judgements about the text itself, drawing on external frames of reference. Readers continually make these kinds of judgments in the course of approaching a text. They need to assess whether the text is appropriate for the task at hand, determining whether it will provide the information they need. They have to make judgments about the truthfulness and reliability of the content. They need to account for any biases they find in the text. And, for some texts, they must make judgments about the quality of the text, both as a crafted object and as a tool for acquiring information.

The term *engaging* in the definition implies the motivation to read. Many people appear to read text only when some task requires them to do so. Others (sometimes) also read for the pleasure it brings them and for general interest. Some read only what others – teachers, employers, governments – make necessary, while others also read things of their own choosing. That is, people differ in how engaged they are with text and how much of a role reading plays in their lives. Volume III, *Learning to Learn*, which looks at reading engagement in detail, shows that reading is an important correlate with the direct cognitive measures. As such, it is important to understand these differences to get a full picture of *reading literacy*. Reading engagement comprises a cluster of affective and behavioural characteristics that include an interest in and enjoyment of reading, a sense of control over what one reads, involvement in the social dimension of reading, and diverse and frequent reading practices.

Written texts comprises texts in a variety of formats, including *continuous* and *non-continuous* texts, and in a variety of text types, such as narrative, expository and interactive. The term *written texts* also comprises texts in a variety of media: hand-written, printed and digital.

Until recently, most reading material was printed on paper. Now, readers also need to access and use text that is displayed on a screen of some kind, whether on a computer, a PDA, an ATM, or a mobile phone. Digital text opens the construct of reading to cover additional types of text and content. Examples of these novel form/content combinations are: interactive texts, such as exchanges in comments sections of blogs or in e-mail response threads; *multiple texts*, whether displayed at the same time on a screen or linked through hypertext; and expandable texts, where a summary can be linked to more detailed information if the user chooses. While one can find examples of similar texts on paper, they are much less common in that form.

The PISA definition of reading encompasses both printed and digital texts, acknowledging that the fundamental competency, regardless of medium, is making meaning from verbal language in its graphic form.

With the words *to achieve one's goals, to develop one's knowledge and potential, and to participate in society*, the second half of the definition is intended to capture the full scope of situations in which *reading literacy* plays a role. To *achieve their goals*, individuals have a range of needs they must address, from basic survival to personal satisfaction, to professional and career development, to participation in society. Reading is increasingly required in meeting those needs, whether simply finding one's way while shopping, or negotiating complex bureaucracies, whose rules are commonly available only in written texts. It is also important in meeting individuals' needs for sociability, for entertainment and leisure, for developing one's community and for work. Reading is also required to *develop one's potential.* This is obviously the case in the contexts of school and post-school education, but surveys suggest that many adults also engage in some kind of learning throughout their life, much of it self-directed and informal. Typically this learning requires some use of text, and as individuals want to improve their life, whether at work or outside, they need to understand, use, and engage with printed and digital texts. The use of *participate in society* underlines the focus on an active role: individuals use text as a way to engage with their social surroundings, to learn about and to actively contribute to life in their community, close to home and more broadly. In this, PISA also recognises the social aspect of *reading literacy*, seeing it as part of the interactions between and among individuals. And of course, for many individuals, reading is essential to their participation in the labour force.

The PISA 2009 framework for assessing *reading literacy*

The PISA framework for assessing literacy has guided the development of the assessment and also sets parameters for reporting. The PISA reading literacy assessment is built on three major characteristics: *texts, aspects* and *situations*. These characteristics are a useful means of analysing and describing the domain, even while it is recognised that the categorisation of texts and tasks is not absolute, since those elements of reading do not exist independently of one another. Figure I.2.7 shows the relationships between the major features of the framework.

All of these elements were systematically manipulated by test developers to construct the tasks that make up the test. Some elements of these framing characteristics are also used as the basis for constructing scales and subscales, and thus for reporting, whereas others ensure that *reading literacy* is adequately covered.

■ Figure I.2.7 ■
Main features of PISA 2009 reading framework

TEXTS What kind of text must students read?	**Medium** In what form does the text appear?	▪ On paper ▪ Digitally
	Environment Can the reader change digital texts?	▪ *Authored* (reader is receptive) ▪ *Message-based* (reader can change)
	Text format How is the text presented?	▪ *Continuous texts* (in sentences) ▪ *Non-continuous texts* (in lists, like this one) ▪ *Mixed texts* (combining these) ▪ *Multiple texts* (brought together from more than one source)
	Text type What is the rhetorical structure of the text?	▪ Descriptive (typically answering "what" questions) ▪ Narration (typically "when") ▪ Exposition (typically "how") ▪ Argumentation (typically "why") ▪ Direction (providing instructions) ▪ Transaction (exchanging information)
ASPECTS What is the reader's purpose and approach to the text?	▪ *Access and retrieve* information in the text ▪ *Integrate and interpret* what they read ▪ *Reflect and evaluate,* standing back from a text and relating it to their own experience	
SITUATIONS What is the intended use of the text, from the author's point of view?	▪ *Personal:* To satisfy one's own interests ▪ *Public:* Relating to wider society ▪ *Educational:* Used in instruction ▪ *Occupational:* Related to the world of work	

The characteristic *texts* covers the range of materials that are read, and is further classified into a number of sub-categorisations: *medium, environment, text format* and *text type*. Text *medium* – print and digital – is an important sub-categorisation in PISA, because it is used as the basis for reporting two separate reading scales. Although the PISA 2009 concept of reading encompasses reading in both print and digital media, and the framework is built to reflect this unitary conceptualisation, the skills and knowledge applied to reading in the two media are not identical. Print reading and digital reading are therefore reported on separate scales to allow countries to explore the differences in reading among their 15-year-olds. The reporting of results in this publication focuses on print reading, while Volume VI, *Students On Line,* explores the results of the assessment of digital reading skills. Text *format* is also used as an organiser for reporting, building subscales for the categories *continuous* and *non-continuous*, which describe two ways in which texts are commonly structured, either in sentences and paragraphs (*continuous*), or in other formats such as lists, diagrams, graphs and tables (*non-continuous*). The other two text classifications are used to ensure an adequate coverage of the definition of *reading literacy*. The *environment* classification applies to digital texts only. It recognises the distinctive feature of a class of digital texts, including e-mails, blogs and forums, that the reader participates in constructing. This kind of text is termed *message-based* in PISA, and is distinguished from *authored* texts, where the text is written by a single author and is read as a completed artefact. Finally, the classification text *type* identifies categories of text that form the basis of many national and some international reading frameworks: *narration, exposition, argumentation* and so on. In PISA they are applied to ensure that reading texts with different rhetorical purposes are included in the assessment.

The second major characteristic, *aspects*, defines the cognitive approach that determines how readers engage with a text. Proficient readers have a repertoire of approaches and purposes for reading. They approach texts in order to access and retrieve information. They are able to interpret texts at the level of words, sentences and larger sections, and integrate information within texts and across *multiple texts*. Proficient readers reflect on texts in order to better understand and extend their own experiences, and in order to evaluate the relevance, utility and quality of the texts themselves. While all of these approaches are integral to proficient reading, the emphasis they are given in reading curricula and pedagogy across schools, systems and countries varies. In PISA 2009 the aspects *access and retrieve*, *integrate and interpret* and *reflect and evaluate* are used as the basis for reporting on reading, to investigate how proficiency in each of them plays out across the participating countries and subgroups of interest.[10]

The third characteristic used to build the PISA reading framework is *situation*, the range of broad contexts for which texts are produced. This characteristic plays a relatively minor role in comparison with *texts* and *aspects*, in that it does not form the basis of reporting scales. However, the specification of *situations* in the framework ensures coverage of the definition of *reading literacy,* so that an appropriate range of contexts with the concomitant sets of vocabulary and linguistic structures is included in the assessment tasks.

In the remaining part of this section the three framework characteristics of *text, aspect* and *situation* are discussed in more detail.

Characteristics of the texts

PISA 2009 categorises texts by the medium through which they are communicated, the environment that establishes whether or not the reader has the potential to influence the content of the text (for digital texts only), the text format and the text type.

Medium

The broadest distinction between texts in the PISA 2009 framework for *reading literacy* is the classification by medium: print or digital.

Print-medium text usually appears on paper in forms such as single sheets, brochures, magazines and books. The physical status of the printed text encourages (though it may not compel) the reader to approach the content of the text in a particular sequence. In essence, printed texts have a fixed or static existence. Moreover, in real life as well as in the assessment context, the extent or amount of the text is immediately visible to the reader.

Digital-medium text for the purposes of PISA corresponds essentially to hypertext: a text or texts with navigation tools and features. Such digital texts have an unfixed, dynamic existence. In the digital medium, typically only a fraction of the available text can be seen at any one time. Often the extent of text available is unknown, and a task may require reference to *multiple texts*. Readers use navigation tools and features such as scroll bars, buttons, menus and tabs. They also use text search functions and global content representation devices such as site maps. A major navigation tool that assists readers in finding their way around a number of texts, and one of the most distinctive features of digital texts, is the hypertext link. (An example of a hypertext link is *www.pisa.oecd.org*.)

The differences between print and digital texts, such as the amount of visible text and the presence of navigation tools and features, imply an expanded set of reading skills and knowledge. Digital texts make possible, and even require, non-sequential reading, with each reader constructing a "customised" text from the information encountered at the links he or she follows. Skilled readers of digital text must be familiar with navigation features and tools that do not exist in the print medium. In addition, typical digital reading activities involve the use of *multiple texts*, sometimes selecting from a virtually infinite pool. Gathering information on the Internet requires skimming and scanning through large amounts of material and immediately evaluating its credibility. Critical thinking, therefore, has become more important than ever in *reading literacy*.[11]

Digital texts extend or emphasise some features of traditional reading, and introduce other features that are new to reading. The inclusion of digital texts in PISA allows the gathering of evidence about student competencies in understanding and using information in the digital medium. It also makes it possible to learn more about how ways of reading in the two media are similar and different in practice, and how various features of texts in the two media impact on the cognitive aspects of reading.

The sample material later in this chapter comprises seven units from the print medium (see Figures I.2.40 to I.2.46) and one from the digital medium (see Figure I.2.47).

Text environment

The distinction by text environment, *authored* or *message-based*, refers to whether or not a digital text can be changed by the reader. Texts with a fixed content are classified as *authored*. Texts with which the reader can interact are classified as *message-based*.

An *authored* environment is one in which the reader is primarily receptive: the content cannot be modified. They are self-contained environments, controlled or published by a commercial company, a government department, an organisation or institution, or an individual. Readers use these sites mainly for obtaining information. Text objects within an *authored* environment include home pages, sites publicising events or goods, government information sites, educational sites containing information for students, news sites and lists of search results.

A *message-based* environment is one in which the reader has the opportunity to add to or change the content, which is to some extent fluid and collaborative. Readers use these sites not only for obtaining information, but also as a way of communicating. Text objects within a *message-based* environment include e-mail messages, blogs, chat rooms, web forums and reviews, and on line forms. In these texts, later entries often cannot be understood without understanding prior contributions.

While *authored* texts more closely resemble traditional print-based texts, *message-based texts* are increasingly prevalent in the digital medium, most prominently for social networking but also in public, educational and work-based contexts. Knowledge of the structures and features of texts in both environments, together with skills in negotiating them and evaluating their authority, are part of the repertoire of proficient readers.

As with many of the variables in the reading framework, the environment classifications are not strictly partitioned, and an individual text may contain elements of both. The digital reading assessment unit *IWANTTOHELP*, which is reproduced in the section containing sample questions at the end of this chapter (see Figure I.2.47), includes tasks that represent both *authored* and *message-based* environments. Two of the questions are based on a blog, the third is based on a series of *authored* web pages and the fourth requires the reader to use both an e-mail message and *authored* web pages.

Text format

Performance on text format subscales were already reported in PISA 2000, where groups of countries showed differential reading performance on *continuous* and *non-continuous texts*, and boys' and girls' results were more similar on the *non-continuous texts* subscale than on *continuous texts* subscale. These results, with their implications for policy, have prompted the inclusion of text format subscales alongside aspect subscales in the reporting of results from the PISA 2009 assessment.

Continuous texts are typically composed of sentences that are, in turn, organised into paragraphs. These may fit into even larger structures such as sections, chapters and books. *Non-continuous texts* are most frequently organised in matrix format, based on combinations of lists. Texts in *continuous* and *non-continuous* format appear in both the print and digital media. *Mixed* and *multiple* format texts are also prevalent in both media, particularly in the digital medium. In *continuous texts*, organisation occurs graphically or visually by the separation of parts of the text into paragraphs, by paragraph indentation, by the breakdown of text into a hierarchy signalled by headings that help readers to recognise the organisation of the text, and by the use of formatting features such as different font sizes, and font types such as italic and boldface. Discourse markers also provide organisational information. These include sequence markers (for example, "first", "second" and "third"), and causal connectors (for example, "therefore", "for this reason" and "since"), which show the relationships between parts of a text. Examples of texts in *continuous text* format in the print medium include newspaper reports, essays, novels, short stories, reviews and letters. In the digital medium the *continuous text* format group includes reviews, blogs and reports in prose. Digital *continuous texts* tend to be short because of the limitations of screen size and the need for piecemeal reading, which make long texts unattractive to many online readers (although this may be changing with the increasing currency of e-books).

Non-continuous texts, also known as documents, are organised differently to *continuous texts*, and therefore require a different kind of reading approach. As the sentence is the smallest unit of *continuous text*, so all *non-continuous texts* can be shown to be composed of a number of lists.[12] Some are single, simple lists, but most consist of several simple lists combined. Examples of *non-continuous texts* are lists, tables, graphs, diagrams, schedules, catalogues, indexes and forms. These texts occur in both print and digital media.

Continuous and *non-continuous texts* require readers to apply different sets of knowledge about the text's distinctive structures and features and somewhat different reading strategies. In everyday tasks, however, readers often need to draw on both sets of knowledge and strategies when they integrate information in different formats and across several texts. The PISA 2009 reading framework has recognised this important part of the reader's repertoire by identifying *mixed* and *multiple texts* as separate text formats.

Mixed texts are defined in PISA as single, coherent objects consisting of a set of elements in both *continuous* and *non-continuous* formats. In well-constructed *mixed texts* the components (for example, a prose explanation including a graph or table) are mutually supportive through coherence and cohesion links at the local and global level. *Mixed text* in the print medium is a common format in magazines, reference books and reports, where authors employ a variety of representations to communicate information. In the digital medium *authored* web pages are typically *mixed texts*, with combinations of lists, paragraphs of prose and often graphics. *Message-based texts* such as online forms, e-mail messages and forums also combine texts that are *continuous* and *non-continuous* in format.

Multiple texts are defined as collections of texts that have been generated independently and each of which makes sense independently. They are juxtaposed for a particular occasion or may have been loosely linked together for the purposes of the assessment. The relationship between the texts may not be obvious; they may be complementary or may contradict one another. For example, a set of websites from different companies providing travel advice may or may not provide similar directions to tourists. *Multiple texts* may all be in one format (for example, *continuous*) or may include both *continuous* and *non-continuous texts*. Given the prevalent use of hypertext in PISA's assessment of digital reading, almost all units in that medium are based on stimulus that consists of *multiple texts*, with the tasks requiring users to read across several texts (which may be different websites or different pages belonging to the same website), each presented in a variety of formats including prose paragraphs, menu lists, diagrams and other graphics.

The sample material at the end of this chapter includes examples representing three of the four text formats, as indicated in Figure I.2.8.[13]

■ Figure I.2.8 ■
Examples of tasks by text format

Text format	Sample questions
Continuous	■ *THE PLAY'S THE THING* – Questions 3, 4 and 7
	■ *TELECOMMUTING* – Question 7
	■ *BRUSHING YOUR TEETH* – Questions 1, 2, 3 and 4
	■ *BLOOD DONATION NOTICE* – Questions 8 and 9
	■ *MISER* – Questions 1, 5 and 7
	■ *IWANTTOHELP* (digital reading assessment) – Question 1
Non-continuous	■ *MOBILE PHONE SAFETY* – Questions 2, 6, 9 and 11
	■ *BALLOON* – Questions 3, 4, 6 and 8
Multiple	■ *TELECOMMUTING* – Question 1
	■ *IWANTTOHELP* (digital reading assessment) – Questions 2, 3 and 8

Text type

All texts in PISA are classified by text type, ascribed according to the main rhetorical purpose of the text, which was primarily used to ensure that the definition of *reading literacy* was adequately covered in the construction of the PISA assessment. It is not conceived of as a variable that influences the difficulty of a task.

Description refers to properties of objects in space, typically answering "what" questions. Impressionistic descriptions present information from the point of view of subjective impressions of relations, qualities, and directions in space. Technical descriptions present information from the point of view of objective observations in space. Examples of *description* include the depiction of a particular place in a travelogue or diary; a catalogue; a geographical map; and a specification of a feature, function or process in a technical manual.

Narration refers to properties of objects in time, typically answering "when" questions. Narratives present change from the point of view of subjective selection and emphasis. Reports present actions and events that can be objectively verified by others. News stories enable readers to form their own independent opinion of facts and events. Examples of narration include novels, short stories, plays, biographies, comic strips, and reports of events in a newspaper.

Exposition presents information as composite concepts or mental constructs, often answering "how" questions. Expository essays provide an explanation of concepts, mental constructs, or conceptions from a subjective point of view. Definitions explain how terms or names are interrelated with mental concepts. Explications are a form of analytic exposition used to explain how a mental concept can be linked with words or terms. Summaries are a form of synthetic exposition used to explain and communicate texts in a shorter form. Minutes are a record of the results of meetings or presentations. Text interpretations are a form of both analytic and synthetic exposition used to explain the abstract concepts which are realised in a particular (fictional or non-fictional) text or group of texts. A scholarly essay, a diagram showing a model of memory, a graph of population trends, a concept map, and an entry in an online encyclopaedia are all examples of expositions.

Argumentation presents the relationship among concepts or propositions, often answering "why" questions. Persuasive and opinionative texts refer to opinions and points of view. Comment relates the concepts of events, objects, and ideas to a private system of thought, values, and beliefs. Scientific *argumentation* relates concepts of events, objects, and ideas to systems of thought and knowledge so that the resulting propositions can be verified as valid or non-valid. A letter to the editor, a poster advertisement, posts in an online forum, and web-based reviews of a book or film are examples of *argumentation*.

Instruction provides directions on what to do. Instructions present directions for certain behaviours in order to complete a task. Rules, regulations and statutes specify requirements for certain behaviours based on impersonal authority, such as practical validity or public authority. Examples of *instruction* are a recipe, a series of diagrams showing a procedure for giving first aid, and guidelines for operating digital software.

Finally, the distinguishing feature of a *transaction* is that it exchanges information in an interaction with the reader. Letters and invitations explore and maintain relationships. Surveys, questionnaires and interviews seek to collect information. Examples of transactional texts are a personal letter to share family news, an e-mail exchange to plan holidays, and a text message to arrange a meeting.

Aspect

The aspects of texts are the second main organisational elements of the PISA 2009 assessment framework. They can be thought of as the mental strategies, approaches or purposes that readers use to negotiate their way into, around and between texts. PISA 2009 distinguishes between three categories – *access and retrieve, integrate and interpret, reflect and evaluate*.[14] These three processes are the basis of subscales measuring performance in PISA, according to students' proficiency in performing each aspect of reading. A fourth category, referred to as *complex,* describes those tasks that inextricably combine and depend on all three of the other processes.

In both the print and digital media, tasks classified as *access and retrieve* involve skills associated with finding, selecting and collecting information. On some occasions readers seek specific pieces of information from a text: What time does the train leave? Who wrote this article? Sometimes finding the needed information is relatively simple, as it is directly and plainly stated in the text. However, *access and retrieve* tasks are not necessarily easy ones. Several factors may contribute to making such tasks challenging. For example, sometimes more than one piece

of information is required or knowledge of text structures and features may be called upon. Tasks in the print medium might require readers to use navigation features such as headings or captions to find their way to the appropriate section of the text before locating the relevant information. In the digital medium, an *access and retrieve* question might involve navigating across several pages of a website, or using menus, lists or tabs to locate relevant information.

The aspect *integrate and interpret* involves processing what is read to make internal sense of a text. Integrating tasks require the reader to understand the relations between different parts of a text. These relations include problem-solution, cause-effect, category-example, equivalency, compare-contrast, and understanding whole-part relationships. To complete such tasks, the reader has to determine what the appropriate connection is. This may be explicitly signalled, as when the text states "the cause of X is Y", or may require an inference by the reader. The parts to be related may be near each other in the text or may be in different paragraphs or even in different texts. Interpreting refers to the process of making meaning from something that is not stated. It may involve recognising a relationship that is not explicit or it may be required at a more local level, for example, to infer (to deduce from evidence and reasoning) the connotation of a phrase or a sentence. When interpreting, a reader is identifying the underlying assumptions or implications of part or all of the text.

Reflect and evaluate tasks involve drawing on knowledge, ideas or values external to the text. In reflecting on a text, readers relate their own experience or knowledge to the text. In evaluating a text, readers make a judgment about it, either drawing on personal experience or on knowledge of the world that may be formal or content-based. Reflecting on and evaluating the content of a text requires the reader to connect information in a text to knowledge from outside sources. To do so, readers must be able to develop an understanding of what is said and intended in a text. They must then test that mental representation against what they know and believe on the basis of either prior information or information found in other texts. Reflecting on and evaluating the form of a text requires readers to stand apart from the text, to consider it objectively and to evaluate its quality and appropriateness. Knowledge of text structure, of the style typical of different kinds of texts and of register play an important role in these tasks. While the kinds of reflection and evaluation called for in the print medium assessment are also required in the digital medium, evaluation in the digital medium takes on a slightly different emphasis. Sources for online information are more varied, ranging from authoritative sources to postings with unknown or uncertain credibility. Because the source of many digital texts is obscure and because it is much easier to distribute them widely and anonymously, such judgments are especially important for digital texts. All information must be evaluated in terms of accuracy, reliability and timeliness, but this is particularly important with online material.

The three broad aspects defined so far are not conceived of as entirely separate and independent, but rather as interrelated and interdependent. Indeed from a cognitive processing perspective they can be considered to be semi-hierarchical: it is not possible to interpret or integrate information without having first retrieved it, and it is not possible to reflect on or evaluate information without having accessed the information, and very likely made some sort of interpretation. In PISA, however, while it is acknowledged that all aspects (as cognitive processes) are likely to play some role in each task, each task is designed to emphasise one or another of the aspects. Generally, the aspect classification for each PISA reading literacy task depends on the objective of the task. For example, retrieving a single piece of explicitly stated information from a web page (such as finding out the number of Internet users worldwide) would be classified as an *access and retrieve* task, even though it might involve a complex series of steps including the evaluation of the relevance of several results on a search result page, comparing and contrasting descriptions and deciding which of several sources is likely to be most authoritative.

A few PISA digital reading tasks are classified as *complex* in terms of aspect. These tasks have been designed to take advantage of the relative freedom of reading in this medium, where the arrangement and organisation given to a print text by the author's ordering of pages, chapters or larger sections is absent, and the sequence of steps to be taken by the reader in completing a task is thus much more fluid. These tasks, which are intended to simulate the uncertainty of negotiating hyperspace, do not allow assigning the task to one of the three aspects in any meaningful way. The most salient feature of such tasks is the interaction between accessing, retrieving, interpreting, integrating and reflecting. Therefore these tasks have been described as *complex* to represent this dynamic cognitive processing.

Figure I.2.9 shows sample tasks that represent each of the aspects. The tasks are reproduced in full at the end of this chapter.

■ Figure I.2.9 ■

Examples of tasks by aspect

Aspects required	Sample questions
Access and retrieve	▪ *BRUSHING YOUR TEETH* – Questions 2 and 3 ▪ *BALLOON* – Question 3 ▪ *MISER* – Question 7 ▪ *IWANTTOHELP* (digital reading assessment) – Questions 1 and 2
Integrate and interpret	▪ *MOBILE PHONE SAFETY* – Questions 2 and 9 ▪ *THE PLAY'S THE THING* – Questions 3, 4 and 7 ▪ *TELECOMMUTING* – Question 1 ▪ *BRUSHING YOUR TEETH* – Question 1 ▪ *BALLOON* – Question 8 ▪ *BLOOD DONATION NOTICE* – Question 8 ▪ *MISER* – Questions 1 and 5 ▪ *IWANTTOHELP* (digital reading assessment) – Question 3
Reflect and evaluate	▪ *MOBILE PHONE SAFETY* – Questions 6 and 11 ▪ *TELECOMMUTING* – Question 7 ▪ *BRUSHING YOUR TEETH* – Question 4 ▪ *BALLOON* – Questions 4 and 6 ▪ *BLOOD DONATION NOTICE* – Question 9
Complex	▪ *IWANTTOHELP* (digital reading assessment) – Question 8

Situation

Situation is used in PISA to define texts and their associated tasks, and refers to the contexts and uses for which the author constructed the text. While content is not used for the purpose of reporting results, by sampling texts across a variety of situations the intent is to maximise the diversity of content included in the PISA reading literacy survey. Each text is assigned to one of the four situations identified in PISA – *personal*, *public*, *educational* and *occupational* – according to its supposed audience and purpose, rather than with regard to the place where the reading activity may be carried out. For example, literary texts, which are often used in classrooms, are generally not written for educational purposes, but rather for readers' personal enjoyment and appreciation. They are therefore classified as *personal*. Conversely, textbooks are read both in schools and in homes, and the process and purpose probably differ little from one setting to another. Such texts are classified as *educational* in PISA.

The *personal* category relates to texts that are intended to satisfy an individual's personal interests, both practical and intellectual. This category also includes texts that are intended to maintain or develop personal connections with other people. It includes personal letters, fiction, biography, and informational texts that are intended to be read to satisfy curiosity, as a part of leisure or recreational activities. In the digital medium it includes personal e-mails, instant messages and diary-style blogs.

The *public* category describes texts that relate to activities and concerns of society as a whole. The category includes official documents as well as information about public events. In general, the texts associated with this category assume a more or less anonymous contact with others; they also include forum-style blogs, news websites and public notices that are encountered both online and in print.

The content of *educational* texts is usually designed specifically for the purpose of instruction. Printed text books and interactive learning software are typical examples of material generated for this kind of reading. Educational reading normally involves acquiring information as part of a larger learning task. The materials are often not chosen by the reader, but instead assigned by an instructor. The model tasks are those usually identified as "reading to learn".

Occupational texts are those associated with the workplace, often texts that support the accomplishment of some immediate task. Such texts might be intended to help readers search for a job, either in a print newspaper's classified advertisement section, or on line, or to follow workplace directions. The tasks addressing this kind of text are often referred to as "reading to do" rather than "reading to learn". Texts written for these purposes, and the tasks based on them, are classified as *occupational* in PISA.

The sample material at the end of this chapter includes examples of texts representing each of the four situations, as shown in Figure I.2.10. Unit names are listed rather than tasks, since in most cases all tasks in a unit are classified under the same situation: that of the stimulus text.

■ Figure I.2.10 ■
Examples of text format by situation

Situation	Sample texts
Personal	■ THE PLAY'S THE THING ■ MISER
Public	■ MOBILE PHONE SAFETY ■ BLOOD DONATION NOTICE
Educational	■ BRUSHING YOUR TEETH ■ BALLOON
Occupational	■ TELECOMMUTING ■ IWANTTOHELP (digital reading assessment)

How the PISA 2009 reading results are reported

How the PISA 2009 reading tests were designed, analysed and scaled

The development of the PISA 2009 reading tasks was co-ordinated by an international consortium of educational research institutions contracted by participating countries through the OECD, under the guidance of a group of reading experts from participating countries. Participating countries contributed stimulus material and questions, which were reviewed, tried out and refined iteratively over the three years leading up to the administration of the assessment in 2009. The development process involved provision for several rounds of commentary from participating countries, as well as small-scale piloting and a formal field trial in which samples of 15-year-olds from all participating countries took part. The reading expert group recommended the final selection of tasks, which included material submitted by 21 of the participating countries. The selection was made with regard to both their technical quality, assessed on the basis of their performance in the field trial, and their cultural appropriateness and interest level for 15-year-olds, as judged by participating countries. Another essential criterion for selection of the set of material as a whole was its fit to the framework described in the previous section, in order to maintain the balance across various categories of text, aspect and situation. Finally, it was ensured that the set of questions covered a range of difficulty, allowing for good measurement and a description of the *reading literacy* of all 15-year-old students, from the least proficient to the highly able.

Over 130 print reading questions were used in PISA 2009, but each student in the sample only saw a proportion of the total pool because different sets of questions were given to different students. The reading questions selected for inclusion in PISA 2009 were organised into half-hour clusters. These, along with clusters of mathematics and science questions, were assembled into booklets containing four clusters each. Each participating student was then given a two-hour assessment. As reading was the focus of the PISA 2009 assessment, every booklet included at least one cluster of reading material. The clusters were rotated so that each cluster appeared in each of the four possible positions in the booklets, and each pair of clusters appeared in at least 1 of the 13 booklets that were used in each country.

This design, similar to those used in previous PISA assessments, makes it possible to construct a single scale of reading proficiency, in which each question is associated with a particular point on the scale that indicates its difficulty, and each student's performance is associated with a particular point on the same scale that indicates his or her estimated proficiency. A description of the modelling technique used to construct this scale can be found in *PISA 2009 Technical Report* (OECD, forthcoming).

The relative difficulty of tasks in a test is estimated by considering the proportion of test takers who answer each question correctly. The relative proficiency of students taking a particular test can be estimated by considering the proportion of test questions they answer correctly. A single continuous scale shows the relationship between the difficulty of questions and the proficiency of students. By constructing a scale that shows the difficulty of each question, it is possible to locate the level of *reading literacy* that the question represents. By showing the proficiency of each student on the same scale, it is possible to describe the level of *reading literacy* that the student possesses.

The location of student proficiency on this scale is set in relation to the particular group of questions used in the assessment, but just as the sample of students taking PISA in 2009 is drawn to represent all the 15-year-olds in the participating countries, so the individual questions used in the assessment are designed to represent the definition of *reading literacy* adequately. Estimates of student proficiency reflect the kinds of tasks they would be expected to perform successfully. This means that students are likely to be able to complete questions successfully at or below the difficulty level associated with their own position on the scale (but they may not always do so). Conversely, they are unlikely to be able to complete questions above the difficulty level associated with their position on the scale successfully (but they may sometimes do so). Figure I.2.11 illustrates how this probabilistic model works.

■ Figure I.2.11 ■
Relationship between questions and students on a proficiency scale

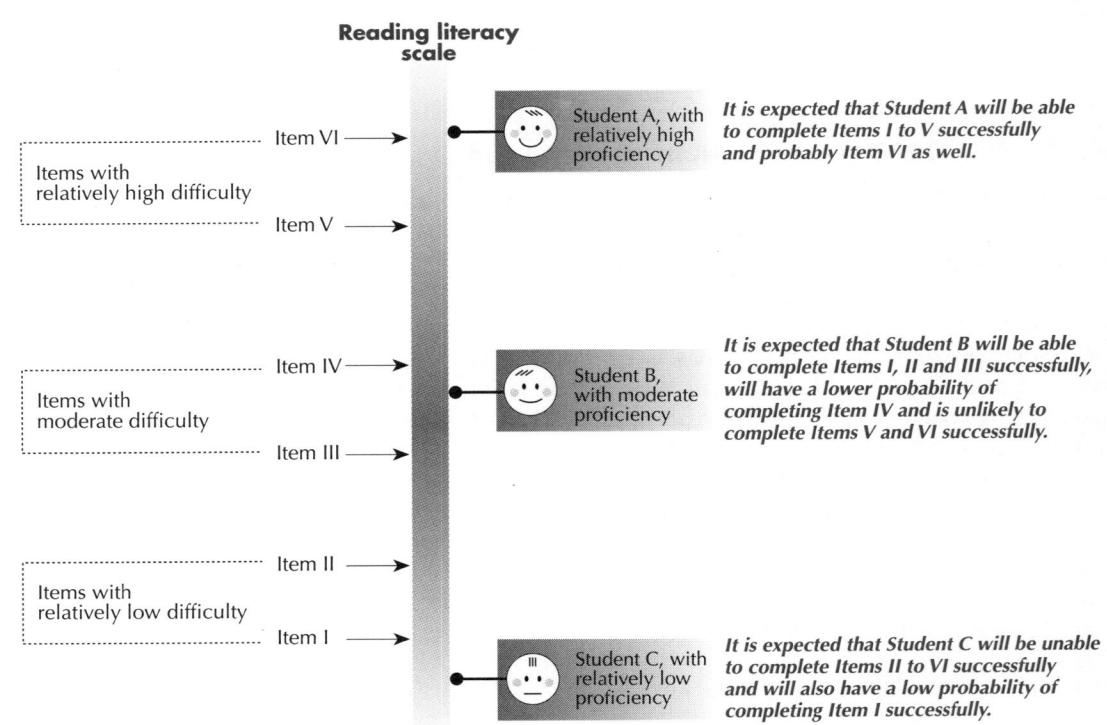

The further a student's proficiency is located above a given question, the more likely he or she is to complete the question (and other questions of similar difficulty) successfully; the further the student's proficiency is located below a given question, the lower the probability that the student will be able to complete the question, and other similarly difficult questions successfully.

How reading proficiency levels are defined in PISA 2009

PISA 2009 provides an overall reading literacy scale for reading texts, drawing on all the questions in the reading assessment, as well as scales for three aspects and two text formats.[15] The metric for the overall reading scale is based on a mean for OECD countries set at 500 in PISA 2000, with a standard deviation of 100. To help in interpreting what students' scores mean in substantive terms, the scale is divided into levels, based on a set of statistical principles. Descriptions are then generated, based on the tasks that are located within each level, to describe the kinds of skills and knowledge needed to complete them successfully.

For PISA 2009, the range of difficulty of tasks allows for the description of seven levels of reading proficiency: Level 1b is the lowest described level, then Level 1a, Level 2, Level 3 and so on up to Level 6.

■ Figure I.2.12 ■
Summary descriptions for the seven levels of proficiency in reading

Level	Lower score limit	Percentage of students able to perform tasks at each level or above (OECD average)	Characteristics of tasks
6	698	0.8% of students across the OECD can perform tasks at Level 6 on the reading scale	Tasks at this level typically require the reader to make multiple inferences, comparisons and contrasts that are both detailed and precise. They require demonstration of a full and detailed understanding of one or more texts and may involve integrating information from more than one text. Tasks may require the reader to deal with unfamiliar ideas, in the presence of prominent competing information, and to generate abstract categories for interpretations. *Reflect and evaluate* tasks may require the reader to hypothesise about or critically evaluate a complex text on an unfamiliar topic, taking into account multiple criteria or perspectives, and applying sophisticated understandings from beyond the text. A salient condition for *access and retrieve* tasks at this level is precision of analysis and fine attention to detail that is inconspicuous in the texts.
5	626	7.6% of students across the OECD can perform tasks at least at Level 5 on the reading scale	Tasks at this level that involve retrieving information require the reader to locate and organise several pieces of deeply embedded information, inferring which information in the text is relevant. Reflective tasks require critical evaluation or hypothesis, drawing on specialised knowledge. Both interpretative and reflective tasks require a full and detailed understanding of a text whose content or form is unfamiliar. For all aspects of reading, tasks at this level typically involve dealing with concepts that are contrary to expectations.
4	553	28.3% of students across the OECD can perform tasks at least at Level 4 on the reading scale	Tasks at this level that involve retrieving information require the reader to locate and organise several pieces of embedded information. Some tasks at this level require interpreting the meaning of nuances of language in a section of text by taking into account the text as a whole. Other interpretative tasks require understanding and applying categories in an unfamiliar context. Reflective tasks at this level require readers to use formal or public knowledge to hypothesise about or critically evaluate a text. Readers must demonstrate an accurate understanding of long or complex texts whose content or form may be unfamiliar.
3	480	57.2% of students across the OECD can perform tasks at least at Level 3 on the reading scale	Tasks at this level require the reader to locate, and in some cases recognise the relationship between, several pieces of information that must meet multiple conditions. Interpretative tasks at this level require the reader to integrate several parts of a text in order to identify a main idea, understand a relationship or construe the meaning of a word or phrase. They need to take into account many features in comparing, contrasting or categorising. Often the required information is not prominent or there is much competing information; or there are other obstacles in the text, such as ideas that are contrary to expectation or negatively worded. Reflective tasks at this level may require connections, comparisons, and explanations, or they may require the reader to evaluate a feature of the text. Some reflective tasks require readers to demonstrate a fine understanding of the text in relation to familiar, everyday knowledge. Other tasks do not require detailed text comprehension but require the reader to draw on less common knowledge.
2	407	81.2% of students across the OECD can perform tasks at least at Level 2 on the reading scale	Some tasks at this level require the reader to locate one or more pieces of information, which may need to be inferred and may need to meet several conditions. Others require recognising the main idea in a text, understanding relationships, or construing meaning within a limited part of the text when the information is not prominent and the reader must make low level inferences. Tasks at this level may involve comparisons or contrasts based on a single feature in the text. Typical reflective tasks at this level require readers to make a comparison or several connections between the text and outside knowledge, by drawing on personal experience and attitudes.
1a	335	94.3% of students across the OECD can perform tasks at least at Level 1a on the reading scale	Tasks at this level require the reader: to locate one or more independent pieces of explicitly stated information; to recognise the main theme or author's purpose in a text about a familiar topic; or to make a simple connection between information in the text and common, everyday knowledge. Typically the required information in the text is prominent and there is little, if any, competing information. The reader is explicitly directed to consider relevant factors in the task and in the text.
1b	262	98.9% of students across the OECD can perform tasks at least at Level 1b on the reading scale	Tasks at this level require the reader to locate a single piece of explicitly stated information in a prominent position in a short, syntactically simple text with a familiar context and text type, such as a narrative or a simple list. The text typically provides support to the reader, such as repetition of information, pictures or familiar symbols. There is minimal competing information. In tasks requiring interpretation the reader may need to make simple connections between adjacent pieces of information.

Students with a proficiency within the range of Level 1b are likely to be able to complete Level 1b tasks successfully, but are unlikely to be able to complete tasks at higher levels. Level 6 reflects tasks that present the greatest challenge in terms of reading skills and knowledge. Students with scores in this range are likely to be able to complete successfully reading tasks located at that level, as well as all the other reading tasks in PISA.

PISA applies a standard methodology for constructing proficiency scales. Based on a student's performance on the tasks in the test, his or her score is generated and located in a specific part of the scale, thus allowing the score to be associated with a defined proficiency level. The level at which the student's score is located is the highest level for which he or she would be expected to answer correctly most of a random selection of questions within the same level. Thus, for example, in an assessment composed of tasks spread uniformly across Level 3, students with a score located within Level 3 would be expected to complete at least 50% of the tasks successfully. Because a level covers a range of difficulty and proficiency, success rates across the band vary. Students near the bottom of the level would be likely to succeed on just over 50% of the tasks spread uniformly across the level, while students at the top of the level would be likely to succeed on well over 70% of the same tasks.

Figure I.2.12 provides details of the nature of the reading skills, knowledge and understanding required at each level of the reading scale.

A profile of PISA reading questions

For an assessment such as PISA, which is conducted every three years, it is necessary to retain a sufficient number of questions from successive surveys to establish reliable trends. Other questions are publicly released after the survey to illustrate the ways in which performance was measured. At the end of this chapter, a selection of the released questions for the 2009 reading assessment is presented to illustrate the framework characteristics and the levels of proficiency described in this volume.

■ Figure I.2.13 ■

Map of selected reading questions in PISA 2009, illustrating the proficiency levels

Level	Lower score limit	Questions
6		*THE PLAY'S THE THING* – Question 3 (730)
	698	
5	626	
4		*MOBILE PHONE SAFETY* – Question 11 (604)
		BALLOON – Question 3.2 (595)
		MOBILE PHONE SAFETY – Question 2 (561)
	553	*THE PLAY'S THE THING* – Question 7 (556)
3		*MISER* – Question 5 (548)
		TELECOMMUTING – Question 1 (537)
		MOBILE PHONE SAFETY – Question 6 (526)
		TELECOMMUTING – Question 7 (514)
		BALLOON – Question 4 (510)
	480	*MOBILE PHONE SAFETY* – Question 9 (488)
2		*THE PLAY'S THE THING* – Question 4 (474)
		BALLOON – Question 3.1 (449)
		BLOOD DONATION NOTICE – Question 8 (438)
	407	*BALLOON* – Question 6 (411)
1a		*BRUSHING YOUR TEETH* – Question 4 (399)
		MISER – Question 1 (373)
		BALLOON – Question 8 (370)
		BLOOD DONATION NOTICE – Question 9 (368)
		BRUSHING YOUR TEETH – Question 2 (358)
	335	*BRUSHING YOUR TEETH* – Question 1 (353)
1b		*MISER* – Question 7 (310)
	262	*BRUSHING YOUR TEETH* – Question 3 (285)

Note: Numbers in brackets refer to the difficulty of the question. Decimal points indicate questions that have a partial credit score (.1) and a full credit score (.2).

Figure I.2.13 shows a map of these questions in relation to their position on the described proficiency scale. The first column shows the proficiency level within which the task is located. The second column indicates the lowest scale score for a task, in terms of its difficulty, that would allow it to be regarded as falling within that level. The last column shows the name of the unit and the task number. It will be noticed that tasks within the same unit can represent a range of difficulties: *THE PLAY'S THE THING*, for example, comprises questions at Levels 2, 4 and 6. Thus a single unit may cover a broad section of the PISA reading difficulty range.

What students can do in reading

PISA summarises student performance on a reading scale that provides an overall picture of students' accumulated reading skills, knowledge and understanding at age 15. Results for this overall reading performance measure are presented below, covering both the average level of reading performance in each country and the distribution of reading proficiency. Detailed results for the different aspects and text formats are presented in subsequent sections.

Students reaching the different levels of proficiency

This section describes performance in terms of the seven levels of reading proficiency that have been constructed for reporting reading in PISA 2009. Beyond Level 5, which was the highest described level of proficiency in previous PISA reading assessments, a new Level 6 has been added to describe very high levels of reading proficiency. The previous bottom level of measured proficiency, Level 1, has been relabelled as Level 1a. A new level, Level 1b, describes students who would previously have been rated as "below Level 1", but who show proficiency in relation to a new set of tasks that is easier than those included in previous PISA assessments. These changes allow countries to know more about what kinds of tasks students with very high and very low reading proficiency are capable of. Apart from the additional levels, the meaning of being proficient at reading Levels 2, 3, 4 and 5 remains the same in PISA 2009 as in previous surveys.

The distribution of student performance across these proficiency levels is shown in Figure I.2.14. Results are presented in terms of the percentage of 15-year-olds within each country reaching the seven proficiency levels described in Figure I.2.12. Table I.2.1 provides figures for the percentage of students at each proficiency level on the reading scale with standard errors.

Proficiency at Level 6 (scores higher than 698 points)

Students proficient at Level 6 on the reading scale are highly-skilled readers. They are capable of conducting fine-grained analysis of texts, which requires detailed comprehension of both explicit information and unstated implications; and capable of reflecting on and evaluating what they read at a more general level. Since students with scale scores at this level have successfully completed almost all of the tasks presented to them in the reading assessment, they have demonstrated that they are capable of dealing with many different types of reading material: they are by implication diversified readers who can assimilate information from unfamiliar content areas presented in atypical formats, as well as being able to engage with more familiar content with typical structures and text features. Another characteristic of the most highly developed readers, as defined by PISA, is also that they can overcome preconceptions in the face of new information, even when that information is contrary to expectations. They are capable of recognising what is provided in a text, both conspicuously and more subtly, while at the same time being able to apply a critical perspective to it, drawing on sophisticated understandings from beyond the text. This combination of a capacity to absorb the new and to evaluate it is greatly valued in knowledge economies, which depend on innovation and nuanced decision making that draw on all the available evidence. The proportion of a population performing at this very high level in reading is therefore of particular interest.

Across OECD countries, less than 1% of students (0.8%) perform at this level, but there is variation among countries. Seven countries have a significantly higher percentage of students performing at Level 6 – more than twice the average: the OECD countries New Zealand, Australia, Japan, Canada and Finland, as well as the partner countries and economies Singapore and Shanghai-China. Three of these are Asian countries and three are English-speaking OECD countries. While in these countries the majority of students perform relatively well, with less than 5% of the students performing below Level 1a, two of these countries show rather wide distributions – Japan and New Zealand – and two have very small spreads of student performance – Finland and Shanghai-China. Israel, which has a mean score well below the average at 474, shows an above-average of 1% of its students (OECD average of 0.8%) performing at Level 6 as well as an above-average 12% of its students (OECD average of 6%) not being proficient above Level 1b. In contrast, some countries with relatively high overall performance did not have a strong representation of students at the highest level of reading proficiency. Among these is Korea, with a mean score of 539, the highest of any OECD country, but with only a just above-average percentage of students reaching Level 6 (1%).

■ Figure I. 2.14 ■
How proficient are students in reading?
Percentage of students at the different levels of reading proficiency

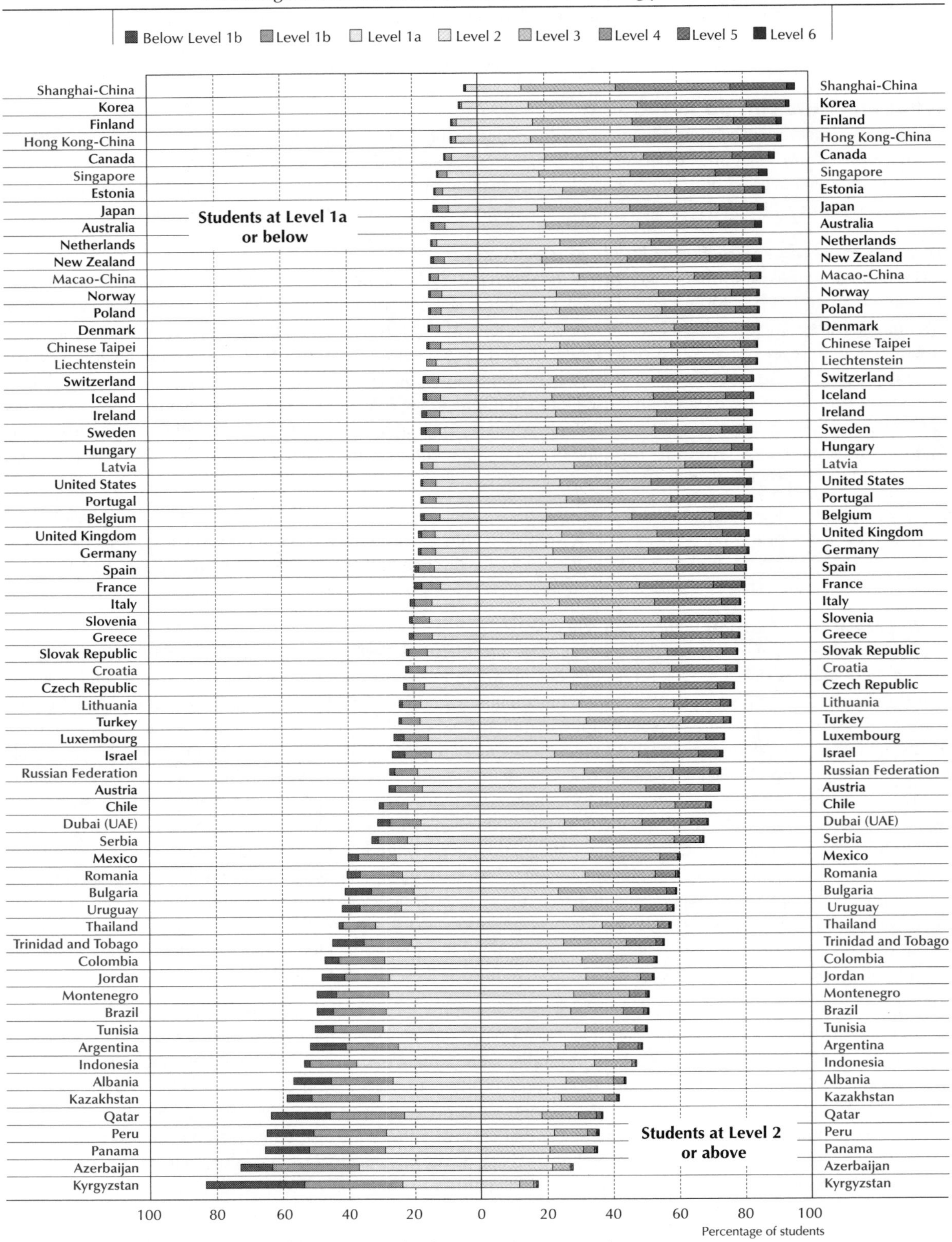

■ Below Level 1b ■ Level 1b □ Level 1a □ Level 2 ■ Level 3 ■ Level 4 ■ Level 5 ■ Level 6

Shanghai-China
Korea
Finland
Hong Kong-China
Canada
Singapore
Estonia
Japan
Australia
Netherlands
New Zealand
Macao-China
Norway
Poland
Denmark
Chinese Taipei
Liechtenstein
Switzerland
Iceland
Ireland
Sweden
Hungary
Latvia
United States
Portugal
Belgium
United Kingdom
Germany
Spain
France
Italy
Slovenia
Greece
Slovak Republic
Croatia
Czech Republic
Lithuania
Turkey
Luxembourg
Israel
Russian Federation
Austria
Chile
Dubai (UAE)
Serbia
Mexico
Romania
Bulgaria
Uruguay
Thailand
Trinidad and Tobago
Colombia
Jordan
Montenegro
Brazil
Tunisia
Argentina
Indonesia
Albania
Kazakhstan
Qatar
Peru
Panama
Azerbaijan
Kyrgyzstan

Students at Level 1a or below

Students at Level 2 or above

100 80 60 40 20 0 20 40 60 80 100

Percentage of students

Countries are ranked in descending order of the percentage of students at Levels 2, 3, 4, 5 and 6.
Source: OECD, *PISA 2009 Database,* Table I.2.1.

StatLink ᴍ⃰ᴤᴾ⃰ http://dx.doi.org/10.1787/888932343133

The very small percentage of students performing at Level 6 illustrates that the PISA scale is capable of distinguishing reading proficiency up to the highest level of excellence that 15-year-olds are capable of attaining. Indeed, this level of proficiency is currently quite aspirational for many: in 18 partner countries and economies less than one-tenth of one per cent of the 15-year-old population performs at this top level.

Proficiency at Level 5 (scores higher than 626 but lower than or equal to 698 points)

Students proficient at Level 5 on the reading literacy scale can handle texts that are unfamiliar in either form or content. They can find information in such texts, demonstrate detailed understanding, and infer which information is relevant to the task. They are also able to critically evaluate such texts and build hypotheses about them, drawing on specialised knowledge and accommodating concepts that may be contrary to expectations. An inspection of the kinds of tasks students at Level 5 are capable of suggests that those who get to this level can be regarded as potential "world class" knowledge workers of tomorrow, making the proportion of a country's students reaching this level relevant for its future economic competitiveness.

Since students proficient at Level 6 can also do Level 5 tasks, the following descriptions use "proficient at Level 5" to mean those whose highest level of performance is either Level 5 or 6. The same terminology is used to refer to the cumulative proportions at lower levels. Students performing at Level 5 or 6 are frequently referred to as "top performers" in this report.

Across OECD countries, 8% of PISA 2009 students are proficient at Level 5 or higher. One country, Shanghai-China, has well over twice the average capable of Level 5 tasks (19% of students). Several other countries had percentages above 12% of students at Level 5 or above: the OECD countries New Zealand, Finland, Japan, Korea, Australia, Canada as well as the partner countries and economies Singapore and Hong Kong-China. All of these countries also perform well in terms of mean proficiency. Conversely, countries with lower average performance also tend to be those with the lowest percentages of students capable of succeeding with Level 5 reading tasks. All of the countries with less than half of one per cent of students performing at Level 5 (the OECD country Mexico as well as the partner countries Azerbaijan, Indonesia, Kyrgyzstan, Albania, Tunisia, Jordan, Thailand, Kazakhstan and Peru) have a mean performance below 407, the cut-score between Levels 1a and 2, with the exception of Mexico and Thailand.

Proficiency at Level 4 (scores higher than 553 but lower than or equal to 626 points)

Students proficient at Level 4 on the reading literacy scale are capable of difficult reading tasks, such as locating embedded information, construing meaning from nuances of language and critically evaluating a text. Tasks at this level that involve retrieving information require students to locate and organise several pieces of embedded information and some tasks require interpreting the meaning of nuances of language in a section of text by taking into account the text as a whole. Other interpretative tasks require understanding and applying categories in an unfamiliar context. Reflective tasks at this level require readers to use formal or public knowledge to hypothesise about or critically evaluate a text. Readers must demonstrate an accurate understanding of long or complex texts whose content or form may be unfamiliar.

Across OECD countries, 28% of PISA 2009 students are proficient at Level 4 or higher. A ranking of countries by the percentage of students performing at Levels 4 and above generally matches the ranking of countries by mean performance, but there are a number of exceptions. Taking into account its mean performance (496), France, for example, has a disproportionately high percentage of students performing at these levels (32%), despite having a mean score not statistically different from the OECD average, while in Denmark, with a similar average to France, the proportion is 26%. Nineteen countries have less than 10% of their population performing at Level 4.

Proficiency at Level 3 (scores higher than 480 but lower than or equal to 553 points)

Students proficient at Level 3 on the reading literacy scale are capable of reading tasks of moderate complexity, such as locating multiple pieces of information, making links between different parts of a text, and relating it to familiar everyday knowledge. Tasks at this level require students to locate, and in some cases recognise the relationship between, several pieces of information that must meet multiple conditions. Interpretative tasks at this level require students to integrate several parts of a text in order to identify a main idea, understand a relationship or construe the meaning of a word or phrase. They need to take into account many features in comparing, contrasting or categorising. Often the required information is not prominent or there is much competing information; or there are other challenges in the text, such as ideas that are contrary to expectation or negatively worded. Reflective tasks at this level may require connections, comparisons, and explanations, or they may require students to evaluate a

feature of the text. Some reflective tasks require readers to demonstrate a fine understanding of the text in relation to familiar, everyday knowledge. Other tasks do not require detailed text comprehension but require the reader to draw on less common knowledge from outside of the text.

Across OECD countries, the majority (57%) of 15-year-old students are proficient at Level 3 or higher. For half of these students (29% of the total), this is the highest level reached, making Level 3 the most common level of highest performance for students across OECD countries. In four countries and economies – Shanghai-China, Korea, Hong Kong-China and Finland – over three quarters of the students can do tasks at least at Level 3. On the other hand, this degree of proficiency is demonstrated by fewer than half of the students in 30 countries, including the OECD countries Luxembourg, the Czech Republic, Austria, Turkey, Chile and Mexico.

Proficiency at Level 2 (scores higher than 407 but lower than or equal to 480 points)

Students proficient at Level 2 on the reading literacy scale are capable of tasks such as locating information that meets several conditions, making comparisons or contrasts around a single feature, working out what a well-defined part of a text means even when the information is not prominent, and making connections between the text and personal experience. Some tasks at this level require students to locate one or more pieces of information, which may need to be inferred and may need to meet several conditions. Others require recognising the main idea in a text, understanding relationships, or construing meaning within a limited part of the text when the information is not prominent and the reader must make low level inferences. Tasks at this level may involve comparisons or contrasts based on a single feature in the text. Typical reflective tasks at this level require students to make a comparison or several connections between the text and outside knowledge, by drawing on personal experience and attitudes.

Level 2 can be considered a baseline level of proficiency, at which students begin to demonstrate the reading literacy competencies that will enable them to participate effectively and productively in life. The follow-up of students who were assessed by PISA in 2000 as part of the Canadian Youth in Transition Survey has shown that students scoring below Level 2 face a disproportionately higher risk of poor post-secondary participation or low labour-market outcomes at age 19, and even more so at age 21, the latest age for which data from this longitudinal study are currently available.[16] For example, of students who performed below Level 2 in PISA reading in 2000, over 60% had not gone on to any post-school education by the age of 21; by contrast, more than half of the students (55%) who had performed at Level 2 as their highest level were at college or university.

Across OECD countries, more than four in five students (81%) are proficient at Level 2 or higher. In Shanghai-China and Korea, only small proportions of students, 4% and 6% respectively, are not proficient at Level 2. At the other extreme, in ten partner countries only a minority could perform at this level. In 18 participating countries and economies, Level 2 was the most common highest level of proficiency for students, including some OECD countries: Mexico and Chile with 33%, and Turkey with 32%. Other countries for which Level 2 had the highest percentage of students included three Latin American countries (Colombia, Uruguay and Argentina) and three Eastern European countries (Romania, the Russian Federation and Bulgaria).

Proficiency at Level 1a (scores higher than 335 but lower than or equal to 407 points)

Students proficient at Level 1a on the reading literacy scale are capable of locating pieces of explicitly stated information that are rather prominent in the text, recognising a main idea in a text about a familiar topic, and recognising the connection between information in such a text and their everyday experience. Tasks at this level require students to locate one or more independent pieces of explicitly stated information, recognise the main theme or author's purpose in a text about a familiar topic, or make a simple connection between information in the text and common, everyday knowledge. Typically the required information in the text is prominent and there is little, if any, competing information. Students are explicitly directed to consider relevant factors in the task and in the text.

Across OECD countries, the great majority of 15-year-old students (94%) are proficient at Level 1a or higher. However, in the five partner countries, Azerbaijan, Peru, Panama, Qatar and Kyrgyzstan, more than one in three students do not reach this level. This does not mean that they are illiterate, but it does mean that they do not display even the very limited range of reading skills needed for Level 1a tasks. Moreover, in a number of partner countries including Indonesia, Azerbaijan, Kazakhstan, Panama, Peru, Brazil, Albania and Qatar, Level 1a is the most common highest level of proficiency.

Proficiency at Level 1b (scores higher than 262 but lower than or equal to 335 points) and below Level 1b (scores lower than or equal 262 points)

Students proficient at Level 1b on the reading literacy scale can find explicitly stated information in short, simple texts with a familiar style and content. They can make low-level inferences such as recognising a causal connection across two sentences even when it is not stated. Tasks at this level require students to locate a single piece of explicitly stated information in a prominent position in a short, syntactically simple text with a familiar context and text type, such as a narrative or a simple list. The text typically provides support to the reader, such as repetition of information, pictures or familiar symbols. There is minimal competing information. In tasks requiring interpretation students may need to make simple connections between adjacent pieces of information.

A small percentage of students across OECD countries – 1.1% – has scores below 262 points on the PISA scale. These students are therefore judged to have performed below Level 1b. This does not mean that they are necessarily completely illiterate, but there is insufficient information on which to base a description of their reading proficiency: only two tasks were used in PISA 2009 whose difficulty matched the proficiency of students below Level 1b – too few tasks on which to base any generalisations about what students performing at this level can do as readers.

The fact that just one in a hundred students across OECD countries cannot perform tasks at Level 1b demonstrates that the PISA reading scale is now able to describe accurately the performance of almost all students. Looked at in another way, 6% of students do not reach Level 1a, and the addition of Level 1b identifies reading tasks that five out of six members of this group can do. Even in the lowest performing countries, with the exception of Kyrgyzstan, this is true of at least half of students who perform below Level 1a. This improved capacity of PISA to describe reading skills at a very low level complements its improved ability to describe very high reading skills, at Level 6.

All countries have some students performing at Level 1b, and every country except Liechtenstein has some proportion – though in some cases, a small one – of students performing below Level 1b. However, in Kyrgyzstan, 59% of students perform below Level 1a, half of them below Level 1b. In four other countries, more than one third of students perform at or below Level 1b: Qatar, Panama, Peru and Azerbaijan. Clearly, finding ways to increase the general population's literacy level in these countries is vital for their development.

Inequality of learning outcomes

Looking at the distribution of performance for each country across the proficiency levels, it becomes apparent that there is wide variation, regardless of average proficiency. A lot of the narrowest gaps between high and low performers are found in Asia as in Korea and in the partner countries and economies Indonesia, Thailand, Macao-China, Shanghai-China and Hong Kong-China. Estonia, Turkey and Chile, as well as the partner countries Azerbaijan, Latvia and Serbia, are also the countries with comparatively narrow gaps between high and low performers. For each of these countries, the gap between the top quarter and the bottom quarter of students in reading performance is at least 15 points less than the average gap, and the gap for all of these countries is also substantially narrower than the average when comparing performance of the bottom 10% and the top 10% of students (see Table I.2.3). The narrow distribution does not appear to be associated with the overall level of performance. For example, one of the top performing OECD countries, Korea, has one of the narrowest distributions of ability, as does Chile, a country performing well below the OECD average.

Countries exhibiting the widest distribution of performance in reading are the OECD countries Israel, Belgium, Austria, New Zealand, Luxembourg and France, as well as the partner countries and economies Qatar, Bulgaria, Trinidad and Tobago, Dubai (UAE) and Argentina, all of which have a gap of at least 15 points between their top quarter and bottom quarter of students wider than the average gap. The difference in performance between the top and bottom quarters in these countries is in the order of, or more than, two full proficiency levels.

As with those countries with a comparatively narrow distribution of student performance, the group of countries with a wide performance range is heterogeneous in mean proficiency in reading, with New Zealand (27 points above the average) and Qatar (122 points below the average) representing the extremes. Possible explanations for the wide variation in proficiency in Belgium, Austria, New Zealand and Luxembourg are the existence of an academically tracked school system (Austria and Belgium) and/or of different ethnic/language groups within the country associated with disparate socio-economic status (Luxembourg and New Zealand). Volume II, *Overcoming Social Background*, and Volume IV, *What Makes a School Successful?*, examine in detail important factors underlying the performance distribution among countries.

■ Figure I.2.15 ■

Comparing countries' performance in reading

	Statistically significantly **above** the OECD average
	Not statistically significantly different from the OECD average
	Statistically significantly **below** the OECD average

Mean	Comparison country	Countries whose mean score is NOT statistically significantly different from that of the comparison country
556	Shanghai-China	
539	Korea	Finland, Hong Kong-China
536	Finland	Korea, Hong Kong-China
533	Hong Kong-China	Korea, Finland
526	Singapore	Canada, New Zealand, Japan
524	Canada	Singapore, New Zealand, Japan
521	New Zealand	Singapore, Canada, Japan, Australia
520	Japan	Singapore, Canada, New Zealand, Australia, Netherlands
515	Australia	New Zealand, Japan, Netherlands
508	Netherlands	Japan, Australia, Belgium, Norway, Estonia, Switzerland, Poland, Iceland, United States, Liechtenstein, Sweden, Germany
506	Belgium	Netherlands, Norway, Estonia, Switzerland, Poland, United States, Liechtenstein
503	Norway	Netherlands, Belgium, Estonia, Switzerland, Poland, Iceland, United States, Liechtenstein, Sweden, Germany, Ireland, France
501	Estonia	Netherlands, Belgium, Norway, Switzerland, Poland, Iceland, United States, Liechtenstein, Sweden, Germany, Ireland, France, Chinese Taipei, Denmark, United Kingdom, Hungary
501	Switzerland	Netherlands, Belgium, Norway, Estonia, Poland, Iceland, United States, Liechtenstein, Sweden, Germany, Ireland, France, Chinese Taipei, Denmark, United Kingdom, Hungary
500	Poland	Netherlands, Belgium, Norway, Estonia, Switzerland, Iceland, United States, Liechtenstein, Sweden, Germany, Ireland, France, Chinese Taipei, Denmark, United Kingdom, Hungary
500	Iceland	Netherlands, Norway, Estonia, Switzerland, Poland, United States, Liechtenstein, Sweden, Germany, Ireland, France, Chinese Taipei, Hungary
500	United States	Netherlands, Belgium, Norway, Estonia, Switzerland, Poland, Iceland, Liechtenstein, Sweden, Germany, Ireland, France, Chinese Taipei, Denmark, United Kingdom, Hungary
499	Liechtenstein	Netherlands, Belgium, Norway, Estonia, Switzerland, Poland, Iceland, United States, Sweden, Germany, Ireland, France, Chinese Taipei, Denmark, United Kingdom, Hungary
497	Sweden	Netherlands, Norway, Estonia, Switzerland, Poland, Iceland, United States, Liechtenstein, Germany, Ireland, France, Chinese Taipei, Denmark, United Kingdom, Hungary, Portugal
497	Germany	Netherlands, Norway, Estonia, Switzerland, Poland, Iceland, United States, Liechtenstein, Sweden, Ireland, France, Chinese Taipei, Denmark, United Kingdom, Hungary
496	Ireland	Norway, Estonia, Switzerland, Poland, Iceland, United States, Liechtenstein, Sweden, Germany, France, Chinese Taipei, Denmark, United Kingdom, Hungary, Portugal
496	France	Norway, Estonia, Switzerland, Poland, Iceland, United States, Liechtenstein, Sweden, Germany, Ireland, Chinese Taipei, Denmark, United Kingdom, Hungary, Portugal
495	Chinese Taipei	Estonia, Switzerland, Poland, Iceland, United States, Liechtenstein, Sweden, Germany, Ireland, France, Denmark, United Kingdom, Hungary, Portugal
495	Denmark	Estonia, Switzerland, Poland, United States, Liechtenstein, Sweden, Germany, Ireland, France, Chinese Taipei, United Kingdom, Hungary, Portugal
494	United Kingdom	Estonia, Switzerland, Poland, United States, Liechtenstein, Sweden, Germany, Ireland, France, Chinese Taipei, Denmark, Hungary, Portugal
494	Hungary	Estonia, Switzerland, Poland, Iceland, United States, Liechtenstein, Sweden, Germany, Ireland, France, Chinese Taipei, Denmark, United Kingdom, Portugal
489	Portugal	Sweden, Ireland, France, Chinese Taipei, Denmark, United Kingdom, Hungary, Macao-China, Italy, Latvia, Slovenia, Greece
487	Macao-China	Portugal, Italy, Latvia, Greece
486	Italy	Portugal, Macao-China, Latvia, Slovenia, Greece, Spain
484	Latvia	Portugal, Macao-China, Italy, Slovenia, Greece, Spain, Czech Republic, Slovak Republic
483	Slovenia	Portugal, Italy, Latvia, Greece, Spain, Czech Republic
483	Greece	Portugal, Macao-China, Italy, Latvia, Slovenia, Spain, Czech Republic, Slovak Republic, Croatia, Israel
481	Spain	Italy, Latvia, Slovenia, Greece, Czech Republic, Slovak Republic, Croatia, Israel
478	Czech Republic	Latvia, Slovenia, Greece, Spain, Slovak Republic, Croatia, Israel, Luxembourg, Austria
477	Slovak Republic	Latvia, Greece, Spain, Czech Republic, Croatia, Israel, Luxembourg
476	Croatia	Greece, Spain, Czech Republic, Slovak Republic, Israel, Luxembourg, Austria, Lithuania
474	Israel	Greece, Spain, Czech Republic, Slovak Republic, Croatia, Luxembourg, Austria, Lithuania, Turkey
472	Luxembourg	Czech Republic, Slovak Republic, Croatia, Israel, Austria, Lithuania
470	Austria	Czech Republic, Slovak Republic, Croatia, Israel, Luxembourg, Lithuania, Turkey
468	Lithuania	Croatia, Israel, Luxembourg, Austria, Turkey
464	Turkey	Israel, Austria, Lithuania, Dubai (UAE), Russian Federation
459	Dubai (UAE)	Turkey, Russian Federation
459	Russian Federation	Turkey, Dubai (UAE)
449	Chile	Serbia
442	Serbia	Chile, Bulgaria
429	Bulgaria	Serbia, Uruguay, Mexico, Romania, Thailand, Trinidad and Tobago
426	Uruguay	Bulgaria, Mexico, Romania, Thailand
425	Mexico	Bulgaria, Uruguay, Romania, Thailand
424	Romania	Bulgaria, Uruguay, Mexico, Thailand, Trinidad and Tobago
421	Thailand	Bulgaria, Uruguay, Mexico, Romania, Trinidad and Tobago, Colombia
416	Trinidad and Tobago	Bulgaria, Romania, Thailand, Colombia, Brazil
413	Colombia	Thailand, Trinidad and Tobago, Brazil, Montenegro, Jordan
412	Brazil	Trinidad and Tobago, Colombia, Montenegro, Jordan
408	Montenegro	Colombia, Brazil, Jordan, Tunisia, Indonesia, Argentina
405	Jordan	Colombia, Brazil, Montenegro, Tunisia, Indonesia, Argentina
404	Tunisia	Montenegro, Jordan, Indonesia, Argentina
402	Indonesia	Montenegro, Jordan, Tunisia, Argentina
398	Argentina	Montenegro, Jordan, Tunisia, Indonesia, Kazakhstan
390	Kazakhstan	Argentina, Albania
385	Albania	Kazakhstan, Panama
372	Qatar	Panama, Peru
371	Panama	Albania, Qatar, Peru, Azerbaijan
370	Peru	Qatar, Panama, Azerbaijan
362	Azerbaijan	Panama, Peru
314	Kyrgyzstan	

Source: OECD, *PISA 2009 Database*.
StatLink ⏷ http://dx.doi.org/10.1787/888932343133

Average level of proficiency

The discussion in the previous section focuses on describing countries' performance at each of the defined proficiency levels. Another way of summarising the difference in performance between countries is to consider their mean performance, both relative to each other and to the OECD mean. For PISA 2009, the OECD mean is 493, with a standard deviation of 93. This establishes the benchmark against which each country's reading performance in PISA 2009 is compared.

Figure I.2.15 shows each country's mean score, and allows readers to see for which pairs of countries the differences between the means shown are statistically similar. For each country shown on the left in the middle column, the list of countries on the right hand column shows countries whose mean scores are not sufficiently different to be distinguished with confidence.[17] For all other cases, one country has a higher performance than another if it is above it in the list in the middle column, and a lower performance if it is below. For example, while Shanghai-China clearly ranks first, the performance of Korea, which comes second on the list, cannot be distinguished with confidence from Finland and Hong Kong-China, which come third and fourth respectively.

Korea and Finland are the highest-performing OECD countries, with mean scores of 539 and 536 points, respectively. The partner economy Shanghai-China is outperforming these two countries by a significant margin, with a mean score of 556. An additional group of OECD countries and partner countries and economies perform around a quarter of a standard deviation or more above the OECD mean: Hong Kong-China (with a mean of 533), Singapore (526), Canada (524), New Zealand (521) and Japan (520). Australia is not far behind with a mean score of 515. The next seven OECD countries and one partner economy have mean scores that can be confidently judged as significantly above the OECD mean: the Netherlands (508), Belgium (506), Norway (503), Estonia (501), Switzerland (501), Poland (500), Iceland (500) and Liechtenstein (499). Nine other OECD countries perform at a level not significantly different from the OECD mean: the United States, Sweden, Germany, Ireland, France, Denmark, the United Kingdom, Hungary and Portugal. One partner economy, Chinese Taipei, is also in this category.

In comparing mean reading performance across countries, there are clear and substantial disparities. The lowest performing OECD country, Mexico, has an average score of 425 points. This means that the gap between the highest and lowest performing OECD countries is 114 points – well over one standard deviation or the equivalent of almost three school years, on average across countries. However, the gap between the partner countries/economies is even larger, with 242 score points – over two and a half standard deviations or the equivalent of more than 6 school years – separating the mean performance of Shanghai-China (556) and Kyrgyzstan (314).

Because the figures are derived from samples, it is not possible to determine a precise rank of a country's performance among the participating countries. It is possible, however, to determine, with confidence, a range of ranks in which the country's performance level lies (Figure I.2.16).

Gender differences in performance on the reading scale

Concern about gender differences in education in much of the 20th century focused on the disadvantage and underachievement of girls. More recently, however, the underachievement of boys in *reading literacy* has become the focus of policy attention. In the PISA 2009 reading assessment, girls outperform boys in every participating country by an average, across OECD countries, of 39 PISA score points: over half a proficiency level and roughly the equivalent of an average school year's progress (see Table A1.2). Figure I.2.17 shows gender differences in reading performance for each country. Tables I.2.2 and I.2.3 provide further details.

While girls outperform boys in reading in every participating country, the gap is much wider in some countries than in others. As shown in Volume III, *Learning to Learn*, these differences closely relate to gender differences in student attitudes and behaviours. With the exception of Denmark, the Northern European countries have above-average gender gaps; the most pronounced of these is in Finland, where the score difference is, at 55 points, the greatest of all OECD countries. The gender differences in East Asian countries and economies tend to cluster just below the average, with Korea, Hong Kong-China, Macao-China and Chinese Taipei all showing gaps of between 33 and 37 points. However, the highest performing among these countries and economies, Shanghai-China, also has a slightly wider gender gap of 40 points.

In each of the country groups described above, the country with the highest or second highest mean overall is also the country with the widest gender gap: in other words, in these countries, girls are disproportionately contributing to the country's high reading proficiency. Strategies to improve boys' reading proficiency would have an accentuated effect on overall achievement.

■ Figure I.2.16 ■
Where countries rank in reading performance

	Statistically significantly **above** the OECD average
	Not statistically significantly different from the OECD average
	Statistically significantly **below** the OECD average

			Reading scale			
			Range of rank			
			OECD countries		All countries/economies	
	Mean Score	S.E.	Upper rank	Lower rank	Upper rank	Lower rank
Shanghai-China	556	(2.4)			1	1
Korea	539	(3.5)	1	2	2	4
Finland	536	(2.3)	1	2	2	4
Hong Kong-China	533	(2.1)			3	4
Singapore	526	(1.1)			5	6
Canada	524	(1.5)	3	4	5	7
New Zealand	521	(2.4)	3	5	6	9
Japan	520	(3.5)	3	6	5	9
Australia	515	(2.3)	5	7	8	10
Netherlands	508	(5.1)	5	13	8	16
Belgium	506	(2.3)	7	10	10	14
Norway	503	(2.6)	7	14	10	18
Estonia	501	(2.6)	8	17	11	21
Switzerland	501	(2.4)	8	17	11	21
Poland	500	(2.6)	8	17	11	22
Iceland	500	(1.4)	9	16	12	19
United States	500	(3.7)	8	20	11	25
Liechtenstein	499	(2.8)			11	23
Sweden	497	(2.9)	10	21	13	26
Germany	497	(2.7)	11	21	14	26
Ireland	496	(3.0)	12	22	15	27
France	496	(3.4)	11	22	14	27
Chinese Taipei	495	(2.6)			17	27
Denmark	495	(2.1)	15	22	18	26
United Kingdom	494	(2.3)	15	22	19	27
Hungary	494	(3.2)	13	22	16	27
Portugal	489	(3.1)	18	24	23	31
Macao-China	487	(0.9)			27	30
Italy	486	(1.6)	22	24	27	31
Latvia	484	(3.0)			27	34
Slovenia	483	(1.0)	23	26	30	33
Greece	483	(4.3)	22	29	27	37
Spain	481	(2.0)	24	28	30	35
Czech Republic	478	(2.9)	24	29	31	37
Slovak Republic	477	(2.5)	25	29	32	37
Croatia	476	(2.9)			33	39
Israel	474	(3.6)	26	31	33	40
Luxembourg	472	(1.3)	29	31	36	39
Austria	470	(2.9)	29	32	36	41
Lithuania	468	(2.4)			38	41
Turkey	464	(3.5)	31	32	39	43
Dubai (UAE)	459	(1.1)			41	43
Russian Federation	459	(3.3)			41	43
Chile	449	(3.1)	33	33	44	44
Serbia	442	(2.4)			45	46
Bulgaria	429	(6.7)			45	50
Uruguay	426	(2.6)			46	50
Mexico	425	(2.0)	34	34	46	49
Romania	424	(4.1)			46	50
Thailand	421	(2.6)			47	51
Trinidad and Tobago	416	(1.2)			50	52
Colombia	413	(3.7)			50	55
Brazil	412	(2.7)			51	54
Montenegro	408	(1.7)			53	56
Jordan	405	(3.3)			53	58
Tunisia	404	(2.9)			54	58
Indonesia	402	(3.7)			54	58
Argentina	398	(4.6)			55	59
Kazakhstan	390	(3.1)			58	60
Albania	385	(4.0)			59	60
Qatar	372	(0.8)			61	63
Panama	371	(6.5)			61	64
Peru	370	(4.0)			61	64
Azerbaijan	362	(3.3)			63	64
Kyrgyzstan	314	(3.2)			65	65

Source: OECD, *PISA 2009 Database*.
StatLink ᛜᚳᛞᛟ http://dx.doi.org/10.1787/888932343133

■ Figure I. 2.17 ■
Gender differences in reading performance

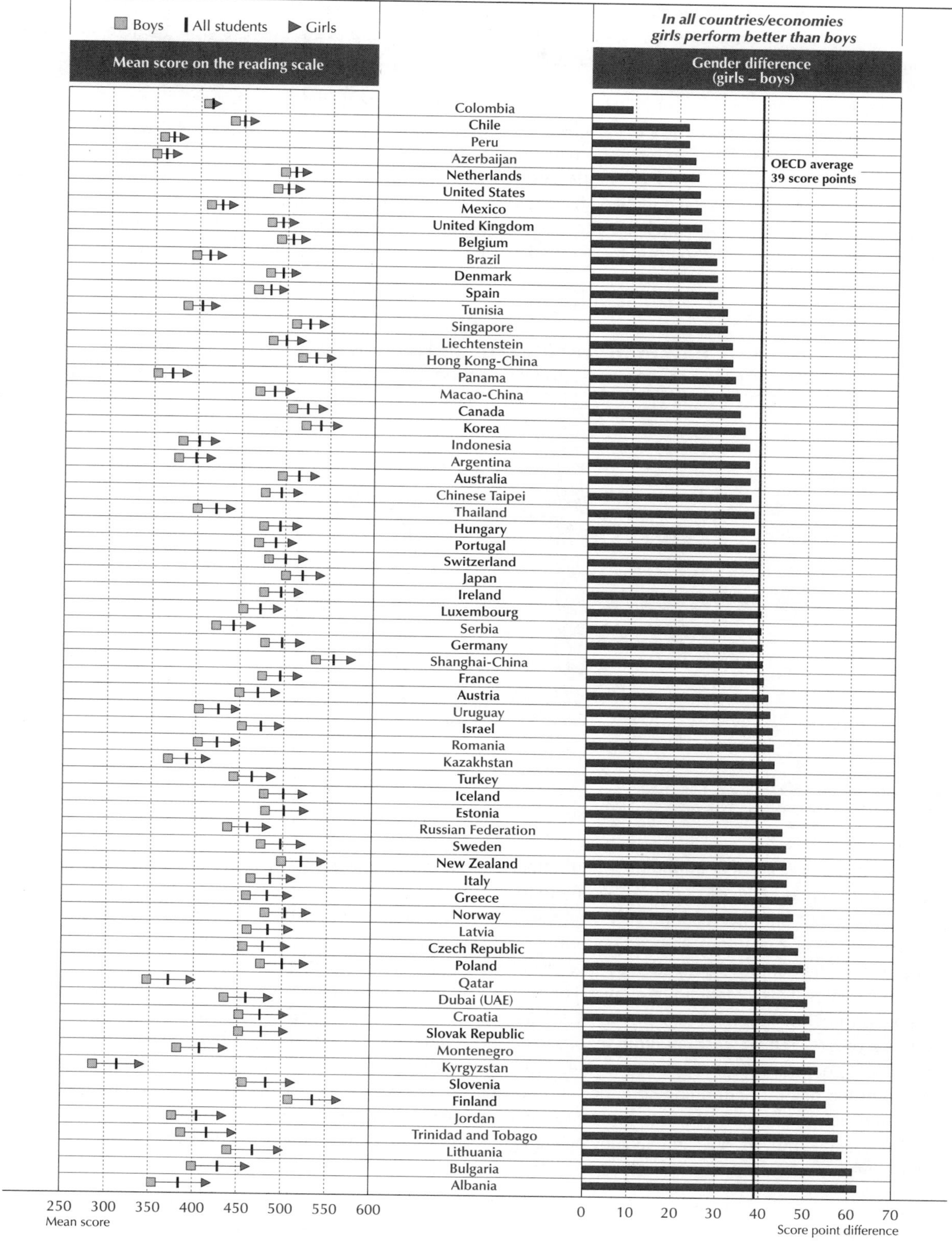

■ Boys ▌ All students ▶ Girls	**In all countries/economies girls perform better than boys**
Mean score on the reading scale	**Gender difference (girls – boys)**

OECD average
39 score points

Colombia
Chile
Peru
Azerbaijan
Netherlands
United States
Mexico
United Kingdom
Belgium
Brazil
Denmark
Spain
Tunisia
Singapore
Liechtenstein
Hong Kong-China
Panama
Macao-China
Canada
Korea
Indonesia
Argentina
Australia
Chinese Taipei
Thailand
Hungary
Portugal
Switzerland
Japan
Ireland
Luxembourg
Serbia
Germany
Shanghai-China
France
Austria
Uruguay
Israel
Romania
Kazakhstan
Turkey
Iceland
Estonia
Russian Federation
Sweden
New Zealand
Italy
Greece
Norway
Latvia
Czech Republic
Poland
Qatar
Dubai (UAE)
Croatia
Slovak Republic
Montenegro
Kyrgyzstan
Slovenia
Finland
Jordan
Trinidad and Tobago
Lithuania
Bulgaria
Albania

Mean score: 250 300 350 400 450 500 550 600
Score point difference: 0 10 20 30 40 50 60 70

Note: All gender differences are statistically significant (see Annex A3).
Countries are ranked in ascending order of the gender score point difference (girls – boys).
Source: OECD, *PISA 2009 Database,* Table I.2.3.
StatLink ᴍˢᴾ http://dx.doi.org/10.1787/888932343133

Yet there is no obvious pattern regarding gender performance among groups of countries with lower performance overall. For example, among the group of Latin American countries, both the highest performing overall (Chile) and the lowest performing (Peru) have the same, relatively small, gender gap (22 points). One of the middle-ranking countries within this group, Colombia, has by far the smallest gender gap of any country, with a difference of only 9 score points between the means for girls and boys.

How large are these gender differences in terms of the average level of proficiency that boys and girls achieve? One way to think of this is to consider where most boys and girls fall in their highest level of proficiency. As can be seen in Figure I.2.18, the most common highest proficiency level for both boys and girls is Level 3, but whereas almost as many boys are at Level 2 as Level 3, for girls, Level 4 is the second most common level attained. Another way to compare performance around the middle of the reading scale is by noting that half of boys (51%) but only a third of girls (34%) fail to reach Level 3, which is associated with being able to perform the kinds of tasks that are commonly demanded of young and older adults in their everyday lives. This represents a major difference in the capabilities of boys and girls at age 15.

■ Figure I.2.18 ■
How proficient are girls and boys in reading?
OECD average percentages of boys and girls who performed at the different levels of reading proficiency

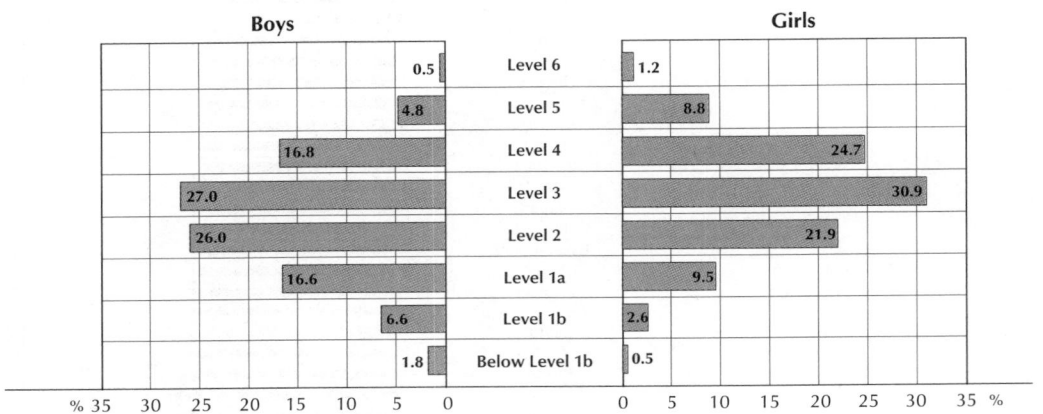

Source: OECD, *PISA 2009 Database,* Table I.2.2.
StatLink ᴍᴤᴾ http://dx.doi.org/10.1787/888932343133

Gender differences are also important when comparing the number of students with particularly low levels of reading proficiency. Eighteen countries had more than 50% of 15-year-old boys performing below Level 2 on the reading scale, but only five countries showed the same proportion of girls at that level. Across OECD countries, only about half as many girls as boys perform below Level 2, but the ratio varies according to overall country performance. In countries with generally low levels of performance in reading, the proportions of girls and boys performing below Level 2 tend to be similar. For example, there are at least four-fifths of the number of girls as boys who perform below Level 2 in Colombia, Kyrgyzstan, Azerbaijan, Peru and Panama, all of which have low mean reading scores overall. In these countries' efforts to develop reading proficiency, boys and girls need to receive equal attention. In contrast, overall, the two countries/economies with the widest gender gap at low levels of performance are two of the highest performing countries and economies. In Finland and Shanghai-China, the number of girls performing below Level 2 is only one-quarter that of the number of boys. These countries might consider examining the obstacles that prevent boys from achieving high proficiency in reading. Some of the differences relate closely to gender differences in attitudes and behaviour, which are discussed in Volume III.

Some of the variations in boys' and girls' proficiency across different aspects and text formats will emerge in the discussion of the reading subscales in the sections that follow. Such variations provide insights into the areas that reading curricula and pedagogy could focus on in an effort to close the gender gap by improving boys' access to and engagement with different kinds of reading tasks and diverse texts. Again, some of these differences are related to gender differences in attitudes and behaviour, which are discussed in Volume III.

STUDENT PERFORMANCE IN DIFFERENT AREAS OF READING ACROSS PARTICIPATING COUNTRIES

This section takes a more nuanced look at reading performance by analysing student performance at the level of the reading subscales – the aspect subscales: *access and retrieve*, *integrate and interpret* and *reflect and evaluate*; and the text-format subscales: *continuous* and *non-continuous*.

Aspect subscales

Student performance on the *access and retrieve* reading subscale

About one-quarter of the questions in the pool of reading tasks in PISA 2009 were assigned to the *access and retrieve* subscale. As noted before, tasks classified as *access and retrieve* involve skills associated with finding, selecting and collecting information. Sometimes finding the required information is relatively simple, as it is directly and plainly stated in the text. However, *access and retrieve* tasks are not necessarily easy ones. For example, sometimes more than one piece of information is required; sometimes knowledge of text structures and features is called upon.

In assessment tasks that call for retrieving information, students usually must match information given in the question with either identically worded or synonymous information in the text, and use this to find the new information requested. Easy retrieval tasks characteristically require a literal match between the words of the task and the words in the text. More difficult retrieval tasks often involve finding synonymous information, forming mental categories to identify what needs to be found, or discriminating between two similar pieces of information. Different levels of proficiency can be measured by systematically varying the elements that contribute to the difficulty of the task.

■ Figure I.2.19 ■

Summary descriptions of the seven proficiency levels on the reading subscale *access and retrieve*

Level	Percentage of students able to perform tasks at each level or above (OECD average)	Characteristics of tasks	Examples of released *access and retrieve* questions
6	1.4% of students across the OECD can perform tasks at Level 6	Combine multiple pieces of independent information, from different parts of a *mixed text,* in an accurate and precise sequence, working in an unfamiliar context.	
5	9.5% of students across the OECD can perform tasks at least at Level 5	Locate and possibly combine multiple pieces of deeply embedded information, some of which may be outside the main body of the text. Deal with strongly distracting competing information.	
4	30.4% of students across the OECD can perform tasks at least at Level 4	Locate several pieces of embedded information, each of which may need to meet multiple criteria, in a text with unfamiliar context or form. Possibly combine verbal and graphical information. Deal with extensive and/or prominent competing information.	*BALLOON* – Question 3.2 (595)
3	57.9% of students across the OECD can perform tasks at least at Level 3	Locate several pieces of information, each of which may need to meet multiple criteria. Combine pieces of information within a text. Deal with competing information.	
2	80.4% of students across the OECD can perform tasks at least at Level 2	Locate one or more pieces of information, each of which may need to meet multiple criteria. Deal with some competing information.	*BALLOON* –Question 3.2 (449)
1a	93.0% of students across the OECD can perform tasks at least at Level 1a	Locate one or more independent pieces of explicitly stated information meeting a single criterion, by making a literal or synonymous match. The target information may not be prominent in the text but there is little or no competing information.	*BRUSHING YOUR TEETH –* Question 2 (358)
1b	98.0% of students across the OECD can perform tasks at least at Level 1b	Locate a single piece of explicitly stated information in a prominent position in a simple text, by making a literal or synonymous match, where there is no competing information. May make simple connections between adjacent pieces of information.	*MISER* – Question 7 (310) *BRUSHING YOUR TEETH –* Question 3 (285)

■ Figure I. 2.20 ■

How well do students *access and retrieve* information from what they read?

Percentage of students at the different levels of proficiency in accessing and retrieving information

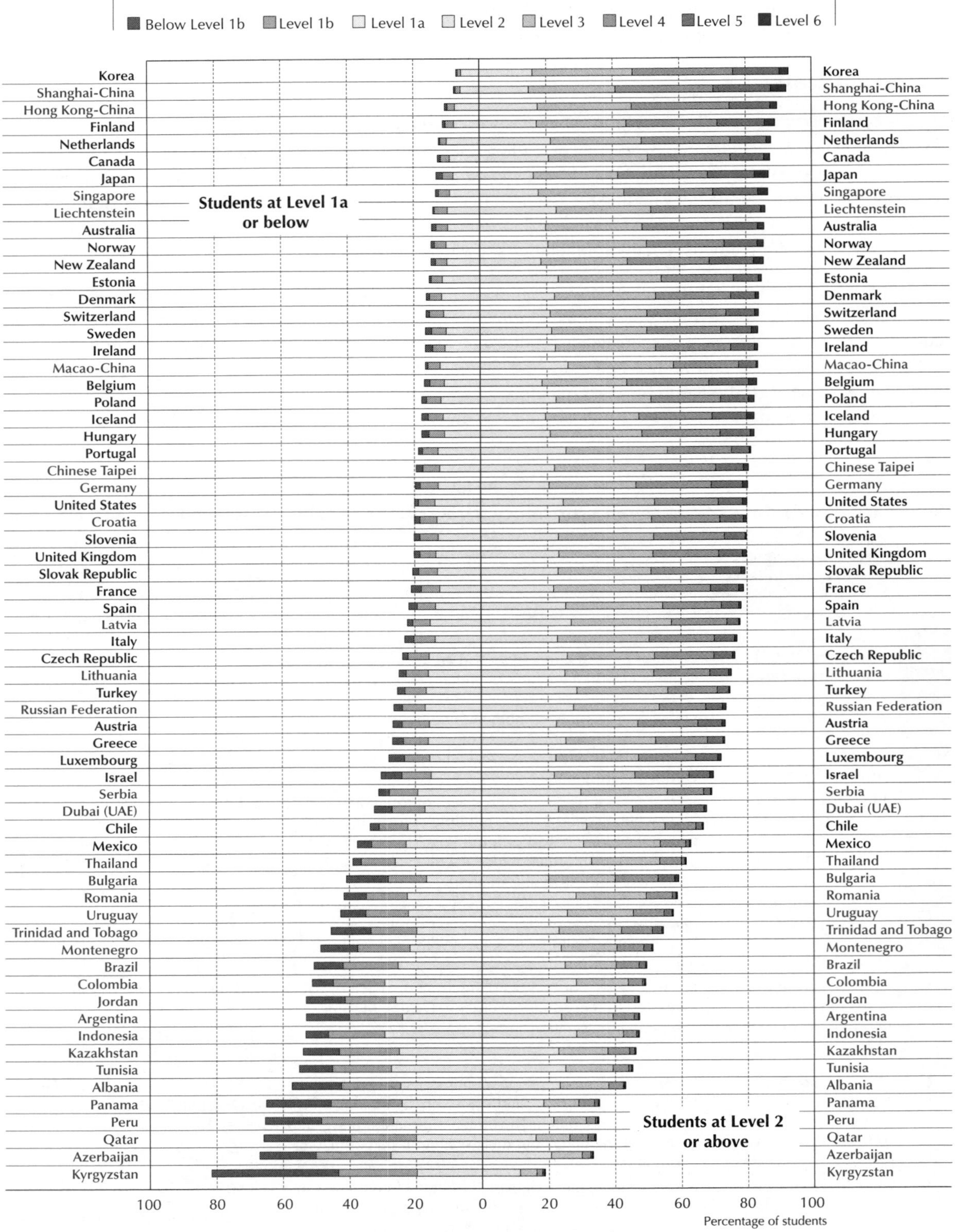

■ Below Level 1b　■ Level 1b　□ Level 1a　□ Level 2　□ Level 3　▨ Level 4　▨ Level 5　■ Level 6

Korea
Shanghai-China
Hong Kong-China
Finland
Netherlands
Canada
Japan
Singapore
Liechtenstein
Australia
Norway
New Zealand
Estonia
Denmark
Switzerland
Sweden
Ireland
Macao-China
Belgium
Poland
Iceland
Hungary
Portugal
Chinese Taipei
Germany
United States
Croatia
Slovenia
United Kingdom
Slovak Republic
France
Spain
Latvia
Italy
Czech Republic
Lithuania
Turkey
Russian Federation
Austria
Greece
Luxembourg
Israel
Serbia
Dubai (UAE)
Chile
Mexico
Thailand
Bulgaria
Romania
Uruguay
Trinidad and Tobago
Montenegro
Brazil
Colombia
Jordan
Argentina
Indonesia
Kazakhstan
Tunisia
Albania
Panama
Peru
Qatar
Azerbaijan
Kyrgyzstan

Students at Level 1a or below

Students at Level 2 or above

100 80 60 40 20 0 20 40 60 80 100

Percentage of students

Countries are ranked in descending order of the percentage of students at Levels 2, 3, 4, 5 and 6.
Source: OECD, *PISA 2009 Database*, Table I.2.4.
StatLink ▨▨▨ http://dx.doi.org/10.1787/888932343133

Figure I.2.19 provides descriptions of the nature of the reading skills, knowledge and understanding required at each level of the scale for the access and retrieve aspect of reading, with the percentage of students across OECD countries who perform at this level in PISA 2009. The right-hand column lists examples of *access and retrieve* questions. Figures I.2.40 to I.2.46 describe these questions and provide commentary on what they show.

Figure I.2.20 shows the percentage of students at each proficiency level on the *access and retrieve* subscale. Details of performance by gender on this subscale are also provided in Table I.2.5.

The mean score for OECD countries on the *access and retrieve* subscale is 495 points, slightly higher than the mean for reading as a whole. The distribution of performance is more dispersed on the *access and retrieve* subscale than on the overall reading scale (the standard deviation was 101 points compared with 93 points for the overall reading scale). The higher mean and wider distribution suggest that more students performed at very high levels on the *access and retrieve* subscale than on the overall reading literacy scale. Five countries or economies yielded more than 3% of students at Level 6: the OECD countries Japan, Finland and New Zealand, as well as the partner countries and economies Shanghai-China and Singapore. In Shanghai-China, 17% of students also performed at Level 5. Although on average countries performed more strongly on the *access and retrieve* subscale, the wider spread of results is evident at the lower end of the scale, in even lower performance by some countries in this aspect than in reading overall. In 13 partner countries – Kyrgyzstan, Azerbaijan, Qatar, Peru, Panama, Albania, Tunisia, Kazakhstan, Indonesia, Argentina, Jordan, Colombia and Brazil – more than 50% of students performed below Level 2.

Figure I.2.21 shows each country's mean score on the *access and retrieve* subscale, and allows readers to see for which pairs of countries the differences between the means shown are statistically significant. For each country shown on the left in the middle column, the list of countries on the right hand column shows countries whose mean scores are not sufficiently different to be distinguished with confidence. For all other cases, one country has higher performance than another if it is above it in the list in the middle column, and lower performance if it is below it.

Table I.2.6 presents the mean score, variation and gender difference for each country on this subscale. As on the overall reading scale, girls performed more strongly than boys on the *access and retrieve* subscale in every country except in Colombia, where the difference is not significant. The mean difference was similar to the reading scale (40 points and 39 points, respectively).

Student performance on the **integrate and interpret** reading subscale

As noted before, the aspect *integrate and interpret* involves processing what is read to make internal sense of a text. Integrating tasks require the reader to understand the relation(s) between different parts of a text. These relations include problem-solution, cause-effect, category-example, equivalency, compare-contrast, and understanding whole-part relationships. To complete such tasks, students had to determine the appropriate connection. In easier tasks this may be explicitly signalled, as when the text states "the cause of X is Y"; in more difficult tasks, an inference may be required by the reader. The parts to be related may be near each other in the text or in different paragraphs or even in different texts. Interpreting refers to the process of making meaning from something that is not stated. It may involve recognising a relationship that is not explicit or inferring, that is deducing from evidence and reasoning, the connotation of a phrase or a sentence. When interpreting, a reader is identifying the underlying assumptions or implications of part or all of the text.

With around half of the questions in the pool of PISA reading tasks assigned to the *integrate and interpret* subscale, it encompasses a wide spectrum both in cognitive characteristics and difficulty. The difficulty of these tasks is determined by the number of pieces of information to be integrated and the number of locations where they are found, as well as by the verbal complexity and the familiarity of the subject.

Figure I.2.22 provides details of the nature of the reading skills, knowledge and understanding required at each level of the described proficiency scale for the *integrate and interpret* aspect of reading, with the percentage of students across OECD countries who performed at this level in PISA 2009. The right hand column shows examples of released *integrate and interpret* questions. Figures I.2.40 to I.2.46 describe these questions and comments on what they show.

■ Figure I.2.21 ■

Comparing countries on *access and retrieve* performance

	Statistically significantly **above** the OECD average
	Not statistically significantly different from the OECD average
	Statistically significantly **below** the OECD average

Mean	Comparison country	Countries whose mean score is NOT statistically significantly different from that of the comparison country
549	Shanghai-China	Korea
542	Korea	Shanghai-China
532	Finland	Japan, Hong Kong-China
530	Japan	Finland, Hong Kong-China, Singapore, Netherlands
530	Hong Kong-China	Finland, Japan, Singapore, Netherlands
526	Singapore	Japan, Hong Kong-China, Netherlands
521	New Zealand	Netherlands, Canada
519	Netherlands	Japan, Hong Kong-China, Singapore, New Zealand, Canada, Belgium, Australia, Norway, Liechtenstein
517	Canada	New Zealand, Netherlands, Belgium, Australia, Norway
513	Belgium	Netherlands, Canada, Australia, Norway, Liechtenstein
513	Australia	Netherlands, Canada, Belgium, Norway, Liechtenstein
512	Norway	Netherlands, Canada, Belgium, Australia, Liechtenstein, Iceland, Switzerland, Sweden
508	Liechtenstein	Netherlands, Belgium, Australia, Norway, Iceland, Switzerland, Sweden, Estonia, Denmark, Hungary, Germany, Poland, Ireland
507	Iceland	Norway, Liechtenstein, Switzerland, Sweden, Estonia, Denmark, Hungary, Germany
505	Switzerland	Norway, Liechtenstein, Iceland, Sweden, Estonia, Denmark, Hungary, Germany, Poland, Ireland
505	Sweden	Norway, Liechtenstein, Iceland, Switzerland, Estonia, Denmark, Hungary, Germany, Poland, Ireland
503	Estonia	Liechtenstein, Iceland, Switzerland, Sweden, Denmark, Hungary, Germany, Poland, Ireland, Chinese Taipei
502	Denmark	Liechtenstein, Iceland, Switzerland, Sweden, Estonia, Hungary, Germany, Poland, Ireland, Chinese Taipei
501	Hungary	Liechtenstein, Iceland, Switzerland, Sweden, Estonia, Denmark, Germany, Poland, Ireland, Chinese Taipei, United States, France
501	Germany	Liechtenstein, Iceland, Switzerland, Sweden, Estonia, Denmark, Hungary, Poland, Ireland, Chinese Taipei, United States, France, Croatia
500	Poland	Liechtenstein, Switzerland, Sweden, Estonia, Denmark, Hungary, Germany, Ireland, Chinese Taipei, United States, France
498	Ireland	Liechtenstein, Switzerland, Sweden, Estonia, Denmark, Hungary, Germany, Poland, Chinese Taipei, Macao-China, United States, France, Croatia, United Kingdom, Slovak Republic
496	Chinese Taipei	Estonia, Denmark, Hungary, Germany, Poland, Ireland, Macao-China, United States, France, Croatia, United Kingdom, Slovak Republic, Portugal
493	Macao-China	Ireland, Chinese Taipei, United States, France, Croatia, United Kingdom, Slovak Republic, Portugal
492	United States	Hungary, Germany, Poland, Ireland, Chinese Taipei, Macao-China, France, Croatia, United Kingdom, Slovak Republic, Slovenia, Portugal
492	France	Hungary, Germany, Poland, Ireland, Chinese Taipei, Macao-China, United States, Croatia, United Kingdom, Slovak Republic, Slovenia, Portugal
492	Croatia	Germany, Ireland, Chinese Taipei, Macao-China, United States, France, United Kingdom, Slovak Republic, Slovenia, Portugal
491	United Kingdom	Ireland, Chinese Taipei, Macao-China, United States, France, Croatia, Slovak Republic, Slovenia, Portugal
491	Slovak Republic	Ireland, Chinese Taipei, Macao-China, United States, France, Croatia, United Kingdom, Slovenia, Portugal
489	Slovenia	United States, France, Croatia, United Kingdom, Slovak Re public, Portugal
488	Portugal	Chinese Taipei, Macao-China, United States, France, Croatia, United Kingdom, Slovak Republic, Slovenia, Italy
482	Italy	Portugal, Spain, Czech Republic, Austria, Lithuania, Latvia
480	Spain	Italy, Czech Republic, Austria, Lithuania, Latvia
479	Czech Republic	Italy, Spain, Austria, Lithuania, Latvia
477	Austria	Italy, Spain, Czech Republic, Lithuania, Latvia, Luxembourg, Russian Federation, Greece, Turkey
476	Lithuania	Italy, Spain, Czech Republic, Austria, Latvia, Luxembourg, Russian Federation, Greece, Turkey
476	Latvia	Italy, Spain, Czech Republic, Austria, Lithuania, Luxembourg, Russian Federation, Greece, Turkey
471	Luxembourg	Austria, Lithuania, Latvia, Russian Federation, Greece, Turkey, Israel
469	Russian Federation	Austria, Lithuania, Latvia, Luxembourg, Greece, Turkey, Israel
468	Greece	Austria, Lithuania, Latvia, Luxembourg, Russian Federation, Turkey, Israel
467	Turkey	Austria, Lithuania, Latvia, Luxembourg, Russian Federation, Greece, Israel
463	Israel	Luxembourg, Russian Federation, Greece, Turkey, Dubai (UAE)
458	Dubai (UAE)	Israel
449	Serbia	Chile
444	Chile	Serbia, Bulgaria
433	Mexico	Thailand, Bulgaria, Romania
431	Thailand	Mexico, Bulgaria, Uruguay, Romania
430	Bulgaria	Chile, Mexico, Thailand, Uruguay, Romania, Trinidad and Tobago
424	Uruguay	Thailand, Bulgaria, Romania
423	Romania	Mexico, Thailand, Bulgaria, Uruguay, Trinidad and Tobago
413	Trinidad and Tobago	Bulgaria, Romania, Brazil
408	Montenegro	Brazil, Colombia, Indonesia
407	Brazil	Trinidad and Tobago, Montenegro, Colombia, Indonesia, Kazakhstan
404	Colombia	Montenegro, Brazil, Indonesia, Kazakhstan, Argentina, Jordan
399	Indonesia	Montenegro, Brazil, Colombia, Kazakhstan, Argentina, Jordan, Tunisia
397	Kazakhstan	Brazil, Colombia, Indonesia, Argentina, Jordan, Tunisia
394	Argentina	Colombia, Indonesia, Kazakhstan, Jordan, Tunisia
394	Jordan	Colombia, Indonesia, Kazakhstan, Argentina, Tunisia
393	Tunisia	Indonesia, Kazakhstan, Argentina, Jordan
380	Albania	Panama
364	Peru	Panama, Azerbaijan
363	Panama	Albania, Peru, Azerbaijan, Qatar
361	Azerbaijan	Peru, Panama, Qatar
354	Qatar	Panama, Azerbaijan
299	Kyrgyzstan	

Source: OECD, *PISA 2009 Database*.
StatLink ⟲ http://dx.doi.org/10.1787/888932343133

■ Figure I.2.22 ■
Summary descriptions of the seven proficiency levels on the reading subscale
integrate and interpret

Level	Percentage of students able to perform tasks at each level or above (OECD average)	Characteristics of tasks	Examples of released *integrate and interpret* questions
6	1.1% of students across the OECD can perform tasks at Level 6	Make multiple inferences, comparisons and contrasts that are both detailed and precise. Demonstrate a full and detailed understanding of the whole text or specific sections. May involve integrating information from more than one text. Deal with unfamiliar abstract ideas, in the presence of prominent competing information. Generate abstract categories for interpretations.	*THE PLAY'S THE THING* – Question 3 (730)
5	8.3% of students across the OECD can perform tasks at least at Level 5	Demonstrate a full and detailed understanding of a text. Construe the meaning of nuanced language. Apply criteria to examples scattered through a text, using high level inference. Generate categories to describe relationships between parts of a text. Deal with ideas that are contrary to expectations.	
4	28.4% of students across the OECD can perform tasks at least at Level 4	Use text-based inferences to understand and apply categories in an unfamiliar context, and to construe the meaning of a section of text by taking into account the text as a whole. Deal with ambiguities and ideas that are negatively worded.	*MOBILE PHONE SAFETY* – Question 2 (561) *THE PLAY'S THE THING* – Question 7 (556)
3	56.6% of students across the OECD can perform tasks at least at Level 3	Integrate several parts of a text in order to identify the main idea, understand a relationship or construe the meaning of a word or phrase. Compare, contrast or categorise taking many criteria into account. Deal with competing information.	*MISER* – Question 5 (548) *TELECOMMUTING* – Question 1 (537) *MOBILE PHONE SAFETY* – Question 9 (488)
2	80.7% of students across the OECD can perform tasks at least at Level 2	Identify the main idea in a text, understand relationships, form or apply simple categories, or construe meaning within a limited part of the text when the information is not prominent and low-level inferences are required.	*THE PLAY'S THE THING* – Question 4 (474) *BLOOD DONATION NOTICE* – Question 8 (438)
1a	94.3% of students across the OECD can perform tasks at least at Level 1a	Recognise the main theme or author's purpose in a text about a familiar topic, when the required information in the text is prominent.	*MISER* – Question 1 (373) *BALLOON* – Question 8 (370) *BRUSHING YOUR TEETH* – Question 1 (353)
1b	98.9% of students across the OECD can perform tasks at least at Level 1b	Either recognise a simple idea that is reinforced several times in the text (possibly with picture cues), or interpret a phrase, in a short text on a familiar topic.	

Figure I.2.23 shows the percentage of students at each proficiency level on the *integrate and interpret* subscale. Details of performance by gender on this subscale are provided in Table I.2.8.

Because such a large proportion – nearly 50% – of the questions in the PISA 2009 reading assessment contributed to this subscale, most of the features of the *integrate and interpret* subscale are similar to those of the overall reading scale. The two are virtually indistinguishable in terms of mean and spread of performance across OECD countries: the average for the *integrate and interpret* subscale has a mean of 493 and standard deviation of 94, while for the overall reading scale, the figures are 493 and 93, respectively.

The spread of performance on the *integrate and interpret* subscale is also very close to that of the overall reading scale. Across OECD countries, the largest percentage of students – 28% – performed at Level 3 on this subscale; the figure for reading is 29%. On this subscale, in New Zealand and in the partner countries and economies Singapore and Shanghai-China, more than 3% of students performed at Level 6. In several countries and economies, substantial percentages of students performed at Levels 5 and 6 combined: over 10% in the OECD countries Finland, New Zealand, Korea, Japan, Canada, Australia, Belgium, France, the Netherlands and the United States, and in the partner countries and economies Shanghai-China, Singapore and Hong Kong-China. The high performance in these countries was not confined to a small elite: for example, in Finland and Korea, and in partner economy Shanghai-China, the largest proportions of students – above 30% in each case – were proficient at Level 4.

■ Figure I. 2.23 ■

How well do students *integrate and interpret* what they read?

Percentage of students at the different proficiency levels in integrating and interpreting what they read

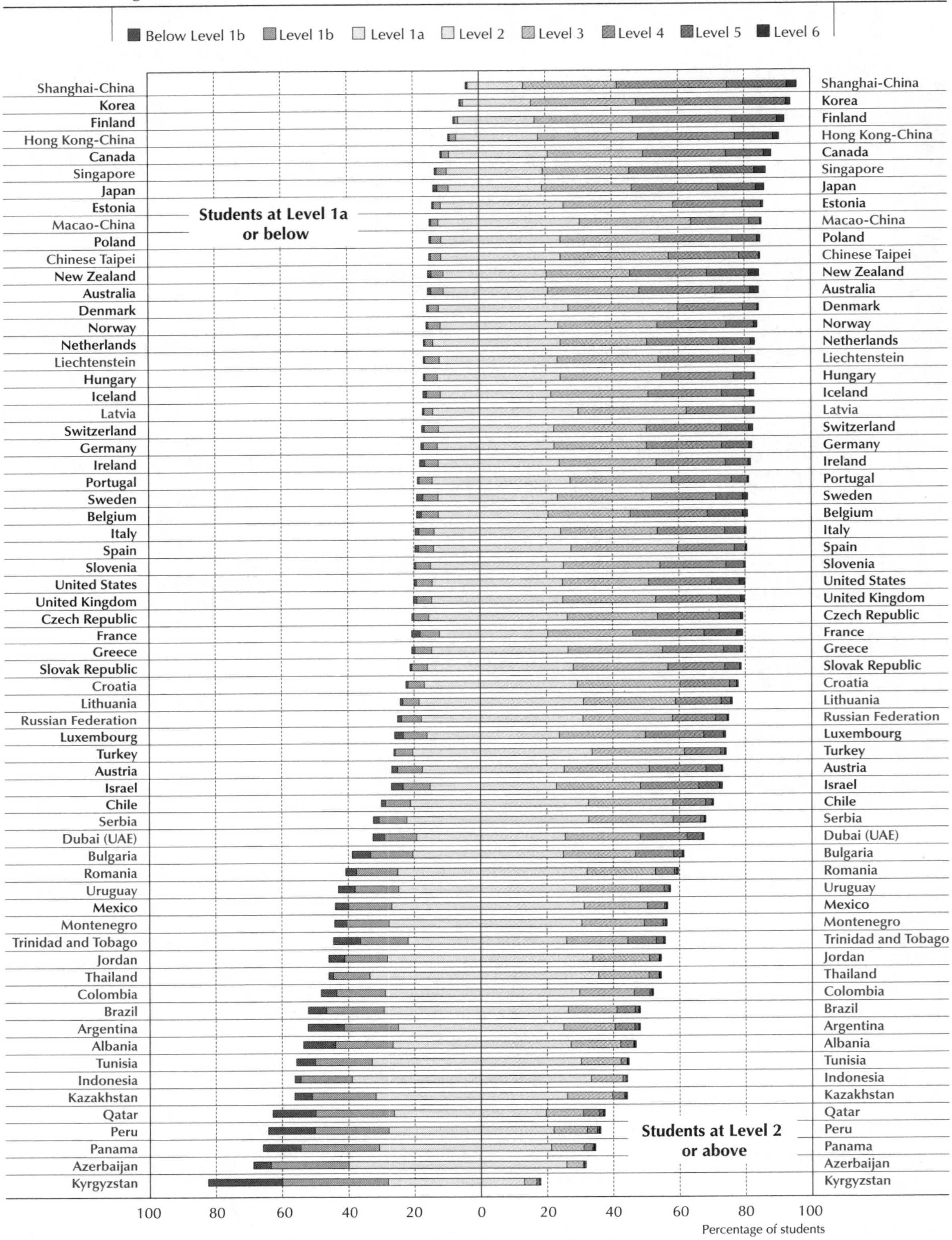

■ Below Level 1b ▨ Level 1b ☐ Level 1a ☐ Level 2 ▨ Level 3 ▨ Level 4 ■ Level 5 ■ Level 6

Shanghai-China
Korea
Finland
Hong Kong-China
Canada
Singapore
Japan
Estonia
Macao-China
Poland
Chinese Taipei
New Zealand
Australia
Denmark
Norway
Netherlands
Liechtenstein
Hungary
Iceland
Latvia
Switzerland
Germany
Ireland
Portugal
Sweden
Belgium
Italy
Spain
Slovenia
United States
United Kingdom
Czech Republic
France
Greece
Slovak Republic
Croatia
Lithuania
Russian Federation
Luxembourg
Turkey
Austria
Israel
Chile
Serbia
Dubai (UAE)
Bulgaria
Romania
Uruguay
Mexico
Montenegro
Trinidad and Tobago
Jordan
Thailand
Colombia
Brazil
Argentina
Albania
Tunisia
Indonesia
Kazakhstan
Qatar
Peru
Panama
Azerbaijan
Kyrgyzstan

Students at Level 1a or below

Students at Level 2 or above

100   80   60   40   20   0   20   40   60   80   100

Percentage of students

Countries are ranked in descending order of the percentage of students at Levels 2, 3, 4, 5 and 6.
Source: OECD, *PISA 2009 Database*, Table I.2.7.
StatLink ⬛ᵢₛ⬛ http://dx.doi.org/10.1787/888932343133

■ Figure I.2.24 ■

Comparing countries on *integrate and interpret* performance

	Statistically significantly **above** the OECD average
	Not statistically significantly different from the OECD average
	Statistically significantly **below** the OECD average

Mean	Comparison country	Countries whose mean score is NOT statistically significantly different from the comparison country
558	Shanghai-China	
541	Korea	Finland
538	Finland	Korea
530	Hong Kong-China	
525	Singapore	Canada, Japan
522	Canada	Singapore, Japan, New Zealand
520	Japan	Singapore, Canada, New Zealand, Australia
517	New Zealand	Canada, Japan, Australia
513	Australia	Japan, New Zealand, Netherlands
504	Netherlands	Australia, Belgium, Poland, Iceland, Norway, Switzerland, Germany, Estonia, Chinese Taipei, Liechtenstein, France, Hungary, United States, Sweden, Ireland
504	Belgium	Netherlands, Poland, Iceland, Norway, Switzerland, Germany, Estonia, Chinese Taipei, Liechtenstein, France, Hungary, United States
503	Poland	Netherlands, Belgium, Iceland, Norway, Switzerland, Germany, Estonia, Chinese Taipei, Liechtenstein, France, Hungary, United States
503	Iceland	Netherlands, Belgium, Poland, Norway, Switzerland, Germany, Estonia, Chinese Taipei, Liechtenstein, France, Hungary, United States
502	Norway	Netherlands, Belgium, Poland, Iceland, Switzerland, Germany, Estonia, Chinese Taipei, Liechtenstein, France, Hungary, United States, Sweden
502	Switzerland	Netherlands, Belgium, Poland, Iceland, Norway, Germany, Estonia, Chinese Taipei, Liechtenstein, France, Hungary, United States, Sweden
501	Germany	Netherlands, Belgium, Poland, Iceland, Norway, Switzerland, Estonia, Chinese Taipei, Liechtenstein, France, Hungary, United States, Sweden, Ireland
500	Estonia	Netherlands, Belgium, Poland, Iceland, Norway, Switzerland, Germany, Chinese Taipei, Liechtenstein, France, Hungary, United States, Sweden, Ireland
499	Chinese Taipei	Netherlands, Belgium, Poland, Iceland, Norway, Switzerland, Germany, Estonia, Liechtenstein, France, Hungary, United States, Sweden, Ireland
498	Liechtenstein	Netherlands, Belgium, Poland, Iceland, Norway, Switzerland, Germany, Estonia, Chinese Taipei, France, Hungary, United States, Sweden, Ireland, Denmark, United Kingdom, Italy
497	France	Netherlands, Belgium, Poland, Iceland, Norway, Switzerland, Germany, Estonia, Chinese Taipei, Liechtenstein, Hungary, United States, Sweden, Ireland, Denmark, United Kingdom, Italy
496	Hungary	Netherlands, Belgium, Poland, Iceland, Norway, Switzerland, Germany, Estonia, Chinese Taipei, Liechtenstein, France, United States, Sweden, Ireland, Denmark, United Kingdom, Italy, Czech Republic
495	United States	Netherlands, Belgium, Poland, Iceland, Norway, Switzerland, Germany, Estonia, Chinese Taipei, Liechtenstein, France, Hungary, Sweden, Ireland, Denmark, United Kingdom, Italy, Slovenia, Macao-China, Czech Republic, Portugal
494	Sweden	Netherlands, Norway, Switzerland, Germany, Estonia, Chinese Taipei, Liechtenstein, France, Hungary, United States, Ireland, Denmark, United Kingdom, Italy, Slovenia, Macao-China, Czech Republic, Portugal
494	Ireland	Netherlands, Germany, Estonia, Chinese Taipei, Liechtenstein, France, Hungary, United States, Sweden, Denmark, United Kingdom, Italy, Slovenia, Macao-China, Czech Republic, Portugal, Greece
492	Denmark	Liechtenstein, France, Hungary, United States, Sweden, Ireland, United Kingdom, Italy, Slovenia, Macao-China, Czech Republic, Portugal, Greece
491	United Kingdom	Liechtenstein, France, Hungary, United States, Sweden, Ireland, Denmark, Italy, Slovenia, Macao-China, Czech Republic, Portugal, Latvia, Greece
490	Italy	Liechtenstein, France, Hungary, United States, Sweden, Ireland, Denmark, United Kingdom, Slovenia, Macao-China, Czech Republic, Portugal, Latvia, Greece
489	Slovenia	United States, Sweden, Ireland, Denmark, United Kingdom, Italy, Macao-China, Czech Republic, Portugal, Latvia, Greece
488	Macao-China	United States, Sweden, Ireland, Denmark, United Kingdom, Italy, Slovenia, Czech Republic, Portugal, Latvia, Greece
488	Czech Republic	Hungary, United States, Sweden, Ireland, Denmark, United Kingdom, Italy, Slovenia, Macao-China, Portugal, Latvia, Greece, Slovak Republic
487	Portugal	United States, Sweden, Ireland, Denmark, United Kingdom, Italy, Slovenia, Macao-China, Czech Republic, Latvia, Greece, Slovak Republic, Spain
484	Latvia	United Kingdom, Italy, Slovenia, Macao-China, Czech Republic, Portugal, Greece, Slovak Republic, Spain
484	Greece	Ireland, Denmark, United Kingdom, Italy, Slovenia, Macao-China, Czech Republic, Portugal, Latvia, Slovak Republic, Spain
481	Slovak Republic	Czech Republic, Portugal, Latvia, Greece, Spain, Israel
481	Spain	Portugal, Latvia, Greece, Slovak Republic
475	Luxembourg	Israel, Croatia, Austria
473	Israel	Slovak Republic, Luxembourg, Croatia, Austria, Lithuania, Russian Federation
472	Croatia	Luxembourg, Israel, Austria, Lithuania, Russian Federation
471	Austria	Luxembourg, Israel, Croatia, Lithuania, Russian Federation
469	Lithuania	Israel, Croatia, Austria, Russian Federation
467	Russian Federation	Israel, Croatia, Austria, Lithuania, Turkey
459	Turkey	Russian Federation, Dubai (UAE), Chile
457	Dubai (UAE)	Turkey, Chile
452	Chile	Turkey, Dubai (UAE), Serbia
445	Serbia	Chile, Bulgaria
436	Bulgaria	Serbia, Romania
425	Romania	Bulgaria, Uruguay, Montenegro, Trinidad and Tobago, Mexico, Thailand
423	Uruguay	Romania, Montenegro, Trinidad and Tobago, Mexico, Thailand
420	Montenegro	Romania, Uruguay, Trinidad and Tobago, Mexico, Thailand
419	Trinidad and Tobago	Romania, Uruguay, Montenegro, Mexico, Thailand, Colombia
418	Mexico	Romania, Uruguay, Montenegro, Trinidad and Tobago, Thailand, Colombia
416	Thailand	Romania, Uruguay, Montenegro, Trinidad and Tobago, Mexico, Colombia, Jordan
411	Colombia	Trinidad and Tobago, Mexico, Thailand, Jordan, Brazil
410	Jordan	Thailand, Colombia, Brazil
406	Brazil	Colombia, Jordan, Argentina
398	Argentina	Brazil, Indonesia, Kazakhstan, Tunisia, Albania
397	Indonesia	Argentina, Kazakhstan, Tunisia, Albania
397	Kazakhstan	Argentina, Indonesia, Tunisia, Albania
393	Tunisia	Argentina, Indonesia, Kazakhstan, Albania
393	Albania	Argentina, Indonesia, Kazakhstan, Tunisia
379	Qatar	Azerbaijan, Panama, Peru
373	Azerbaijan	Qatar, Panama, Peru
372	Panama	Qatar, Azerbaijan, Peru
371	Peru	Qatar, Azerbaijan, Panama
327	Kyrgyzstan	

Source: OECD, *PISA 2009 Database*.
StatLink ⌐⌐⌐ http://dx.doi.org/10.1787/888932343133

At the other end of the proficiency range, few countries had very large numbers of students performing below the range of described levels in PISA, but there were several partner countries with more than 10% of students performing below Level 1b: Kyrgyzstan, Peru, Qatar, Panama and Argentina. The modal performance of a substantial number of countries on the reading scale was at Level 1a on the *integrate and interpret* subscale, and several partner countries showed over 30% of students performing at this level: Azerbaijan, Indonesia, Thailand, Tunisia, Kazakhstan and Panama.

Figure I.2.24 shows each country's mean score on the *integrate and interpret* subscale, and shows for which pairs of countries the differences between the means shown are statistically significant. For each country shown on the left in the middle column, the list of countries on the right hand column shows countries whose mean scores are not sufficiently different to be distinguished with confidence. For all other cases, one country has higher performance than another if it is above it in the list in the middle column, and lower performance if it is below.

Table I.2.9 presents the mean score, variation and gender difference for each country on this subscale. As on the overall reading scale, girls performed more strongly than boys in every country on the *integrate and interpret* subscale. There is a slightly smaller gap between girls' and boys' performance on this subscale (36 compared with 39). Nevertheless, in 36 countries the gap was more than half of one proficiency level, and in seven of these (the OECD countries Finland and Slovenia, and the partner countries Albania, Lithuania, Bulgaria, Jordan and Trinidad and Tobago), it is over 50 points. The appearance of Finland in this group indicates that extreme gender inequality in performance can co-exist with high overall performance. The mean performance of boys in Finland on this subscale (513), as on the overall reading scale (508), is still well above the OECD average. Colombia exhibits by far the smallest gender gap here as elsewhere in reading, with girls outperforming boys by only eight points.

■ Figure I.2.25 ■
Summary descriptions of the seven proficiency levels on the reading subscale *reflect and evaluate*

Level	Percentage of students able to perform tasks at each level or above (OECD average)	Characteristics of tasks	Examples of released *reflect and evaluate* questions
6	1.2% of students across the OECD can perform tasks at Level 6	Hypothesise about or critically evaluate a complex text on an unfamiliar topic, taking into account multiple criteria or perspectives, and applying sophisticated understandings from beyond the text. Generate categories for evaluating text features in terms of appropriateness for an audience.	
5	8.8% of students across the OECD can perform tasks at least at Level 5	Hypothesise about a text, drawing on specialised knowledge, and on deep understanding of long or complex texts that contain ideas contrary to expectations. Critically analyse and evaluate potential or real inconsistencies, either within the text or between the text and ideas outside the text.	
4	29.5% of students across the OECD can perform tasks at least at Level 4	Use formal or public knowledge to hypothesise about or critically evaluate a text. Show accurate understanding of long or complex texts.	*MOBILE PHONE SAFETY* – Question 11 (604)
3	57.7% of students across the OECD can perform tasks at least at Level 3	Make connections or comparisons, give explanations, or evaluate a feature of a text. Demonstrate a detailed understanding of the text in relation to familiar, everyday knowledge, or draw on less common knowledge.	*MOBILE PHONE SAFETY* – Question 6 (526) *TELECOMMUTING* – Question 7 (514) *BALLOON* – Question 4 (510)
2	80.7% of students across the OECD can perform tasks at least at Level 2	Make a comparison or connections between the text and outside knowledge, or explain a feature of the text by drawing on personal experience or attitudes.	*BALLOON* – Question 6 (411)
1a	93.5% of students across the OECD can perform tasks at least at Level 1a	Make a simple connection between information in the text and common, everyday knowledge.	*BRUSHING YOUR TEETH* – Question 4 (399) *BLOOD DONATION NOTICE* – Question 9 (368)
1b	98.4% of students across the OECD can perform tasks at least at Level 1b	There are no questions at this level in the existing reading question pool.	

Student performance on the **reflect and evaluate** reading subscale

Reflect and evaluate tasks involve engaging with a text while drawing on information, ideas or values external to the text. In *reflecting* on a text, readers relate their own experience or knowledge to the text. In *evaluating* a text, readers make a judgement about it, either drawing on personal experience or on knowledge of the world that may be formal or content-based. Reflecting on and evaluating the content of a text requires the reader to connect information in a text to knowledge from outside sources. To do so, readers must be able to understand what is said and intended in a text. They must then test that mental representation against what they know and believe on the basis of either prior information or information found in other texts. Reflecting on and evaluating the form of a text requires readers to stand apart from the text, consider it objectively and evaluate its quality and appropriateness. Knowledge of text structure, the style typical of different kinds of texts and register play an important role in these tasks.

About one-quarter of the questions in the pool of reading tasks for PISA 2009 address the *reflect and evaluate* aspect. The difficulty of questions with this classification is determined by several factors, including the quantity and explicitness of information to support reflection and evaluation, and the extent to which the information is common knowledge. Easier tasks require the reader to relate a text dealing with a familiar topic to familiar and personal knowledge. For such tasks, the question provides a clear direction to the reader about the criterion that should form the basis of the connection. At the other end of the scale, difficult *reflect and evaluate* tasks, which typically relate to more complex texts on topics that are not within the reader's immediate experience, require the reader to evaluate the structure or content of the text drawing on formal standards, or to hypothesise about some element of the text, such as why it is presented in a particular form, using criteria that are not provided. Readers need to generate their own terms of reference using internalised standards of relevance and plausibility.

Figure I.2.25 provides details of the nature of the reading skills, knowledge and understanding required at each level of the proficiency scale for the *reflect and evaluate* aspect of reading, along with the percentage of students across OECD countries who perform at this level in PISA 2009. The right hand column shows examples of released *reflect and evaluate* questions. Figures I.2.40 to I.2.46 describe these questions and provide commentary on what they show.

Figure I.2.26 shows the percentage of students at each proficiency level on the *reflect and evaluate* subscale. Details of performance by gender on this subscale are also provided in Table I.2.11.

Mean performance across OECD countries was slightly higher on the *reflect and evaluate* subscale than on the overall reading scale (494 compared with 493 points), and was also slightly more dispersed (a standard deviation of 97 compared with 93). Some high performing countries on the overall reading literacy scale show particularly strong performance at the top end of the scale. In the OECD countries, nearly 5% of students in New Zealand attained Level 6 (more than the proportion reaching Level 6 for any other country in any aspect of reading), and over 2% of students did so in Japan, Australia, Canada, the United States, New Zealand and Korea and in the partner countries and economies Singapore and Shanghai-China. At the other end of the scale, those countries that performed poorly overall also performed poorly on this subscale, though *reflect and evaluate* appears to be a particularly problematic aspect for several low-to-moderate performing countries from Eastern Europe: the Slovak Republic, the Czech Republic and Slovenia, and the partner countries Serbia and the Russian Federation. With mean scores on the overall reading scale between 442 and 483, these countries all have significantly lower means on the *reflect and evaluate subscale*, by at least 12 points, and at least 3% more students performing at or below Level 1b.

Figure I.2.27 shows each country's mean score on the *reflect and evaluate* subscale, and shows for which pairs of countries the differences between the means shown are statistically significant. For each country shown on the left in the middle column, the list of countries on the right hand column shows countries whose mean scores are not sufficiently different to be distinguished with confidence. For all other cases, one country has higher performance than another if it is above it in the list in the middle column, and lower performance if it is below it.

Table I.2.12 presents the mean and standard deviation overall, means for boys and girls and gender difference, percentiles score, variation and gender difference for each country on this subscale. As on the overall reading scale, girls universally performed better than boys in every country on the *reflect and evaluate* subscale. There is a larger average gap between girls' and boys' performance on this subscale than on the overall reading scale (44 compared with 39). The scale also shows the largest gaps over all in countries, of up to 70 points – almost a full proficiency level. The OECD country Slovenia and 7 partner countries have a gender gap of at least 60 points: Albania, Bulgaria, Trinidad and Tobago, Jordan, Lithuania, Croatia and Montenegro. Five of these eight countries are in southeastern Europe, where there appears to be some tendency for boys to be particularly weak in reflection and evaluation relative to girls. As an example, in Bulgaria, only 24% of boys but 43% of girls achieve at least Level 3.

■ Figure I. 2.26 ■
How well do students *reflect on and evaluate* what they read?
Percentage of students at the different proficiency levels in reflecting and evaluating what they read

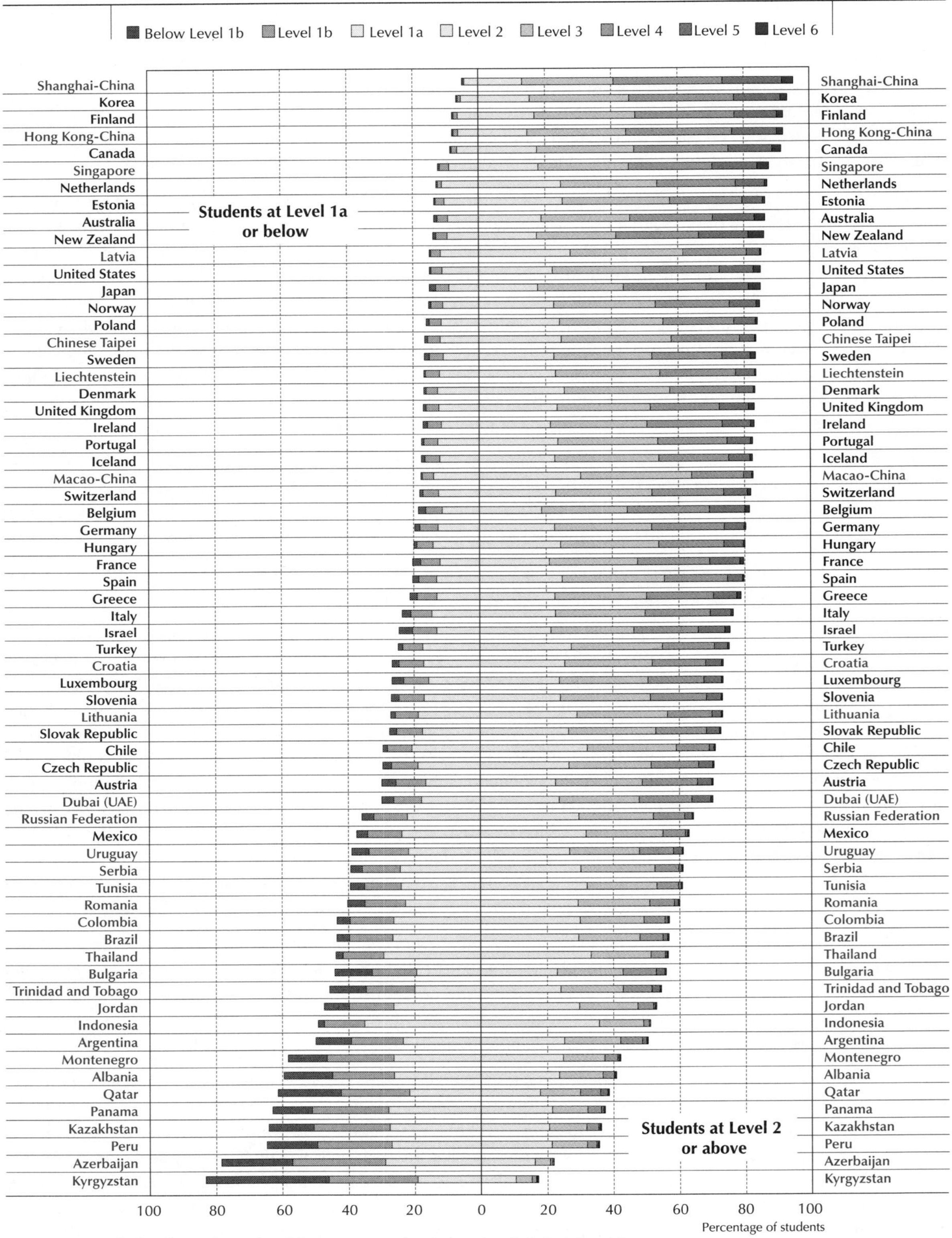

■ Below Level 1b   ▨ Level 1b   ☐ Level 1a   ☐ Level 2   ▨ Level 3   ▨ Level 4   ▨ Level 5   ■ Level 6

Shanghai-China
Korea
Finland
Hong Kong-China
Canada
Singapore
Netherlands
Estonia
Australia
New Zealand
Latvia
United States
Japan
Norway
Poland
Chinese Taipei
Sweden
Liechtenstein
Denmark
United Kingdom
Ireland
Portugal
Iceland
Macao-China
Switzerland
Belgium
Germany
Hungary
France
Spain
Greece
Italy
Israel
Turkey
Croatia
Luxembourg
Slovenia
Lithuania
Slovak Republic
Chile
Czech Republic
Austria
Dubai (UAE)
Russian Federation
Mexico
Uruguay
Serbia
Tunisia
Romania
Colombia
Brazil
Thailand
Bulgaria
Trinidad and Tobago
Jordan
Indonesia
Argentina
Montenegro
Albania
Qatar
Panama
Kazakhstan
Peru
Azerbaijan
Kyrgyzstan

Students at Level 1a or below

Students at Level 2 or above

100   80   60   40   20   0   20   40   60   80   100
Percentage of students

Countries are ranked in descending order of the percentage of students at Levels 2, 3, 4, 5 and 6.
Source: OECD, *PISA 2009 Database,* Table I.2.10.
StatLink ⟨⟩ http://dx.doi.org/10.1787/888932343133

■ Figure I.2.27 ■
Comparing countries on *reflect and evaluate* performance

Statistically significantly **above** the OECD average
Not statistically significantly different from the OECD average
Statistically significantly **below** the OECD average

Mean	Comparison country	Countries whose mean score is NOT statistically significantly different from that of the comparison country
557	Shanghai-China	
542	Korea	Hong Kong-China, Finland, Canada
540	Hong Kong-China	Korea, Finland, Canada
536	Finland	Korea, Hong Kong-China, Canada, New Zealand
535	Canada	Korea, Hong Kong-China, Finland, New Zealand
531	New Zealand	Finland, Canada, Singapore
529	Singapore	New Zealand
523	Australia	Japan
521	Japan	Australia, United States, Netherlands
512	United States	Japan, Netherlands, Belgium, Norway, Ireland
510	Netherlands	Japan, United States, Belgium, Norway, United Kingdom, Estonia, Ireland, Sweden
505	Belgium	United States, Netherlands, Norway, United Kingdom, Estonia, Ireland, Sweden, Liechtenstein
505	Norway	United States, Netherlands, Belgium, United Kingdom, Estonia, Ireland, Sweden, Poland, Liechtenstein
503	United Kingdom	Netherlands, Belgium, Norway, Estonia, Ireland, Sweden, Poland, Liechtenstein, Switzerland, Portugal, France
503	Estonia	Netherlands, Belgium, Norway, United Kingdom, Ireland, Sweden, Poland, Liechtenstein, Switzerland, Portugal, France
502	Ireland	United States, Netherlands, Belgium, Norway, United Kingdom, Estonia, Sweden, Poland, Liechtenstein, Switzerland, Portugal, Iceland, France
502	Sweden	Netherlands, Belgium, Norway, United Kingdom, Estonia, Ireland, Poland, Liechtenstein, Switzerland, Portugal, Iceland, France
498	Poland	Norway, United Kingdom, Estonia, Ireland, Sweden, Liechtenstein, Switzerland, Portugal, Iceland, France, Denmark, Chinese Taipei, Latvia, Germany, Greece
498	Liechtenstein	Belgium, Norway, United Kingdom, Estonia, Ireland, Sweden, Poland, Switzerland, Portugal, Iceland, France, Denmark, Chinese Taipei, Latvia, Germany, Greece, Hungary
497	Switzerland	United Kingdom, Estonia, Ireland, Sweden, Poland, Liechtenstein, Portugal, Iceland, France, Denmark, Chinese Taipei, Latvia, Germany, Greece, Hungary
496	Portugal	United Kingdom, Estonia, Ireland, Sweden, Poland, Liechtenstein, Switzerland, Iceland, France, Denmark, Chinese Taipei, Latvia, Germany, Greece, Hungary
496	Iceland	Ireland, Sweden, Poland, Liechtenstein, Switzerland, Portugal, France, Denmark, Chinese Taipei, Latvia, Germany, Greece
495	France	United Kingdom, Estonia, Ireland, Sweden, Poland, Liechtenstein, Switzerland, Portugal, Iceland, Denmark, Chinese Taipei, Latvia, Germany, Greece, Hungary
493	Denmark	Poland, Liechtenstein, Switzerland, Portugal, Iceland, France, Chinese Taipei, Latvia, Germany, Greece, Hungary
493	Chinese Taipei	Poland, Liechtenstein, Switzerland, Portugal, Iceland, France, Denmark, Latvia, Germany, Greece, Hungary
492	Latvia	Poland, Liechtenstein, Switzerland, Portugal, Iceland, France, Denmark, Chinese Taipei, Germany, Greece, Hungary, Israel
491	Germany	Poland, Liechtenstein, Switzerland, Portugal, Iceland, France, Denmark, Chinese Taipei, Latvia, Greece, Hungary, Israel
489	Greece	Poland, Liechtenstein, Switzerland, Portugal, Iceland, France, Denmark, Chinese Taipei, Latvia, Germany, Hungary, Spain, Israel, Italy, Macao-China
489	Hungary	Liechtenstein, Switzerland, Portugal, France, Denmark, Chinese Taipei, Latvia, Germany, Greece, Spain, Israel, Italy
483	Spain	Greece, Hungary, Israel, Italy, Macao-China
483	Israel	Latvia, Germany, Greece, Hungary, Spain, Italy, Macao-China, Turkey
482	Italy	Greece, Hungary, Spain, Israel, Macao-China
481	Macao-China	Greece, Spain, Israel, Italy
473	Turkey	Israel, Croatia, Luxembourg, Slovenia, Slovak Republic, Dubai (UAE), Austria
471	Croatia	Turkey, Luxembourg, Slovenia, Slovak Republic, Dubai (UAE), Lithuania, Austria, Czech Republic
471	Luxembourg	Turkey, Croatia, Slovenia, Slovak Republic
470	Slovenia	Turkey, Croatia, Luxembourg, Slovak Republic
466	Slovak Republic	Turkey, Croatia, Luxembourg, Slovenia, Dubai (UAE), Lithuania, Austria, Czech Republic
466	Dubai (UAE)	Turkey, Croatia, Slovak Republic, Lithuania, Austria, Czech Republic
463	Lithuania	Croatia, Slovak Republic, Dubai (UAE), Austria, Czech Republic
463	Austria	Turkey, Croatia, Slovak Republic, Dubai (UAE), Lithuania, Czech Republic
462	Czech Republic	Croatia, Slovak Republic, Dubai (UAE), Lithuania, Austria
452	Chile	
441	Russian Federation	Uruguay
436	Uruguay	Russian Federation, Mexico, Serbia, Romania
432	Mexico	Uruguay, Serbia, Tunisia, Romania
430	Serbia	Uruguay, Mexico, Tunisia, Romania, Brazil, Colombia, Bulgaria
427	Tunisia	Mexico, Serbia, Romania, Brazil, Colombia, Thailand, Bulgaria
426	Romania	Uruguay, Mexico, Serbia, Tunisia, Brazil, Colombia, Thailand, Bulgaria
424	Brazil	Serbia, Tunisia, Romania, Colombia, Thailand, Bulgaria
422	Colombia	Serbia, Tunisia, Romania, Brazil, Thailand, Bulgaria, Trinidad and Tobago
420	Thailand	Tunisia, Romania, Brazil, Colombia, Bulgaria
417	Bulgaria	Serbia, Tunisia, Romania, Brazil, Colombia, Thailand, Trinidad and Tobago, Indonesia, Jordan, Argentina
413	Trinidad and Tobago	Colombia, Bulgaria, Indonesia, Jordan
409	Indonesia	Bulgaria, Trinidad and Tobago, Jordan, Argentina
407	Jordan	Bulgaria, Trinidad and Tobago, Indonesia, Argentina
402	Argentina	Bulgaria, Indonesia, Jordan
383	Montenegro	Panama, Albania
377	Panama	Montenegro, Albania, Qatar, Kazakhstan, Peru
376	Albania	Montenegro, Panama, Qatar, Kazakhstan, Peru
376	Qatar	Panama, Albania, Kazakhstan, Peru
373	Kazakhstan	Panama, Albania, Qatar, Peru
368	Peru	Panama, Albania, Qatar, Kazakhstan
335	Azerbaijan	
300	Kyrgyzstan	

Source: OECD, *PISA 2009 Database*.
StatLink ⟐ http://dx.doi.org/10.1787/888932343133

■ Figure I.2.28 ■
Comparing countries on the different aspect subscales

Country performance on the subscale is between 0 to 3 score points **higher** than on the combined reading scale
Country performance on the subscale is between 3 to 10 score points **higher** than on the combined reading scale
Country performance on the subscale is 10 or more score points **higher** than on the combined reading scale

Country performance on the subscale is between 0 to 3 score points **lower** than on the combined reading scale
Country performance on the subscale is between 3 to 10 score points **lower** than on the combined reading scale
Country performance on the subscale is 10 or more score points **lower** than on the combined reading scale

	Reading score	Performance difference between the combined reading scale and each *aspect* subscale		
		Access and retrieve	*Integrate and interpret*	*Reflect and evaluate*
Shanghai-China	556	-7	2	1
Korea	539	2	1	3
Finland	536	-4	2	0
Hong Kong-China	533	-4	-3	6
Singapore	526	0	-1	3
Canada	524	-8	-2	11
New Zealand	521	0	-4	10
Japan	520	10	0	1
Australia	515	-2	-2	8
Netherlands	508	11	-4	2
Belgium	506	7	-2	-1
Norway	503	9	-1	2
Estonia	501	2	-1	2
Switzerland	501	5	1	-3
Poland	500	0	2	-3
Iceland	500	6	2	-4
United States	500	-8	-5	12
Liechtenstein	499	8	-2	-2
Sweden	497	7	-3	5
Germany	497	3	3	-6
Ireland	496	2	-2	7
France	496	-4	2	0
Chinese Taipei	495	1	4	-2
Denmark	495	7	-3	-2
United Kingdom	494	-3	-4	9
Hungary	494	7	2	-5
Portugal	489	-1	-3	7
Macao-China	487	6	2	-6
Italy	486	-4	4	-4
Latvia	484	-8	0	8
Slovenia	483	6	6	-13
Greece	483	-15	2	7
Spain	481	-1	0	2
Czech Republic	478	1	9	-16
Slovak Republic	477	13	4	-12
Croatia	476	16	-3	-5
Israel	474	-11	-1	9
Luxembourg	472	-2	3	-2
Austria	470	7	1	-7
Lithuania	468	8	0	-5
Turkey	464	3	-5	8
Dubai (UAE)	459	-1	-3	6
Russian Federation	459	9	7	-19
Chile	449	-5	3	3
Serbia	442	7	3	-12
Bulgaria	429	0	7	-12
Uruguay	426	-1	-3	10
Mexico	425	7	-7	7
Romania	424	-2	0	2
Thailand	421	10	-5	-1
Trinidad and Tobago	416	-3	2	-3
Colombia	413	-9	-2	9
Brazil	412	-5	-6	12
Montenegro	408	0	13	-25
Jordan	405	-11	5	2
Tunisia	404	-10	-10	23
Indonesia	402	-3	-4	7
Argentina	398	-4	-1	4
Kazakhstan	390	7	6	-18
Albania	385	-5	8	-9
Qatar	372	-18	7	4
Panama	371	-7	1	6
Peru	370	-6	2	-2
Azerbaijan	362	0	12	-27
Kyrgyzstan	314	-15	13	-14
OECD average	493	2	0	1

Source: OECD, *PISA 2009 Database*, Tables I.2.3, I.2.6, I.2.9 and I.2.12.
StatLink ᴍᴤᴾ http://dx.doi.org/10.1787/888932343133

The relative strengths and weaknesses of countries in different aspects of reading

Figure I.2.28 shows the mean performance of each participating country on the overall reading scale and compares it with its mean performance on the *access and retrieve, integrate and interpret* and *reflect and evaluate* subscales, showing the difference in points between the overall scale and each of the aspect subscales.

Some OECD countries performed consistently across the aspect subscales, with no more than three score points separating the mean proficiencies across the three aspects. These countries were Estonia, Korea, Luxembourg, Poland and Spain. More typically, however, there was some variation in performance across the aspect subscales.

Some countries performed significantly lower on the *reflect and evaluate* subscales – by at least 10 points – than on one or more of the other two aspect subscales. In this group are the OECD countries the Czech Republic, Slovenia, the Slovak Republic, and the partner countries Azerbaijan, Montenegro, the Russian Federation, Kazakhstan, Kyrgyzstan, Serbia and Bulgaria. Students in these countries appear to be less accustomed to critically evaluating and reflecting upon what they read, and more accustomed to using texts to find and analyse information.

Conversely, distinguishable groups of countries performed better on the *reflect and evaluate* aspect than on one or both of the other aspects. Apart from Ireland, all English-speaking countries (Australia, Canada, New Zealand, the United Kingdom and the United States) have a mean score at least 10 points higher on the *reflect and evaluate* subscale than on one or both of the other subscales. The same is true of Hong Kong-China. Another distinguishable group with this profile comprises several of the Latin American partner countries: Brazil, Colombia, Panama and Uruguay. The remaining Latin American countries – the OECD countries Chile and Mexico, and the partner country Argentina – also performed comparatively well on the *reflect and evaluate* subscale. Students in these countries demonstrate strength in expressing views about texts and discerning their structure and purpose, but a comparative deficit in attentive and accurate information-focused reading.

In addition to comparing mean scores for each of the aspects, another way of looking at countries' relative strength or weakness in aspects of reading is by examining their rank in each aspect. The range of ranks for each country in each aspect is listed in Figure I.2.29.

Gender disparities in the different aspects of reading

Figures I.2.30a, I.2.30b and I.2.30c show the distribution of student performance on each aspect subscale for each country, marked with the mean performance of girls and boys.

While girls outperformed boys in every aspect of reading as well as on the overall reading scale, there are some variations across the aspect subscales. The smallest variation between girls and boys is on the *integrate and interpret* subscale (36 points) and the largest on the *reflect and evaluate* subscale (44 points). This relative disparity is reflected in every part of the distribution of performance on the aspect subscales.

For example, on the *integrate and interpret* subscale, 2% or more of girls in eight OECD countries and three partner countries and economies performed at Level 6, with the highest percentage of 4.2% in Shanghai-China, New Zealand, and Singapore. On the same aspect subscale, the only countries in which more than 2% of boys performed at Level 6 are the OECD countries New Zealand and Australia (both 2.1%) and the partner country Singapore (2.8%). These figures can be compared with the parallel results on the *reflect and evaluate* subscale, where the picture is similar but more pronounced. On the *reflect and evaluate* subscale, over 2% of girls in ten OECD countries and three partner countries and economies attained proficiency Level 6, with New Zealand yielding 6.5% at this level. Only in the OECD countries New Zealand, Japan and Australia, and in the partner country Singapore did more than 2% of boys achieve Level 6 on the *reflect and evaluate* subscale.

At the other end of the performance spectrum, the ratio between girls' and boys' performance was similar across the three aspect subscales: roughly half as many girls as boys performed below Level 2 on each of the aspect subscales across OECD countries. On the *access and retrieve* subscale, 13.5% of girls and 25.6% of boys performed below Level 2; on the *integrate and interpret* subscale, 13.4% of girls and 25.1% of boys; on the *reflect and evaluate* subscale, 12.6% of girls and 25.9% of boys performed below this level.

■ Figure I.2.29 [Part 1/3] ■

Where countries rank in different aspects of reading performance

Statistically significantly **above** the OECD average
Not statistically significantly different from the OECD average
Statistically significantly **below** the OECD average

	Mean Score	S.E.	OECD countries		All countries/economies	
			Upper rank	Lower rank	Upper rank	Lower rank
Shanghai-China	549	(2.9)			1	1
Korea	542	(3.6)	1	1	1	2
Finland	532	(2.7)	2	3	3	5
Japan	530	(3.8)	2	4	3	7
Hong Kong-China	530	(2.7)			3	6
Singapore	526	(1.4)			5	7
New Zealand	521	(2.4)	4	6	6	9
Netherlands	519	(5.1)	3	9	5	12
Canada	517	(1.5)	5	8	8	11
Belgium	513	(2.4)	5	9	8	13
Australia	513	(2.4)	5	9	8	13
Norway	512	(2.8)	6	11	9	14
Liechtenstein	508	(4.0)			10	20
Iceland	507	(1.6)	9	13	12	17
Switzerland	505	(2.7)	9	16	12	20
Sweden	505	(2.9)	9	16	13	21
Estonia	503	(3.0)	10	18	13	22
Denmark	502	(2.6)	11	18	14	22
Hungary	501	(3.7)	10	19	13	23
Germany	501	(3.5)	11	19	14	24
Poland	500	(2.8)	12	19	16	24
Ireland	498	(3.3)	12	20	16	26
Chinese Taipei	496	(2.8)			19	28
Macao-China	493	(1.2)			23	28
United States	492	(3.6)	17	24	22	31
France	492	(3.8)	17	24	21	31
Croatia	492	(3.1)			22	31
United Kingdom	491	(2.5)	19	24	23	31
Slovak Republic	491	(3.0)	19	24	23	31
Slovenia	489	(1.1)	20	24	27	31
Portugal	488	(3.3)	19	25	24	32
Italy	482	(1.8)	24	27	31	35
Spain	480	(2.1)	25	28	32	36
Czech Republic	479	(3.2)	25	29	32	37
Austria	477	(3.2)	25	29	32	38
Lithuania	476	(3.0)			32	38
Latvia	476	(3.6)			32	39
Luxembourg	471	(1.3)	29	31	37	40
Russian Federation	469	(3.9)			37	42
Greece	468	(4.4)	29	32	36	42
Turkey	467	(4.1)	29	32	37	42
Israel	463	(4.1)	30	32	39	43
Dubai (UAE)	458	(1.4)			42	43
Serbia	449	(3.1)			44	45
Chile	444	(3.4)	33	33	44	46
Mexico	433	(2.1)	34	34	46	48
Thailand	431	(3.5)			46	49
Bulgaria	430	(8.3)			45	50
Uruguay	424	(2.9)			48	50
Romania	423	(4.7)			47	50
Trinidad and Tobago	413	(1.6)			50	52
Montenegro	408	(2.3)			52	54
Brazil	407	(3.3)			52	55
Colombia	404	(3.7)			52	56
Indonesia	399	(4.7)			53	59
Kazakhstan	397	(3.7)			54	59
Argentina	394	(4.8)			55	59
Jordan	394	(4.0)			55	59
Tunisia	393	(3.3)			55	59
Albania	380	(4.7)			60	61
Peru	364	(4.3)			61	63
Panama	363	(7.7)			61	64
Azerbaijan	361	(4.5)			61	64
Qatar	354	(1.0)			63	64
Kyrgyzstan	299	(4.0)			65	65

Table heading: **Access and retrieve subscale** — Range of rank

Source: OECD, *PISA 2009 Database*.
StatLink ■■■ http://dx.doi.org/10.1787/888932343133

■ Figure I.2.29 [Part 2/3] ■

Where countries rank in different aspects of reading performance

Statistically significantly **above** the OECD average
Not statistically significantly different from the OECD average
Statistically significantly **below** the OECD average

	Mean Score	S.E.	Integrate and interpret subscale			
			Range of rank			
			OECD countries		All countries/economies	
			Upper rank	Lower rank	Upper rank	Lower rank
Shanghai-China	558	(2.5)			1	1
Korea	541	(3.4)	1	2	2	3
Finland	538	(2.3)	1	2	2	3
Hong Kong-China	530	(2.2)			4	4
Singapore	525	(1.2)			5	6
Canada	522	(1.5)	3	4	5	7
Japan	520	(3.5)	3	6	5	9
New Zealand	517	(2.4)	4	6	7	9
Australia	513	(2.4)	5	7	8	10
Netherlands	504	(5.4)	6	17	9	22
Belgium	504	(2.5)	7	14	10	17
Poland	503	(2.8)	7	15	10	19
Iceland	503	(1.5)	7	13	10	17
Norway	502	(2.7)	7	15	10	19
Switzerland	502	(2.5)	7	15	10	19
Germany	501	(2.8)	7	16	10	21
Estonia	500	(2.8)	8	17	11	22
Chinese Taipei	499	(2.5)			12	23
Liechtenstein	498	(4.0)			10	25
France	497	(3.6)	9	21	12	26
Hungary	496	(3.2)	11	22	14	27
United States	495	(3.7)	12	24	15	30
Sweden	494	(3.0)	13	23	17	29
Ireland	494	(3.0)	14	24	17	29
Denmark	492	(2.1)	16	23	20	29
United Kingdom	491	(2.4)	17	25	22	32
Italy	490	(1.6)	19	25	24	31
Slovenia	489	(1.1)	21	25	25	31
Macao-China	488	(0.8)			26	31
Czech Republic	488	(2.9)	19	27	24	34
Portugal	487	(3.0)	20	27	25	34
Latvia	484	(2.8)			28	35
Greece	484	(4.0)	21	29	25	35
Slovak Republic	481	(2.5)	25	28	32	36
Spain	481	(2.0)	26	28	32	35
Luxembourg	475	(1.1)	29	31	36	38
Israel	473	(3.4)	28	31	36	41
Croatia	472	(2.9)			36	41
Austria	471	(2.9)	29	31	36	41
Lithuania	469	(2.4)			38	41
Russian Federation	467	(3.1)			38	42
Turkey	459	(3.3)	32	33	41	43
Dubai (UAE)	457	(1.3)			42	44
Chile	452	(3.1)	32	33	43	45
Serbia	445	(2.4)			45	46
Bulgaria	436	(6.4)			45	47
Romania	425	(4.0)			46	50
Uruguay	423	(2.6)			47	51
Montenegro	420	(1.6)			47	51
Trinidad and Tobago	419	(1.4)			48	52
Mexico	418	(2.0)	34	34	48	52
Thailand	416	(2.6)			49	53
Colombia	411	(3.8)			51	55
Jordan	410	(3.1)			52	55
Brazil	406	(2.7)			53	56
Argentina	398	(4.7)			55	60
Indonesia	397	(3.5)			56	60
Kazakhstan	397	(3.0)			56	60
Tunisia	393	(2.7)			57	60
Albania	393	(3.8)			56	60
Qatar	379	(0.9)			61	62
Azerbaijan	373	(2.9)			62	64
Panama	372	(5.9)			61	64
Peru	371	(4.0)			62	64
Kyrgyzstan	327	(2.9)			65	65

Source: OECD, *PISA 2009 Database.*
StatLink http://dx.doi.org/10.1787/888932343133

■ Figure I.2.29 [Part 3/3] ■

Where countries rank in different aspects of reading performance

Statistically significantly **above** the OECD average
Not statistically significantly different from the OECD average
Statistically significantly **below** the OECD average

			Reflect and evaluate subscale			
			\(Range of rank\)			
			OECD countries		All countries/economies	
	Mean Score	S.E.	Upper rank	Lower rank	Upper rank	Lower rank
Shanghai-China	557	(2.4)			1	1
Korea	542	(3.9)	1	2	2	4
Hong Kong-China	540	(2.5)			2	4
Finland	536	(2.2)	1	4	3	6
Canada	535	(1.6)	2	4	3	6
New Zealand	531	(2.5)	3	5	4	7
Singapore	529	(1.1)			6	7
Australia	523	(2.5)	5	6	8	9
Japan	521	(3.9)	5	7	8	10
United States	512	(4.0)	6	10	9	13
Netherlands	510	(5.0)	6	13	9	16
Belgium	505	(2.5)	8	14	11	17
Norway	505	(2.7)	8	14	11	17
United Kingdom	503	(2.4)	9	16	12	19
Estonia	503	(2.6)	9	16	11	19
Ireland	502	(3.1)	8	16	11	20
Sweden	502	(3.0)	9	17	11	20
Poland	498	(2.8)	12	20	15	26
Liechtenstein	498	(3.2)			14	26
Switzerland	497	(2.7)	13	21	16	26
Portugal	496	(3.3)	13	22	15	27
Iceland	496	(1.4)	15	20	18	25
France	495	(3.4)	14	23	17	29
Denmark	493	(2.6)	16	23	20	29
Chinese Taipei	493	(2.8)			20	29
Latvia	492	(3.0)			20	29
Germany	491	(2.8)	18	24	22	30
Greece	489	(4.9)	16	26	20	33
Hungary	489	(3.3)	19	25	23	31
Spain	483	(2.2)	23	26	29	33
Israel	483	(4.0)	22	27	28	34
Italy	482	(1.8)	24	26	30	33
Macao-China	481	(0.8)			31	33
Turkey	473	(4.0)	26	30	33	39
Croatia	471	(3.5)			34	40
Luxembourg	471	(1.1)	27	29	34	37
Slovenia	470	(1.2)	27	30	34	37
Slovak Republic	466	(2.9)	28	32	36	42
Dubai (UAE)	466	(1.1)			37	41
Lithuania	463	(2.5)			38	42
Austria	463	(3.4)	30	32	37	42
Czech Republic	462	(3.1)	30	32	38	42
Chile	452	(3.2)	33	33	43	43
Russian Federation	441	(3.7)			44	45
Uruguay	436	(2.9)			44	47
Mexico	432	(1.9)	34	34	45	48
Serbia	430	(2.6)			45	49
Tunisia	427	(3.0)			46	51
Romania	426	(4.5)			46	53
Brazil	424	(2.7)			48	53
Colombia	422	(4.2)			48	54
Thailand	420	(2.8)			49	53
Bulgaria	417	(7.1)			48	57
Trinidad and Tobago	413	(1.3)			53	55
Indonesia	409	(3.8)			53	57
Jordan	407	(3.4)			54	57
Argentina	402	(4.8)			55	57
Montenegro	383	(1.9)			58	59
Panama	377	(6.3)			58	63
Albania	376	(4.6)			58	63
Qatar	376	(1.0)			59	62
Kazakhstan	373	(3.4)			59	63
Peru	368	(4.2)			61	63
Azerbaijan	335	(3.8)			64	64
Kyrgyzstan	300	(4.0)			65	65

Source: OECD, *PISA 2009 Database*.
StatLink ᵐˢᵖ http://dx.doi.org/10.1787/888932343133

■ Figure I. 2.30a ■
Gender differences in the ability to *access and retrieve* information from reading

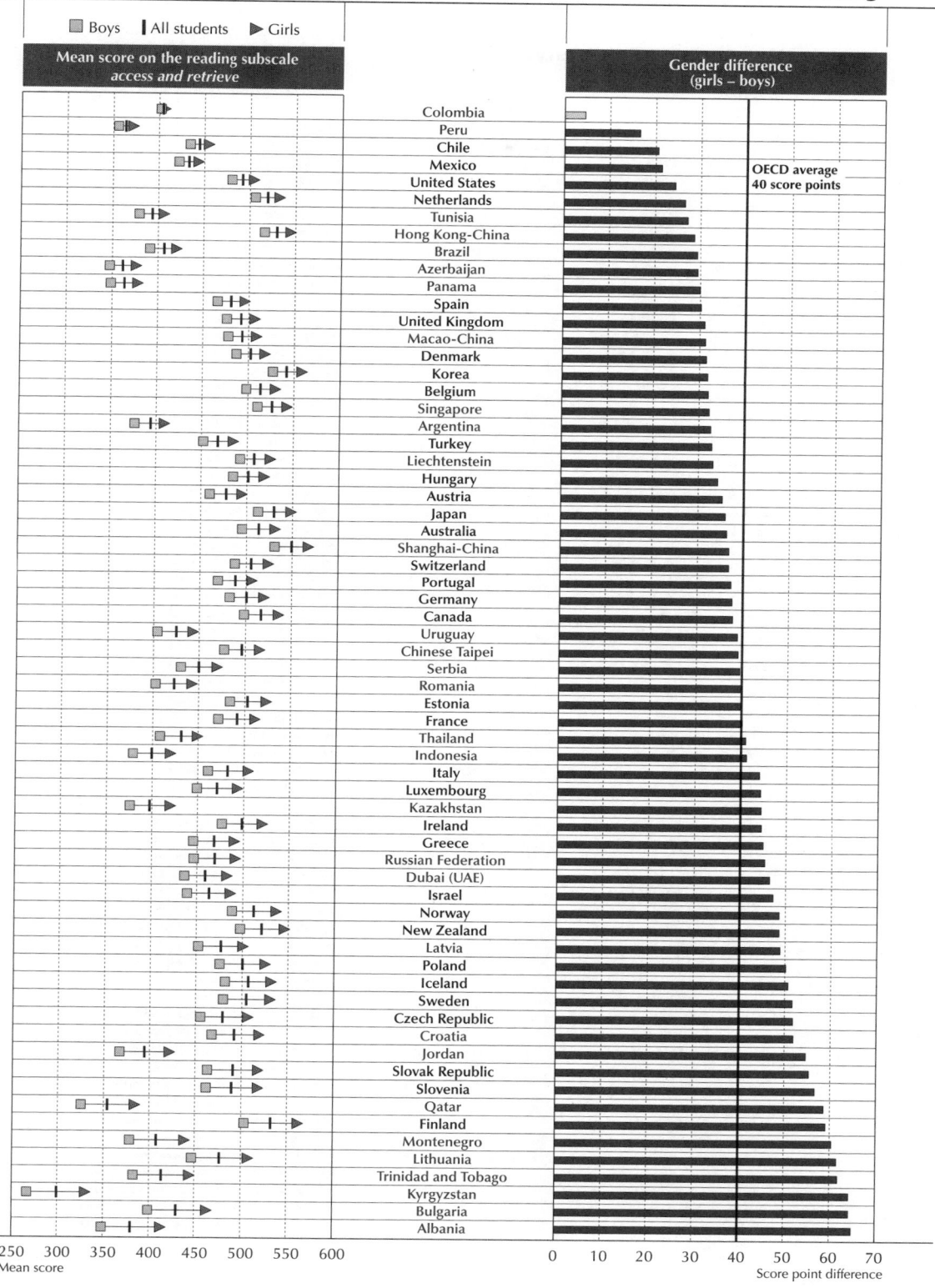

Note: Statistically significant gender differences are marked in a darker tone (see Annex A3).
Countries are ranked in ascending order of the gender score point difference (girls – boys).
Source: OECD, *PISA 2009 Database,* Table I.2.6.
StatLink ⬛ᵐˢᵖ⬛ http://dx.doi.org/10.1787/888932343133

■ Figure I. 2.30b ■

Gender differences in the ability to *integrate and interpret* information from reading

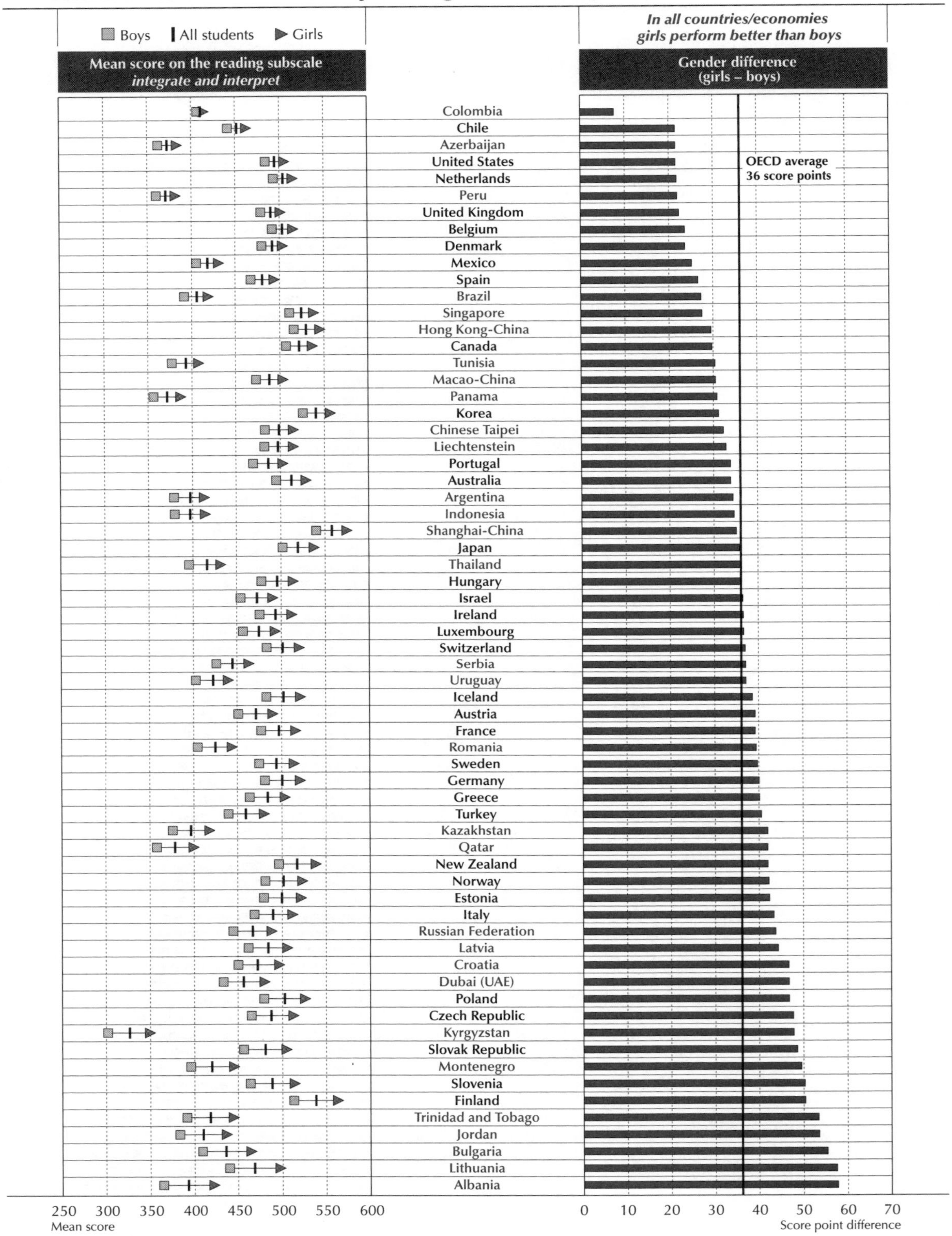

☐ Boys | All students   ▶ Girls

In all countries/economies girls perform better than boys

| Mean score on the reading subscale *integrate and interpret* | Gender difference (girls – boys) |

OECD average 36 score points

Colombia
Chile
Azerbaijan
United States
Netherlands
Peru
United Kingdom
Belgium
Denmark
Mexico
Spain
Brazil
Singapore
Hong Kong-China
Canada
Tunisia
Macao-China
Panama
Korea
Chinese Taipei
Liechtenstein
Portugal
Australia
Argentina
Indonesia
Shanghai-China
Japan
Thailand
Hungary
Israel
Ireland
Luxembourg
Switzerland
Serbia
Uruguay
Iceland
Austria
France
Romania
Sweden
Germany
Greece
Turkey
Kazakhstan
Qatar
New Zealand
Norway
Estonia
Italy
Russian Federation
Latvia
Croatia
Dubai (UAE)
Poland
Czech Republic
Kyrgyzstan
Slovak Republic
Montenegro
Slovenia
Finland
Trinidad and Tobago
Jordan
Bulgaria
Lithuania
Albania

250   300   350   400   450   500   550   600
Mean score

0   10   20   30   40   50   60   70
Score point difference

Note: All gender differences are statistically significant (see Annex A3).
Countries are ranked in ascending order of the gender score point difference (girls – boys).
Source: OECD, *PISA 2009 Database,* Table I.2.9.
StatLink ▒▒▒ http://dx.doi.org/10.1787/888932343133

Figure I. 2.30c

Gender differences in the ability to *reflect on and evaluate* information from reading

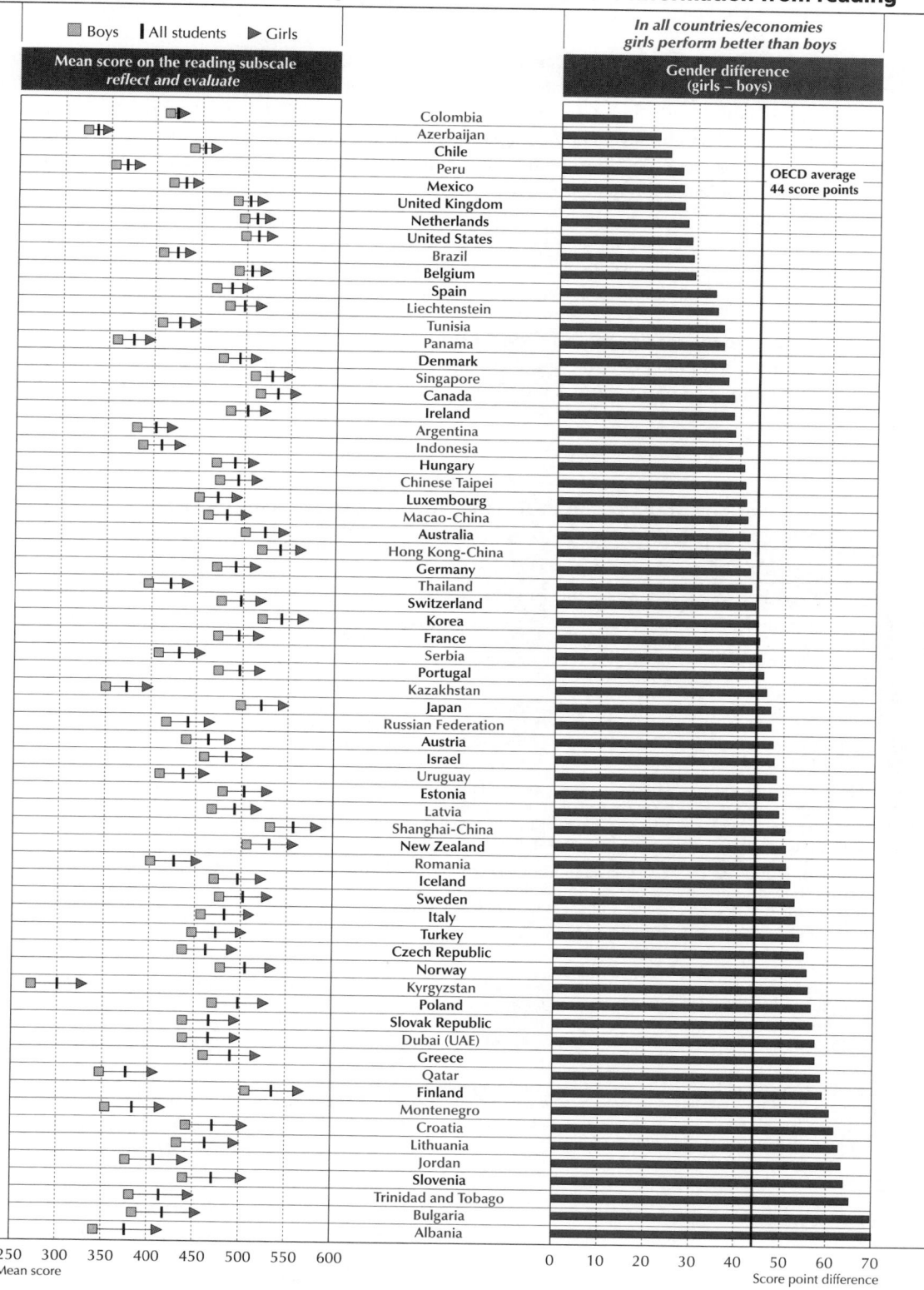

Note: All gender differences are statistically significant (see Annex A3).
Countries are ranked in ascending order of the gender score point difference (girls – boys).
Source: OECD, *PISA 2009 Database,* Table I.2.12.
StatLink http://dx.doi.org/10.1787/888932343133

Text format subscales

The reading framework identifies four text formats, *continuous, non-continuous, mixed* and *multiple.* Two of these are used as the basis for building text-format subscales: *continuous texts* and *non-continuous texts*.

A little under two-thirds of the questions are classified as *continuous.* These are questions based on stimulus in prose (complete sentences and paragraphs), or on the prose section of texts in a format comprising a mix of *continuous* and *non-continuous* parts. A little under one-third of the questions in PISA 2009 are classified as *non-continuous.* These are questions based on stimulus in *non-continuous* format, such as tables, graphs, maps, forms and diagrams, or on the *non-continuous* section of a text with a *mixed* format. Five percent of questions are classified as *mixed format.* These questions require the reader to draw equally on *continuous* and *non-continuous* parts of a *mixed format* text. These questions have not been included in either the *continuous-* or *non-continuous text* subscales. A number of *multiple texts* are used as stimulus in PISA 2009, but in these cases the texts comprising each set of stimuli are all in *continuous* format, so the 5% of questions classified as *multiple texts*, where the reader is required to draw on more than one text, are included in the construction of the *continuous texts* subscale.

Student performance on the reading subscale **continuous texts**

With 65% of questions from the PISA 2009 pool of reading tasks contributing to the *continuous texts* subscale, a wide variety of tasks and text characteristics must be accounted for in describing increasing levels of proficiency.

■ Figure I.2.31 ■

Summary descriptions of the seven proficiency levels on the reading subscale *continuous texts*

Level	Percentage of students able to perform tasks at each level or above (OECD average)	Characteristics of tasks	Examples of released *continuous texts* questions
6	1.0% of students across the OECD can perform tasks at Level 6	Negotiate single or multiple texts that may be long, dense or deal with highly abstract and implicit meanings. Relate information in texts to multiple, complex or counterintuitive ideas.	*THE PLAY'S THE THING* – Question 3 (730)
5	8.2% of students across the OECD can perform tasks at least at Level 5	Negotiate texts whose discourse structure is not obvious or clearly marked, in order to discern the relationship of specific parts of the text to the implicit theme or intention.	
4	28.8% of students across the OECD can perform tasks at least at Level 4	Follow linguistic or thematic links over several paragraphs, often in the absence of clear discourse markers, in order to locate, interpret or evaluate embedded information.	*THE PLAY'S THE THING* – Question 7 (556)
3	57.2% of students across the OECD can perform tasks at least at Level 3	Use conventions of text organisation, where present, and follow implicit or explicit logical links such as cause and effect relationships across sentences or paragraphs in order to locate, interpret or evaluate information.	*MISER* – Question 5 (548) *TELECOMMUTING* – Question 1 (537) *TELECOMMUTING* – Question 7 (514)
2	80.9% of students across the OECD can perform tasks at least at Level 2	Follow logical and linguistic connections within a paragraph in order to locate or interpret information; or synthesise information across texts or parts of a text in order to infer the author's purpose.	*THE PLAY'S THE THING* – Question 4 (474) *BLOOD DONATION NOTICE* – Question 8 (438)
1a	94.1% of students across the OECD can perform tasks at least at Level 1a	Use redundancy, paragraph headings or common print conventions to identify the main idea of the text, or to locate information stated explicitly within a short section of text.	*BRUSHING YOUR TEETH* – Question 4 (399) *MISER* – Question 1 (373) *BLOOD DONATION NOTICE* – Question 9 (368) *BRUSHING YOUR TEETH* – Question 2 (358) *BRUSHING YOUR TEETH* – Question 1 (353)
1b	98.7% of students across the OECD can perform tasks at least at Level 1b	Recognise information in short, syntactically simple texts that have a familiar context and text type, and include ideas that are reinforced by pictures or by repeated verbal cues.	*MISER* – Question 7 (310) *BRUSHING YOUR TEETH* – Question 3 (285)

At the lowest levels, tasks are based on short, simple texts in a familiar form, with verbal repetition and/or non-verbal support such as a picture. As tasks become more difficult, the syntactic structure of the associated texts increases in complexity, the content becomes less familiar and more abstract, and the reader is required to focus on ever larger sections of the text or on more widely scattered information. At the upper levels, tasks require the reader to extract and process information from long or dense texts in an unfamiliar format, where there are few, if any, explicit markers as to the location of the needed information, and the reader is required to construct meaning from what is implied rather than stated.

Figure I.2.31 provides descriptions of the nature of the reading skills, knowledge and understanding required at each level of the scale for the *continuous texts* aspect of reading, with the percentage of students across OECD countries who perform at this level in PISA 2009. The right-hand column lists examples of released *continuous texts* questions. Figures I.2.40 to I.2.46 describe these questions and provide commentary on what they show.

Figure I.2.32 shows the percentage of students at each proficiency level on the *continuous texts* subscale. Details of performance by gender on this subscale are also provided in Table I.2.15.

With such a large percentage of the questions contributing to the *continuous texts* subscale, it is not surprising that the profile of performance by reading level is very similar to that for the overall reading scale: the difference at each level, on average, is less than 0.5 of a percentage point. Figure I.2.32 shows that across countries, there is a relatively small percentage of students who are proficient at the very highest levels of performance (for OECD countries, on average, 7.2% and 1% at Levels 5 and 6, respectively). Nevertheless, more than 15% of students attain one of these levels in the OECD country New Zealand (15.9%) and the partner countries and economies Shanghai-China (23.7%), Hong Kong-China (15.4%) and Singapore (15.2%). At the other end of the spectrum, on average across OECD countries, almost 19% of students perform below Level 2, and the figure is greater than 50% in the partner countries Kyrgyzstan, Azerbaijan, Panama, Peru, Qatar, Kazakhstan, Albania, Indonesia and Argentina. This indicates that in these countries, the majority of 15-year-olds are likely to find it difficult to use *continuous texts* unless the texts are short and clearly sign-posted; and even with such texts, they are unlikely to be able to do more than identify a main idea or find explicitly stated information.

Figure I.2.33 shows each country's mean score on the *continuous texts* subscale, and shows for which pairs of countries the differences between the means shown are statistically significant. For each country shown on the left in the middle column, the list of countries on the right hand column shows countries whose mean scores are not sufficiently different to be distinguished with confidence. For all other cases, one country has a higher performance than another if it is above it in the list in the middle column, and a lower performance if it is below.

Table I.2.16 presents the mean score, variation and gender difference for each country on the *continuous texts* subscale. Girls outperformed boys in every country on the *continuous texts* subscale; indeed the gap is even slightly wider than on the overall reading scale (42 compared with 39). In 51 countries, the gap is more than half of one proficiency level (more than 36 points). The biggest gap is between boys and girls in the partner country Albania (67 points) while, as in the overall scale and the aspect subscales, the partner country Colombia has the smallest gender gap, with only 14 points separating boys and girls.

Student performance on the reading subscale **non-continuous texts**

Traditionally, reading has been associated mainly with *continuous texts*. In many school systems, especially in language-of-instruction classes, reading is typically confined to literature and expository prose. In other parts of the curriculum, however, proficiency in understanding and using *non-continuous texts* is at least equally important: for example, students need to be able to read and interpret maps and tables in the social sciences, and diagrams and graphs in the sciences. In adult life, a large part of everyday reading involves *non-continuous texts*, such as tax forms, timetables, graphed reports of household energy consumption, and lists of safety instructions in the workplace. Given the prevalence of *non-continuous texts*, a substantial proportion of tasks in the PISA 2009 pool of reading tasks – nearly 30% – are dedicated to assessing students' proficiency in reading these kinds of texts.

All *non-continuous texts* can be analysed as comprising one or more lists, the easiest tasks on this subscale are based on a single, simple list and require the reader to focus on a single explicit and prominently placed piece of information. Increasing difficulty on the scale is associated with tasks based on texts with more complex list structures, such as combined lists, and those with less familiar forms of presentation. In addition, more difficult tasks require readers to integrate information from multiple parts of a document or even to translate information presented in different *non-continuous* formats, thus implicitly involving a deep understanding of the structures of several texts.

■ Figure I. 2.32 ■

How well do students read *continuous texts*?

Percentage of students at the different levels of proficiency in reading continuous texts

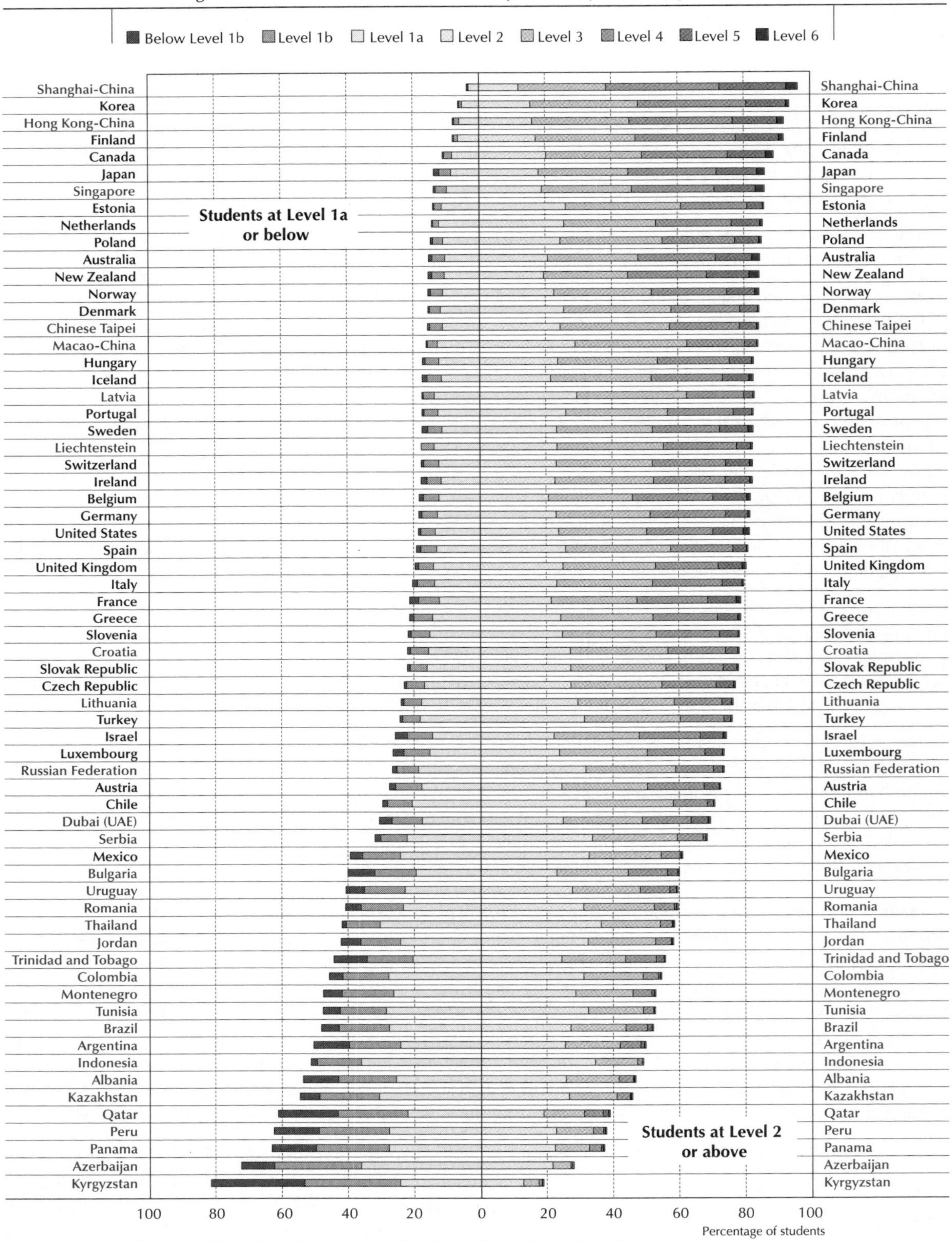

■ Below Level 1b ▨ Level 1b ☐ Level 1a ☐ Level 2 ▨ Level 3 ▨ Level 4 ▨ Level 5 ■ Level 6

Students at Level 1a or below

Students at Level 2 or above

| Shanghai-China |
| Korea |
| Hong Kong-China |
| Finland |
| Canada |
| Japan |
| Singapore |
| Estonia |
| Netherlands |
| Poland |
| Australia |
| New Zealand |
| Norway |
| Denmark |
| Chinese Taipei |
| Macao-China |
| Hungary |
| Iceland |
| Latvia |
| Portugal |
| Sweden |
| Liechtenstein |
| Switzerland |
| Ireland |
| Belgium |
| Germany |
| United States |
| Spain |
| United Kingdom |
| Italy |
| France |
| Greece |
| Slovenia |
| Croatia |
| Slovak Republic |
| Czech Republic |
| Lithuania |
| Turkey |
| Israel |
| Luxembourg |
| Russian Federation |
| Austria |
| Chile |
| Dubai (UAE) |
| Serbia |
| Mexico |
| Bulgaria |
| Uruguay |
| Romania |
| Thailand |
| Jordan |
| Trinidad and Tobago |
| Colombia |
| Montenegro |
| Tunisia |
| Brazil |
| Argentina |
| Indonesia |
| Albania |
| Kazakhstan |
| Qatar |
| Peru |
| Panama |
| Azerbaijan |
| Kyrgyzstan |

100 80 60 40 20 0 20 40 60 80 100

Percentage of students

Countries are ranked in descending order of the percentage of students at Levels 2, 3, 4, 5 and 6.
Source: OECD, *PISA 2009 Database,* Table I.2.14.
StatLink ⬛⬛ http://dx.doi.org/10.1787/888932343133

■ Figure I.2.33 ■

Comparing countries' performance in reading *continuous texts*

	Statistically significantly **above** the OECD average
	Not statistically significantly different from the OECD average
	Statistically significantly **below** the OECD average

Mean	Comparison country	Countries whose mean score is NOT statistically significantly different from that of the comparison country
564	Shanghai-China	
538	Korea	Hong Kong-China, Finland
538	Hong Kong-China	Korea, Finland
535	Finland	Korea, Hong Kong-China
524	Canada	Singapore, Japan
522	Singapore	Canada, Japan, New Zealand
520	Japan	Canada, Singapore, New Zealand, Australia
518	New Zealand	Singapore, Japan, Australia
513	Australia	Japan, New Zealand, Netherlands
506	Netherlands	Australia, Norway, Belgium, Poland, Iceland, United States, Sweden, Switzerland, Estonia, Hungary, Ireland, Chinese Taipei, Denmark, Germany
505	Norway	Netherlands, Belgium, Poland, Iceland, United States, Sweden
504	Belgium	Netherlands, Norway, Poland, Iceland, United States, Sweden, Switzerland, Estonia, Hungary, Ireland
502	Poland	Netherlands, Norway, Belgium, Iceland, United States, Sweden, Switzerland, Estonia, Hungary, Ireland, Chinese Taipei, Denmark, Germany, Liechtenstein
501	Iceland	Netherlands, Norway, Belgium, Poland, United States, Sweden, Switzerland, Estonia, Hungary, Ireland, Chinese Taipei, Denmark, Germany, Liechtenstein
500	United States	Netherlands, Norway, Belgium, Poland, Iceland, Sweden, Switzerland, Estonia, Hungary, Ireland, Chinese Taipei, Denmark, Germany, Liechtenstein, France, Portugal, United Kingdom
499	Sweden	Netherlands, Norway, Belgium, Poland, Iceland, United States, Switzerland, Estonia, Hungary, Ireland, Chinese Taipei, Denmark, Germany, Liechtenstein, France, Portugal, United Kingdom
498	Switzerland	Netherlands, Belgium, Poland, Iceland, United States, Sweden, Estonia, Hungary, Ireland, Chinese Taipei, Denmark, Germany, Liechtenstein, France, Portugal, United Kingdom
497	Estonia	Netherlands, Belgium, Poland, Iceland, United States, Sweden, Switzerland, Hungary, Ireland, Chinese Taipei, Denmark, Germany, Liechtenstein, France, Portugal, United Kingdom
497	Hungary	Netherlands, Belgium, Poland, Iceland, United States, Sweden, Switzerland, Estonia, Ireland, Chinese Taipei, Denmark, Germany, Liechtenstein, France, Portugal, United Kingdom, Greece
497	Ireland	Netherlands, Belgium, Poland, Iceland, United States, Sweden, Switzerland, Estonia, Hungary, Chinese Taipei, Denmark, Germany, Liechtenstein, France, Portugal, United Kingdom, Greece
496	Chinese Taipei	Netherlands, Poland, Iceland, United States, Sweden, Switzerland, Estonia, Hungary, Ireland, Denmark, Germany, Liechtenstein, France, Portugal, United Kingdom
496	Denmark	Netherlands, Poland, Iceland, United States, Sweden, Switzerland, Estonia, Hungary, Ireland, Chinese Taipei, Germany, Liechtenstein, France, Portugal, United Kingdom
496	Germany	Netherlands, Poland, Iceland, United States, Sweden, Switzerland, Estonia, Hungary, Ireland, Chinese Taipei, Denmark, Liechtenstein, France, Portugal, United Kingdom, Greece
495	Liechtenstein	Poland, Iceland, United States, Sweden, Switzerland, Estonia, Hungary, Ireland, Chinese Taipei, Denmark, Germany, France, Portugal, United Kingdom, Italy, Greece
492	France	United States, Sweden, Switzerland, Estonia, Hungary, Ireland, Chinese Taipei, Denmark, Germany, Liechtenstein, Portugal, United Kingdom, Italy, Macao-China, Greece, Spain, Latvia
492	Portugal	United States, Sweden, Switzerland, Estonia, Hungary, Ireland, Chinese Taipei, Denmark, Germany, Liechtenstein, France, United Kingdom, Italy, Macao-China, Greece, Spain, Latvia
492	United Kingdom	United States, Sweden, Switzerland, Estonia, Hungary, Ireland, Chinese Taipei, Denmark, Germany, Liechtenstein, France, Portugal, Italy, Macao-China, Greece
489	Italy	Liechtenstein, France, Portugal, United Kingdom, Macao-China, Greece, Spain, Latvia
488	Macao-China	France, Portugal, United Kingdom, Italy, Greece, Spain, Latvia
487	Greece	Hungary, Ireland, Germany, Liechtenstein, France, Portugal, United Kingdom, Italy, Macao-China, Spain, Slovenia, Latvia, Slovak Republic, Czech Republic, Croatia, Israel
484	Spain	France, Portugal, Italy, Macao-China, Greece, Slovenia, Latvia, Slovak Republic, Czech Republic, Croatia, Israel
484	Slovenia	Greece, Spain, Latvia, Slovak Republic, Czech Republic, Israel
484	Latvia	France, Portugal, Italy, Macao-China, Greece, Spain, Slovenia, Slovak Republic, Czech Republic, Croatia, Israel
479	Slovak Republic	Greece, Spain, Slovenia, Latvia, Czech Republic, Croatia, Israel
479	Czech Republic	Greece, Spain, Slovenia, Latvia, Slovak Republic, Croatia, Israel
478	Croatia	Greece, Spain, Latvia, Slovak Republic, Czech Republic, Israel, Austria
477	Israel	Greece, Spain, Slovenia, Latvia, Slovak Republic, Czech Republic, Croatia, Luxembourg, Lithuania, Austria
471	Luxembourg	Israel, Lithuania, Austria, Turkey
470	Lithuania	Israel, Luxembourg, Austria, Turkey
470	Austria	Croatia, Israel, Luxembourg, Lithuania, Turkey
466	Turkey	Luxembourg, Lithuania, Austria, Dubai (UAE), Russian Federation
461	Dubai (UAE)	Turkey, Russian Federation
461	Russian Federation	Turkey, Dubai (UAE), Chile
453	Chile	Russian Federation
444	Serbia	Bulgaria
433	Bulgaria	Serbia, Uruguay, Mexico, Romania, Thailand
429	Uruguay	Bulgaria, Mexico, Romania, Thailand
426	Mexico	Bulgaria, Uruguay, Romania, Thailand
423	Romania	Bulgaria, Uruguay, Mexico, Thailand, Trinidad and Tobago, Jordan, Colombia, Brazil
423	Thailand	Bulgaria, Uruguay, Mexico, Romania, Trinidad and Tobago, Jordan, Colombia
418	Trinidad and Tobago	Romania, Thailand, Jordan, Colombia, Brazil
417	Jordan	Romania, Thailand, Trinidad and Tobago, Colombia, Brazil, Montenegro
415	Colombia	Romania, Thailand, Trinidad and Tobago, Jordan, Brazil, Montenegro, Tunisia, Indonesia
414	Brazil	Romania, Trinidad and Tobago, Jordan, Colombia, Montenegro, Tunisia, Indonesia
411	Montenegro	Jordan, Colombia, Brazil, Tunisia, Indonesia
408	Tunisia	Colombia, Brazil, Montenegro, Indonesia, Argentina
405	Indonesia	Colombia, Brazil, Montenegro, Tunisia, Argentina, Kazakhstan
400	Argentina	Tunisia, Indonesia, Kazakhstan, Albania
399	Kazakhstan	Indonesia, Argentina, Albania
392	Albania	Argentina, Kazakhstan
375	Qatar	Kazakhstan, Peru
374	Peru	Qatar, Panama
373	Panama	Qatar, Peru, Azerbaijan
362	Azerbaijan	Panama
319	Kyrgyzstan	

Source: OECD, *PISA 2009 Database*.
StatLink ᴍᴤ◖ http://dx.doi.org/10.1787/888932343133

Figure I.2.34 provides descriptions of the nature of the reading skills, knowledge and understanding required at each level of the scale for the *non-continuous texts* aspect of reading, with the percentage of students across OECD countries who performed at this level in PISA 2009. The right-hand column lists examples of released *non-continuous texts* questions. Figures I.2.40 to I.2.46 describe these questions and provide commentary on what they show.

■ Figure I.2.34 ■

Summary descriptions of the seven proficiency levels on the reading subscale
non-continuous texts

Level	Percentage of students able to perform tasks at each level or above (OECD average)	Characteristics of tasks	Examples of released *non-continuous texts* questions
6	1.0% of students across the OECD can perform tasks at least at Level 6	Identify and combine information from different parts of a complex document that has unfamiliar content, sometimes drawing on features that are external to the display, such as footnotes, labels and other organisers. Demonstrate a full understanding of the text structure and its implications.	
5	8.0% of students across the OECD can perform tasks at least at Level 5	Identify patterns among many pieces of information presented in a display that may be long and detailed, sometimes by referring to information that is in an unexpected place in the text or outside the text.	
4	28.5% of students across the OECD can perform tasks at least at Level 4	Scan a long, detailed text in order to find relevant information, often with little or no assistance from organisers such as labels or special formatting, to locate several pieces of information to be compared or combined.	*MOBILE PHONE SAFETY* – Question 11 (604) *BALLOON* – Question 3.2 (595) *MOBILE PHONE SAFETY* – Question 2 (561)
3	57.3% of students across the OECD can perform tasks at least at Level 3	Consider one display in the light of a second, separate document or display, possibly in a different format, or draw conclusions by combining several pieces of graphical, verbal and numeric information.	*MOBILE PHONE SAFETY* – Question 6 (526) *BALLOON* – Question 4 (510) *BALLOON* – Question 3.1 (449) *MOBILE PHONE SAFETY* – Question 9 (488)
2	80.9% of students across the OECD can perform tasks at least at Level 2	Demonstrate a grasp of the underlying structure of a visual display such as a simple tree diagram or table, or combine two pieces of information from a graph or table.	*BALLOON* – Question 6 (411)
1a	93.7% of student across the OECD can perform tasks at least at Level 1a	Focus on discrete pieces of information, usually within a single display such as a simple map, a line graph or bar graph that presents only a small amount of information in a straightforward way, and in which most of the verbal text is limited to a small number of words or phrases.	*BALLOON* – Question 8 (370)
1b	98.5% of student across the OECD can perform tasks at least at Level 1b	Identify information in a short text with a simple list structure and a familiar format.	

Figure I.2.35 shows the percentage of students at each proficiency level on the *non-continuous texts* subscale. Details of performance by gender on this subscale are also provided in Table I.2.18.

Mean performance across OECD countries is the same on the *non-continuous texts* subscale as on the overall reading scale (493 points), but is slightly more dispersed (a standard deviation of 95 compared with 93). For almost half of the participating countries, including most OECD countries, the modal level is Level 3. The exceptions are in the OECD countries Finland, Korea and New Zealand, all of which have a modal level of Level 4, as well as in the partner countries and economies Shanghai-China and Singapore. Among the OECD countries, Chile, Mexico and Turkey are also exceptions, with more students performing at Level 2 than at any other level.

■ Figure I. 2.35 ■
How well do students read *non-continuous texts*?
Percentage of students at the different levels of proficiency in reading non-continuous texts

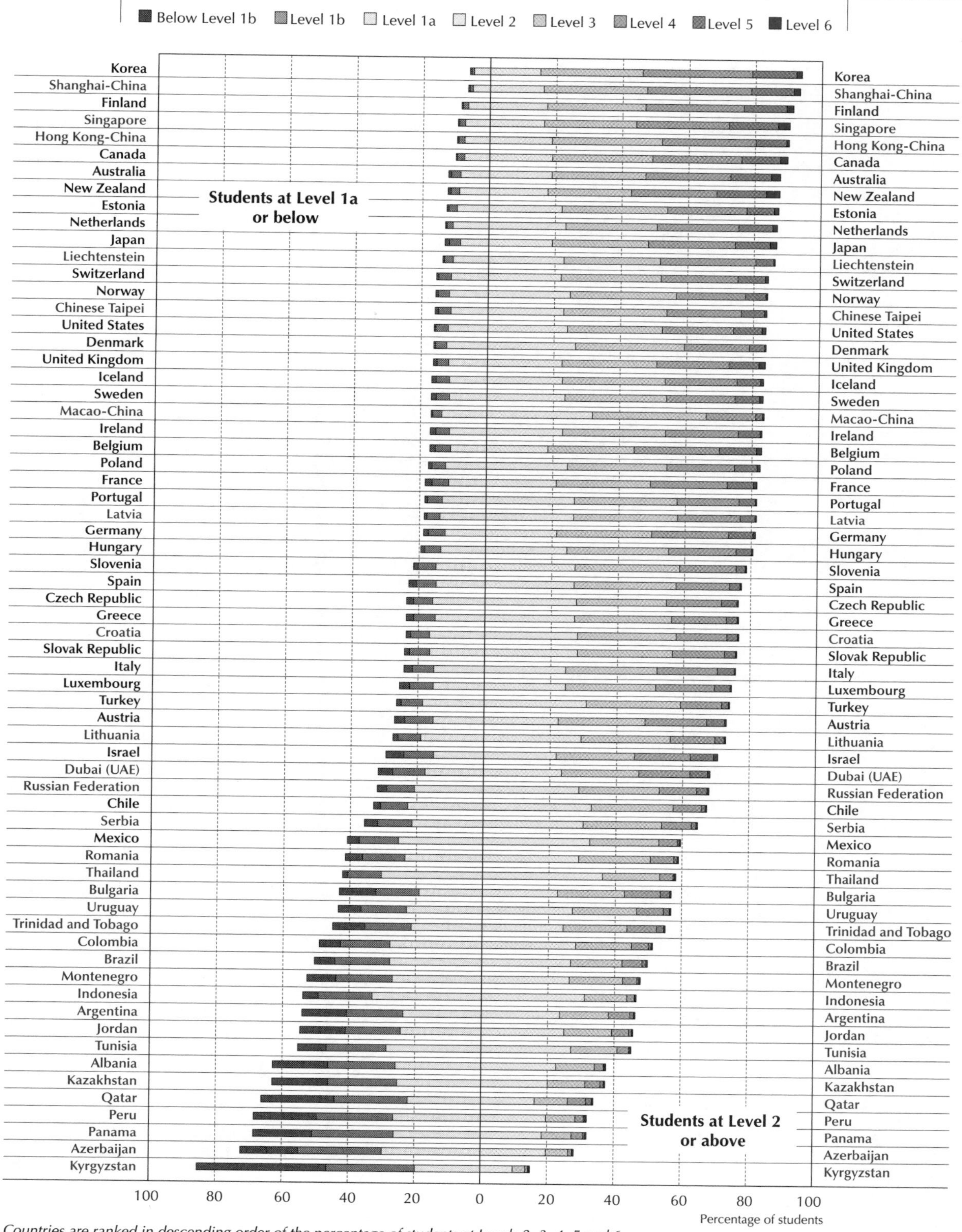

■ Below Level 1b ■ Level 1b □ Level 1a □ Level 2 ▨ Level 3 ▨ Level 4 ▨ Level 5 ■ Level 6

Korea	Korea
Shanghai-China	Shanghai-China
Finland	Finland
Singapore	Singapore
Hong Kong-China	Hong Kong-China
Canada	Canada
Australia	Australia
New Zealand	New Zealand
Estonia	Estonia
Netherlands	Netherlands
Japan	Japan
Liechtenstein	Liechtenstein
Switzerland	Switzerland
Norway	Norway
Chinese Taipei	Chinese Taipei
United States	United States
Denmark	Denmark
United Kingdom	United Kingdom
Iceland	Iceland
Sweden	Sweden
Macao-China	Macao-China
Ireland	Ireland
Belgium	Belgium
Poland	Poland
France	France
Portugal	Portugal
Latvia	Latvia
Germany	Germany
Hungary	Hungary
Slovenia	Slovenia
Spain	Spain
Czech Republic	Czech Republic
Greece	Greece
Croatia	Croatia
Slovak Republic	Slovak Republic
Italy	Italy
Luxembourg	Luxembourg
Turkey	Turkey
Austria	Austria
Lithuania	Lithuania
Israel	Israel
Dubai (UAE)	Dubai (UAE)
Russian Federation	Russian Federation
Chile	Chile
Serbia	Serbia
Mexico	Mexico
Romania	Romania
Thailand	Thailand
Bulgaria	Bulgaria
Uruguay	Uruguay
Trinidad and Tobago	Trinidad and Tobago
Colombia	Colombia
Brazil	Brazil
Montenegro	Montenegro
Indonesia	Indonesia
Argentina	Argentina
Jordan	Jordan
Tunisia	Tunisia
Albania	Albania
Kazakhstan	Kazakhstan
Qatar	Qatar
Peru	Peru
Panama	Panama
Azerbaijan	Azerbaijan
Kyrgyzstan	Kyrgyzstan

Students at Level 1a or below

Students at Level 2 or above

100 80 60 40 20 0 20 40 60 80 100

Percentage of students

Countries are ranked in descending order of the percentage of students at Levels 2, 3, 4, 5 and 6.
Source: OECD, *PISA 2009 Database*, Table I.2.17.
StatLink ᴍᴙᴨᴩ http://dx.doi.org/10.1787/888932343133

■ Figure I.2.36 ■

Comparing countries' performance in reading *non-continuous texts*

	Statistically significantly **above** the OECD average
	Not statistically significantly different from the OECD average
	Statistically significantly **below** the OECD average

Mean	Comparison country	Countries whose mean score is NOT statistically significantly different from that of the comparison country
542	Korea	Shanghai-China, Singapore, Finland
539	Shanghai-China	Korea, Singapore, Finland
539	Singapore	Korea, Shanghai-China, Finland
535	Finland	Korea, Shanghai-China, Singapore, New Zealand
532	New Zealand	Finland, Canada
527	Canada	New Zealand, Australia, Hong Kong-China
524	Australia	Canada, Hong Kong-China, Japan, Netherlands
522	Hong Kong-China	Canada, Australia, Japan, Netherlands
518	Japan	Australia, Hong Kong-China, Netherlands, Estonia, Belgium
514	Netherlands	Australia, Hong Kong-China, Japan, Estonia, Belgium, Liechtenstein, United Kingdom, Switzerland, United States
512	Estonia	Japan, Netherlands, Belgium, Liechtenstein, United Kingdom, Switzerland
511	Belgium	Japan, Netherlands, Estonia, Liechtenstein, United Kingdom, Switzerland, United States
506	Liechtenstein	Netherlands, Estonia, Belgium, United Kingdom, Switzerland, United States, Chinese Taipei, France, Sweden
506	United Kingdom	Netherlands, Estonia, Belgium, Liechtenstein, Switzerland, United States, Chinese Taipei, France
505	Switzerland	Netherlands, Estonia, Belgium, Liechtenstein, United Kingdom, United States, Chinese Taipei, France, Sweden
503	United States	Netherlands, Belgium, Liechtenstein, United Kingdom, Switzerland, Chinese Taipei, Iceland, France, Sweden, Norway, Germany, Ireland, Poland
500	Chinese Taipei	Liechtenstein, United Kingdom, Switzerland, United States, Iceland, France, Sweden, Norway, Germany, Ireland, Poland
499	Iceland	United States, Chinese Taipei, France, Sweden, Norway, Germany, Ireland, Poland
498	France	Liechtenstein, United Kingdom, Switzerland, United States, Chinese Taipei, Iceland, Sweden, Norway, Germany, Ireland, Poland, Denmark
498	Sweden	Liechtenstein, Switzerland, United States, Chinese Taipei, Iceland, France, Norway, Germany, Ireland, Poland, Denmark
498	Norway	United States, Chinese Taipei, Iceland, France, Sweden, Germany, Ireland, Poland, Denmark
497	Germany	United States, Chinese Taipei, Iceland, France, Sweden, Norway, Ireland, Poland, Denmark
496	Ireland	United States, Chinese Taipei, Iceland, France, Sweden, Norway, Germany, Poland, Denmark, Portugal
496	Poland	United States, Chinese Taipei, Iceland, France, Sweden, Norway, Germany, Ireland, Denmark, Portugal, Hungary
493	Denmark	France, Sweden, Norway, Germany, Ireland, Poland, Portugal, Hungary, Latvia
488	Portugal	Ireland, Poland, Denmark, Hungary, Latvia
487	Hungary	Poland, Denmark, Portugal, Latvia, Macao-China
487	Latvia	Denmark, Portugal, Hungary, Macao-China
481	Macao-China	Hungary, Latvia, Czech Republic
476	Italy	Slovenia, Czech Republic, Spain, Austria, Greece, Croatia, Slovak Republic
476	Slovenia	Italy, Czech Republic, Spain, Austria, Greece, Croatia, Slovak Republic
474	Czech Republic	Macao-China, Italy, Slovenia, Spain, Austria, Greece, Croatia, Luxembourg, Slovak Republic, Israel
473	Spain	Italy, Slovenia, Czech Republic, Austria, Greece, Croatia, Luxembourg, Slovak Republic, Israel
472	Austria	Italy, Slovenia, Czech Republic, Spain, Greece, Croatia, Luxembourg, Slovak Republic, Israel
472	Greece	Italy, Slovenia, Czech Republic, Spain, Austria, Croatia, Luxembourg, Slovak Republic, Israel, Lithuania, Turkey
472	Croatia	Italy, Slovenia, Czech Republic, Spain, Austria, Greece, Luxembourg, Slovak Republic, Israel
472	Luxembourg	Czech Republic, Spain, Austria, Greece, Croatia, Slovak Republic, Israel
471	Slovak Republic	Italy, Slovenia, Czech Republic, Spain, Austria, Greece, Croatia, Luxembourg, Israel
467	Israel	Czech Republic, Spain, Austria, Greece, Croatia, Luxembourg, Slovak Republic, Lithuania, Turkey, Dubai (UAE)
462	Lithuania	Greece, Israel, Turkey, Dubai (UAE)
461	Turkey	Greece, Israel, Lithuania, Dubai (UAE), Russian Federation
460	Dubai (UAE)	Israel, Lithuania, Turkey, Russian Federation
452	Russian Federation	Turkey, Dubai (UAE), Chile
444	Chile	Russian Federation, Serbia
438	Serbia	Chile
424	Mexico	Romania, Thailand, Bulgaria, Uruguay
424	Romania	Mexico, Thailand, Bulgaria, Uruguay, Trinidad and Tobago
423	Thailand	Mexico, Romania, Bulgaria, Uruguay
421	Bulgaria	Mexico, Romania, Thailand, Uruguay, Trinidad and Tobago, Colombia, Brazil
421	Uruguay	Mexico, Romania, Thailand, Bulgaria, Trinidad and Tobago
417	Trinidad and Tobago	Romania, Bulgaria, Uruguay, Colombia
409	Colombia	Bulgaria, Trinidad and Tobago, Brazil, Indonesia
408	Brazil	Bulgaria, Colombia, Indonesia
399	Indonesia	Colombia, Brazil, Montenegro, Tunisia, Argentina, Jordan
398	Montenegro	Indonesia, Tunisia, Argentina
393	Tunisia	Indonesia, Montenegro, Argentina, Jordan
391	Argentina	Indonesia, Montenegro, Tunisia, Jordan
387	Jordan	Indonesia, Tunisia, Argentina
371	Kazakhstan	Albania, Panama
366	Albania	Kazakhstan, Qatar, Panama, Peru
361	Qatar	Albania, Panama, Peru
359	Panama	Kazakhstan, Albania, Qatar, Peru, Azerbaijan
356	Peru	Albania, Qatar, Panama, Azerbaijan
351	Azerbaijan	Panama, Peru
293	Kyrgyzstan	

Source: OECD, *PISA 2009 Database*.
StatLink ᵃᵐˢᵖ http://dx.doi.org/10.1787/888932343133

For many of the partner countries and economies, Level 2 is also the modal level, while several have more students performing at Level 1a than at any other level: Albania, Argentina, Azerbaijan, Brazil, Indonesia, Kazakhstan, Montenegro, Panama, Peru, Qatar and Tunisia. In Kyrgyzstan, the modal level was below Level 1b.

Figure I.2.36 shows each country's mean score on the *non-continuous* subscale, and the statistically significant differences between them. For each country shown on the left in the middle column, the list of countries on the right hand column shows countries whose mean scores are not sufficiently different to be distinguished with confidence. For all other cases, one country has a higher performance than another if it is above it in the list in the middle column, and a lower performance if it is below.

Table I.2.19 presents the mean score, variation and gender difference for each country on the *non-continuous texts* subscale. While girls outperform boys in every country on this subscale, the gap is generally narrower than on the overall reading scale, with an average difference of 36 points compared with 39 points. A notable group, in which the gap between boys and girls is less than 20 scale score points, includes several Latin American countries: the OECD countries Chile and Mexico, and the partner countries Colombia, Peru and Brazil. The gap between boys' and girls' performance in Colombia is only 5 points. The only other country with a similarly small gap between boys' and girls' performance is the partner country Azerbaijan. A few countries are exceptions to this trend of a narrower gap between boys and girls. In the OECD countries Belgium and the United Kingdom, as well as the partner countries Jordan and Kazakhstan, the difference in performance is greater on the *non-continuous texts* subscale than on the overall scale, and in the OECD countries the Netherlands, Germany, Spain and Sweden, and in the partner countries Liechtenstein, the Russian Federation and Serbia, the gender differences are the same for the *non-continuous texts* subscale and the overall scale.

The relative strengths and weaknesses of countries in text-format subscales

The PISA reading assessment was designed so that the sets of tasks based on texts in each text format covered a similar range of difficulties, question formats (selected response and constructed response) and aspects, and related to a wide variety of text types. This was intended to ensure that any differences in performance on the text-format subscales could be confidently attributed to the text format variable rather than to the effects of other variables.

Figure I.2.37 shows the differences between countries' scores on the *continuous* and *non-continuous texts* subscales.

The average performance in *continuous* and *non-continuous* tasks is almost identical, at 494 and 493 score points, respectively. Nevertheless, there is variation across countries. Some countries perform consistently across the text-format subscales, showing a similar marginal difference in performance in favour of *continuous texts* to the average difference of one point, or an even smaller difference than the average difference. The OECD countries Finland, Luxembourg and Ireland, and the partner countries Thailand and Trinidad and Tobago are in the latter category. However, some variation in performance on the two text-format subscales is more common within countries.

Seventeen countries perform significantly better – by at least 10 points – on the *continuous texts* subscale than on the *non-continuous* scale, including two very high-performing partner economies, Shanghai-China and Hong Kong-China, and some very low-performing partner countries, including Kyrgyzstan, Azerbaijan, Peru, Panama, Qatar, Albania and Kazakhstan. Despite their apparent heterogeneity in the overall level of performance, the countries in this category may place more emphasis in their curricula on reading *continuous texts*, rather than reading a more diverse array of texts. There are fewer countries with substantially higher performance (by more than 10 points) on the *non-continuous* than on the *continuous* subscale.

Gender differences in the text-format subscales

When compared with the overall reading scale, girls perform consistently better on the *continuous* subscale while the gap generally narrows somewhat between boys and girls on the *non-continuous* tasks. The differences in gender performance are quite marked when comparing the two subscales directly.

The previous section identified countries in which there are comparatively large differences in performance, in either direction, on the two text-format subscales. Often, apparently small differences in performance overall can mask large differences between proficiency of boys and girls on the subscales within a country. For example, although the mean score difference between the two text-format subscales in the partner country Romania is less than two points, boys performed better on the *non-continuous texts* subscale than on the *continuous* by almost eight points, while girls performed worse on the *non-continuous texts* subscale than on the *continuous texts* subscale by five points.

■ Figure I.2.37 ■
Comparing countries on the different text format subscales

	Country performance on the subscale is between 0 to 3 score points **higher** than on the combined reading scale
	Country performance on the subscale is between 3 to 10 score points **higher** than on the combined reading scale
	Country performance on the subscale is 10 or more score points **higher** than on the combined reading scale
	Country performance on the subscale is between 0 to 3 score points **lower** than on the combined reading scale
	Country performance on the subscale is between 3 to 10 score points **lower** than on the combined reading scale
	Country performance on the subscale is 10 or more score points **lower** than on the combined reading scale

	Reading score	Performance difference between the combined reading scale and each *text format* subscale	
		Continuous texts	*Non-continuous texts*
Shanghai-China	556	8	-16
Korea	539	-1	3
Finland	536	-1	-1
Hong Kong-China	533	5	-11
Singapore	526	-4	13
Canada	524	0	3
New Zealand	521	-3	11
Japan	520	1	-2
Australia	515	-2	9
Netherlands	508	-2	6
Belgium	506	-2	5
Norway	503	2	-6
Estonia	501	-4	11
Switzerland	501	-2	5
Poland	500	2	-5
Iceland	500	0	-1
United States	500	0	3
Liechtenstein	499	-5	7
Sweden	497	2	0
Germany	497	-2	0
Ireland	496	1	1
France	496	-4	3
Chinese Taipei	495	1	5
Denmark	495	1	-2
United Kingdom	494	-3	11
Hungary	494	3	-7
Portugal	489	3	-1
Macao-China	487	1	-6
Italy	486	3	-10
Latvia	484	0	3
Slovenia	483	1	-7
Greece	483	4	-11
Spain	481	3	-9
Czech Republic	478	1	-4
Slovak Republic	477	2	-6
Croatia	476	2	-4
Israel	474	3	-7
Luxembourg	472	-1	-1
Austria	470	0	2
Lithuania	468	2	-6
Turkey	464	2	-3
Dubai (UAE)	459	1	0
Russian Federation	459	1	-7
Chile	449	4	-6
Serbia	442	2	-4
Bulgaria	429	4	-8
Uruguay	426	3	-5
Mexico	425	1	-1
Romania	424	-1	0
Thailand	421	2	2
Trinidad and Tobago	416	1	0
Colombia	413	2	-4
Brazil	412	2	-3
Montenegro	408	4	-10
Jordan	405	12	-18
Tunisia	404	4	-11
Indonesia	402	4	-3
Argentina	398	2	-7
Kazakhstan	390	8	-20
Albania	385	7	-18
Qatar	372	4	-10
Panama	371	3	-12
Peru	370	4	-13
Azerbaijan	362	0	-11
Kyrgyzstan	314	5	-21
OECD average	494	0	0

Source: OECD, *PISA 2009 Database*, Tables I.2.3, I.2.16 and I.2.19.
StatLink ⫘⫘ http://dx.doi.org/10.1787/888932343133

■ Figure I.2.38 ■

Where countries rank in reading *continuous* and *non-continuous texts*

Statistically significantly **above** the OECD average
Not statistically significantly different from the OECD average
Statistically significantly **below** the OECD average

Continuous texts subscale

	Mean Score	S.E.	OECD countries Upper rank	OECD countries Lower rank	All countries/ economies Upper rank	All countries/ economies Lower rank
Shanghai-China	564	(2.5)			1	1
Korea	538	(3.5)	1	2	2	4
Hong Kong-China	538	(2.3)			2	4
Finland	535	(2.3)	1	2	2	4
Canada	524	(1.5)	3	4	5	6
Singapore	522	(1.1)			5	7
Japan	520	(3.6)	3	5	5	8
New Zealand	518	(2.4)	4	6	6	9
Australia	513	(2.5)	5	7	8	10
Netherlands	506	(5.0)	5	14	8	18
Norway	505	(2.6)	7	12	10	15
Belgium	504	(2.4)	7	12	10	15
Poland	502	(2.7)	7	15	10	19
Iceland	501	(1.6)	9	15	12	19
United States	500	(3.7)	7	19	10	24
Sweden	499	(3.0)	8	19	11	24
Switzerland	498	(2.5)	10	20	13	24
Estonia	497	(2.7)	10	20	13	25
Hungary	497	(3.3)	10	22	13	27
Ireland	497	(3.3)	10	22	13	27
Chinese Taipei	496	(2.6)			14	26
Denmark	496	(2.1)	12	21	15	25
Germany	496	(2.7)	12	22	15	27
Liechtenstein	495	(3.0)			16	28
France	492	(3.5)	15	25	18	31
Portugal	492	(3.2)	15	24	19	31
United Kingdom	492	(2.4)	17	24	21	30
Italy	489	(1.6)	20	24	25	30
Macao-China	488	(0.9)			27	31
Greece	487	(4.3)	19	28	23	35
Spain	484	(2.1)	23	27	28	34
Slovenia	484	(1.1)	24	27	30	34
Latvia	484	(3.0)			28	36
Slovak Republic	479	(2.6)	26	29	32	37
Czech Republic	479	(2.9)	25	29	32	37
Croatia	478	(2.9)			33	38
Israel	477	(3.6)	26	31	32	39
Luxembourg	471	(1.2)	29	31	37	40
Lithuania	470	(2.5)			37	41
Austria	470	(2.9)	29	32	37	41
Turkey	466	(3.5)	30	32	38	43
Dubai (UAE)	461	(1.2)			41	43
Russian Federation	461	(3.1)			41	43
Chile	453	(3.1)	33	33	43	44
Serbia	444	(2.3)			45	46
Bulgaria	433	(6.8)			45	50
Uruguay	429	(2.7)			46	49
Mexico	426	(2.0)	34	34	47	50
Romania	423	(4.0)			46	52
Thailand	423	(2.8)			47	51
Trinidad and Tobago	418	(1.3)			50	53
Jordan	417	(3.2)			50	55
Colombia	415	(3.7)			50	56
Brazil	414	(2.8)			51	56
Montenegro	411	(1.8)			53	56
Tunisia	408	(2.9)			54	58
Indonesia	405	(3.7)			55	59
Argentina	400	(4.6)			56	60
Kazakhstan	399	(3.1)			57	60
Albania	392	(4.1)			59	60
Qatar	375	(0.9)			61	63
Peru	374	(3.9)			61	63
Panama	373	(6.7)			61	64
Azerbaijan	362	(3.3)			63	64
Kyrgyzstan	319	(3.2)			65	65

Non-continuous texts subscale

	Mean Score	S.E.	OECD countries Upper rank	OECD countries Lower rank	All countries/ economies Upper rank	All countries/ economies Lower rank
Korea	542	(3.6)	1	1	1	3
Shanghai-China	539	(2.4)			1	4
Singapore	539	(1.1)			1	3
Finland	535	(2.4)	2	3	3	5
New Zealand	532	(2.3)	2	4	4	6
Canada	527	(1.6)	4	5	5	7
Australia	524	(2.3)	4	6	6	9
Hong Kong-China	522	(2.3)			7	9
Japan	518	(3.5)	5	8	7	11
Netherlands	514	(5.1)	5	10	7	14
Estonia	512	(2.7)	6	10	9	13
Belgium	511	(2.2)	7	10	10	13
Liechtenstein	506	(3.2)			11	18
United Kingdom	506	(2.3)	9	13	12	17
Switzerland	505	(2.5)	9	13	12	17
United States	503	(3.5)	9	17	12	22
Chinese Taipei	500	(2.8)			14	23
Iceland	499	(1.5)	12	17	16	22
France	498	(3.4)	11	20	15	25
Sweden	498	(2.8)	12	20	16	25
Norway	498	(2.6)	12	19	16	25
Germany	497	(2.8)	12	20	16	25
Ireland	496	(3.0)	12	20	17	26
Poland	496	(2.8)	13	20	18	26
Denmark	493	(2.3)	16	21	22	27
Portugal	488	(3.2)	20	22	24	28
Hungary	487	(3.3)	20	22	25	29
Latvia	487	(3.4)			25	29
Macao-China	481	(1.1)			28	30
Italy	476	(1.7)	23	27	30	34
Slovenia	476	(1.1)	23	26	30	33
Czech Republic	474	(3.4)	23	30	29	38
Spain	473	(2.1)	24	30	31	38
Austria	472	(3.2)	23	31	30	39
Greece	472	(4.3)	23	31	30	40
Croatia	472	(3.0)			31	39
Luxembourg	472	(1.2)	26	30	33	38
Slovak Republic	471	(2.8)	24	31	31	39
Israel	467	(3.9)	27	32	34	42
Lithuania	462	(2.6)			39	42
Turkey	461	(3.8)	31	32	39	43
Dubai (UAE)	460	(1.3)			40	42
Russian Federation	452	(3.9)			42	44
Chile	444	(3.2)	33	33	44	45
Serbia	438	(2.9)			44	45
Mexico	424	(2.0)	34	34	46	49
Romania	424	(4.5)			46	50
Thailand	423	(2.7)			46	50
Bulgaria	421	(7.2)			46	52
Uruguay	421	(2.7)			47	51
Trinidad and Tobago	417	(1.4)			49	51
Colombia	409	(4.1)			51	54
Brazil	408	(2.8)			51	53
Indonesia	399	(4.5)			53	57
Montenegro	398	(1.9)			54	56
Tunisia	393	(3.3)			55	58
Argentina	391	(5.2)			54	58
Jordan	387	(4.1)			56	58
Kazakhstan	371	(3.9)			59	60
Albania	366	(4.6)			59	62
Qatar	361	(0.9)			60	62
Panama	359	(6.5)			60	64
Peru	356	(4.4)			61	64
Azerbaijan	351	(4.2)			62	64
Kyrgyzstan	293	(3.7)			65	65

Source: OECD, *PISA 2009 Database*.
StatLink ᐧᐧᐧ http://dx.doi.org/10.1787/888932343133

■ Figure I. 2.39a ■
Gender differences in reading *continuous texts*

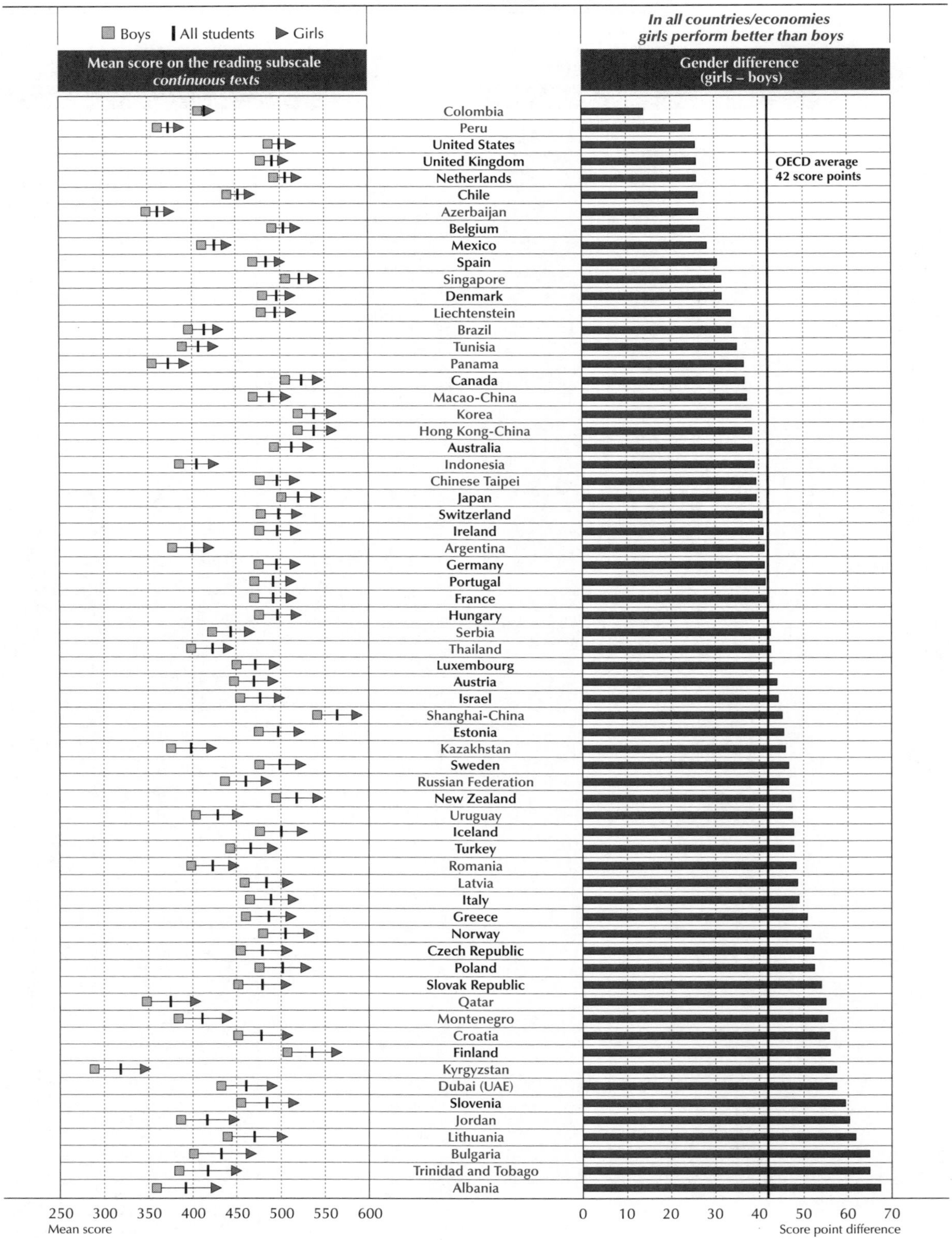

| ☐ Boys | ❙ All students | ▶ Girls |

In all countries/economies girls perform better than boys

Mean score on the reading subscale continuous texts

Gender difference (girls – boys)

OECD average 42 score points

Colombia
Peru
United States
United Kingdom
Netherlands
Chile
Azerbaijan
Belgium
Mexico
Spain
Singapore
Denmark
Liechtenstein
Brazil
Tunisia
Panama
Canada
Macao-China
Korea
Hong Kong-China
Australia
Indonesia
Chinese Taipei
Japan
Switzerland
Ireland
Argentina
Germany
Portugal
France
Hungary
Serbia
Thailand
Luxembourg
Austria
Israel
Shanghai-China
Estonia
Kazakhstan
Sweden
Russian Federation
New Zealand
Uruguay
Iceland
Turkey
Romania
Latvia
Italy
Greece
Norway
Czech Republic
Poland
Slovak Republic
Qatar
Montenegro
Croatia
Finland
Kyrgyzstan
Dubai (UAE)
Slovenia
Jordan
Lithuania
Bulgaria
Trinidad and Tobago
Albania

250 300 350 400 450 500 550 600
Mean score

0   10   20   30   40   50   60   70
Score point difference

Note: All gender differences are statistically significant (see Annex A3).
Countries are ranked in ascending order of the gender score point difference (girls – boys).
Source: OECD, *PISA 2009 Database,* Table I.2.16.
StatLink ᴍˢᴾ http://dx.doi.org/10.1787/888932343133

■ Figure I. 2.39b ■
Gender differences in reading *non-continuous texts*

□ Boys | All students ▶ Girls

Mean score on the reading subscale *non-continuous texts*		Gender difference (girls – boys)

Colombia
Chile
Peru
Azerbaijan
Mexico
Brazil
United States
Tunisia
Netherlands
United Kingdom
Hong Kong-China
Denmark
Panama
Macao-China
Argentina
Singapore
Spain
Belgium
Thailand
Uruguay
Hungary
Liechtenstein
Korea
Canada
Portugal
Luxembourg
Australia
Shanghai-China
Romania
Indonesia
Turkey
Chinese Taipei
France
Switzerland
Austria
Japan
Ireland
Serbia
Israel
Germany
Dubai (UAE)
Iceland
Greece
Norway
Estonia
Italy
New Zealand
Russian Federation
Croatia
Czech Republic
Kyrgyzstan
Sweden
Poland
Latvia
Slovenia
Slovak Republic
Kazakhstan
Montenegro
Qatar
Trinidad and Tobago
Finland
Lithuania
Albania
Bulgaria
Jordan

OECD average
36 score points

250 300 350 400 450 500 550 600
Mean score

0 10 20 30 40 50 60 70
Score point difference

Note: Statistically significant gender differences are marked in a darker tone (see Annex A3).
Countries are ranked in ascending order of the gender score point difference (girls – boys).
Source: OECD, *PISA 2009 Database,* Table I.2.19.

StatLink ⏺ http://dx.doi.org/10.1787/888932343133

Thus, the gender gap in performance on the *non-continuous texts* subscale is less than the gap between boys and girls on the *continuous texts* subscale by about 13 points. Other countries that show a similar pattern of performance, where boys performed better on the *non-continuous texts* scale than on the *continuous* and girls performed worse, with a difference of more than 10 points, are the OECD country Turkey and the partner countries and economies Dubai (UAE), Uruguay, Trinidad and Tobago, Brazil and Thailand. In other countries in which the gap narrows substantially between boys' and girls' performance on the *non-continuous texts* subscale, compared with the gap between them on the *continuous texts* subscale, a different pattern is evident: here, both boys and girls performed better on the *continuous texts* subscale, but girls perform much better – by more than 10 points. The OECD countries Slovenia, Chile and Hungary, and the partner countries and economies Argentina, Hong Kong-China, Kyrgyzstan, Croatia, Tunisia and Albania fit this description. Conversely, in some countries, both boys and girls perform better on the *non-continuous texts* than on the *continuous texts* subscale. As well as the six countries named previously as performing better overall on *non-continuous texts* than on the *continuous texts* subscale (the OECD countries Estonia, New Zealand, United Kingdom and Australia, as well as the partner countries Singapore and Liechtenstein), this category includes the OECD countries the Netherlands, Switzerland, Belgium, France, Korea, Canada and the United States, and the partner countries and economies Chinese Taipei and Latvia. In all of these countries except the United Kingdom and Belgium, boys' results contribute more to the superior performance on the *non-continuous texts* subscale than do girls' results.

In sum, boys tend to do better in handling *non-continuous* rather than *continuous texts*. This may be associated with the kinds of reading preferred by boys and girls, which is examined in Volume III. The results in Volume III show, for example, that while substantial numbers of both girls and boys do not read much for pleasure at all, among those who do, girls tend to favour longer texts, such as prose fiction and some non-fiction books, whereas boys spend more time reading newspapers and comics. How accustomed the two gender groups are to these different kinds of texts may help explain their different performance on the *continuous* and *non-continuous texts* subscales.

Examples of the PISA 2009 reading units

The questions are presented in the order in which they appeared within the unit in the main survey. Percentages of student responses are not provided in the tabulation of framework characteristics (as they were in the parallel material in the 2006 international report) because several of the units were only administered by some of the countries, and the comparison of percentages between questions in those units and other units might lead to a misinterpretation of task difficulty.

■ Figure I.2.40 ■

BRUSHING YOUR TEETH

Do our teeth become cleaner and cleaner the longer and harder we brush them?

British researchers say no. They have actually tried out many different alternatives, and ended up with the perfect way to brush your teeth. A two minute brush, without brushing too hard, gives the best result. If you brush hard, you harm your tooth enamel and your gums without loosening food remnants or plaque.

Bente Hansen, an expert on tooth brushing, says that it is a good idea to hold the toothbrush the way you hold a pen. "Start in one corner and brush your way along the whole row," she says. "Don't forget your tongue either! It can actually contain loads of bacteria that may cause bad breath."

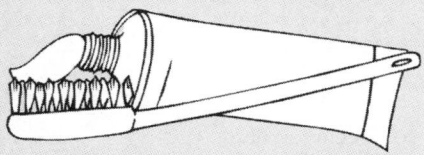

"Brushing your Teeth" is an article from a Norwegian magazine.

Use "Brushing Your Teeth" above to answer the questions that follow.

BRUSHING YOUR TEETH – QUESTION 1

Situation: *Educational*
Text format: *Continuous*
Text type: *Exposition*
Aspect: *Integrate and interpret – Form a broad understanding*
Question format: *Multiple choice*
Difficulty: *353 (1a)* ■

698	Level 6
626	Level 5
553	Level 4
480	Level 3
407	Level 2
335	Level 1a
262	Level 1b
	Below Level 1b

What is this article about?

A. The best way to brush your teeth.

B. The best kind of toothbrush to use.

C. The importance of good teeth.

D. The way different people brush their teeth.

Scoring

Full Credit: The best way to brush your teeth.

Comment

This task requires the reader to recognise the main idea of a short descriptive text. The text is not only short, but about the very familiar, everyday topic of brushing one's teeth. The language is quite idiomatic ("loads of bacteria", "bad breath"), and the text is composed of short paragraphs and familiar syntactic structures, with a straightforward heading and a supporting illustration. All of these features combine to make the text very approachable.

The difficulty of this question is located towards bottom of Level 1a, among the easier PISA reading questions. The question stem is rather open and broad, directing the reader to look for a broad generalisation as an answer. The words of the key ("The best way to brush your teeth") include a term that is part of the title ("brush(ing) your teeth"), and if – drawing on knowledge about the conventional structures and features of texts – there is an expectation that a title is likely to summarise a text, the reader need go no further than the title to find the key. Should confirmation be sought, the first three sentences of the body of the text also encapsulate the main idea, and it is repeated by illustration and elaboration in what little remains of this short piece. Thus the required information is both prominent and repeated in a short and simple text: all markers of relatively easy reading tasks.

BRUSHING YOUR TEETH – *QUESTION 2*

Situation: *Educational*
Text format: *Continuous*
Text type: *Exposition*
Aspect: *Access and retrieve – Retrieve information*
Question format: *Multiple choice*
Difficulty: *358 (1a)* •

698	Level 6
626	Level 5
553	Level 4
480	Level 3
407	Level 2
335	Level 1a
262	Level 1b
	Below Level 1b

What do the British researchers recommend?

A. That you brush your teeth as often as possible.

B. That you do not try to brush your tongue.

C. That you do not brush your teeth too hard.

D. That you brush your tongue more often than your teeth.

Scoring

Full Credit: C. That you do not brush your teeth too hard.

Comment

Another question located at Level 1a, this task requires readers to retrieve a specific piece of information from the text rather than recognise a broad generalisation (as in the previous task); the question is therefore classified as **access and retrieve** *by aspect. The task explicitly directs the reader to the second paragraph with the literal match to "British researchers". It nevertheless requires some synthesis and some inference, to understand that the British researchers referred to at the beginning of paragraph 2 are those giving the advice throughout the paragraph, and that "gives the best results" is synonymous with "recommend". Performance on this task showed that the distractor providing most competition for the key is the first one, "That you brush your teeth as often as possible", presumably because it draws on a plausible misconception based on prior knowledge.*

BRUSHING YOUR TEETH – *QUESTION 3*

Situation: *Educational*
Text format: *Continuous*
Text type: *Exposition*
Aspect: *Access and retrieve – Retrieve information*
Question format: *Short response*
Difficulty: *285 (1b)* •

698	Level 6
626	Level 5
553	Level 4
480	Level 3
407	Level 2
335	Level 1a
262	Level 1b
	Below Level 1b

Why should you brush your tongue, according to Bente Hansen?

....

....

Scoring

Full Credit: Refers either to the <u>bacteria</u> OR <u>getting rid of bad breath</u>, OR <u>both</u>. Response may paraphrase or quote directly from the text.

- To get rid of bacteria.
- Your tongue can contain bacteria.
- Bacteria.
- Because you can avoid bad breath.
- Bad breath.
- To remove bacteria and therefore stop you from having bad breath. *[both]*
- It can actually contain loads of bacteria that may cause bad breath. *[both]*
- Bacteria can cause bad breath.

Comment

The wording of the question provides two terms that can be used literally to find the relevant section of the text: "Bente Hansen" and "tongue". Moreover, the term "Bente Hansen" occurs in a prominent position at the very beginning of the last paragraph. In the same paragraph the term "tongue" occurs, giving an even more precise clue for locating the exact place in which the required information is to be found. Each of these terms occurs only once in the text, so the reader does not need to deal with any competing information when matching the question to the relevant part of the text.

With a difficulty located in the lowest described level, Level 1b, this is one of the easiest questions in the PISA 2009 reading assessment. It does nevertheless require a low level of inference, since the reader has to understand that "it" in the last sentence refers to "your tongue". A further element that might be expected to contribute to difficulty is that the focus of the question is relatively abstract: the reader is asked to identify a cause ("Why?"). Mitigating this potential difficulty, however, is the fact that the word "cause" is explicitly used in the text ("that may cause bad breath"), providing a clear pointer to the required answer, so long as the reader infers the semantic relationship between "why" and "cause". It is worth noting that tasks at this lowest described level of PISA reading still demand some reading skill beyond mere decoding. It follows that students described as performing at Level 1b have demonstrated that they can read with a degree of **understanding**, in a manner consistent with the PISA definition of reading.

BRUSHING YOUR TEETH – QUESTION 4

Situation: *Educational*
Text format: *Continuous*
Text type: *Exposition*
Aspect: *Reflect and evaluate – Reflect on and evaluate the form of a text*
Question format: *Multiple choice*
Difficulty: *399 (Level 1a)*

Why is a pen mentioned in the text?

A. To help you understand how to hold a toothbrush.

B. Because you start in one corner with both a pen and a toothbrush.

C. To show that you can brush your teeth in many different ways.

D. Because you should take tooth brushing as seriously as writing.

Scoring

Full Credit: A. To help you understand how to hold a toothbrush.

Comment

The last of the tasks in this unit is located near the top of Level 1a in difficulty. Its aspect is **reflect and evaluate** because it requires standing back from the text and considering the intention of one part of it. Although this is a relatively abstract task in comparison with others in this unit, the wording of both the question stem and the key gives substantial support. The reference to "pen" in the stem directs the reader to the third paragraph. The wording of the key has a direct match with the wording in the relevant part of the text: "how to hold a toothbrush" and "hold the toothbrush the way …" respectively. The task requires the reader to recognises an analogy, but the analogical thinking is, again, explicitly there in the text: "hold the toothbrush the way you hold a pen".

The familiar content and the brevity of the text help to explain why this question is relatively easy, while its somewhat abstract focus accounts for the fact that it is the most difficult of the unit.

■ Figure I.2.41 ■

MOBILE PHONE SAFETY

Are mobile phones dangerous?

Key points

- Conflicting reports about the health risks of mobile phones appeared in the late 1990s.
- Millions of pounds have now been invested in scientific research to investigate the effects of mobile phones.

Yes	No
1. Radio waves given off by mobile phones can heat up body tissue, having damaging effects.	Radio waves are not powerful enough to cause heat damage to the body.
2. Magnetic fields created by mobile phones can affect the way that your body cells work.	The magnetic fields are incredibly weak, and so unlikely to affect cells in our body.
3. People who make long mobile phone calls sometimes complain of fatigue, headaches, and loss of concentration.	These effects have never been observed under laboratory conditions and may be due to other factors in modern lifestyles.
4. Mobile phone users are 2.5 times more likely to develop cancer in areas of the brain adjacent to their phone ears.	Researchers admit it's unclear this increase is linked to using mobile phones.
5. The International Agency for Research on Cancer found a link between childhood cancer and power lines. Like mobile phones, power lines also emit radiation.	The radiation produced by power lines is a different kind of radiation, with much more energy than that coming from mobile phones.
6. Radio frequency waves similar to those in mobile phones altered the gene expression in nematode worms.	Worms are not humans, so there is no guarantee that our brain cells will react in the same way.

If you use a mobile phone …

Key points

- Given the immense numbers of mobile phone users, even small adverse effects on health could have major public health implications.
- In 2000, the Stewart Report (a British report) found no known health problems caused by mobile phones, but advised caution, especially among the young, until more research was carried out. A further report in 2004 backed this up.

Do	Don't
Keep the calls short.	Don't use your mobile phone when the reception is weak, as the phone needs more power to communicate with the base station, and so the radio-wave emissions are higher.
Carry the mobile phone away from your body when it is on standby.	Don't buy a mobile phone with a high "SAR" value[1]. This means that it emits more radiation.
Buy a mobile phone with a long "talk time". It is more efficient, and has less powerful emissions.	Don't buy protective gadgets unless they have been independently tested.

1. SAR (specific absorption rate) is a measurement of how much electromagnetic radiation is absorbed by body tissue whilst using a mobile phone.

"Mobile Phone Safety" on the previous two pages is from a website.

Use "Mobile Phone Safety" to answer the questions that follow.

MOBILE PHONE SAFETY – *QUESTION 2*

Situation: *Public*
Text format: *Non-continuous*
Text type: *Exposition*
Aspect: *Integrate and interpret – Form a broad understanding*
Question format: *Multiple choice*
Difficulty: *561 (Level 4)* •

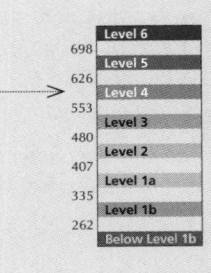

698	Level 6
626	Level 5
553	Level 4
480	Level 3
407	Level 2
335	Level 1a
262	Level 1b
	Below Level 1b

What is the purpose of the Key points?

A. To describe the dangers of using mobile phones.

B. To suggest that debate about mobile phone safety is ongoing.

C. To describe the precautions that people who use mobile phones should take.

D. To suggest that there are no known health problems caused by mobile phones.

Scoring

Full Credit: To suggest that debate about mobile phone safety is ongoing.

Comment

Classified as a **form a broad understanding task** within the **integrate** and interpret aspect, this task focuses on detecting a theme from the repetition of a particular category of information, in this case the "Key Points", a series of four boxed snippets ranged down the left hand side of the two-page text. Tasks addressing the broad understanding category are typically fairly easy, as they tend to focus on repeated and often prominent ideas in a text. However, several features of this text and task conspire to make it comparatively difficult, at Level 4. The four short Key Points tell their own story: they are related to but do not summarise the information in the body of the two main tables, so the reader needs to focus on what appears as a peripheral part of the text structure. Moreover, while all of the boxes have the caption "Key Points" the content is diverse in terms of text type, making the task of summary more difficult. The first two Key Points give a brief history of the controversy about mobile phones, the third makes a conditional proposition, and the fourth reports an equivocal finding. The fact that ambiguity, uncertainty and opposing ideas are the content of the Key Points is likely, of itself, to make the task more difficult. Here, identifying the "purpose" (which in this context is equivalent to the main theme) means establishing a hierarchy among ideas presented in the Key Points, and choosing the one that is most general and overarching. Options A and C represent different details of the Key Points, but not a single idea that could be described as overarching. Option D lifts a clause (out of context) from the fourth Key Point. Only option B, selected by 45% of students from across the OECD countries, presents a statement that synthesises the heterogeneous elements of the Key Points.

MOBILE PHONE SAFETY – QUESTION 11

Situation: *Public*
Text format: *Non-continuous*
Text type: *Exposition*
Aspect: *Reflect and evaluate – Reflect on and evaluate the content of a text*
Question format: *Multiple choice*
Difficulty: *604 (Level 4)* •

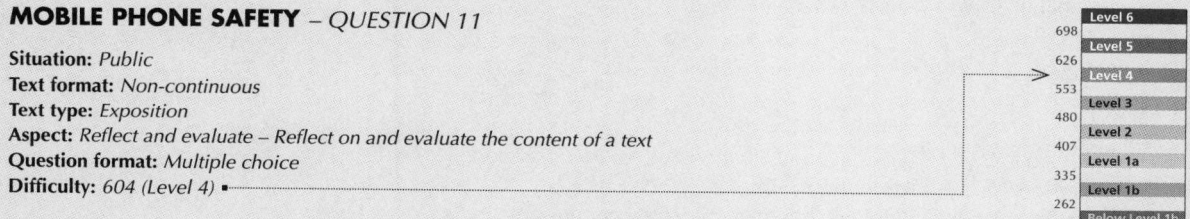

	Level 6
698	
	Level 5
626	
	Level 4
553	
	Level 3
480	
	Level 2
407	
	Level 1a
335	
	Level 1b
262	
	Below Level 1b

"It is difficult to prove that one thing has definitely caused another."

What is the relationship of this piece of information to the Point 4 **Yes** and **No** statements in the table **Are mobile phones dangerous?**

A. It supports the Yes argument but does not prove it.

B. It proves the Yes argument.

C. It supports the No argument but does not prove it.

D. It shows that the No argument is wrong.

Scoring

Full Credit: C. It supports the No argument but does not prove it.

Comment

This task requires the reader to recognise the relationship between a generalised statement external to the text and a pair of statements in a table. It is classified as **reflect and evaluate** in terms of aspect because of this external reference point. This is the most difficult task in the **MOBILE PHONE SAFETY** unit, right on the border of Level 4 and Level 5. The degree of difficulty is influenced by a number of factors. First, the stem statement uses abstract terminology ("It is difficult to prove that one thing has definitely caused another"). Secondly – a relatively straightforward part of the task – the reader needs to work out which of the two tables is relevant to this task (the first one) and which point to look at (Point 4). Thirdly, the reader needs to assimilate the structure of the relevant table: namely, that it presents opposing statements in its two columns; as we have already noted, contrary ideas are intrinsically more difficult to deal with than complementary ones. Then, the reader needs to discern precisely how the NO statement challenges the YES statement in a particular instance. Finally, logical relationship between the YES and NO statements in Point 4 must be matched, again at an abstracted level, with one of the options presented in the multiple-choice format of the task. With all these challenges intrinsic to the task, it is not surprising therefore that only a little over one-third of students across OECD countries gained credit for it.

MOBILE PHONE SAFETY – *QUESTION 6*

Situation: *Public*
Text format: *Non-continuous*
Text type: *Exposition*
Aspect: *Reflect and evaluate – Reflect on and evaluate the content of a text*
Question format: *Open constructed response*
Difficulty: *526 (Level 3)* ▪

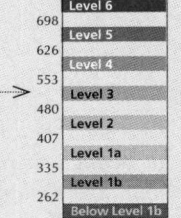

Look at Point 3 in the **No** column of the table. In this context, what might one of these "other factors" be? Give a reason for your answer.

....

Scoring

Full Credit

Identifies a <u>factor in modern lifestyles that could be related to fatigue, headaches, or loss of concentration</u>. The explanation may be self-evident, or explicitly stated. For example:

- Not getting enough sleep. If you don't, you will be tired.
- Being too busy. That makes you tired.
- Too much homework, that makes you tired AND gives you headaches.
- Noise – that gives you a headache.
- Stress.
- Working late.
- Exams.
- The world is just too loud.
- People don't take time to relax anymore.
- People don't prioritise the things that matter, so they get grumpy and sick.
- Computers.
- Pollution.
- Watching too much TV.
- Drugs.
- Microwave ovens.
- Too much emailing.

Comment

Another task in which the reader needs to reflect on and evaluate the content of a text, this task calls on the ability to relate the text to knowledge external to the text. Readers must give an example from their own experience of a factor in modern life, other than mobile phones, that could explain "fatigue, headaches and loss of concentration". As in the previous task, one step in completing this task successfully is to locate the relevant information using a number reference (here, "Point 3"). The reader's subsequent steps are less complex than in the previous task, since only the YES part of Point 3 need be taken into account. In addition, the external information that needs to be drawn on is directly related to personal experience, rather than to an abstracted logical statement.

A wide range of responses earn full credit for this task. Full credit is given for producing a factor and providing an explanation as to why this might cause fatigue, headaches and loss of concentration. An example of this kind of response is "Not getting enough sleep. If you don't, you will be fatigued." Full credit is also given if it is considered that the explanation is implicit in the statement of the factor, in which case no explicit explanation is required. An example of this kind of response is "stress". On the other hand, a response such as "lifestyle" is judged too vague, without a supporting explanation or elaboration, and so is given no credit.

Towards the top of Level 3, this task was successfully completed by just over half of the students in OECD countries.

MOBILE PHONE SAFETY – *QUESTION 9*

Situation: *Public*
Text format: *Non-continuous*
Text type: *Exposition*
Aspect: *Integrate and interpret – Develop an interpretation*
Question format: *Multiple choice*
Difficulty: *488 (Level 3)* ▪

Level 6
698
Level 5
626
Level 4
553
Level 3
480
Level 2
407
Level 1a
335
Level 1b
262
Below Level 1b

Look at the table with the heading **If you use a mobile phone ...**

Which of these ideas is the table based on?

A. There is no danger involved in using mobile phones.

B. There is a proven risk involved in using mobile phones.

C. There may or may not be danger involved in using mobile phones, but it is worth taking precautions.

D. There may or may not be danger involved in using mobile phones, but they should not be used until we know for sure.

E. The **Do** instructions are for those who take the threat seriously, and the **Don't** instructions are for everyone else.

Scoring

Full Credit: C. There may or may not be danger involved in using mobile phones, but it is worth taking precautions.

Comment

In this task the reader is explicitly directed to look at the second table, and to recognise its underlying assumption. In fact, the assumption is indicated in the last boxed Key Point: that in the absence of decisive evidence about the danger of mobile phones, it is advisable to take caution. The task asks readers to infer the consequences of this judgment, which can be done by checking that the table's contents are consistent with the Key Point. Alternatively, the reader can consult only the table and draw an independent conclusion from it. Option A is incorrect since it flatly contradicts the substance of the Key Point, and is inconsistent with the import of a set of injunctions that neither embargoes nor gives carte blanche to mobile phone use. Option B is rather more plausible, but the word "proven" makes it wrong in light of the information in the Key Point that no known health problems caused by mobile phones were found in the two studies that were cited. Option C presents itself as the best answer, consistent with both the Key Point and all the detail of the DO and DON'T columns. Option D can be dismissed as nothing more than the heading of a table that reads: "If you use a mobile phone ...", and option E sets up a specious opposition that has no support in the text. Just under two-thirds of students selected the correct response, making it the easiest of the four tasks related to this challenging stimulus.

■ Figure I.2.42 ■
BALLOON

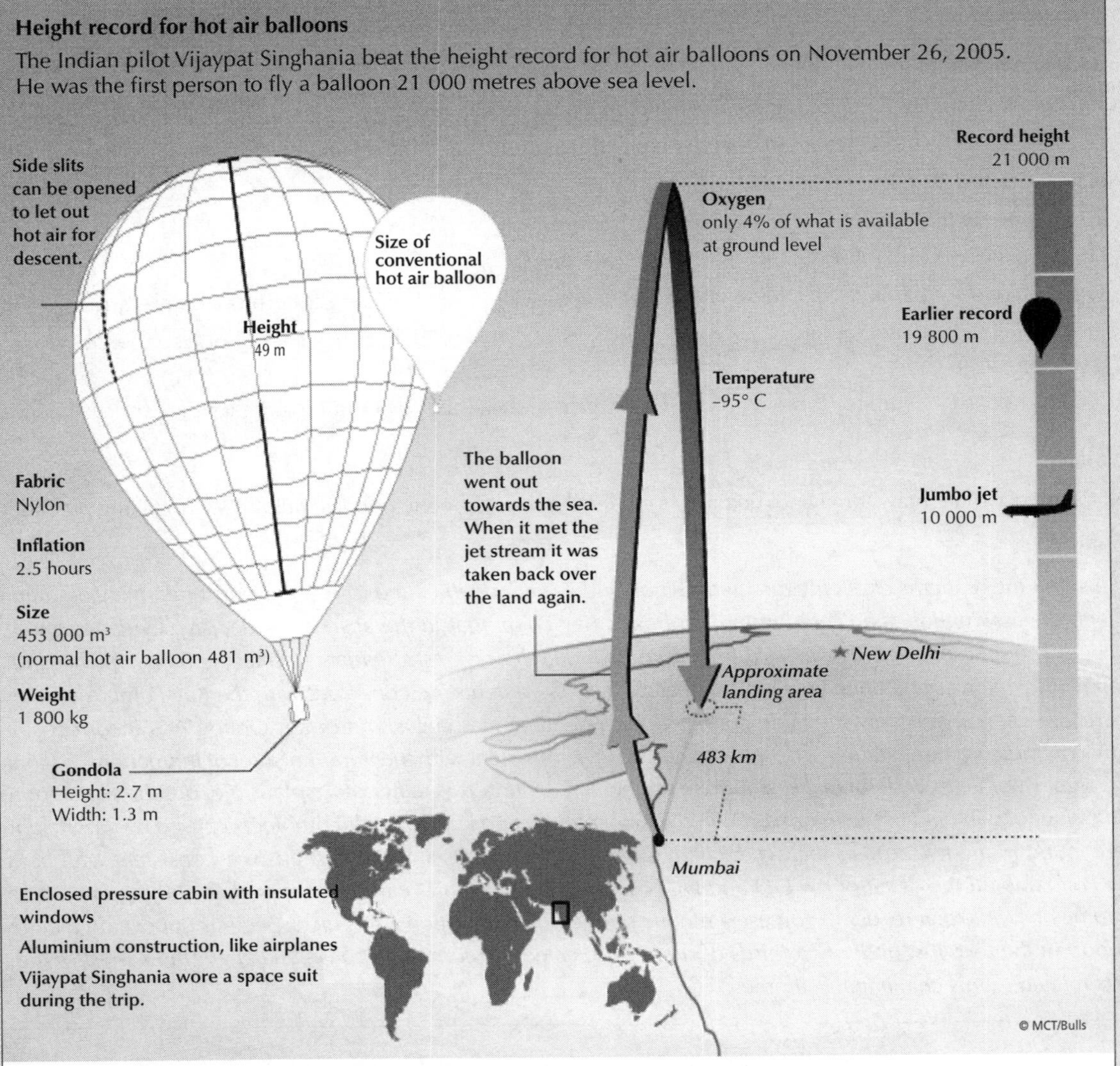

Height record for hot air balloons

The Indian pilot Vijaypat Singhania beat the height record for hot air balloons on November 26, 2005.
He was the first person to fly a balloon 21 000 metres above sea level.

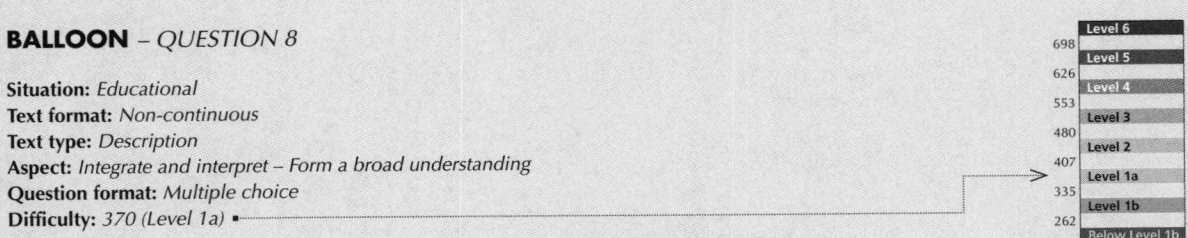

Record height
21 000 m

Oxygen
only 4% of what is available
at ground level

Earlier record
19 800 m

Temperature
−95° C

Jumbo jet
10 000 m

Side slits
can be opened
to let out
hot air for
descent.

**Size of
conventional
hot air balloon**

Height
49 m

Fabric
Nylon

Inflation
2.5 hours

Size
453 000 m³
(normal hot air balloon 481 m³)

Weight
1 800 kg

Gondola
Height: 2.7 m
Width: 1.3 m

The balloon
went out
towards the sea.
When it met the
jet stream it was
taken back over
the land again.

★ *New Delhi*

*Approximate
landing area*

483 km

Mumbai

Enclosed pressure cabin with insulated
windows

Aluminium construction, like airplanes

Vijaypat Singhania wore a space suit
during the trip.

© MCT/Bulls

Use "Balloon" on the previous page to answer the questions that follow.

BALLOON – *QUESTION 8*

Level 6	698
Level 5	626
Level 4	553
Level 3	480
Level 2	407
Level 1a	335
Level 1b	262
Below Level 1b	

Situation: *Educational*
Text format: *Non-continuous*
Text type: *Description*
Aspect: *Integrate and interpret – Form a broad understanding*
Question format: *Multiple choice*
Difficulty: *370 (Level 1a)* ■

What is the main idea of this text?

A. Singhania was in danger during his balloon trip.

B. Singhania set a new world record.

C. Singhania travelled over both sea and land.

D. Singhania's balloon was enormous.

Scoring

Full Credit: B. Singhania set a new world record.

Comment

The main idea of this non-continuous text is stated explicitly and prominently several times, including in the title, "Height record for hot air balloon". The prominence and repetition of the required information helps to explains its easiness: it is located in the lower half of Level 1a.

Although the main idea is explicitly stated, the question is classified as integrate and interpret, with the sub-classification forming a broad understanding, because it involves distinguishing the most significant and general from subordinate information in the text. The first option – "Singhania was in danger during his balloon trip" – is a plausible speculation, but it is not supported by anything in the text, and so cannot qualify as a main idea. The third option – "Singhania travelled over both sea and land" – accurately paraphrases information from the text, but it is a detail rather than the main idea. The fourth option – "Singhania's balloon was enormous" – refers to a conspicuous graphic feature in the text but, again, it is subordinate to the main idea.

BALLOON – QUESTION 3

Situation: Educational
Text format: Non-continuous
Text type: Description
Aspect: Access and retrieve – Retrieve information
Question format: Short response
Difficulty: Full credit 595 (Level 4); Partial credit 449 (Level 2)

698	Level 6
626	Level 5
553	Level 4
480	Level 3
407	Level 2
335	Level 1a
262	Level 1b
	Below Level 1b

Vijaypat Singhania used technologies found in two other types of transport. Which types of transport?

1. ....

2. ....

Scoring

Full Credit: Refers to <u>BOTH airplanes AND spacecraft</u> (in either order, can include both answers on one line). For example:

- 1. Aircraft
  2. Spacecraft
- 1. Airplanes
  2. Space ships
- 1. Air travel
  2. Space travel
- 1. Planes
  2. Space rockets
- 1. Jets
  2. Rockets

Partial Credit: Refers to EITHER <u>airplanes OR spacecraft</u>. For example:

- Spacecraft
- Space travel
- Space rockets
- Rockets
- Aircraft
- Airplanes
- Air travel
- Jets

Comment

In this task full credit is given for responses that lists the two required types of transport, and partial credit is given to responses that listed one type. The scoring rules reproduced above demonstrate that credit is available for several different paraphrases of the terms "airplanes" and "spacecraft".

The partial credit score is located in the upper half of Level 2 while the full credit score is located at Level 4, illustrating the fact that **access and retrieve** questions can create a significant challenge. The difficulty of the task is particularly influenced by a number of features of the text. The layout, with several different kinds of graphs and multiple captions, is quite a common type of non-continuous presentation often seen in magazines and modern textbooks, but because it does not have a conventional ordered structure (unlike, for example, a table or graph), finding specific pieces of discrete information is relatively inefficient. Captions ("Fabric", "Record height", and so on) give some support to the reader in navigating the text, but the information specific required for this task does not have a caption, so that readers have to generate their own categorisation of the relevant information as they search. Having once found the required information, inconspicuously located at the bottom left-hand corner of the diagram, the reader needs to recognise that the "aluminium construction, like airplanes" and the "space suit" are associated with categories of transport. In order to obtain credit for this question, the response needs to refer to a form or forms of transport, rather than simply transcribing an approximate section of text. Thus "space travel" is credited, but "space suit" is not. A significant piece of competing information in the text constitutes a further difficulty: many students referred to a "jumbo jet" in their answer. Although "air travel" or "airplane" or "jet" is given credit, "jumbo jet" is deemed to refer specifically to the image and caption on the right of the diagram. This answer is not given credit as the jumbo jet in the illustration is not included in the material with reference to technology used for Singhania's balloon.

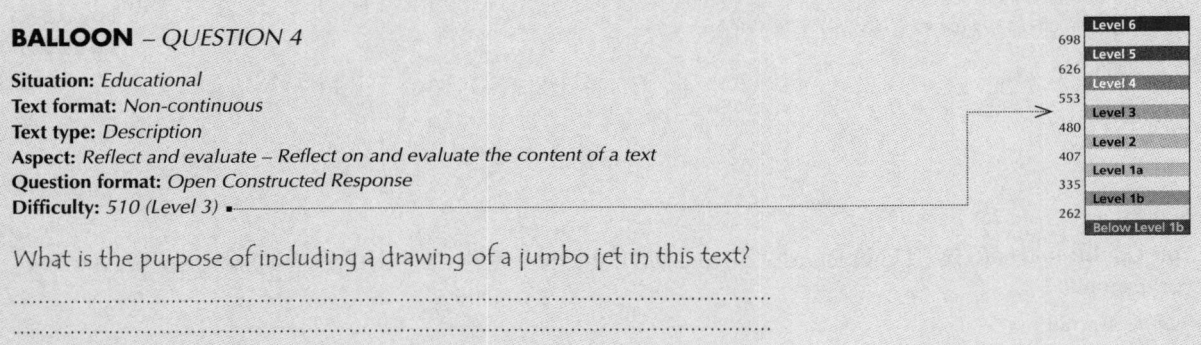

BALLOON – *QUESTION 4*

Situation: *Educational*
Text format: *Non-continuous*
Text type: *Description*
Aspect: *Reflect and evaluate – Reflect on and evaluate the content of a text*
Question format: *Open Constructed Response*
Difficulty: *510 (Level 3)*

What is the purpose of including a drawing of a jumbo jet in this text?

....

....

Scoring

Full Credit: Refers explicitly or implicitly to the <u>height of the balloon</u> OR to <u>the record</u>. May refer to comparison between the jumbo jet and the balloon.

- To show how high the balloon went.
- To emphasise the fact that the balloon went really, really high.
- To show how impressive his record really was – he went higher than jumbo jets!
- As a point of reference regarding height.
- To show how impressive his record really was. [minimal]

Comment

The main idea of the text is to describe the height record set by Vijaypat Singhania in his extraordinary balloon. The diagram on the right-hand side of the graphic, which includes the jumbo jet, implicitly contributes to the "wow!" factor of the text, showing just how impressive the height achieved by Singhania was by comparing it with what we usually associate with grand height: a jumbo jet's flight. In order to gain credit for this task, students must recognise the persuasive intent of including the illustration of the jumbo jet. For this reason the task is classified as **reflect and evaluate,** with the sub-category **reflect on and evaluate the content of a text**. At the upper end of Level 3, this question is moderately difficult.

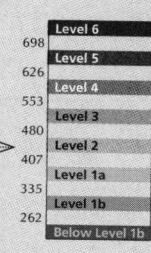

BALLOON – QUESTION 6

Situation: *Educational*
Text format: *Non-continuous*
Text type: *Description*
Aspect: *Reflect and evaluate – Reflect on and evaluate the content of a text*
Question format: *Multiple choice*
Difficulty: *411 (Level 2)* •

698   Level 6
Level 5
626   Level 4
553   Level 3
480   Level 2
407   Level 1a
335   Level 1b
262   Below Level 1b

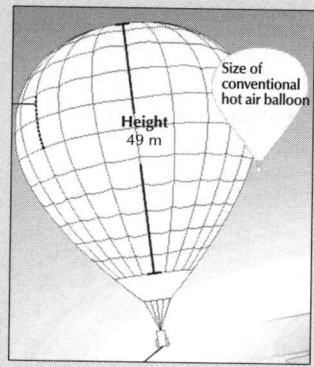

Why does the drawing show two balloons?

A. To compare the size of Singhania's balloon before and after it was inflated.

B. To compare the size of Singhania's balloon with that of other hot air balloons.

C. To show that Singhania's balloon looks small from the ground.

D. To show that Singhania's balloon almost collided with another balloon.

Scoring

Full Credit: B. To compare the size of Singhania's balloon with that of other hot air balloons.

Comment

It is important for readers to be aware that texts are not randomly occurring artefacts, but are constructed deliberately and with intent, and that part of the meaning of a text is found in the elements that authors choose to include. Like the previous task, this task is classified under **reflect and evaluate** *because it asks about authorial intent. It focuses on a graphic element – here the illustration of two balloons – and asks students to consider the purpose of this inclusion. In the context of the over-arching idea of the text, to describe (and celebrate) Singhania's flight, the balloon illustration sends the message, "This is a really big balloon!", just as the jumbo jet illustration sends the message, "This is a really high flight!" The caption on the smaller balloon ("Size of a conventional hot air balloon") makes it obvious that this is a different balloon to Singhania's, and therefore, for attentive readers, renders options A and C implausible. Option D has no support in the text. With a difficulty near the bottom of Level 2, this is a rather easy task.*

■ Figure I.2.43 ■
BLOOD DONATION

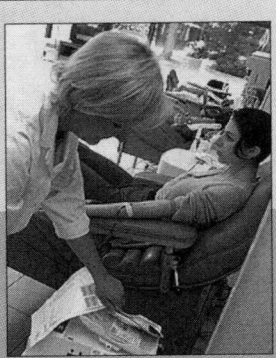

Blood donation is essential.

There is no product that can fully substitute for human blood. Blood donation is thus irreplaceable and essential to save lives.

In France, each year, 500,000 patients benefit from a blood transfusion.

The instruments for taking the blood are sterile and single-use (syringe, tubes, bags).

There is no risk in giving your blood.

Blood donation

It is the best-known kind of donation, and takes from 45 minutes to 1 hour.

A 450-ml bag is taken as well as some small samples on which tests and checks will be done.
- A man can give his blood five times a year, a woman three times.
- Donors can be from 18 to 65 years old.

An 8-week interval is compulsory between each donation.

"Blood Donation Notice" on the previous page is from a French website.

Use "Blood Donation Notice" to answer the questions that follow.

BLOOD DONATION NOTICE – QUESTION 8

Situation: *Public*
Text format: *Continuous*
Text type: *Argumentation*
Aspect: *Integrate and interpret – Develop an interpretation*
Question format: *Open constructed response*
Difficulty: *438 (Level 2)*

698	Level 6
626	Level 5
553	Level 4
480	Level 3
407	Level 2
335	Level 1a
262	Level 1b
	Below Level 1b

An eighteen-year-old woman who has given her blood twice in the last twelve months wants to give blood again. According to "Blood Donation Notice", on what condition will she be allowed to give blood again?

....

....

Scoring

Full Credit: Identifies that <u>enough time must have elapsed</u> since her last donation.
- Depends whether it has been 8 weeks since her last donation or not.
- She can if it has been long enough, otherwise she can't.

Comment

At a level of difficulty around the middle of Level 2, this task asks the reader to apply the information in the text to a practical case. This is the kind of reading activity that is typically associated with such a text in everyday life, and thus meets one of PISA's aims in answering questions about how well young people at the end of compulsory schooling are equipped to meet the challenges of their future lives.

The reader must match the case described in the question stem with four pieces of information provided in the second half of the text: the age and sex of the prospective donor, the number of times a person is allowed to give blood, and the interval required between donations. Reference to this last piece of information is needed in order to meet the task's requirement to stipulate the "condition" under which the young woman can give blood. As evidenced in the two examples of full credit responses, students are given credit for either a specific answer that includes reference to the interval of eight weeks between donations, or for a more generalised answer, such as "She can if it has been long enough, otherwise she can't".

BLOOD DONATION NOTICE – *QUESTION 9*

Situation: *Public*
Text format: *Continuous*
Text type: *Argumentation*
Aspect: *Reflect and evaluate – Reflect on and evaluate the content of a text*
Question format: *Multiple choice*
Difficulty: *368 (Level 1a)*

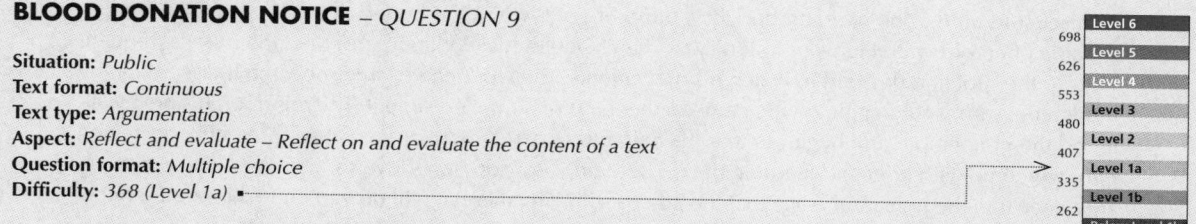

The text says: "The instruments for taking the blood are sterile and single-use ... "

Why does the text include this information?

A. To reassure you that blood donation is safe.

B. To emphasise that blood donation is essential.

C. To explain the uses of your blood.

D. To give details of the tests and checks.

Scoring

QUESTION INTENT:

Reflect and evaluate: Reflect on and evaluate the content of a text.

Recognise the persuasive purpose of a phrase in an advertisement.

Full Credit: A. To reassure you that blood donation is safe.

Comment

*To gain credit for this task, students must recognise the persuasive purpose of part of an advertisement. The task is classified as **reflect and evaluate** because students need to consider the wider context of what appears to be a simple statement of fact in order to recognise the underlying purpose for its inclusion.*

The relative easiness of this task, which is located in the lower half of Level 1a, can be attributed to the brevity of the text and also to the fact that it deals with an everyday topic. Another characteristic of relatively easy questions exemplified here is that they typically draw on information that is consistent with common preconceptions: there is nothing contrary to expectations in the notion that people are encouraged to donate blood and reassured that donation involves no risk. Although the persuasive intent of this text is not stated explicitly in the words of the blood donation notice, the idea that it is encouraging people to donate blood and reassuring them about the safety of blood donation can be inferred from several statements. The text begins with "Blood donation is essential", a notion that is repeated and elaborated in the second paragraph ("irreplaceable and essential"). The text also refers to the absence of risk immediately after the section of text in focus in this task, though the logical connection between the two paragraphs – evidence: conclusion – must be inferred.

■ Figure I.2.44 ■

MISER

THE MISER AND HIS GOLD

A fable by Aesop

A miser sold all that he had and bought a lump of gold, which he buried in a hole in the ground by the side of an old wall. He went to look at it daily. One of his workmen observed the miser's frequent visits to the spot and decided to watch his movements. The workman soon discovered the secret of the hidden treasure, and digging down, came to the lump of gold, and stole it. The miser, on his next visit, found the hole empty and began to tear his hair and to make loud lamentations. A neighbour, seeing him overcome with grief and learning the cause, said, "Pray do not grieve so; but go and take a stone, and place it in the hole, and fancy that the gold is still lying there. It will do you quite the same service; for when the gold was there, you had it not, as you did not make the slightest use of it."

Use the fable "The Miser and his Gold" on the previous page to answer the questions that follow.

MISER – QUESTION 1

Situation: *Personal*
Text format: *Continuous*
Text type: *Narration*
Aspect: *Integrate and interpret – Develop an interpretation*
Question format: *Closed constructed response*
Difficulty: *373 (Level 1a)* ∎

	Level 6
698	Level 5
626	Level 4
553	Level 3
480	Level 2
407	Level 1a
335	Level 1b
262	Below Level 1b

Read the sentences below and number them according to the sequence of events in the text.

☐ The miser decided to turn all his money into a lump of gold.

☐ A man stole the miser's gold.

☐ The miser dug a hole and hid his treasure in it.

☐ The miser's neighbour told him to replace the gold with a stone.

Scoring

Full Credit: All four correct: 1, 3, 2, 4 in that order.

Comment

Fables are a popular and respected text type in many cultures and they are a favourite text type in reading assessments for similar reasons: they are short, self-contained, morally instructive and have stood the test of time. While perhaps not the most common reading material for young adults in OECD countries they are nevertheless likely to be familiar from childhood, and the pithy, often acerbic observations of a fable can pleasantly surprise even a blasé 15-year-old. MISER is typical of its genre: it captures and satirises a particular human weakness in a neat economical story, executed in a single paragraph.

*Since **narrations** are defined as referring to properties of objects in time, typically answering "when" questions, it is appropriate to include a task based on a narrative text that asks for a series of statements about the story to be put into the correct sequence. With such a short text, and with statements in the task that are closely matched with the terms of the story, this is an easy task, around the middle of Level 1a. On the other hand, the language of the text is rather formal and has some old-fashioned locutions. (Translators were asked to reproduce the fable-like style of the source versions.) This characteristic of the text is likely to have added to the difficulty of the question.*

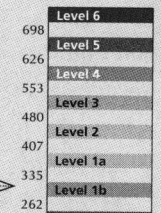

MISER – *QUESTION 7*

Situation: *Personal*
Text format: *Continuous*
Text type: *Narration*
Aspect: *Access and retrieve – Retrieve information*
Question format: *Short response*
Difficulty: *310 (Level 1b)* ■

698	Level 6
626	Level 5
553	Level 4
480	Level 3
407	Level 2
335	Level 1a
262	Level 1b
	Below Level 1b

How did the miser get a lump of gold?

....

Scoring

Full Credit: States that he <u>sold everything he had</u>. May paraphrase or quote directly from the text.

- He sold all he had.

- He sold all his stuff.

- He bought it. *[implicit connection to selling everything he had]*

Comment

This is one of the easiest tasks in PISA reading, with a difficulty in the middle of Level 1b. The reader is required to **access and retrieve** *a piece of explicitly stated information in the opening sentence of a very short text. To gain full credit, the response can either quote directly from the text – "He sold all that he had" – or provide a paraphrase such as "He sold all his stuff". The formal language of the text, which is likely to have added difficulty in other tasks in the unit, is unlikely to have much impact here because the required information is located at the very beginning of the text. Although this is an extremely easy question in PISA's frame of reference, it still requires a small degree of inference, beyond the absolutely literal: the reader must infer that there is a causal connection between the first proposition (that the miser sold all he had) and the second (that he bought gold).*

MISER – *QUESTION 5*

Situation: *Personal*
Text format: *Continuous*
Text type: *Narration*
Aspect: *Integrate and interpret – Develop an interpretation*
Question format: *Open constructed response*
Difficulty: *548 (Level 3)* ■

698	Level 6
626	Level 5
553	Level 4
480	Level 3
407	Level 2
335	Level 1a
262	Level 1b
	Below Level 1b

Here is part of a conversation between two people who read "The Miser and his Gold".

Speaker 1

The neighbour was nasty. He could have recommended replacing the gold with something better than a stone.

No he couldn't. The stone was important in the story.

Speaker 2

What could Speaker 2 say to support his point of view?

....

....

Scoring

Full Credit

Recognises that the message of the story depends on the gold being replaced by something useless or worthless.

- It needed to be replaced by something worthless to make the point.
- The stone is important in the story, because the whole point is he might as well have buried a stone for all the good the gold did him.
- If you replaced it with something better than a stone, it would miss the point because the thing buried needs to be something really useless.
- A stone is useless, but for the miser, so was the gold!
- Something better would be something he could use – he didn't use the gold, that's what the guy was pointing out.
- Because stones can be found anywhere. The gold and the stone are the same to the miser. *["can be found anywhere" implies that the stone is of no special value]*

Comment

This task takes the form of setting up a dialogue between two imaginary readers, to represent two conflicting interpretations of the story. In fact only the second speaker's position is consistent with the overall implication of the text, so that in providing a supporting explanation readers demonstrate that they have understood the "punch line" – the moral import – of the fable. The relative difficulty of the task, near the top of Level 3, is likely to be influenced by the fact that readers needs to do a good deal of work to generate a full credit response. First they must make sense of the neighbour's speech in the story, which is expressed in a formal register. (As noted, translators were asked to reproduce the fable-like style.) Secondly, the relationship between the question stem and the required information is not obvious: there is little or no support in the stem ("What could Speaker 2 say to support his point of view?") to guide the reader in interpreting the task, though the reference to the stone and the neighbour by the speakers should point the reader to the end of the fable.

As shown in examples of responses, to gain full credit, students could express, in a variety of ways, the key idea that wealth has no value unless it is used. Vague gestures at meaning, such as "the stone had a symbolic value", are not given credit.

■ Figure I.2.45 ■

THE PLAY'S THE THING

Takes place in a castle by the beach in Italy.

FIRST ACT

Ornate guest room in a very nice beachside castle. Doors on the right and left. Sitting
5 *room set in the middle of the stage: couch, table, and two armchairs. Large windows at the back. Starry night. It is dark on the stage. When the curtain goes up we hear men conversing loudly behind the door on the left.*
10 *The door opens and three tuxedoed gentlemen enter. One turns the light on immediately. They walk to the centre in silence and stand around the table. They sit down together, Gál in the armchair to the left, Turai in the one on*
15 *the right, Ádám on the couch in the middle. Very long, almost awkward silence. Comfortable stretches. Silence. Then:*

GÁL
Why are you so deep in thought?

20 **TURAI**
I'm thinking about how difficult it is to begin a play. To introduce all the principal characters in the beginning, when it all starts.

ÁDÁM
25 I suppose it must be hard.

TURAI
It is – devilishly hard. The play starts. The audience goes quiet. The actors enter the stage and the torment begins. It's an eternity,
30 sometimes as much as a quarter of an hour before the audience finds out who's who and what they are all up to.

GÁL
Quite a peculiar brain you've got. Can't you
35 forget your profession for a single minute?

TURAI
That cannot be done.

GÁL
Not half an hour passes without you
40 discussing theatre, actors, plays. There are other things in this world.

TURAI
There aren't. I am a dramatist. That is my curse.

45 **GÁL**
You shouldn't become such a slave to your profession.

TURAI
If you do not master it, you are its slave.
50 There is no middle ground. Trust me, it's no joke starting a play well. It is one of the toughest problems of stage mechanics. Introducing your characters promptly. Let's look at this scene here, the three of
55 us. Three gentlemen in tuxedoes. Say they enter not this room in this lordly castle, but rather a stage, just when a play begins. They would have to chat about a whole lot of uninteresting topics until it came out

60 who we are. Wouldn't it be much easier to start all this by standing up and introducing ourselves? Stands up. Good evening. The three of us are guests in this castle. We have just arrived from the
65 dining room where we had an excellent dinner and drank two bottles of champagne. My name is Sándor TURAI, I'm a playwright, I've been writing plays for thirty years, that's my profession. Full stop.
70 Your turn.

GÁL
Stands up. My name is GÁL, I'm also a playwright. I write plays as well, all of them in the company of this gentleman
75 here. We are a famous playwright duo. All playbills of good comedies and operettas read: written by GÁL and TURAI. Naturally, this is my profession as well.

GÁL and **TURAI**
80 *Together.* And this young man …

ÁDÁM
Stands up. This young man is, if you allow me, Albert ÁDÁM, twenty-five years old, composer. I wrote the music for these kind
85 gentlemen for their latest operetta. This is my first work for the stage. These two elderly angels have discovered me and now, with their help, I'd like to become famous. They got me invited to this castle. They got
90 my dress-coat and tuxedo made. In other words, I am poor and unknown, for now. Other than that I'm an orphan and my grandmother raised me. My grandmother has passed away. I am all alone in this world. I
95 have no name, I have no money.

TURAI
But you are young.

GÁL
And gifted.

100 **ÁDÁM**
And I am in love with the soloist.

TURAI
You shouldn't have added that. Everyone in the audience would figure that out anyway.

105 *They all sit down.*

TURAI
Now wouldn't this be the easiest way to start a play?

GÁL
110 If we were allowed to do this, it would be easy to write plays.

TURAI
Trust me, it's not that hard. Just think of this whole thing as …

115 **GÁL**
All right, all right, all right, just don't start talking about the theatre again. I'm fed up with it. We'll talk tomorrow, if you wish.

"The Play's the Thing" is the beginning of a play by the Hungarian dramatist Ferenc Molnár.

Use "The Play's the Thing" on the previous two pages to answer the questions that follow. (Note that line numbers are given in the margin of the script to help you find parts that are referred to in the questions.)

THE PLAY'S THE THING – *QUESTION 3*

Situation: *Personal*
Text format: *Continuous*
Text type: *Narration*
Aspect: *Integrate and interpret – Develop an interpretation*
Question format: *Short response*
Difficulty: *730 (Level 6)* •

698	Level 6
626	Level 5
553	Level 4
480	Level 3
407	Level 2
335	Level 1a
262	Level 1b
	Below Level 1b

What were the characters in the play doing **just before** the curtain went up?

....

Scoring

Full Credit: Refers to <u>dinner</u> or <u>drinking champagne</u>. May paraphrase or quote the text directly.

- They have just had dinner and champagne.
- "We have just arrived from the dining room where we had an excellent dinner." *[direct quotation]*
- "An excellent dinner and drank two bottles of champagne." *[direct quotation]*
- Dinner and drinks.
- Dinner.
- Drank champagne.
- Had dinner and drank.
- They were in the dining room.

Comment

This task illustrates several features of the most difficult tasks in PISA reading. The text is long by PISA standards, and it may be supposed that the fictional world depicted is remote from the experience of most 15-year-olds. The introduction to the unit tells students that the stimulus of **THE PLAY'S THE THING** *is the beginning of a play by the Hungarian dramatist Ferenc Molnár, but there is no other external orientation. The setting ("a castle by the beach in Italy") is likely to be exotic to many, and the situation is only revealed gradually through the dialogue itself. While individual pieces of vocabulary are not particularly difficult, and the tone is often chatty, the register of the language is a little mannered. Perhaps most importantly a level of unfamiliarity is introduced by the abstract theme of the discussion: a sophisticated conversation between characters about the relationship between life and art, and the challenges of writing for the theatre. The text is classified as narration because this theme is dealt with as part of the play's narrative.*

While all the tasks in this unit acquire a layer of difficulty associated with the challenges of the text, the cognitive demand of this task in particular is also attributable to the high level of interpretation required to define the meaning of the question's terms, in relation to the text. The reader needs to be alert to the distinction between characters and actors. The question refers to what the characters (not the actors) were doing "just before the curtain went up". This is potentially confusing since it requires recognition of a shift between the real world of a stage in a theatre, which has a curtain, and the imaginary world of Gal, Turai and Adam, who were in the dining room having dinner just before they entered the guest room (the stage setting). A question that assesses students' capacity to distinguish between real and fictional worlds seems particularly appropriate in relation to a text whose theme is about just that, so that the complexity of the question is aligned with the content of the text.

A further level of the task's difficulty is introduced by the fact that the required information is in an unexpected location. The question refers to the action "before the curtain went up", which would typically lead one to search at the opening of the scene, the beginning of the extract. On the contrary, the information is actually found about half-way through the extract, when Turai reveals that he and his friends "have just arrived from the dining room". While the scoring for the question shows that several kinds of response are acceptable, to be given full credit readers must demonstrate that they have found this inconspicuous piece of information. The need to assimilate information that is contrary to expectations – where the reader needs to give full attention to the text in defiance of preconceptions – is highly characteristic of the most demanding reading tasks in PISA.

THE PLAY'S THE THING – QUESTION 4

Situation: *Personal*
Text format: *Continuous*
Text type: *Narration*
Aspect: *Integrate and interpret – Develop an interpretation*
Question format: *Multiple choice*
Difficulty: *474 (Level 2)* •

698	Level 6
626	Level 5
553	Level 4
480	Level 3
407	Level 2
335	Level 1a
262	Level 1b
	Below Level 1b

"It's an eternity, sometimes as much as a quarter of an hour … " (lines 29-30)
According to Turai, why is a quarter of an hour "an eternity"?

A. It is a long time to expect an audience to sit still in a crowded theatre.

B. It seems to take forever for the situation to be clarified at the beginning of a play.

C. It always seems to take a long time for a dramatist to write the beginning of a play.

D. It seems that time moves slowly when a significant event is happening in a play.

Scoring

Full Credit: B. It seems to take forever for the situation to be clarified at the beginning of a play.

Comment

Near the borderline between Level 2 and Level 3, this question together with the previous one illustrates the fact that questions covering a wide range of difficulties can be based on a single text.

Unlike in the previous task, the stem of this task directs the reader to the relevant section in the play, even quoting the lines, thus relieving the reader of any challenge in figuring out where the necessary information is to be found. Nevertheless, the reader needs to understand the context in which the line is uttered in order to respond successfully. In fact, the implication of "It seems to take forever for the situation to be clarified at the beginning of a play" underpins much of the rest of this extract, which enacts the solution of characters explicitly introducing themselves at the beginning of a play instead of waiting for the action to reveal who they are. Insofar as the utterance that is quoted in the stem prompts most of the rest of this extract, repetition and emphasis support the reader in integrating and interpreting the quotation. In that respect too, this task clearly differs from Question 3, in which the required information is only provided once, and is buried in an unexpected part of the text.

THE PLAY'S THE THING – QUESTION 7

Situation: *Personal*
Text format: *Continuous*
Text type: *Narration*
Aspect: *Integrate and interpret – Form a broad understanding*
Question format: *Multiple choice*
Difficulty: *556 (Level 4)* •

698	Level 6
626	Level 5
553	Level 4
480	Level 3
407	Level 2
335	Level 1a
262	Level 1b
	Below Level 1b

Overall, what is the dramatist Molnár doing in this extract?

A. He is showing the way that each character will solve his own problems.

B. He is making his characters demonstrate what an eternity in a play is like.

C. He is giving an example of a typical and traditional opening scene for a play.

D. He is using the characters to act out one of his own creative problems.

Scoring

Full Credit: D. He is using the characters to act out one of his own creative problems.

Comment

In this task the reader is asked to take a global perspective, **form a broad understanding** *by integrating and interpreting the implications of the dialogue across the text. The task involves recognising the conceptual theme of a section of a play, where the theme is literary and abstract. This relatively unfamiliar territory for most 15-year-olds is likely to constitute the difficulty of the task, which is located at Level 4. A little under half of the students in OECD countries gained full credit for this task, with the others divided fairly evenly across the three distractors.*

■ Figure I.2.46 ■
TELECOMMUTING

The way of the future

Just imagine how wonderful it would be to "telecommute"[1] to work on the electronic highway, with all your work done on a computer or by phone! No longer would you have to jam your body into crowded buses or trains or waste hours and hours travelling to and from work. You could work wherever you want to – just think of all the job opportunities this would open up!

Molly

Disaster in the making

Cutting down on commuting hours and reducing the energy consumption involved is obviously a good idea. But such a goal should be accomplished by improving public transportation or by ensuring that workplaces are located near where people live. The ambitious idea that telecommuting should be part of everyone's way of life will only lead people to become more and more self-absorbed. Do we really want our sense of being part of a community to deteriorate even further?

Richard

---

1. "Telecommuting" is a term coined by Jack Nilles in the early 1970s to describe a situation in which workers work on a computer away from a central office (for example, at home) and transmit data and documents to the central office via telephone lines.

Use "Telecommuting" above to answer the questions that follow.

TELECOMMUTING – *QUESTION 1*

Situation: *Occupational*
Text format: *Multiple*
Text type: *Argumentation*
Aspect: *Integrate and interpret – Form a broad understanding*
Question format: *Multiple choice*
Difficulty: *537 (Level 3)*

698	Level 6
626	Level 5
553	Level 4
480	Level 3
407	Level 2
335	Level 1a
262	Level 1b
	Below Level 1b

What is the relationship between "The way of the future" and "Disaster in the making"?

A. They use different arguments to reach the same general conclusion.

B. They are written in the same style but they are about completely different topics.

C. They express the same general point of view, but arrive at different conclusions.

D. They express opposing points of view on the same topic.

Scoring

Full Credit: D. They express opposing points of view on the same topic.

Comment

The stimulus for the unit **TELECOMMUTING** *is two short texts that offer contrasting opinions on telecommuting, defined in a footnote to the text as "working on a computer away from a central office". The only addition to the originally submitted text that was made by PISA test developers was this footnote. It was assumed that the term "telecommuting" would be unfamiliar to most 15-year-olds. The footnote was included in order to avoid giving an advantage to students whose language would allow them to unpack the meaning of this compound word. For example, students tested in English may have been able to infer the meaning of the word by combining the meaning of "tele" (distant) and "commute". By contrast, some countries in which English is not the testing language used the English term or a transliteration, which would not provide the same clues to the meaning.*

The purpose of each of the short texts in the stimulus is to persuade readers to a point of view, so the stimulus is classified as **argumentation**. *Given that the purpose of the stimulus material is to discuss an issue related to working life, the text is classified as occupational in terms of situation. The two pieces that make up the stimulus are both continuous, but because they were generated independently and juxtaposed for the purpose of the assessment, the text format classification of this text is* **multiple**.

This question requires students to recognise the relationship between the two short texts. To answer correctly, students must first form a global understanding of each of the short texts, and then identify the relationship between them: that is, that they express contrasting points of view on the same topic. A factor contributing to the difficulty of this question is the level of interpretation required to identify the position that is expressed in each text. In the first text the author's position is signalled clearly early in the text ("Just imagine how wonderful it would be to 'telecommute' to work …") and reinforced throughout. In contrast the second piece contains no direct statement of the author's own position: instead, it is written as a series of responses to arguments that the author opposes, so understanding the position of the second author requires a greater level of interpretation than understanding the position of the first author. Once the work of interpreting the position of each author has been done, recognising that the positions are contrasting is relatively straightforward. The weakest students chose option B. These students fail to recognise that the two texts are about the same topic. Students who chose options A and C recognise that the two texts are about the same topic, but fail to identify that they express contrasting views. At Level 3, just over one-half of the students in OECD countries gained credit for this question.

TELECOMMUTING – *QUESTION 7*

Situation: *Occupational*
Text format: *Continuous*
Text type: *Argumentation*
Aspect: *Reflect and evaluate – Reflect on and evaluate the content of a text*
Question format: *Open constructed response*
Difficulty: *514 (Level 3)*

698	Level 6
626	Level 5
553	Level 4
480	Level 3
407	Level 2
335	Level 1a
262	Level 1b
	Below Level 1b

What is one kind of work for which it would be difficult to telecommute? Give a reason for your answer.

....

....

....

....

Scoring

QUESTION INTENT:

Reflect and evaluate: Reflect on and evaluate the content of a text

Use prior knowledge to generate an example that fits a category described in a text

Full Credit: <u>Identifies a kind of work</u> and gives a <u>plausible explanation as to why a person who does that kind of work could not telecommute</u>. Responses MUST indicate (explicitly or implicitly) that it is necessary to be physically present for the specific work.

- Building. It's hard to work with the wood and bricks from just anywhere.

- Sportsperson. You need to really be there to play the sport.

- Plumber. You can't fix someone else's sink from your home!

- Digging ditches because you need to be there.

- Nursing – it's hard to check if patients are ok over the Internet.

Comment

This question requires students to generate an example (a profession) that fits a given category. The textual information required for this question is found in the footnote definition of telecommuting. Therefore, although the stimulus is comprised of multiple texts, this question is classified as **continuous** *in terms of text format because it only refers to one text element.*

To provide an example of a job in which telecommuting would be difficult, students must link their comprehension of the text (the definition of telecommuting) with outside knowledge, since no specific profession is mentioned in the text. This question is therefore classified as **reflect and evaluate**, *with the sub-category* **reflect on and evaluate the content of a text.**

In order to gain credit for this question, students needed to give an example and to justify why their example fitted the given category, and the explanation needed to refer either explicitly or implicitly to the fact that the worker would need to be physically present in order to perform their job. Although the range of responses eligible for full credit was very wide, many students failed to gain credit because they did not provide an explanation at all, or they gave an explanation that did not show that they understood that the job they listed would require the worker's physical presence. An example of the latter is, "Digging ditches because it would be hard work." Compare this with the credited response, "Digging ditches because you need to be there."

Nearly 60% of students gained full credit for this question.

Example of a digital reading task

One task from the PISA 2009 assessment of reading of digital texts, comprising four items, is reproduced in this section. Screen shots are used to illustrate parts of the stimulus relevant to each question. The digital version of this unit and other released tasks are available at *www.pisa.oecd.org.*

■ Figure I.2.47 ■
IWANTTOHELP

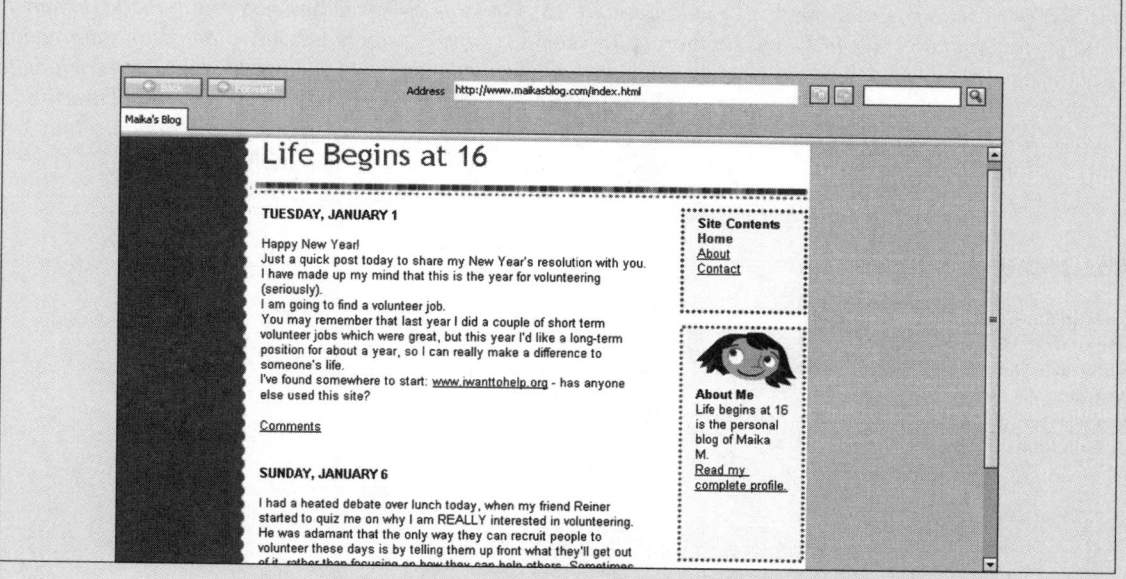

IWANTTOHELP – QUESTION 1

Situation: *Occupational*
Environment: *Message-based*
Text format: *Continuous*
Text type: *Description*
Aspect: *Access and retrieve – Retrieve information*
Question format: *Multiple choice*

Read Maika's blog entry for January 1. What does the entry say about Maika's experience of volunteering?

A. She has been a volunteer for many years.

B. She only volunteers in order to be with her friends.

C. She has done a little volunteering but would like to do more.

D. She has tried volunteering but does not think it is worthwhile.

Scoring

Full Credit: C. She has done a little volunteering but would like to do more.

Comment

*The first page that students see in this unit is the home page of the blog (Life Begins at 16) of a young person named Maika. This page contains two entries from the blog, for January 1 and January 6. Although this kind of text often appears on a social networking site, the specific content describes Maika's interest in and plans for doing voluntary work, so this question (and later questions in this unit) are classified as falling within the **occupational** context.*

Fifteen-year-old students may not have much experience of volunteering, but the concept is quite concrete, and the text is made accessible by the use of language that is relatively simple and colloquial ("Just a quick post", "(seriously)"), and addressed directly to the audience who may be reading it ("share my New Year's resolution with you", "You may remember", "has anyone else used this site?"). The page contains features typical of social networking sites, with four links available within the site ("About", "Contact", "Read my complete profile", "Comments") and one link to an external site (www.iwanttohelp.org).

This task requires the reader to identify information about Maika's experience of volunteering. Students need to read the short text entry for January 1 in order to locate the answer. It is not necessary to scroll down to see the remainder of the entry for January 6, nor for any other kind of navigation. The second and third sentences of the text give an indication of Maika's desire to work as a volunteer, which discounts option D and guides the reader towards the second part of the key ("would like to do more"). The key is a simple paraphrase of two pieces of information in the following sentence: "... last year I did a couple of short term voluntary jobs ..., but this year I'd like a long-term position ...". Given the relative prominence of the information in this short text, the direct and relatively simple language, the lack of need to navigate, and the straightforward way in which terms in the question and key to expressions they locate in the text are related, this has all the features of an easy question.

IWANTTOHELP – *QUESTION 2*

Situation: *Educational*
Environment: *Message-based*
Text format: *Multiple*
Text type: *Description*
Aspect: *Access and retrieve – Retrieve information*
Question format: *Multiple choice*

Go to Maika's "About" page.

What kind of work does Maika want to do when she leaves school?

A. Photography.

B. Web design.

C. Banking.

D. Social work.

Scoring

Full Credit: B. Web design.

Comment

This question also starts on the home page of the blog, but the question directs students to navigate to a second page. Therefore, in contrast to all print reading tasks , the information needed to answer the question cannot be obtained from the material initially presented: the student needs to locate an additional text by clicking on the link. In this instance, selecting the correct link from the five available is easy because there is a literal match between the term in the task and the name of the link ("About"), and because the link is prominent.

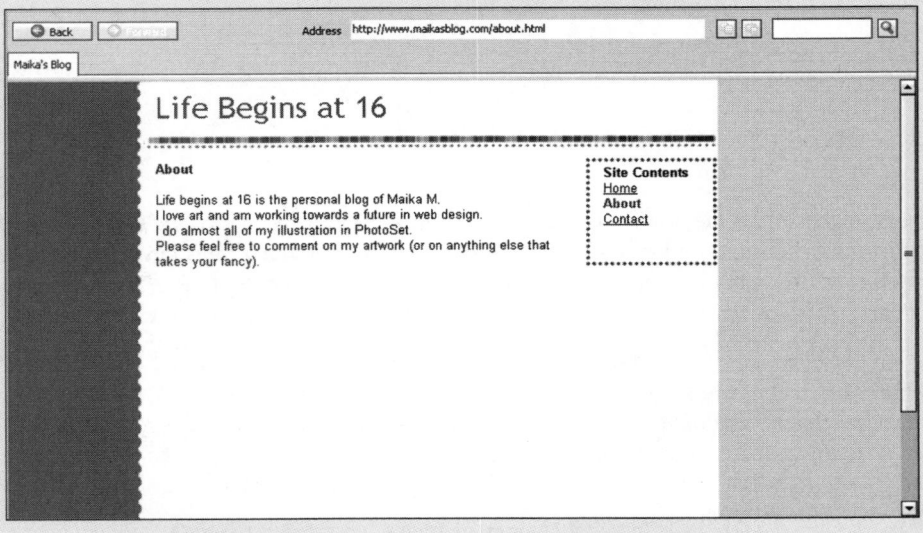

Once students click on this link, a second text appears, hiding the first text – this is one of the strongest distinctions between print and digital texts. This new text is very brief, containing a small amount of background information about the personal life of the writer of the blog. It can be considered as dealing with information of a kind likely to be fairly familiar to most 15-year-olds. There is minor distracting information in option A, with reference to "PhotoSet" in the text, while option D is also plausible, given the information on the first text (the home page) about Maika's expressed desire to do voluntary work and to make a difference to someone's life. Answering this question relies on making a literal match between the key and one of the terms in the text, "web design". The brevity of the text, its simple language, and the literal matches make this question relatively comprehensible; it appears that the need for one navigation step adds an element of difficulty, making it slightly more difficult than the previous question.

IWANTTOHELP – *QUESTION 3*

Situation: *Educational*
Environment: *Authored*
Text format: *Multiple*
Text type: *Argumentation*
Aspect: *Integrate and interpret – Form a broad understanding*
Question format: *Multiple choice*

Open the link that Maika refers to in her January 1 post. What is the main function of this website?

A. To encourage people to buy **iwanttohelp** products.

B. To encourage people to give money to people in need.

C. To explain how you can make money by volunteering.

D. To provide people with information about ways to volunteer.

E. To tell people in need where they can find help.

Scoring

Full Credit: D. To provide people with information about ways to volunteer.

Comment

In this task students are required to recognise the main idea of a text, but in order to do this, they first need to find the text. In order to view the necessary text, they have to click on a link, as indicated in the task. Only one of the hyperlinks on this page occurs within the blog entry for January 1, so the direction in the task is explicit, but four other links available on the page act as distractors. Clicking on the correct link takes the reader not only to a new page, but also to an entirely new website, the home page for an organisation called iwanttohelp. This page opens in a new tab, so that it is possible for students to click on the tab "Maika's Blog" if they wish to return to the first text, although that is not necessary for this task. The content of the new website is more abstract, employing terms that may be relatively unfamiliar to students, such as "non-profit organisation", "opportunity" and ".org", and is addressed to a large anonymous audience rather than operating at the personal level of a blog.

This text is classified as argumentation because it encourages readers to take action, either by contacting other organisations ("Find an Opportunity Now") or by making donations ("We rely on public donations"). Four links to other part of the website are available on this page, if students wish to explore the site in order to obtain a broader picture of the organisation. This however would be time consuming and inefficient. Such opportunities always exist for anyone reading material on the Internet, so one feature of reading in this environment is being able to judge when it is necessary to open new links, thus expanding the number of available texts.

In this case, in order to answer this broad understanding question, students need to read the short description of the organisation provided in the box on the left of the home page, supported by the prominent question and link above the photograph. It is not possible to make any literal matches between the task and the key: some (relatively low) level of inference is needed to recognise that this site provides information explaining how people could volunteer. The distractors all have some degree of plausibility, because of their references to the iwanttohelp site, to money and people in need, to volunteering, and to giving information about help.

This task is somewhat harder than the previous task, although it is still relatively easy. The comparative difficulty is explained by the need to navigate to the text with the required information using the correct link; the amount of potentially distracting information available through irrelevant links on the web pages; the somewhat abstract and unfamiliar information and language used; and the need for a level of inference to answer the question.

IWANTTOHELP – *QUESTION 4*

Situation: *Educational*
Environment: *Mixed*
Text format: *Multiple*
Text type: *Not specified*
Aspect: *Complex*
Question format: *Constructed response*

Read Maika's blog for January 1. Go to the iwanttohelp site and find an opportunity for Maika. Use the e-mail button on the "Opportunity Details" page for this opportunity to tell Maika about it. Explain in the e-mail why the opportunity is suitable for her. Then send your e-mail by clicking on the "Send" button.

Scoring

Full Credit: Selects Graphic Artist or Upway Primary School and writes a message in the e-mail text box with a relevant explanation that matches Maika's criteria.

E-mail message for Graphic Artist

Refers to ongoing position or future or web design or art.
- You're a great artist and it is ongoing – you said you wanted a longer type of work right?
- It's ongoing and it would help you get experience for your future.
- You are obviously interested in graphic design, and want to pursue this when you finish school, and you would also love to volunteer. This would be a great opportunity to do both these things, and will look great on your CV too!.

OR

E-mail message for Upway Primary School

Refers to ongoing position or making a difference.
- This would be a good job – ongoing and you get to help some kids.
- Here's a job where you'll really make a difference.

Partial Credit: Selects Graphic Artist or Upway Primary School and writes a message in the e-mail text box with no explanation or an irrelevant explanation.

E-mail message for Graphic Artist

Gives insufficient or vague answer.
- You'd like it.

Shows inaccurate comprehension of the opportunity or gives an implausible or irrelevant answer.

- You'd be working with kids a lot. *[Irrelevant, not one of Maika's criteria.]*
- It gives you a chance to get out and about.

OR

E-mail message for Upway Primary School

Gives insufficient or vague answer.

- You need an hour a week but it sounds like this could be what you're looking for. *[Lacks reference to job criteria, repeats part of stem.]*
- You'd like it.

Shows <u>inaccurate comprehension of the opportunity</u> or gives an <u>implausible or irrelevant</u> answer.

- It gives you a chance to get out and about.

Comment

This is an example of a complex task, which involves all three aspects of reading. It also has a substantial navigation requirement. This complexity highlights a number of differences between print and digital reading tasks. The overall task requires students to construct a short e-mail message after integrating and reflecting upon information located in several texts. The text type has not been specified because the task requires the reader to integrate information from several types of text: argumentation (the iwanttohelp website), description (Maika's blog) and transaction (the e-mail).

Beginning with an interpretation of information given on Maika's blog, students are then required to locate a number of pages on the iwanttohelp website, to evaluate information on these pages in relation to what they have read on the blog, and to use the evaluation to send Maika a simple message. There is no single pathway for navigation, and two different texts can be used to formulate responses that receive credit. This variability is typical of navigation in the digital environment.

The task requires students to navigate from the starting page, Maika's blog, to the Latest Opportunities page shown below. To see the whole page, scrolling is required.

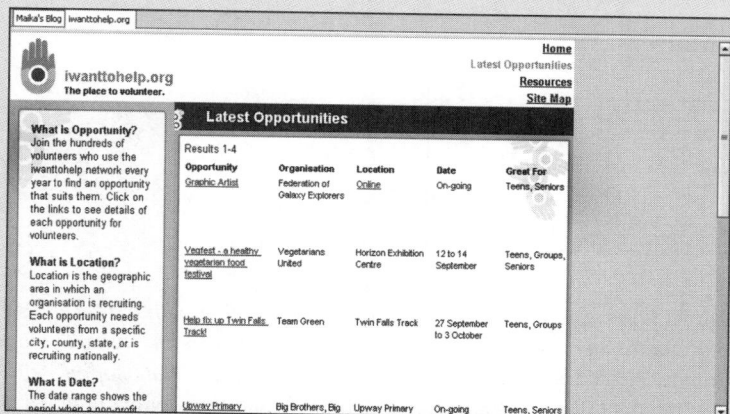

This page offers four opportunities for students to evaluate on Maika's behalf, each with links providing additional information. Students may open as many of the links as they consider necessary. The page for the Upway Primary School opportunity is shown below.

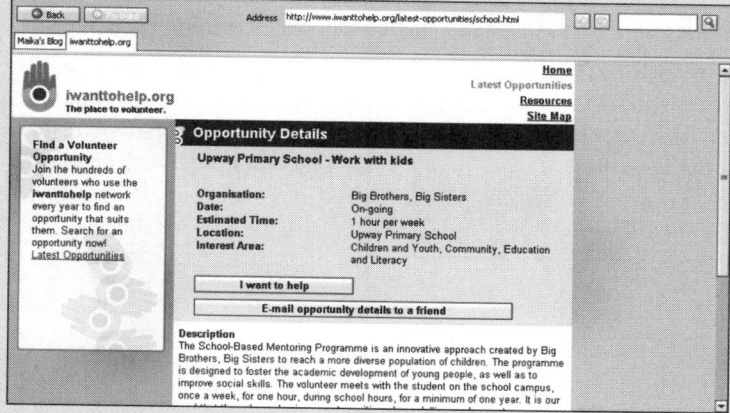

This text is fairly short, but relatively dense, with quite complex vocabulary ("an innovative approach", "a more diverse population", "foster the academic development", "academic support"). Having located the opportunities, students need to compare descriptions of the opportunities with the criteria given on Maika's blog. They may click on the tab to re-read her entry for January 1, where she refers to wanting "a long-term position" in which she can "make a difference". A broad understanding of the Upway Primary School text would support the evaluation that working here would fit Maika's criteria. This interpretation is supported by expressions such as "The volunteer meets with the student ... for a minimum of one year" and "through academic support, positive role modelling, and a one-to-one friendship, students will succeed".

Some students may also use the link "Read my complete profile" or "About", which refers to her interest in "a future in web design" and to her "artwork". The information here supports the selection of the Graphic Artist opportunity.

Students may use the "Back" and "Forward" buttons, the links on each page and the scroll bar to navigate back and forth between descriptions of various opportunities until they have selected the one that they judge to be most suitable. In each case it is necessary to scroll down to see a full description of the opportunity.

Once students have chosen an opportunity, they need to construct an e-mail message to send to Maika. They do this by opening yet another link, "E-mail opportunity details to a friend", in accordance with the task instructions.

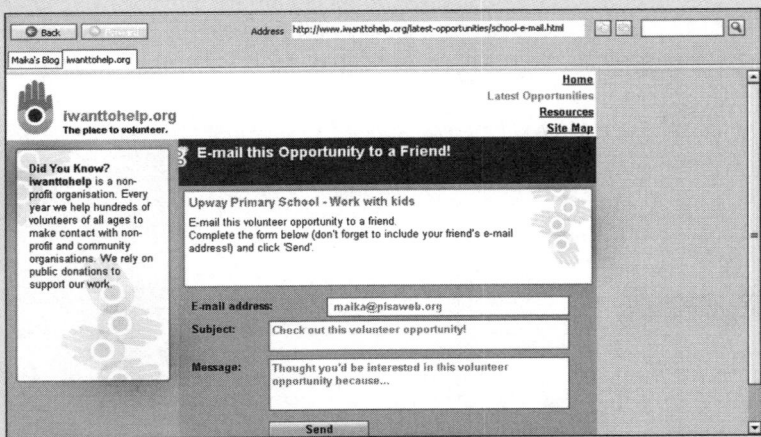

The page where they do this has the e-mail address and subject lines already completed, together with the beginning of a message: "Thought you'd be interested in this volunteer opportunity because...". To receive credit, students must select either the Graphic Artist or the Upway Primary School opportunity. Students who recommend the Graphic Artist opportunity receive full credit if they refer to the fact that this opportunity is an ongoing position; or comment that it is relevant to her future or to her interest in web design or art. Students who recommend Upway Primary School receive full credit if they refer either to the fact that this is an ongoing position or to the idea of making a difference.

Students who select one of these two opportunities but do not write a message that refers to the criteria Maika is seeking nevertheless receive partial credit for having successfully completed much of this complex task: accessing relevant information, comparing information from different texts and making a judgment about which opportunity is suitable.

In summary, in order to obtain full credit for this task, students need to go through a series of processes, involving multiple navigation steps to access a series of texts. Some of the navigation steps are made explicit in the task instructions, but readers need to make multiple evaluations of the available links to decide which ones would allow the most efficient way of completing the task. Students need to make multiple interpretations of texts, from Maika's blog as well as various pages on the iwanttohelp website, and to compare ideas and information across these texts, in support of the reflection and evaluation that the task requires.

Notes

1. For a full description of the PISA 2009 assessment framework, see OECD (2010c).

2. See Stiglitz, J.E., A. Sen and J.P. Fitoussi (2009).

3. See OECD (2010b).

4. See OECD (2010a).

5. The GDP values represent GDP per capita in 2009 at current prices, adjusted for differences in purchasing power between OECD countries.

6. It should be borne in mind, however, that the number of countries involved in this comparison is small and that the trend line is therefore strongly affected by the particular characteristics of the countries included in this comparison.

7. Spending per student is approximated by multiplying public and private expenditure on educational institutions per student in 2009 at each level of education by the theoretical duration of education at the respective level, up to the age of 15. Cumulative expenditure for a given country is approximated as follows: let $n(0)$, $n(1)$ and $n(2)$ be the typical number of years spent by a student from the age of 6 up to the age of 15 years in primary, lower secondary and upper secondary education. Let $E(0)$, $E(1)$ and $E(2)$ be the annual expenditure per student in USD converted using purchasing power parities in primary, lower secondary and upper secondary education, respectively. The cumulative expenditure is then calculated by multiplying current annual expenditure E by the typical duration of study n for each level of education i using the following formula:

$$CE = \sum_{i=0}^{2} n(i) * E(i)$$

8. For this purpose, the respective data were standardised across countries and then averaged over the different aspects.

9. For further detail see Butler, J. and R.J. Adams (2007).

10. These three aspects also formed the basis of reporting on reading subscales in PISA 2000. The names of the aspects have been modified for PISA 2009 in order to make them applicable to the digital medium as well as to the print medium. *Access and retrieve* is an expanded version of *retrieving information*; and *integrate and interpret* of *interpreting texts*. *Reflect and evaluate* is synonymous with PISA 2000's *reflecting upon and evaluating texts*.

11. Halpern, D.F. (1989); Shetzer, H. and M. Warschauer (2000); Warschauer, M. (1999).

12. Kirsch, I. and P.B. Mosenthal (1990).

13. For examples of tasks based on the fourth text format, mixed texts, see AFRICAN TREK in OECD (2010c).

14. In PISA 2000, PISA 2003 and PISA 2006 these three broad aspects were called "Retrieving information", "Interpreting texts" and "Reflection and evaluation", respectively. The terms have been changed for PISA 2009 to better accommodate the aspects in relation to digital texts.

15. A separate digital reading literacy scale has also been constructed: see Volume VI, *Students On Line*.

16. The standard deviation is a measure for the variability of performance. As a rule of thumb, the range between the mean minus one standard deviation and the mean plus one standard deviation contains about 70% of the students. The mean plus/minus two standard deviations contains about 95% of students and the mean plus/minus three standard deviations contains 99% of students.

17. Confidence level 95%.

3

A Profile of Student Performance in Mathematics and Science

What can 15-year-old students do in mathematics and science? This chapter examines student performance in these two subjects as measured by PISA 2009. It provides examples of assessment questions, relating them to each PISA proficiency level, discusses gender differences in student performance, and compares countries' mean performance. As the global demand for highly skilled workers grows, the chapter also highlights today's top performers in reading, mathematics and science.

WHAT STUDENTS CAN DO IN MATHEMATICS

PISA defines *mathematical literacy* as an individual's capacity to formulate, employ and interpret mathematics in a variety of contexts. This includes reasoning mathematically and using mathematical concepts, procedures, facts and tools to describe, explain and predict phenomena. *Mathematical literacy* also helps individuals recognise the role that mathematics plays in the world and make the well-founded judgements and decisions needed by constructive, engaged and reflective citizens. In the PISA assessments, *mathematical literacy* is demonstrated through students' ability to analyse, reason and communicate effectively as they pose, solve and interpret mathematical problems that involve quantitative, spatial, probabilistic or other mathematical concepts.

Mathematics was the focus of the PISA 2003 survey, and the mean score on the PISA 2003 mathematics scale was set at 500 for OECD countries at that point. This mean score is the benchmark against which mathematics performances in PISA 2006 and PISA 2009 are compared. In PISA 2009, mathematics was given a smaller amount of assessment time than in PISA 2003. Ninety minutes of the assessment time were devoted to mathematics in 2009, allowing for only an update on overall performance rather than the kind of in-depth analysis of knowledge and skills shown in the PISA 2003 report (OECD, 2004).

A profile of PISA mathematics questions

A selection of sample questions is included in the following section to illustrate the type of tasks students encounter in the PISA mathematics assessment. Each task presented includes the text, as seen by the students. The sample questions described here were released following the implementation of the PISA 2003 survey. A map of these selected questions is shown below in Figure I.3.1. The selected questions have been ordered according to their difficulty, with the most difficult at the top, and the least difficult at the bottom.

■ Figure I.3.1 ■
Map of selected mathematics questions in PISA 2009, illustrating the proficiency levels

Level	Lower score limit	Questions
6	669	*CARPENTER* – Question 1 (687)
5	607	*TEST SCORES* – Question 16 (620)
4	545	*EXCHANGE RATE* – Question 11 (586)
3	482	*GROWING UP* – Question 7 (525)
2	420	*STAIRCASE* – Question 2 (421)
1	358	*EXCHANGE RATE* – Question 9 (406)

Towards the top of the scale, the tasks typically involve a number of different elements, and require high levels of interpretation. Usually, the situations described are unfamiliar and so require some degree of thoughtful reflection and creativity. Questions generally demand some form of argument, often in the form of an explanation. Typical activities involved include: interpreting complex and unfamiliar data; imposing a mathematical construction on a complex real-world situation; and using mathematical modelling processes. At this level of the scale, questions tend to have several elements that need to be linked by students, and successful negotiation typically requires a strategic approach to several interrelated steps. For example, Question 1 from *CARPENTER* (Figure I.3.2) presents students with four diagrams and the students have to ascertain which of these (there could be more than one) would be suitable for a garden bed, given a certain length of timber for the perimeter. The question requires geometrical understanding and application.

Around the middle of the scale, questions require substantial interpretation, frequently of situations that are relatively unfamiliar or unpractised. Students may be required to restate the situation, often in more formal mathematical representations, in order to understand and analyse it. This often involves a chain of reasoning or a sequence of calculations. Students may also be required to express their reasoning through a simple explanation. Typical activities include: interpreting a set of related graphs; interpreting text, relating this to information in a table or graph, extracting the relevant information and performing some calculations; using scale conversions to calculate distances on a map; and using spatial reasoning and geometric knowledge to perform distance, speed and time calculations. For example, *GROWING UP* presents students with a graph of the average height of young males and young females from the ages of 10 to 20 years. Question 7 from *GROWING UP* (Figure I.3.5) asks students to identify the period of time when females are on average taller than males of the same age. Students must interpret the graph to understand exactly what is being displayed. They also have to relate the graphs for males and females to each other and determine how the specified period of time is shown, then accurately read the relevant values from the horizontal scale.

Near the bottom of the scale, questions set in simple and relatively familiar contexts require only the most limited interpretation of a situation and direct application of well-known mathematical concepts. Typical activities include: reading a value directly from a graph or table; performing a very simple and straightforward arithmetic calculation; ordering a small set of numbers correctly; counting familiar objects; using a simple currency exchange rate; and identifying and listing simple combinatorial outcomes. For example, Question 9 from *EXCHANGE RATE* (Figure I.3.7) presents students with a simple rate for converting Singapore dollars (SGD) into South African rand (ZAR), namely 1 SGD = 4.2 ZAR. The question requires students to apply the rate to convert 3000 SGD into ZAR. The rate is presented in the form of a familiar equation, and the mathematical step required is direct and reasonably obvious.

■ Figure I.3.2 ■
CARPENTER

A carpenter has 32 metres of timber and wants to make a border around a garden bed. He is considering the following designs for the garden bed.

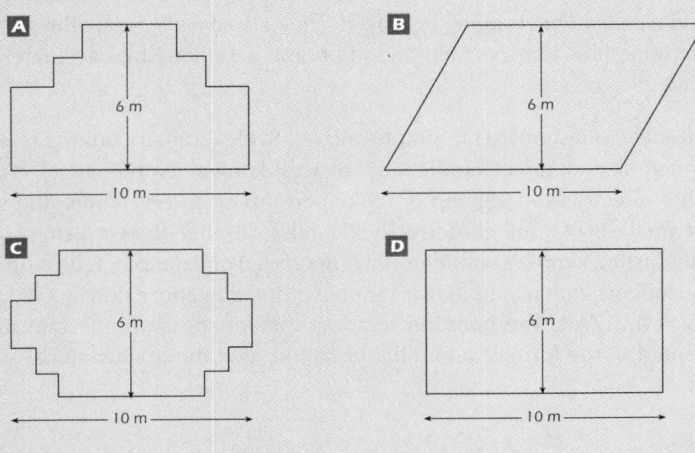

CARPENTER – QUESTION 1

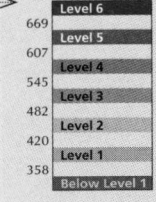

Content area: *Space and shape*
Difficulty: *687* •
**Percentage of correct answers (OECD countries): 20.2%*

Circle either "Yes" or "No" for each design to indicate whether the garden bed can be made with 32 metres of timber.

Garden bed design	Using this design, can the garden bed be made with 32 metres of timber?
Design A	Yes / No
Design B	Yes / No
Design C	Yes / No
Design D	Yes / No

Scoring

Full Credit: Yes, No, Yes, Yes, in that order.

Comment

This complex multiple-choice item is situated in an educational context, since it is the kind of quasi-realistic problem that would typically be seen in a mathematics class, rather than being a genuine problem likely to be met in an occupational setting. A small number of such problems have been included in PISA, though they are not typical. That being said, the competencies needed for this problem are certainly relevant and part of mathematical literacy. This item illustrates Level 6 with a difficulty of 687 score points. The item belongs to the space and shape content area. The students need the competence to recognise that the two-dimensional shapes A, C and D have the same perimeter, and therefore they need to decode the visual information and see similarities and differences. The students need to see whether or not a certain border-shape can be made with 32 metres of timber. In three cases this is rather evident because of the rectangular shapes. But the fourth is a parallelogram, requiring more than 32 metres. This use of geometrical insight, argumentation skills and some technical geometrical knowledge puts this item at Level 6.

■ Figure I.3.3 ■
TEST SCORES

The diagram shows the results on a science test for two groups, labelled as Group A and Group B. The mean score for Group A is 62.0 and the mean for Group B is 64.5. Students pass this test when their score is 50 or above.

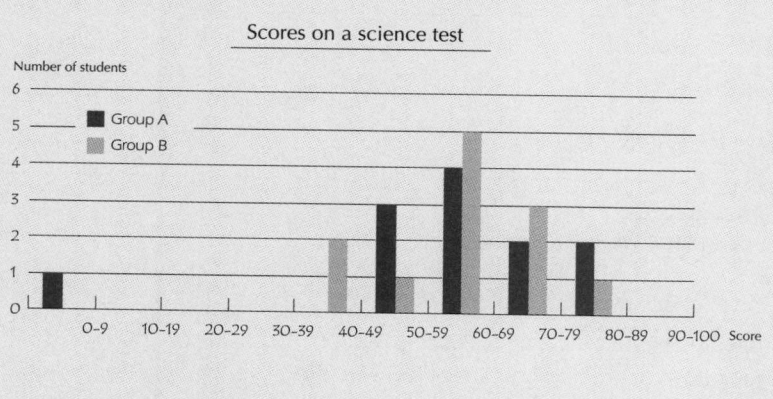

Scores on a science test

TEST SCORE – *QUESTION 16*

Content area: *Uncertainty*
Difficulty: *620* ■
**Percentage of correct answers (OECD countries): 32.7%*

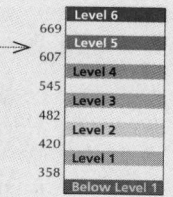

Looking at the diagram, the teacher claims that Group B did better than Group A in this test.

The students in Group A don't agree with their teacher. They try to convince the teacher that Group B may not necessarily have done better.

Give one mathematical argument, using the graph that the students in Group A could use.

Comment

This open-constructed response item is situated in an educational context. It has a difficulty of 620 score points. The educational context of this item is one that all students are familiar with: comparing test scores. In this case a science test has been administered to two groups of students: A and B. The results are given to the students in two different ways: in words with some data embedded and by means of two graphs in one grid. Students must find arguments that support the statement that Group A actually did better than Group B, given the counter-argument of one teacher that Group B did better – on the grounds of the higher mean for Group B. The item falls into the content area of uncertainty. Knowledge of this area of mathematics is essential, as data and graphical representations play a major role in the media and in other aspects of daily experiences. The students have a choice of at least three arguments here: the first one is that more students in Group A pass the test; a second one is the distorting effect of the outlier in the results of Group A; and a final argument is that Group A has more students that scored 80 or above. Students who are successful have applied statistical knowledge in a problem situation that is somewhat structured and where the mathematical representation is partially apparent. They need reasoning and insight to interpret and analyse the given information, and they must communicate their reasons and arguments. Therefore the item clearly illustrates Level 5.

■ Figure I.3.4 ■
EXCHANGE RATE – *Question 11*

Mei-Ling from Singapore was preparing to go to South Africa for 3 months as an exchange student. She needed to change some Singapore dollars (SGD) into South African rand (ZAR).

EXCHANGE RATE – *QUESTION 11*

Content area: Quantity
Difficulty: 586
Percentage of correct answers (OECD countries): 40.5%

669	Level 6
607	Level 5
545	Level 4
482	Level 3
420	Level 2
358	Level 1
	Below Level 1

During these 3 months the exchange rate had changed from 4.2 to 4.0 ZAR per SGD.

Was it in Mei-Ling's favour that the exchange rate now was 4.0 ZAR instead of 4.2 ZAR, when she changed her South African rand back to Singapore dollars? Give an explanation to support your answer.

Scoring

Full Credit: Yes, with adequate explanation.

Comment

This open-constructed response item is situated in a public context and has a difficulty of 586 score points. As far as the mathematics content is concerned students need to apply procedural knowledge involving number operations: multiplication and division, which along with the quantitative context, place the item in the quantity area. The competencies needed to solve the problem are not trivial. Students need to reflect on the concept of exchange rate and its consequences in this particular situation. The mathematisation required is of a rather high level, although all the required information is explicitly presented: not only is the identification of the relevant mathematics somewhat complex, but the reduction of it to a problem within the mathematical world also places significant demands on the student. The competency needed to solve this problem can be described as using flexible reasoning and reflection. Explaining the results requires some communication skills as well. The combination of familiar context, complex situation, non-routine problem and the need for reasoning, insight and communication places the item at Level 4.

■ Figure I.3.5 ■
GROWING UP

In 1998 the average height of both young males and young females in the Netherlands is represented in this graph.

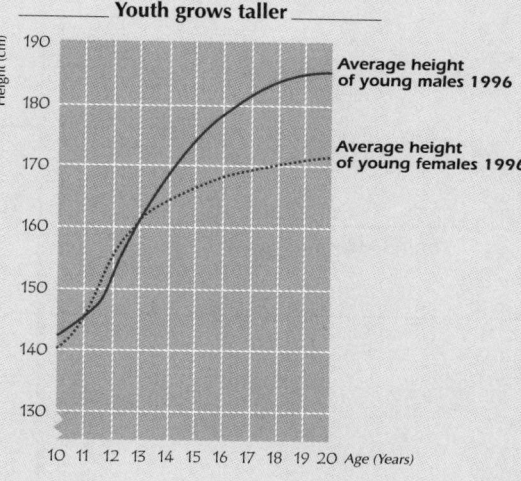

Youth grows taller

Height (cm)

Average height of young males 1996

Average height of young females 1996

Age (Years)

GROWING UP – QUESTION 7

Content area: *Change and relationships*
Difficulty: *525* ●
Percentage of correct answers (OECD countries): *54.8%*

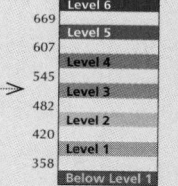

Level 6	669
Level 5	607
Level 4	545
Level 3	482
Level 2	420
Level 1	358
Below Level 1	

According to this graph, on average, during which period in their life are females taller than males of the same age?

Scoring

Full Credit: Responses giving the correct interval (from 11 to 13 years) or stating that girls are taller than boys when they are 11 and 12 years old.

Comment

This item, with its focus on age and height, lies in the change and relationships *content area, and has a difficulty of 420 (Level 1). The students are asked to compare characteristics of two datasets, interpret these datasets and draw conclusions. The competencies needed to successfully solve the problem involve the interpretation and decoding of reasonably familiar and standard representations of well-known mathematical objects. Students need thinking and reasoning competencies to answer the question: "Where do the graphs have common points?" and argumentation and communication competencies to explain the role these points play in finding the desired answer. Students who score partial credit are able to show well-directed reasoning and/or insight, but they fail to come up with a full, comprehensive answer. They properly identify ages 11 and/or 12 and/or 13 as being part of an answer but fail to identify the continuum from 11 to 13 years. The item provides a good illustration of the boundary between Level 1 and Level 2. The full credit response to this item illustrates Level 3, as it has a difficulty of 525 score points. Students who score full credit not only show well-directed reasoning and/or insight, but they also come up with a full, comprehensive answer. Students who solve the problem successfully are adept at using graphical representations, making conclusions and communicating their findings.*

■ Figure I.3.6 ■
STAIRCASE

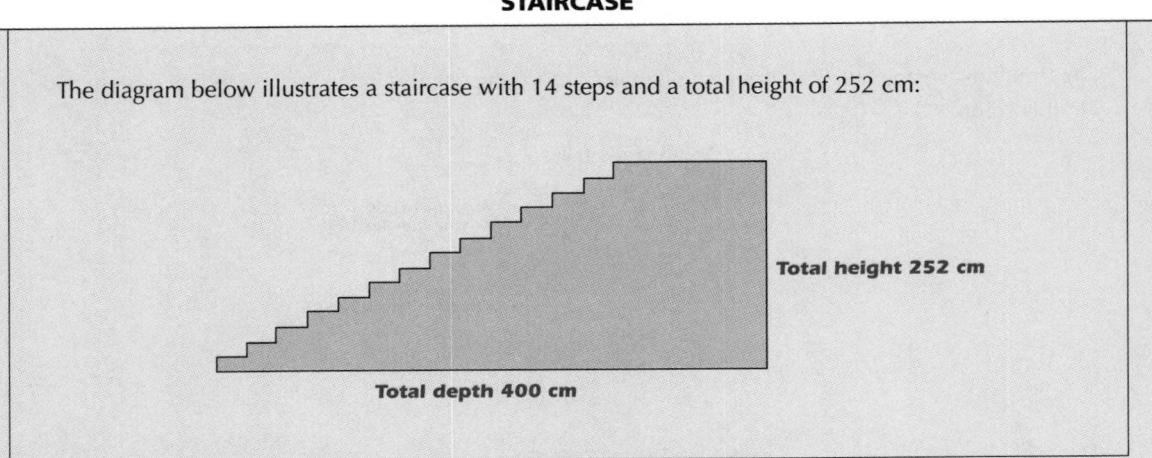

The diagram below illustrates a staircase with 14 steps and a total height of 252 cm:

Total height 252 cm

Total depth 400 cm

STAIRCASE – QUESTION 2

Content area: *Space and shape*
Difficulty: *421* ■
**Percentage of correct answers (OECD countries): 78.3%*

669 — Level 6
Level 5
607
Level 4
545
Level 3
482
Level 2
420
Level 1
358
Below Level 1

What is the height of each of the 14 steps?

Height: ....cm.

Scoring

Full Credit: 18

Comment

This short open-constructed response item is situated in a daily life context for carpenters and is therefore classified as having an occupational context. It has a difficulty of 421 score points. One does not need to be a carpenter to understand the relevant information; it is clear that an informed citizen should be able to interpret and solve a problem like this that uses two different representation modes: language, including numbers, and a graphical representation. But the illustration serves a simple and non-essential function: students know what stairs look like. This item is noteworthy because it has redundant information (the height is 252 cm) that is sometimes considered to be confusing by students; but such redundancy is common in real-world problem solving. The context of the stairs places the item in the space and shape content area, but the actual procedure to carry out is simple division. All the required information, and even more than that, is presented in a recognisable situation, and the students can extract the relevant information from a single source. In essence, the item makes use of a single representational mode, and with the application of a basic algorithm, this item fits, although barely, at Level 2.

■ Figure I.3.7 ■
EXCHANGE RATE – *Question 9*

Mei-Ling from Singapore was preparing to go to South Africa for 3 months as an exchange student. She needed to change some Singapore dollars (SGD) into South African rand (ZAR).

EXCHANGE RATE – *QUESTION 9*

Content area: Quantity
Difficulty: 406 ■
Percentage of correct answers (OECD countries): 79.9%

Mei-Ling found out that the exchange rate between Singapore dollars and South African rand was:
1 SGD = 4.2 ZAR

Mei-Ling changed 3000 Singapore dollars into South African rand at this exchange rate.

How much money in South African rand did Mei-Ling get?

Scoring

Full Credit: 12 600 ZAR (unit not required).

Comment

This short open-constructed response item is situated in a public context. It has a difficulty of 406 score points. Experience in using exchange rates may not be common to all students, but the concept can be seen as belonging to skills and knowledge for citizenship. The mathematics content is restricted to just one of the four basic operations: multiplication. This places the item in the quantity area, and more specifically, in operations with numbers. As far as the competencies are concerned, a very limited form of mathematisation is needed for understanding a simple text and linking the given information to the required calculation. All the required information is explicitly presented. Thus the competency needed to solve this problem can be described as the performance of a routine procedure and/or application of a standard algorithm. The combination of a familiar context, a clearly defined question and a routine procedure places the item at Level 1.

STUDENT PERFORMANCE IN MATHEMATICS

The six proficiency levels used in mathematics in the PISA 2009 assessment are the same as those established for mathematics in 2003 when it was the major area of assessment. The process used to produce proficiency levels in mathematics is similar to that used to produce proficiency levels in reading, as described in Volume I, Chapter 2.

■ Figure I.3.8 ■
Summary descriptions for the six levels of proficiency in mathematics

Level	Lower score limit	What students can typically do
6	669	At Level 6 students can conceptualise, generalise and utilise information based on their investigations and modelling of complex problem situations. They can link different information sources and representations and flexibly translate between them. Students at this level are capable of advanced mathematical thinking and reasoning. These students can apply this insight and understanding along with a mastery of symbolic and formal mathematical operations and relationships to develop new approaches and strategies for attacking novel situations. Students at this level can formulate and precisely communicate their actions and reflections regarding their findings, interpretations, arguments, and the appropriateness of these to the original situations.
5	607	At Level 5 students can develop and work with models for complex situations, identifying constraints and specifying assumptions. They can select, compare, and evaluate appropriate problem-solving strategies for dealing with complex problems related to these models. Students at this level can work strategically using broad, well-developed thinking and reasoning skills, appropriately linked representations, symbolic and formal characterisations, and insight pertaining to these situations. They can reflect on their actions and formulate and communicate their interpretations and reasoning.
4	545	At Level 4 students can work effectively with explicit models for complex concrete situations that may involve constraints or call for making assumptions. They can select and integrate different representations, including symbolic representations, linking them directly to aspects of real-world situations. Students at this level can utilise well-developed skills and reason flexibly, with some insight, in these contexts. They can construct and communicate explanations and arguments based on their interpretations, arguments and actions.
3	482	At Level 3 students can execute clearly described procedures, including those that require sequential decisions. They can select and apply simple problem-solving strategies. Students at this level can interpret and use representations based on different information sources and reason directly from them. They can develop short communications reporting their interpretations, results and reasoning.
2	420	At Level 2 students can interpret and recognise situations in contexts that require no more than direct inference. They can extract relevant information from a single source and make use of a single representational mode. Students at this level can employ basic algorithms, formulae, procedures, or conventions. They are capable of direct reasoning and literal interpretations of the results.
1	358	At Level 1 students can answer questions involving familiar contexts where all relevant information is present and the questions are clearly defined. They are able to identify information and to carry out routine procedures according to direct instructions in explicit situations. They can perform actions that are obvious and follow immediately from the given stimuli.

Proficiency at Level 6 (scores higher than 669 points)

Students proficient at Level 6 on the mathematics scale can conceptualise, generalise, and utilise information based on their investigations and modelling of complex problem situations. They can link different information sources and representations and flexibly translate them. They are capable of advanced mathematical thinking and reasoning. These students can apply insight and understanding, along with a mastery of symbolic and formal mathematical operations and relationships, to develop new approaches and strategies for addressing novel situations. Students at this level can formulate and accurately communicate their actions and reflections regarding their findings, interpretations, arguments, and the appropriateness of these to the given situations.

Across OECD countries, an average of 3.1% of students perform at Level 6 in mathematics. In Korea and Switzerland, around 8% of students are at this level, and more than 5% of students in Japan, Belgium and New Zealand perform at this level. Among the partner countries and economies, in Shanghai-China, more than one-quarter of students perform at Level 6, while in Singapore, Chinese Taipei and Hong Kong-China the proportion is 15.6%, 11.3% and 10.8%, respectively. In contrast, less than 1% of students in Mexico, Chile, Greece and Ireland reach Level 6, and in the partner countries Kyrgyzstan, Indonesia, Colombia, Jordan, Albania, Tunisia and Panama, the percentage is close to zero.

■ Figure I.3.9 ■

How proficient are students in mathematics?

Percentage of students at the different levels of mathematics proficiency

■ Below Level 1   ■ Level 1   □ Level 2   ■ Level 3   ■ Level 4   ■ Level 5   ■ Level 6

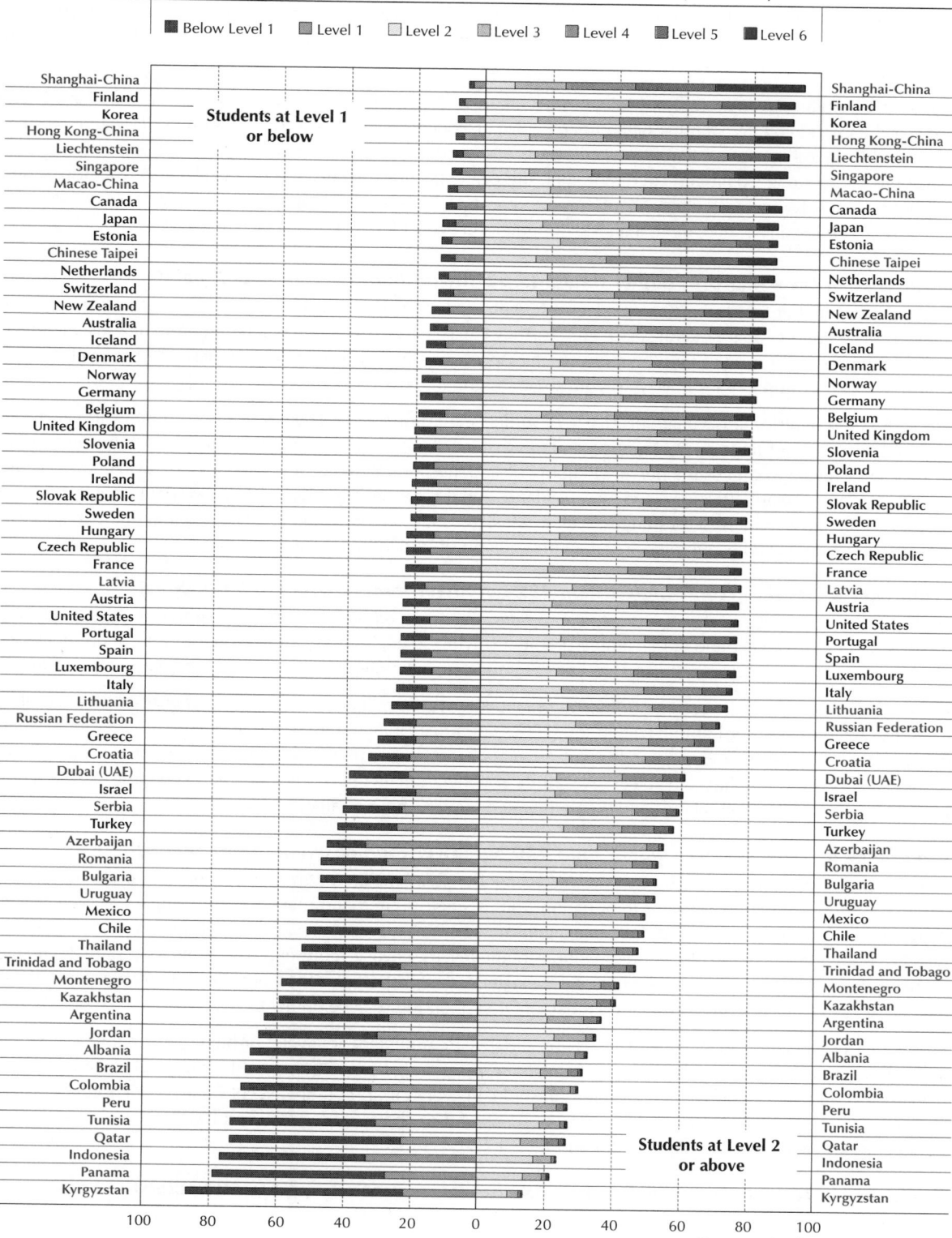

Countries are ranked in descending order of the percentage of students at Levels 2, 3, 4, 5 and 6.
Source: OECD, *PISA 2009 Database*, Table I.3.1.

StatLink 🔗 http://dx.doi.org/10.1787/888932343152

Proficiency at Level 5 (scores higher than 607 but lower than or equal to 669 points)

Students proficient at Level 5 can develop and work with models in complex situations, identifying constraints and specifying assumptions. They can select, compare, and evaluate appropriate problem-solving strategies for dealing with complex problems related to these models. Students at this level can work strategically using broad, well-developed thinking and reasoning skills, appropriately linked representations, symbolic and formal characterisations, and insight pertaining to these situations.

Across OECD countries, an average of 12.7% of students are proficient at Level 5 or higher (Figure I.3.9 and Table I.3.1). Korea is the OECD country with the highest percentage of students – 25.6% – at Level 5 or 6. Switzerland, Finland, Japan and Belgium have more than 20% of students at these levels, while in the partner countries and economies Singapore, Hong Kong-China and Chinese Taipei, the percentage of students at these levels is 35.6%, 30.7% and 28.6%, respectively, and in Shanghai-China, more than half of all students perform at least at Level 5. With the exception of Chile and Mexico, more than 5% of students in every OECD country reach at least Level 5.

Proficiency at Level 4 (scores higher than 545 but lower than or equal to 607 points)

Students proficient at Level 4 can work effectively with explicit models for complex concrete situations that may involve constraints or call for making assumptions. They can select and integrate different representations, including symbolic representations, and link them directly to aspects of real-world situations. Students at this level can use well-developed skills and reason flexibly, with some insight, in these contexts.

Across OECD countries, an average of 31.6% of students are proficient at Level 4 or higher (that is, at Level 4, 5 or 6) (Figure I.3.9 and Table I.3.1). In Korea and the partner countries and economies Shanghai-China, Singapore, Hong Kong-China and Chinese Taipei, the majority of students perform at this level. In Finland, Switzerland, Japan, the Netherlands, Canada, Belgium, and New Zealand, and the partner countries and economies Liechtenstein and Macao-China, more than 40% do so. However, in Mexico, Chile, Turkey, Israel and Greece, and in the majority of the partner countries and economies, less than one-quarter of students attain at least Level 4.

Proficiency at Level 3 (scores higher than 482 but lower than or equal to 545 points)

Students proficient at Level 3 can execute clearly described procedures, including those that require sequential decisions. They can select and apply simple problem-solving strategies and can interpret and use representations based on different information sources. They can communicate their interpretations, results and reasoning succinctly.

Across OECD countries, an average of 56.0% of students are proficient at Level 3 or higher (that is, at Level 3, 4, 5 or 6) (Figure I.3.9 and Table I.3.1). In the OECD countries Finland and Korea, and the partner countries and economies Shanghai-China, Hong Kong-China, Singapore and Liechtenstein, over three-quarters of 15-year-olds are proficient at Level 3 or higher, and at least two-thirds of students attain this level in the OECD countries Switzerland, Japan, Canada and the Netherlands and the partner economies Chinese Taipei and Macao-China.

Proficiency at Level 2 (scores higher than 420 but lower than or equal to 482 points)

Students proficient at Level 2 can interpret and recognise situations in contexts that require no more than direct inference. They can extract relevant information from a single source and make use of a single representational mode. Students at this level can employ basic algorithms, formulae, procedures or conventions. They are capable of direct reasoning and making literal interpretations of the results. Level 2 represents a baseline level of mathematics proficiency on the PISA scale at which students begin to demonstrate the kind of skills that enable them to use mathematics in ways that are considered fundamental for their future development.

Across OECD countries, an average of 78.0% of students are proficient at Level 2 or higher. In Finland and Korea, and in the partner countries and economies Shanghai-China, Hong Kong-China, Liechtenstein and Singapore, more than 90% of students perform at or above this threshold. In every OECD country except Chile, Mexico, Turkey, Israel and Greece, at least three-quarters of students are at Level 2 or above, and in Chile and Mexico more than half of all students are below Level 2 (Figure I.3.9 and Table I.3.1).

Proficiency at Level 1 (scores higher than 358 but lower than or equal to 420 points) or below

Students proficient at Level 1 can answer questions involving familiar contexts where all relevant information is present and the questions are clearly defined. They are able to identify information and to carry out routine procedures according to direct instructions in explicit situations. They can perform obvious actions that follow immediately from the given stimuli.

Students performing below 358 score points – that is, below Level 1 – usually do not succeed at the most basic mathematical tasks that PISA measures. Their pattern of answers is such that they would be expected to solve fewer than half of the tasks in a test made up of questions drawn solely from Level 1. Such students are likely to have serious difficulties using mathematics to benefit from further education and learning opportunities throughout life.

Across OECD countries, an average of 14.0% of students perform at Level 1, and 8.0% perform below Level 1, but there are wide differences between countries. In Finland and Korea, and in the partner countries and economies Shanghai-China, Hong Kong-China, Liechtenstein and Singapore, less than 10% of students perform at or below Level 1. In all other OECD countries, the percentage of students performing at or below Level 1 ranges from 11.5% in Canada to 51.0% in Chile (Figure I.3.9 and Table I.3.1).

Mean country performance in mathematics

The discussion above has focused on comparisons of the distributions of student performance between countries. Another way to summarise student performance and to compare the relative standing of countries in mathematics is by way of countries' mean scores on the PISA assessment. Countries with high average performance will have a considerable economic and social advantage. As explained before, because mathematics was the focus of the PISA 2003 survey, the PISA 2003 mean score for OECD countries was set at 500. This score establishes the benchmark against which mathematics performance in PISA 2006 and PISA 2009 are compared. The average score in mathematics in PISA 2009 (496 score points) appears to be slightly lower than the score of 500 in PISA 2003, but this difference is not statistically significant.

When interpreting mean performance, only those differences between countries that are statistically significant should be taken into account. Figure I.3.10 shows each country's mean score and also for which pairs of countries the differences between the means shown are statistically significant. For each country shown on the left in the middle column, the list of countries in the right hand column shows countries whose mean scores are not statistically significantly different. For all other cases, one country has a higher performance than another if it is above it in the list in the middle column, and lower performance if it is below it. For example: Shanghai-China ranks first, Singapore second and Hong Kong-China third, but the performance of Korea, which appears fourth on the list, cannot be distinguished with confidence from that of Chinese Taipei.

Korea, with a country mean of 546 score points in mathematics, is the highest performing OECD country. Three partner countries and economies, Shanghai-China, Singapore and Hong Kong-China, have a mean score that is around one proficiency level or more above the average of 496 score points in PISA 2009. Other OECD countries with mean performances above the average include Finland (541), Switzerland (534), Japan (529), Canada (527), the Netherlands (526), New Zealand (519), Belgium (515), Australia (514), Germany (513), Estonia (512), Iceland (507), Denmark (503) and Slovenia (501). Three partner countries and economies perform above the average: Chinese Taipei (543), Liechtenstein (536) and Macao-China (525). Nine OECD countries perform around the average: Norway, France, the Slovak Republic, Austria, Poland, Sweden, the Czech Republic, the United Kingdom and Hungary.

Among OECD countries, performance differences are large; 128 score points separate the mean scores of the highest and lowest performing OECD countries, and when the partner countries and economies are considered along with the OECD countries, this range amounts to 269 score points.

Because the figures are derived from samples, it is not possible to determine a precise rank of the performance of a country among the participating countries. It is, however, possible to determine, with confidence, a range of ranks in which the country's performance level lies (Figure I.3.11).

The performance range between the highest- and lowest-performing students is shown in Table I.3.3. Finland, which is one of the highest-performing OECD countries, shows one of the narrowest distributions between the 5th percentile, the point on the PISA mathematics scale which the 5% lowest-performing students attain, and the 95th percentile, the point which 5% of the best-performing students attain, with a difference equivalent to 270 score points. Among the partner countries and economies, some of the lower-performing countries, such as Indonesia, Colombia and Tunisia, have a narrow distribution, ranging from 233 to 252 score points. Among the partner countries and economies, Singapore, Chinese Taipei and Shanghai-China have the largest differences in the performances of their students between the 5th and the 95th percentiles, but are among the 5 countries with the highest performance in mathematics. In the OECD area, Israel, Belgium, Switzerland, France, Luxembourg and Germany also show a wide performance range. In Israel and Belgium, this partly reflects the performance differences between different communities.

■ Figure I.3.10 ■

Comparing countries' performance in mathematics

Statistically significantly **above** the OECD average
Not statistically significantly different from the OECD average
Statistically significantly **below** the OECD average

Mean	Comparison country	Countries whose mean score is NOT statistically significantly different from that of the comparison country
600	Shanghai-China	
562	Singapore	
555	Hong Kong-China	Korea
546	Korea	Hong Kong-China, Chinese Taipei, Finland, Liechtenstein
543	Chinese Taipei	Korea, Finland, Liechtenstein, Switzerland
541	Finland	Korea, Chinese Taipei, Liechtenstein, Switzerland
536	Liechtenstein	Korea, Chinese Taipei, Finland, Switzerland, Japan, Netherlands
534	Switzerland	Chinese Taipei, Finland, Liechtenstein, Japan, Canada, Netherlands
529	Japan	Liechtenstein, Switzerland, Canada, Netherlands, Macao-China
527	Canada	Switzerland, Japan, Netherlands, Macao-China
526	Netherlands	Liechtenstein, Switzerland, Japan, Canada, Macao-China, New Zealand
525	Macao-China	Japan, Canada, Netherlands
519	New Zealand	Netherlands, Belgium, Australia, Germany
515	Belgium	New Zealand, Australia, Germany, Estonia
514	Australia	New Zealand, Belgium, Germany, Estonia
513	Germany	New Zealand, Belgium, Australia, Estonia, Iceland
512	Estonia	Belgium, Australia, Germany, Iceland
507	Iceland	Germany, Estonia, Denmark
503	Denmark	Iceland, Slovenia, Norway, France, Slovak Republic
501	Slovenia	Denmark, Norway, France, Slovak Republic, Austria
498	Norway	Denmark, Slovenia, France, Slovak Republic, Austria, Poland, Sweden, Czech Republic, United Kingdom, Hungary
497	France	Denmark, Slovenia, Norway, Slovak Republic, Austria, Poland, Sweden, Czech Republic, United Kingdom, Hungary
497	Slovak Republic	Denmark, Slovenia, Norway, France, Austria, Poland, Sweden, Czech Republic, United Kingdom, Hungary
496	Austria	Slovenia, Norway, France, Slovak Republic, Poland, Sweden, Czech Republic, United Kingdom, Hungary, United States
495	Poland	Norway, France, Slovak Republic, Austria, Sweden, Czech Republic, United Kingdom, Hungary, Luxembourg, United States, Portugal
494	Sweden	Norway, France, Slovak Republic, Austria, Poland, Czech Republic, United Kingdom, Hungary, Luxembourg, United States, Ireland, Portugal
493	Czech Republic	Norway, France, Slovak Republic, Austria, Poland, Sweden, United Kingdom, Hungary, Luxembourg, United States, Ireland, Portugal
492	United Kingdom	Norway, France, Slovak Republic, Austria, Poland, Sweden, Czech Republic, Hungary, Luxembourg, United States, Ireland, Portugal
490	Hungary	Norway, France, Slovak Republic, Austria, Poland, Sweden, Czech Republic, United Kingdom, Luxembourg, United States, Ireland, Portugal, Spain, Italy, Latvia
489	Luxembourg	Poland, Sweden, Czech Republic, United Kingdom, Hungary, United States, Ireland, Portugal
487	United States	Austria, Poland, Sweden, Czech Republic, United Kingdom, Hungary, Luxembourg, Ireland, Portugal, Spain, Italy, Latvia
487	Ireland	Sweden, Czech Republic, United Kingdom, Hungary, Luxembourg, United States, Portugal, Spain, Italy, Latvia
487	Portugal	Poland, Sweden, Czech Republic, United Kingdom, Hungary, Luxembourg, United States, Ireland, Spain, Italy, Latvia
483	Spain	Hungary, United States, Ireland, Portugal, Italy, Latvia
483	Italy	Hungary, United States, Ireland, Portugal, Spain, Latvia
482	Latvia	Hungary, United States, Ireland, Portugal, Spain, Italy, Lithuania
477	Lithuania	Latvia
468	Russian Federation	Greece, Croatia
466	Greece	Russian Federation, Croatia
460	Croatia	Russian Federation, Greece
453	Dubai (UAE)	Israel, Turkey
447	Israel	Dubai (UAE), Turkey, Serbia
445	Turkey	Dubai (UAE), Israel, Serbia
442	Serbia	Israel, Turkey
431	Azerbaijan	Bulgaria, Romania, Uruguay
428	Bulgaria	Azerbaijan, Romania, Uruguay, Chile, Thailand, Mexico
427	Romania	Azerbaijan, Bulgaria, Uruguay, Chile, Thailand
427	Uruguay	Azerbaijan, Bulgaria, Romania, Chile
421	Chile	Bulgaria, Romania, Uruguay, Thailand, Mexico
419	Thailand	Bulgaria, Romania, Chile, Mexico, Trinidad and Tobago
419	Mexico	Bulgaria, Chile, Thailand
414	Trinidad and Tobago	Thailand
405	Kazakhstan	Montenegro
403	Montenegro	Kazakhstan
388	Argentina	Jordan, Brazil, Colombia, Albania
387	Jordan	Argentina, Brazil, Colombia, Albania
386	Brazil	Argentina, Jordan, Colombia, Albania
381	Colombia	Argentina, Jordan, Brazil, Albania, Indonesia
377	Albania	Argentina, Jordan, Brazil, Colombia, Tunisia, Indonesia
371	Tunisia	Albania, Indonesia, Qatar, Peru, Panama
371	Indonesia	Colombia, Albania, Tunisia, Qatar, Peru, Panama
368	Qatar	Tunisia, Indonesia, Peru, Panama
365	Peru	Tunisia, Indonesia, Qatar, Panama
360	Panama	Tunisia, Indonesia, Qatar, Peru
331	Kyrgyzstan	

Source: OECD, *PISA 2009 Database*.
StatLink ᆗᇜ http://dx.doi.org/10.1787/888932343152

■ Figure I.3.11 ■
Where countries rank in mathematics performance

- ▢ Statistically significantly **above** the OECD average
- ▨ Not statistically significantly different from the OECD average
- ▤ Statistically significantly **below** the OECD average

			Mathematics			
			Range of rank			
			OECD countries		All countries/economies	
	Mean Score	S.E.	Upper rank	Lower rank	Upper rank	Lower rank
Shanghai-China	600	(2.8)			1	1
Singapore	562	(1.4)			2	2
Hong Kong-China	555	(2.7)			3	4
Korea	546	(4.0)	1	2	3	6
Chinese Taipei	543	(3.4)			4	7
Finland	541	(2.2)	1	3	4	7
Liechtenstein	536	(4.1)			5	9
Switzerland	534	(3.3)	2	4	6	9
Japan	529	(3.3)	3	6	8	12
Canada	527	(1.6)	4	6	9	12
Netherlands	526	(4.7)	3	7	8	13
Macao-China	525	(0.9)			10	12
New Zealand	519	(2.3)	6	8	12	14
Belgium	515	(2.3)	7	11	13	17
Australia	514	(2.5)	7	11	13	17
Germany	513	(2.9)	8	12	13	17
Estonia	512	(2.6)	8	11	14	17
Iceland	507	(1.4)	11	13	17	19
Denmark	503	(2.6)	12	16	18	21
Slovenia	501	(1.2)	13	15	19	21
Norway	498	(2.4)	13	20	19	26
France	497	(3.1)	13	22	19	28
Slovak Republic	497	(3.1)	13	22	19	28
Austria	496	(2.7)	14	22	20	28
Poland	495	(2.8)	15	24	21	29
Sweden	494	(2.9)	15	24	21	30
Czech Republic	493	(2.8)	16	25	22	31
United Kingdom	492	(2.4)	17	25	23	31
Hungary	490	(3.5)	18	28	23	34
Luxembourg	489	(1.2)	22	26	28	33
United States	487	(3.6)	21	29	26	36
Ireland	487	(2.5)	22	29	28	35
Portugal	487	(2.9)	22	29	28	36
Spain	483	(2.1)	26	29	32	36
Italy	483	(1.9)	26	29	32	36
Latvia	482	(3.1)			32	37
Lithuania	477	(2.6)			36	38
Russian Federation	468	(3.3)			38	39
Greece	466	(3.9)	30	30	38	40
Croatia	460	(3.1)			39	40
Dubai (UAE)	453	(1.1)			41	42
Israel	447	(3.3)	31	32	42	44
Turkey	445	(4.4)	31	32	41	44
Serbia	442	(2.9)			42	44
Azerbaijan	431	(2.8)			45	47
Bulgaria	428	(5.9)			45	51
Romania	427	(3.4)			45	49
Uruguay	427	(2.6)			45	49
Chile	421	(3.1)	33	34	47	51
Thailand	419	(3.2)			48	52
Mexico	419	(1.8)	33	34	49	51
Trinidad and Tobago	414	(1.3)			51	52
Kazakhstan	405	(3.0)			53	54
Montenegro	403	(2.0)			53	54
Argentina	388	(4.1)			55	58
Jordan	387	(3.7)			55	58
Brazil	386	(2.4)			55	58
Colombia	381	(3.2)			56	59
Albania	377	(4.0)			57	61
Tunisia	371	(3.0)			59	63
Indonesia	371	(3.7)			59	63
Qatar	368	(0.7)			61	63
Peru	365	(4.0)			61	64
Panama	360	(5.2)			62	64
Kyrgyzstan	331	(2.9)			65	65

Source: OECD, *PISA 2009 Database*.
StatLink ᔕᒣᔕ http://dx.doi.org/10.1787/888932343152

■ Figure I.3.12 ■
Gender differences in mathematics performance

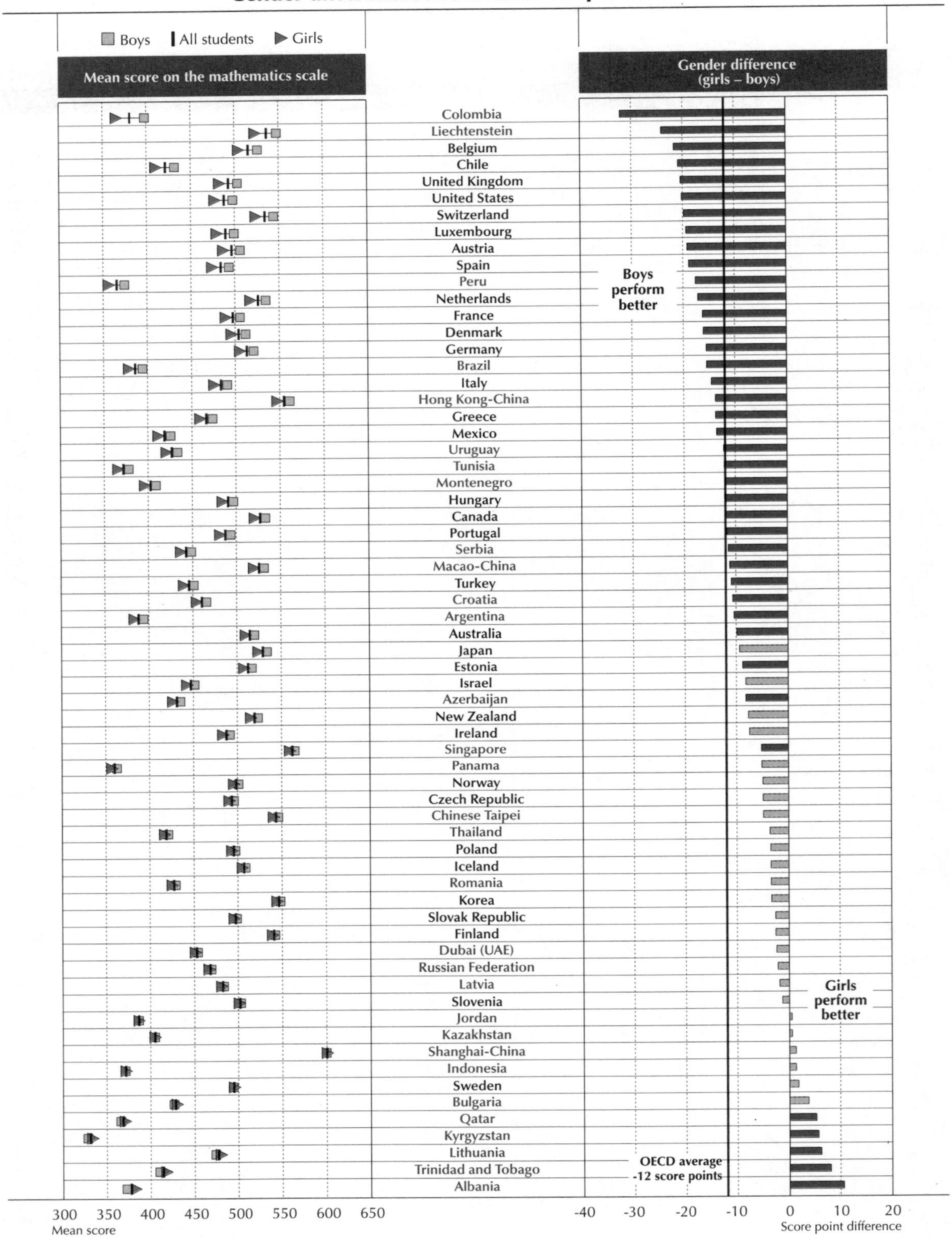

☐ Boys   ┃ All students   ▶ Girls

Mean score on the mathematics scale		Gender difference (girls – boys)

Colombia
Liechtenstein
Belgium
Chile
United Kingdom
United States
Switzerland
Luxembourg
Austria
Spain
Peru
Netherlands
France
Denmark
Germany
Brazil
Italy
Hong Kong-China
Greece
Mexico
Uruguay
Tunisia
Montenegro
Hungary
Canada
Portugal
Serbia
Macao-China
Turkey
Croatia
Argentina
Australia
Japan
Estonia
Israel
Azerbaijan
New Zealand
Ireland
Singapore
Panama
Norway
Czech Republic
Chinese Taipei
Thailand
Poland
Iceland
Romania
Korea
Slovak Republic
Finland
Dubai (UAE)
Russian Federation
Latvia
Slovenia
Jordan
Kazakhstan
Shanghai-China
Indonesia
Sweden
Bulgaria
Qatar
Kyrgyzstan
Lithuania
Trinidad and Tobago
Albania

Boys perform better

Girls perform better

OECD average -12 score points

300 350 400 450 500 550 600 650
Mean score

-40   -30   -20   -10   0   10   20
Score point difference

Note: Statistically significant gender differences are marked in a darker tone (see Annex A3).
Countries are ranked in ascending order of the gender score point difference (girls – boys).
Source: OECD, *PISA 2009 Database*, Table I.3.3.
StatLink ⧉ http://dx.doi.org/10.1787/888932343152

Gender differences in mathematics

On average across OECD countries, boys outperformed girls, with an advantage of 12 score points.

Of all 65 participating countries there are 35 countries with an advantage for boys and 5 with an advantage for girls. For the countries with an advantage for boys on the mathematics scale, gender differences vary widely, even if they tend to be much smaller than corresponding gender differences observed on the reading scale. The largest gender differences are observed in Belgium, Chile, the United Kingdom and the United States, with an advantage of 20 score points or more for boys and a difference of 32 and 24 score points, respectively, in the partner countries and economies Colombia and Liechtenstein. Japan, New Zealand, Ireland, Norway, the Czech Republic, Poland, Iceland, Korea, the Slovak Republic, Finland, Slovenia and Sweden, as well as the partner countries and economies Panama, Chinese Taipei, Thailand, Romania, Dubai (UAE), the Russian Federation, Latvia, Jordan, Kazakhstan, Shanghai-China, Indonesia and Bulgaria do not show measurable differences between the scores for boys and girls. In the partner countries and economies Qatar, Kyrgyzstan, Lithuania, Trinidad and Tobago and Albania, girls outperformed boys in mathematics by between 5 and 11 score points (Table I.3.3).

WHAT STUDENTS CAN DO IN SCIENCE

An understanding of science and technology is central to a young person's preparedness for life in modern society. This understanding also empowers individuals to participate in determining public policy where issues of science and technology affect their lives. PISA defines *scientific literacy* as an individual's scientific knowledge, and use of that knowledge, to identify questions, acquire new knowledge, explain scientific phenomena and draw evidence-based conclusions about science-related issues; their understanding of the characteristic features of science as a form of human knowledge and enquiry; their awareness of how science and technology shape our material, intellectual and cultural environments; and their willingness to engage in science-related issues, and with the ideas of science, as a reflective citizen.

PISA examines both the cognitive and affective aspects of students' competencies in science. The cognitive aspects include students' knowledge and capacity to use this knowledge effectively, as they carry out certain cognitive processes that are characteristic of science and scientific enquiries of personal, social, or global relevance. Science was the focus of the PISA 2006 survey, and the PISA 2006 science mean score for OECD countries was set at 498 then (500 in PISA 2006 with the 30 OECD countries, but 498 after taking into account the 4 new OECD countries). This mean score is the benchmark against which science performance in PISA 2009 is compared and will be the benchmark for such comparisons in the future. However, in PISA 2009, science was given a smaller amount of assessment time than in PISA 2006. Ninety minutes of the assessment time were devoted to science in 2009, allowing for only an update on overall performance rather than the kind of in-depth analysis of knowledge and skills shown in the PISA 2006 report (OECD, 2007). The average score in science in PISA 2009 is set at 501.

A profile of PISA science questions

Figure I.3.13 shows a map of a selection of PISA science questions and scores (in parentheses) to illustrate broadly what is required at different difficulty levels. The sample questions described in the following section were released following the implementation of the PISA 2006 survey. The selected questions have been ordered according to their difficulty, with the most difficult at the top, and the least difficult at the bottom.

■ Figure I.3.13 ■

Map of selected science questions in PISA 2009, illustrating the proficiency levels

Level	Lower score limit	Questions
6	708	*GREENHOUSE* – Question 5 (709)
5	633	*GREENHOUSE* – Question 4.2 (659) (full credit)
4	559	*CLOTHES* – Question 1 (567)
3	484	*MARY MONTAGU* – Question 4 (507)
2	409	*GENETICALLY MODIFIED CROPS* – Question 3 (421)
1	335	*PHYSICAL EXERCISE* – Question 3 (386)

Factors that determine the difficulty of questions assessing science performance include: the level of familiarity of the scientific ideas, processes and terminology involved; the length of the train of logic required to respond to a question, that is, the number of steps needed to arrive at an adequate response and how much one step depends on the previous one; the degree to which abstract scientific ideas or concepts are required in forming a response; and the level of reasoning, insight and generalisation involved in forming judgements, conclusions and explanations.

Typical questions near the top of the scale involve interpreting complex and unfamiliar data, imposing a scientific explanation on a complex real-world situation, and applying scientific processes to unfamiliar problems. At this part of the scale, questions tend to have several scientific or technological elements that need to be linked by students, requiring several interrelated steps. The construction of evidence-based arguments also requires critical thinking and abstract reasoning. Question 5 from GREENHOUSE (Figure I.3.14) is an example of Level 6 and of the competency to explain phenomena scientifically. In this question, students must analyse a conclusion to account for other factors that could influence the greenhouse effect. As a first step to solving this problem, the student must be able to identify the change and measured variables and have sufficient understanding of the methods of investigation to recognise the influence of other factors. In addition, the student needs to recognise the scenario and identify its major components. This involves identifying a number of abstract concepts and their relationships in order to determine what "other" factors might affect the relationship between Earth's temperature and the amount of carbon dioxide emissions in the atmosphere. Thus, in order to respond correctly, a student must understand the need to control factors outside the changed and measured variables and must possess sufficient knowledge of "Earth systems" to identify at least one of the factors that should be controlled. Sufficient knowledge of "Earth systems" is considered the critical scientific skill involved, so this question is categorised as explaining phenomena scientifically.

Around the middle of the scale, questions require substantially more interpretation, frequently in situations that are relatively unfamiliar. Sometimes they demand the use of knowledge from different scientific disciplines, including more formal scientific or technological representation, and the thoughtful synthesis of those disciplines in order to promote understanding and facilitate analysis. Sometimes they involve a chain of reasoning and require students to express their reasoning in a simple explanation. Typical activities include interpreting aspects of a scientific investigation, explaining certain procedures used in an experiment and providing evidence-based reasons for a recommendation. An example of a question in the middle of the scale is Question 4 from MARY MONTAGU (Figure I.3.16). This question requires the student to identify why young children and old people are more at risk of the effects of influenza than others in the population. Directly, or by inference, the reason is attributed to the weaker immune systems among young children and old people. The issue is community control of disease, so the setting is social. A correct explanation involves applying several pieces of knowledge that are well established in the community. The question stem also provides a clue to the groups' different levels of resistance to disease.

On the bottom of the scale, questions require less scientific knowledge and are applied in familiar contexts, with easy scientific explanations that arise directly from given evidence. Question 3 of PHYSICAL EXERCISE (Figure I.3.18) is an example of an easy question, located at Level 1 on the PISA science scale below the baseline of *scientific literacy*. To gain credit, a student must recall knowledge about the operation of muscles and formation of fat in the body correctly, particularly the facts that when muscles are exercised they receive an increased flow of blood and fats are not formed. This knowledge enables students to accept the first statement of this complex multiple-choice question and reject the second one. In this question, no context needs to be analysed: the knowledge required has widespread currency and no relationships need to be investigated or established.

■ Figure I.3.14 ■
GREENHOUSE

Read the texts and answer the questions that follow.

THE GREENHOUSE EFFECT: FACT OR FICTION?

Living things need energy to survive. The energy that sustains life on the Earth comes from the Sun, which radiates energy into space because it is so hot. A tiny proportion of this energy reaches the Earth.

The Earth's atmosphere acts like a protective blanket over the surface of our planet, preventing the variations in temperature that would exist in an airless world.

Most of the radiated energy coming from the Sun passes through the Earth's atmosphere. The Earth absorbs some of this energy, and some is reflected back from the Earth's surface. Part of this reflected energy is absorbed by the atmosphere.

As a result of this the average temperature above the Earth's surface is higher than it would be if there were no atmosphere. The Earth's atmosphere has the same effect as a greenhouse, hence the term greenhouse effect.

The greenhouse effect is said to have become more pronounced during the twentieth century.

It is a fact that the average temperature of the Earth's atmosphere has increased. In newspapers and periodicals the increased carbon dioxide emission is often stated as the main source of the temperature rise in the twentieth century.

A student named André becomes interested in the possible relationship between the average temperature of the Earth's atmosphere and the carbon dioxide emission on the Earth.

In a library he comes across the following two graphs.

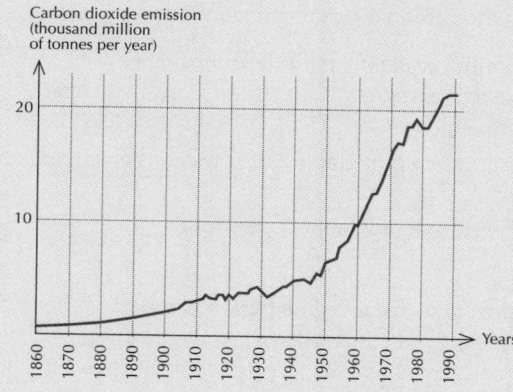
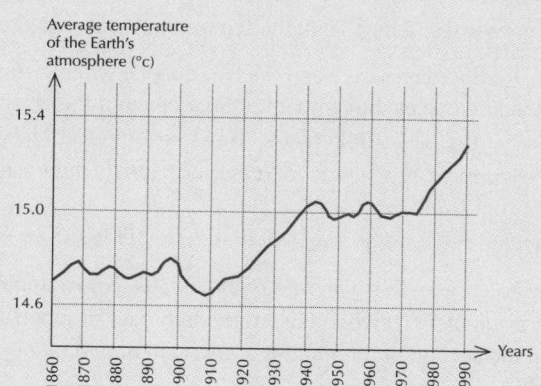

André concludes from these two graphs that it is certain that the increase in the average temperature of the Earth's atmosphere is due to the increase in the carbon dioxide emission.

GREENHOUSE – QUESTION 4

Question type: Open-constructed response
Competency: Using scientific evidence
Knowledge category: "Scientific explanations" (knowledge about science)
Application area: "Environment"
Setting: Global
Difficulty: Full credit 659; Partial credit 568
Percentage of correct answers (OECD countries): 34.5%

Level 6 / 708 / Level 5 / 633 / Level 4 / 559 / Level 3 / 484 / Level 2 / 409 / Level 1 / 335 / Below Level 1

Another student, Jeanne, disagrees with André's conclusion. She compares the two graphs and says that some parts of the graphs do not support his conclusion.

Give an example of a part of the graphs that does not support André's conclusion. Explain your answer.

Scoring

Full Credit:

Refers to one particular part of the graphs in which the curves are not both descending or both climbing and gives the corresponding explanation. For example:

- In 1900–1910 (about) CO_2 was increasing, whilst the temperature was going down.
- In 1980–1983 carbon dioxide went down and the temperature rose.
- The temperature in the 1800s is much the same but the first graph keeps climbing.
- Between 1950 and 1980 the temperature didn't increase but the CO_2 did.
- From 1940 until 1975 the temperature stays about the same but the carbon dioxide emission shows a sharp rise.
- In 1940 the temperature is a lot higher than in 1920 and they have similar carbon dioxide emissions.

Partial Credit:

Mentions a correct period, without any explanation. For example:

- 1930–1933.
- before 1910.

Mentions only one particular year (not a period of time), with an acceptable explanation. For example:

- In 1980 the emissions were down but the temperature still rose.

Gives an example that doesn't support André's conclusion but makes a mistake in mentioning the period. *[Note: There should be evidence of this mistake – e.g. an area clearly illustrating a correct answer is marked on the graph and then a mistake made in transferring this information to the text.]* For example:

- Between 1950 and 1960 the temperature decreased and the carbon dioxide emission increased.

Refers to differences between the two curves, without mentioning a specific period. For example:

- At some places the temperature rises even if the emission decreases.
- Earlier there was little emission but nevertheless high temperature.
- When there is a steady increase in graph 1, there isn't an increase in graph 2, it stays constant. *[Note: It stays constant "overall".]*
- Because at the start the temperature is still high where the carbon dioxide was very low.

Refers to an irregularity in one of the graphs. For example:

- It is about 1910 when the temperature had dropped and went on for a certain period of time.
- In the second graph there is a decrease in temperature of the Earth's atmosphere just before 1910.

Indicates difference in the graphs, but explanation is poor. For example:

- In the 1940s the heat was very high but the carbon dioxide very low. *[Note: The explanation is very poor, but the difference that is indicated is clear.]*

Comment

Another example from GREENHOUSE centres on the competency using scientific evidence and asks students to identify a portion of a graph that does not provide evidence supporting a conclusion. This question requires the student to look for specific differences that vary from positively correlated general trends in these two graphical datasets. Students must locate a portion where curves are not both ascending or descending and provide this finding as part of a justification for a conclusion. As a consequence it involves a greater amount of insight and analytical skill than is required for Question 3. Rather than a generalisation about the relation between the graphs, the student is asked to accompany the nominated period of difference with an explanation of that difference in order to gain full credit.

The ability to effectively compare the detail of two datasets and give a critique of a given conclusion locates the full credit question at Level 5 of the scientific literacy scale. If the student understands what the question requires of them and correctly identifies a difference in the two graphs, but is unable to explain this difference, the student gains partial credit for the question and is identified at Level 4 of the scientific literacy scale.

This environmental issue is global which defines the setting. The skill required by students is to interpret data graphically presented so the question belongs in the "Scientific explanations" category.

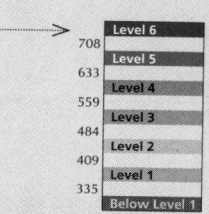

GREENHOUSE – *QUESTION 5*

Question type: *Open-constructed response*
Competency: *Explaining phenomena scientifically*
Knowledge category: *"Earth and space systems" (knowledge of science)*
Application area: *"Environment"*
Setting: *Global*
Difficulty: *709* ▪
Percentage of correct answers (OECD countries): *18.9%*

	Level 6
708	Level 5
633	Level 4
559	Level 3
484	Level 2
409	Level 1
335	Below Level 1

André persists in his conclusion that the average temperature rise of the Earth's atmosphere is caused by the increase in the carbon dioxide emission. But Jeanne thinks that his conclusion is premature. She says: "Before accepting this conclusion you must be sure that other factors that could influence the greenhouse effect are constant".
Name one of the factors that Jeanne means.

....

....

Scoring

Full Credit:

Gives a factor referring to the energy/radiation coming from the Sun. For example:

- The sun heating and maybe the earth changing position.
- Energy reflected back from Earth. *[Assuming that by "Earth" the student means "the ground".]*

Gives a factor referring to a natural component or a potential pollutant. For example:

- Water vapour in the air.
- Clouds.
- The things such as volcanic eruptions.
- Atmospheric pollution (gas, fuel).
- The amount of exhaust gas.
- CFC's.
- The number of cars.
- Ozone (as a component of air). *[Note: for references to depletion, use Code 03.]*

Comment

Question 5 of GREENHOUSE is an example of Level 6 and of the competency explaining phenomena scientifically. *In this question, students must analyse a conclusion to account for other factors that could influence the greenhouse effect. This question combines aspects of the two competencies* identifying scientific issues *and* explaining phenomena scientifically. *The student needs to understand the necessity of controlling factors outside the change and measured variables and to recognise those variables. The student must possess sufficient knowledge of "Earth systems" to be able to identify at least one of the factors that should be controlled. The latter criterion is considered the critical scientific skill involved so this question is categorised as* explaining phenomena scientifically. *The effects of this environmental issue are global, which defines the setting.*

As a first step in gaining credit for this question the student must be able to identify the change and measured variables and have sufficient understanding of methods of investigation to recognise the influence of other factors. However, the student also needs to recognise the scenario in context and identify its major components. This involves a number of abstract concepts and their relationships in determining what "other" factors might affect the relationship between the Earth's temperature and the amount of carbon dioxide emissions into the atmosphere. This locates the question near the boundary between Level 5 and 6 in the explaining phenomena scientifically *category.*

■ Figure I.3.15 ■
CLOTHES

Read the text and answer the questions that follow.

CLOTHES TEXT

A team of British scientists is developing "intelligent" clothes that will give disabled children the power of "speech". Children wearing waistcoats made of a unique electrotextile, linked to a speech synthesiser, will be able to make themselves understood simply by tapping on the touch-sensitive material.

The material is made up of normal cloth and an ingenious mesh of carbon-impregnated fibres that can conduct electricity. When pressure is applied to the fabric, the pattern of signals that passes through the conducting fibres is altered and a computer chip can work out where the cloth has been touched. It then can trigger whatever electronic device is attached to it, which could be no bigger than two boxes of matches.

"The smart bit is in how we weave the fabric and how we send signals through it – and we can weave it into existing fabric designs so you cannot see it's in there," says one of the scientists.

Without being damaged, the material can be washed, wrapped around objects or scrunched up. The scientist also claims it can be mass-produced cheaply.

Source: Steve Farrer, "Interactive fabric promises a material gift of the garb", *The Australian*, 10 August 1998.

CLOTHES – *QUESTION 1*

Question type: Complex multiple choice
Competency: Identifying scientific issues
Knowledge category: "Scientific enquiry" (knowledge about science)
Application area: "Frontiers of science and technology"
Setting: Social
Difficulty: 567 •
Percentage of correct answers (OECD countries): 47.9%

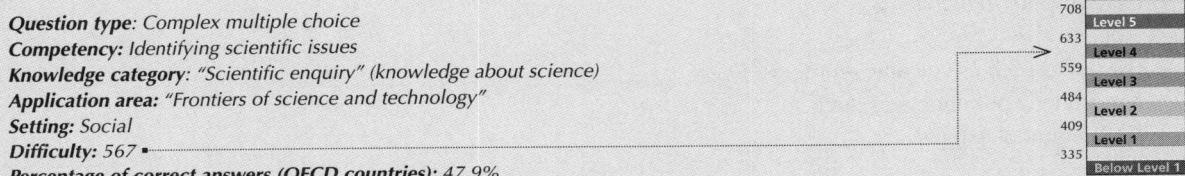

	Level 6
708	
	Level 5
633	
	Level 4
559	
	Level 3
484	
	Level 2
409	
	Level 1
335	
	Below Level 1

Can these claims made in the article be tested through scientific investigation in the laboratory?
Circle either "Yes" or "No" for each.

The material can be	Can the claim be tested through scientific investigation in the laboratory?
washed without being damaged.	Yes / No
wrapped around objects without being damaged.	Yes / No
scrunched up without being damaged.	Yes / No
mass-produced cheaply.	Yes / No

Scoring

Full Credit: Yes, Yes, Yes, No, in that order.

Comment

The question requires the student to identify the change and measured variables associated with testing a claim about the clothing. It also involves an assessment of whether there are techniques to quantify the measured variable and whether other variables can be controlled. This process then needs to be accurately applied for all four claims. The issue of "intelligent" clothes is in the category "Frontiers of science and technology" and is a community issue addressing a need for disabled children so the setting is social. The scientific skills applied are concerned with the nature of investigation which places the question in the "Scientific enquiry" category.

The need to identify change and measured variables, together with an appreciation of what would be involved in carrying out measurement and controlling variables, locates the question at Level 4.

■ Figure I.3.16 ■
MARY MONTAGU

Read the following newspaper article and answer the questions that follow.

THE HISTORY OF VACCINATION

Mary Montagu was a beautiful woman. She survived an attack of smallpox in 1715 but she was left covered with scars. While living in Turkey in 1717, she observed a method called inoculation that was commonly used there. This treatment involved scratching a weak type of smallpox virus into the skin of healthy young people who then became sick, but in most cases only with a mild form of the disease.

Mary Montagu was so convinced of the safety of these inoculations that she allowed her son and daughter to be inoculated.

In 1796, Edward Jenner used inoculations of a related disease, cowpox, to produce antibodies against smallpox. Compared with the inoculation of smallpox, this treatment had less side effects and the treated person could not infect others. The treatment became known as vaccination.

MARY MONTAGU – QUESTION 2

Question type: Multiple choice
Competency: Explaining phenomena scientifically
Knowledge category: "Living systems" (knowledge of science)
Application area: "Health"
Setting: Social
Difficulty: 436 ▪

Percentage of correct answers (OECD countries): 74.9%

708	Level 6
633	Level 5
559	Level 4
484	Level 3
409	Level 2
335	Level 1
	Below Level 1

What kinds of diseases can people be vaccinated against?

A. Inherited diseases like haemophilia.

B. Diseases that are caused by viruses, like polio.

C. Diseases from the malfunctioning of the body, like diabetes.

D. Any sort of disease that has no cure.

Scoring

Full Credit: B. Diseases that are caused by viruses, like polio.

Comment

To gain credit the student must recall a specific piece of knowledge that vaccination helps prevent diseases, the cause for which is external to normal body components. This fact is then applied in the selection of the correct explanation and the rejection of other explanations. The term "virus" appears in the stimulus text and provides a hint for students. This lowered the difficulty of the question. Recalling an appropriate, tangible scientific fact and its application in a relatively simple context locates the question at Level 2.

MARY MONTAGU – QUESTION 3

Question type: Multiple choice
Competency: Explaining phenomena scientifically
Knowledge category: "Living systems" (knowledge of science)
Application area: "Health"
Setting: Social
Difficulty: 431 ▪

Percentage of correct answers (OECD countries): 75.1%

708	Level 6
633	Level 5
559	Level 4
484	Level 3
409	Level 2
335	Level 1
	Below Level 1

If animals or humans become sick with an infectious bacterial disease and then recover, the type of bacteria that caused the disease does not usually make them sick again.

What is the reason for this?

A. The body has killed all bacteria that may cause the same kind of disease.

B. The body has made antibodies that kill this type of bacteria before they multiply.

C. The red blood cells kill all bacteria that may cause the same kind of disease.

D. The red blood cells capture and get rid of this type of bacteria from the body.

Scoring

Full Credit: B. The body has made antibodies that kill this type of bacteria before they multiply.

Comment

To correctly answer this question the student must recall that the body produces antibodies that attack foreign bacteria, the cause of bacterial disease. Its application involves the further knowledge that these antibodies provide resistance to subsequent infections of the same bacteria. The issue is community control of disease, so the setting is social.

In selecting the appropriate explanation the student is recalling a tangible scientific fact and applying it in a relatively simple context. Consequently, the question is located at Level 2.

MARY MONTAGU – QUESTION 4

Question type: *Open-constructed response*
Competency: *Explaining phenomena scientifically*
Knowledge category: *"Living systems" (knowledge of science)*
Application area: *"Health"*
Setting: *Social*
Difficulty: 507 ∎
Percentage of correct answers (OECD countries): *61.7%*

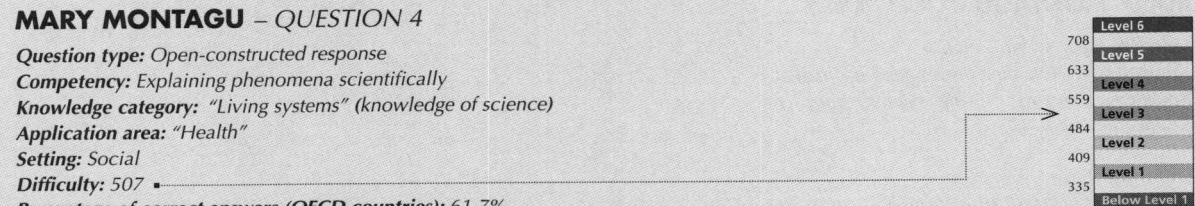

Give one reason why it is recommended that young children and old people, in particular, should be vaccinated against influenza (flu).

....
....
....

Scoring

Full Credit: Responses referring to young and/or old people having weaker immune systems than other people, or similar. For example:

> These people have less resistance to getting sick.
> The young and old can't fight off disease as easily as others.
> They are more likely to catch the flu.
> If they get the flu the effects are worse in these people.
> Because organisms of young children and older people are weaker.
> Old people get sick more easily.

Comment

This question requires the student to identify why young children and old people are more at risk of the effects of influenza than others in the population. Directly, or by inference, the reason is attributed to young children and old people having weaker immune systems. The issue is community control of disease, so the setting is social.

A correct explanation involves applying several pieces of knowledge that are well established in the community. The question stem also provides a cue to the groups having different resistance to disease. This puts the question at Level 3.

■ Figure I.3.17 ■
GENETICALLY MODIFIED CROPS

GM CORN SHOULD BE BANNED

Wildlife conservation groups are demanding that a new genetically modified (GM) corn be banned.

This GM corn is designed to be unaffected by a powerful new herbicide that kills conventional corn plants. This new herbicide will kill most of the weeds that grow in cornfields.

The conservationists say that because these weeds are feed for small animals, especially insects, the use of the new herbicide with the GM corn will be bad for the environment. Supporters of the use of the GM corn say that a scientific study has shown that this will not happen.

Here are details of the scientific study mentioned in the above article:

- Corn was planted in 200 fields across the country.
- Each field was divided into two. The genetically modified (GM) corn treated with the powerful new herbicide was grown in one half, and the conventional corn treated with a conventional herbicide was grown in the other half.
- The number of insects found in the GM corn, treated with the new herbicide, was about the same as the number of insects in the conventional corn, treated with the conventional herbicide.

GENETICALLY MODIFIED CROPS – QUESTION 3

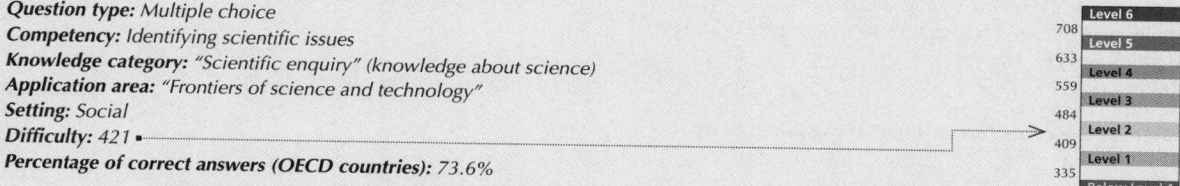

Question type: Multiple choice
Competency: Identifying scientific issues
Knowledge category: "Scientific enquiry" (knowledge about science)
Application area: "Frontiers of science and technology"
Setting: Social
Difficulty: 421
Percentage of correct answers (OECD countries): 73.6%

708	Level 6
633	Level 5
559	Level 4
484	Level 3
409	Level 2
335	Level 1
	Below Level 1

Corn was planted in 200 fields across the country. Why did the scientists use more than one site?

A. So that many farmers could try the new GM corn.

B. To see how much GM corn they could grow.

C. To cover as much land as possible with the GM crop.

D. To include various growth conditions for corn.

Scoring

Full Credit: D. To include various growth conditions for corn.

Comment

Towards the bottom of the scale, typical questions for Level 2 are exemplified by Question 3 from the unit GENETICALLY MODIFIED CROPS, which is for the competency identifying scientific issues. Question 3 asks a simple question about varying conditions in a scientific investigation and students are required to demonstrate knowledge about the design of science experiments.

To answer this question correctly in the absence of cues, the student needs to be aware that the effect of the treatment (different herbicides) on the outcome (insect numbers) could depend on environmental factors. Thus, by repeating the test in 200 locations the chance of a specific set of environmental factors giving rise to a spurious outcome can be accounted for. Since the question focuses on the methodology of the investigation it is categorised as "Scientific enquiry". The application area of genetic modification places this at the "Frontiers of science and technology" and given its restriction to one country it can be said to have a social setting.

In the absence of cues this question has the characteristics of Level 4, i.e. the student shows an awareness of the need to account for varying environmental factors and is able to recognise an appropriate way of dealing with that issue. However, the question actually performed at Level 2. This can be accounted for by the cues given in the three distractors. Students likely are able to easily eliminate these as options thus leaving the correct explanation as the answer. The effect is to reduce the difficulty of the question.

■ Figure I.3.18 ■
PHYSICAL EXERCISE

Regular but moderate physical exercise is good for our health.

PHYSICAL EXERCISE – QUESTION 3

Question type: *Complex multiple choice*
Competency: *Explaining phenomena scientifically*
Knowledge category: *"Living systems" (knowledge of science)*
Application area: *"Health"*
Setting: *Personal*
Difficulty: *386* •
Percentage of correct answers (OECD countries): *82.4%*

Level 6	
	708
Level 5	
	633
Level 4	
	559
Level 3	
	484
Level 2	
	409
Level 1	
	335
Below Level 1	

What happens when muscles are exercised? Circle "Yes" or "No" for each statement.

Does this happen when muscles are exercised?	Yes or No?
Muscles get an increased flow of blood.	Yes / No
Fats are formed in the muscles.	Yes / No

Scoring

Full Credit: Both correct: Yes, No, in that order.

Comment

For this question, to gain credit a student has to correctly recall knowledge about the operation of muscles and about the formation of fat in the body, i.e. students must have knowledge of the science fact that active muscles get an increased flow of blood and that fats are not formed when muscles are exercised. This enables the student to accept the first explanation of this complex multiple-choice question and reject the second explanation.

The two simple factual explanations contained in the question are not related to each other. Each is accepted or rejected as an effect of the exercise of muscles and the knowledge has widespread currency. Consequently, the question is located at Level 1. PHYSICAL EXERCISE, CLOTHES and GRAND CANYON are at Level 1 (below the cut-point), at the very bottom of the scale for the competency explaining phenomena scientifically.

STUDENT PERFORMANCE IN SCIENCE

When science was the major subject in 2006, six proficiency levels were defined on the science scale. These same proficiency levels are used for reporting science results in PISA 2009. The process used to produce proficiency levels in science is similar to that used to produce proficiency levels in reading and mathematics, as described in Volume I, Chapter 2.

Figure I.3.19 presents a description of the scientific knowledge and skills which students possess at the various proficiency levels, with Level 6 being the highest level of proficiency.

■ Figure I.3.19 ■
Summary descriptions for the six levels of proficiency in science

Level	Lower score limit	What students can typically do
6	708	At Level 6, students can consistently identify, explain and apply scientific knowledge and *knowledge about science* in a variety of complex life situations. They can link different information sources and explanations and use evidence from those sources to justify decisions. They clearly and consistently demonstrate advanced scientific thinking and reasoning, and they demonstrate willingness to use their scientific understanding in support of solutions to unfamiliar scientific and technological situations. Students at this level can use scientific knowledge and develop arguments in support of recommendations and decisions that centre on *personal, social* or *global* situations.
5	633	At Level 5, students can identify the scientific components of many complex life situations, apply both scientific concepts and *knowledge about science* to these situations, and can compare, select and evaluate appropriate scientific evidence for responding to life situations. Students at this level can use well-developed inquiry abilities, link knowledge appropriately and bring critical insights to situations. They can construct explanations based on evidence and arguments based on their critical analysis.
4	559	At Level 4, students can work effectively with situations and issues that may involve explicit phenomena requiring them to make inferences about the role of science or technology. They can select and integrate explanations from different disciplines of science or technology and link those explanations directly to aspects of life situations. Students at this level can reflect on their actions and they can communicate decisions using scientific knowledge and evidence.
3	484	At Level 3, students can identify clearly described scientific issues in a range of contexts. They can select facts and knowledge to explain phenomena and apply simple models or inquiry strategies. Students at this level can interpret and use scientific concepts from different disciplines and can apply them directly. They can develop short statements using facts and make decisions based on scientific knowledge.
2	409	At Level 2, students have adequate scientific knowledge to provide possible explanations in familiar contexts or draw conclusions based on simple investigations. They are capable of direct reasoning and making literal interpretations of the results of scientific inquiry or technological problem solving.
1	335	At Level 1, students have such a limited scientific knowledge that it can only be applied to a few, familiar situations. They can present scientific explanations that are obvious and follow explicitly from given evidence.

Proficiency at Level 6 (scores higher than 708 points)

Students proficient at Level 6 on the science scale can consistently identify, explain and apply scientific knowledge and *knowledge about science* in a variety of complex life situations. They can link different information sources and explanations and use evidence from those sources to justify decisions. They clearly and consistently demonstrate advanced scientific thinking and reasoning, and they use their scientific understanding to solve unfamiliar scientific and technological situations. Students at this level can use scientific knowledge and develop arguments in support of recommendations and decisions that centre on personal, social, or global situations.

Across OECD countries, an average of 1.1% of students perform at Level 6. Between 2% and 5% of the students are at this level in New Zealand (3.6%), Finland (3.3%), Australia (3.1%) and Japan (2.6%) as well as in the partner countries and economies Singapore (4.6%), Shanghai-China (3.9%) and Hong Kong-China (2.0%). In Mexico, Chile and Turkey, 0% of students reach this level, and the situation is similar in half of the partner countries, namely Indonesia, Azerbaijan, Kyrgyzstan, Montenegro, Panama, Albania, Colombia, Tunisia, Jordan, Romania, Brazil, Kazakhstan, Peru, Serbia, Thailand and Argentina.

Proficiency at Level 5 (scores higher than 633 but lower than or equal to 708 points)

Students proficient at Level 5 can identify the scientific components of many complex life situations, apply both scientific concepts and *knowledge about science* to these situations, and can compare, select and evaluate appropriate scientific evidence for responding to life situations. Students at this level can use well-developed inquiry abilities, link knowledge appropriately and bring critical insights to situations. They can construct explanations based on evidence and arguments that emerge from their critical analysis.

Across OECD countries, 8.5% of students are proficient at Levels 5 or 6 (Figure I.3.21 and Table I.3.4). More than 15% of students are in either of these levels in Finland (18.7%), New Zealand (17.6%) and Japan (16.9 %), as well as in the partner countries and economies Shanghai-China (24.3%), Singapore (19.9%) and Hong Kong-China (16.2%). In three partner countries, Indonesia, Azerbaijan and Kyrgyzstan, 0% of students reach at least Level 5. Those countries with 0.5% or less of students at these levels are Mexico (0.2%) and the partner countries Albania (0.1%), Colombia (0.1%), Tunisia (0.2%), Peru (0.2%), Panama (0.2%), Montenegro (0.2%), Kazakhstan (0.3%), Romania (0.4%) and Jordan (0.5%).

Proficiency at Level 4 (scores higher than 559 but lower than or equal to 633 points)

Students proficient at Level 4 work effectively with situations and issues that may involve explicit phenomena requiring them to make inferences about the role of science or technology. They can select and integrate explanations from different disciplines of science or technology and link those explanations directly to aspects of life situations. Students at this level can reflect on their actions and can communicate decisions using scientific knowledge and evidence.

Across OECD countries, an average of 29.1% of students is proficient at Level 4 or higher (Level 4, 5 or 6) (Figure I.3.21 and Table I.3.4). Half of all students in Finland perform at Level 4, 5 or 6, and more than 60% do so in the partner economy Shanghai-China. Between 35% and 49% of students perform at one of these levels in Japan (46.4%), New Zealand (42.8%), Korea (42.0%), Australia (39.0%), Canada (38.3%), the Netherlands (38.1%), Germany (37.8%) and Estonia (36.1%), as well as in the partner countries and economies Hong Kong-China (48.9%), Singapore (45.6%) and Liechtenstein (35.1%). In contrast, less than 5% of students reach Level 4, 5 or 6 in Mexico (3.3%) and in the partner countries Indonesia (0.5%), Kyrgyzstan (0.8%), Azerbaijan (0.8%), Peru (2.0%), Albania (2.1%), Tunisia (2.3%), Panama (2.4%), Colombia (2.6%), Montenegro (3.4%), Kazakhstan (3.9%), Brazil (4.4%), Jordan (4.6%) and Romania (4.8%).

Proficiency at Level 3 (scores higher than 484 but lower than or equal to 559 points)

Students proficient at Level 3 can identify clearly described scientific issues in a range of contexts. They can select facts and tap knowledge to explain phenomena and apply simple models or inquiry strategies. Students at this level can interpret and use scientific concepts from different disciplines and can apply them directly. They can develop short statements using facts and make decisions based on scientific knowledge.

Across OECD countries, 57.7% of students are proficient to Level 3 or higher (Level 3, 4, 5 or 6) on the science scale (Figure I.3.21 and Table I.3.4). In the OECD countries Finland (78.7%) and Korea (75.2%), as well as in the partner economies Shanghai-China (86.3%) and Hong Kong-China (78.3%), over three-quarters of 15-year-olds are proficient to Level 3 or higher, and at least two-thirds of students in the OECD countries Japan (73.1%), Estonia (70.4%), Canada (69.6%), New Zealand (68.6%) and Australia (67.5%), and in the partner countries and economies Singapore (71.0%) and Chinese Taipei (67.8%) perform at least at this level.

Proficiency at Level 2 (scores higher than 409 but lower than or equal to 484 points)

Students proficient at Level 2 have adequate scientific knowledge to provide possible explanations in familiar contexts or to draw conclusions based on simple investigations. They are capable of direct reasoning and making literal interpretations of the results of scientific inquiry or technological problem solving. Level 2 has been established as the baseline level, defining the level of achievement on the PISA scale at which students begin to demonstrate the science competencies that will enable them to participate actively in life situations related to science and technology.

Across OECD countries, an average of 82% of students are proficient at Level 2 or higher. In Finland (94.0%), Korea (93.7%), Estonia (91.7%) and Canada (90.4%), as well as in the partner economies Shanghai-China (96.8%), Hong Kong-China (93.4%) and Macao-China (90.4%), more than 90% of students perform at or above this threshold. In every country except the three partner countries Kyrgyzstan (18.0%), Azerbaijan (30.0%) and Peru (31.7%), at least two-thirds of students are at Level 2 or above (Figure I.3.21 and Table I.3.4).

■ Figure I.3.20 ■
How proficient are students in science?
Percentage of students at the different levels of science proficiency

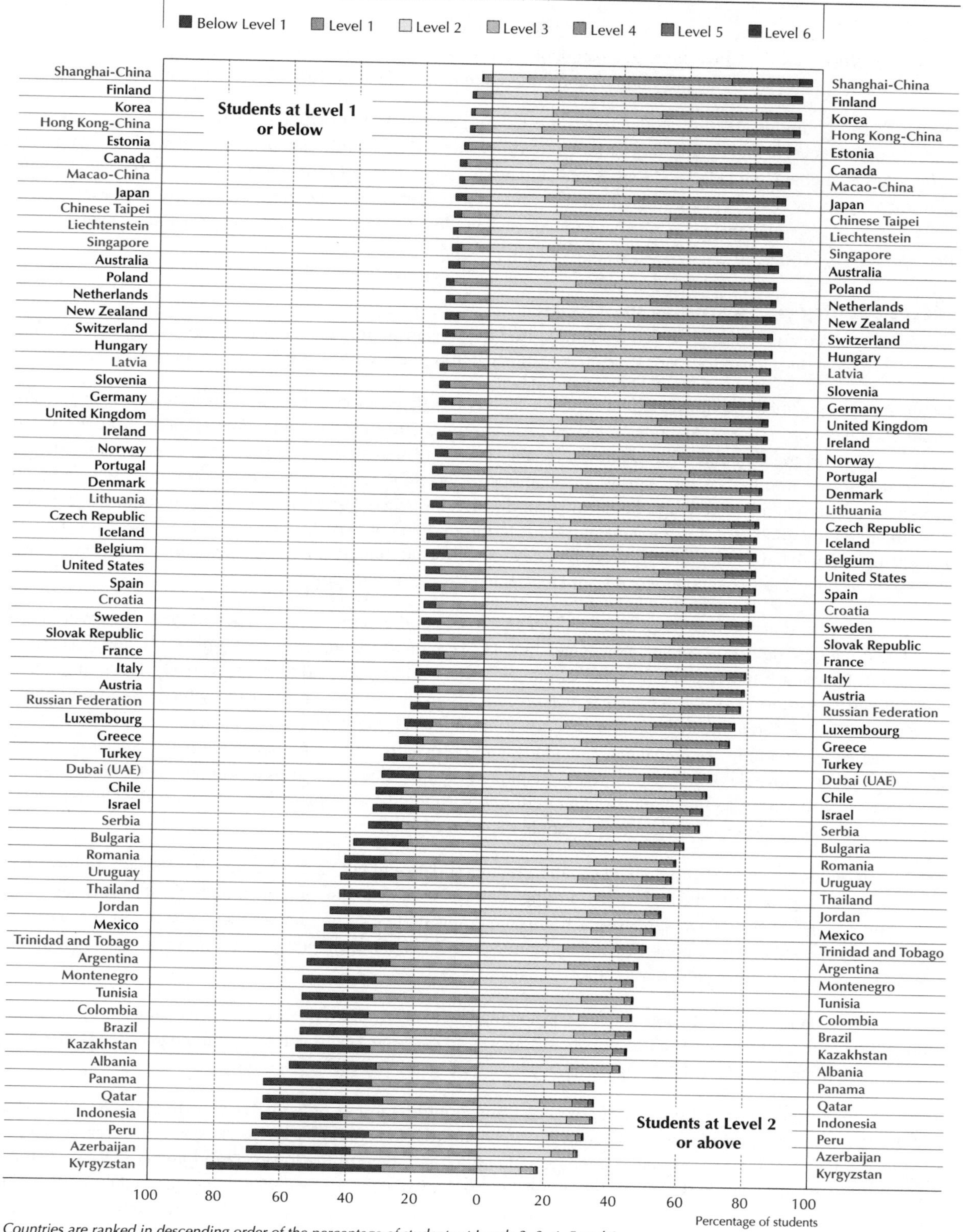
Below Level 1
Level 1
Level 2
Level 3
Level 4
Level 5
Level 6
Students at Level 1 or below
Students at Level 2 or above
Shanghai-China
Finland
Korea
Hong Kong-China
Estonia
Canada
Macao-China
Japan
Chinese Taipei
Liechtenstein
Singapore
Australia
Poland
Netherlands
New Zealand
Switzerland
Hungary
Latvia
Slovenia
Germany
United Kingdom
Ireland
Norway
Portugal
Denmark
Lithuania
Czech Republic
Iceland
Belgium
United States
Spain
Croatia
Sweden
Slovak Republic
France
Italy
Austria
Russian Federation
Luxembourg
Greece
Turkey
Dubai (UAE)
Chile
Israel
Serbia
Bulgaria
Romania
Uruguay
Thailand
Jordan
Mexico
Trinidad and Tobago
Argentina
Montenegro
Tunisia
Colombia
Brazil
Kazakhstan
Albania
Panama
Qatar
Indonesia
Peru
Azerbaijan
Kyrgyzstan
100
80
60
40
20
0
20
40
60
80
100
Percentage of students

Countries are ranked in descending order of the percentage of students at Levels 2, 3, 4, 5 and 6.
Source: OECD, *PISA 2009 Database*, Table I.3.4.
StatLink http://dx.doi.org/10.1787/888932343152

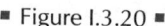

Proficiency at Level 1 (scores higher than 335 but lower than or equal to 409 points) or below

Students proficient at Level 1 have such limited scientific knowledge that it can only be applied to a few, familiar situations. They can present scientific explanations that are obvious and follow explicitly from given evidence.

Students performing below 335 score points – that is, below Level 1 – usually do not succeed at the most basic levels of science that PISA measures. Such students will have serious difficulties in using science to benefit from further education and learning opportunities and participate in life situations related to science and technology.

Across OECD countries, 18% of students perform below Level 2, 13% of students perform at Level 1 and 5% perform below Level 1. In Finland (6.0%), Korea (6.3%), Estonia (8.3%) and Canada (9.6%), as well as the partner economies Shanghai-China (3.2%), Hong Kong-China (6.6%) and Macao-China (9.6%), less than 10% of students perform at or below Level 1. In all other OECD countries, the percentage of students performing at or below Level 1 ranges from 10.7% in Japan to 47.4% in Mexico. More than three-quarters of students perform above Level 2 in the partner country Kyrgyzstan (82.0%) (Figure I.3.21 and Table I.3.4).

Mean country performance in science

Countries' performance in science can be summarised by a mean score. Science was the focus of the PISA 2006 survey. The mean in science for OECD countries was set at 498 in PISA 2006 and at 501 in PISA 2009.

When interpreting mean performance, only those differences between countries that are statistically significant should be taken into account. Figure I.3.21 shows each country's mean score, and allows readers to see for which pairs of countries the differences between the means shown are statistically significant. For each country shown on the left in the middle column, the list of countries in the right hand column shows countries whose mean scores are not sufficiently different to be distinguished with confidence. For all other cases, one country has higher performance than another if it is above it in the list in the middle column, and lower performance if it is below. For example: Shanghai-China, ranks first on the PISA science scale, but Finland, which appears second on the list, cannot be distinguished with confidence from Hong Kong-China, which appears third.

Three countries and economies outperform all other countries and economies in science in PISA 2009 with more than half a standard deviation above the average: the OECD country Finland, with 554 score points, and the partner economies Shanghai-China and Hong Kong-China, with 575 and 549 score points, respectively. Japan and Korea and the partner country Singapore have mean scores of 539, 538 and 542, respectively, which are around half a proficiency level or above the average of 501 score points in PISA 2009. Other countries with mean performances above the average include New Zealand, Canada, Estonia, Australia, the Netherlands, Germany, Switzerland, the United Kingdom, Slovenia, Poland, Ireland and Belgium, and the partner countries and economies Chinese Taipei, Liechtenstein and Macao-China. Countries that performed around the average include Hungary, the United States, the Czech Republic, Norway, Denmark and France.

The gap in performance between the highest and the lowest performing OECD countries is 138 score points. That is, while the average score of the highest performing country, Finland, is 554, or more than half a standard deviation above the average, Mexico's average score of 416 score points is almost one standard deviation below the average. But the gap among the partner countries and economies is even larger, with 245 score points of difference between Shanghai-China (575) and Kyrgyzstan (330).

Because the figures are derived from samples, it is not possible to determine a precise rank of a country's performance among the participating countries. It is possible, however, to determine with confidence a range of ranks in which the country's performance level lies (Figure I.3.22).

The performance difference between students within countries and economies is shown in Table I.3.6. The distribution of student performance in science within countries and economies is even larger than in mathematics, ranging from 227 to 358 score points. Among OECD countries, some of the lower performing countries, such as Mexico, Turkey and Chile, show the narrowest distributions between the 5th and 95th percentile in the OECD, with this difference equivalent to 254, 265 and 268 score points, respectively. However, Korea shows a difference of 266 score points, but is among the 3 highest-performing OECD countries. In the same way, Shanghai-China, with the best score in science for PISA 2009, has a narrow distribution, with only 270 score points.

■ Figure I.3.21 ■

Comparing countries' performance in science

	Statistically significantly **above** the OECD average
	Not statistically significantly different from the OECD average
	Statistically significantly **below** the OECD average

Mean	Comparison country	Countries whose mean score is NOT statistically significantly different from that comparison country
575	Shanghai-China	
554	Finland	Hong Kong-China
549	Hong Kong-China	Finland
542	Singapore	Japan, Korea
539	Japan	Singapore, Korea, New Zealand
538	Korea	Singapore, Japan, New Zealand
532	New Zealand	Japan, Korea, Canada, Estonia, Australia, Netherlands
529	Canada	New Zealand, Estonia, Australia, Netherlands
528	Estonia	New Zealand, Canada, Australia, Netherlands, Germany, Liechtenstein
527	Australia	New Zealand, Canada, Estonia, Netherlands, Chinese Taipei, Germany, Liechtenstein
522	Netherlands	New Zealand, Canada, Estonia, Australia, Chinese Taipei, Germany, Liechtenstein, Switzerland, United Kingdom, Slovenia
520	Chinese Taipei	Australia, Netherlands, Germany, Liechtenstein, Switzerland, United Kingdom
520	Germany	Estonia, Australia, Netherlands, Chinese Taipei, Liechtenstein, Switzerland, United Kingdom
520	Liechtenstein	Estonia, Australia, Netherlands, Chinese Taipei, Germany, Switzerland, United Kingdom
517	Switzerland	Netherlands, Chinese Taipei, Germany, Liechtenstein, United Kingdom, Slovenia, Macao-China
514	United Kingdom	Netherlands, Chinese Taipei, Germany, Liechtenstein, Switzerland, Slovenia, Macao-China, Poland, Ireland
512	Slovenia	Netherlands, Switzerland, United Kingdom, Macao-China, Poland, Ireland, Belgium
511	Macao-China	Switzerland, United Kingdom, Slovenia, Poland, Ireland, Belgium
508	Poland	United Kingdom, Slovenia, Macao-China, Ireland, Belgium, Hungary, United States
508	Ireland	United Kingdom, Slovenia, Macao-China, Poland, Belgium, Hungary, United States, Czech Republic, Norway
507	Belgium	Slovenia, Macao-China, Poland, Ireland, Hungary, United States, Czech Republic, Norway, France
503	Hungary	Poland, Ireland, Belgium, United States, Czech Republic, Norway, Denmark, France, Sweden, Austria
502	United States	Poland, Ireland, Belgium, Hungary, Czech Republic, Norway, Denmark, France, Iceland, Sweden, Austria, Latvia, Portugal
500	Czech Republic	Ireland, Belgium, Hungary, United States, Norway, Denmark, France, Iceland, Sweden, Austria, Latvia, Portugal
500	Norway	Ireland, Belgium, Hungary, United States, Czech Republic, Denmark, France, Iceland, Sweden, Austria, Latvia, Portugal
499	Denmark	Hungary, United States, Czech Republic, Norway, France, Iceland, Sweden, Austria, Latvia, Portugal
498	France	Belgium, Hungary, United States, Czech Republic, Norway, Denmark, Iceland, Sweden, Austria, Latvia, Portugal, Lithuania, Slovak Republic
496	Iceland	United States, Czech Republic, Norway, Denmark, France, Sweden, Austria, Latvia, Portugal, Lithuania, Slovak Republic
495	Sweden	Hungary, United States, Czech Republic, Norway, Denmark, France, Iceland, Austria, Latvia, Portugal, Lithuania, Slovak Republic, Italy
494	Austria	Hungary, United States, Czech Republic, Norway, Denmark, France, Iceland, Sweden, Latvia, Portugal, Lithuania, Slovak Republic, Italy, Spain, Croatia
494	Latvia	United States, Czech Republic, Norway, Denmark, France, Iceland, Sweden, Austria, Portugal, Lithuania, Slovak Republic, Italy, Spain, Croatia
493	Portugal	United States, Czech Republic, Norway, Denmark, France, Iceland, Sweden, Austria, Latvia, Lithuania, Slovak Republic, Italy, Spain, Croatia
491	Lithuania	France, Iceland, Sweden, Austria, Latvia, Portugal, Slovak Republic, Italy, Spain, Croatia
490	Slovak Republic	France, Iceland, Sweden, Austria, Latvia, Portugal, Lithuania, Italy, Spain, Croatia
489	Italy	Sweden, Austria, Latvia, Portugal, Lithuania, Slovak Republic, Spain, Croatia
488	Spain	Austria, Latvia, Portugal, Lithuania, Slovak Republic, Italy, Croatia, Luxembourg
486	Croatia	Austria, Latvia, Portugal, Lithuania, Slovak Republic, Italy, Spain, Luxembourg, Russian Federation
484	Luxembourg	Spain, Croatia, Russian Federation
478	Russian Federation	Croatia, Luxembourg, Greece
470	Greece	Russian Federation, Dubai (UAE)
466	Dubai (UAE)	Greece
455	Israel	Turkey, Chile
454	Turkey	Israel, Chile
447	Chile	Israel, Turkey, Serbia, Bulgaria
443	Serbia	Chile, Bulgaria
439	Bulgaria	Chile, Serbia, Romania, Uruguay
428	Romania	Bulgaria, Uruguay, Thailand
427	Uruguay	Bulgaria, Romania, Thailand
425	Thailand	Romania, Uruguay
416	Mexico	Jordan
415	Jordan	Mexico, Trinidad and Tobago
410	Trinidad and Tobago	Jordan, Brazil
405	Brazil	Trinidad and Tobago, Colombia, Montenegro, Argentina, Tunisia, Kazakhstan
402	Colombia	Brazil, Montenegro, Argentina, Tunisia, Kazakhstan
401	Montenegro	Brazil, Colombia, Argentina, Tunisia, Kazakhstan
401	Argentina	Brazil, Colombia, Montenegro, Tunisia, Kazakhstan, Albania
401	Tunisia	Brazil, Colombia, Montenegro, Argentina, Kazakhstan
400	Kazakhstan	Brazil, Colombia, Montenegro, Argentina, Tunisia, Albania
391	Albania	Argentina, Kazakhstan, Indonesia
383	Indonesia	Albania, Qatar, Panama, Azerbaijan
379	Qatar	Indonesia, Panama
376	Panama	Indonesia, Qatar, Azerbaijan, Peru
373	Azerbaijan	Indonesia, Panama, Peru
369	Peru	Panama, Azerbaijan
330	Kyrgyzstan	

Source: OECD, *PISA 2009 Database*.
StatLink ▀▄▅ http://dx.doi.org/10.1787/888932343152

■ Figure I.3.22 ■

Where countries rank in science performance

	Statistically significantly **above** the OECD average
	Not statistically significantly different from the OECD average
	Statistically significantly **below** the OECD average

			Science			
			Range of rank			
			OECD countries		**All countries/economies**	
	Mean Score	**S.E.**	**Upper rank**	**Lower rank**	**Upper rank**	**Lower rank**
Shanghai-China	575	(2.3)			1	1
Finland	554	(2.3)	1	1	2	3
Hong Kong-China	549	(2.8)			2	3
Singapore	542	(1.4)			4	6
Japan	539	(3.4)	2	3	4	6
Korea	538	(3.4)	2	4	4	7
New Zealand	532	(2.6)	3	6	6	9
Canada	529	(1.6)	4	7	7	10
Estonia	528	(2.7)	4	8	7	11
Australia	527	(2.5)	4	8	7	11
Netherlands	522	(5.4)	4	11	7	16
Chinese Taipei	520	(2.6)			11	15
Germany	520	(2.8)	7	10	10	15
Liechtenstein	520	(3.4)			10	16
Switzerland	517	(2.8)	8	12	12	17
United Kingdom	514	(2.5)	9	13	14	19
Slovenia	512	(1.1)	10	13	16	19
Macao-China	511	(1.0)			16	19
Poland	508	(2.4)	12	16	17	22
Ireland	508	(3.3)	11	17	16	23
Belgium	507	(2.5)	12	17	18	24
Hungary	503	(3.1)	13	21	19	27
United States	502	(3.6)	13	22	19	29
Czech Republic	500	(3.0)	15	23	21	29
Norway	500	(2.6)	16	23	21	29
Denmark	499	(2.5)	16	23	22	30
France	498	(3.6)	16	25	22	33
Iceland	496	(1.4)	20	25	26	32
Sweden	495	(2.7)	19	26	25	34
Austria	494	(3.2)	19	28	25	36
Latvia	494	(3.1)			25	35
Portugal	493	(2.9)	21	28	27	36
Lithuania	491	(2.9)			28	37
Slovak Republic	490	(3.0)	23	29	29	37
Italy	489	(1.8)	25	28	32	37
Spain	488	(2.1)	25	29	32	37
Croatia	486	(2.8)			33	39
Luxembourg	484	(1.2)	28	29	37	39
Russian Federation	478	(3.3)			38	40
Greece	470	(4.0)	30	30	39	41
Dubai (UAE)	466	(1.2)			40	41
Israel	455	(3.1)	31	32	42	43
Turkey	454	(3.6)	31	33	42	44
Chile	447	(2.9)	32	33	43	45
Serbia	443	(2.4)			44	46
Bulgaria	439	(5.9)			44	47
Romania	428	(3.4)			47	49
Uruguay	427	(2.6)			47	49
Thailand	425	(3.0)			47	49
Mexico	416	(1.8)	34	34	50	51
Jordan	415	(3.5)			50	52
Trinidad and Tobago	410	(1.2)			51	53
Brazil	405	(2.4)			52	56
Colombia	402	(3.6)			53	58
Montenegro	401	(2.0)			54	58
Argentina	401	(4.6)			53	59
Tunisia	401	(2.7)			53	58
Kazakhstan	400	(3.1)			53	58
Albania	391	(3.9)			58	60
Indonesia	383	(3.8)			59	62
Qatar	379	(0.9)			60	62
Panama	376	(5.7)			60	64
Azerbaijan	373	(3.1)			62	64
Peru	369	(3.5)			62	64
Kyrgyzstan	330	(2.9)			65	65

Source: OECD, *PISA 29 Database*.
StatLink ⧉ http://dx.doi.org/10.1787/888932343152

■ Figure I.3.23 ■
Gender differences in science performance

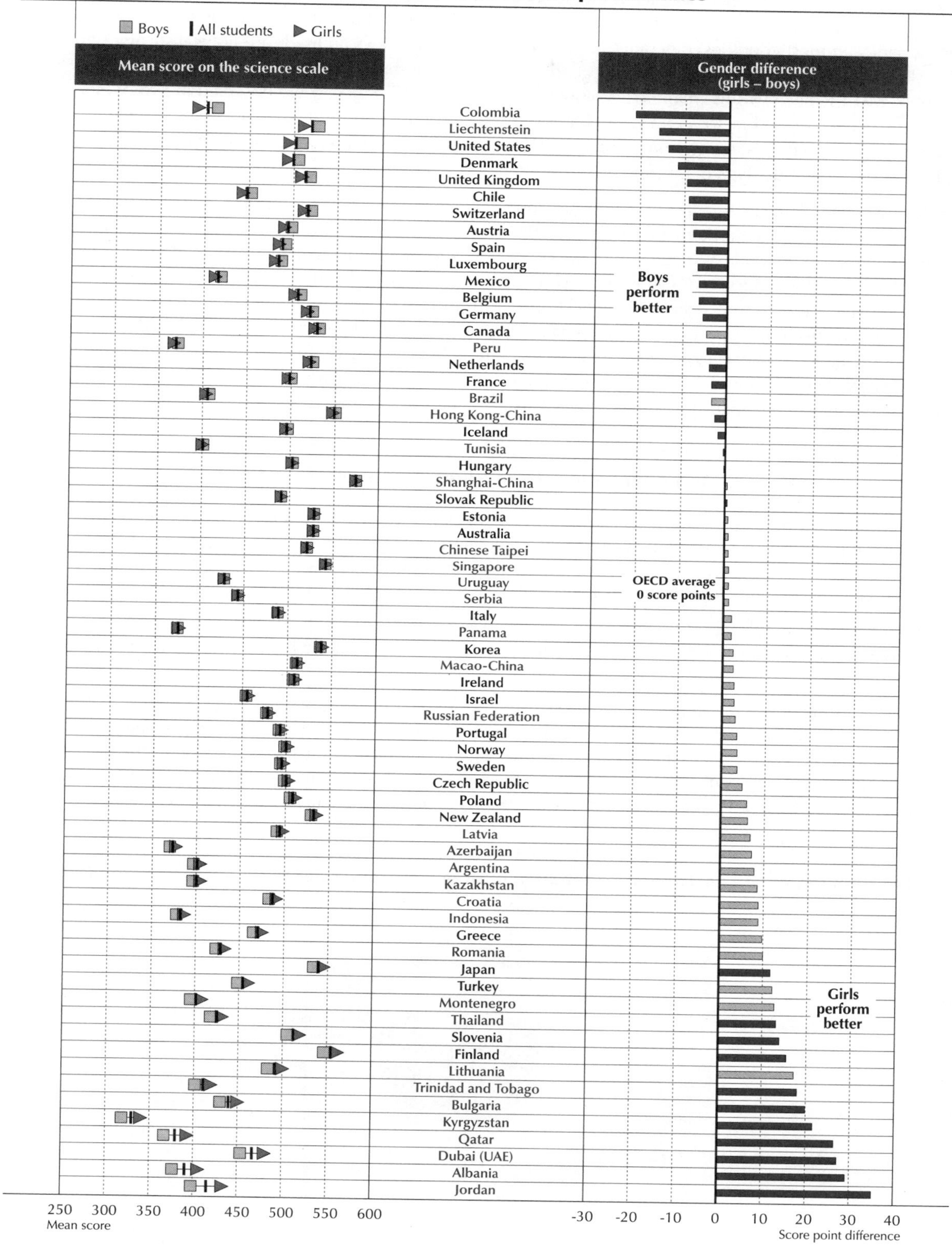

■ Boys ❚ All students ▶ Girls

Mean score on the science scale		Gender difference (girls – boys)

Colombia
Liechtenstein
United States
Denmark
United Kingdom
Chile
Switzerland
Austria
Spain
Luxembourg
Mexico
Belgium
Germany
Canada
Peru
Netherlands
France
Brazil
Hong Kong-China
Iceland
Tunisia
Hungary
Shanghai-China
Slovak Republic
Estonia
Australia
Chinese Taipei
Singapore
Uruguay
Serbia
Italy
Panama
Korea
Macao-China
Ireland
Israel
Russian Federation
Portugal
Norway
Sweden
Czech Republic
Poland
New Zealand
Latvia
Azerbaijan
Argentina
Kazakhstan
Croatia
Indonesia
Greece
Romania
Japan
Turkey
Montenegro
Thailand
Slovenia
Finland
Lithuania
Trinidad and Tobago
Bulgaria
Kyrgyzstan
Qatar
Dubai (UAE)
Albania
Jordan

Boys perform better

OECD average 0 score points

Girls perform better

250 300 350 400 450 500 550 600
Mean score

-30 -20 -10 0 10 20 30 40
Score point difference

Note: Statistically significant gender differences are marked in a darker tone (see Annex A3).
Countries are ranked in ascending order of the gender score point difference (girls – boys).
Source: OECD, *PISA 2009 Database,* Table I.3.6.
StatLink ⟨ms⟩ http://dx.doi.org/10.1787/888932343152

Gender differences in science

Across OECD countries, gender differences in science performance tend to be small, both in absolute terms and when compared with the large gender gap in reading performance and the more moderate gender differences in mathematics. In most countries, differences in the average score for boys and girls are not statistically significant. This shows that science is a subject where gender equality is closer to reality than in mathematics or reading. In 2006, when science was the main focus of assessment, gender differences were observed in two of the science processes being assessed: across OECD countries, girls scored higher in the area of *identifying scientific issues*, while boys outscored girls in *explaining phenomena scientifically*. The shorter assessment time in science in 2009, did not allow for a re-analysis of this finding.

The largest gender differences in favour of boys are observed in the United States and Denmark, with 14 and 12 score points, respectively, and in the partner countries Colombia and Liechtenstein, with 21 and 16 score points, respectively. In the United Kingdom, Chile, Switzerland, Spain, Luxembourg, Mexico and Canada, boys outperform girls in science with a difference that ranges from five to nine score points. On the other hand, girls outperform boys in science in Finland, Slovenia, Turkey and Greece, with a difference of 10 to 15 score points, and in Poland with a difference of 6 score points. In the partner countries Jordan, Albania, Dubai (UAE), Qatar, Kyrgyzstan, Bulgaria, Trinidad and Tobago, Lithuania, Thailand, Montenegro and Romania, which perform below the average, the advantage of girls ranges from 10 to 35 score points. This is also the case for the partner countries Indonesia, Kazakhstan, Argentina, Azerbaijan and Latvia, with a smaller difference that varies between six and nine score points (Table I.3.6).

Box I.3.1 **Top performers in reading, mathematics or science**

The rapidly growing demand for highly skilled workers has led to a global competition for talent. High-level skills are critical for creating new knowledge, technologies and innovation and, as such, are key to economic growth and social development. Looking at the top performing students in reading, mathematics and science allows countries to estimate their future talent pool. [See (OECD, 2009)]

"Top performers" in reading, mathematics or science refer to students who attain Level 5 or 6 in these subjects, *i.e.* perform higher than 626 score points in reading, 607 score points in mathematics, or 633 score points in science.

Figure I.3.a shows the proportion of top performers in the three subject areas across OECD countries. Parts in the diagram in blue represent the percentage of 15-year-old students who are top performers in just one of the three assessment subject areas, that is, in either reading, mathematics or science. The parts in grey show the percentage of students who are top performers in two of the subject areas, while the white part in the centre of the diagram shows the percentage of 15-year-old students who are top performers in all three assessment subject areas.

■ Figure I.3.a ■

Overlapping of top performers in reading, mathematics and science on average in the OECD

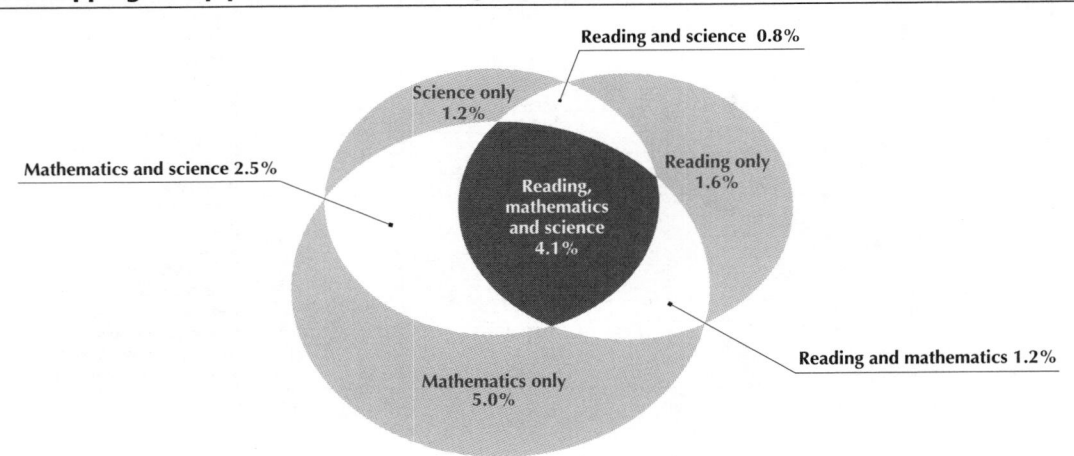

Note: Non-top performers in any of the three domains: 83.7%.
Source: OECD, *PISA 2009 Database,* Table I.3.7.
StatLink http://dx.doi.org/10.1787/888932343152

■ Figure I.3.b ■
Top performers in reading, mathematics and science
Percentage of students reaching the two highest levels of proficiency

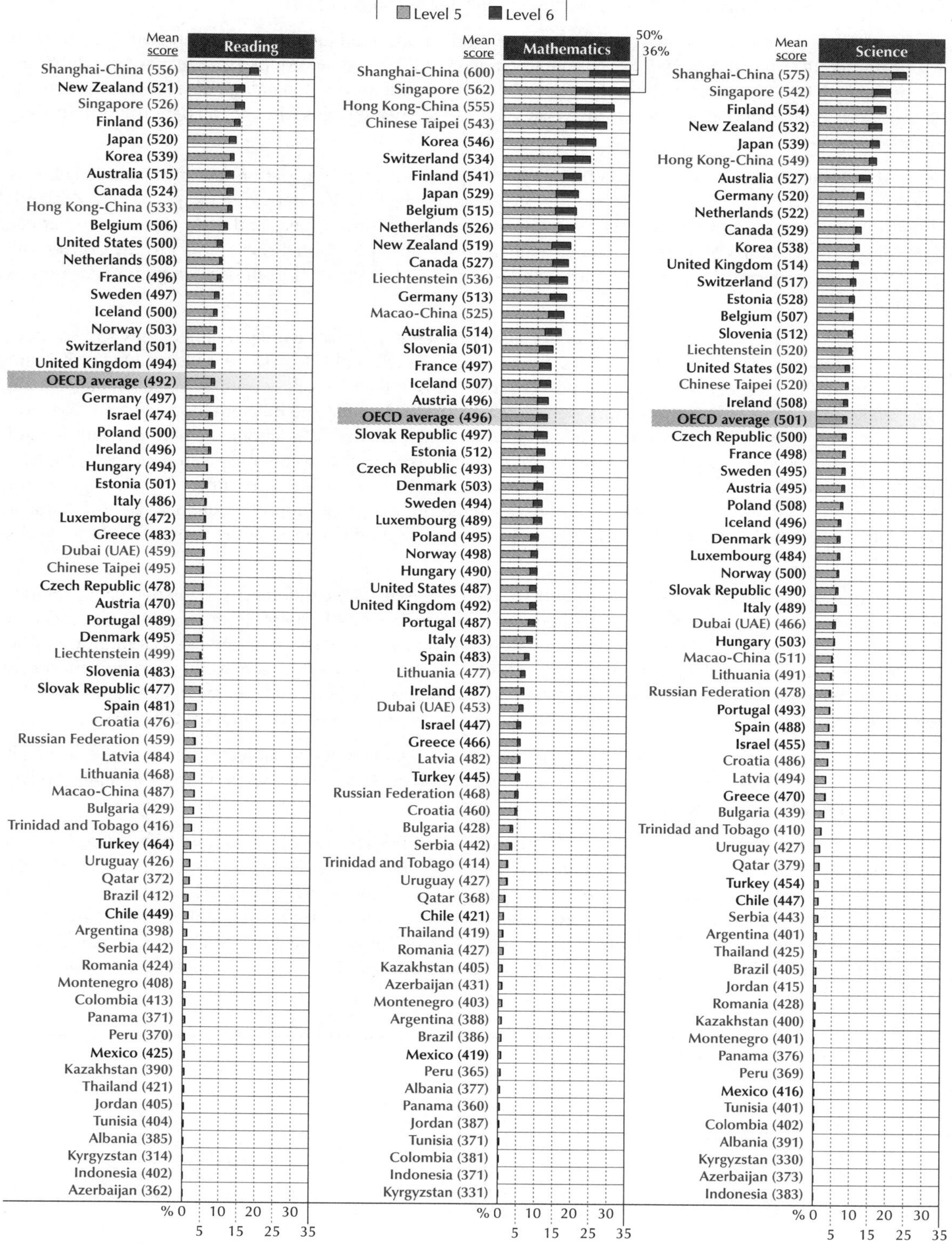

Level 5 ■ Level 6

Reading

Country (Mean score)
Shanghai-China (556)
New Zealand (521)
Singapore (526)
Finland (536)
Japan (520)
Korea (539)
Australia (515)
Canada (524)
Hong Kong-China (533)
Belgium (506)
United States (500)
Netherlands (508)
France (496)
Sweden (497)
Iceland (500)
Norway (503)
Switzerland (501)
United Kingdom (494)
OECD average (492)
Germany (497)
Israel (474)
Poland (500)
Ireland (496)
Hungary (494)
Estonia (501)
Italy (486)
Luxembourg (472)
Greece (483)
Dubai (UAE) (459)
Chinese Taipei (495)
Czech Republic (478)
Austria (470)
Portugal (489)
Denmark (495)
Liechtenstein (499)
Slovenia (483)
Slovak Republic (477)
Spain (481)
Croatia (476)
Russian Federation (459)
Latvia (484)
Lithuania (468)
Macao-China (487)
Bulgaria (429)
Trinidad and Tobago (416)
Turkey (464)
Uruguay (426)
Qatar (372)
Brazil (412)
Chile (449)
Argentina (398)
Serbia (442)
Romania (424)
Montenegro (408)
Colombia (413)
Panama (371)
Peru (370)
Mexico (425)
Kazakhstan (390)
Thailand (421)
Jordan (405)
Tunisia (404)
Albania (385)
Kyrgyzstan (314)
Indonesia (402)
Azerbaijan (362)

Mathematics — 50% / 36%

Country (Mean score)
Shanghai-China (600)
Singapore (562)
Hong Kong-China (555)
Chinese Taipei (543)
Korea (546)
Switzerland (534)
Finland (541)
Japan (529)
Belgium (515)
Netherlands (526)
New Zealand (519)
Canada (527)
Liechtenstein (536)
Germany (513)
Macao-China (525)
Australia (514)
Slovenia (501)
France (497)
Iceland (507)
Austria (496)
OECD average (496)
Slovak Republic (497)
Estonia (512)
Czech Republic (493)
Denmark (503)
Sweden (494)
Luxembourg (489)
Poland (495)
Norway (498)
Hungary (490)
United States (487)
United Kingdom (492)
Portugal (487)
Italy (483)
Spain (483)
Lithuania (477)
Ireland (487)
Dubai (UAE) (453)
Israel (447)
Greece (466)
Latvia (482)
Turkey (445)
Russian Federation (468)
Croatia (460)
Bulgaria (428)
Serbia (442)
Trinidad and Tobago (414)
Uruguay (427)
Qatar (368)
Chile (421)
Thailand (419)
Romania (427)
Kazakhstan (405)
Azerbaijan (431)
Montenegro (403)
Argentina (388)
Brazil (386)
Mexico (419)
Peru (365)
Albania (377)
Panama (360)
Jordan (387)
Tunisia (371)
Colombia (381)
Indonesia (371)
Kyrgyzstan (331)

Science

Country (Mean score)
Shanghai-China (575)
Singapore (542)
Finland (554)
New Zealand (532)
Japan (539)
Hong Kong-China (549)
Australia (527)
Germany (520)
Netherlands (522)
Canada (529)
Korea (538)
United Kingdom (514)
Switzerland (517)
Estonia (528)
Belgium (507)
Slovenia (512)
Liechtenstein (520)
United States (502)
Chinese Taipei (520)
Ireland (508)
OECD average (501)
Czech Republic (500)
France (498)
Sweden (495)
Austria (495)
Poland (508)
Iceland (496)
Denmark (499)
Luxembourg (484)
Norway (500)
Slovak Republic (490)
Italy (489)
Dubai (UAE) (466)
Hungary (503)
Macao-China (511)
Lithuania (491)
Russian Federation (478)
Portugal (493)
Spain (488)
Israel (455)
Croatia (486)
Latvia (494)
Greece (470)
Bulgaria (439)
Trinidad and Tobago (410)
Uruguay (427)
Qatar (379)
Turkey (454)
Chile (447)
Serbia (443)
Argentina (401)
Thailand (425)
Brazil (405)
Jordan (415)
Romania (428)
Kazakhstan (400)
Montenegro (401)
Panama (376)
Peru (369)
Mexico (416)
Tunisia (401)
Colombia (402)
Albania (391)
Kyrgyzstan (330)
Azerbaijan (373)
Indonesia (383)

% 0   10   20   30   (5   15   25   35)

Countries are ranked in descending order of the percentage of top performers (Level 5 or 6).
Source: OECD, *PISA 2009 Database,* Tables I.2.1, I.3.1 and I.3.4.
StatLink ⟐⟐⟐ http://dx.doi.org/10.1787/888932343152

....

On average across OECD countries, 16.3% of students are top performers in at least one of the subject areas of science, mathematics or reading. However, only 4.1% of 15-year-old students are top performers in all three assessment subject areas. This shows that excellence is not simply strong performance in all areas, but rather that it can be found among a wide range of students in various subject areas.

About 1.2% of students are top performers in both reading and mathematics but not in science, less than 1% of students (0.8%) are top performers in both reading and science but not in mathematics, and 2.4% are top performers in both mathematics and science but not in reading. The percentage of students who are top performers in both mathematics and science is greater than the percentages who are top performers in reading and mathematics or in reading and science.

There is substantial variation among countries in the percentages of top performers in the three subjects (see Table I.3.7). Top performers comprise between 8% and 10% of 15-year-old students in New Zealand, Finland, Japan and Australia, and in the partner economy Hong Kong-China, and even more in the partner countries and economies Shanghai-China and Singapore, with 14.6% and 12.3%, respectively. Conversely, in 3 OECD countries and 21 partner countries and economies, less than 1% of students are top performers in all 3 domains.

Figure I.3.b shows the proportions of top performers for each country in reading, mathematics and science. Although on average across OECD countries, slightly less than 7% and 1% of 15-year-olds reach Level 5 and Level 6 in reading, respectively, these proportions vary substantially across countries. For example, among OECD countries, New Zealand, Finland, Japan, Korea, Australia, Canada and Belgium have at least 10% of top performers in reading, whereas Mexico, Chile and Turkey have less than 3%. Among the partner countries and economies, the overall proportion of these top performers also varies considerably from country to country, with students in many countries not achieving Level 6 in reading. At the same time, 2 partner countries and economies, Shanghai-China and Singapore, have the highest proportion of students at Level 5. Similar variations are shown in mathematics and science, with only slight differences in the patterns of these results among countries.

Among countries with similar mean scores in PISA, there are remarkable differences in the percentage of top-performing students. For example, Liechtenstein has a mean score of 499 points in reading in PISA 2009 and less than 5% of students at high proficiency levels in reading, which is less than the average of around 8%. Sweden has a similar mean reading score of 497 points, but 9% of its students achieve high proficiency levels in reading, which is more than the average. Although Liechtenstein has a small percentage of students at the lowest levels, the results could indicate the absence of a highly educated talent pool for the future.

Despite similarities across countries for each subject area, a high rank in one subject is no guarantee of a high rank in the others. For example, Switzerland has one of the highest shares of top performers in mathematics, but just an average share of top performers in reading.

Across the three subjects and countries, girls are as likely to be top performers as boys. On average across OECD countries, the proportion of top performers across subject areas is similar between boys and girls: 4.4% of girls and 3.8% of boys are top performers in all three subject areas, and 15.6% of girls and 17.0% of boys are top performers in at least one subject area (see Table I.3.8). However, while the gender gap among students who are top performers is small only in science (1.0% of girls and 1.5% of boys), it is large among top performers in reading only (2.8% of girls and 0.5% of boys) and in mathematics only (3.4% of girls and 6.6% of boys).

Policy Implications

Evidence of the importance of *reading literacy* for the success of individuals, economies and societies has never been stronger. After nearly a decade of PISA studies, those participating countries that have conducted longitudinal studies have shown that the reading skills which PISA measures are a strong predictor of positive outcomes for young adults, influencing the chance that they will participate in post-secondary education and their expected future earnings. Assessments of adult literacy have also found that the adult population's measured literacy levels can do far more to explain a country's economic success than the length of time that they have spent in education.

Not surprisingly, the percentages of young people who display very low and very high levels of literacy and the gap between them, which reflects the amount of inequality among populations or subgroups, have profound implications for a nation's prospective economic and social development.

The results of PISA 2009 show wide differences between countries in the knowledge and skills of 15-year-olds in *reading literacy*. The equivalent of an average of six years of schooling, 242 score points, separates the highest and lowest average performances of the countries that took part in the PISA 2009 reading assessment. Differences *between* countries, however, represent only a fraction of overall variation in student performance. The difference in reading performances *within* countries is generally even greater, with often over 300 point separating the highest and lowest performers in a country. Addressing the educational needs of such diverse populations and narrowing the observed gaps in student performance remains a formidable challenge for all countries.

To what extent is the observed variation in student performance on the PISA 2009 assessments a reflection of a possible innate distribution of students' abilities, and thus a challenge for education systems that cannot be influenced directly by education policy? The analysis in this volume shows that not only do the magnitude of within-country disparities in reading performance vary widely between countries, but also that large disparities in performance are not necessary for a country to attain a high level of overall performance. Although more general contextual factors need to be considered when such disparities are compared between countries, public policy has the potential to make an important contribution to providing equal opportunities and equitable learning outcomes for all students. Countries differ not just in their mean performance, but also in the extent to which they are able to close the gap between the students with the lowest and the highest levels of performance, and to reduce some of the barriers to equitable distribution of learning outcomes. These findings are relevant to policy makers.

Many factors contribute to variation in student performance. Disparities can result from the socio-economic backgrounds of students and schools, from the human and financial resources available to schools, from curricular differences, and from the way in which teaching is organised and delivered. As the causes of variation in student performance differ, so too do the approaches chosen by different countries to address the challenge. Some countries have non-selective school systems that seek to provide all students with the same opportunities for learning and require each school to cater to a full range of student performances. Other countries respond to diversity by forming groups of students with similar levels of performance through selection either within or between schools, with the aim of serving students according to their specific needs. Volume IV examines in greater detail how such policies and practices relate to the performance of students and schools in reading.

TACKLING LOW PERFORMANCE

Countries with large numbers of students who struggle to master basic reading literacy skills at age 15 are likely to be held back in the future due to substantial proportions of the adult population lacking skills that are needed in the modern workplace and society. Among those who fail to reach Level 2 on the PISA reading scale, the majority can be expected not to continue with education beyond school age, and therefore risk facing difficulties using reading for learning throughout their lives. Level 2 can be considered a baseline level of proficiency, at which students begin to demonstrate the reading skills that will enable them to participate effectively and productively in life. Students who do not reach Level 2 have difficulties locating basic information that meets several conditions, making comparisons or contrasts around a single feature, working out what a well-defined part of a text means when the information is not prominent, or making connections between the text and outside knowledge by drawing on personal experience and attitudes. The proportion of 15-year-olds in this situation varies widely across countries, from fewer than one student out of ten in four countries and economies to the majority of students in ten countries. Even in the average OECD country, where nearly one student out of five does not reach Level 2, tackling such low performance remains a major challenge.

The 2009 PISA assessment improved the measurement of low performance by separating performance below Level 2 into two sub-levels. Some low-performing students show the ability to find and process simple information at proficiency Level 1a. Among those unable even to do these tasks, the majority nevertheless still demonstrate technical reading skills, by solving easier tasks at the lower Level 1b, which only require students to retrieve very simple and explicit information from texts. In all but six countries in PISA 2009, over 90% of students can read at least to this level. This shows that while countries hoping to compete in the world economy need to reduce the number of students who do not reach Level 2, in most cases they have at least something to build on. The policy challenge is to improve students' proficiency by raising their ability to find, interpret and reflect on information in different kinds of text. Those countries that have achieved marked improvements among their lowest performers in reading over the last decade demonstrate that this can be done. Volume V shows, for example, that in Chile the proportion of students performing below Level 2 fell from nearly half in 2000 to below one third in 2009.

Reducing the proportion of students performing below Level 2 also has an important economic dimension. The magnitude of this gain is illustrated by a model which estimates that bringing all students to Level 2 could boost the combined economic output of OECD countries by around USD 200 trillion. While such estimates will always be associated with considerable uncertainty, they suggest that the cost of educational improvement is just a fraction of the high cost of low educational performance.

In tackling low performance, countries need to look at a range of associated factors identified by PISA. The significance of social background is examined in Volume II of this series, of attitudes to learning in Volume III and of school policies, practices and resources in Volume IV. Another important factor is gender: on average in OECD countries, one girl in eight and one boy in four failed to reach Level 2 in PISA 2009. This significant gender gap in underperformance is particularly large in some high-performing countries where almost all remaining underperformance exists among boys. In Finland, for example, only 3% of girls do not reach Level 2, but among boys it is 13%. Some other countries with performance slightly below the OECD average still have very few girls performing poorly, but overall performance is brought down by the large number of boys at low proficiency levels: in Latvia, 9% of girls and 27% of boys do not reach Level 2, and in the Slovak Republic that proportionately is 13% and 32%, respectively. While the situation is less extreme elsewhere, in many OECD countries it is clear that a focus on underperformance needs to target boys. This is particularly so as the gender gap has significantly widened over the last decade.

The fact that performance differences within the genders are significantly larger than between the genders suggests that this challenge can be successfully addressed.

PURSUING EXCELLENCE

At the other end of the proficiency spectrum, a small proportion of students attains Level 5 or higher. These students will be at the forefront of a competitive, knowledge-based global economy, and in each country their numbers will be important. They are able to retrieve information by locating and organising several pieces of deeply embedded information, inferring which information in the text is relevant; critically evaluate information and build hypotheses drawing on specialised knowledge; develop a full and detailed understanding of a text whose content or form is unfamiliar; and deal with concepts that are contrary to expectations.

Results from the PISA 2009 assessment show that nurturing high performance and tackling low performance need not be mutually exclusive. The countries with the very highest overall reading performance in PISA 2009, Finland and Korea, as well as the partner economies Hong Kong-China and Shanghai-China, also have among the lowest variation in student scores. Equally importantly, since 2009, Korea has been able to raise its already high reading performance by more than doubling the percentage of students reaching Level 5 or higher.

On average across OECD countries, 7.6% of students attain at least Level 5, but in Singapore, New Zealand and Shanghai-China this percentage is around twice the OECD average. For some countries, developing even a small corps of high-performing students remains an aspiration; in 16 countries, fewer than 1% of students reach Level 5.

STRENGTHS AND WEAKNESSES IN DIFFERENT KINDS OF READING

To read with understanding, students need to be able to retrieve, interpret and reflect on written information. This is true not just of advanced reading, but is evident at every developmental level, more so than ever in the age of the Internet. Faced with what seems like an infinite amount of online information in their future adult lives, they will need the skills necessary to find the information that they want, critically evaluate its reliability and relevance, and integrate and apply this information to solve their information needs. Only with a combination of these skills will they be able to use reading to function effectively across the different aspects of their lives.

In some countries, student performance varies between different aspects of reading in significant ways. Such variation may be related to differences in the ways in which reading skills are taught and learned in different cultures, to variations in curriculum emphasis or to the effectiveness with which different aspects of the school curriculum is delivered.

One reason for thinking that these differences could be linked to some deep-seated features of national cultures or curricula is that there are marked patterns of variation across different groups of countries. This is true in particular of the relative performance shown by students, on the one hand, on the *reflect and evaluate* subscale and, on the other, on the other two reading subscales – *access and retrieve* and *integrate and interpret*. In all predominantly English-speaking countries and in eight out of nine Latin American countries in PISA, the subscale where students showed the greatest strength was *reflect and evaluate*, and in most of these cases the difference with other subscales was substantial. In contrast, among 19 PISA countries in Eastern Europe, Southeast Europe and Central Asia, there were some significant differences in subscale results in 17 countries, and in all but 2 of these, the *reflect and evaluate* subscale was the weakest. This suggests that in some cultures, students are better at getting to grips with more direct reading tasks requiring them to obtain information from a text and work out what it means, while in others, they are relatively better at reflecting on the implications of its content. Since both types of skill are needed to be a good reader, these differences should help inform education systems in different cultures where extra effort may be needed.

Similarly, there are marked differences between countries in their performance in reading texts in different formats. In the 17 countries with substantially better performance in reading *continuous texts* than *non-continuous texts*, it may be that there is a more traditional language-of-instruction curriculum, in which little attention is paid to analysing and reflecting on non-prose material. It is noteworthy that the six countries in which performance on *non-continuous texts* was stronger than on *continuous texts* were all relatively high-performing countries over all. Moreover, given the association between the relatively strong performance of boys on *non-continuous texts,* and their propensity (explored in Volume III) to engage with texts of diverse formats, it would appear that exposure to a variety of texts in different formats is likely to raise reading proficiency as a whole. And taking into account the importance of understanding and using *non-continuous texts* in adult life, a pedagogical implication of these findings is that, in the classroom, young people should be exposed to and learn to negotiate a variety of texts in different formats.

STUDENT PERFORMANCE IN MATHEMATICS AND SCIENCE

As in reading, PISA 2009 shows large contrasts between some countries with outstanding performance in mathematics and science, and others with very large numbers of students who have limited proficiency in these domains. In both mathematics and science, students in some East Asian countries and economies did particularly well in 2009. The highest average performance in mathematics was seen in five countries and economies in this region, Shanghai-China, Singapore, Hong Kong-China, Korea and Chinese Taipei. Students in Shanghai-China had a mean performance of 600 points, equivalent to nearly the top of Level 4. In contrast, the mean performance in the highest country outside

this region, Finland, was at the top of Level 3, and the OECD average was near the bottom of Level 3. Similarly, in science, five of the best-performing six countries and economies, Shanghai-China, Hong Kong-China, Singapore, Japan and Korea, were from East Asia. On the other hand, in both mathematics and science, the lowest-performing countries were up to two proficiency levels below the OECD average, with 11 partner countries in mathematics and 7 in science at average scores below 400.

One feature of these wide differences in performance is a wide divide across countries in the proportion of students who lack basic skills in mathematics and science, which they will require to operate effectively in today's world. In both subjects, about one student in five in OECD countries does not progress beyond a very basic level of understanding at Level 1. This means for example that they can only perform mathematical tasks in very familiar contexts and can only show understanding of science at a very basic level in a limited range of situations. Such students will have difficulties thinking mathematically and scientifically in a world that demands this of them in their working lives and as active citizens. While in all but five OECD countries, at least three-quarters of students get above this level in mathematics, in Chile and Mexico half are below it; this is also the case in 15 partner countries. In science, 13 partner countries and economies (but no OECD countries) have a majority of students below Level 2. These countries still need to work hard to enable the majority of their population to understand a world in which scientific issues are part of public debate.

At the other end of the proficiency scale, the number of students reaching Level 5 or 6 in mathematics and science will be particularly important for countries wishing to create a pool of workers able to advance the frontiers of scientific and technological knowledge in the future and compete in the global economy. Here again, the contrasts are stark. In Chile and Mexico, and 16 partner countries and economies, fewer than one in 50 students reach this high level of mathematics proficiency. In all other OECD countries it is at least 1 student in 20, on average in OECD countries it is 1 in 8, and in Korea and Switzerland, the OECD countries with the highest proportion of students proficient in mathematics at least at Level 5, it is 1 in 4. While the last two countries are clearly at an advantage with twice the proportion of students highly proficient in mathematics than the average for the OECD, several East Asian countries and economies show that this is by no means an upper limit. Around one in three students in Hong Kong-China and Singapore, and a half of those in Shanghai-China are at Level 5 or 6 in mathematics. This creates a challenge to all OECD countries, showing that it is possible to develop a population where high mathematical proficiency becomes the norm, allowing broadly-based participation at the high end of the knowledge economy. In the case of science, there are similar patterns but the differences are not as wide: Shanghai-China has 24% of students at Level 5 or 6, compared to 19% in Finland, the highest OECD country.

In mathematics and science, gender differences are less important than in reading. In most countries, there is no difference in science, and while boys are ahead in mathematics, in 37 out of 65 PISA countries, most differences are relatively small. The exceptions are in Belgium, Chile, the United Kingdom, the United States and partner countries and economies Colombia and Liechtenstein, where boys are at least 20 score points ahead of girls. It is noticeable that in none of the highest-performing countries in mathematics are there large gender differences, and in Finland, Korea and partner countries and economies Chinese Taipei and Shanghai-China, all among the highest performers, gender differences are not significant.

These results show countries where boys are still more likely than girls to perform well overall in mathematics that there is no absolute barrier preventing girls from performing well. The picture for high performance is less clear-cut. In OECD countries most of those reaching the very highest proficiency level, Level 6, are boys: on average 4% of boys reach this level, compared to 2% of girls. However, in the partner countries and economies Chinese Taipei and Shanghai-China, similarly high numbers of boys and girls reach Level 6. Indeed, in these countries and in Singapore, at least 10% of girls reach Level 6. Even among boys, there is only one OECD country – Switzerland – where one in ten reaches Level 6. Thus, there is no "ceiling" of mathematical performance above which girls are bound to do worse than boys, and the barriers that exist appear to be related to cultural factors rather than the distribution of natural ability.

THE POTENTIAL TO IMPROVE PERFORMANCE ACROSS THE WORLD

The balance of proficiency in some of the richer countries in PISA looks very different from that of some of the poorer countries. In reading, for example, the ten countries for which the majority of students are at Level 1 or below, all in poorer parts of the world, contrast starkly in profile with the 34 OECD countries, where on average a majority reach at least Level 3. However, the fact that the best-performing country or economy in the 2009 assessment is Shanghai-China, with a GDP per capita well below the OECD average, underlines that low national income is

not incompatible with strong educational performance. Indeed, while there is a correlation between GDP per capita and educational performance, this correlation only predicts 6% of the differences between average student performance across countries. The other 94% of differences reflect the fact that two countries of similar prosperity can produce very different educational results. The results are similarly variable when substituting spending per student, relative poverty or the share of students with an immigrant background for GDP per capita.

This finding represents both a warning and an opportunity. It is a warning to countries in the "developed" world that they cannot take for granted that they will forever have "human capital" superior to other parts of the world. At a time of intensified global competition, these countries will need to work hard to maintain a knowledge and skill base that keeps up with changing demands. In particular, PISA underlines the extent to which these countries need to tackle underperformance among some students, to ensure that as many as possible of their future workforces are equipped with at least the levels of proficiency that enables them to participate in social and economic development. The high social and economic cost of poor educational performance in advanced economies risks becoming a significant drag on economic development in high-wage countries.

At the same time, the findings show that poor literacy skills are not an inevitable consequence of relatively low national income – an encouraging outcome for less developed countries that currently have large numbers of students performing at low levels. Indeed, Volume V, looks at trends in PISA and identifies a number of poorer countries that have made substantial inroads into educational performance in a relatively short space of time. Overall, PISA shows that an image of a world divided neatly into rich and well-educated countries and poor and badly-educated countries is well out-of-date.

References

Bertschy, K., M. Alejandrea Cattaneo and **Stefan C. Wolter** (2009), "PISA and the Transition into the Labour Market", *LABOUR: Review of Labour Economics and Industrial Relations,* Vol. 23, pp. 111-137.

Butler, J. and **R.J. Adams** (2007), "The Impact of Differential Investment of Student Effort on the Outcomes of International Studies", *Journal of Applied Measurement,* Vol. 3, No. 8, pp. 279-304.

Friedman, T.L. (2005), *The World is Flat: A Brief History of the Twenty-First Century,* Farrar, Straus and Giroux, New York.

Ganzeboom, H.B. G., P.M. De Graaf and **D.J. Treiman** (1992), "A Standard International Socio-Economic Index of Occupational Status", *Social Science Research* (21-1), pp. 1-56.

Halpern, D.F. (1989), *Thought and Knowledge: An Introduction to Critical Thinking,* Lawrence Erlbaum Associates, Hillsdale, New Jersey.

Hanushek, E.A. and **L. Wößmann** (2007), *Education Quality and Economic Growth,* The International Bank for Reconstruction and Development/The World Bank, Washington, DC.

ILO (International Labour Organization) (1990), *International Standard Classification of Occupations* (ISCO-88), Geneva.

International Telecommunications Union (2010), *ICT Statistics Database, www.itu.int/ITU-D/icteye/Indicators.aspx,* retrieved 14 March 2010.

Kirsch, I. and **P.B. Mosenthal** (1990), "Exploring Document Literacy: Variables Underlying the Performance of Young Adults", *Reading Research Quarterly,* Vol. 1, No. 25, pp. 5-30.

Marks, G.N. (2007), "Do Schools Matter for Early School Leaving? Individual and School Influences in Australia", *School Effectiveness and School Implementation,* Vol. 18, No. 4, University of Melbourne, Australian Council for Educational Research, Australia, pp. 429-450.

OECD (1999), *Classifying Educational Programmes: Manual for ISCED-97 Implemention in OECD Countries,* OECD Publishing.

OECD (2001), *Knowledge and Skills for Life: First Results from PISA 2000,* OECD Publishing.

OECD (2001), *Understanding the Digital Divide,* OECD Publishing.

OECD (2002), *Reading for Change: Performance and Engagement across Countries – Results from PISA 2000,* OECD Publishing.

OECD (2004), *Learning for Tomorrow's World: First results from PISA 2003,* OECD Publishing.

OECD (2007), *PISA 2006: Science Competencies for Tomorrow's World,* OECD Publishing.

OECD (2009), *Top of the Class,* OECD Publishing.

OECD (2010a), *Pathways to Success: How Knowledge and Skills at Age 15 Shape Future Lives in Canada,* OECD Publishing.

OECD (2010b), *The High Cost of Low Educational Performance,* OECD Publishing.

OECD (2010c), *PISA 2009 Framework: Key Competencies in Reading, Mathematics and Science,* OECD Publishing, Paris.

OECD (2010d), *Education at a Glance 2010: OECD Indicators,* OECD Publishing.

OECD (forthcoming), *PISA 2009 Technical Report,* OECD Publishing.

Shetzer, H. and **M. Warschauer** (2000), "An Electronic Literacy Approach to Network-Based Language Teaching", in M. Warschauer and R. Kem (eds.), *Network-Based Language Teaching: Concepts and Practice,* Cambridge University Press, New York, pp. 171-185.

Stiglitz, J.E., A. Sen and **J.P. Fitoussi** (2009), "Report by the Commission on the Measurement of Economic Performance and Social Progress", retrieved 14 September 2009.

Warschauer, M. (1999), *Electronic Literacies: Language Culture and Power in Online Education,* Lawrence Erlbaum Associates, Mahwah, New Jersey.

Werlich, E. (1976), *A Text Grammar of English,* Quelle and Meyer, Heidelberg.

Annex A

TECHNICAL BACKGROUND

All tables in Annex A are available on line

ANNEX A1
INDICES FROM THE STUDENT, SCHOOL AND PARENT CONTEXT QUESTIONNAIRES

Explanation of indices

This section explains the indices derived from the student, school and parent context questionnaires used in PISA 2009. However in Volume I, only few student indices have been used.

Several PISA measures reflect indices that summarise responses from students, their parents or school representatives (typically principals) to a series of related questions. The questions were selected from larger pool of questions on the basis of theoretical considerations and previous research. Structural equation modelling was used to confirm the theoretically expected behaviour of the indices and to validate their comparability across countries. For this purpose, a model was estimated separately for each country and collectively for all OECD countries.

For a detailed description of other PISA indices and details on the methods, see the *PISA 2009 Technical Report* (OECD, forthcoming).

There are two types of indices: simple indices and scale indices.

Simple indices are the variables that are constructed through the arithmetic transformation or recoding of one or more items, in exactly the same way across assessments. Here, item responses are used to calculate meaningful variables, such as the recoding of the four-digit ISCO-88 codes into 'Highest parents' socio-economic index (HISEI)' or, teacher-student ratio based on information from the school questionnaire.

Scale indices are the variables constructed through the scaling of multiple items. Unless otherwise indicated, the index was scaled using a weighted maximum likelihood estimate (WLE) (Warm, 1985), using a one-parameter item response model (a partial credit model was used in the case of items with more than two categories). The scaling was done in three stages:

- The item parameters were estimated from equal-sized subsamples of students from each OECD country.

- The estimates were computed for all students and all schools by anchoring the item parameters obtained in the preceding step.

- The indices were then standardised so that the mean of the index value for the OECD student population was zero and the standard deviation was one (countries being given equal weight in the standardisation process).

Sequential codes were assigned to the different response categories of the questions in the sequence in which the latter appeared in the student, school or parent questionnaires. Where indicated in this section, these codes were inverted for the purpose of constructing indices or scales. It is important to note that negative values for an index do not necessarily imply that students responded negatively to the underlying questions. A negative value merely indicates that the respondents answered less positively than all respondents did on average across OECD countries. Likewise, a positive value on an index indicates that the respondents answered more favourably, or more positively, than respondents did, on average, in OECD countries.

Terms enclosed in brackets < > in the following descriptions were replaced in the national versions of the student, school and parent questionnaires by the appropriate national equivalent. For example, the term <qualification at ISCED level 5A> was translated in the United States into "Bachelor's degree, post-graduate certificate program, Master's degree program or first professional degree program". Similarly the term <classes in the language of assessment> in Luxembourg was translated into "German classes" or "French classes" depending on whether students received the German or French version of the assessment instruments.

In addition to simple and scaled indices described in this annex, there are a number of variables from the questionnaires that correspond to single items not used to construct indices. These non-recoded variables have prefix of "ST" for the questionnaire items in the student questionnaire, "SC" for the items in the school questionnaire, and "PA" for the items in the parent questionnaire. All the context questionnaires as well as the PISA international database, including all variables, are available through *www.pisa. oecd.org*.

Student-level simple indices

Study programme

In PISA 2009, study programmes available to 15-year-old students in each country were collected both through the student tracking form and the student questionnaire (ST02). All study programmes were classified using ISCED (OECD, 1999). In the PISA international database, all national programmes are indicated in a variable (PROGN) where the first three digits are the ISO code for a country, the fourth digit the sub-national category and the last two digits the nationally specific programme code.

The following internationally comparable indices were derived from the data on study programmes:

- Programme level (ISCEDL) indicates whether students are (1) primary education level (ISCED 1); (2) lower secondary education level; or (3) upper secondary education level.

- Programme designation (ISCEDD) indicates the designation of the study programme: (1) = "A" (general programmes designed to give access to the next programme level); (2) = "B" (programmes designed to give access to vocational studies at the next programme level); (3) = "C" (programmes designed to give direct access to the labour market); or (4) = "M" (modular programmes that combine any or all of these characteristics).

- Programme orientation (ISCEDO) indicates whether the programme's curricular content is (1) general; (2) pre-vocational; (3) vocational; or (4) modular programmes that combine any or all of these characteristics.

Occupational status of parents

Occupational data for both a student's father and a student's mother were obtained by asking open-ended questions in the student questionnaire (ST9a, ST9b, ST12, ST13a, ST13b and ST16). The responses were coded to four-digit ISCO codes (ILO, 1990) and then mapped to Ganzeboom *et al.*'s SEI index (Ganzeboom, de Graaf and Treiman, 1992). Higher scores of SEI indicate higher levels of occupational status. The following three indices are obtained:

- Mother's occupational status (BMMJ).

- Father's occupational status (BFMJ).

- The highest occupational level of parents (HISEI) corresponds to the higher SEI score of either parent or to the only available parent's SEI score.

Educational level of parents

The educational level of parents is classified using ISCED (OECD, 1999) based on students' responses in the student questionnaire (ST10, ST11, ST14 and ST15). Please note that the question format for school education in PISA 2009 differs from the one used in PISA 2000, 2003 and 2006 but the method used to compute parental education is the same.

As in PISA 2000, 2003 and 2006, indices were constructed by selecting the highest level for each parent and then assigning them to the following categories: (0) None, (1) ISCED 1 (primary education), (2) ISCED 2 (lower secondary), (3) ISCED Level 3B or 3C (vocational/pre-vocational upper secondary), (4) ISCED 3A (upper secondary) and/or ISCED 4 (non-tertiary post-secondary), (5) ISCED 5B (vocational tertiary), (6) ISCED 5A, 6 (theoretically oriented tertiary and post-graduate). The following three indices with these categories are developed:

- Mother's educational level (MISCED).

- Father's educational level (FISCED).

- Highest educational level of parents (HISCED) corresponds to the higher ISCED level of either parent.

Highest educational level of parents was also converted into the number of years of schooling (PARED). For the conversion of level of education into years of schooling, see Table A1.1.

Relative grade

Data on the student's grade are obtained both from the student questionnaire (ST01) and from the student tracking form. As with all variables that are on both the tracking form and the questionnaire, inconsistencies between the two sources are reviewed and resolved during data-cleaning. In order to capture between-country variation, the relative grade index (GRADE) indicates whether students are at the modal grade in a country (value of 0), or whether they are below or above the modal grade level (+ x grades, - x grades).

The relationship between the grade and student performance was estimated through a multilevel model accounting for the following background variables: *i)* the **PISA index of economic, social and cultural status**; *ii)* the **PISA index of economic, social and cultural status** squared; *iii)* the school mean of the **PISA index of economic, social and cultural status**; *iv)* an indicator as to whether students were foreign born first-generation students; *v)* the percentage of first-generation students in the school; and *vi)* students' gender.

Table A1.2 presents the results of the multilevel model. Column 1 in Table A1.2 estimates the score point difference that is associated with one grade level (or school year). This difference can be estimated for the 32 OECD countries in which a sizeable number of 15-year-olds in the PISA samples were enrolled in at least two different grades. Since 15-year-olds cannot be assumed to be distributed at random across the grade levels, adjustments had to be made for the above-mentioned contextual factors that may relate to the assignment of students to the different grade levels. These adjustments are documented in columns 2 to 7 of the table.

[Part 1/1]

Table A1.1 Levels of parental education converted into years of schooling

	Did not go to school	Completed ISCED Level 1 (primary education)	Completed ISCED Level 2 (lower secondary education)	Completed ISCED Levels 3B or 3C (upper secondary education providing direct access to the labor market or to ISCED 5B programmes)	Completed ISCED Level 3A (upper secondary education providing access to ISCED 5A and 5B programmes) and/or ISCED Level 4 (non-tertiary post-secondary)	Completed ISCED Level 5A (university level tertiary education) or ISCED Level 6 (advanced research programmes)	Completed ISCED Level 5B (non-university tertiary education)
OECD							
Australia	0.0	6.0	10.0	11.0	12.0	15.0	14.0
Austria	0.0	4.0	9.0	12.0	12.5	17.0	15.0
Belgium	0.0	6.0	9.0	12.0	12.0	17.0	14.5
Canada	0.0	6.0	9.0	12.0	12.0	17.0	15.0
Chile	0.0	6.0	8.0	12.0	12.0	17.0	16.0
Czech Republic	0.0	5.0	9.0	11.0	13.0	16.0	16.0
Denmark	0.0	6.0	9.0	12.0	12.0	17.0	15.0
Estonia	0.0	4.0	9.0	12.0	12.0	16.0	15.0
Finland	0.0	6.0	9.0	12.0	12.0	16.5	14.5
France	0.0	5.0	9.0	12.0	12.0	15.0	14.0
Germany	0.0	4.0	10.0	13.0	13.0	18.0	15.0
Greece	0.0	6.0	9.0	11.5	12.0	17.0	15.0
Hungary	0.0	4.0	8.0	10.5	12.0	16.5	13.5
Iceland	0.0	7.0	10.0	13.0	14.0	18.0	16.0
Ireland	0.0	6.0	9.0	12.0	12.0	16.0	14.0
Israel	0.0	6.0	9.0	12.0	12.0	15.0	15.0
Italy	0.0	5.0	8.0	12.0	13.0	17.0	16.0
Japan	0.0	6.0	9.0	12.0	12.0	16.0	14.0
Korea	0.0	6.0	9.0	12.0	12.0	16.0	14.0
Luxembourg	0.0	6.0	9.0	12.0	13.0	17.0	16.0
Mexico	0.0	6.0	9.0	12.0	12.0	16.0	14.0
Netherlands	0.0	6.0	10.0	a	12.0	16.0	a
New Zealand	0.0	5.5	10.0	11.0	12.0	15.0	14.0
Norway	0.0	6.0	9.0	12.0	12.0	16.0	14.0
Poland	0.0	a	8.0	11.0	12.0	16.0	15.0
Portugal	0.0	6.0	9.0	12.0	12.0	17.0	15.0
Scotland	0.0	7.0	11.0	13.0	13.0	16.0	16.0
Slovak Republic	0.0	4.5	8.5	12.0	12.0	17.5	13.5
Slovenia	0.0	4.0	8.0	11.0	12.0	16.0	15.0
Spain	0.0	5.0	8.0	10.0	12.0	16.5	13.0
Sweden	0.0	6.0	9.0	11.5	12.0	15.5	14.0
Switzerland	0.0	6.0	9.0	12.5	12.5	17.5	14.5
Turkey	0.0	5.0	8.0	11.0	11.0	15.0	13.0
United Kingdom	0.0	6.0	9.0	12.0	13.0	16.0	15.0
United States	0.0	6.0	9.0	a	12.0	16.0	14.0
Partners							
Albania	0.0	6.0	9.0	12.0	12.0	16.0	16.0
Argentina	0.0	6.0	10.0	12.0	12.0	17.0	14.5
Azerbaijan	0.0	4.0	9.0	11.0	11.0	17.0	14.0
Brazil	0.0	4.0	8.0	11.0	11.0	16.0	14.5
Bulgaria	0.0	4.0	8.0	12.0	12.0	17.5	15.0
Colombia	0.0	5.0	9.0	11.0	11.0	15.5	14.0
Croatia	0.0	4.0	8.0	11.0	12.0	17.0	15.0
Dubai (UAE)	0.0	5.0	9.0	12.0	12.0	16.0	15.0
Hong Kong- China	0.0	6.0	9.0	11.0	13.0	16.0	14.0
Indonesia	0.0	6.0	9.0	12.0	12.0	15.0	14.0
Jordan	0.0	6.0	10.0	12.0	12.0	16.0	14.5
Kazakhstan	0.0	4.0	9.0	11.5	12.5	15.0	14.0
Kyrgyzstan	0.0	4.0	8.0	11.0	10.0	15.0	13.0
Latvia	0.0	3.0	8.0	11.0	11.0	16.0	16.0
Liechtenstein	0.0	5.0	9.0	11.0	13.0	17.0	14.0
Lithuania	0.0	3.0	8.0	11.0	11.0	16.0	15.0
Macao-China	0.0	6.0	9.0	11.0	12.0	16.0	15.0
Montenegro	0.0	4.0	8.0	11.0	12.0	16.0	15.0
Panama	0.0	6.0	9.0	12.0	12.0	16.0	a
Peru	0.0	6.0	9.0	11.0	11.0	17.0	14.0
Qatar	0.0	6.0	9.0	12.0	12.0	16.0	15.0
Romania	0.0	4.0	8.0	11.5	12.5	16.0	14.0
Russian Federation	0.0	4.0	9.0	11.5	12.0	15.0	a
Serbia	0.0	4.0	8.0	11.0	12.0	17.0	14.5
Shanghai-China	0.0	6.0	9.0	12.0	12.0	16.0	15.0
Singapore	0.0	6.0	8.0	10.5	10.5	12.5	12.5
Chinese Taipei	0.0	6.0	9.0	12.0	12.0	16.0	14.0
Thailand	0.0	6.0	9.0	12.0	12.0	16.0	14.0
Trinidad and Tobago	0.0	5.0	9.0	12.0	12.0	16.0	15.0
Tunisia	0.0	6.0	9.0	12.0	13.0	17.0	16.0
Uruguay	0.0	6.0	9.0	12.0	12.0	17.0	15.0

StatLink ᗰ᛬ᛋ᠍ http://dx.doi.org/10.1787/888932343171

[Part 1/1]

Table A1.2 **A multilevel model to estimate grade effects in reading accounting for some background variables**

	Grade		Index of economic, social and cultural status		Index of economic, social and cultural status squared		School mean index of economic, social and cultural status		First Generation students		School percentage of first generation students		Gender – student is a female		Intercept	
	Coeff	S.E.	Coeff	S.E.	Coeff	S.E.	Coeff	S.E.	Coeff	S.E.	Coeff	S.E.	Coeff	S.E.	Coeff	S.E.
OECD																
Australia	33.2	(1.95)	30.0	(1.36)	-3.8	(1.05)	66.4	(1.87)	-7.4	(2.82)	0.1	(0.07)	32.9	(1.91)	466.0	(1.39)
Austria	35.3	(2.18)	11.4	(1.66)	-0.5	(1.00)	89.7	(3.86)	-33.1	(6.11)	1.4	(0.13)	19.9	(2.67)	467.9	(2.45)
Belgium	48.9	(1.98)	10.0	(1.12)	-0.1	(0.63)	79.9	(1.73)	-3.2	(5.18)	0.3	(0.11)	11.3	(1.81)	507.0	(1.70)
Canada	45.0	(2.14)	19.4	(1.52)	1.5	(0.91)	33.9	(2.28)	-13.7	(3.18)	0.3	(0.04)	30.4	(1.60)	483.4	(1.76)
Chile	35.5	(1.55)	8.6	(1.52)	0.3	(0.63)	37.4	(1.61)	c	c	c	c	13.8	(2.33)	478.6	(1.60)
Czech Republic	44.6	(3.39)	13.4	(1.89)	-2.3	(1.47)	111.5	(3.12)	-8.9	(12.29)	0.4	(0.33)	32.3	(2.84)	460.7	(2.39)
Denmark	36.1	(3.02)	27.9	(1.51)	-2.8	(1.10)	35.1	(2.91)	-37.5	(5.97)	0.0	(0.14)	25.5	(2.59)	474.0	(1.95)
Estonia	44.4	(2.74)	14.1	(1.80)	1.6	(1.43)	52.1	(4.52)	-18.7	(14.08)	-3.3	(0.44)	36.7	(2.45)	485.8	(2.02)
Finland	37.3	(3.60)	27.7	(1.66)	-2.5	(1.30)	10.4	(3.28)	-56.0	(13.09)	-0.1	(0.29)	51.5	(2.26)	500.6	(2.02)
France	47.1	(5.14)	12.5	(1.70)	-1.9	(1.12)	81.6	(4.04)	-11.6	(9.24)	0.2	(0.15)	25.9	(2.67)	516.5	(2.35)
Germany	34.4	(1.74)	9.2	(1.23)	-1.6	(0.74)	109.1	(2.16)	-13.2	(4.80)	0.2	(0.12)	27.2	(1.92)	458.0	(1.46)
Greece	22.6	(10.86)	15.9	(1.46)	1.5	(1.07)	41.2	(2.84)	-15.0	(7.82)	0.0	(0.18)	36.2	(2.55)	469.0	(2.04)
Hungary	25.6	(2.19)	8.3	(1.39)	0.9	(0.87)	74.8	(2.09)	2.8	(7.92)	0.0	(0.27)	21.4	(2.22)	494.1	(1.65)
Iceland	c	c	29.8	(2.56)	-5.1	(1.56)	-3.8	(5.12)	-52.2	(11.45)	-1.3	(0.40)	44.9	(2.59)	469.1	(4.23)
Ireland	18.2	(1.94)	29.7	(1.78)	-3.5	(1.44)	43.6	(2.68)	-32.8	(6.52)	-0.1	(0.20)	33.9	(3.62)	474.8	(2.77)
Israel	36.6	(3.85)	19.9	(1.90)	3.4	(1.04)	104.7	(2.10)	-11.0	(6.13)	1.5	(0.08)	29.4	(2.81)	460.1	(2.13)
Italy	36.1	(1.67)	4.5	(0.69)	-1.4	(0.42)	76.4	(1.07)	-29.7	(3.36)	0.2	(0.08)	24.0	(1.29)	491.4	(0.85)
Japan	a	a	4.1	(1.51)	0.1	(1.47)	144.2	(2.40)	c	c	c	c	27.9	(2.43)	508.6	(1.58)
Korea	31.2	(9.77)	12.9	(1.42)	1.9	(1.18)	64.9	(2.24)	a	a	a	a	30.6	(3.21)	537.7	(2.08)
Luxembourg	45.3	(1.95)	16.6	(1.31)	-2.6	(1.08)	62.0	(2.89)	-10.4	(5.11)	-0.2	(0.10)	33.0	(2.22)	435.7	(2.40)
Mexico	32.6	(1.59)	7.5	(0.92)	0.8	(0.34)	27.8	(0.80)	-41.9	(6.36)	-1.8	(0.15)	17.9	(1.03)	473.7	(1.02)
Netherlands	26.6	(2.04)	6.0	(1.52)	-1.2	(1.02)	106.7	(2.32)	-11.6	(5.72)	1.7	(0.14)	15.3	(1.85)	484.5	(2.33)
New Zealand	44.2	(4.15)	38.9	(1.82)	-1.7	(1.44)	56.3	(3.35)	-12.2	(3.84)	0.0	(0.10)	44.8	(2.62)	496.5	(2.44)
Norway	37.6	(18.19)	34.2	(2.00)	-3.4	(1.62)	31.1	(4.32)	-33.4	(7.52)	0.4	(0.25)	48.3	(2.56)	453.2	(2.87)
Poland	73.8	(4.44)	29.4	(1.59)	-1.8	(1.21)	19.4	(2.99)	c	c	c	c	44.2	(2.41)	498.9	(1.89)
Portugal	48.9	(1.71)	12.0	(0.94)	1.0	(0.64)	21.3	(1.33)	-5.3	(5.75)	0.0	(0.23)	22.9	(1.84)	518.6	(1.92)
Slovak Republic	34.2	(3.85)	14.7	(1.44)	-3.2	(0.98)	64.3	(6.30)	c	c	c	c	39.1	(2.58)	483.2	(2.33)
Slovenia	22.8	(3.41)	4.8	(1.28)	0.0	(1.25)	100.2	(2.74)	-23.4	(7.48)	-0.2	(0.24)	27.7	(2.16)	452.4	(1.63)
Spain	61.7	(1.22)	9.8	(0.83)	0.4	(0.64)	22.7	(1.25)	-29.7	(2.86)	0.4	(0.04)	18.0	(1.42)	511.3	(1.07)
Sweden	63.8	(6.69)	31.4	(1.82)	-1.3	(1.04)	49.0	(6.55)	-38.8	(8.53)	0.3	(0.34)	43.2	(2.41)	454.4	(3.62)
Switzerland	45.5	(2.75)	18.2	(1.27)	-1.0	(1.23)	59.5	(2.95)	-25.1	(3.99)	-0.7	(0.11)	27.0	(2.00)	488.8	(1.50)
Turkey	33.7	(1.96)	7.7	(1.50)	0.3	(0.61)	46.3	(1.70)	c	c	c	c	27.9	(1.74)	524.0	(1.59)
United Kingdom	35.9	(6.21)	27.7	(2.01)	-0.3	(1.51)	65.7	(2.49)	-13.6	(8.49)	-0.3	(0.13)	23.1	(2.48)	468.7	(1.73)
United States	36.3	(2.17)	23.5	(1.70)	4.4	(1.15)	50.4	(2.56)	-5.6	(5.57)	0.8	(0.14)	25.4	(2.36)	463.5	(2.01)
Partners																
Albania	11.9	(5.07)	20.8	(3.04)	3.2	(1.35)	43.0	(2.47)	c	c	c	c	56.5	(3.40)	421.5	(3.44)
Argentina	33.6	(2.50)	11.2	(1.96)	0.9	(0.87)	52.6	(2.03)	-27.0	(10.55)	0.5	(0.20)	24.0	(2.38)	439.7	(2.32)
Azerbaijan	13.2	(1.78)	10.5	(1.67)	1.3	(0.90)	36.4	(2.00)	-9.8	(12.34)	-0.3	(0.49)	22.6	(2.16)	390.9	(2.12)
Brazil	36.1	(1.23)	7.7	(1.54)	1.3	(0.57)	38.3	(1.25)	-71.7	(17.16)	-0.9	(0.47)	20.2	(1.63)	445.5	(1.33)
Bulgaria	27.8	(5.08)	15.7	(1.93)	0.2	(1.29)	75.7	(3.99)	c	c	c	c	42.1	(3.51)	423.7	(2.61)
Colombia	33.2	(1.12)	6.9	(2.01)	0.9	(0.72)	39.4	(1.53)	c	c	c	c	3.2	(2.17)	477.7	(1.83)
Croatia	31.8	(2.33)	10.3	(1.36)	-4.0	(0.99)	75.3	(2.01)	-13.0	(5.71)	-0.1	(0.22)	31.4	(2.56)	472.8	(1.69)
Dubai (UAE)	34.6	(1.56)	15.2	(1.52)	3.2	(1.03)	25.9	(3.13)	21.5	(3.25)	1.1	(0.05)	28.2	(3.94)	362.4	(2.92)
Hong Kong-China	33.6	(2.03)	-0.9	(1.70)	-1.0	(0.76)	41.9	(1.64)	23.4	(3.70)	-0.4	(0.06)	21.9	(2.42)	575.8	(1.83)
Indonesia	14.4	(2.00)	4.7	(2.44)	0.9	(0.62)	29.1	(1.83)	c	c	c	c	28.0	(1.48)	430.8	(2.46)
Jordan	47.6	(6.38)	17.7	(1.52)	0.7	(0.81)	26.9	(1.55)	-11.5	(7.50)	-0.2	(0.20)	48.1	(2.73)	415.5	(2.04)
Kazakhstan	22.2	(2.42)	16.2	(2.12)	-1.7	(1.31)	55.7	(2.70)	-12.2	(6.78)	0.0	(0.10)	38.1	(2.23)	411.1	(1.57)
Kyrgyzstan	20.8	(2.92)	18.3	(2.23)	1.7	(1.10)	75.2	(2.03)	-23.4	(21.78)	3.3	(0.50)	46.0	(2.45)	345.7	(1.83)
Latvia	43.8	(3.07)	16.2	(1.89)	-0.8	(1.35)	37.0	(2.77)	c	c	c	c	38.9	(2.36)	479.6	(1.77)
Liechtenstein	23.8	(7.40)	2.1	(4.18)	-5.3	(3.07)	112.5	(12.17)	-12.6	(10.22)	-0.7	(0.44)	20.3	(6.86)	499.8	(8.42)
Lithuania	27.4	(2.87)	18.1	(1.56)	0.2	(1.04)	44.0	(2.45)	c	c	c	c	51.1	(2.34)	447.6	(1.87)
Macao-China	36.7	(1.01)	1.8	(1.61)	-1.1	(0.78)	1.0	(4.75)	16.7	(2.17)	-0.1	(0.23)	14.1	(1.51)	511.0	(3.47)
Montenegro	22.9	(3.44)	12.1	(1.38)	-0.3	(1.05)	64.2	(6.54)	-1.8	(6.69)	-1.2	(0.32)	39.3	(2.63)	409.5	(2.58)
Panama	32.6	(3.41)	7.9	(2.42)	1.2	(0.79)	45.8	(2.60)	-3.4	(10.77)	-1.4	(0.16)	15.8	(4.48)	431.3	(3.22)
Peru	27.5	(1.23)	10.5	(2.05)	0.9	(0.64)	47.2	(1.46)	c	c	c	c	8.3	(2.17)	445.6	(1.29)
Qatar	30.7	(1.70)	5.3	(0.98)	0.4	(0.85)	12.7	(2.91)	31.5	(2.98)	1.7	(0.07)	31.4	(3.71)	302.5	(2.94)
Romania	19.6	(4.19)	10.7	(1.63)	-0.3	(0.79)	63.9	(2.34)	c	c	c	c	13.7	(2.56)	446.4	(1.70)
Russian Federation	31.0	(2.01)	18.2	(1.93)	-1.6	(1.40)	38.8	(3.32)	-9.1	(5.88)	-0.4	(0.22)	38.7	(2.28)	452.9	(1.89)
Serbia	21.3	(4.48)	9.2	(1.25)	-0.8	(0.74)	55.1	(3.42)	1.2	(5.65)	0.3	(0.13)	27.1	(2.22)	425.1	(1.60)
Shanghai-China	21.8	(3.34)	4.6	(1.41)	0.1	(0.85)	57.3	(1.48)	c	c	c	c	29.3	(1.98)	583.5	(2.04)
Singapore	28.9	(2.09)	22.2	(2.19)	-2.8	(1.14)	104.7	(2.86)	0.4	(4.21)	-1.0	(0.13)	24.6	(2.57)	590.2	(2.76)
Chinese Taipei	15.4	(4.12)	15.5	(1.50)	-1.2	(1.05)	82.8	(3.06)	c	c	c	c	36.8	(2.25)	515.6	(2.03)
Thailand	22.1	(2.05)	10.4	(1.54)	2.4	(0.66)	28.8	(1.31)	a	a	a	a	31.3	(1.78)	454.6	(1.67)
Trinidad and Tobago	35.3	(1.60)	-0.6	(2.00)	-0.2	(0.91)	123.2	(3.42)	-9.2	(13.59)	-0.7	(0.28)	40.4	(2.90)	484.9	(2.77)
Tunisia	49.7	(1.57)	3.7	(1.76)	0.7	(0.56)	17.8	(1.25)	c	c	c	c	14.4	(1.84)	449.6	(1.63)
Uruguay	41.4	(1.49)	12.4	(1.58)	0.5	(0.75)	29.7	(1.58)	c	c	c	c	30.1	(2.48)	464.2	(2.29)

StatLink ⛓️📈 http://dx.doi.org/10.1787/888932343171

While it is possible to estimate the typical performance difference among students in two adjacent grades net of the effects of selection and contextual factors, this difference cannot automatically be equated with the progress that students have made over the last school year but should be interpreted as a lower boundary of the progress achieved. This is not only because different students were assessed but also because the content of the PISA assessment was not expressly designed to match what students had learned in the preceding school year but more broadly to assess the cumulative outcome of learning in school up to age 15. For example, if the curriculum of the grades in which 15-year-olds are enrolled mainly includes material other than that assessed by PISA (which, in turn, may have been included in earlier school years) then the observed performance difference will underestimate student progress.

Immigration

Information on the country of birth of students and their parents (ST17) is collected in a similar manner as in PISA 2000, PISA 2003 and PISA 2006 by using nationally specific ISO coded variables. The ISO codes of the country of birth for students and their parents are available in the PISA international database (COBN_S, COBN_M, and COBN_F).

The index on immigrant background (IMMIG) has the following categories: (1) native students (those students born in the country of assessment, or those with at least one parent born in that country; students who were born abroad with at least one parent born in the country of assessment are also classified as 'native' students), (2) second-generation students (those born in the country of assessment but whose parents were born in another country) , and (3) first-generation students (those born outside the country of assessment and whose parents were also born in another country). Students with missing responses for either the student or for both parents, or for all three questions have been given missing values for this variable.

Student-level scale indices

Family wealth

The index of family wealth (WEALTH) is based on the students' responses on whether they had the following at home: a room of their own, a link to the Internet, a dishwasher (treated as a country-specific item), a DVD player, and three other country-specific items (some items in ST20); and their responses on the number of cellular phones, televisions, computers, cars and the rooms with a bath or shower (ST21).

Home educational resources

The index of home educational resources (HEDRES) is based on the items measuring the existence of educational resources at home including a desk and a quiet place to study, a computer that students can use for schoolwork, educational software, books to help with students' school work, technical reference books and a dictionary (some items in ST20).

Cultural possessions

The index of cultural possessions (CULTPOSS) is based on the students' responses to whether they had the following at home: classic literature, books of poetry and works of art (some items in ST20).

Economic, social and cultural status

The PISA index of economic, social and cultural status (ESCS) was derived from the following three indices: highest occupational status of parents (HISEI), highest educational level of parents in years of education according to ISCED (PARED), and home possessions (HOMEPOS). The index of home possessions (HOMEPOS) comprises all items on the indices of WEALTH, CULTPOSS and HEDRES, as well as books in the home recoded into a four-level categorical variable (0-10 books, 11-25 or 26-100 books, 101-200 or 201-500 books, more than 500 books).

The PISA index of economic, social and cultural status (ESCS) was derived from a principal component analysis of standardised variables (each variable has an OECD mean of zero and a standard deviation of one), taking the factor scores for the first principal component as measures of the index of economic, social and cultural status.

Principal component analysis was also performed for each participating country to determine to what extent the components of the index operate in similar ways across countries. The analysis revealed that patterns of factor loading were very similar across countries, with all three components contributing to a similar extent to the index. For the occupational component, the average factor loading was 0.80, ranging from 0.66 to 0.87 across countries. For the educational component, the average factor loading was 0.79, ranging from 0.69 to 0.87 across countries. For the home possession component, the average factor loading was 0.73, ranging from 0.60 to 0.84 across countries. The reliability of the index ranged from 0.41 to 0.81. These results support the cross-national validity of the PISA index of economic, social and cultural status.

The imputation of components for students missing data on one component was done on the basis of a regression on the other two variables, with an additional random error component. The final values on the PISA index of economic, social and cultural status (ESCS) have an OECD mean of zero and a standard deviation of one.

ANNEX A2
THE PISA TARGET POPULATION, THE PISA SAMPLES AND THE DEFINITION OF SCHOOLS

Definition of the PISA target population

PISA 2009 provides an assessment of the cumulative yield of education and learning at a point at which most young adults are still enrolled in initial education.

A major challenge for an international survey is to ensure that international comparability of national target populations is guaranteed in such a venture.

Differences between countries in the nature and extent of pre-primary education and care, the age of entry into formal schooling and the institutional structure of educational systems do not allow the definition of internationally comparable grade levels of schooling. Consequently, international comparisons of educational performance typically define their populations with reference to a target age group. Some previous international assessments have defined their target population on the basis of the grade level that provides maximum coverage of a particular age cohort. A disadvantage of this approach is that slight variations in the age distribution of students across grade levels often lead to the selection of different target grades in different countries, or between education systems within countries, raising serious questions about the comparability of results across, and at times within, countries. In addition, because not all students of the desired age are usually represented in grade-based samples, there may be a more serious potential bias in the results if the unrepresented students are typically enrolled in the next higher grade in some countries and the next lower grade in others. This would exclude students with potentially higher levels of performance in the former countries and students with potentially lower levels of performance in the latter.

In order to address this problem, PISA uses an age-based definition for its target population, *i.e.* a definition that is not tied to the institutional structures of national education systems. PISA assesses students who were aged between 15 years and 3 (complete) months and 16 years and 2 (complete) months at the beginning of the assessment period, plus or minus a 1 month allowable variation, and who were enrolled in an educational institution with Grade 7 or higher, regardless of the grade levels or type of institution in which they were enrolled, and regardless of whether they were in full-time or part-time education. Educational institutions are generally referred to as schools in this publication, although some educational institutions (in particular, some types of vocational education establishments) may not be termed schools in certain countries. As expected from this definition, the average age of students across OECD countries was 15 years and 9 months. The range in country means was 2 months and 5 days (0.18 years), from the minimum country mean of 15 years and 8 months to the maximum country mean of 15 years and 10 months.

Given this definition of population, PISA makes statements about the knowledge and skills of a group of individuals who were born within a comparable reference period, but who may have undergone different educational experiences both in and outside of schools. In PISA, these knowledge and skills are referred to as the yield of education at an age that is common across countries. Depending on countries' policies on school entry, selection and promotion, these students may be distributed over a narrower or a wider range of grades across different education systems, tracks or streams. It is important to consider these differences when comparing PISA results across countries, as observed differences between students at age 15 may no longer appear as students' educational experiences converge later on.

If a country's scale scores in reading, scientific or mathematical literacy are significantly higher than those in another country, it cannot automatically be inferred that the schools or particular parts of the education system in the first country are more effective than those in the second. However, one can legitimately conclude that the cumulative impact of learning experiences in the first country, starting in early childhood and up to the age of 15, and embracing experiences both in school, home and beyond, have resulted in higher outcomes in the literacy domains that PISA measures.

The PISA target population did not include residents attending schools in a foreign country. It does, however, include foreign nationals attending schools in the country of assessment.

To accommodate countries that desired grade-based results for the purpose of national analyses, PISA 2009 provided a sampling option to supplement age-based sampling with grade-based sampling.

Population coverage

All countries attempted to maximise the coverage of 15-year-olds enrolled in education in their national samples, including students enrolled in special educational institutions. As a result, PISA 2009 reached standards of population coverage that are unprecedented in international surveys of this kind.

The sampling standards used in PISA permitted countries to exclude up to a total of 5% of the relevant population either by excluding schools or by excluding students within schools. All but 5 countries, Denmark (8.17%), Luxembourg (8.15%), Canada (6.00%), Norway (5.93%) and the United States (5.16%), achieved this standard, and in 36 countries and economies, the overall exclusion rate was less than 2%. When language exclusions were accounted for (*i.e.* removed from the overall exclusion rate), the United States no longer had an exclusion rate greater than 5%. For details, see *www.pisa.oecd.org*.

Exclusions within the above limits include:

- *At the school level: i)* schools that were geographically inaccessible or where the administration of the PISA assessment was not considered feasible; and *ii)* schools that provided teaching only for students in the categories defined under "within-school exclusions", such as schools for the blind. The percentage of 15-year-olds enrolled in such schools had to be less than 2.5% of the nationally desired target population [0.5% maximum for *i)* and 2% maximum for *ii)*]. The magnitude, nature and justification of school-level exclusions are documented in the *PISA 2009 Technical Report* (OECD, forthcoming).

- *At the student level: i)* students with an intellectual disability; *ii)* students with a functional disability; *iii)* students with limited assessment language proficiency; *iv)* other – a category defined by the national centres and approved by the international centre; and *v)* students taught in a language of instruction for the main domain for which no materials were available. Students could not be excluded solely because of low proficiency or common discipline problems. The percentage of 15-year-olds excluded within schools had to be less than 2.5% of the nationally desired target population.

Table A2.1 describes the target population of the countries participating in PISA 2009. Further information on the target population and the implementation of PISA sampling standards can be found in the *PISA 2009 Technical Report* (OECD, forthcoming).

- **Column 1** shows the **total number of 15-year-olds** according to the most recent available information, which in most countries meant the year 2008 as the year before the assessment.

- **Column 2** shows the number of 15-year-olds enrolled in schools in Grade 7 or above (as defined above), which is referred to as the **eligible population**.

- **Column 3** shows the **national desired target population**. Countries were allowed to exclude up to 0.5% of students *a priori* from the eligible population, essentially for practical reasons. The following *a priori* exclusions exceed this limit but were agreed with the PISA Consortium: Canada excluded 1.1% of its population from Territories and Aboriginal reserves; France excluded 1.7% of its students in its *territoires d'outre-mer* and other institutions; Indonesia excluded 4.7% of its students from four provinces because of security reasons; Kyrgyzstan excluded 2.3% of its population in remote, inaccessible schools; and Serbia excluded 2% of its students taught in Serbian in Kosovo.

- **Column 4** shows the **number of students enrolled in schools that were excluded from the national desired target population** either from the sampling frame or later in the field during data collection.

- **Column 5** shows the **size of the national desired target population after subtracting the students enrolled in excluded schools**. This is obtained by subtracting Column 4 from Column 3.

- **Column 6** shows the **percentage of students enrolled in excluded schools**. This is obtained by dividing Column 4 by Column 3 and multiplying by 100.

- **Column 7** shows the **number of students participating in PISA 2009**. Note that in some cases this number does not account for 15-year-olds assessed as part of additional national options.

- **Column 8** shows the **weighted number of participating students**, *i.e.* the number of students in the nationally defined target population that the PISA sample represents.

- Each country attempted to maximise the coverage of PISA's target population within the sampled schools. In the case of each sampled school, all eligible students, namely those 15 years of age, regardless of grade, were first listed. Sampled students who were to be excluded had still to be included in the sampling documentation, and a list drawn up stating the reason for their exclusion. **Column 9** indicates the **total number of excluded students,** which is further described and classified into specific categories in Table A2.2. **Column 10** indicates the **weighted number of excluded students,** *i.e.* the overall number of students in the nationally defined target population represented by the number of students excluded from the sample, which is also described and classified by exclusion categories in Table A2.2. Excluded students were excluded based on five categories: *i)* students with an intellectual disability – the student has a mental or emotional disability and is cognitively delayed such that he/she cannot perform in the PISA testing situation; *ii)* students with a functional disability – the student has a moderate to severe permanent physical disability such that he/she cannot perform in the PISA testing situation; *iii)* students with a limited assessment language proficiency – the student is unable to read or speak any of the languages of the assessment in the country and would be unable to overcome the language barrier in the testing situation (typically a student who has received less than one year of instruction in the languages of the assessment may be excluded); *iv)* other – a category defined by the national centres and approved by the international centre; and *v)* students taught in a language of instruction for the main domain for which no materials were available.

- **Column 11** shows the **percentage of students excluded within schools**. This is calculated as the weighted number of excluded students (Column 10), divided by the weighted number of excluded and participating students (Column 8 plus Column 10), then multiplied by 100.

[Part 1/2]

Table A2.1 PISA target populations and samples

		Population and sample information						
		Total population of 15-year-olds	Total enrolled population of 15-year-olds at Grade 7 or above	Total in national desired target population	Total school-level exclusions	Total in national desired target population after all school exclusions and before within-school exclusions	School-level exclusion rate (%)	Number of participating students	Weighted number of participating students
		(1)	(2)	(3)	(4)	(5)	(6)	(7)	(8)
OECD	Australia	286 334	269 669	269 669	7 057	262 612	2.62	14 251	240 851
	Austria	99 818	94 192	94 192	115	94 077	0.12	6 590	87 326
	Belgium	126 377	126 335	126 335	2 474	123 861	1.96	8 501	119 140
	Canada	430 791	426 590	422 052	2 370	419 682	0.56	23 207	360 286
	Chile	290 056	265 542	265 463	2 594	262 869	0.98	5 669	247 270
	Czech Republic	122 027	116 153	116 153	1 619	114 534	1.39	6 064	113 951
	Denmark	70 522	68 897	68 897	3 082	65 815	4.47	5 924	60 855
	Estonia	14 248	14 106	14 106	436	13 670	3.09	4 727	12 978
	Finland	66 198	66 198	66 198	1 507	64 691	2.28	5 810	61 463
	France	749 808	732 825	720 187	18 841	701 346	2.62	4 298	677 620
	Germany	852 044	852 044	852 044	7 138	844 906	0.84	4 979	766 993
	Greece	102 229	105 664	105 664	696	104 968	0.66	4 969	93 088
	Hungary	121 155	118 387	118 387	3 322	115 065	2.81	4 605	105 611
	Iceland	4 738	4 738	4 738	20	4 718	0.42	3 646	4 410
	Ireland	56 635	55 464	55 446	276	55 170	0.50	3 937	52 794
	Israel	122 701	112 254	112 254	1 570	110 684	1.40	5 761	103 184
	Italy	586 904	573 542	573 542	2 694	570 848	0.47	30 905	506 733
	Japan	1 211 642	1 189 263	1 189 263	22 955	1 166 308	1.93	6 088	1 113 403
	Korea	717 164	700 226	700 226	2 927	697 299	0.42	4 989	630 030
	Luxembourg	5 864	5 623	5 623	186	5 437	3.31	4 622	5 124
	Mexico	2 151 771	1 425 397	1 425 397	5 825	1 419 572	0.41	38 250	1 305 461
	Netherlands	199 000	198 334	198 334	6 179	192 155	3.12	4 760	183 546
	New Zealand	63 460	60 083	60 083	645	59 438	1.07	4 643	55 129
	Norway	63 352	62 948	62 948	1 400	61 548	2.22	4 660	57 367
	Poland	482 500	473 700	473 700	7 650	466 050	1.61	4 917	448 866
	Portugal	115 669	107 583	107 583	0	107 583	0.00	6 298	96 820
	Slovak Republic	72 826	72 454	72 454	1 803	70 651	2.49	4 555	69 274
	Slovenia	20 314	19 571	19 571	174	19 397	0.89	6 155	18 773
	Spain	433 224	425 336	425 336	3 133	422 203	0.74	25 887	387 054
	Sweden	121 486	121 216	121 216	2 323	118 893	1.92	4 567	113 054
	Switzerland	90 623	89 423	89 423	1 747	87 676	1.95	11 812	80 839
	Turkey	1 336 842	859 172	859 172	8 569	850 603	1.00	4 996	757 298
	United Kingdom	786 626	786 825	786 825	17 593	769 232	2.24	12 179	683 380
	United States	4 103 738	4 210 475	4 210 475	15 199	4 195 276	0.36	5 233	3 373 264
Partners	Albania	55 587	42 767	42 767	372	42 395	0.87	4 596	34 134
	Argentina	688 434	636 713	636 713	2 238	634 475	0.35	4 774	472 106
	Azerbaijan	185 481	184 980	184 980	1 886	183 094	1.02	4 727	105 886
	Brazil	3 292 022	2 654 489	2 654 489	15 571	2 638 918	0.59	20 127	2 080 159
	Bulgaria	80 226	70 688	70 688	1 369	69 319	1.94	4 507	57 833
	Colombia	893 057	582 640	582 640	412	582 228	0.07	7 921	522 388
	Croatia	48 491	46 256	46 256	535	45 721	1.16	4 994	43 065
	Dubai (UAE)	10 564	10 327	10 327	167	10 160	1.62	5 620	9 179
	Hong Kong-China	85 000	78 224	78 224	809	77 415	1.03	4 837	75 548
	Indonesia	4 267 801	3 158 173	3 010 214	10 458	2 999 756	0.35	5 136	2 259 118
	Jordan	117 732	107 254	107 254	0	107 254	0.00	6 486	104 056
	Kazakhstan	281 659	263 206	263 206	7 210	255 996	2.74	5 412	250 657
	Kyrgyzstan	116 795	93 989	91 793	1 149	90 644	1.25	4 986	78 493
	Latvia	28 749	28 149	28 149	943	27 206	3.35	4 502	23 162
	Liechtenstein	399	360	360	5	355	1.39	329	355
	Lithuania	51 822	43 967	43 967	522	43 445	1.19	4 528	40 530
	Macao-China	7 500	5 969	5 969	3	5 966	0.05	5 952	5 978
	Montenegro	8 500	8 493	8 493	10	8 483	0.12	4 825	7 728
	Panama	57 919	43 623	43 623	501	43 122	1.15	3 969	30 510
	Peru	585 567	491 514	490 840	984	489 856	0.20	5 985	427 607
	Qatar	10 974	10 665	10 665	114	10 551	1.07	9 078	9 806
	Romania	152 084	152 084	152 084	679	151 405	0.45	4 776	151 130
	Russian Federation	1 673 085	1 667 460	1 667 460	25 012	1 642 448	1.50	5 308	1 290 047
	Serbia	85 121	75 128	73 628	1 580	72 048	2.15	5 523	70 796
	Shanghai-China	112 000	100 592	100 592	1 287	99 305	1.28	5 115	97 045
	Singapore	54 982	54 212	54 212	633	53 579	1.17	5 283	51 874
	Chinese Taipei	329 249	329 189	329 189	1 778	327 411	0.54	5 831	297 203
	Thailand	949 891	763 679	763 679	8 438	755 241	1.10	6 225	691 916
	Trinidad and Tobago	19 260	17 768	17 768	0	17 768	0.00	4 778	14 938
	Tunisia	153 914	153 914	153 914	0	153 914	0.00	4 955	136 545
	Uruguay	53 801	43 281	43 281	30	43 251	0.07	5 957	33 971

Note: For a full explanation of the details in this table, please refer to the *PISA 2009 Technical Report* (OECD, forthcoming). The figure for total national population of 15-year-olds enrolled in Column 1 may occasionally be larger than the total number of 15-year-olds in Column 2 due to differing data sources. In Greece, Column 1 does not include immigrants but Column 2 does.

StatLink ᵃˢᵖ http://dx.doi.org/10.1787/888932343190

[Part 2/2]

Table A2.1 **PISA target populations and samples**

	Population and sample information				Coverage indices		
	Number of excluded students	Weighted number of excluded students	Within-school exclusion rate (%)	Overall exclusion rate (%)	Coverage index 1: Coverage of national desired population	Coverage index 2: Coverage of national enrolled population	Coverage index 3: Coverage of 15-year-old population
	(9)	(10)	(11)	(12)	(13)	(14)	(15)
OECD							
Australia	313	4 389	1.79	4.36	0.956	0.956	0.841
Austria	45	607	0.69	0.81	0.992	0.992	0.875
Belgium	30	292	0.24	2.20	0.978	0.978	0.943
Canada	1 607	20 837	5.47	6.00	0.940	0.930	0.836
Chile	15	620	0.25	1.22	0.988	0.987	0.852
Czech Republic	24	423	0.37	1.76	0.982	0.982	0.934
Denmark	296	2 448	3.87	8.17	0.918	0.918	0.863
Estonia	32	97	0.74	3.81	0.962	0.962	0.911
Finland	77	717	1.15	3.40	0.966	0.966	0.928
France	1	304	0.04	2.66	0.973	0.957	0.904
Germany	28	3 591	0.47	1.30	0.987	0.987	0.900
Greece	142	2 977	3.10	3.74	0.963	0.963	0.911
Hungary	10	361	0.34	3.14	0.969	0.969	0.872
Iceland	187	189	4.10	4.50	0.955	0.955	0.931
Ireland	136	1 492	2.75	3.23	0.968	0.967	0.932
Israel	86	1 359	1.30	2.68	0.973	0.973	0.841
Italy	561	10 663	2.06	2.52	0.975	0.975	0.863
Japan	0	0	0.00	1.93	0.981	0.981	0.919
Korea	16	1 748	0.28	0.69	0.993	0.993	0.879
Luxembourg	196	270	5.01	8.15	0.919	0.919	0.874
Mexico	52	1 951	0.15	0.56	0.994	0.994	0.607
Netherlands	19	648	0.35	3.46	0.965	0.965	0.922
New Zealand	184	1 793	3.15	4.19	0.958	0.958	0.869
Norway	207	2 260	3.79	5.93	0.941	0.941	0.906
Poland	15	1 230	0.27	1.88	0.981	0.981	0.930
Portugal	115	1 544	1.57	1.57	0.984	0.984	0.837
Slovak Republic	106	1 516	2.14	4.58	0.954	0.954	0.951
Slovenia	43	138	0.73	1.61	0.984	0.984	0.924
Spain	775	12 673	3.17	3.88	0.961	0.961	0.893
Sweden	146	3 360	2.89	4.75	0.953	0.953	0.931
Switzerland	209	940	1.15	3.08	0.969	0.969	0.892
Turkey	11	1 497	0.20	1.19	0.988	0.988	0.566
United Kingdom	318	17 094	2.44	4.62	0.954	0.954	0.869
United States	315	170 542	4.81	5.16	0.948	0.948	0.822
Partners							
Albania	0	0	0.00	0.87	0.991	0.991	0.614
Argentina	14	1 225	0.26	0.61	0.994	0.994	0.686
Azerbaijan	0	0	0.00	1.02	0.990	0.990	0.571
Brazil	24	2 692	0.13	0.72	0.993	0.993	0.632
Bulgaria	0	0	0.00	1.94	0.981	0.981	0.721
Colombia	11	490	0.09	0.16	0.998	0.998	0.585
Croatia	34	273	0.63	1.78	0.982	0.982	0.888
Dubai (UAE)	5	7	0.07	1.69	0.983	0.983	0.869
Hong Kong-China	9	119	0.16	1.19	0.988	0.988	0.889
Indonesia	0	0	0.00	0.35	0.997	0.950	0.529
Jordan	24	443	0.42	0.42	0.996	0.996	0.884
Kazakhstan	82	3 844	1.51	4.21	0.958	0.958	0.890
Kyrgyzstan	86	1 384	1.73	2.96	0.970	0.948	0.672
Latvia	19	102	0.43	3.77	0.962	0.962	0.813
Liechtenstein	0	0	0.00	1.39	0.986	0.986	0.890
Lithuania	74	632	1.53	2.70	0.973	0.973	0.782
Macao-China	0	0	0.00	0.05	0.999	0.999	0.797
Montenegro	0	0	0.00	0.12	0.999	0.999	0.909
Panama	0	0	0.00	1.15	0.989	0.989	0.527
Peru	9	558	0.13	0.33	0.997	0.995	0.730
Qatar	28	28	0.28	1.35	0.986	0.986	0.894
Romania	0	0	0.00	0.45	0.996	0.996	0.994
Russian Federation	59	15 247	1.17	2.65	0.973	0.973	0.771
Serbia	10	133	0.19	2.33	0.977	0.957	0.832
Shanghai-China	7	130	0.13	1.41	0.986	0.986	0.866
Singapore	48	417	0.80	1.96	0.980	0.980	0.943
Chinese Taipei	32	1 662	0.56	1.09	0.989	0.989	0.903
Thailand	6	458	0.07	1.17	0.988	0.988	0.728
Trinidad and Tobago	11	36	0.24	0.24	0.998	0.998	0.776
Tunisia	7	184	0.13	0.13	0.999	0.999	0.887
Uruguay	14	67	0.20	0.26	0.997	0.997	0.631

Note: For a full explanation of the details in this table please refer to the *PISA 2009 Technical Report* (OECD, forthcoming). The figure for total national population of 15-year-olds enrolled in Column 1 may occasionally be larger than the total number of 15-year-olds in Column 2 due to differing data sources. In Greece, Column 1 does not include immigrants but Column 2 does include immigrants.

StatLink ⌨️ http://dx.doi.org/10.1787/888932343190

[Part 1/1]
Table A2.2 **Exclusions**

	Student exclusions (unweighted)						Student exclusion (weighted)					
	Number of excluded students with a disability (Code 1)	Number of excluded students with a disability (Code 2)	Number of excluded students because of language (Code 3)	Number of excluded students for other reasons (Code 4)	Number of excluded students because of no materials available in the language of instruction (Code 5)	Total number of excluded students	Weighted number of excluded students with a disability (Code 1)	Weighted number of excluded students with a disability (Code 2)	Weighted number of excluded students because of language (Code 3)	Weighted number of excluded students for other reasons (Code 4)	Number of excluded students because of no materials available in the language of instruction (Code 5)	Total weighted number of excluded students
	(1)	(2)	(3)	(4)	(5)	(6)	(7)	(8)	(9)	(10)	(11)	(12)
OECD												
Australia	24	210	79	0	0	313	272	2 834	1 283	0	0	4 389
Austria	0	26	19	0	0	45	0	317	290	0	0	607
Belgium	3	17	10	0	0	30	26	171	95	0	0	292
Canada	49	1 458	100	0	0	1 607	428	19 082	1 326	0	0	20 837
Chile	5	10	0	0	0	15	177	443	0	0	0	620
Czech Republic	8	7	9	0	0	24	117	144	162	0	0	423
Denmark	13	182	35	66	0	296	165	1 432	196	656	0	2 448
Estonia	3	28	1	0	0	32	8	87	2	0	0	97
Finland	4	48	12	11	2	77	38	447	110	99	23	717
France	1	0	0	0	0	1	304	0	0	0	0	304
Germany	6	20	2	0	0	28	864	2 443	285	0	0	3 591
Greece	7	11	7	117	0	142	172	352	195	2 257	0	2 977
Hungary	0	1	0	9	0	10	0	48	0	313	0	361
Iceland	3	78	64	38	1	187	3	78	65	39	1	189
Ireland	4	72	25	35	0	136	51	783	262	396	0	1 492
Israel	10	69	7	0	0	86	194	1 049	116	0	0	1 359
Italy	45	348	168	0	0	561	748	6 241	3 674	0	0	10 663
Japan	0	0	0	0	0	0	0	0	0	0	0	0
Korea	7	9	0	0	0	16	994	753	0	0	0	1 748
Luxembourg	2	132	62	0	0	196	2	206	62	0	0	270
Mexico	25	25	2	0	0	52	1 010	905	36	0	0	1 951
Netherlands	6	13	0	0	0	19	178	470	0	0	0	648
New Zealand	19	84	78	0	3	184	191	824	749	0	29	1 793
Norway	8	160	39	0	0	207	90	1 756	414	0	0	2 260
Poland	2	13	0	0	0	15	169	1 061	0	0	0	1 230
Portugal	2	100	13	0	0	115	25	1 322	197	0	0	1 544
Slovak Republic	12	37	1	56	0	106	171	558	19	768	0	1 516
Slovenia	6	10	27	0	0	43	40	32	66	0	0	138
Spain	45	441	289	0	0	775	1 007	7 141	4 525	0	0	12 673
Sweden	115	0	31	0	0	146	2 628	0	732	0	0	3 360
Switzerland	11	106	92	0	0	209	64	344	532	0	0	940
Turkey	3	3	5	0	0	11	338	495	665	0	0	1 497
United Kingdom	40	247	31	0	0	318	2 438	13 482	1 174	0	0	17 094
United States	29	236	40	10	0	315	15 367	127 486	21 718	5 971	0	170 542
Partners												
Albania	0	0	0	0	0	0	0	0	0	0	0	0
Argentina	4	10	0	0	0	14	288	937	0	0	0	1 225
Azerbaijan	0	0	0	0	0	0	0	0	0	0	0	0
Brazil	21	3	0	0	0	24	2 495	197	0	0	0	2 692
Bulgaria	0	0	0	0	0	0	0	0	0	0	0	0
Colombia	7	2	2	0	0	11	200	48	242	0	0	490
Croatia	4	30	0	0	0	34	34	239	0	0	0	273
Dubai (UAE)	1	1	3	0	0	5	2	2	3	0	0	7
Hong Kong-China	0	9	0	0	0	9	0	119	0	0	0	119
Indonesia	0	0	0	0	0	0	0	0	0	0	0	0
Jordan	11	7	6	0	0	24	166	149	127	0	0	443
Kazakhstan	10	17	0	0	55	82	429	828	0	0	2 587	3 844
Kyrgyzstan	68	13	5	0	0	86	1 093	211	80	0	0	1 384
Latvia	6	8	5	0	0	19	25	44	33	0	0	102
Liechtenstein	0	0	0	0	0	0	0	0	0	0	0	0
Lithuania	4	69	1	0	0	74	33	590	9	0	0	632
Macao-China	0	0	0	0	0	0	0	0	0	0	0	0
Montenegro	0	0	0	0	0	0	0	0	0	0	0	0
Panama	0	0	0	0	0	0	0	0	0	0	0	0
Peru	4	5	0	0	0	9	245	313	0	0	0	558
Qatar	9	18	1	0	0	28	9	18	1	0	0	28
Romania	0	0	0	0	0	0	0	0	0	0	0	0
Russian Federation	11	47	1	0	0	59	2 081	13 010	157	0	0	15 247
Serbia	4	5	0	0	1	10	66	53	0	0	13	133
Shanghai-China	1	6	0	0	0	7	19	111	0	0	0	130
Singapore	2	22	24	0	0	48	17	217	182	0	0	417
Chinese Taipei	13	19	0	0	0	32	684	977	0	0	0	1 662
Thailand	0	5	1	0	0	6	0	260	198	0	0	458
Trinidad and Tobago	1	10	0	0	0	11	3	33	0	0	0	36
Tunisia	4	1	2	0	0	7	104	21	58	0	0	184
Uruguay	2	9	3	0	0	14	14	34	18	0	0	67

Exclusion codes:
Code 1 Functional disability – student has a moderate to severe permanent physical disability.
Code 2 Intellectual disability – student has a mental or emotional disability and has either been tested as cognitively delayed or is considered in the professional opinion of qualified staff to be cognitively delayed.
Code 3 Limited assessment language proficiency – student is not a native speaker of any of the languages of the assessment in the country and has been resident in the country for less than one year.
Code 4 Other defined by the national centres and approved by the international centre.
Code 5 No materials available in the language of instruction.
Note: For a full explanation of other details in this table, please refer to the *PISA 2009 Technical Report* (OECD, forthcoming).
StatLink ⛯⛯ http://dx.doi.org/10.1787/888932343190

- *Column 12* shows the **overall exclusion rate**, which represents the weighted percentage of the national desired target population excluded from PISA either through school-level exclusions or through the exclusion of students within schools. It is calculated as the school-level exclusion rate (Column 6 divided by 100) plus within-school exclusion rate (Column 11 divided by 100) multiplied by 1 minus the school-level exclusion rate (Column 6 divided by 100). This result is then multiplied by 100. Five countries, Denmark, Luxembourg, Canada, Norway and the United States, had exclusion rates higher than 5%. When language exclusions were accounted for (*i.e.* removed from the overall exclusion rate), the United States no longer had an exclusion rate greater than 5%.

- *Column 13* presents an **index of the extent to which the national desired target population is covered by the PISA sample**. Denmark, Luxembourg, Canada, Norway and the United States were the only countries where the coverage is below 95%.

- *Column 14* presents an **index of the extent to which 15-year-olds enrolled in schools are covered by the PISA sample**. The index measures the overall proportion of the national enrolled population that is covered by the non-excluded portion of the student sample. The index takes into account both school-level and student-level exclusions. Values close to 100 indicate that the PISA sample represents the entire education system as defined for PISA 2009. The index is the weighted number of participating students (Column 8) divided by the weighted number of participating and excluded students (Column 8 plus Column 10), times the nationally defined target population (Column 5) divided by the eligible population (Column 2) (times 100).

- *Column 15* presents an **index of the coverage of the 15-year-old population**. This index is the weighted number of participating students (Column 8) divided by the total population of 15-year-old students (Column 1).

This high level of coverage contributes to the comparability of the assessment results. For example, even assuming that the excluded students would have systematically scored worse than those who participated, and that this relationship is moderately strong, an exclusion rate in the order of 5% would likely lead to an overestimation of national mean scores of less than 5 score points (on a scale with an international mean of 500 score points and a standard deviation of 100 score points). This assessment is based on the following calculations: if the correlation between the propensity of exclusions and student performance is 0.3, resulting mean scores would likely be overestimated by 1 score point if the exclusion rate is 1%, by 3 score points if the exclusion rate is 5%, and by 6 score points if the exclusion rate is 10%. If the correlation between the propensity of exclusions and student performance is 0.5, resulting mean scores would be overestimated by 1 score point if the exclusion rate is 1%, by 5 score points if the exclusion rate is 5%, and by 10 score points if the exclusion rate is 10%. For this calculation, a model was employed that assumes a bivariate normal distribution for performance and the propensity to participate. For details, see the *PISA 2009 Technical Report* (OECD, forthcoming).

Sampling procedures and response rates

The accuracy of any survey results depends on the quality of the information on which national samples are based as well as on the sampling procedures. Quality standards, procedures, instruments and verification mechanisms were developed for PISA that ensured that national samples yielded comparable data and that the results could be compared with confidence.

Most PISA samples were designed as two-stage stratified samples (where countries applied different sampling designs, these are documented in the *PISA 2009 Technical Report* [OECD, forthcoming]). The first stage consisted of sampling individual schools in which 15-year-old students could be enrolled. Schools were sampled systematically with probabilities proportional to size, the measure of size being a function of the estimated number of eligible (15-year-old) students enrolled. A minimum of 150 schools were selected in each country (where this number existed), although the requirements for national analyses often required a somewhat larger sample. As the schools were sampled, replacement schools were simultaneously identified, in case a sampled school chose not to participate in PISA 2009.

In the case of Iceland, Liechtenstein, Luxembourg, Macao-China and Qatar, all schools and all eligible students within schools were included in the sample.

Experts from the PISA Consortium performed the sample selection process for most participating countries and monitored it closely in those countries that selected their own samples. The second stage of the selection process sampled students within sampled schools. Once schools were selected, a list of each sampled school's 15-year-old students was prepared. From this list, 35 students were then selected with equal probability (all 15-year-old students were selected if fewer than 35 were enrolled). The number of students to be sampled per school could deviate from 35, but could not be less than 20.

Data-quality standards in PISA required minimum participation rates for schools as well as for students. These standards were established to minimise the potential for response biases. In the case of countries meeting these standards, it was likely that any bias resulting from non-response would be negligible, *i.e.* typically smaller than the sampling error.

A minimum response rate of 85% was required for the schools initially selected. Where the initial response rate of schools was between 65 and 85%, however, an acceptable school response rate could still be achieved through the use of replacement schools. This procedure brought with it a risk of increased response bias. Participating countries were, therefore, encouraged to persuade as many of the schools in the original sample as possible to participate. Schools with a student participation rate between 25% and 50% were not regarded as participating schools, but data from these schools were included in the database and contributed to the various estimations. Data from schools with a student participation rate of less than 25% were excluded from the database.

[Part 1/2]

Table A2.3 **Response rates**

		Initial sample – before school replacement					Final sample – after school replacement		
		Weighted school participation rate before replacement (%)	Weighted number of responding schools (weighted also by enrolment)	Weighted number of schools sampled (responding and non-responding) (weighted also by enrolment)	Number of responding schools (unweighted)	Number of responding and non-responding schools (unweighted)	Weighted school participation rate after replacement (%)	Weighted number of responding schools (weighted also by enrolment)	Weighted number of schools sampled (responding and non-responding) (weighted also by enrolment)
		(1)	(2)	(3)	(4)	(5)	(6)	(7)	(8)
OECD	Australia	97.78	265 659	271 696	342	357	98.85	268 780	271 918
	Austria	93.94	88 551	94 261	280	291	93.94	88 551	94 261
	Belgium	88.76	112 594	126 851	255	292	95.58	121 291	126 899
	Canada	88.04	362 152	411 343	893	1 001	89.64	368 708	411 343
	Chile	94.34	245 583	260 331	189	201	99.04	257 594	260 099
	Czech Republic	83.09	94 696	113 961	226	270	97.40	111 091	114 062
	Denmark	83.94	55 375	65 967	264	325	90.75	59 860	65 964
	Estonia	100.00	13 230	13 230	175	175	100.00	13 230	13 230
	Finland	98.65	62 892	63 751	201	204	100.00	63 748	63 751
	France	94.14	658 769	699 776	166	177	94.14	658 769	699 776
	Germany	98.61	826 579	838 259	223	226	100.00	838 259	838 259
	Greece	98.19	98 710	100 529	181	184	99.40	99 925	100 529
	Hungary	98.21	101 523	103 378	184	190	99.47	103 067	103 618
	Iceland	98.46	4 488	4 558	129	141	98.46	4 488	4 558
	Ireland	87.18	48 821	55 997	139	160	88.44	49 526	55 997
	Israel	92.03	103 141	112 069	170	186	95.40	106 918	112 069
	Italy	94.27	532 432	564 811	1 054	1 108	99.08	559 546	564 768
	Japan	87.77	999 408	1 138 694	171	196	94.99	1 081 662	1 138 694
	Korea	100.00	683 793	683 793	157	157	100.00	683 793	683 793
	Luxembourg	100.00	5 437	5 437	39	39	100.00	5 437	5 437
	Mexico	95.62	1 338 291	1 399 638	1 512	1 560	97.71	1 367 668	1 399 730
	Netherlands	80.40	154 471	192 140	155	194	95.54	183 555	192 118
	New Zealand	84.11	49 917	59 344	148	179	91.00	54 130	59 485
	Norway	89.61	55 484	61 920	183	207	96.53	59 759	61 909
	Poland	88.16	409 513	464 535	159	187	97.70	453 855	464 535
	Portugal	93.61	102 225	109 205	201	216	98.43	107 535	109 251
	Slovak Republic	93.33	67 284	72 092	180	191	99.01	71 388	72 105
	Slovenia	98.36	19 798	20 127	337	352	98.36	19 798	20 127
	Spain	99.53	422 692	424 705	888	892	99.53	422 692	424 705
	Sweden	99.91	120 693	120 802	189	191	99.91	120 693	120 802
	Switzerland	94.25	81 005	85 952	413	429	98.71	84 896	86 006
	Turkey	100.00	849 830	849 830	170	170	100.00	849 830	849 830
	United Kingdom	71.06	523 271	736 341	418	549	87.35	643 027	736 178
	United States	67.83	2 673 852	3 941 908	140	208	77.50	3 065 651	3 955 606
Partners	Albania	97.29	39 168	40 259	177	182	99.37	39 999	40 253
	Argentina	97.18	590 215	607 344	194	199	99.42	603 817	607 344
	Azerbaijan	99.86	168 646	168 890	161	162	100.00	168 890	168 890
	Brazil	93.13	2 435 250	2 614 824	899	976	94.75	2 477 518	2 614 806
	Bulgaria	98.16	56 922	57 991	173	178	99.10	57 823	58 346
	Colombia	90.21	507 649	562 728	260	285	94.90	533 899	562 587
	Croatia	99.19	44 561	44 926	157	159	99.86	44 862	44 926
	Dubai (UAE)	100.00	10 144	10 144	190	190	100.00	10 144	10 144
	Hong Kong-China	69.19	53 800	77 758	108	156	96.75	75 232	77 758
	Indonesia	94.54	2 337 438	2 472 502	172	183	100.00	2 473 528	2 473 528
	Jordan	100.00	105 906	105 906	210	210	100.00	105 906	105 906
	Kazakhstan	100.00	257 427	257 427	199	199	100.00	257 427	257 427
	Kyrgyzstan	98.53	88 412	89 733	171	174	99.47	89 260	89 733
	Latvia	97.46	26 986	27 689	180	185	99.39	27 544	27 713
	Liechtenstein	100.00	356	356	12	12	100.00	356	356
	Lithuania	98.13	41 759	42 555	192	197	99.91	42 526	42 564
	Macao-China	100.00	5 966	5 966	45	45	100.00	5 966	5 966
	Montenegro	100.00	8 527	8 527	52	52	100.00	8 527	8 527
	Panama	82.58	33 384	40 426	180	220	83.76	33 779	40 329
	Peru	100.00	480 640	480 640	240	240	100.00	480 640	480 640
	Qatar	97.30	10 223	10 507	149	154	97.30	10 223	10 507
	Romania	100.00	150 114	150 114	159	159	100.00	150 114	150 114
	Russian Federation	100.00	1 392 765	1 392 765	213	213	100.00	1 392 765	1 392 765
	Serbia	99.21	70 960	71 524	189	191	99.97	71 504	71 524
	Shanghai-China	99.32	98 841	99 514	151	152	100.00	99 514	99 514
	Singapore	96.19	51 552	53 592	168	175	97.88	52 454	53 592
	Chinese Taipei	99.34	322 005	324 141	157	158	100.00	324 141	324 141
	Thailand	98.01	737 225	752 193	225	230	100.00	752 392	752 392
	Trinidad and Tobago	97.21	17 180	17 673	155	160	97.21	17 180	17 673
	Tunisia	100.00	153 198	153 198	165	165	100.00	153 198	153 198
	Uruguay	98.66	42 820	43 400	229	233	98.66	42 820	43 400

StatLink ᐦᒫᐦ http://dx.doi.org/10.1787/888932343190

[Part 2/2]

Table A2.3 **Response rates**

		Final sample – after school replacement		Final sample – students within schools after school replacement				
		Number of responding schools (unweighted)	Number of responding and non-responding schools (unweighted)	Weighted student participation rate after replacement (%)	Number of students assessed (weighted)	Number of students sampled (assessed and absent) (weighted)	Number of students assessed (unweighted)	Number of students sampled (assessed and absent) (unweighted)
		(9)	(10)	(11)	(12)	(13)	(14)	(15)
OECD	Australia	345	357	86.05	205 234	238 498	14 060	16 903
	Austria	280	291	88.63	72 793	82 135	6 568	7 587
	Belgium	275	292	91.38	104 263	114 097	8 477	9 245
	Canada	908	1 001	79.52	257 905	324 342	22 383	27 603
	Chile	199	201	92.88	227 541	244 995	5 663	6 097
	Czech Republic	260	270	90.75	100 685	110 953	6 049	6 656
	Denmark	285	325	89.29	49 236	55 139	5 924	6 827
	Estonia	175	175	94.06	12 208	12 978	4 727	5 023
	Finland	203	204	92.27	56 709	61 460	5 810	6 309
	France	166	177	87.12	556 054	638 284	4 272	4 900
	Germany	226	226	93.93	720 447	766 993	4 979	5 309
	Greece	183	184	95.95	88 875	92 631	4 957	5 165
	Hungary	187	190	93.25	97 923	105 015	4 605	4 956
	Iceland	129	141	83.91	3 635	4 332	3 635	4 332
	Ireland	141	160	83.81	39 248	46 830	3 896	4 654
	Israel	176	186	89.45	88 480	98 918	5 761	6 440
	Italy	1 095	1 108	92.13	462 655	502 190	30 876	33 390
	Japan	185	196	95.32	1 010 801	1 060 382	6 077	6 377
	Korea	157	157	98.76	622 187	630 030	4 989	5 057
	Luxembourg	39	39	95.57	4 897	5 124	4 622	4 833
	Mexico	1 531	1 560	95.13	1 214 827	1 276 982	38 213	40 125
	Netherlands	185	194	89.78	157 912	175 897	4 747	5 286
	New Zealand	161	179	84.65	42 452	50 149	4 606	5 476
	Norway	197	207	89.92	49 785	55 366	4 660	5 194
	Poland	179	187	85.87	376 767	438 739	4 855	5 674
	Portugal	212	216	87.11	83 094	95 386	6 263	7 169
	Slovak Republic	189	191	93.03	63 854	68 634	4 555	4 898
	Slovenia	337	352	90.92	16 777	18 453	6 135	6 735
	Spain	888	892	89.60	345 122	385 164	25 871	28 280
	Sweden	189	191	92.97	105 026	112 972	4 567	4 912
	Switzerland	425	429	93.58	74 712	79 836	11 810	12 551
	Turkey	170	170	97.85	741 029	757 298	4 996	5 108
	United Kingdom	481	549	86.96	520 121	598 110	12 168	14 046
	United States	160	208	86.99	2 298 889	2 642 598	5 165	5 951
Partners	Albania	181	182	95.39	32 347	33 911	4 596	4 831
	Argentina	198	199	88.25	414 166	469 285	4 762	5 423
	Azerbaijan	162	162	99.14	105 095	106 007	4 691	4 727
	Brazil	926	976	89.04	1 767 872	1 985 479	19 901	22 715
	Bulgaria	176	178	97.34	56 096	57 630	4 499	4 617
	Colombia	274	285	92.83	462 602	498 331	7 910	8 483
	Croatia	158	159	93.76	40 321	43 006	4 994	5 326
	Dubai (UAE)	190	190	90.39	8 297	9 179	5 620	6 218
	Hong Kong-China	151	156	93.19	68 142	73 125	4 837	5 195
	Indonesia	183	183	96.91	2 189 287	2 259 118	5 136	5 313
	Jordan	210	210	95.85	99 734	104 056	6 486	6 777
	Kazakhstan	199	199	98.49	246 872	250 657	5 412	5 489
	Kyrgyzstan	173	174	98.04	76 523	78 054	4 986	5 086
	Latvia	184	185	91.27	21 241	23 273	4 502	4 930
	Liechtenstein	12	12	92.68	329	355	329	355
	Lithuania	196	197	93.36	37 808	40 495	4 528	4 854
	Macao-China	45	45	99.57	5 952	5 978	5 952	5 978
	Montenegro	52	52	95.43	7 375	7 728	4 825	5 062
	Panama	183	220	88.67	22 666	25 562	3 913	4 449
	Peru	240	240	96.35	412 011	427 607	5 985	6 216
	Qatar	149	154	93.63	8 990	9 602	8 990	9 602
	Romania	159	159	99.47	150 331	151 130	4 776	4 803
	Russian Federation	213	213	96.77	1 248 353	1 290 047	5 308	5 502
	Serbia	190	191	95.37	67 496	70 775	5 522	5 804
	Shanghai-China	152	152	98.89	95 966	97 045	5 115	5 175
	Singapore	171	175	91.04	46 224	50 775	5 283	5 809
	Chinese Taipei	158	158	95.30	283 239	297 203	5 831	6 108
	Thailand	230	230	97.37	673 688	691 916	6 225	6 396
	Trinidad and Tobago	155	160	85.92	12 275	14 287	4 731	5 518
	Tunisia	165	165	96.93	132 354	136 545	4 955	5 113
	Uruguay	229	233	87.03	29 193	33 541	5 924	6 815

StatLink ⏋⫯⬌⌐ http://dx.doi.org/10.1787/888932343190

PISA 2009 also required a minimum participation rate of 80% of students within participating schools. This minimum participation rate had to be met at the national level, not necessarily by each participating school. Follow-up sessions were required in schools in which too few students had participated in the original assessment sessions. Student participation rates were calculated over all original schools, and also over all schools, whether original sample or replacement schools, and from the participation of students in both the original assessment and any follow-up sessions. A student who participated in the original or follow-up cognitive sessions was regarded as a participant. Those who attended only the questionnaire session were included in the international database and contributed to the statistics presented in this publication if they provided at least a description of their father's or mother's occupation.

Table A2.3 shows the response rates for students and schools, before and after replacement.

- *Column 1* shows the **weighted participation rate of schools before replacement**. This is obtained by dividing Column 2 by Column 3.

- *Column 2* shows the **weighted number of responding schools before school replacement** (weighted by student enrolment).

- *Column 3* shows the **weighted number of sampled schools before school replacement** (including both responding and non-responding schools, weighted by student enrolment).

- *Column 4* shows the unweighted number **of responding schools before school replacement**.

- *Column 5* shows the unweighted **number of responding and non-responding schools before school replacement**.

- *Column 6* shows the **weighted participation rate of schools after replacement**. This is obtained by dividing Column 7 by Column 8.

- *Column 7* shows the **weighted number of responding schools after school replacement** (weighted by student enrolment).

- *Column 8* shows the **weighted number of schools sampled after school replacement** (including both responding and non-responding schools, weighted by student enrolment).

- *Column 9* shows the unweighted number of responding schools after school replacement.

- *Column 10* shows the unweighted number of responding and non-responding schools after school replacement.

- *Column 11* shows the **weighted student participation rate after replacement**. This is obtained by dividing Column 12 by Column 13.

- *Column 12* shows the **weighted number of students assessed**.

- *Column 13* shows the **weighted number of students sampled** (including both students who were assessed and students who were absent on the day of the assessment).

- *Column 14* shows the **unweighted number of students assessed.** Note that any students in schools with student-response rates less than 50% were not included in these rates (both weighted and unweighted).

- *Column 15* shows the **unweighted number of students sampled** (including both students that were assessed and students who were absent on the day of the assessment). Note that any students in schools where fewer than half of the eligible students were assessed were not included in these rates (neither weighted nor unweighted).

Definition of schools

In some countries, sub-units within schools were sampled instead of schools and this may affect the estimation of the between-school variance components. In Austria, the Czech Republic, Germany, Hungary, Japan, Romania and Slovenia, schools with more than one study programme were split into the units delivering these programmes. In the Netherlands, for schools with both lower and upper secondary programmes, schools were split into units delivering each programme level. In the Flemish Community of Belgium, in the case of multi-campus schools, implantations (campuses) were sampled, whereas in the French Community, in the case of multi-campus schools, the larger administrative units were sampled. In Australia, for schools with more than one campus, the individual campuses were listed for sampling. In Argentina, Croatia and Dubai (UAE), schools that had more than one campus had the locations listed for sampling. In Spain, the schools in the Basque region with multi-linguistic models were split into linguistic models for sampling.

Grade levels

Students assessed in PISA 2009 are at various grade levels. The percentage of students at each grade level is presented by country in Table A2.4a and by gender within each country in Table A2.4b.

[Part 1/1]

Table A2.4a **Percentage of students at each grade level**

		7th grade		8th grade		9th grade		10th grade		11th grade		12th grade	
		%	S.E.	%	S.E.	%	S.E.	%	S.E.	%	S.E.	%	S.E.
OECD	Australia	0.0	(0.0)	0.1	(0.0)	10.4	(0.6)	70.8	(0.6)	18.6	(0.6)	0.1	(0.0)
	Austria	0.7	(0.2)	6.2	(1.0)	42.4	(0.9)	50.7	(1.0)	0.0	(0.0)	0.0	c
	Belgium	0.4	(0.2)	5.5	(0.5)	32.0	(0.6)	60.8	(0.7)	1.2	(0.1)	0.0	(0.0)
	Canada	0.0	(0.0)	1.2	(0.2)	13.6	(0.5)	84.1	(0.5)	1.1	(0.1)	0.0	(0.0)
	Chile	1.0	(0.2)	3.9	(0.5)	20.5	(0.8)	69.4	(1.0)	5.2	(0.3)	0.0	(0.0)
	Czech Republic	0.5	(0.2)	3.8	(0.3)	48.9	(1.0)	46.7	(1.1)	0.0	c	0.0	c
	Denmark	0.1	(0.0)	14.7	(0.6)	83.5	(0.8)	1.7	(0.5)	0.0	c	0.0	c
	Estonia	1.6	(0.3)	24.0	(0.7)	72.4	(0.9)	1.8	(0.3)	0.1	(0.1)	0.0	c
	Finland	0.5	(0.1)	11.8	(0.5)	87.3	(0.5)	0.0	c	0.4	(0.1)	0.0	c
	France	1.3	(0.9)	3.6	(0.7)	34.4	(1.2)	56.6	(1.5)	4.0	(0.7)	0.1	(0.0)
	Germany	1.2	(0.2)	11.0	(0.5)	54.8	(0.8)	32.5	(0.8)	0.4	(0.1)	0.0	(0.0)
	Greece	0.4	(0.2)	1.4	(0.5)	5.5	(0.8)	92.7	(1.0)	0.0	c	0.0	c
	Hungary	2.8	(0.6)	7.6	(1.1)	67.1	(1.4)	22.4	(0.9)	0.1	(0.1)	0.0	(0.0)
	Iceland	0.0	c	0.0	c	0.0	(0.0)	98.3	(0.1)	1.7	(0.1)	0.0	c
	Ireland	0.1	(0.0)	2.4	(0.3)	59.1	(1.0)	24.0	(1.4)	14.4	(1.1)	0.0	c
	Israel	0.0	c	0.3	(0.1)	17.9	(1.0)	81.3	(1.0)	0.5	(0.2)	0.0	(0.0)
	Italy	0.1	(0.1)	1.4	(0.3)	16.9	(0.4)	78.4	(0.6)	3.2	(0.3)	0.0	c
	Japan	0.0	c	0.0	c	0.0	c	100.0	(0.0)	0.0	c	0.0	c
	Korea	0.0	c	0.0	(0.0)	4.2	(0.9)	95.1	(0.9)	0.7	(0.1)	0.0	c
	Luxembourg	0.6	(0.1)	11.6	(0.2)	51.6	(0.3)	36.0	(0.2)	0.3	(0.0)	0.0	c
	Mexico	1.7	(0.1)	7.4	(0.3)	34.5	(0.8)	55.6	(0.9)	0.7	(0.2)	0.0	(0.0)
	Netherlands	0.2	(0.2)	2.7	(0.3)	46.2	(1.1)	50.5	(1.1)	0.5	(0.1)	0.0	c
	New Zealand	0.0	c	0.0	c	0.0	(0.0)	5.9	(0.4)	88.8	(0.5)	5.3	(0.3)
	Norway	0.0	c	0.0	c	0.5	(0.1)	99.3	(0.2)	0.2	(0.1)	0.0	c
	Poland	1.0	(0.2)	4.5	(0.4)	93.6	(0.6)	0.9	(0.3)	0.0	c	0.0	c
	Portugal	2.3	(0.3)	9.0	(0.8)	27.9	(1.6)	60.4	(2.2)	0.4	(0.1)	0.0	c
	Slovak Republic	1.0	(0.2)	2.6	(0.3)	35.7	(1.4)	56.9	(1.6)	3.8	(0.8)	0.0	(0.0)
	Slovenia	0.0	c	0.1	(0.1)	3.0	(0.7)	90.7	(0.7)	6.2	(0.2)	0.0	c
	Spain	0.1	(0.0)	9.9	(0.4)	26.5	(0.6)	63.4	(0.7)	0.0	(0.0)	0.0	c
	Sweden	0.1	(0.1)	3.2	(0.3)	95.1	(0.6)	1.6	(0.5)	0.0	c	0.0	c
	Switzerland	0.6	(0.1)	15.5	(0.9)	61.7	(1.3)	21.0	(1.1)	1.2	(0.5)	0.0	(0.0)
	Turkey	0.7	(0.1)	3.5	(0.8)	25.2	(1.3)	66.6	(1.5)	3.8	(0.3)	0.2	(0.1)
	United Kingdom	0.0	c	0.0	c	0.0	c	1.2	(0.1)	98.0	(0.1)	0.8	(0.0)
	United States	0.0	c	0.1	(0.1)	10.9	(0.8)	68.5	(1.0)	20.3	(0.7)	0.1	(0.1)
	OECD average	0.8	(0.1)	5.8	(0.1)	37.0	(0.2)	52.9	(0.2)	9.9	(0.1)	0.5	(0.0)
Partners	Albania	0.4	(0.1)	2.2	(0.3)	50.9	(2.0)	46.4	(2.0)	0.1	(0.0)	0.0	c
	Argentina	4.7	(0.9)	12.9	(1.3)	20.4	(1.2)	57.8	(2.1)	4.3	(0.5)	0.0	c
	Azerbaijan	0.6	(0.2)	5.3	(0.5)	49.4	(1.3)	44.3	(1.3)	0.4	(0.1)	0.0	c
	Brazil	6.8	(0.4)	18.0	(0.7)	37.5	(0.8)	35.7	(0.8)	2.1	(0.1)	0.0	c
	Bulgaria	1.5	(0.3)	6.1	(0.6)	88.7	(0.9)	3.8	(0.6)	0.0	c	0.0	c
	Colombia	4.4	(0.5)	10.3	(0.7)	22.1	(0.8)	42.3	(1.0)	21.0	(1.0)	0.0	c
	Croatia	0.0	c	0.2	(0.2)	77.5	(0.4)	22.3	(0.4)	0.0	c	0.0	c
	Dubai (UAE)	1.1	(0.1)	3.4	(0.1)	14.8	(0.4)	56.9	(0.5)	22.9	(0.4)	0.9	(0.1)
	Hong Kong-China	1.7	(0.2)	7.2	(0.5)	25.2	(0.5)	65.9	(0.9)	0.1	(0.0)	0.0	c
	Indonesia	1.5	(0.5)	6.5	(0.8)	46.0	(3.1)	40.5	(3.2)	5.0	(0.8)	0.5	(0.4)
	Jordan	0.1	(0.1)	1.3	(0.2)	7.0	(0.5)	91.6	(0.6)	0.0	c	0.0	c
	Kazakhstan	0.4	(0.1)	6.4	(0.4)	73.3	(1.9)	19.7	(2.0)	0.1	(0.0)	0.0	c
	Kyrgyzstan	0.2	(0.1)	7.9	(0.5)	71.4	(1.3)	19.8	(1.4)	0.7	(0.1)	0.0	c
	Latvia	2.7	(0.5)	15.5	(0.7)	79.4	(0.9)	2.4	(0.3)	0.1	(0.1)	0.0	(0.0)
	Liechtenstein	0.8	(0.5)	17.5	(1.1)	71.3	(0.8)	10.4	(1.0)	0.0	c	0.0	c
	Lithuania	0.5	(0.1)	10.2	(0.9)	80.9	(0.8)	8.4	(0.6)	0.0	(0.0)	0.0	c
	Macao-China	6.7	(0.1)	19.2	(0.2)	34.9	(0.1)	38.7	(0.1)	0.5	(0.1)	0.0	c
	Montenegro	0.0	c	2.5	(1.7)	82.7	(1.5)	14.8	(0.3)	0.0	c	0.0	c
	Panama	2.9	(0.8)	10.6	(1.6)	30.6	(3.3)	49.8	(4.5)	6.1	(1.4)	0.0	c
	Peru	4.0	(0.4)	8.9	(0.6)	17.1	(0.7)	44.6	(1.1)	25.4	(0.8)	0.0	c
	Qatar	1.7	(0.1)	3.6	(0.1)	13.5	(0.2)	62.6	(0.2)	18.2	(0.2)	0.4	(0.1)
	Romania	0.0	c	7.2	(1.0)	88.6	(1.1)	4.3	(0.6)	0.0	c	0.0	c
	Russian Federation	0.9	(0.2)	10.0	(0.7)	60.1	(1.8)	28.1	(1.6)	0.9	(0.2)	0.0	c
	Serbia	0.2	(0.1)	2.1	(0.5)	96.0	(0.6)	1.7	(0.2)	0.0	c	0.0	c
	Shanghai-China	1.0	(0.2)	4.1	(0.4)	37.4	(0.8)	57.1	(0.9)	0.4	(0.2)	0.0	(0.0)
	Singapore	1.0	(0.2)	2.6	(0.2)	34.7	(0.4)	61.6	(0.3)	0.0	c	0.0	(0.0)
	Chinese Taipei	0.0	c	0.1	(0.0)	34.4	(0.9)	65.5	(0.9)	0.0	(0.0)	0.0	c
	Thailand	0.1	(0.0)	0.5	(0.1)	23.2	(1.1)	73.5	(1.1)	2.7	(0.4)	0.0	c
	Trinidad and Tobago	2.1	(0.2)	8.8	(0.4)	25.3	(0.4)	56.1	(0.4)	7.7	(0.3)	0.0	c
	Tunisia	6.4	(0.4)	13.4	(0.6)	23.9	(0.9)	50.9	(1.4)	5.4	(0.4)	0.0	c
	Uruguay	7.1	(0.8)	10.6	(0.6)	21.5	(0.8)	56.2	(1.1)	4.6	(0.4)	0.0	c

StatLink ᵐˢᵖ http://dx.doi.org/10.1787/888932343190

[Part 1/2]

Table A2.4b **Percentage of students at each grade level, by gender**

		Boys – grade level										
		7th grade		8th grade		9th grade		10th grade		11th grade		12th grade	
		%	S.E.	%	S.E.	%	S.E.	%	S.E.	%	S.E.	%	S.E.
OECD	Australia	0.0	c	0.1	(0.0)	13.1	(0.9)	69.6	(1.1)	17.1	(0.8)	0.1	(0.0)
	Austria	0.7	(0.2)	7.4	(1.2)	42.6	(1.3)	49.3	(1.3)	0.0	(0.0)	0.0	c
	Belgium	0.6	(0.2)	6.4	(0.7)	34.6	(0.9)	57.3	(1.0)	1.1	(0.2)	0.0	(0.0)
	Canada	0.0	(0.0)	1.4	(0.3)	14.6	(0.6)	82.9	(0.6)	1.1	(0.1)	0.0	(0.0)
	Chile	1.3	(0.3)	4.9	(0.6)	23.2	(1.0)	65.9	(1.3)	4.7	(0.3)	0.0	c
	Czech Republic	0.7	(0.2)	4.5	(0.5)	52.5	(2.2)	42.3	(2.4)	0.0	c	0.0	c
	Denmark	0.1	(0.0)	19.5	(0.9)	79.5	(1.0)	0.8	(0.3)	0.0	c	0.0	c
	Estonia	2.4	(0.5)	27.0	(1.0)	69.6	(1.1)	1.0	(0.3)	0.0	c	0.0	c
	Finland	0.6	(0.2)	14.0	(0.8)	85.2	(0.8)	0.0	c	0.2	(0.1)	0.0	c
	France	1.3	(0.9)	4.0	(0.6)	39.6	(1.5)	51.4	(1.9)	3.6	(0.8)	0.0	(0.0)
	Germany	1.4	(0.3)	13.1	(0.7)	56.1	(1.0)	28.8	(0.9)	0.6	(0.1)	0.0	c
	Greece	0.5	(0.2)	1.9	(0.5)	6.2	(1.2)	91.4	(1.5)	0.0	c	0.0	c
	Hungary	3.2	(0.8)	9.3	(1.3)	68.8	(1.6)	18.7	(0.9)	0.0	(0.0)	0.0	(0.0)
	Iceland	0.0	c	0.0	c	0.0	c	98.7	(0.2)	1.3	(0.2)	0.0	c
	Ireland	0.1	(0.0)	2.8	(0.5)	60.9	(1.3)	22.4	(1.5)	13.8	(1.4)	0.0	c
	Israel	0.0	c	0.5	(0.2)	19.9	(1.1)	78.7	(1.2)	1.0	(0.4)	0.0	c
	Italy	0.1	(0.1)	1.7	(0.4)	20.1	(0.6)	75.7	(0.7)	2.5	(0.3)	0.0	c
	Japan	0.0	c	0.0	c	0.0	c	100.0	(0.0)	0.0	c	0.0	c
	Korea	0.0	c	0.1	(0.1)	4.7	(1.3)	94.5	(1.4)	0.7	(0.2)	0.0	c
	Luxembourg	0.8	(0.2)	12.5	(0.4)	52.4	(0.5)	34.0	(0.4)	0.3	(0.1)	0.0	c
	Mexico	2.0	(0.2)	8.8	(0.5)	37.6	(0.9)	51.0	(0.9)	0.5	(0.2)	0.0	c
	Netherlands	0.4	(0.3)	3.0	(0.4)	48.9	(1.3)	47.3	(1.3)	0.3	(0.1)	0.0	c
	New Zealand	0.0	c	0.0	c	0.0	c	6.9	(0.5)	87.9	(0.6)	5.2	(0.5)
	Norway	0.0	c	0.0	c	0.5	(0.1)	99.2	(0.2)	0.3	(0.2)	0.0	c
	Poland	1.5	(0.3)	6.5	(0.6)	91.6	(0.7)	0.5	(0.2)	0.0	c	0.0	c
	Portugal	3.4	(0.5)	10.5	(0.9)	30.9	(2.0)	54.9	(2.6)	0.4	(0.1)	0.0	c
	Slovak Republic	1.4	(0.3)	3.7	(0.5)	40.1	(1.9)	51.6	(2.1)	3.3	(0.7)	0.0	c
	Slovenia	0.0	c	0.1	(0.1)	4.0	(1.2)	91.1	(1.2)	4.7	(0.4)	0.0	c
	Spain	0.1	(0.0)	12.2	(0.6)	28.7	(0.8)	58.9	(0.9)	0.0	(0.0)	0.0	c
	Sweden	0.0	(0.0)	4.1	(0.4)	94.7	(0.6)	1.1	(0.3)	0.0	c	0.0	c
	Switzerland	0.8	(0.2)	18.0	(1.2)	60.7	(1.8)	19.4	(1.8)	1.0	(0.4)	0.1	(0.1)
	Turkey	1.0	(0.2)	4.0	(0.9)	30.2	(1.4)	61.3	(1.7)	3.2	(0.3)	0.2	(0.1)
	United Kingdom	0.0	c	0.0	c	0.0	c	1.3	(0.2)	98.0	(0.2)	0.7	(0.1)
	United States	0.0	c	0.1	(0.0)	13.2	(1.0)	68.6	(1.4)	17.9	(0.9)	0.1	(0.1)
	OECD average	1.0	(0.1)	7.0	(0.1)	40.8	(0.2)	50.8	(0.2)	9.8	(0.1)	0.7	(0.0)
Partners	Albania	0.5	(0.2)	2.6	(0.4)	54.0	(2.0)	42.9	(2.1)	0.0	(0.0)	0.0	c
	Argentina	5.9	(1.1)	15.4	(1.4)	22.7	(1.5)	52.5	(2.4)	3.5	(0.5)	0.0	c
	Azerbaijan	0.6	(0.2)	4.7	(0.5)	47.8	(1.4)	46.5	(1.5)	0.3	(0.1)	0.0	c
	Brazil	8.4	(0.6)	21.0	(0.9)	37.8	(0.8)	31.1	(0.9)	1.7	(0.2)	0.0	c
	Bulgaria	2.0	(0.4)	7.4	(0.9)	86.9	(1.2)	3.7	(0.6)	0.0	c	0.0	c
	Colombia	5.5	(0.9)	11.5	(0.9)	21.9	(1.1)	42.4	(1.4)	18.7	(1.2)	0.0	c
	Croatia	0.0	c	0.1	(0.1)	79.1	(0.6)	20.7	(0.6)	0.0	c	0.0	c
	Dubai (UAE)	1.6	(0.2)	4.5	(0.3)	16.0	(0.2)	53.6	(0.7)	23.1	(0.6)	1.1	(0.2)
	Hong Kong-China	1.9	(0.3)	7.3	(0.6)	26.6	(0.7)	64.1	(1.0)	0.1	(0.1)	0.0	c
	Indonesia	1.8	(0.7)	8.2	(1.0)	49.3	(3.4)	36.2	(3.6)	4.0	(0.9)	0.5	(0.3)
	Jordan	0.1	(0.1)	1.2	(0.4)	7.5	(0.8)	91.2	(0.9)	0.0	c	0.0	c
	Kazakhstan	0.5	(0.1)	7.1	(0.6)	75.2	(2.2)	17.2	(2.3)	0.1	(0.0)	0.0	c
	Kyrgyzstan	0.2	(0.1)	8.9	(0.7)	72.9	(1.6)	17.4	(1.6)	0.5	(0.2)	0.0	c
	Latvia	3.6	(0.9)	19.9	(1.1)	74.7	(1.4)	1.6	(0.4)	0.1	(0.1)	0.0	(0.0)
	Liechtenstein	1.1	(0.7)	19.7	(1.6)	68.9	(1.2)	10.3	(1.2)	0.0	c	0.0	c
	Lithuania	0.6	(0.2)	12.3	(1.2)	80.0	(1.2)	7.2	(0.7)	0.0	c	0.0	c
	Macao-China	8.9	(0.2)	22.0	(0.2)	34.9	(0.2)	33.6	(0.2)	0.5	(0.1)	0.0	c
	Montenegro	0.0	c	3.0	(2.0)	85.0	(1.8)	12.0	(0.4)	0.0	c	0.0	c
	Panama	3.4	(1.1)	13.6	(2.5)	32.6	(4.4)	45.7	(5.5)	4.7	(1.8)	0.0	c
	Peru	4.9	(0.5)	11.2	(0.8)	18.8	(1.0)	42.3	(1.4)	22.9	(0.9)	0.0	c
	Qatar	1.9	(0.1)	4.3	(0.2)	14.8	(0.3)	60.4	(0.3)	18.2	(0.2)	0.4	(0.1)
	Romania	0.0	c	6.3	(1.1)	89.9	(1.3)	3.9	(0.7)	0.0	c	0.0	c
	Russian Federation	1.4	(0.3)	10.4	(0.9)	61.2	(1.9)	26.3	(1.9)	0.8	(0.2)	0.0	c
	Serbia	0.3	(0.1)	2.7	(0.7)	95.6	(0.8)	1.4	(0.2)	0.0	c	0.0	c
	Shanghai-China	1.2	(0.3)	5.1	(0.6)	38.8	(1.2)	54.7	(1.4)	0.2	(0.1)	0.0	c
	Singapore	0.8	(0.2)	2.9	(0.3)	35.7	(0.6)	60.6	(0.5)	0.0	c	0.0	c
	Chinese Taipei	0.0	c	0.2	(0.1)	35.2	(1.5)	64.7	(1.5)	0.0	c	0.0	c
	Thailand	0.2	(0.1)	0.8	(0.2)	26.3	(1.4)	70.5	(1.4)	2.2	(0.5)	0.0	c
	Trinidad and Tobago	2.7	(0.3)	10.7	(0.5)	28.4	(0.6)	51.0	(0.5)	7.1	(0.4)	0.0	c
	Tunisia	8.9	(0.6)	16.8	(0.9)	24.4	(1.1)	45.3	(1.5)	4.7	(0.5)	0.0	c
	Uruguay	9.1	(1.0)	12.0	(0.8)	24.9	(0.8)	50.4	(1.3)	3.6	(0.4)	0.0	c

StatLink http://dx.doi.org/10.1787/888932343190

[Part 2/2]

Table A2.4b   **Percentage of students at each grade level, by gender**

	Girls – Grade level											
	7th grade		8th grade		9th grade		10th grade		11th grade		12th grade	
	%	S.E.	%	S.E.	%	S.E.	%	S.E.	%	S.E.	%	S.E.
OECD												
Australia	0.0	(0.0)	0.1	(0.0)	7.9	(0.5)	72.0	(0.8)	20.0	(0.8)	0.1	(0.0)
Austria	0.6	(0.4)	5.0	(1.2)	42.2	(1.4)	52.1	(1.5)	0.0	(0.0)	0.0	c
Belgium	0.3	(0.1)	4.5	(0.5)	29.3	(1.1)	64.5	(1.1)	1.3	(0.2)	0.0	(0.0)
Canada	0.0	(0.0)	1.0	(0.2)	12.5	(0.5)	85.3	(0.5)	1.1	(0.1)	0.0	(0.0)
Chile	0.7	(0.1)	2.9	(0.5)	17.7	(0.9)	73.0	(1.1)	5.6	(0.4)	0.0	(0.0)
Czech Republic	0.3	(0.2)	3.1	(0.4)	44.8	(1.9)	51.8	(1.9)	0.0	c	0.0	c
Denmark	0.1	(0.0)	10.0	(0.7)	87.3	(0.9)	2.5	(0.8)	0.0	c	0.0	c
Estonia	0.9	(0.3)	20.8	(0.9)	75.4	(1.1)	2.7	(0.5)	0.2	(0.2)	0.0	c
Finland	0.4	(0.1)	9.6	(0.6)	89.4	(0.6)	0.0	c	0.6	(0.2)	0.0	c
France	1.3	(0.9)	3.2	(0.9)	29.4	(1.5)	61.6	(1.7)	4.4	(0.8)	0.1	(0.1)
Germany	1.1	(0.2)	8.8	(0.6)	53.4	(1.1)	36.4	(1.1)	0.3	(0.1)	0.0	(0.0)
Greece	0.2	(0.2)	0.9	(0.5)	4.9	(0.7)	94.0	(0.9)	0.0	c	0.0	c
Hungary	2.3	(0.7)	5.9	(1.1)	65.4	(1.6)	26.2	(1.2)	0.2	(0.1)	0.0	c
Iceland	0.0	c	0.0	c	0.0	(0.1)	97.9	(0.2)	2.1	(0.2)	0.0	c
Ireland	0.1	(0.1)	2.0	(0.4)	57.3	(1.5)	25.7	(2.0)	15.1	(1.5)	0.0	c
Israel	0.0	c	0.1	(0.1)	15.9	(1.0)	83.8	(1.1)	0.2	(0.1)	0.0	(0.0)
Italy	0.2	(0.1)	1.0	(0.2)	13.5	(0.6)	81.4	(0.7)	3.9	(0.3)	0.0	c
Japan	0.0	c	0.0	c	0.0	c	100.0	(0.0)	0.0	c	0.0	c
Korea	0.0	c	0.0	c	3.6	(1.0)	95.6	(1.0)	0.8	(0.1)	0.0	c
Luxembourg	0.4	(0.1)	10.6	(0.3)	50.8	(0.4)	38.0	(0.3)	0.2	(0.1)	0.0	c
Mexico	1.5	(0.2)	6.1	(0.4)	31.5	(0.9)	60.1	(1.0)	0.8	(0.3)	0.0	(0.0)
Netherlands	0.1	(0.1)	2.3	(0.4)	43.4	(1.4)	53.5	(1.3)	0.7	(0.2)	0.0	c
New Zealand	0.0	c	0.0	c	0.1	(0.1)	4.8	(0.5)	89.8	(0.6)	5.4	(0.5)
Norway	0.0	c	0.0	c	0.4	(0.1)	99.4	(0.2)	0.1	(0.1)	0.0	c
Poland	0.6	(0.2)	2.5	(0.3)	95.6	(0.7)	1.3	(0.6)	0.0	c	0.0	c
Portugal	1.4	(0.2)	7.7	(0.8)	25.1	(1.4)	65.4	(1.9)	0.4	(0.1)	0.0	c
Slovak Republic	0.7	(0.2)	1.5	(0.3)	31.4	(1.8)	62.1	(2.1)	4.3	(0.9)	0.0	(0.0)
Slovenia	0.0	c	0.0	c	1.9	(0.7)	90.3	(0.8)	7.8	(0.5)	0.0	c
Spain	0.1	(0.1)	7.6	(0.4)	24.2	(0.7)	68.0	(0.8)	0.0	(0.0)	0.0	c
Sweden	0.1	(0.1)	2.3	(0.3)	95.4	(0.7)	2.2	(0.7)	0.0	c	0.0	c
Switzerland	0.4	(0.1)	12.9	(0.9)	62.6	(1.8)	22.7	(2.0)	1.4	(0.6)	0.0	c
Turkey	0.4	(0.1)	2.9	(0.8)	19.8	(1.3)	72.3	(1.6)	4.4	(0.4)	0.2	(0.1)
United Kingdom	0.0	c	0.0	c	0.0	c	1.0	(0.1)	98.1	(0.1)	0.9	(0.1)
United States	0.0	c	0.2	(0.2)	8.5	(0.7)	68.4	(1.1)	22.8	(1.0)	0.1	(0.1)
OECD average	0.6	(0.1)	5.0	(0.1)	35.6	(0.2)	55.0	(0.2)	10.2	(0.1)	0.5	(0.0)
Partners												
Albania	0.2	(0.1)	1.8	(0.4)	47.6	(2.3)	50.2	(2.3)	0.2	(0.1)	0.0	c
Argentina	3.6	(0.9)	10.7	(1.5)	18.4	(1.2)	62.3	(2.2)	4.9	(0.6)	0.0	c
Azerbaijan	0.6	(0.3)	5.8	(0.6)	51.0	(1.5)	42.1	(1.4)	0.4	(0.1)	0.0	c
Brazil	5.4	(0.4)	15.3	(0.6)	37.1	(0.9)	39.7	(0.9)	2.5	(0.2)	0.0	c
Bulgaria	0.9	(0.3)	4.6	(0.7)	90.6	(1.0)	3.9	(0.7)	0.0	c	0.0	c
Colombia	3.3	(0.4)	9.1	(0.8)	22.4	(1.0)	42.2	(1.1)	23.0	(1.1)	0.0	c
Croatia	0.0	c	0.2	(0.2)	75.8	(0.6)	24.1	(0.5)	0.0	c	0.0	c
Dubai (UAE)	0.6	(0.1)	2.2	(0.2)	13.5	(0.5)	60.4	(0.6)	22.7	(0.7)	0.6	(0.1)
Hong Kong-China	1.5	(0.2)	7.1	(0.6)	23.5	(0.6)	67.9	(1.0)	0.0	c	0.0	c
Indonesia	1.2	(0.3)	4.9	(0.8)	42.7	(3.7)	44.6	(3.8)	6.0	(1.1)	0.6	(0.5)
Jordan	0.1	(0.0)	1.3	(0.3)	6.5	(0.7)	92.1	(0.9)	0.0	c	0.0	c
Kazakhstan	0.4	(0.1)	5.7	(0.5)	71.5	(2.0)	22.3	(2.1)	0.2	(0.1)	0.0	c
Kyrgyzstan	0.1	(0.1)	7.1	(0.6)	69.9	(1.5)	22.0	(1.6)	0.9	(0.2)	0.0	c
Latvia	1.7	(0.4)	11.2	(0.6)	83.9	(0.8)	3.1	(0.4)	0.1	(0.1)	0.0	c
Liechtenstein	0.6	(0.6)	15.0	(1.5)	74.0	(1.2)	10.4	(1.6)	0.0	c	0.0	c
Lithuania	0.3	(0.1)	8.1	(0.8)	81.9	(0.9)	9.6	(0.7)	0.0	(0.0)	0.0	c
Macao-China	4.4	(0.1)	16.3	(0.2)	34.9	(0.2)	43.9	(0.2)	0.5	(0.1)	0.0	c
Montenegro	0.0	c	2.0	(1.4)	80.3	(1.3)	17.8	(0.4)	0.0	c	0.0	c
Panama	2.4	(0.6)	7.7	(1.1)	28.7	(3.0)	53.8	(4.0)	7.5	(1.6)	0.0	c
Peru	3.2	(0.4)	6.5	(0.6)	15.4	(0.8)	47.0	(1.2)	27.9	(1.2)	0.0	c
Qatar	1.4	(0.1)	3.0	(0.1)	12.1	(0.2)	64.9	(0.2)	18.1	(0.2)	0.5	(0.1)
Romania	0.0	c	8.1	(1.5)	87.3	(1.5)	4.7	(0.6)	0.0	c	0.0	c
Russian Federation	0.5	(0.1)	9.7	(0.8)	59.0	(2.0)	29.8	(1.8)	1.0	(0.2)	0.0	c
Serbia	0.1	(0.1)	1.4	(0.5)	96.4	(0.6)	2.0	(0.2)	0.0	c	0.0	c
Shanghai-China	0.8	(0.2)	3.0	(0.4)	36.1	(1.0)	59.5	(1.0)	0.6	(0.2)	0.0	(0.0)
Singapore	1.2	(0.2)	2.3	(0.3)	33.7	(0.5)	62.7	(0.4)	0.0	(0.0)	0.0	(0.0)
Chinese Taipei	0.0	c	0.0	(0.0)	33.7	(1.5)	66.3	(1.5)	0.0	(0.0)	0.0	c
Thailand	0.0	c	0.3	(0.1)	20.9	(1.4)	75.8	(1.4)	3.0	(0.4)	0.0	c
Trinidad and Tobago	1.5	(0.3)	6.9	(0.5)	22.3	(0.6)	61.0	(0.6)	8.3	(0.4)	0.0	c
Tunisia	4.2	(0.4)	10.3	(0.5)	23.4	(1.0)	56.1	(1.4)	6.0	(0.5)	0.0	c
Uruguay	5.4	(0.6)	9.4	(0.5)	18.5	(0.9)	61.4	(1.2)	5.4	(0.6)	0.0	c

StatLink ⟶ http://dx.doi.org/10.1787/888932343190

Students in or out of the regular education system in Argentina

The low performance of 15-year-old students in Argentina is, to some extent, influenced by a fairly large proportion of 15-year-olds enrolled in programmes outside the regular education system. Table A2.5 shows the proportion of students inside and outside the regular education system, alongside their performance in PISA 2009.

Table A2.5 **Percentage of students and mean scores in reading, mathematics and science, according to whether students are in or out of the regular education system in Argentina**

| | Percentage of students | | Mean performance | | | | | |
| | | | Reading | | Mathematics | | Science | |
	%	S.E.	Mean	S.E.	Mean	S.E.	Mean	S.E.
Students in the regular educational system[1]	60.9	2.2	439	5.1	421	4.8	439	4.9
Students out of the regular educational system[2]	39.1	2.2	335	8.0	337	6.7	341	8.3

1. Students who are not in grade 10 or 11 and in programme 3, 4, 5, 6, 7 or 8.
2. Students who are in grade 10 or 11 and in programme 3, 4, 5, 6, 7 or 8.
StatLink ᐧᐧᐧ http://dx.doi.org/10.1787/888932343190

ANNEX A3
STANDARD ERRORS, SIGNIFICANCE TESTS AND SUB-GROUP COMPARISONS

The statistics in this report represent estimates of national performance based on samples of students, rather than values that could be calculated if every student in every country had answered every question. Consequently, it is important to measure the degree of uncertainty of the estimates. In PISA, each estimate has an associated degree of uncertainty, which is expressed through a standard error. The use of confidence intervals provides a way to make inferences about the population means and proportions in a manner that reflects the uncertainty associated with the sample estimates. From an observed sample statistic and assuming a normal distribution, it can be inferred that the corresponding population result would lie within the confidence interval in 95 out of 100 replications of the measurement on different samples drawn from the same population.

In many cases, readers are primarily interested in whether a given value in a particular country is different from a second value in the same or another country, *e.g.* whether girls in a country perform better than boys in the same country. In the tables and figures used in this report, differences are labelled as statistically significant when a difference of that size, smaller or larger, would be observed less than 5% of the time, if there were actually no difference in corresponding population values. Similarly, the risk of reporting a correlation as significant if there is, in fact, no correlation between two measures, is contained at 5%.

Throughout the report, significance tests were undertaken to assess the statistical significance of the comparisons made.

Gender differences
Gender differences in student performance or other indices were tested for statistical significance. Positive differences indicate higher scores for boys, while negative differences indicate higher scores for girls. Generally, differences marked in bold in the tables in this volume are statistically significant at the 95% confidence level.

Performance differences between the top and bottom quartiles of PISA indices and scales
Differences in average performance between the top and bottom quarters of the PISA indices and scales were tested for statistical significance. Data marked in bold indicate that performance between the top and bottom quarters of students on the respective index is statistically significantly different at the 95% confidence level.

ANNEX A4
QUALITY ASSURANCE

Quality assurance procedures were implemented in all parts of PISA 2009, as was done for all previous PISA surveys.

The consistent quality and linguistic equivalence of the PISA 2009 assessment instruments were facilitated by providing countries with equivalent source versions of the assessment instruments in English and French, and requiring countries (other than those assessing students in English and French) to prepare and consolidate two independent translations using both source versions. Precise translation and adaptation guidelines were supplied, also including instructions for selecting and training the translators. For each country, the translation and format of the assessment instruments (including test materials, marking guides, questionnaires and manuals) were verified by expert translators appointed by the PISA Consortium before they were used in the PISA 2009 Field Trial and Main Study. These translators' mother tongue was the language of instruction in the country concerned and they were knowledgeable about education systems. For further information on the PISA translation procedures, see the *PISA 2009 Technical Report* (OECD, forthcoming).

The survey was implemented through standardised procedures. The PISA Consortium provided comprehensive manuals that explained the implementation of the survey, including precise instructions for the work of School Co-ordinators and scripts for Test Administrators to use during the assessment sessions. Proposed adaptations to survey procedures, or proposed modifications to the assessment session script, were submitted to the PISA Consortium for approval prior to verification. The PISA Consortium then verified the national translation and adaptation of these manuals.

To establish the credibility of PISA as valid and unbiased, and to encourage uniformity in administering the assessment sessions, Test Administrators in participating countries were selected using the following criteria: it was required that the Test Administrator not be the reading, mathematics or science instructor of any students in the sessions he or she would administer for PISA; it was recommended that the Test Administrator not be a member of the staff of any school where he or she would administer for PISA; and it was considered preferable that the Test Administrator not be a member of the staff of any school in the PISA sample. Participating countries organised an in-person training session for Test Administrators.

Participating countries were required to ensure that: Test Administrators worked with the School Co-ordinator to prepare the assessment session, including updating student tracking forms and identifying excluded students; no extra time was given for the cognitive items (while it was permissible to give extra time for the student questionnaire); no instrument was administered before the two one-hour parts of the cognitive session; Test Administrators recorded the student participation status on the student tracking forms and filled in a Session Report Form; no cognitive instrument was permitted to be photocopied; no cognitive instrument could be viewed by school staff before the assessment session; and Test Administrators returned the material to the National Centre immediately after the assessment sessions.

National Project Managers were encouraged to organise a follow-up session when more than 15% of the PISA sample was not able to attend the original assessment session.

National Quality Monitors from the PISA Consortium visited all National Centres to review data-collection procedures. Finally, School Quality Monitors from the PISA Consortium visited a sample of 15 schools during the assessment. For further information on the field operations, see the *PISA 2009 Technical Report* (OECD, forthcoming).

Marking procedures were designed to ensure consistent and accurate application of the marking guides outlined in the PISA Operations Manuals. National Project Managers were required to submit proposed modifications to these procedures to the Consortium for approval. Reliability studies to analyse the consistency of marking were implemented, these are discussed in more detail below.

Software specially designed for PISA facilitated data entry, detected common errors during data entry, and facilitated the process of data cleaning. Training sessions familiarised National Project Managers with these procedures.

For a description of the quality assurance procedures applied in PISA and in the results, see the *PISA 2009 Technical Report* (OECD, forthcoming).

The results of data adjudication show that the PISA Technical Standards were fully met in all countries and economies that participated in PISA 2009, though for one country, some serious doubts were raised. Analysis of the data for Azerbaijan suggest that the PISA Technical Standards may not have been fully met for the following four main reasons: i) the order of difficulty of the clusters is inconsistent with previous experience and the ordering varies across booklets; ii) the percentage correct on some items is higher than that of the highest scoring countries; iii) the difficulty of the clusters varies widely across booklets; and iv) the coding of items in Azerbaijan is at an extremely high level of agreement between independent coders, and was judged, on some items, to be too lenient. However, further investigation of the survey instruments, the procedures for test implementation and coding of student responses at the national level did not provide sufficient evidence of systematic errors or violations of the PISA Technical Standards. Azerbaijan's data are, therefore, included in the PISA 2009 international dataset.

For the PISA 2009 assessment in Austria, a dispute between teacher unions and the education minister has led to the announcement of a boycott of PISA which was withdrawn after the first week of testing. The boycott required the OECD to remove identifiable cases from the dataset. Although the Austrian dataset met the PISA 2009 technical standards after the removal of these cases, the negative atmosphere in regard to educational assessment has affected the conditions under which the assessment was administered and could have adversely affected student motivation to respond to the PISA tasks. The comparability of the 2009 data with data from earlier PISA assessments can therefore not be ensured and data for Austria have therefore been excluded from trend comparisons.

ANNEX A5
DEVELOPMENT OF THE PISA ASSESSMENT INSTRUMENTS

The development of the PISA 2009 assessment instruments was an interactive process between the PISA Consortium, various international expert groups working under the auspices of the OECD, the PISA Governing Board and national experts. A panel of international experts led, in close consultation with participating countries, the identification of the range of skills and competencies in the respective assessment domains that were considered to be crucial for an individual's capacity to fully participate in and contribute to a successful modern society. A description of the assessment domains – the assessment framework – was then used by participating countries, and other test development professionals, as they contributed assessment materials. The development of this assessment framework involved the following steps:

- Development of a working definition for the assessment area and description of the assumptions that underlay that definition;

- Evaluation of how to organise the set of tasks constructed in order to report to policy-makers and researchers on performance in each assessment area among 15-year-old students in participating countries;

- Identification of a set of key characteristics to be taken into account when assessment tasks were constructed for international use;

- Operationalisation of the set of key characteristics to be used in test construction, with definitions based on existing literature and the experience of other large-scale assessments;

- Validation of the variables, and assessment of the contribution that each made to the understanding of task difficulty in participating countries; and

- Preparation of an interpretative scheme for the results.

The frameworks were agreed at both scientific and policy levels and subsequently provided the basis for the development of the assessment instruments. The frameworks are described in *Assessing Scientific, Reading and Mathematical Literacy: A Framework for PISA 2009* (OECD 2009a). They provided a common language and a vehicle for participating countries to develop a consensus as to the measurement goals of PISA.

Assessment items were then developed to reflect the intentions of the frameworks and were piloted in a Field Trial in all participating countries before a final set of items was selected for the PISA 2009 Main Study. Tables A5.1, A5.2 and A5.3 show the distribution of PISA 2009 assessment items according to the various dimensions of the PISA frameworks.

Due attention was paid to reflecting the national, cultural and linguistic variety among OECD countries. As part of this effort the PISA Consortium used professional test item development teams in several different countries. In addition to the items that were developed by the international experts working with the PISA Consortium, assessment material was contributed by participating countries. The Consortium's multi-national team of test developers deemed a substantial amount of this submitted material as appropriate given the requirements laid out by the PISA assessment frameworks. As a result, the item pool included assessment items from Australia, Belgium, Canada, China, Colombia, Finland, France, Germany, Greece, Hungary, Japan, Korea, Mexico, the Netherlands, New Zealand, Norway, Portugal, Serbia, Sweden, Switzerland and the United States.

[Part 1/1]

Table A5.1 **Distribution of items by the dimensions of the PISA framework for the assessment of reading**

	Number of items	Number of multiple-choice items	Number of complex multiple-choice items	Number of closed-constructed response items	Number of open-constructed response items	Number of short response items
Distribution of reading items by format						
Continuous	81	36	6	4	31	4
Non-continuous	38	10	3	7	12	6
Mixed	7	4	1	0	1	1
Multiple	5	0	2	2	1	0
Total	**131**	**50**	**12**	**13**	**45**	**11**
Distribution of reading items by aspect of reading task						
Access and retrieve	31	6	3	9	3	10
Integrate and interpret	67	38	6	4	18	1
Reflect and evaluate	33	8	1	0	24	0
Total	**131**	**52**	**10**	**13**	**45**	**11**
Distribution of reading items by situation						
Personal	37	10	2	5	17	3
Public	35	19	2	2	10	2
Occupational	21	4	3	3	10	1
Educational	38	19	3	3	8	5
Total	**131**	**52**	**10**	**13**	**45**	**11**

StatLink ▄□▄ http://dx.doi.org/10.1787/888932343247

[Part 1/1]

Table A5.2   Distribution of items by the dimensions of the PISA framework for the assessment of mathematics

	Number of items	Number of multiple-choice items	Number of complex multiple-choice items	Number of closed-constructed response items	Number of open-constructed response items	Number of short response items
Distribution of mathematics items by topic						
Quantity	11	3	2	2	0	4
Space and shape	8	2	1	1	3	1
Change and relationships	9	1	2	0	5	1
Uncertainty	7	3	2	0	0	2
Total	35	9	7	3	8	8
Distribution of mathematics items by competency cluster						
Reproduction	9	5	0	1	1	2
Connection	18	1	6	1	4	6
Reflection	8	3	1	1	3	0
Total	35	9	7	3	8	8
Distribution of mathematics items by situation or context						
Personal	4	3	1	0	0	0
Public	13	5	2	1	2	3
Occupational	1	0	0	0	0	1
Educational	4	0	2	2	0	0
Scientific	12	1	2	0	5	4
Intra-mathematical	1	0	0	0	1	0
Total	35	9	7	3	8	8

StatLink ⫘ http://dx.doi.org/10.1787/888932343247

[Part 1/1]

Table A5.3   Distribution of items by the dimensions of the PISA framework for the assessment of science

	Number of items	Number of multiple-choice items	Number of complex multiple-choice items	Number of closed-constructed response items	Number of open-constructed response items	Number of short response items
Distribution of science items by content area						
Knowledge of science "Physical systems"	6	3	2	1	0	0
Knowledge of science "Living systems"	9	2	3	0	4	0
Knowledge of science "Earth and space"	7	3	2	0	2	0
Knowledge of science "Technology systems"	4	1	2	0	1	0
Knowledge about science "Scientific enquiry"	14	4	6	0	4	0
Knowledge about science "Scientific explanations"	13	5	2	0	6	0
Total	53	18	17	1	17	0
Distribution of science items by science competencies						
Identifying scientific issues	13	4	6	0	3	0
Explaining phenomena scientifically	22	8	7	1	6	0
Using scientific evidence	18	6	4	0	8	0
Total	53	18	17	1	17	0
Distribution of science items by situation or context						
Personal	12	5	4	1	2	0
Social	30	10	8	0	12	0
Global	11	3	5	0	3	0
Total	53	18	17	1	17	0
Total	131	52	10	13	45	11

StatLink ⫘ http://dx.doi.org/10.1787/888932343247

Each item included in the assessment pool was rated by each country: *i)* for potential cultural, gender or other bias; *ii)* for relevance to 15-year-olds in school and non-school contexts; and *iii)* for familiarity and level of interest. A first consultation of countries on the item pool was undertaken as part of the process of developing the Field Trial assessment instruments. A second consultation was undertaken after the Field Trial to assist in the final selection of items for the Main Study.

Following the Field Trial, in which all items were tested in all participating countries, test developers and expert groups considered a variety of aspects in selecting the items for the Main Study: *i)* the results from the Field Trial, *ii)* the outcome of the item review from countries, and *iii)* queries received during the Field Trial marking process. The test developers and expert groups selected a final set of items in September 2008 which, following a period of negotiation, was adopted by participating countries at both scientific and policy levels.

The Main Survey included 37 reading units with 131 test items. 19 of these units originated from material submitted by participating countries. 16 of the units came from one or other of the Consortium teams, and two originated as IALS material. The Main Survey instruments also included 24 mathematics units (35 items) and 18 science units (53 items).

Five item types were used in the PISA assessment instruments:

- *Open-constructed response items:* These items required students to construct a longer response, allowing for the possibility of a broad range of divergent, individual responses and differing viewpoints. These items usually asked students to relate information or ideas in the stimulus text to their own experience or opinions, with the acceptability depending less on the position taken by the student than on the ability to use what they had read when justifying or explaining that position. For selected items, partial credit was awarded for partially correct or less complete answers. All of these items were marked by hand.

- *Closed-constructed response items:* These items required students to construct their own responses, there being a limited range of acceptable answers. Most of these items were scored dichotomously with a few items included in the marking process.

- *Short-response items:* These items required students to provide a brief answer, as in the closed-constructed response items, but here there was a wider range of possible answers. These items were marked by hand, thus allowing for partial credit as well as dichotomous scoring.

- *Complex multiple-choice items:* These items required students to make a series of choices, usually binary. Students indicated their answer by circling a word or short phrase (for example "yes" or "no") for each point. These items were scored dichotomously for each choice, yielding the possibility of full or partial credit for the whole item.

- *Multiple-choice items:* These items required students to circle a letter to indicate one choice among four or five alternatives, each of which might be a number, a word, a phrase or a sentence. They were scored dichotomously.

PISA 2009 was designed to yield group-level information in a broad range of content. The PISA assessment of reading included material allowing for a total of 270 minutes of assessment time. The mathematics and science assessments each comprised 90 minutes of assessment time. Each student, however, sat assessments lasting a total of 120 minutes.

In order to cover the intended broad range of content while meeting the limit of 120 minutes of individual assessment time, the assessment in each assessment area was divided into clusters, organised into thirteen booklets for each country. There were seven 30-minute reading clusters, three 30-minute clusters for mathematics and three 30-minute clusters for science. Since reading was the major domain in PISA 2009, every student was administered some reading items as part of the assessment.

Countries that had demonstrated a low mean proficiency in reading in previous PISA cycles (or, if they were new countries, were expected to perform at a relatively low level on the basis of their Field Trial results) were offered the option of replacing two of the standard reading clusters with two easier clusters of reading items. Nevertheless, because five of the seven reading clusters were administered in common across all countries, the performance of countries opting for the easier clusters could be measured on the same scale as that of the countries administering the standard assessments.

This assessment design was balanced so that each item cluster appeared four times, once in each of four possible locations in a booklet. Further, each cluster appeared once with each other cluster. The final design, therefore, ensured that a representative sample responded to each cluster of items.

For further information on the development of the PISA assessment instruments and the PISA assessment design, see the PISA 2009 Technical Report (OECD, forthcoming).

ANNEX A6
RELIABILITY OF THE CODING OF RESPONSES TO OPEN-ENDED ITEMS

The PISA assessment instruments contain assessment items presented in a mixture of format-types, including items for which student responses can be scored automatically (such as multiple-choice items) and open-ended items for which a trained coder must intervene manually to assign student responses to the pre-defined response categories. This requirement for manual coding of student responses to certain assessment items, performed by coders trained at the national level, introduces the possibility of national-level bias in the resulting PISA scores: coders in Country A may interpret and apply the coding instructions more or less leniently or harshly in comparison with coders in Country B.

The process of coding responses to open-ended items was an important step in ensuring the quality and comparability of PISA results.

Detailed guidelines contributed to a response coding process that was accurate and consistent across countries. The coding guidelines consisted of coding manuals, training materials for recruiting coders, and workshop materials used for training of national coders. Before national training, the PISA Consortium organised training sessions to present the material and to train the coding co-ordinators from the participating countries. The latter were then responsible for training their national coders.

For each assessment item, the relevant coding manual described the aim of the question and how to code students' responses to each item. This description included the credit labels – full credit, partial credit or no credit – attached to the possible categories of responses. PISA 2009 also included a system of double-digit coding for some mathematics and science items in which the first digit represented the score and the second digit represented different strategies or approaches that students used to solve the problem. The second digit generated national profiles of student strategies and misconceptions. By way of illustration, the coding manuals also included real examples of students' responses (drawn from the Field Trial) accompanied by a rationale for their classification.

In each country, a sub-sample of 100 assessment booklets of each type was coded independently by 4 coders and examined by the PISA Consortium. In order to examine the consistency of this coding process in more detail, the PISA Consortium conducted an inter-coder reliability study on the sub-sample of these 100 booklets. For details, see the *PISA 2009 Technical Report* (OECD, forthcoming).

At the between-country level, an International Coding Review (ICR) was implemented to check on the consistency of applying response coding standards across all participating countries. The objective of this study was to estimate potential bias (either leniency or harshness) in the coding standards applied in each National Centre, and to express this potential bias in "PISA units". The ICR was implemented in two stages as described below.

Overview of International Coding Review procedures

An International Coding Review (ICR) was conducted as one of the PISA 2009 quality control procedures in order to investigate the possibility of systematic differences among countries in the coding of open-ended items. The objective of this review was to estimate potential bias (either leniency or harshness) in each country's PISA reading literacy results, and to express this potential bias in the same units that are used to report country performance on the PISA reading scales.

For the PISA 2009 ICR, the Consortium identified a set of items for inclusion in the study. Two booklets were chosen: Booklet 8 (containing eight manually coded reading items from Cluster R2) and Booklet 12 (containing six manually coded reading items from Cluster R7). These items were also among those used previously in the multiple-coding study and had been coded four times by national coders as part of that study. The code assigned by the fourth national coder was entered into PISA data and is referred to as the "reported code".

For each country-by-language unit from a National Centre's data, up to 80 PISA records[1] (excluding those with a high number of missing responses for the multiple-coded items) were selected by the PISA Consortium from the data from Booklets 8 and 12. The student IDs of the selected records were sent to the National Centres in an Excel file.

In the PISA National Centres, the corresponding booklets were located and scanned and these scanned images were sent to the PISA Consortium's linguistic verification expert. Where scanning was not possible, the original booklets were sent by post. The PISA Consortium's linguistic verification expert then erased the national coders' marks on all received copies of the booklets.

Coding of each student's response was then carried out a fifth time by a member of a team of independent reviewers who had been trained specifically for this task. These independent reviewers had previously been involved as part of the international translation verification team. The code assigned by the independent reviewer is referred to as the "verifier code".

. . . .

1. For some adjudicated entities or certain languages all booklets were selected if, for a variety of reasons, there were fewer than 80 PISA records per booklet per country-by-language unit in the multiple coding exercise.

Reported and verifier scores were then calculated. These were obtained by scaling all the ICR students' data from all countries from Cluster R2 in Booklet 8 and Cluster R7 in Booklet 12 (including automatically scored and open-ended responses). Scaling using the reported code for the open-ended responses produced the "reported score". Scaling using the verifier code for the open-ended responses produced the "verifier score".

Each country's scores were then extracted and the reported scores and the verifier scores were compared. This comparison involved calculating the mean difference between the reported scores and the verified scores for each country for both booklets.[2] A 95% confidence interval was then calculated around the mean difference. If the confidence interval contained 0, the differences in score were considered as not statistically significant. Two hypothetical examples in Table A6.1 show that Country A was initially found to be lenient (CNT aaa: positive confidence interval: [5.93; 24.41]) and Country B was found to be neither lenient nor harsh (CNT bbb confidence interval [-7.16; 4.641] contains 0).

Table A6.1 Examples of an initially lenient result and a neutral result

CNT	Language	Mean difference between reported and verifier scores	N	Standard deviation	Confidence interval		Leniency(+) Harshness(-)
					Low	High	
aaa	aaaa	15.17	80	41.53	5.93	24.41	
bbb	bbbb	-1.26	78	26.17	-7.16	4.641	+

StatLink ⟡⟡⟡ http://dx.doi.org/10.1787/888932343266

In addition, two types of inconsistencies between national codes and verifier codes were flagged:

- when the verifier code was compared with each of the four national codes and fewer than two matches were observed; and
- when the average raw score of the four national coders was at least 0.5 points higher or lower than the score based on the verifier code.

Cases are flagged if at least one of these conditions were met. Examples of flagged cases are given in Table A6.2.

Table A6.2 Examples of flagged cases

CNT	StudentID	Question	Coder 1	Coder 2	Coder 3	Coder 4	Verifier	Flag (Y/N)
xxx	Xxxxx00001	R104Q05	0	1	1	1	1	N
xxx	Xxxxx00012	R104Q05	1	1	1	1	0	Y
xxx	Xxxxx00031	R104Q05	1	1	1	0	0	Y
xxx	Xxxxx00014	R104Q05	0	1	1	2	0	Y
xxx	Xxxxx00020	R104Q05	1	0	2	1	2	Y
xxx	Xxxxx00025	R104Q05	2	0	2	0	2	Y

StatLink ⟡⟡⟡ http://dx.doi.org/10.1787/888932343266

For each country, the percentage of flagged cases (Y) was calculated for each item in each booklet. If more than 10% of cases were flagged for a country, the item was highlighted. In Table A6.3, two hypothetical countries are presented. Country A (aaa) has a high percentage of flagged records for four out of six items. This often corresponds to either leniency or harshness of coding. Country B (bbb) has only two items with a comparatively high percentage of flagged records. This usually does not translate into leniency or harshness.

Table A6.3 Hypothetical examples of percentages of flagged cases for Booklet 12

Country	R432Q05	R446Q06	R456Q02	R456Q06	R460Q01	R466Q02	Total	N
aaa	26.25	8.75	15.00	11.25	17.50	2.50	13.54	80
bbb	5.13	11.54	10.26	1.28	7.69	1.28	6.20	78

StatLink ⟡⟡⟡ http://dx.doi.org/10.1787/888932343266

Items R111Q02B and R111Q06B in Booklet 8 had a high percentage of disagreement in nearly all countries. Therefore these items were excluded from calculations of leniency/harshness and they were investigated separately.

After excluding Items R111Q02B and R111Q06B, a country was selected for further adjudication if it was found initially to be lenient or harsh for both booklets. This involved additional coding by senior Consortium staff of a random sample of 30 students' responses from each identified country. The sampled student responses were translated back into English, and the responses together with the four national codes and the verifier code for these selected cases were reviewed by the international adjudicator.

The systematic harshness or leniency of coder on the national PISA score for each domain is confirmed if the percentage of agreement between verifier and adjudicator is above 50% for each booklet. The results of the International Coding Review will be reported in the *PISA 2009 Technical Report* (OECD, forthcoming).

• •

2. These results are further investigated by a Consortium adjudicator to confirm that the leniency or harshness was found to be on the national coder's side rather than a lenient or harsh international verifier.

Annex B

TABLES OF RESULTS
All tables in Annex B are available on line

Annex B1: Results for countries and economies

Annex B2: Results for regions within countries

Adjudicated regions
Data for which adherence to the PISA sampling
standards and international comparability
was internationally adjudicated.

Non-adjudicated regions
Data for which adherence to the PISA sampling
standards at subnational levels was assessed
by the countries concerned.

In these countries, adherence to the PISA sampling
standards and international comparability was
internationally adjudicated only for the combined set
of all subnational entities.

Note: Unless otherwise specified, all the data contained in the following tables are drawn from the OECD PISA Database.

ANNEX B1
RESULTS FOR COUNTRIES AND ECONOMIES

[Part 1/1]

Table I.2.1 **Percentage of students at each proficiency level on the reading scale**

	Below Level 1b (less than 262.04 score points)		Level 1b (from 262.04 to less than 334.75 score points)		Level 1a (from 334.75 to less than 407.47 score points)		Level 2 (from 407.47 to less than 480.18 score points)		Level 3 (from 480.18 to less than 552.89 score points)		Level 4 (from 552.89 to less than 625.61 score points)		Level 5 (from 625.61 to less than 698.32 score points)		Level 6 (above 698.32 score points)	
	%	S.E.	%	S.E.	%	S.E.	%	S.E.	%	S.E.	%	S.E.	%	S.E.	%	S.E.
OECD																
Australia	1.0	(0.1)	3.3	(0.3)	10.0	(0.4)	20.4	(0.6)	28.5	(0.7)	24.1	(0.7)	10.7	(0.5)	2.1	(0.3)
Austria	1.9	(0.4)	8.1	(0.8)	17.5	(1.0)	24.1	(1.0)	26.0	(0.9)	17.4	(0.9)	4.5	(0.4)	0.4	(0.1)
Belgium	1.1	(0.3)	4.7	(0.5)	11.9	(0.6)	20.3	(0.7)	25.8	(0.9)	24.9	(0.7)	10.1	(0.5)	1.1	(0.2)
Canada	0.4	(0.1)	2.0	(0.2)	7.9	(0.3)	20.2	(0.6)	30.0	(0.7)	26.8	(0.6)	11.0	(0.4)	1.8	(0.2)
Chile	1.3	(0.2)	7.4	(0.8)	21.9	(1.0)	33.2	(1.1)	25.6	(1.1)	9.3	(0.7)	1.3	(0.2)	0.0	(0.0)
Czech Republic	0.8	(0.3)	5.5	(0.6)	16.8	(1.1)	27.4	(1.0)	27.0	(1.0)	17.4	(1.0)	4.7	(0.5)	0.4	(0.1)
Denmark	0.4	(0.1)	3.1	(0.3)	11.7	(0.7)	26.0	(0.9)	33.1	(1.2)	20.9	(1.1)	4.4	(0.4)	0.3	(0.1)
Estonia	0.3	(0.1)	2.4	(0.4)	10.6	(0.9)	25.6	(1.3)	33.8	(1.0)	21.2	(0.8)	5.4	(0.5)	0.6	(0.2)
Finland	0.2	(0.1)	1.5	(0.2)	6.4	(0.4)	16.7	(0.6)	30.1	(0.8)	30.6	(0.9)	12.9	(0.7)	1.6	(0.2)
France	2.3	(0.5)	5.6	(0.5)	11.8	(0.8)	21.1	(1.0)	27.2	(1.0)	22.4	(1.1)	8.5	(0.8)	1.1	(0.3)
Germany	0.8	(0.2)	4.4	(0.5)	13.3	(0.8)	22.2	(0.9)	28.8	(1.1)	22.8	(0.9)	7.0	(0.6)	0.6	(0.2)
Greece	1.4	(0.4)	5.6	(0.9)	14.3	(1.1)	25.6	(1.1)	29.3	(1.2)	18.2	(1.0)	5.0	(0.5)	0.6	(0.2)
Hungary	0.6	(0.2)	4.7	(0.8)	12.3	(1.0)	23.8	(1.2)	31.0	(1.3)	21.6	(1.1)	5.8	(0.7)	0.3	(0.1)
Iceland	1.1	(0.2)	4.2	(0.4)	11.5	(0.7)	22.2	(0.8)	30.6	(0.9)	21.9	(0.8)	7.5	(0.6)	1.0	(0.2)
Ireland	1.5	(0.4)	3.9	(0.5)	11.8	(0.7)	23.3	(1.0)	30.6	(0.9)	21.9	(0.9)	6.3	(0.5)	0.7	(0.2)
Israel	3.9	(0.7)	8.0	(0.7)	14.7	(0.6)	22.5	(1.0)	25.5	(0.9)	18.1	(0.7)	6.4	(0.5)	1.0	(0.2)
Italy	1.4	(0.2)	5.2	(0.3)	14.4	(0.5)	24.0	(0.5)	28.9	(0.6)	20.2	(0.5)	5.4	(0.3)	0.4	(0.1)
Japan	1.3	(0.4)	3.4	(0.5)	8.9	(0.7)	18.0	(0.8)	28.0	(0.9)	27.0	(0.9)	11.5	(0.7)	1.9	(0.4)
Korea	0.2	(0.2)	0.9	(0.3)	4.7	(0.6)	15.4	(1.0)	33.0	(1.2)	32.9	(1.4)	11.9	(1.0)	1.0	(0.2)
Luxembourg	3.1	(0.3)	7.3	(0.4)	15.7	(0.6)	24.0	(0.7)	27.0	(0.6)	17.3	(0.6)	5.2	(0.4)	0.5	(0.2)
Mexico	3.2	(0.3)	11.4	(0.5)	25.5	(0.6)	33.0	(0.6)	21.2	(0.6)	5.3	(0.4)	0.4	(0.1)	0.0	(0.0)
Netherlands	0.1	(0.1)	1.8	(0.3)	12.5	(1.4)	24.7	(1.5)	27.6	(1.2)	23.5	(1.7)	9.1	(1.0)	0.7	(0.2)
New Zealand	0.9	(0.2)	3.2	(0.4)	10.2	(0.6)	19.3	(0.8)	25.8	(0.8)	24.8	(0.8)	12.9	(0.8)	2.9	(0.4)
Norway	0.5	(0.1)	3.4	(0.4)	11.0	(0.7)	23.6	(0.8)	30.9	(0.9)	22.1	(1.2)	7.6	(0.9)	0.8	(0.2)
Poland	0.6	(0.1)	3.1	(0.3)	11.3	(0.7)	24.5	(1.1)	31.0	(1.0)	22.3	(1.0)	6.5	(0.5)	0.7	(0.1)
Portugal	0.6	(0.1)	4.0	(0.4)	13.0	(1.0)	26.4	(1.1)	31.6	(1.1)	19.6	(0.9)	4.6	(0.5)	0.2	(0.1)
Slovak Republic	0.8	(0.3)	5.6	(0.6)	15.9	(0.8)	28.1	(1.0)	28.5	(1.1)	16.7	(0.8)	4.2	(0.5)	0.3	(0.1)
Slovenia	0.8	(0.1)	5.2	(0.3)	15.2	(0.5)	25.6	(0.7)	29.2	(0.9)	19.3	(0.8)	4.3	(0.5)	0.3	(0.1)
Spain	1.2	(0.2)	4.7	(0.4)	13.6	(0.6)	26.8	(0.8)	32.6	(1.0)	17.7	(0.7)	3.2	(0.3)	0.2	(0.1)
Sweden	1.5	(0.3)	4.3	(0.4)	11.7	(0.7)	23.5	(1.0)	29.8	(1.0)	20.3	(0.9)	7.7	(0.6)	1.3	(0.3)
Switzerland	0.7	(0.2)	4.1	(0.4)	12.1	(0.6)	22.7	(0.7)	29.7	(0.8)	22.6	(0.8)	7.4	(0.7)	0.7	(0.2)
Turkey	0.8	(0.2)	5.6	(0.6)	18.1	(1.0)	32.2	(1.2)	29.1	(1.1)	12.4	(1.1)	1.8	(0.4)	0.0	(0.0)
United Kingdom	1.0	(0.2)	4.1	(0.4)	13.4	(0.6)	24.9	(0.7)	28.8	(0.8)	19.8	(0.8)	7.0	(0.5)	1.0	(0.2)
United States	0.6	(0.1)	4.0	(0.4)	13.1	(0.8)	24.4	(0.9)	27.6	(0.8)	20.6	(0.9)	8.4	(0.8)	1.5	(0.4)
OECD total	1.1	(0.1)	4.8	(0.1)	13.8	(0.3)	24.4	(0.3)	27.9	(0.3)	19.9	(0.3)	7.0	(0.2)	1.0	(0.1)
OECD average	1.1	(0.0)	4.6	(0.1)	13.1	(0.1)	24.0	(0.2)	28.9	(0.2)	20.7	(0.2)	6.8	(0.1)	0.8	(0.0)
Partners																
Albania	11.3	(0.9)	18.7	(1.3)	26.6	(1.2)	25.6	(1.3)	14.4	(1.2)	3.1	(0.5)	0.2	(0.1)	0.0	c
Argentina	10.8	(1.1)	15.8	(1.3)	25.0	(1.3)	25.4	(1.2)	16.0	(1.0)	6.0	(0.8)	0.9	(0.2)	0.1	(0.1)
Azerbaijan	9.7	(1.1)	26.1	(1.1)	36.9	(1.2)	21.5	(1.2)	5.3	(0.8)	0.5	(0.2)	0.0	(0.0)	0.0	c
Brazil	5.0	(0.4)	16.0	(0.7)	28.6	(0.8)	27.1	(0.8)	15.9	(0.9)	6.1	(0.5)	1.2	(0.2)	0.1	(0.1)
Bulgaria	8.0	(1.1)	12.9	(1.4)	20.1	(1.4)	23.4	(1.1)	21.8	(1.4)	11.0	(1.1)	2.6	(0.5)	0.2	(0.1)
Colombia	4.2	(0.7)	13.9	(1.0)	29.0	(1.2)	30.6	(1.1)	17.1	(1.0)	4.6	(0.5)	0.5	(0.2)	0.0	(0.0)
Croatia	1.0	(0.2)	5.0	(0.4)	16.5	(1.0)	27.4	(1.0)	30.6	(1.2)	16.4	(1.0)	3.1	(0.4)	0.1	(0.1)
Dubai (UAE)	3.7	(0.2)	9.4	(0.5)	17.9	(0.5)	25.4	(0.7)	23.5	(0.8)	14.8	(0.7)	4.8	(0.5)	0.5	(0.2)
Hong Kong-China	0.2	(0.1)	1.5	(0.3)	6.6	(0.6)	16.1	(0.8)	31.4	(0.9)	31.8	(0.9)	11.2	(0.7)	1.2	(0.3)
Indonesia	1.7	(0.4)	14.1	(1.3)	37.6	(1.6)	34.3	(1.4)	11.2	(1.3)	1.0	(0.3)	0.0	c	0.0	c
Jordan	6.9	(0.6)	13.6	(0.8)	27.6	(1.0)	31.8	(1.0)	16.5	(1.0)	3.4	(0.4)	0.2	(0.1)	0.0	c
Kazakhstan	7.5	(0.7)	20.4	(1.0)	30.7	(0.9)	24.1	(0.9)	13.1	(0.9)	3.7	(0.5)	0.4	(0.1)	0.0	c
Kyrgyzstan	29.8	(1.2)	29.7	(0.9)	23.8	(0.9)	11.5	(0.8)	4.2	(0.6)	1.0	(0.3)	0.1	(0.1)	0.0	c
Latvia	0.4	(0.1)	3.3	(0.6)	13.9	(1.0)	28.8	(1.5)	33.5	(1.2)	17.2	(1.0)	2.9	(0.4)	0.1	c
Liechtenstein	0.0	c	2.8	(1.2)	12.8	(1.8)	24.0	(2.8)	31.1	(2.8)	24.6	(2.3)	4.2	(1.4)	0.4	c
Lithuania	0.9	(0.3)	5.5	(0.6)	17.9	(0.9)	30.0	(1.0)	28.6	(0.9)	14.1	(0.8)	2.8	(0.4)	0.1	(0.1)
Macao-China	0.3	(0.1)	2.6	(0.3)	12.0	(0.4)	30.6	(0.6)	34.8	(0.7)	16.9	(0.5)	2.8	(0.2)	0.1	(0.1)
Montenegro	5.9	(0.5)	15.8	(0.8)	27.8	(0.8)	28.0	(0.9)	16.8	(0.8)	5.0	(0.5)	0.6	(0.2)	0.0	c
Panama	13.3	(1.8)	23.1	(1.8)	28.9	(1.8)	20.7	(1.4)	10.1	(1.4)	3.4	(0.7)	0.5	(0.2)	0.0	c
Peru	14.1	(0.9)	22.0	(1.0)	28.7	(1.1)	22.1	(0.9)	10.1	(0.9)	2.6	(0.5)	0.4	(0.2)	0.0	(0.0)
Qatar	17.8	(0.3)	22.4	(0.5)	23.2	(0.6)	18.3	(0.4)	11.1	(0.5)	5.4	(0.3)	1.5	(0.2)	0.2	(0.1)
Romania	4.1	(0.7)	12.7	(1.1)	23.6	(1.2)	31.6	(1.3)	21.2	(1.3)	6.1	(0.7)	0.7	(0.2)	0.0	c
Russian Federation	1.6	(0.3)	6.8	(0.6)	19.0	(0.8)	31.6	(1.0)	26.8	(0.9)	11.1	(0.7)	2.8	(0.4)	0.3	(0.1)
Serbia	2.0	(0.4)	8.8	(0.7)	22.1	(0.9)	33.2	(1.0)	25.3	(1.0)	7.9	(0.6)	0.8	(0.2)	0.0	(0.0)
Shanghai-China	0.1	(0.0)	0.6	(0.1)	3.4	(0.5)	13.3	(0.8)	28.5	(1.2)	34.7	(1.0)	17.0	(1.0)	2.4	(0.4)
Singapore	0.4	(0.1)	2.7	(0.3)	9.3	(0.5)	18.5	(0.6)	27.6	(0.8)	25.7	(0.7)	13.1	(0.5)	2.6	(0.3)
Chinese Taipei	0.7	(0.2)	3.5	(0.4)	11.4	(0.6)	24.6	(0.8)	33.5	(1.1)	21.0	(1.0)	4.8	(0.8)	0.4	(0.2)
Thailand	1.2	(0.3)	9.9	(0.8)	31.7	(1.1)	36.8	(1.2)	16.7	(0.8)	3.3	(0.5)	0.3	(0.2)	0.0	c
Trinidad and Tobago	9.6	(0.5)	14.2	(0.6)	21.0	(0.8)	25.0	(0.9)	19.0	(0.9)	8.9	(0.5)	2.1	(0.3)	0.2	(0.1)
Tunisia	5.5	(0.5)	15.0	(0.8)	29.6	(1.1)	31.5	(1.2)	15.1	(1.0)	3.1	(0.5)	0.2	(0.1)	0.0	c
Uruguay	5.5	(0.6)	12.5	(0.7)	23.9	(0.7)	28.0	(0.7)	20.3	(0.7)	8.1	(0.5)	1.7	(0.3)	0.1	(0.1)

StatLink 🔗 http://dx.doi.org/10.1787/888932343285

[Part 1/2]

Table I.2.2 **Percentage of students at each proficiency level on the reading scale, by gender**

	Boys – Proficiency levels															
	Below Level 1b (less than 262.04 score points)		Level 1b (from 262.04 to less than 334.75 score points)		Level 1a (from 334.75 to less than 407.47 score points)		Level 2 (from 407.47 to less than 480.18 score points)		Level 3 (from 480.18 to less than 552.89 score points)		Level 4 (from 552.89 to less than 625.61 score points)		Level 5 (from 625.61 to less than 698.32 score points)		Level 6 (above 698.32 score points)	
	%	S.E.	%	S.E.	%	S.E.	%	S.E.	%	S.E.	%	S.E.	%	S.E.	%	S.E.
OECD																
Australia	1.5	(0.2)	4.9	(0.5)	13.2	(0.6)	22.5	(0.8)	27.4	(0.8)	20.6	(0.9)	8.3	(0.6)	1.6	(0.3)
Austria	3.1	(0.6)	10.8	(1.2)	21.3	(1.4)	25.1	(1.3)	23.2	(1.2)	13.7	(1.3)	2.7	(0.5)	0.1	(0.1)
Belgium	1.7	(0.3)	6.2	(0.7)	13.7	(0.8)	22.0	(0.9)	24.7	(1.0)	22.4	(1.0)	8.6	(0.7)	0.8	(0.3)
Canada	0.6	(0.1)	3.0	(0.3)	10.8	(0.6)	22.9	(0.8)	29.7	(0.9)	23.5	(0.7)	8.3	(0.5)	1.0	(0.2)
Chile	1.9	(0.4)	9.4	(1.1)	24.8	(1.2)	32.1	(1.4)	22.7	(1.4)	8.1	(0.8)	1.0	(0.3)	0.0	(0.0)
Czech Republic	1.4	(0.4)	7.7	(0.9)	21.7	(1.6)	29.9	(1.7)	24.4	(1.5)	12.2	(1.0)	2.6	(0.4)	0.2	(0.1)
Denmark	0.6	(0.2)	4.3	(0.5)	14.1	(1.1)	29.2	(1.3)	31.6	(1.5)	17.0	(1.4)	3.0	(0.6)	0.2	(0.1)
Estonia	0.6	(0.3)	3.7	(0.6)	14.6	(1.3)	30.3	(1.5)	32.0	(1.4)	15.4	(1.0)	3.1	(0.6)	0.2	(0.1)
Finland	0.3	(0.1)	2.5	(0.4)	10.1	(0.7)	22.7	(1.0)	32.3	(1.3)	23.9	(1.2)	7.5	(0.8)	0.6	(0.2)
France	3.4	(0.7)	8.1	(0.9)	14.1	(1.2)	23.3	(1.4)	25.4	(1.5)	18.6	(1.3)	6.3	(0.8)	0.7	(0.3)
Germany	1.3	(0.4)	6.3	(0.7)	16.4	(1.1)	24.3	(1.3)	28.5	(1.4)	18.8	(1.3)	4.1	(0.5)	0.3	(0.1)
Greece	2.4	(0.6)	8.6	(1.2)	18.7	(1.4)	27.3	(1.2)	26.1	(1.9)	13.5	(1.2)	3.2	(0.7)	0.2	(0.1)
Hungary	0.9	(0.4)	6.6	(1.1)	16.1	(1.4)	25.6	(1.7)	29.7	(1.4)	17.3	(1.4)	3.8	(0.7)	0.1	(0.1)
Iceland	1.8	(0.3)	6.6	(0.6)	15.5	(0.9)	24.4	(1.1)	28.2	(1.1)	18.0	(1.1)	5.1	(0.7)	0.6	(0.3)
Ireland	2.5	(0.6)	5.7	(0.7)	15.0	(1.3)	25.0	(1.6)	29.5	(1.3)	17.8	(1.6)	4.1	(0.7)	0.4	(0.2)
Israel	6.2	(1.1)	10.8	(1.0)	17.0	(1.0)	22.9	(1.1)	21.6	(1.0)	15.1	(1.0)	5.5	(0.8)	0.8	(0.2)
Italy	2.3	(0.4)	7.7	(0.5)	18.9	(0.7)	25.9	(0.8)	25.4	(0.7)	15.9	(0.6)	3.6	(0.3)	0.2	(0.1)
Japan	2.0	(0.7)	5.0	(0.8)	11.9	(1.0)	20.3	(1.2)	26.7	(1.5)	24.1	(1.4)	8.9	(0.9)	1.2	(0.4)
Korea	0.4	(0.3)	1.4	(0.5)	7.0	(1.0)	19.3	(1.6)	34.3	(1.6)	28.4	(1.9)	8.7	(1.1)	0.7	(0.2)
Luxembourg	4.7	(0.5)	9.8	(0.7)	18.4	(1.1)	23.9	(1.2)	25.2	(0.9)	14.4	(0.8)	3.5	(0.4)	0.2	(0.1)
Mexico	4.4	(0.5)	14.2	(0.6)	27.6	(0.7)	31.5	(0.7)	17.8	(0.7)	4.2	(0.4)	0.3	(0.1)	0.0	(0.0)
Netherlands	0.1	(0.1)	2.7	(0.5)	15.1	(1.4)	26.5	(1.6)	26.9	(1.5)	20.9	(1.7)	7.3	(1.0)	0.5	(0.2)
New Zealand	1.7	(0.4)	5.1	(0.7)	13.9	(0.9)	21.3	(1.0)	25.7	(1.1)	20.6	(1.1)	10.1	(1.1)	1.8	(0.4)
Norway	1.0	(0.3)	5.5	(0.6)	14.9	(0.9)	27.4	(1.2)	28.8	(1.1)	17.4	(1.1)	4.5	(0.8)	0.5	(0.2)
Poland	1.2	(0.3)	5.4	(0.6)	16.1	(1.0)	28.3	(1.3)	27.9	(1.3)	16.9	(1.0)	4.0	(0.7)	0.3	(0.2)
Portugal	1.1	(0.2)	6.1	(0.7)	17.5	(1.2)	28.3	(1.3)	28.3	(1.4)	15.4	(1.2)	3.1	(0.5)	0.2	(0.1)
Slovak Republic	1.1	(0.4)	8.9	(1.0)	22.0	(1.3)	30.6	(1.6)	23.4	(1.5)	11.5	(0.9)	2.5	(0.4)	0.1	(0.1)
Slovenia	1.5	(0.2)	8.4	(0.6)	21.3	(0.8)	27.3	(0.9)	25.4	(1.0)	14.0	(0.8)	1.9	(0.5)	0.2	(0.2)
Spain	1.7	(0.3)	6.2	(0.5)	16.5	(0.8)	28.9	(0.9)	30.0	(1.2)	14.2	(0.8)	2.4	(0.3)	0.1	(0.0)
Sweden	2.3	(0.4)	6.5	(0.6)	15.4	(1.1)	25.8	(1.4)	27.8	(1.2)	16.3	(1.0)	5.3	(0.6)	0.7	(0.2)
Switzerland	1.0	(0.2)	5.7	(0.6)	15.3	(0.9)	25.7	(1.0)	28.7	(1.0)	18.4	(1.0)	4.6	(0.6)	0.5	(0.2)
Turkey	1.2	(0.3)	8.6	(0.9)	23.6	(1.4)	32.8	(1.6)	24.5	(1.5)	8.4	(1.1)	0.8	(0.3)	0.0	c
United Kingdom	1.5	(0.3)	5.6	(0.6)	16.0	(1.0)	25.8	(1.1)	27.0	(1.1)	17.2	(1.1)	6.1	(0.6)	0.9	(0.3)
United States	0.9	(0.3)	5.4	(0.7)	15.2	(1.0)	25.6	(1.3)	25.8	(1.1)	19.0	(1.3)	7.2	(0.8)	0.9	(0.5)
OECD total	1.7	(0.1)	6.6	(0.2)	16.7	(0.4)	25.9	(0.4)	26.0	(0.4)	17.1	(0.4)	5.4	(0.2)	0.6	(0.1)
OECD average	1.8	(0.1)	6.6	(0.1)	16.6	(0.2)	26.0	(0.2)	27.0	(0.2)	16.8	(0.2)	4.8	(0.1)	0.5	(0.0)
Partners																
Albania	17.5	(1.5)	24.4	(1.7)	27.2	(1.6)	19.7	(1.8)	9.7	(1.3)	1.5	(0.5)	0.0	(0.0)	0.0	c
Argentina	14.8	(1.5)	18.1	(1.9)	25.9	(1.6)	23.0	(1.3)	12.9	(1.2)	4.5	(0.8)	0.7	(0.2)	0.0	(0.1)
Azerbaijan	12.7	(1.3)	29.7	(1.4)	35.1	(1.5)	17.8	(1.5)	4.3	(0.7)	0.4	(0.2)	0.0	(0.0)	0.0	c
Brazil	7.1	(0.6)	19.5	(1.1)	29.9	(1.0)	24.2	(1.2)	13.2	(0.9)	5.1	(0.5)	0.9	(0.2)	0.1	(0.1)
Bulgaria	12.4	(1.6)	16.9	(1.6)	22.7	(1.7)	21.8	(1.5)	17.2	(1.6)	7.6	(1.0)	1.4	(0.5)	0.1	(0.1)
Colombia	4.6	(1.0)	14.8	(1.5)	30.1	(2.0)	30.0	(1.5)	15.9	(1.3)	4.1	(0.6)	0.5	(0.2)	0.0	(0.0)
Croatia	1.7	(0.4)	7.9	(0.7)	21.7	(1.4)	29.9	(1.5)	26.0	(1.6)	11.5	(1.1)	1.4	(0.3)	0.0	(0.1)
Dubai (UAE)	6.5	(0.4)	13.6	(0.8)	20.8	(0.8)	23.5	(1.0)	20.0	(1.3)	11.6	(1.1)	3.7	(0.6)	0.3	(0.2)
Hong Kong-China	0.4	(0.2)	2.1	(0.5)	8.8	(1.0)	18.7	(1.2)	33.2	(1.4)	27.9	(1.4)	8.1	(0.9)	0.8	(0.3)
Indonesia	2.8	(0.9)	19.5	(1.8)	43.2	(1.8)	27.2	(1.8)	6.9	(1.3)	0.4	(0.2)	0.0	c	0.0	c
Jordan	10.9	(1.1)	18.6	(1.2)	32.1	(1.5)	26.7	(1.7)	10.0	(1.1)	1.7	(0.4)	0.1	(0.1)	0.0	c
Kazakhstan	11.4	(0.9)	25.8	(1.3)	30.3	(1.1)	20.2	(1.1)	9.7	(0.9)	2.4	(0.4)	0.2	(0.1)	0.0	c
Kyrgyzstan	41.1	(1.7)	29.2	(1.2)	18.2	(1.1)	8.2	(0.8)	2.7	(0.5)	0.6	(0.3)	0.0	(0.0)	0.0	c
Latvia	0.7	(0.3)	5.6	(0.9)	20.3	(1.6)	31.8	(1.8)	29.0	(1.9)	11.1	(1.2)	1.5	(0.4)	0.0	(0.1)
Liechtenstein	0.0	c	4.5	(1.9)	16.8	(3.0)	26.2	(4.5)	29.3	(3.2)	20.2	(2.7)	2.9	(1.4)	0.2	(0.5)
Lithuania	1.6	(0.4)	9.0	(0.9)	24.8	(1.3)	32.7	(1.7)	22.8	(1.3)	8.1	(0.7)	0.9	(0.3)	0.0	(0.0)
Macao-China	0.4	(0.1)	3.9	(0.5)	16.2	(0.8)	33.8	(0.9)	31.7	(0.8)	12.3	(0.7)	1.6	(0.3)	0.1	(0.1)
Montenegro	9.4	(0.7)	20.8	(0.8)	31.3	(1.2)	23.9	(1.2)	11.6	(1.1)	2.8	(0.5)	0.3	(0.3)	0.0	c
Panama	16.2	(2.4)	26.0	(2.3)	29.4	(2.6)	19.3	(2.1)	7.0	(1.2)	1.8	(0.6)	0.3	(0.2)	0.0	c
Peru	16.2	(1.1)	24.4	(1.3)	29.1	(1.4)	19.9	(1.2)	7.8	(0.8)	2.1	(0.5)	0.5	(0.3)	0.1	(0.1)
Qatar	24.6	(0.6)	25.6	(0.7)	22.0	(0.8)	13.6	(0.6)	8.3	(0.6)	4.6	(0.4)	1.2	(0.2)	0.2	(0.1)
Romania	6.1	(1.1)	17.6	(1.6)	27.0	(1.4)	28.6	(1.9)	16.3	(1.4)	4.1	(0.6)	0.3	(0.2)	0.0	c
Russian Federation	2.6	(0.6)	10.0	(1.0)	23.8	(1.1)	32.7	(1.8)	22.0	(1.2)	7.3	(0.9)	1.5	(0.4)	0.2	(0.1)
Serbia	3.2	(0.6)	12.4	(1.0)	27.0	(1.4)	31.5	(1.7)	19.8	(1.2)	5.6	(0.6)	0.5	(0.2)	0.0	(0.0)
Shanghai-China	0.2	(0.1)	0.9	(0.3)	5.5	(0.8)	17.8	(1.2)	31.5	(1.5)	30.9	(1.4)	11.7	(0.8)	1.4	(0.3)
Singapore	0.7	(0.2)	4.2	(0.4)	11.3	(0.7)	20.3	(0.9)	27.6	(1.0)	23.8	(0.9)	10.6	(0.7)	1.6	(0.4)
Chinese Taipei	1.3	(0.3)	5.5	(0.6)	14.9	(1.0)	27.0	(1.3)	31.0	(1.4)	17.2	(1.2)	3.1	(0.7)	0.2	(0.2)
Thailand	2.3	(0.5)	16.1	(1.3)	37.1	(1.6)	30.9	(1.5)	11.6	(1.2)	2.0	(0.5)	0.1	(0.1)	0.0	c
Trinidad and Tobago	14.3	(0.8)	18.3	(0.8)	22.8	(1.1)	22.4	(1.1)	15.5	(1.0)	5.9	(0.6)	0.8	(0.3)	0.0	c
Tunisia	8.4	(0.8)	18.9	(1.1)	30.3	(1.1)	27.9	(1.2)	12.2	(1.2)	2.1	(0.6)	0.1	(0.1)	0.0	(0.0)
Uruguay	8.8	(0.9)	16.4	(1.0)	26.2	(1.0)	25.1	(1.1)	16.4	(1.0)	6.0	(0.7)	1.1	(0.2)	0.0	(0.1)

StatLink ㎝ http://dx.doi.org/10.1787/888932343285

[Part 2/2]

Table I.2.2 Percentage of students at each proficiency level on the reading scale, by gender

Girls – Proficiency levels

	Below Level 1b (less than 262.04 score points)		Level 1b (from 262.04 to less than 334.75 score points)		Level 1a (from 334.75 to less than 407.47 score points)		Level 2 (from 407.47 to less than 480.18 score points)		Level 3 (from 480.18 to less than 552.89 score points)		Level 4 (from 552.89 to less than 625.61 score points)		Level 5 (from 625.61 to less than 698.32 score points)		Level 6 (above 698.32 score points)	
	%	S.E.	%	S.E.	%	S.E.	%	S.E.	%	S.E.	%	S.E.	%	S.E.	%	S.E.
OECD																
Australia	0.4	(0.1)	1.8	(0.2)	6.8	(0.5)	18.4	(0.8)	29.5	(1.0)	27.4	(0.8)	13.0	(0.7)	2.6	(0.4)
Austria	0.9	(0.4)	5.6	(0.9)	13.8	(1.1)	23.1	(1.4)	28.7	(1.3)	21.1	(1.2)	6.3	(0.7)	0.6	(0.2)
Belgium	0.6	(0.2)	3.2	(0.6)	10.0	(0.9)	18.5	(0.9)	27.1	(1.1)	27.6	(1.1)	11.6	(0.8)	1.4	(0.3)
Canada	0.1	(0.0)	0.9	(0.2)	5.0	(0.4)	17.5	(0.7)	30.2	(0.8)	30.1	(0.8)	13.6	(0.6)	2.6	(0.3)
Chile	0.7	(0.3)	5.2	(0.7)	18.9	(1.2)	34.4	(1.5)	28.7	(1.5)	10.6	(1.2)	1.5	(0.4)	0.0	(0.0)
Czech Republic	0.2	(0.2)	3.0	(0.6)	11.1	(1.1)	24.6	(1.4)	30.0	(1.3)	23.3	(1.4)	7.2	(0.8)	0.6	(0.2)
Denmark	0.2	(0.1)	2.0	(0.3)	9.3	(0.8)	22.9	(1.2)	34.6	(1.7)	24.8	(1.3)	5.7	(0.6)	0.4	(0.2)
Estonia	0.0	(0.0)	1.0	(0.4)	6.3	(0.8)	20.6	(1.5)	35.6	(1.4)	27.5	(1.2)	7.8	(0.8)	1.1	(0.4)
Finland	0.1	(0.1)	0.5	(0.2)	2.6	(0.4)	10.7	(0.8)	27.8	(1.1)	37.3	(1.1)	18.3	(1.0)	2.7	(0.4)
France	1.3	(0.5)	3.3	(0.6)	9.6	(0.8)	19.0	(1.2)	28.9	(1.4)	25.9	(1.4)	10.6	(1.2)	1.5	(0.4)
Germany	0.3	(0.2)	2.4	(0.4)	9.9	(0.9)	20.1	(1.0)	29.2	(1.3)	27.0	(1.1)	10.0	(0.9)	1.0	(0.3)
Greece	0.5	(0.3)	2.6	(0.7)	10.1	(1.1)	23.9	(1.5)	32.4	(1.3)	22.8	(1.3)	6.7	(0.8)	1.0	(0.3)
Hungary	0.2	(0.2)	2.8	(0.8)	8.4	(1.1)	21.9	(1.7)	32.5	(1.9)	26.0	(1.7)	7.8	(1.0)	0.5	(0.2)
Iceland	0.4	(0.2)	1.9	(0.5)	7.6	(0.9)	19.9	(1.0)	33.1	(1.6)	25.7	(1.4)	9.9	(1.0)	1.4	(0.4)
Ireland	0.6	(0.2)	2.1	(0.5)	8.6	(0.8)	21.4	(1.4)	31.6	(1.1)	26.2	(1.3)	8.6	(0.9)	1.0	(0.4)
Israel	1.5	(0.4)	5.2	(0.6)	12.5	(0.7)	22.1	(1.4)	29.2	(1.5)	20.9	(1.1)	7.3	(0.7)	1.2	(0.3)
Italy	0.5	(0.1)	2.6	(0.3)	9.6	(0.5)	22.1	(0.8)	32.5	(0.7)	24.8	(0.7)	7.2	(0.5)	0.6	(0.1)
Japan	0.6	(0.3)	1.6	(0.4)	5.7	(0.7)	15.5	(1.2)	29.4	(1.3)	30.2	(1.3)	14.2	(1.2)	2.7	(0.6)
Korea	0.1	(0.1)	0.3	(0.1)	2.1	(0.5)	11.1	(1.3)	31.6	(1.7)	38.0	(1.9)	15.4	(1.4)	1.5	(0.3)
Luxembourg	1.5	(0.3)	4.7	(0.7)	12.9	(1.1)	24.1	(1.1)	28.9	(1.1)	20.3	(1.0)	7.0	(0.6)	0.7	(0.3)
Mexico	2.1	(0.3)	8.6	(0.5)	23.4	(0.7)	34.4	(0.8)	24.6	(0.7)	6.4	(0.5)	0.5	(0.1)	0.0	(0.0)
Netherlands	0.0	c	0.9	(0.3)	9.8	(1.3)	23.0	(1.8)	28.3	(1.4)	26.2	(1.9)	10.8	(1.2)	1.0	(0.3)
New Zealand	0.2	(0.1)	1.3	(0.4)	6.3	(0.6)	17.3	(1.0)	25.9	(1.1)	29.3	(1.1)	15.8	(1.4)	4.0	(0.7)
Norway	0.1	(0.1)	1.3	(0.3)	7.0	(0.8)	19.6	(1.0)	33.1	(1.4)	27.0	(1.6)	10.8	(1.2)	1.2	(0.3)
Poland	0.1	(0.1)	0.9	(0.2)	6.5	(0.8)	20.7	(1.3)	34.1	(1.3)	27.6	(1.5)	9.1	(0.9)	1.0	(0.2)
Portugal	0.1	(0.1)	2.0	(0.5)	8.7	(1.0)	24.5	(1.3)	34.8	(1.2)	23.6	(1.2)	5.9	(0.8)	0.3	(0.2)
Slovak Republic	0.4	(0.3)	2.3	(0.5)	9.8	(0.8)	25.7	(1.2)	33.6	(1.4)	21.8	(1.2)	5.9	(0.8)	0.4	(0.2)
Slovenia	0.1	(0.1)	1.8	(0.3)	8.8	(0.7)	23.8	(1.1)	33.3	(1.2)	24.9	(1.3)	6.9	(0.9)	0.4	(0.2)
Spain	0.7	(0.2)	3.2	(0.4)	10.7	(0.7)	24.7	(1.1)	35.2	(1.1)	21.2	(0.9)	4.0	(0.3)	0.3	(0.1)
Sweden	0.7	(0.3)	2.0	(0.5)	7.8	(0.7)	21.1	(1.1)	31.8	(1.3)	24.5	(1.3)	10.2	(0.9)	2.0	(0.4)
Switzerland	0.3	(0.1)	2.4	(0.4)	8.7	(0.8)	19.5	(1.0)	30.8	(1.2)	27.0	(1.2)	10.2	(1.0)	1.0	(0.3)
Turkey	0.3	(0.1)	2.4	(0.5)	12.3	(1.2)	31.5	(1.9)	33.9	(1.5)	16.6	(1.5)	2.9	(0.6)	0.1	(0.1)
United Kingdom	0.5	(0.2)	2.7	(0.4)	10.8	(0.8)	24.0	(1.0)	30.6	(1.0)	22.4	(1.1)	8.0	(0.7)	1.1	(0.3)
United States	0.2	(0.1)	2.5	(0.4)	10.9	(1.0)	23.1	(1.3)	29.4	(1.6)	22.2	(1.3)	9.5	(1.0)	2.1	(0.6)
OECD total	0.6	(0.1)	3.0	(0.1)	10.8	(0.3)	22.9	(0.5)	29.9	(0.6)	22.9	(0.5)	8.6	(0.3)	1.4	(0.2)
OECD average	0.5	(0.0)	2.6	(0.1)	9.5	(0.1)	21.9	(0.2)	30.9	(0.2)	24.7	(0.2)	8.8	(0.1)	1.2	(0.1)
Partners																
Albania	4.9	(0.7)	12.8	(1.3)	26.0	(1.7)	31.9	(1.9)	19.4	(1.6)	4.8	(0.9)	0.3	(0.2)	0.0	(0.0)
Argentina	7.2	(1.0)	13.8	(1.1)	24.3	(1.6)	27.4	(1.5)	18.7	(1.5)	7.4	(1.1)	1.1	(0.4)	0.1	(0.1)
Azerbaijan	6.6	(1.0)	22.4	(1.5)	38.8	(1.6)	25.4	(1.5)	6.2	(1.1)	0.5	(0.2)	0.0	(0.0)	0.0	c
Brazil	3.1	(0.4)	12.9	(0.9)	27.4	(1.2)	29.7	(1.0)	18.3	(1.1)	6.9	(0.7)	1.4	(0.2)	0.1	(0.1)
Bulgaria	3.3	(0.7)	8.5	(1.3)	17.3	(1.5)	25.2	(1.4)	26.8	(1.6)	14.6	(1.5)	3.9	(0.7)	0.3	(0.2)
Colombia	3.9	(0.6)	13.0	(1.1)	28.1	(1.3)	31.2	(1.3)	18.2	(1.2)	5.1	(0.7)	0.6	(0.2)	0.0	(0.0)
Croatia	0.2	(0.1)	1.8	(0.4)	10.6	(1.1)	24.6	(1.2)	35.7	(1.5)	22.0	(1.5)	4.9	(0.7)	0.2	(0.1)
Dubai (UAE)	0.9	(0.2)	4.9	(0.4)	14.9	(0.7)	27.5	(1.2)	27.1	(1.3)	18.0	(0.8)	6.0	(0.7)	0.7	(0.2)
Hong Kong-China	0.0	(0.0)	0.8	(0.2)	4.1	(0.7)	13.1	(0.9)	29.4	(1.2)	36.2	(1.2)	14.7	(1.0)	1.7	(0.4)
Indonesia	0.6	(0.2)	8.8	(1.2)	32.1	(2.0)	41.2	(1.8)	15.5	(1.8)	1.6	(0.5)	0.0	(0.1)	0.0	c
Jordan	2.8	(0.5)	8.4	(1.1)	23.0	(1.3)	37.0	(1.2)	23.1	(1.5)	5.3	(0.7)	0.4	(0.1)	0.0	(0.0)
Kazakhstan	3.6	(0.6)	14.9	(1.2)	31.2	(1.4)	28.1	(1.3)	16.6	(1.2)	5.1	(0.7)	0.5	(0.2)	0.0	(0.0)
Kyrgyzstan	19.1	(1.4)	30.1	(1.5)	29.0	(1.4)	14.7	(1.3)	5.5	(0.8)	1.4	(0.3)	0.2	(0.1)	0.0	c
Latvia	0.0	(0.0)	1.1	(0.4)	7.6	(1.0)	25.9	(1.7)	37.9	(1.5)	23.1	(1.3)	4.2	(0.6)	0.1	(0.1)
Liechtenstein	0.0	c	1.0	(1.0)	8.4	(2.4)	21.6	(3.2)	33.0	(4.3)	29.6	(4.0)	5.8	(2.3)	0.6	(0.8)
Lithuania	0.2	(0.2)	2.0	(0.4)	10.8	(0.9)	27.2	(1.2)	34.5	(1.3)	20.3	(1.3)	4.7	(0.7)	0.3	(0.1)
Macao-China	0.1	(0.1)	1.3	(0.2)	7.6	(0.6)	27.2	(0.8)	38.0	(1.0)	21.6	(0.7)	4.0	(0.4)	0.1	(0.1)
Montenegro	2.2	(0.5)	10.6	(1.2)	24.2	(1.3)	32.4	(1.2)	22.4	(1.1)	7.2	(0.7)	0.9	(0.3)	0.0	(0.0)
Panama	10.4	(1.7)	20.2	(2.1)	28.4	(1.9)	22.1	(1.4)	13.2	(1.9)	4.8	(1.0)	0.8	(0.4)	0.1	(0.1)
Peru	12.0	(1.0)	19.6	(1.2)	28.2	(1.4)	24.3	(1.3)	12.4	(1.3)	3.1	(0.7)	0.4	(0.2)	0.0	(0.0)
Qatar	10.7	(0.5)	19.2	(0.7)	24.5	(0.9)	23.3	(0.7)	14.0	(0.6)	6.3	(0.4)	1.8	(0.2)	0.2	(0.2)
Romania	2.1	(0.5)	8.0	(0.9)	20.3	(1.6)	34.5	(1.8)	25.9	(1.7)	8.0	(1.0)	1.1	(0.3)	0.0	(0.0)
Russian Federation	0.6	(0.2)	3.8	(0.6)	14.2	(1.0)	30.4	(1.4)	31.5	(1.2)	14.9	(1.0)	4.1	(0.7)	0.5	(0.2)
Serbia	0.7	(0.3)	5.1	(0.7)	17.1	(1.2)	35.0	(1.3)	30.8	(1.3)	10.1	(0.8)	1.1	(0.2)	0.0	(0.1)
Shanghai-China	0.0	(0.0)	0.2	(0.1)	1.3	(0.3)	8.8	(0.8)	25.5	(1.5)	38.4	(1.5)	22.3	(1.4)	3.4	(0.7)
Singapore	0.1	(0.1)	1.3	(0.3)	7.3	(0.6)	16.7	(0.9)	27.6	(1.2)	27.7	(1.0)	15.6	(0.8)	3.7	(0.6)
Chinese Taipei	0.1	(0.1)	1.5	(0.3)	7.9	(0.8)	22.2	(1.2)	36.2	(1.5)	24.9	(1.5)	6.5	(1.2)	0.6	(0.4)
Thailand	0.4	(0.2)	5.2	(0.7)	27.6	(1.5)	41.4	(1.6)	20.7	(1.3)	4.3	(0.8)	0.4	(0.2)	0.0	(0.0)
Trinidad and Tobago	5.0	(0.5)	10.3	(0.7)	19.2	(1.1)	27.6	(1.2)	22.4	(1.2)	11.9	(0.7)	3.4	(0.4)	0.3	(0.1)
Tunisia	2.9	(0.5)	11.5	(1.0)	29.0	(1.6)	34.7	(1.7)	17.6	(1.3)	3.9	(0.6)	0.3	(0.2)	0.0	(0.0)
Uruguay	2.6	(0.4)	9.1	(0.8)	21.9	(0.9)	30.5	(1.2)	23.7	(1.0)	10.0	(0.7)	2.1	(0.4)	0.1	(0.1)

StatLink ⟨⟩ http://dx.doi.org/10.1787/888932343285

[Part 1/1]
Table I.2.3 Mean score, variation and gender differences in student performance on the reading scale

		All students				Gender differences						Percentiles											
		Mean score		Standard deviation		Boys		Girls		Difference (B – G)		5th		10th		25th		75th		90th		95th	
		Mean	S.E.	S.D.	S.E.	Mean score	S.E.	Mean score	S.E.	Score dif.	S.E.	Score	S.E.	Score	S.E.	Score	S.E.	Score	S.E.	Score	S.E.	Score	S.E.
OECD	Australia	515	(2.3)	99	(1.4)	496	(2.9)	533	(2.6)	**-37**	(3.1)	343	(3.8)	384	(3.1)	450	(2.9)	584	(2.7)	638	(3.2)	668	(3.9)
	Austria	470	(2.9)	100	(2.0)	449	(3.8)	490	(4.0)	**-41**	(5.5)	299	(5.2)	334	(6.1)	399	(4.3)	545	(3.3)	596	(3.4)	625	(4.3)
	Belgium	506	(2.3)	102	(1.7)	493	(3.4)	520	(2.9)	**-27**	(4.4)	326	(6.1)	368	(4.3)	436	(3.8)	583	(2.2)	631	(2.7)	657	(2.9)
	Canada	524	(1.5)	90	(0.9)	507	(1.8)	542	(1.7)	**-34**	(1.9)	368	(2.9)	406	(2.7)	464	(1.9)	588	(1.7)	637	(1.9)	664	(2.1)
	Chile	449	(3.1)	83	(1.7)	439	(3.9)	461	(3.6)	**-22**	(4.1)	310	(5.1)	342	(5.0)	393	(4.1)	506	(3.3)	556	(3.6)	584	(5.1)
	Czech Republic	478	(2.9)	92	(1.6)	456	(3.7)	504	(3.0)	**-48**	(4.1)	325	(4.8)	357	(4.9)	413	(4.2)	545	(3.3)	598	(3.2)	627	(3.6)
	Denmark	495	(2.1)	84	(1.2)	480	(2.5)	509	(2.5)	**-29**	(2.9)	350	(3.8)	383	(3.7)	440	(2.9)	554	(2.8)	599	(3.0)	624	(2.9)
	Estonia	501	(2.6)	83	(1.7)	480	(2.9)	524	(2.8)	**-44**	(2.5)	359	(5.3)	392	(4.4)	446	(3.3)	559	(2.8)	605	(3.6)	633	(4.1)
	Finland	536	(2.3)	86	(1.0)	508	(2.6)	563	(2.4)	**-55**	(2.3)	382	(3.4)	419	(3.6)	481	(2.7)	597	(2.2)	642	(2.6)	666	(2.6)
	France	496	(3.4)	106	(2.8)	475	(4.3)	515	(3.4)	**-40**	(3.7)	305	(8.2)	352	(7.0)	429	(4.7)	572	(4.0)	624	(3.9)	651	(4.6)
	Germany	497	(2.7)	95	(1.8)	478	(3.6)	518	(2.9)	**-40**	(3.9)	333	(4.8)	367	(5.1)	432	(4.5)	567	(2.8)	615	(3.2)	640	(3.1)
	Greece	483	(4.3)	95	(2.4)	459	(5.5)	506	(3.5)	**-47**	(4.3)	318	(7.8)	355	(8.0)	420	(6.3)	550	(3.1)	601	(3.7)	630	(3.7)
	Hungary	494	(3.2)	90	(2.4)	475	(3.9)	513	(3.6)	**-38**	(4.0)	332	(7.4)	371	(6.9)	435	(4.3)	559	(3.6)	607	(3.5)	632	(4.0)
	Iceland	500	(1.4)	96	(1.2)	478	(2.1)	522	(1.9)	**-44**	(2.8)	331	(4.9)	371	(4.1)	439	(2.9)	567	(2.0)	619	(2.6)	648	(3.9)
	Ireland	496	(3.0)	95	(2.2)	476	(4.2)	515	(3.1)	**-39**	(4.7)	330	(7.8)	373	(4.7)	435	(3.9)	562	(2.8)	611	(2.8)	638	(3.2)
	Israel	474	(3.6)	112	(2.7)	452	(5.2)	495	(3.4)	**-42**	(5.2)	277	(8.8)	322	(7.8)	401	(4.4)	554	(3.4)	611	(4.0)	643	(4.3)
	Italy	486	(1.6)	96	(1.4)	464	(2.3)	510	(1.9)	**-46**	(2.8)	320	(3.7)	358	(2.6)	422	(2.3)	556	(1.7)	604	(1.7)	631	(2.1)
	Japan	520	(3.5)	100	(2.9)	501	(5.6)	540	(3.7)	**-39**	(6.8)	339	(9.8)	386	(7.1)	459	(4.8)	590	(3.0)	639	(3.6)	667	(4.6)
	Korea	539	(3.5)	79	(2.1)	523	(4.9)	558	(3.8)	**-35**	(5.9)	400	(7.6)	435	(5.9)	490	(4.1)	595	(3.4)	635	(3.0)	658	(3.8)
	Luxembourg	472	(1.3)	104	(0.9)	453	(1.9)	492	(1.5)	**-39**	(2.3)	288	(3.6)	332	(3.5)	403	(2.4)	547	(1.7)	600	(2.0)	630	(3.7)
	Mexico	425	(2.0)	85	(1.2)	413	(2.1)	438	(2.1)	**-25**	(1.6)	281	(3.9)	314	(2.9)	370	(2.4)	485	(1.9)	531	(2.2)	557	(2.4)
	Netherlands	508	(5.1)	89	(1.6)	496	(5.1)	521	(5.3)	**-24**	(2.4)	365	(4.7)	390	(5.0)	442	(6.1)	575	(5.4)	625	(4.6)	650	(4.0)
	New Zealand	521	(2.4)	103	(1.7)	499	(3.6)	544	(2.6)	**-46**	(4.3)	344	(5.8)	383	(4.5)	452	(3.1)	595	(2.8)	649	(2.7)	678	(3.7)
	Norway	503	(2.6)	91	(1.2)	480	(3.0)	527	(2.9)	**-47**	(2.9)	346	(4.5)	382	(4.0)	443	(3.6)	568	(2.9)	619	(3.9)	647	(4.4)
	Poland	500	(2.6)	89	(1.3)	476	(2.8)	525	(2.9)	**-50**	(2.5)	346	(5.6)	382	(4.2)	441	(3.4)	565	(3.2)	613	(3.3)	640	(3.6)
	Portugal	489	(3.1)	87	(1.6)	470	(3.5)	508	(2.9)	**-38**	(2.4)	338	(4.8)	373	(4.9)	432	(4.4)	551	(3.4)	599	(3.5)	624	(3.6)
	Slovak Republic	477	(2.5)	90	(1.9)	452	(3.5)	503	(2.8)	**-51**	(3.5)	324	(6.1)	358	(5.2)	416	(4.1)	543	(2.7)	594	(3.2)	621	(4.3)
	Slovenia	483	(1.0)	91	(0.9)	456	(1.6)	511	(1.4)	**-55**	(2.3)	326	(2.9)	359	(2.1)	421	(1.9)	550	(1.7)	598	(2.9)	623	(3.9)
	Spain	481	(2.0)	88	(1.1)	467	(2.2)	496	(2.2)	**-29**	(2.0)	326	(4.2)	364	(3.5)	426	(3.3)	543	(2.0)	588	(2.0)	613	(2.4)
	Sweden	497	(2.9)	99	(1.5)	475	(3.2)	521	(3.1)	**-46**	(2.7)	326	(5.3)	368	(5.5)	437	(3.3)	565	(3.2)	620	(3.7)	651	(3.9)
	Switzerland	501	(2.4)	93	(1.4)	481	(2.9)	520	(2.7)	**-39**	(2.5)	337	(4.1)	374	(4.0)	437	(3.6)	569	(3.0)	617	(3.3)	645	(4.4)
	Turkey	464	(3.5)	82	(1.7)	443	(3.7)	486	(4.1)	**-43**	(3.7)	325	(5.1)	356	(4.3)	409	(3.8)	522	(4.5)	569	(5.2)	596	(5.4)
	United Kingdom	494	(2.3)	95	(1.2)	481	(3.5)	507	(2.9)	**-25**	(4.5)	334	(4.1)	370	(3.1)	430	(2.8)	561	(3.2)	616	(2.6)	646	(3.7)
	United States	500	(3.7)	97	(1.6)	488	(4.2)	513	(3.8)	**-25**	(3.4)	339	(4.2)	372	(3.9)	433	(4.0)	569	(4.6)	625	(5.0)	656	(5.8)
	OECD total	492	(1.2)	98	(0.6)	475	(1.4)	508	(1.2)	**-33**	(1.2)	326	(1.8)	363	(1.5)	426	(1.4)	561	(1.4)	615	(1.5)	645	(1.8)
	OECD average	493	(0.5)	93	(0.3)	474	(0.6)	513	(0.5)	**-39**	(0.6)	332	(1.0)	369	(0.8)	432	(0.7)	560	(0.5)	610	(0.6)	637	(0.7)
Partners	Albania	385	(4.0)	100	(1.9)	355	(5.1)	417	(3.9)	**-62**	(4.4)	212	(6.9)	254	(5.4)	319	(4.9)	458	(4.8)	509	(4.9)	538	(5.5)
	Argentina	398	(4.6)	108	(3.4)	379	(5.1)	415	(4.9)	**-37**	(3.8)	209	(11.3)	257	(8.3)	329	(5.8)	473	(6.3)	535	(7.1)	568	(6.7)
	Azerbaijan	362	(3.3)	76	(1.8)	350	(3.7)	374	(3.3)	**-24**	(2.4)	235	(5.7)	263	(4.7)	311	(4.3)	413	(4.0)	458	(4.4)	485	(6.2)
	Brazil	412	(2.7)	94	(1.5)	397	(2.9)	425	(2.8)	**-29**	(1.7)	262	(3.0)	293	(3.2)	348	(2.7)	474	(3.9)	537	(4.2)	572	(4.6)
	Bulgaria	429	(6.7)	113	(2.5)	400	(7.3)	461	(5.8)	**-61**	(4.7)	234	(8.4)	276	(7.8)	351	(8.5)	512	(6.5)	572	(7.3)	603	(6.7)
	Colombia	413	(3.7)	87	(1.9)	408	(4.5)	418	(4.0)	-9	(3.8)	269	(6.4)	302	(5.2)	355	(4.4)	473	(3.9)	524	(4.1)	554	(4.0)
	Croatia	476	(2.9)	88	(1.6)	452	(3.4)	503	(3.7)	**-51**	(4.6)	327	(4.9)	359	(3.6)	416	(4.5)	539	(3.1)	586	(3.5)	611	(3.8)
	Dubai (UAE)	459	(1.1)	107	(0.9)	435	(1.7)	485	(1.5)	**-51**	(2.3)	277	(3.4)	317	(2.8)	386	(2.4)	536	(2.4)	596	(2.7)	628	(3.1)
	Hong Kong-China	533	(2.1)	84	(1.7)	518	(3.3)	550	(2.8)	**-33**	(4.4)	380	(5.5)	418	(4.5)	482	(3.0)	592	(2.5)	634	(2.9)	659	(3.1)
	Indonesia	402	(3.7)	66	(2.0)	383	(3.8)	420	(3.9)	**-37**	(3.3)	291	(5.8)	315	(5.0)	357	(4.1)	447	(4.6)	487	(5.0)	510	(5.8)
	Jordan	405	(3.3)	91	(2.0)	377	(4.7)	434	(4.1)	**-57**	(6.2)	243	(6.6)	284	(5.0)	350	(4.1)	468	(3.5)	515	(3.9)	542	(4.7)
	Kazakhstan	390	(3.1)	91	(1.6)	369	(3.2)	412	(3.4)	**-43**	(2.7)	245	(3.8)	275	(3.8)	327	(3.1)	452	(4.2)	513	(5.0)	545	(5.2)
	Kyrgyzstan	314	(3.2)	99	(2.1)	287	(3.8)	340	(3.2)	**-53**	(2.7)	155	(5.6)	190	(4.7)	249	(4.1)	377	(4.2)	441	(6.4)	483	(7.5)
	Latvia	484	(3.0)	80	(1.5)	460	(3.4)	507	(3.1)	**-47**	(3.2)	348	(6.3)	379	(4.2)	429	(3.8)	541	(3.3)	584	(3.2)	610	(4.3)
	Liechtenstein	499	(2.8)	83	(3.5)	484	(4.5)	516	(4.5)	**-32**	(7.1)	355	(12.1)	385	(10.6)	442	(6.5)	560	(4.5)	600	(8.4)	626	(11.8)
	Lithuania	468	(2.4)	86	(1.6)	439	(2.8)	498	(2.6)	**-59**	(2.8)	324	(4.5)	353	(4.1)	409	(3.3)	530	(3.1)	580	(3.4)	608	(4.1)
	Macao-China	487	(0.9)	76	(0.8)	470	(1.3)	504	(1.2)	**-34**	(1.7)	357	(2.7)	388	(1.8)	437	(1.4)	540	(1.4)	582	(1.8)	608	(1.8)
	Montenegro	408	(1.7)	93	(1.1)	382	(2.1)	434	(2.1)	**-53**	(2.6)	254	(4.2)	288	(3.8)	345	(2.6)	473	(2.4)	526	(2.7)	558	(4.1)
	Panama	371	(6.5)	99	(3.5)	354	(7.0)	387	(7.3)	**-33**	(6.7)	209	(12.0)	246	(10.0)	304	(7.4)	436	(7.7)	502	(9.3)	540	(10.0)
	Peru	370	(4.0)	98	(2.4)	359	(4.2)	381	(4.9)	**-22**	(4.7)	209	(5.0)	241	(3.9)	302	(4.3)	437	(5.2)	496	(6.4)	530	(7.0)
	Qatar	372	(0.8)	115	(0.8)	347	(1.3)	397	(1.0)	**-50**	(1.8)	196	(2.4)	228	(2.2)	288	(1.4)	450	(1.4)	529	(2.1)	573	(2.8)
	Romania	424	(4.1)	90	(2.3)	403	(4.6)	445	(4.3)	**-43**	(4.4)	271	(6.9)	304	(5.7)	365	(6.0)	488	(4.7)	537	(4.0)	564	(4.6)
	Russian Federation	459	(3.3)	90	(2.0)	437	(3.6)	482	(3.4)	**-45**	(2.7)	310	(5.8)	344	(5.5)	401	(3.6)	519	(3.2)	572	(4.5)	607	(5.6)
	Serbia	442	(2.4)	84	(1.5)	422	(3.3)	462	(2.5)	**-39**	(3.0)	299	(4.9)	331	(3.8)	388	(3.2)	501	(2.5)	547	(2.7)	572	(3.3)
	Shanghai-China	556	(2.4)	80	(1.7)	536	(3.0)	576	(2.3)	**-40**	(2.9)	417	(5.2)	450	(4.8)	504	(3.5)	613	(2.8)	654	(2.7)	679	(3.3)
	Singapore	526	(1.1)	97	(1.0)	511	(1.7)	542	(1.5)	**-31**	(2.3)	357	(3.4)	394	(3.1)	460	(2.0)	597	(2.1)	648	(2.8)	676	(2.7)
	Chinese Taipei	495	(2.6)	86	(1.9)	477	(3.7)	514	(3.6)	**-37**	(5.3)	343	(4.6)	380	(3.9)	439	(3.2)	555	(2.9)	600	(4.6)	627	(6.3)
	Thailand	421	(2.6)	72	(1.9)	400	(3.3)	438	(3.1)	**-38**	(3.8)	305	(4.9)	331	(3.8)	373	(3.2)	469	(2.6)	514	(4.0)	542	(5.5)
	Trinidad and Tobago	416	(1.2)	113	(1.3)	387	(1.9)	445	(1.6)	**-58**	(2.5)	220	(5.8)	265	(3.9)	339	(2.5)	496	(2.3)	559	(2.5)	594	(3.0)
	Tunisia	404	(2.9)	85	(1.8)	387	(3.2)	418	(3.0)	**-31**	(2.2)	258	(4.4)	293	(3.8)	348	(3.4)	462	(3.4)	510	(4.8)	538	(5.2)
	Uruguay	426	(2.6)	99	(1.9)	404	(3.2)	445	(2.8)	**-42**	(3.1)	257	(5.2)	297	(4.2)	359	(3.4)	495	(3.1)	552	(3.3)	584	(4.5)

Note: Values that are statistically significant are indicated in bold (see Annex A3).
StatLink http://dx.doi.org/10.1787/888932343285

[Part 1/1]

Table I.2.4 **Percentage of students at each proficiency level on the reading subscale *access and retrieve***

| | Proficiency levels | | | | | | | | | | | | | | | |
| | Below Level 1b (less than 262.04 score points) | | Level 1b (from 262.04 to less than 334.75 score points) | | Level 1a (from 334.75 to less than 407.47 score points) | | Level 2 (from 407.47 to less than 480.18 score points) | | Level 3 (from 480.18 to less than 552.89 score points) | | Level 4 (from 552.89 to less than 625.61 score points) | | Level 5 (from 625.61 to less than 698.32 score points) | | Level 6 (above 698.32 score points) | |
	%	S.E.	%	S.E.	%	S.E.	%	S.E.	%	S.E.	%	S.E.	%	S.E.	%	S.E.
Australia	1.3	(0.1)	3.5	(0.3)	9.7	(0.5)	19.8	(0.6)	29.0	(0.6)	24.5	(0.6)	10.2	(0.5)	2.0	(0.3)
Austria	2.7	(0.4)	8.2	(0.7)	15.7	(1.1)	22.5	(1.2)	24.5	(1.0)	18.1	(0.9)	7.2	(0.7)	1.0	(0.3)
Belgium	1.7	(0.3)	4.3	(0.4)	10.9	(0.6)	18.6	(0.6)	25.5	(0.8)	24.7	(0.7)	11.9	(0.6)	2.5	(0.3)
Canada	0.9	(0.1)	2.7	(0.2)	9.0	(0.4)	20.7	(0.6)	29.8	(0.6)	24.9	(0.5)	10.1	(0.4)	1.8	(0.2)
Chile	2.7	(0.5)	8.6	(0.7)	22.2	(1.2)	31.6	(1.0)	23.5	(1.0)	9.3	(0.7)	1.9	(0.3)	0.1	(0.1)
Czech Republic	1.6	(0.4)	6.3	(0.7)	15.7	(0.7)	25.8	(0.9)	26.3	(0.8)	17.9	(1.0)	5.6	(0.5)	0.7	(0.2)
Denmark	1.0	(0.2)	3.7	(0.4)	11.6	(0.8)	22.4	(0.7)	30.4	(1.0)	22.6	(1.2)	7.3	(0.6)	1.0	(0.3)
Estonia	0.6	(0.2)	3.3	(0.5)	11.4	(0.8)	23.5	(1.0)	31.0	(1.2)	21.7	(0.9)	7.5	(0.7)	0.9	(0.3)
Finland	0.8	(0.1)	2.5	(0.3)	7.8	(0.5)	17.2	(0.9)	27.0	(0.8)	27.4	(0.8)	14.2	(0.7)	3.1	(0.4)
France	3.0	(0.6)	5.5	(0.6)	12.5	(0.9)	21.8	(1.0)	26.3	(1.2)	20.9	(1.2)	8.5	(0.9)	1.4	(0.3)
Germany	1.5	(0.3)	5.4	(0.4)	12.8	(0.8)	20.6	(1.0)	26.1	(0.9)	22.7	(0.9)	9.4	(0.7)	1.5	(0.3)
Greece	3.3	(0.7)	7.5	(0.9)	16.0	(0.8)	25.3	(0.8)	27.0	(1.1)	15.6	(0.9)	4.6	(0.4)	0.6	(0.1)
Hungary	2.1	(0.5)	4.7	(0.6)	10.8	(0.8)	21.0	(0.9)	27.6	(1.1)	23.6	(1.1)	9.0	(0.7)	1.2	(0.3)
Iceland	2.0	(0.2)	4.5	(0.3)	11.2	(0.6)	19.6	(0.9)	28.1	(0.9)	22.1	(1.1)	10.3	(0.8)	2.3	(0.3)
Ireland	2.2	(0.5)	3.7	(0.4)	10.6	(0.7)	22.6	(0.9)	30.2	(1.0)	22.6	(1.1)	7.2	(0.8)	0.9	(0.2)
Israel	6.2	(0.9)	8.8	(0.6)	15.2	(0.8)	21.8	(0.9)	24.3	(0.8)	16.3	(0.7)	6.2	(0.5)	1.1	(0.2)
Italy	2.8	(0.3)	6.3	(0.3)	13.9	(0.4)	22.9	(0.5)	27.6	(0.5)	19.7	(0.5)	6.1	(0.3)	0.7	(0.1)
Japan	1.9	(0.4)	3.2	(0.5)	8.0	(0.7)	16.2	(0.7)	25.4	(1.0)	27.0	(1.0)	14.1	(0.7)	4.2	(0.5)
Korea	0.3	(0.1)	1.2	(0.3)	5.5	(0.7)	15.9	(1.0)	30.1	(1.0)	30.3	(1.2)	13.9	(1.1)	2.7	(0.4)
Luxembourg	4.7	(0.4)	7.6	(0.4)	15.6	(0.6)	22.4	(0.9)	24.9	(0.8)	17.1	(0.7)	6.7	(0.4)	1.1	(0.2)
Mexico	4.3	(0.4)	10.3	(0.4)	22.8	(0.6)	30.7	(0.6)	23.0	(0.6)	7.6	(0.4)	1.2	(0.1)	0.1	(0.0)
Netherlands	0.2	(0.1)	2.1	(0.4)	10.0	(0.9)	21.4	(1.7)	27.4	(1.3)	26.7	(1.5)	10.8	(1.2)	1.4	(0.3)
New Zealand	1.3	(0.2)	3.4	(0.3)	10.0	(0.6)	18.4	(0.7)	26.0	(0.8)	24.6	(0.8)	13.3	(0.7)	3.0	(0.3)
Norway	1.0	(0.2)	3.5	(0.4)	10.2	(0.6)	20.5	(0.7)	29.6	(0.8)	23.4	(0.9)	9.9	(0.6)	1.9	(0.3)
Poland	1.5	(0.2)	4.3	(0.4)	11.9	(0.6)	22.7	(0.8)	28.6	(0.8)	21.0	(0.8)	8.3	(0.5)	1.8	(0.3)
Portugal	1.2	(0.2)	4.6	(0.5)	12.8	(0.8)	25.7	(1.2)	30.5	(1.3)	19.3	(1.1)	5.3	(0.6)	0.5	(0.2)
Slovak Republic	1.8	(0.4)	5.6	(0.6)	13.1	(0.7)	23.2	(1.0)	28.0	(1.2)	19.6	(0.9)	7.5	(0.6)	1.2	(0.3)
Slovenia	1.8	(0.1)	5.5	(0.4)	12.8	(0.7)	23.3	(0.7)	28.6	(0.9)	21.3	(0.8)	6.2	(0.5)	0.4	(0.1)
Spain	2.5	(0.3)	5.5	(0.4)	13.7	(0.6)	25.4	(0.7)	29.2	(0.7)	17.7	(0.6)	5.2	(0.3)	0.7	(0.1)
Sweden	1.8	(0.3)	4.4	(0.5)	10.3	(0.7)	21.5	(0.8)	28.6	(0.8)	22.3	(1.1)	9.2	(0.9)	1.9	(0.3)
Switzerland	1.0	(0.2)	4.3	(0.4)	11.0	(0.6)	21.1	(0.7)	29.1	(0.8)	23.8	(0.7)	8.6	(0.9)	1.1	(0.3)
Turkey	2.3	(0.5)	6.4	(0.6)	16.6	(0.9)	28.8	(1.1)	27.3	(1.0)	14.9	(1.1)	3.4	(0.6)	0.3	(0.2)
United Kingdom	1.7	(0.3)	4.8	(0.4)	13.6	(0.6)	23.4	(0.9)	28.3	(0.9)	19.8	(0.9)	7.1	(0.6)	1.2	(0.2)
United States	1.2	(0.3)	4.9	(0.4)	13.8	(0.8)	24.8	(0.8)	27.5	(1.0)	19.2	(0.9)	7.2	(0.7)	1.3	(0.3)
OECD total	1.9	(0.1)	5.3	(0.2)	13.5	(0.3)	23.4	(0.3)	27.0	(0.3)	19.7	(0.3)	7.6	(0.2)	1.5	(0.1)
OECD average	2.0	(0.1)	5.0	(0.1)	12.6	(0.1)	22.4	(0.2)	27.5	(0.2)	20.9	(0.2)	8.1	(0.1)	1.4	(0.0)
Albania	14.8	(1.2)	17.9	(1.3)	24.6	(1.1)	23.4	(1.1)	14.7	(1.2)	4.3	(0.7)	0.3	(0.2)	0.0	(0.0)
Argentina	12.9	(1.1)	16.0	(1.0)	24.0	(1.3)	23.8	(1.2)	15.6	(1.2)	6.4	(0.8)	1.2	(0.3)	0.1	(0.1)
Azerbaijan	16.9	(1.4)	22.5	(1.1)	27.6	(1.0)	20.7	(1.0)	9.3	(0.7)	2.6	(0.4)	0.4	(0.2)	0.0	(0.0)
Brazil	8.7	(0.6)	16.5	(0.6)	25.3	(0.9)	24.9	(0.8)	15.4	(0.7)	6.9	(0.6)	1.9	(0.3)	0.2	(0.1)
Bulgaria	12.6	(1.5)	11.5	(0.9)	16.6	(1.1)	20.1	(1.2)	20.0	(1.3)	12.9	(1.2)	5.0	(0.7)	1.2	(0.3)
Colombia	6.3	(0.8)	15.5	(1.0)	29.3	(1.1)	28.4	(1.0)	15.6	(0.9)	4.3	(0.5)	0.6	(0.2)	0.0	(0.0)
Croatia	1.7	(0.3)	5.1	(0.5)	13.2	(0.8)	23.6	(1.0)	27.8	(1.3)	20.6	(1.0)	7.1	(0.6)	1.0	(0.2)
Dubai (UAE)	5.3	(0.4)	9.9	(0.8)	17.1	(0.5)	23.1	(0.7)	22.3	(0.7)	15.5	(0.6)	6.0	(0.4)	0.8	(0.2)
Hong Kong-China	0.8	(0.2)	2.3	(0.3)	7.4	(0.6)	17.5	(0.7)	28.3	(0.9)	29.5	(0.9)	12.2	(0.7)	2.0	(0.4)
Indonesia	6.8	(0.9)	17.0	(1.2)	29.3	(1.3)	28.4	(1.1)	14.1	(1.1)	3.9	(0.9)	0.5	(0.2)	0.0	(0.0)
Jordan	11.7	(0.8)	15.3	(0.8)	26.0	(1.0)	25.4	(0.8)	15.2	(0.8)	5.2	(0.5)	1.0	(0.2)	0.2	(0.1)
Kazakhstan	10.8	(0.8)	18.1	(0.8)	25.0	(0.9)	23.0	(0.9)	14.9	(0.8)	6.5	(0.7)	1.5	(0.3)	0.2	(0.1)
Kyrgyzstan	38.1	(1.3)	23.7	(0.9)	19.7	(0.8)	11.4	(0.8)	5.0	(0.6)	1.7	(0.3)	0.4	(0.2)	0.1	(0.0)
Latvia	1.6	(0.3)	5.2	(0.5)	15.4	(1.0)	27.0	(1.0)	30.2	(1.2)	16.7	(1.1)	3.5	(0.5)	0.3	(0.1)
Liechtenstein	0.5	(0.5)	3.9	(1.1)	9.8	(1.9)	23.0	(2.9)	28.5	(3.0)	25.3	(2.5)	7.8	(1.5)	1.3	(0.7)
Lithuania	2.1	(0.3)	6.7	(0.6)	16.0	(0.8)	25.1	(0.9)	26.7	(0.9)	16.9	(0.8)	5.6	(0.5)	0.9	(0.2)
Macao-China	0.7	(0.1)	3.7	(0.3)	12.1	(0.5)	26.3	(0.6)	31.7	(0.6)	19.6	(0.5)	5.3	(0.3)	0.4	(0.1)
Montenegro	11.2	(0.7)	15.7	(1.0)	21.7	(0.7)	23.8	(0.7)	16.8	(0.7)	8.0	(0.5)	2.4	(0.2)	0.4	(0.2)
Panama	19.4	(2.2)	21.3	(1.7)	24.2	(1.5)	18.4	(1.2)	10.6	(1.3)	4.7	(0.9)	1.1	(0.3)	0.2	(0.1)
Peru	16.9	(1.1)	21.7	(1.2)	26.8	(1.2)	21.4	(1.1)	9.8	(0.8)	2.7	(0.5)	0.6	(0.2)	0.1	(0.1)
Qatar	26.0	(0.5)	19.8	(0.5)	19.9	(0.6)	16.1	(0.6)	10.2	(0.4)	5.5	(0.2)	2.0	(0.2)	0.5	(0.1)
Romania	6.8	(0.9)	12.3	(1.1)	22.5	(1.1)	28.3	(1.1)	21.1	(1.2)	7.8	(0.8)	1.1	(0.3)	0.1	(0.1)
Russian Federation	2.6	(0.4)	6.8	(0.7)	16.9	(1.0)	27.7	(0.9)	25.8	(0.8)	14.0	(0.8)	5.0	(0.5)	1.1	(0.3)
Serbia	3.2	(0.5)	8.5	(0.6)	19.3	(0.9)	29.9	(1.2)	26.0	(0.9)	11.0	(0.9)	2.1	(0.3)	0.1	(0.1)
Shanghai-China	0.5	(0.1)	1.5	(0.3)	5.7	(0.6)	14.8	(0.8)	26.1	(0.9)	29.5	(1.1)	17.3	(0.9)	4.6	(0.4)
Singapore	0.9	(0.2)	3.3	(0.4)	9.0	(0.6)	17.7	(1.0)	25.8	(0.9)	26.8	(0.9)	13.5	(0.6)	3.0	(0.3)
Chinese Taipei	2.0	(0.3)	5.0	(0.5)	12.4	(0.6)	22.2	(0.8)	27.3	(1.0)	21.2	(0.8)	8.3	(0.7)	1.6	(0.3)
Thailand	2.6	(0.5)	10.2	(0.9)	26.1	(1.1)	33.0	(1.1)	20.5	(1.1)	6.5	(0.7)	1.1	(0.3)	0.1	(0.1)
Trinidad and Tobago	12.1	(0.6)	13.7	(0.7)	19.7	(0.9)	23.1	(0.7)	18.8	(0.6)	9.3	(0.5)	2.8	(0.3)	0.5	(0.1)
Tunisia	9.9	(0.7)	17.7	(0.9)	27.4	(0.9)	25.1	(1.0)	14.3	(1.0)	4.7	(0.6)	0.9	(0.2)	0.1	(0.1)
Uruguay	7.6	(0.6)	12.8	(0.7)	22.2	(1.0)	25.7	(0.8)	19.9	(0.8)	9.2	(0.6)	2.4	(0.3)	0.3	(0.1)

StatLink ⌹⌹⌹ http://dx.doi.org/10.1787/888932343285

[Part 1/2]

Table I.2.5 **Percentage of students at each proficiency level on the reading subscale *access and retrieve*, by gender**

Boys – Proficiency levels

	Below Level 1b (less than 262.04 score points)		Level 1b (from 262.04 to less than 334.75 score points)		Level 1a (from 334.75 to less than 407.47 score points)		Level 2 (from 407.47 to less than 480.18 score points)		Level 3 (from 480.18 to less than 552.89 score points)		Level 4 (from 552.89 to less than 625.61 score points)		Level 5 (from 625.61 to less than 698.32 score points)		Level 6 (above 698.32 score points)	
	%	S.E.	%	S.E.	%	S.E.	%	S.E.	%	S.E.	%	S.E.	%	S.E.	%	S.E.
Australia	2.2	(0.3)	5.2	(0.4)	12.4	(0.7)	22.0	(0.8)	27.7	(0.8)	21.0	(0.8)	8.2	(0.6)	1.4	(0.3)
Austria	3.8	(0.6)	10.5	(1.0)	18.2	(1.4)	23.6	(1.3)	22.4	(1.4)	15.4	(1.2)	5.5	(0.7)	0.7	(0.2)
Belgium	2.6	(0.4)	5.5	(0.6)	12.9	(0.8)	20.1	(0.8)	24.8	(1.0)	22.6	(1.0)	9.7	(0.9)	1.9	(0.4)
Canada	1.5	(0.2)	4.1	(0.4)	12.3	(0.6)	23.1	(0.9)	28.6	(1.0)	21.6	(0.7)	7.5	(0.5)	1.2	(0.2)
Chile	4.0	(0.7)	10.4	(1.0)	24.0	(1.4)	29.8	(1.4)	21.3	(1.2)	8.8	(0.9)	1.6	(0.5)	0.2	(0.1)
Czech Republic	2.5	(0.6)	9.0	(1.1)	19.9	(1.2)	28.0	(1.4)	23.7	(1.2)	13.2	(1.2)	3.2	(0.5)	0.4	(0.2)
Denmark	1.6	(0.3)	4.8	(0.6)	14.3	(0.9)	24.7	(1.1)	29.0	(1.2)	19.8	(1.2)	5.3	(0.7)	0.6	(0.3)
Estonia	1.0	(0.3)	4.5	(0.6)	15.6	(1.1)	25.9	(1.3)	29.6	(1.6)	17.8	(1.0)	5.2	(0.7)	0.4	(0.2)
Finland	1.2	(0.2)	4.1	(0.5)	11.6	(1.1)	22.6	(1.7)	28.0	(1.2)	21.8	(1.1)	8.9	(0.8)	1.7	(0.4)
France	4.5	(0.8)	7.8	(0.8)	15.2	(1.2)	23.3	(1.4)	23.9	(1.5)	17.6	(1.4)	6.9	(0.9)	0.9	(0.3)
Germany	2.2	(0.5)	6.8	(1.1)	15.5	(1.0)	22.6	(1.1)	26.0	(1.2)	19.0	(1.2)	7.0	(0.9)	0.8	(0.2)
Greece	5.0	(0.9)	10.2	(1.5)	19.5	(1.4)	26.6	(1.3)	23.5	(1.4)	11.9	(1.0)	3.2	(0.5)	0.2	(0.1)
Hungary	3.0	(0.6)	6.4	(0.9)	13.6	(1.0)	22.2	(1.3)	26.5	(1.4)	20.3	(1.4)	7.0	(0.8)	0.9	(0.3)
Iceland	3.1	(0.5)	6.8	(0.7)	15.1	(1.2)	21.8	(1.4)	26.2	(1.3)	18.3	(1.6)	7.7	(1.0)	1.1	(0.3)
Ireland	3.5	(0.7)	5.1	(0.7)	13.8	(1.1)	24.9	(1.6)	29.4	(1.2)	18.4	(1.2)	4.3	(0.6)	0.5	(0.2)
Israel	10.0	(1.5)	11.7	(0.9)	16.8	(1.3)	21.1	(1.2)	20.6	(1.0)	13.6	(1.0)	5.4	(0.8)	0.9	(0.3)
Italy	4.3	(0.4)	8.8	(0.5)	17.1	(0.6)	24.2	(0.7)	24.7	(0.8)	15.9	(0.6)	4.5	(0.4)	0.5	(0.1)
Japan	2.9	(0.8)	4.5	(0.8)	10.3	(1.9)	18.0	(1.3)	24.6	(1.4)	24.6	(1.2)	12.0	(1.0)	3.2	(0.7)
Korea	0.5	(0.3)	1.8	(0.5)	7.7	(1.0)	19.3	(1.5)	30.5	(1.3)	26.7	(1.5)	11.6	(1.2)	2.0	(0.5)
Luxembourg	7.0	(0.5)	9.5	(0.8)	17.9	(1.0)	22.6	(1.2)	23.9	(1.2)	13.8	(0.9)	4.7	(0.5)	0.6	(0.2)
Mexico	5.6	(0.5)	12.0	(0.6)	24.9	(0.8)	29.3	(0.8)	20.4	(0.8)	6.7	(0.5)	1.1	(0.2)	0.1	(0.0)
Netherlands	0.4	(0.2)	2.9	(0.6)	12.4	(1.2)	23.3	(1.9)	27.5	(1.6)	23.5	(1.9)	9.0	(1.1)	1.0	(0.3)
New Zealand	2.3	(0.4)	5.2	(0.7)	13.5	(0.9)	20.6	(1.0)	25.4	(1.2)	21.0	(1.2)	10.3	(0.8)	1.7	(0.3)
Norway	1.8	(0.4)	5.3	(0.7)	14.1	(0.9)	23.4	(1.1)	28.4	(1.2)	19.0	(1.3)	6.9	(0.7)	1.1	(0.3)
Poland	2.6	(0.4)	6.8	(0.7)	15.8	(1.3)	25.8	(1.2)	25.3	(1.1)	16.9	(0.9)	5.9	(0.6)	1.0	(0.3)
Portugal	2.1	(0.4)	6.9	(0.9)	16.8	(1.0)	26.8	(1.7)	27.4	(1.4)	15.9	(1.2)	4.0	(0.6)	0.2	(0.2)
Slovak Republic	2.9	(0.6)	8.4	(0.9)	17.8	(1.3)	26.7	(1.7)	24.4	(1.3)	14.5	(1.1)	4.5	(0.5)	0.7	(0.3)
Slovenia	3.2	(0.3)	8.6	(0.7)	17.5	(1.0)	25.8	(1.0)	25.1	(1.2)	16.0	(1.0)	3.5	(0.6)	0.2	(0.2)
Spain	3.3	(0.4)	6.9	(0.5)	16.5	(0.8)	26.3	(0.8)	27.7	(0.8)	14.8	(0.6)	4.0	(0.3)	0.4	(0.1)
Sweden	3.0	(0.5)	6.6	(0.8)	13.9	(1.2)	24.5	(1.2)	26.3	(1.0)	19.0	(1.3)	5.8	(0.8)	1.0	(0.3)
Switzerland	1.5	(0.2)	5.8	(0.6)	14.0	(0.9)	23.9	(1.1)	27.9	(1.2)	20.0	(1.3)	6.4	(1.0)	0.6	(0.3)
Turkey	3.4	(0.7)	8.9	(0.8)	19.7	(1.5)	28.2	(1.5)	24.1	(1.5)	12.7	(1.3)	2.9	(0.5)	0.2	(0.1)
United Kingdom	2.7	(0.4)	6.6	(0.6)	16.4	(0.9)	24.2	(1.1)	26.5	(1.3)	16.8	(1.1)	5.9	(0.8)	1.0	(0.3)
United States	1.6	(0.4)	6.7	(0.7)	15.5	(1.1)	25.1	(1.0)	26.8	(1.2)	17.1	(1.1)	6.2	(0.8)	0.9	(0.3)
OECD total	2.8	(0.2)	7.0	(0.2)	15.9	(0.4)	24.4	(0.4)	25.5	(0.4)	17.1	(0.3)	6.2	(0.3)	1.0	(0.1)
OECD average	3.0	(0.1)	6.9	(0.1)	15.7	(0.2)	24.1	(0.1)	25.8	(0.3)	17.5	(0.2)	6.0	(0.1)	0.9	(0.0)
Albania	22.2	(1.7)	22.2	(1.6)	24.0	(1.4)	18.5	(1.4)	9.9	(1.3)	2.9	(0.8)	0.2	(0.2)	0.0	c
Argentina	16.6	(1.4)	18.0	(1.2)	24.1	(1.7)	22.3	(1.6)	13.3	(1.5)	4.6	(1.0)	1.0	(0.4)	0.0	c
Azerbaijan	20.5	(1.7)	24.8	(1.4)	26.7	(1.4)	17.9	(1.6)	7.7	(1.0)	2.0	(0.4)	0.3	(0.2)	0.0	(0.1)
Brazil	12.1	(0.9)	19.1	(0.9)	25.7	(1.0)	21.9	(1.0)	13.3	(0.7)	6.1	(0.6)	1.7	(0.4)	0.2	(0.1)
Bulgaria	18.5	(2.1)	13.8	(1.1)	18.0	(1.5)	18.5	(1.7)	16.4	(1.4)	10.4	(1.2)	3.4	(0.8)	0.9	(0.3)
Colombia	7.1	(1.1)	15.5	(1.4)	29.8	(1.5)	27.4	(1.5)	15.3	(1.3)	4.2	(0.6)	0.7	(0.2)	0.0	(0.0)
Croatia	2.7	(0.4)	7.7	(0.7)	17.4	(1.1)	25.7	(0.9)	25.4	(1.5)	15.8	(1.0)	4.8	(0.5)	0.5	(0.2)
Dubai (UAE)	8.8	(0.7)	13.4	(1.1)	18.8	(0.8)	20.5	(1.0)	19.2	(0.9)	13.7	(0.8)	4.9	(0.5)	0.7	(0.2)
Hong Kong-China	1.2	(0.3)	2.9	(0.5)	9.4	(0.8)	19.4	(1.1)	29.3	(1.5)	26.3	(1.3)	9.7	(0.9)	1.8	(0.4)
Indonesia	9.4	(1.3)	21.2	(1.6)	32.0	(1.4)	25.5	(1.7)	9.6	(1.0)	2.0	(0.5)	0.2	(0.1)	0.0	(0.0)
Jordan	17.4	(1.4)	18.8	(1.1)	26.5	(1.5)	21.8	(1.1)	11.1	(1.0)	3.6	(0.6)	0.6	(0.2)	0.1	(0.1)
Kazakhstan	15.3	(1.3)	21.7	(1.2)	25.0	(1.0)	20.1	(1.1)	12.1	(1.1)	4.6	(0.9)	1.1	(0.3)	0.2	(0.1)
Kyrgyzstan	49.4	(1.7)	22.3	(1.4)	15.5	(1.2)	8.2	(0.9)	3.5	(0.8)	1.0	(0.3)	0.3	(0.1)	0.0	(0.0)
Latvia	2.6	(0.6)	8.5	(1.1)	20.1	(1.3)	29.2	(1.3)	25.1	(1.6)	12.0	(1.2)	2.3	(0.5)	0.2	(0.1)
Liechtenstein	0.9	(0.9)	5.1	(1.9)	11.8	(2.7)	26.0	(4.0)	27.8	(4.0)	22.1	(2.9)	5.4	(2.1)	0.9	(0.8)
Lithuania	3.5	(0.6)	10.4	(1.1)	21.1	(1.2)	27.3	(1.4)	22.7	(1.1)	11.6	(0.9)	3.1	(0.6)	0.4	(0.2)
Macao-China	1.1	(0.2)	5.2	(0.5)	15.6	(0.8)	28.5	(1.1)	28.7	(1.0)	16.5	(0.8)	4.0	(0.4)	0.4	(0.2)
Montenegro	16.1	(1.0)	19.4	(1.5)	23.7	(1.1)	21.2	(1.2)	12.5	(1.1)	5.2	(0.6)	1.5	(0.4)	0.3	(0.2)
Panama	22.3	(2.8)	23.4	(2.1)	23.9	(1.7)	17.6	(2.0)	8.4	(1.4)	3.3	(0.8)	0.8	(0.3)	0.2	(0.1)
Peru	18.6	(1.5)	23.5	(1.7)	26.6	(1.4)	20.1	(1.2)	8.2	(0.8)	2.3	(0.5)	0.5	(0.2)	0.1	(0.1)
Qatar	35.0	(0.7)	20.5	(0.6)	17.6	(0.8)	12.0	(0.6)	7.8	(0.5)	4.9	(0.4)	1.7	(0.2)	0.5	(0.2)
Romania	10.0	(1.5)	15.7	(1.4)	24.4	(1.3)	25.7	(1.4)	17.6	(1.6)	5.8	(0.7)	0.8	(0.3)	0.0	(0.0)
Russian Federation	4.1	(0.7)	9.5	(1.1)	20.5	(1.5)	28.5	(1.3)	23.3	(1.3)	10.3	(0.8)	3.2	(0.5)	0.7	(0.2)
Serbia	4.9	(0.8)	11.9	(1.0)	22.9	(1.3)	28.7	(1.8)	21.4	(1.2)	8.5	(1.0)	1.6	(0.4)	0.1	(0.1)
Shanghai-China	0.8	(0.3)	2.1	(0.5)	8.0	(0.9)	18.4	(1.0)	27.1	(1.6)	26.5	(1.7)	14.0	(1.2)	3.1	(0.5)
Singapore	1.5	(0.3)	4.7	(0.6)	10.8	(0.9)	19.4	(1.2)	25.7	(0.9)	24.6	(1.1)	11.1	(0.7)	2.1	(0.5)
Chinese Taipei	3.1	(0.5)	6.9	(0.7)	15.4	(1.0)	23.5	(1.4)	25.3	(1.1)	18.2	(1.0)	6.5	(0.8)	1.0	(0.3)
Thailand	4.8	(0.9)	14.9	(1.3)	30.6	(1.6)	29.7	(1.6)	15.0	(1.3)	4.2	(0.7)	0.6	(0.3)	0.0	(0.0)
Trinidad and Tobago	18.0	(0.9)	16.7	(1.0)	20.8	(1.5)	20.9	(1.2)	15.1	(0.9)	6.5	(0.6)	1.6	(0.3)	0.2	(0.1)
Tunisia	13.5	(1.1)	19.6	(1.5)	26.9	(1.2)	22.8	(1.3)	12.5	(1.1)	3.8	(0.8)	0.8	(0.3)	0.1	(0.1)
Uruguay	11.6	(1.0)	15.5	(1.1)	22.9	(1.5)	23.5	(1.0)	16.6	(0.9)	7.6	(0.9)	1.9	(0.3)	0.2	(0.1)

StatLink ⟍⟍ http://dx.doi.org/10.1787/888932343285

[Part 2/2]

Table I.2.5 **Percentage of students at each proficiency level on the reading subscale *access and retrieve*, by gender**

	Girls – Proficiency levels															
	Below Level 1b (less than 262.04 score points)		Level 1b (from 262.04 to less than 334.75 score points)		Level 1a (from 334.75 to less than 407.47 score points)		Level 2 (from 407.47 to less than 480.18 score points)		Level 3 (from 480.18 to less than 552.89 score points)		Level 4 (from 552.89 to less than 625.61 score points)		Level 5 (from 625.61 to less than 698.32 score points)		Level 6 (above 698.32 score points)	
	%	S.E.	%	S.E.	%	S.E.	%	S.E.	%	S.E.	%	S.E.	%	S.E.	%	S.E.
Australia	0.5	(0.1)	1.8	(0.2)	7.1	(0.6)	17.7	(0.6)	30.3	(0.8)	27.9	(0.7)	12.1	(0.7)	2.5	(0.4)
Austria	1.7	(0.5)	6.0	(0.9)	13.3	(1.4)	21.5	(1.9)	26.5	(1.3)	20.8	(1.2)	8.8	(0.9)	1.4	(0.4)
Belgium	0.8	(0.2)	3.1	(0.5)	8.7	(0.8)	17.0	(0.9)	26.2	(1.1)	27.0	(1.0)	14.2	(0.8)	3.1	(0.4)
Canada	0.3	(0.1)	1.3	(0.2)	5.7	(0.3)	18.4	(0.6)	31.0	(0.7)	28.1	(0.7)	12.8	(0.6)	2.4	(0.3)
Chile	1.3	(0.4)	6.8	(0.9)	20.4	(1.5)	33.4	(1.4)	25.9	(1.2)	9.9	(0.9)	2.1	(0.4)	0.1	(0.1)
Czech Republic	0.6	(0.2)	3.3	(0.6)	11.0	(0.9)	23.3	(1.4)	29.2	(1.4)	23.2	(1.4)	8.3	(0.8)	1.2	(0.3)
Denmark	0.4	(0.2)	2.5	(0.4)	8.9	(0.8)	20.1	(1.0)	31.8	(1.5)	25.4	(1.8)	9.4	(0.9)	1.4	(0.4)
Estonia	0.2	(0.2)	2.1	(0.6)	6.8	(0.7)	21.0	(1.3)	32.5	(1.6)	26.0	(1.3)	10.0	(1.3)	1.5	(0.5)
Finland	0.3	(0.2)	1.0	(0.2)	3.9	(0.6)	11.7	(0.9)	25.9	(1.1)	33.0	(1.3)	19.5	(1.3)	4.6	(0.5)
France	1.6	(0.6)	3.4	(0.7)	9.9	(0.9)	20.3	(1.3)	28.7	(1.4)	24.1	(1.3)	10.0	(1.0)	2.0	(0.5)
Germany	0.7	(0.2)	3.9	(0.7)	10.0	(1.0)	18.4	(1.2)	26.2	(1.3)	26.6	(1.4)	11.9	(1.0)	2.3	(0.5)
Greece	1.6	(0.6)	4.8	(0.8)	12.7	(1.0)	24.2	(1.3)	30.5	(1.1)	19.3	(1.4)	6.0	(0.8)	0.9	(0.2)
Hungary	1.3	(0.6)	2.9	(0.6)	8.1	(1.0)	19.7	(1.2)	28.6	(1.5)	26.8	(1.6)	11.1	(1.2)	1.4	(0.3)
Iceland	0.8	(0.2)	2.2	(0.5)	7.4	(0.7)	17.4	(0.9)	29.9	(1.1)	25.8	(1.2)	12.9	(1.2)	3.5	(0.6)
Ireland	0.9	(0.3)	2.2	(0.5)	7.3	(0.8)	20.3	(1.2)	31.0	(1.6)	26.9	(1.6)	10.1	(1.2)	1.4	(0.4)
Israel	2.6	(0.6)	5.9	(0.7)	13.7	(0.8)	22.6	(1.0)	27.8	(1.1)	19.0	(1.0)	7.0	(0.6)	1.3	(0.4)
Italy	1.2	(0.2)	3.7	(0.4)	10.5	(0.5)	21.5	(0.6)	30.6	(0.6)	23.7	(0.7)	7.7	(0.4)	1.0	(0.2)
Japan	1.0	(0.3)	1.8	(0.4)	5.5	(0.7)	14.3	(1.1)	26.3	(1.3)	29.7	(1.4)	16.2	(1.0)	5.2	(0.8)
Korea	0.0	(0.0)	0.5	(0.2)	3.2	(0.7)	12.2	(1.2)	29.8	(1.3)	34.2	(1.6)	16.5	(1.5)	3.5	(0.7)
Luxembourg	2.3	(0.4)	5.6	(0.7)	13.3	(0.7)	22.1	(1.1)	25.9	(1.1)	20.5	(0.9)	8.8	(0.6)	1.6	(0.3)
Mexico	3.1	(0.4)	8.6	(0.5)	20.8	(0.6)	32.0	(0.7)	25.6	(0.7)	8.6	(0.4)	1.3	(0.2)	0.1	(0.0)
Netherlands	0.1	(0.1)	1.4	(0.5)	7.5	(0.9)	19.4	(1.8)	27.2	(1.4)	29.9	(1.6)	12.6	(1.6)	1.8	(0.5)
New Zealand	0.4	(0.2)	1.4	(0.3)	6.3	(0.7)	16.0	(0.9)	26.6	(1.2)	28.5	(1.2)	16.4	(1.1)	4.4	(0.6)
Norway	0.2	(0.2)	1.5	(0.3)	6.1	(0.6)	17.4	(1.2)	30.9	(1.1)	28.1	(1.5)	13.0	(0.9)	2.7	(0.6)
Poland	0.3	(0.1)	1.8	(0.3)	8.1	(0.7)	19.7	(1.0)	31.9	(1.1)	25.0	(1.3)	10.8	(0.8)	2.5	(0.5)
Portugal	0.5	(0.1)	2.5	(0.5)	9.0	(0.8)	24.5	(1.7)	33.5	(1.9)	22.6	(1.2)	6.6	(0.8)	0.7	(0.4)
Slovak Republic	0.7	(0.3)	2.9	(0.5)	8.5	(0.8)	19.7	(1.4)	31.4	(1.5)	24.6	(1.3)	10.4	(1.0)	1.7	(0.5)
Slovenia	0.3	(0.1)	2.2	(0.3)	8.0	(0.6)	20.7	(0.9)	32.3	(1.1)	26.9	(1.2)	9.0	(0.8)	0.6	(0.2)
Spain	1.7	(0.3)	4.1	(0.4)	10.8	(0.7)	24.5	(1.0)	30.7	(1.0)	20.7	(0.8)	6.6	(0.6)	1.0	(0.2)
Sweden	0.7	(0.3)	2.1	(0.5)	6.5	(0.6)	18.4	(1.0)	31.1	(1.2)	25.6	(1.5)	12.7	(1.3)	2.9	(0.5)
Switzerland	0.5	(0.2)	2.8	(0.5)	7.9	(0.9)	18.2	(1.1)	30.3	(1.0)	27.8	(1.2)	10.9	(1.1)	1.6	(0.4)
Turkey	1.0	(0.4)	3.7	(0.6)	13.3	(1.1)	29.4	(1.5)	30.6	(1.4)	17.3	(1.4)	4.0	(0.8)	0.5	(0.3)
United Kingdom	0.8	(0.2)	3.1	(0.5)	10.9	(0.8)	22.7	(1.1)	30.1	(1.3)	22.8	(1.4)	8.2	(0.8)	1.4	(0.4)
United States	0.7	(0.2)	3.0	(0.4)	12.0	(0.9)	24.5	(1.3)	28.3	(1.3)	21.4	(1.2)	8.3	(0.9)	1.8	(0.5)
OECD total	1.1	(0.1)	3.5	(0.2)	11.0	(0.3)	22.5	(0.4)	28.5	(0.4)	22.4	(0.4)	9.1	(0.3)	1.9	(0.2)
OECD average	0.9	(0.1)	3.1	(0.1)	9.5	(0.1)	20.7	(0.2)	29.3	(0.2)	24.4	(0.2)	10.2	(0.2)	1.9	(0.1)
Albania	7.0	(1.0)	13.3	(1.6)	25.2	(1.9)	28.4	(2.0)	19.7	(2.0)	5.8	(1.1)	0.5	(0.2)	0.0	(0.0)
Argentina	9.8	(1.1)	14.2	(1.3)	24.0	(1.6)	25.1	(1.4)	17.5	(1.2)	7.8	(0.9)	1.5	(0.4)	0.1	(0.1)
Azerbaijan	13.1	(1.4)	20.1	(1.3)	28.5	(1.3)	23.6	(1.3)	11.0	(0.9)	3.2	(0.6)	0.5	(0.2)	0.0	(0.1)
Brazil	5.8	(0.4)	14.3	(0.8)	25.1	(1.1)	27.6	(1.0)	17.3	(0.8)	7.6	(0.8)	2.1	(0.4)	0.3	(0.1)
Bulgaria	6.3	(0.9)	9.1	(1.0)	15.2	(1.3)	21.8	(1.6)	24.0	(1.7)	15.6	(1.4)	6.6	(0.9)	1.6	(0.4)
Colombia	5.5	(1.0)	15.6	(1.2)	28.9	(1.6)	29.2	(1.4)	15.8	(1.0)	4.3	(0.6)	0.6	(0.3)	0.1	(0.1)
Croatia	0.6	(0.2)	2.1	(0.4)	8.5	(1.0)	21.1	(1.6)	30.5	(1.6)	26.0	(1.4)	9.6	(1.0)	1.6	(0.4)
Dubai (UAE)	1.7	(0.3)	6.2	(0.7)	15.3	(0.8)	25.8	(1.3)	25.5	(1.2)	17.4	(0.8)	7.2	(0.6)	1.0	(0.2)
Hong Kong-China	0.3	(0.2)	1.6	(0.3)	5.3	(0.7)	15.3	(1.1)	27.2	(1.1)	33.0	(1.2)	15.1	(0.9)	2.4	(0.5)
Indonesia	4.2	(0.8)	12.9	(1.3)	26.7	(1.8)	31.3	(1.5)	18.4	(1.5)	5.7	(1.1)	0.7	(0.2)	0.1	(0.1)
Jordan	5.8	(0.9)	11.7	(1.0)	25.5	(1.3)	29.1	(1.3)	19.4	(1.3)	6.9	(0.8)	1.3	(0.3)	0.2	(0.1)
Kazakhstan	6.3	(0.8)	14.4	(1.3)	25.0	(1.5)	25.9	(1.1)	17.6	(1.0)	8.4	(0.9)	2.0	(0.4)	0.3	(0.1)
Kyrgyzstan	27.5	(1.5)	25.0	(1.1)	23.7	(1.3)	14.4	(1.0)	6.4	(0.7)	2.4	(0.5)	0.6	(0.3)	0.1	(0.1)
Latvia	0.6	(0.3)	2.0	(0.4)	10.8	(1.1)	25.0	(1.3)	35.1	(1.3)	21.3	(1.5)	4.7	(0.7)	0.4	(0.2)
Liechtenstein	0.0	c	2.5	(1.5)	7.5	(2.5)	19.7	(3.8)	29.2	(3.9)	28.9	(4.3)	10.4	(2.9)	1.8	(1.2)
Lithuania	0.6	(0.2)	2.8	(0.4)	10.7	(0.9)	22.9	(1.5)	30.9	(1.3)	22.5	(1.1)	8.2	(0.7)	1.4	(0.3)
Macao-China	0.4	(0.2)	2.0	(0.3)	8.5	(0.6)	24.1	(1.2)	34.9	(1.1)	22.9	(0.8)	6.6	(0.5)	0.6	(0.2)
Montenegro	5.9	(0.9)	11.8	(0.8)	19.5	(0.9)	26.5	(1.1)	21.4	(1.0)	11.0	(1.0)	3.3	(0.4)	0.6	(0.3)
Panama	16.5	(2.1)	19.3	(2.4)	24.5	(2.3)	19.3	(1.9)	12.7	(1.9)	6.1	(1.2)	1.4	(0.5)	0.2	(0.2)
Peru	15.1	(1.3)	19.9	(1.5)	26.9	(1.3)	22.7	(1.3)	11.5	(1.2)	3.2	(0.7)	0.7	(0.3)	0.0	(0.1)
Qatar	16.7	(0.5)	19.2	(0.7)	22.3	(0.7)	20.2	(0.8)	12.5	(0.6)	6.2	(0.3)	2.3	(0.3)	0.5	(0.1)
Romania	3.7	(0.7)	9.1	(1.2)	20.6	(1.4)	30.9	(1.5)	24.5	(1.4)	9.7	(1.1)	1.4	(0.3)	0.1	(0.1)
Russian Federation	1.1	(0.3)	4.2	(0.6)	13.4	(1.1)	26.8	(1.2)	28.3	(1.1)	17.7	(1.1)	6.8	(0.7)	1.6	(0.4)
Serbia	1.5	(0.4)	5.1	(0.6)	15.6	(1.0)	31.0	(1.3)	30.5	(1.5)	13.5	(1.2)	2.5	(0.5)	0.2	(0.2)
Shanghai-China	0.2	(0.1)	0.9	(0.2)	3.5	(0.5)	11.3	(0.8)	25.2	(1.1)	32.4	(1.2)	20.6	(1.1)	6.1	(0.6)
Singapore	0.4	(0.1)	1.9	(0.4)	7.2	(0.4)	15.8	(1.3)	25.8	(1.1)	29.0	(1.1)	16.0	(1.0)	4.0	(0.7)
Chinese Taipei	0.9	(0.3)	3.1	(0.5)	9.2	(0.6)	20.8	(1.0)	29.3	(1.4)	24.3	(1.1)	10.1	(1.1)	2.2	(0.5)
Thailand	0.9	(0.3)	6.6	(0.8)	22.6	(1.2)	35.6	(1.2)	24.7	(1.2)	8.2	(1.0)	1.4	(0.4)	0.1	(0.1)
Trinidad and Tobago	6.2	(0.7)	10.7	(0.8)	18.6	(1.0)	25.3	(1.0)	22.5	(1.0)	12.0	(0.7)	3.9	(0.5)	0.8	(0.2)
Tunisia	6.6	(0.7)	16.1	(1.0)	27.8	(1.2)	27.1	(1.1)	15.9	(1.2)	5.5	(0.8)	0.9	(0.3)	0.1	(0.1)
Uruguay	4.1	(0.5)	10.3	(0.8)	21.5	(1.0)	27.5	(1.1)	22.8	(1.0)	10.6	(0.7)	2.8	(0.5)	0.3	(0.2)

StatLink http://dx.doi.org/10.1787/888932343285

[Part 1/1]

Table I.2.6 **Mean score, variation and gender differences in student performance on the reading subscale *access and retrieve***

		All students				Gender differences						Percentiles											
		Mean score		Standard deviation		Boys		Girls		Difference (B – G)		5th		10th		25th		75th		90th		95th	
		Mean	S.E.	S.D.	S.E.	Mean score	S.E.	Mean score	S.E.	Score dif.	S.E.	Score	S.E.	Score	S.E.	Score	S.E.	Score	S.E.	Score	S.E.	Score	S.E.
OECD	Australia	513	(2.4)	100	(1.3)	495	(2.9)	531	(2.7)	**-36**	(2.8)	337	(4.5)	381	(3.5)	451	(2.7)	583	(2.6)	635	(3.4)	665	(3.6)
	Austria	477	(3.2)	109	(2.2)	459	(4.1)	494	(4.3)	**-35**	(5.8)	291	(5.9)	329	(4.9)	402	(5.1)	557	(3.8)	616	(4.7)	646	(4.7)
	Belgium	513	(2.4)	108	(1.8)	498	(3.5)	530	(3.0)	**-32**	(4.6)	323	(6.2)	368	(4.6)	444	(3.5)	591	(2.8)	643	(3.0)	673	(3.4)
	Canada	517	(1.5)	95	(1.0)	498	(1.9)	536	(1.6)	**-38**	(2.0)	353	(3.2)	393	(2.7)	456	(2.0)	583	(2.0)	634	(2.3)	664	(2.7)
	Chile	444	(3.4)	91	(2.0)	434	(4.4)	454	(3.4)	**-20**	(4.1)	290	(6.5)	328	(5.7)	384	(4.3)	506	(3.7)	559	(4.3)	591	(4.5)
	Czech Republic	479	(3.2)	99	(1.7)	455	(4.4)	506	(3.5)	**-52**	(4.8)	309	(6.2)	349	(5.6)	412	(4.3)	551	(3.5)	605	(3.7)	635	(3.6)
	Denmark	502	(2.6)	94	(1.4)	486	(3.1)	518	(2.9)	**-31**	(3.1)	339	(5.6)	376	(4.4)	440	(3.5)	569	(3.1)	619	(3.1)	648	(4.8)
	Estonia	503	(3.0)	91	(1.7)	484	(3.4)	523	(3.2)	**-40**	(3.3)	345	(4.8)	381	(4.0)	444	(3.6)	567	(3.6)	617	(4.0)	647	(4.1)
	Finland	532	(2.7)	99	(1.2)	503	(3.1)	562	(2.8)	**-59**	(2.5)	357	(5.6)	401	(4.0)	470	(3.6)	602	(2.9)	653	(3.1)	682	(3.7)
	France	492	(3.8)	110	(3.2)	471	(4.7)	511	(3.6)	**-40**	(3.8)	298	(9.5)	347	(7.6)	422	(4.7)	571	(4.5)	625	(4.6)	656	(5.0)
	Germany	501	(3.5)	104	(2.2)	482	(4.5)	520	(3.8)	**-38**	(4.4)	318	(7.2)	358	(6.0)	429	(5.3)	578	(4.0)	630	(4.1)	658	(4.5)
	Greece	468	(4.4)	103	(2.5)	445	(5.5)	490	(4.1)	**-45**	(4.9)	285	(9.5)	330	(8.5)	401	(6.3)	540	(4.0)	595	(3.8)	627	(3.6)
	Hungary	501	(3.7)	104	(3.1)	484	(4.4)	519	(4.4)	**-34**	(4.6)	315	(11.0)	362	(8.6)	437	(5.0)	576	(4.0)	627	(4.0)	654	(4.4)
	Iceland	507	(1.6)	108	(1.4)	481	(2.4)	532	(2.3)	**-51**	(3.4)	319	(5.5)	363	(3.8)	439	(3.4)	580	(2.7)	639	(3.0)	672	(4.1)
	Ireland	498	(3.3)	99	(2.4)	476	(4.5)	521	(3.4)	**-44**	(4.6)	321	(9.7)	372	(5.4)	439	(4.1)	567	(2.8)	616	(4.0)	643	(4.1)
	Israel	463	(4.1)	120	(3.1)	439	(6.2)	486	(3.7)	**-47**	(6.2)	247	(12.1)	299	(8.7)	386	(5.5)	548	(3.7)	610	(4.1)	643	(4.8)
	Italy	482	(1.8)	105	(1.5)	460	(2.6)	504	(2.2)	**-44**	(3.1)	295	(4.7)	341	(3.2)	415	(2.6)	557	(1.7)	609	(1.7)	639	(2.1)
	Japan	530	(3.8)	110	(3.2)	512	(6.1)	548	(4.0)	**-36**	(7.2)	333	(10.4)	386	(7.9)	464	(4.8)	605	(3.3)	658	(4.7)	691	(4.9)
	Korea	542	(3.6)	87	(2.3)	527	(5.0)	558	(3.9)	**-32**	(5.9)	391	(7.8)	429	(6.3)	486	(4.2)	602	(3.6)	650	(3.7)	677	(4.8)
	Luxembourg	471	(1.3)	115	(1.1)	449	(2.0)	493	(1.6)	**-44**	(2.5)	266	(5.7)	318	(3.2)	396	(2.9)	553	(2.3)	612	(2.3)	645	(3.9)
	Mexico	433	(2.1)	94	(1.4)	422	(2.4)	443	(2.2)	**-21**	(1.8)	271	(4.4)	311	(3.4)	373	(2.6)	498	(2.0)	548	(2.3)	577	(2.7)
	Netherlands	519	(5.1)	92	(1.6)	506	(5.0)	532	(5.4)	**-26**	(2.5)	364	(6.7)	396	(5.2)	453	(5.8)	588	(5.5)	634	(5.0)	661	(6.3)
	New Zealand	521	(2.4)	106	(1.7)	497	(3.5)	546	(2.7)	**-49**	(4.2)	338	(4.9)	381	(4.4)	452	(3.4)	597	(2.8)	650	(3.0)	680	(3.3)
	Norway	512	(2.8)	99	(1.6)	488	(3.5)	537	(3.0)	**-49**	(3.4)	340	(5.2)	382	(4.5)	449	(3.5)	580	(3.4)	634	(3.6)	665	(4.1)
	Poland	500	(2.8)	101	(1.4)	475	(3.1)	525	(3.1)	**-50**	(2.9)	326	(5.0)	369	(4.0)	435	(3.6)	569	(2.9)	626	(3.9)	660	(4.2)
	Portugal	488	(3.3)	93	(2.0)	469	(3.9)	506	(3.2)	**-37**	(3.0)	326	(6.2)	367	(5.5)	430	(4.3)	553	(3.6)	602	(4.5)	631	(4.6)
	Slovak Republic	491	(3.0)	103	(2.6)	463	(4.3)	518	(3.3)	**-55**	(4.3)	311	(8.5)	353	(7.0)	423	(4.0)	563	(3.4)	619	(3.7)	648	(4.6)
	Slovenia	489	(1.1)	98	(0.8)	461	(1.7)	518	(1.5)	**-57**	(2.5)	314	(4.0)	355	(2.7)	426	(2.2)	561	(1.8)	610	(3.2)	635	(3.3)
	Spain	480	(2.1)	100	(1.2)	465	(2.2)	495	(2.5)	**-30**	(2.2)	303	(4.3)	350	(3.4)	419	(2.8)	549	(2.3)	602	(2.5)	632	(2.7)
	Sweden	505	(2.9)	104	(1.5)	479	(3.3)	531	(3.2)	**-52**	(2.9)	321	(5.9)	368	(4.7)	440	(3.5)	577	(3.1)	631	(4.7)	664	(3.9)
	Switzerland	505	(2.7)	97	(1.5)	487	(3.3)	524	(2.8)	**-37**	(2.9)	331	(5.3)	375	(4.6)	443	(4.2)	576	(2.9)	625	(3.8)	653	(4.1)
	Turkey	467	(4.1)	95	(2.2)	451	(4.5)	484	(4.6)	**-33**	(4.2)	303	(7.9)	343	(5.6)	407	(4.2)	534	(4.8)	586	(4.8)	614	(6.0)
	United Kingdom	491	(2.5)	101	(1.6)	476	(3.9)	507	(2.9)	**-31**	(4.6)	321	(4.6)	361	(4.4)	426	(3.3)	561	(2.8)	617	(3.5)	650	(4.2)
	United States	492	(3.6)	99	(1.5)	480	(4.0)	504	(3.8)	**-24**	(3.4)	325	(5.0)	363	(4.6)	425	(4.0)	561	(4.4)	618	(4.4)	650	(5.4)
	OECD total	491	(1.2)	104	(0.6)	475	(1.4)	507	(1.3)	**-32**	(1.2)	313	(1.9)	355	(1.7)	423	(1.4)	564	(1.3)	621	(1.5)	653	(1.8)
	OECD average	495	(0.5)	101	(0.3)	475	(0.7)	515	(0.6)	**-40**	(0.7)	318	(1.2)	361	(0.9)	430	(0.7)	566	(0.6)	619	(0.6)	649	(0.7)
Partners	Albania	380	(4.7)	112	(2.1)	348	(5.9)	413	(4.4)	**-65**	(4.7)	182	(8.2)	232	(6.7)	307	(5.7)	461	(5.4)	520	(5.8)	550	(6.6)
	Argentina	394	(4.8)	115	(3.1)	376	(5.2)	409	(5.2)	**-33**	(4.1)	193	(11.0)	242	(7.0)	321	(5.7)	474	(6.1)	539	(6.2)	574	(6.4)
	Azerbaijan	361	(4.5)	103	(2.4)	347	(4.9)	376	(4.6)	**-29**	(2.7)	189	(7.5)	227	(7.2)	293	(5.5)	432	(5.1)	493	(5.4)	528	(6.0)
	Brazil	407	(3.3)	107	(1.9)	391	(3.5)	420	(3.4)	**-29**	(2.2)	232	(4.6)	270	(4.2)	334	(3.3)	478	(4.6)	546	(5.5)	587	(6.1)
	Bulgaria	430	(8.3)	139	(3.3)	399	(9.3)	463	(7.0)	**-64**	(5.6)	183	(10.1)	239	(12.7)	339	(10.3)	530	(8.1)	599	(8.8)	637	(9.8)
	Colombia	404	(3.7)	91	(2.0)	402	(4.6)	406	(4.0)	-4	(4.5)	251	(6.8)	286	(6.3)	344	(4.5)	467	(3.9)	522	(3.7)	553	(4.4)
	Croatia	492	(3.1)	101	(1.9)	467	(3.7)	519	(3.9)	**-52**	(4.8)	318	(5.8)	359	(5.3)	427	(4.5)	563	(3.4)	616	(3.3)	646	(4.8)
	Dubai (UAE)	458	(1.4)	117	(1.3)	436	(1.9)	482	(1.8)	**-46**	(2.5)	258	(5.3)	304	(2.7)	380	(2.5)	543	(2.2)	606	(2.9)	639	(3.6)
	Hong Kong-China	530	(2.7)	94	(1.9)	516	(4.1)	545	(3.2)	**-28**	(4.8)	361	(5.9)	404	(4.8)	471	(3.4)	596	(2.7)	642	(3.5)	669	(5.2)
	Indonesia	399	(4.7)	91	(2.4)	378	(4.9)	419	(5.0)	**-41**	(4.4)	248	(7.6)	281	(6.1)	338	(5.6)	461	(5.3)	515	(7.0)	547	(7.3)
	Jordan	394	(4.0)	110	(2.2)	367	(5.7)	421	(5.0)	**-55**	(7.5)	195	(7.6)	249	(6.2)	328	(4.8)	469	(4.4)	529	(4.7)	564	(5.0)
	Kazakhstan	397	(3.7)	110	(2.0)	375	(3.8)	420	(4.2)	**-44**	(3.1)	218	(6.2)	257	(4.8)	321	(4.3)	473	(4.9)	542	(6.7)	580	(6.4)
	Kyrgyzstan	299	(4.0)	122	(2.4)	266	(5.0)	330	(4.0)	**-64**	(3.8)	95	(7.7)	143	(5.7)	218	(4.9)	380	(5.2)	457	(7.0)	503	(8.7)
	Latvia	476	(3.6)	92	(1.9)	452	(4.2)	501	(3.6)	**-49**	(3.7)	319	(6.7)	356	(5.4)	416	(4.7)	542	(3.8)	590	(4.0)	617	(4.2)
	Liechtenstein	508	(4.0)	93	(3.8)	492	(6.2)	525	(6.5)	**-33**	(9.9)	344	(21.4)	385	(10.2)	448	(9.8)	574	(6.5)	621	(7.7)	650	(11.9)
	Lithuania	476	(3.0)	102	(1.9)	446	(3.8)	508	(2.7)	**-61**	(3.2)	303	(5.8)	343	(5.5)	408	(4.1)	548	(3.1)	605	(3.7)	637	(3.7)
	Macao-China	493	(1.2)	88	(0.9)	477	(1.6)	509	(1.3)	**-31**	(1.8)	342	(3.3)	379	(2.0)	435	(2.3)	554	(1.5)	603	(2.3)	630	(2.3)
	Montenegro	408	(2.3)	119	(1.6)	378	(2.4)	438	(3.4)	**-60**	(3.6)	206	(6.1)	253	(4.5)	328	(4.0)	490	(3.0)	558	(3.8)	597	(4.2)
	Panama	363	(7.7)	119	(4.2)	348	(8.8)	378	(8.0)	**-30**	(7.6)	167	(12.5)	211	(12.7)	283	(7.9)	443	(8.6)	521	(10.8)	565	(11.4)
	Peru	364	(4.3)	106	(2.7)	356	(4.3)	372	(5.5)	**-16**	(5.0)	184	(6.6)	226	(5.2)	293	(4.5)	436	(4.7)	497	(6.8)	534	(8.0)
	Qatar	354	(1.0)	135	(0.9)	325	(1.6)	384	(1.2)	**-58**	(2.0)	140	(2.5)	181	(2.9)	258	(2.1)	445	(2.1)	536	(2.6)	586	(4.3)
	Romania	423	(4.7)	102	(2.7)	402	(5.6)	442	(4.6)	**-40**	(5.1)	243	(8.6)	287	(6.9)	357	(6.1)	494	(4.8)	548	(4.7)	576	(5.7)
	Russian Federation	469	(3.9)	103	(2.0)	446	(4.2)	491	(4.1)	**-45**	(2.9)	297	(7.7)	339	(6.1)	403	(4.7)	536	(4.4)	599	(4.6)	636	(6.1)
	Serbia	449	(3.1)	95	(2.0)	430	(4.2)	469	(3.1)	**-39**	(4.1)	284	(6.4)	324	(5.6)	389	(3.8)	515	(3.2)	567	(3.9)	595	(3.9)
	Shanghai-China	549	(2.9)	96	(1.9)	531	(3.7)	568	(2.6)	**-37**	(3.3)	382	(5.9)	423	(5.3)	489	(3.8)	617	(3.0)	666	(3.4)	695	(4.1)
	Singapore	526	(1.4)	103	(1.2)	510	(2.0)	543	(1.9)	**-32**	(2.8)	345	(5.3)	388	(3.4)	459	(2.5)	599	(1.6)	651	(3.5)	680	(3.6)
	Chinese Taipei	496	(2.8)	105	(1.8)	477	(4.0)	516	(3.8)	**-39**	(5.7)	312	(6.0)	358	(4.1)	429	(3.9)	570	(3.6)	625	(3.8)	656	(4.4)
	Thailand	431	(3.5)	86	(2.1)	408	(4.2)	449	(3.7)	**-41**	(4.1)	290	(6.5)	322	(5.5)	374	(3.8)	488	(3.4)	540	(4.6)	573	(5.5)
	Trinidad and Tobago	413	(1.6)	125	(1.4)	382	(2.3)	444	(1.9)	**-62**	(2.7)	192	(4.8)	246	(4.4)	332	(3.3)	501	(3.0)	567	(3.2)	607	(3.6)
	Tunisia	393	(3.3)	102	(1.7)	379	(3.7)	406	(3.5)	**-27**	(2.7)	221	(5.7)	263	(5.0)	327	(4.1)	463	(4.3)	523	(5.1)	559	(6.7)
	Uruguay	424	(2.9)	110	(1.7)	404	(3.5)	443	(3.1)	**-39**	(3.5)	235	(6.4)	280	(5.0)	352	(3.9)	502	(3.2)	563	(4.2)	599	(4.7)

Note: Values that are statistically significant are indicated in bold (see Annex A3).
StatLink http://dx.doi.org/10.1787/888932343285

[Part 1/1]

Table I.2.7 Percentage of students at each proficiency level on the reading subscale *integrate and interpret*

	Below Level 1b (less than 262.04 score points)		Level 1b (from 262.04 to less than 334.75 score points)		Level 1a (from 334.75 to less than 407.47 score points)		Level 2 (from 407.47 to less than 480.18 score points)		Level 3 (from 480.18 to less than 552.89 score points)		Level 4 (from 552.89 to less than 625.61 score points)		Level 5 (from 625.61 to less than 698.32 score points)		Level 6 (above 698.32 score points)	
	%	S.E.	%	S.E.	%	S.E.	%	S.E.	%	S.E.	%	S.E.	%	S.E.	%	S.E.
OECD																
Australia	1.0	(0.1)	3.7	(0.2)	10.9	(0.5)	20.7	(0.5)	27.6	(0.7)	22.9	(0.6)	10.5	(0.5)	2.7	(0.4)
Austria	1.8	(0.3)	7.5	(0.6)	17.6	(0.9)	25.2	(1.3)	25.7	(1.0)	17.1	(1.0)	4.7	(0.5)	0.4	(0.1)
Belgium	1.4	(0.3)	5.1	(0.4)	12.6	(0.6)	20.5	(0.7)	24.9	(0.7)	23.3	(0.8)	10.6	(0.6)	1.5	(0.3)
Canada	0.4	(0.1)	2.3	(0.2)	9.1	(0.4)	20.7	(0.6)	28.8	(0.6)	25.0	(0.5)	11.4	(0.4)	2.3	(0.2)
Chile	1.3	(0.2)	7.5	(0.7)	21.2	(1.1)	32.6	(1.2)	25.5	(1.0)	9.9	(0.8)	1.9	(0.4)	0.1	(0.1)
Czech Republic	0.6	(0.2)	4.5	(0.5)	15.5	(0.9)	26.3	(1.1)	27.3	(1.1)	18.7	(1.2)	6.4	(0.6)	0.7	(0.2)
Denmark	0.5	(0.1)	3.1	(0.3)	12.3	(0.6)	26.8	(0.9)	33.0	(0.9)	19.8	(0.9)	4.4	(0.5)	0.2	(0.1)
Estonia	0.2	(0.1)	2.4	(0.4)	11.6	(0.8)	25.4	(1.1)	33.2	(1.1)	20.9	(0.9)	5.6	(0.5)	0.6	(0.2)
Finland	0.2	(0.1)	1.3	(0.2)	6.3	(0.4)	16.8	(0.6)	29.7	(0.8)	30.0	(0.8)	13.6	(0.8)	2.2	(0.3)
France	2.6	(0.5)	5.8	(0.6)	12.3	(0.8)	20.4	(1.0)	25.7	(1.1)	21.6	(1.0)	9.9	(0.8)	1.8	(0.3)
Germany	0.7	(0.2)	4.2	(0.4)	12.8	(0.8)	22.4	(0.9)	27.9	(1.2)	22.7	(1.2)	8.3	(0.7)	0.9	(0.2)
Greece	1.0	(0.3)	5.0	(0.7)	14.7	(1.1)	26.5	(0.9)	28.5	(1.1)	18.5	(1.1)	5.1	(0.5)	0.6	(0.2)
Hungary	0.5	(0.2)	3.7	(0.6)	12.8	(0.9)	24.3	(1.3)	30.7	(1.2)	21.7	(1.2)	6.0	(0.7)	0.4	(0.1)
Iceland	1.1	(0.2)	4.1	(0.5)	11.9	(0.8)	21.5	(0.7)	29.4	(0.9)	22.2	(0.8)	8.5	(0.6)	1.3	(0.3)
Ireland	1.5	(0.4)	4.1	(0.6)	12.6	(0.8)	24.0	(1.0)	29.3	(1.1)	20.9	(0.9)	6.9	(0.6)	0.8	(0.2)
Israel	3.5	(0.6)	8.2	(0.7)	15.2	(0.7)	22.9	(0.9)	25.4	(1.0)	17.7	(0.7)	6.2	(0.5)	0.9	(0.2)
Italy	1.1	(0.2)	4.6	(0.3)	13.9	(0.4)	24.4	(0.6)	29.2	(0.6)	20.4	(0.5)	5.9	(0.3)	0.6	(0.1)
Japan	1.2	(0.3)	3.4	(0.5)	9.3	(0.7)	18.9	(0.8)	27.1	(0.9)	26.2	(1.1)	11.3	(0.7)	2.6	(0.5)
Korea	0.2	(0.1)	0.9	(0.4)	4.8	(0.6)	15.7	(1.0)	31.7	(1.1)	32.4	(1.3)	12.9	(1.1)	1.4	(0.2)
Luxembourg	2.6	(0.3)	7.2	(0.4)	16.2	(0.6)	23.8	(0.8)	26.0	(0.7)	17.7	(0.6)	5.9	(0.4)	0.7	(0.2)
Mexico	4.0	(0.4)	13.0	(0.6)	26.9	(0.6)	31.3	(0.6)	19.1	(0.6)	5.1	(0.4)	0.5	(0.1)	0.0	(0.0)
Netherlands	0.1	(0.1)	2.7	(0.4)	14.1	(1.5)	24.4	(1.2)	26.2	(1.2)	21.7	(1.7)	9.6	(0.9)	1.3	(0.3)
New Zealand	1.0	(0.2)	3.6	(0.5)	10.9	(0.5)	20.3	(0.7)	25.2	(0.8)	23.3	(0.8)	12.5	(0.8)	3.1	(0.4)
Norway	0.6	(0.2)	3.7	(0.4)	11.9	(0.7)	23.7	(1.1)	30.0	(1.1)	20.9	(1.0)	8.2	(0.6)	1.1	(0.2)
Poland	0.5	(0.1)	3.1	(0.4)	11.5	(0.7)	24.5	(1.0)	29.9	(1.0)	22.0	(0.9)	7.5	(0.6)	1.0	(0.2)
Portugal	0.5	(0.2)	3.9	(0.4)	14.4	(0.9)	27.2	(0.9)	30.6	(1.2)	18.1	(0.8)	4.8	(0.5)	0.3	(0.2)
Slovak Republic	0.6	(0.3)	4.7	(0.6)	16.0	(0.8)	28.1	(1.0)	28.6	(1.2)	17.2	(0.9)	4.5	(0.5)	0.4	(0.1)
Slovenia	0.4	(0.1)	4.5	(0.4)	15.0	(0.7)	25.2	(1.0)	29.2	(0.8)	20.0	(0.8)	5.4	(0.4)	0.4	(0.1)
Spain	1.1	(0.1)	4.5	(0.5)	14.0	(0.7)	27.5	(0.7)	32.2	(0.9)	17.2	(0.6)	3.3	(0.2)	0.2	(0.1)
Sweden	1.9	(0.3)	4.6	(0.6)	12.7	(0.9)	23.4	(1.0)	28.5	(1.0)	19.4	(1.0)	8.1	(0.6)	1.5	(0.3)
Switzerland	0.8	(0.2)	4.3	(0.4)	12.5	(0.7)	22.4	(0.7)	28.0	(0.9)	22.7	(1.0)	8.2	(0.7)	1.2	(0.3)
Turkey	0.4	(0.1)	5.3	(0.6)	20.5	(1.0)	33.8	(1.1)	27.8	(1.2)	11.0	(1.1)	1.2	(0.3)	0.0	(0.0)
United Kingdom	1.0	(0.2)	4.5	(0.4)	14.6	(0.7)	25.0	(0.8)	28.1	(0.8)	18.5	(0.7)	7.1	(0.4)	1.2	(0.2)
United States	0.7	(0.2)	4.7	(0.5)	14.5	(0.8)	24.9	(0.8)	26.0	(0.8)	19.1	(0.9)	8.2	(0.7)	1.8	(0.4)
OECD total	1.2	(0.1)	5.2	(0.2)	14.6	(0.3)	24.6	(0.3)	26.8	(0.3)	19.1	(0.3)	7.2	(0.2)	1.3	(0.1)
OECD average	1.1	(0.0)	4.6	(0.1)	13.6	(0.1)	24.2	(0.2)	28.1	(0.2)	20.2	(0.2)	7.2	(0.1)	1.1	(0.0)
Partners																
Albania	9.6	(0.8)	17.4	(1.0)	26.6	(1.3)	27.1	(1.0)	15.1	(1.2)	3.9	(0.5)	0.3	(0.1)	0.0	(0.0)
Argentina	10.9	(1.1)	16.4	(1.0)	25.0	(1.1)	25.0	(1.3)	15.5	(1.1)	6.0	(0.8)	1.2	(0.3)	0.1	(0.1)
Azerbaijan	5.3	(0.7)	23.4	(1.4)	40.0	(1.2)	25.8	(1.4)	5.1	(0.7)	0.3	(0.1)	0.0	(0.0)	0.0	c
Brazil	5.5	(0.4)	17.4	(0.7)	29.3	(0.8)	26.3	(0.8)	14.7	(0.8)	5.5	(0.5)	1.1	(0.2)	0.1	(0.1)
Bulgaria	5.6	(0.8)	12.8	(1.3)	20.5	(1.4)	24.9	(1.4)	21.8	(1.5)	11.4	(1.1)	2.7	(0.5)	0.3	(0.1)
Colombia	4.7	(0.7)	14.7	(1.1)	28.9	(1.2)	29.8	(1.1)	16.5	(1.0)	4.7	(0.5)	0.6	(0.2)	0.0	(0.0)
Croatia	0.6	(0.1)	4.9	(0.6)	16.9	(1.1)	29.3	(1.0)	30.9	(1.1)	15.0	(1.0)	2.2	(0.3)	0.1	(0.0)
Dubai (UAE)	3.5	(0.3)	9.7	(0.6)	19.3	(0.6)	25.5	(0.9)	22.7	(0.8)	14.1	(0.6)	4.6	(0.5)	0.6	(0.2)
Hong Kong-China	0.4	(0.2)	2.0	(0.3)	7.0	(0.6)	17.8	(0.9)	30.2	(1.0)	29.3	(1.2)	11.5	(0.7)	1.8	(0.2)
Indonesia	1.8	(0.4)	15.4	(1.3)	39.0	(1.6)	33.3	(1.5)	9.5	(1.2)	0.9	(0.3)	0.0	(0.0)	0.0	c
Jordan	4.8	(0.6)	13.0	(0.9)	28.2	(1.1)	33.9	(1.0)	17.1	(1.0)	3.0	(0.4)	0.1	(0.1)	0.0	(0.0)
Kazakhstan	5.2	(0.4)	19.3	(1.3)	31.8	(1.1)	26.0	(0.9)	13.7	(0.9)	3.6	(0.5)	0.4	(0.1)	0.0	(0.0)
Kyrgyzstan	22.5	(1.3)	32.0	(1.4)	28.1	(0.9)	13.0	(0.8)	3.7	(0.4)	0.7	(0.2)	0.0	(0.0)	0.0	c
Latvia	0.4	(0.1)	2.7	(0.5)	14.2	(1.0)	29.8	(1.2)	32.7	(1.1)	17.1	(1.0)	3.0	(0.4)	0.1	(0.1)
Liechtenstein	0.4	(0.4)	4.4	(1.2)	12.2	(2.1)	23.5	(2.5)	30.5	(3.2)	23.2	(2.7)	5.2	(1.8)	0.7	(0.6)
Lithuania	0.8	(0.2)	4.9	(0.5)	18.5	(0.9)	31.2	(1.3)	27.7	(1.0)	13.8	(0.8)	2.9	(0.4)	0.1	(0.1)
Macao-China	0.2	(0.1)	2.5	(0.2)	12.4	(0.4)	30.4	(0.7)	33.7	(0.7)	17.5	(0.5)	3.3	(0.3)	0.1	(0.1)
Montenegro	3.7	(0.3)	12.8	(0.7)	27.8	(0.9)	30.6	(0.8)	18.8	(0.7)	5.7	(0.4)	0.7	(0.3)	0.0	(0.0)
Panama	11.3	(1.6)	23.7	(1.8)	30.8	(1.8)	21.2	(1.6)	9.9	(1.4)	2.7	(0.6)	0.4	(0.1)	0.0	(0.0)
Peru	14.0	(1.0)	22.4	(1.1)	27.9	(1.1)	21.9	(0.9)	10.1	(0.8)	3.1	(0.5)	0.6	(0.2)	0.1	(0.1)
Qatar	12.9	(0.4)	23.7	(0.6)	26.3	(0.6)	19.6	(0.7)	11.3	(0.3)	4.8	(0.3)	1.2	(0.2)	0.1	(0.1)
Romania	3.4	(0.5)	12.4	(1.0)	25.1	(1.3)	33.2	(1.1)	20.6	(1.3)	5.7	(0.7)	0.7	(0.2)	0.0	(0.0)
Russian Federation	1.2	(0.2)	6.0	(0.6)	17.9	(0.9)	31.0	(1.0)	27.0	(1.1)	13.0	(1.0)	3.6	(0.5)	0.4	(0.1)
Serbia	1.7	(0.3)	8.4	(0.6)	22.3	(0.9)	32.7	(0.8)	25.4	(0.8)	8.4	(0.6)	1.1	(0.2)	0.0	(0.0)
Shanghai-China	0.0	(0.0)	0.5	(0.1)	3.4	(0.5)	13.3	(0.8)	28.3	(1.1)	33.2	(0.9)	18.0	(0.9)	3.1	(0.4)
Singapore	0.6	(0.1)	3.0	(0.3)	9.9	(0.5)	19.2	(0.7)	26.2	(0.7)	24.8	(0.9)	12.9	(0.5)	3.5	(0.3)
Chinese Taipei	0.4	(0.2)	3.2	(0.4)	11.6	(0.6)	24.5	(0.8)	32.7	(1.0)	21.3	(0.9)	5.9	(0.5)	0.5	(0.2)
Thailand	1.4	(0.3)	11.1	(0.9)	33.5	(1.1)	35.6	(1.2)	15.2	(0.8)	3.0	(0.5)	0.2	(0.1)	0.0	(0.0)
Trinidad and Tobago	8.2	(0.6)	14.3	(0.6)	22.0	(0.8)	25.9	(1.0)	18.5	(0.8)	8.6	(0.6)	2.2	(0.3)	0.2	(0.1)
Tunisia	5.6	(0.6)	17.2	(1.0)	32.9	(1.3)	30.3	(1.3)	11.9	(0.8)	1.9	(0.4)	0.1	(0.1)	0.0	(0.0)
Uruguay	5.1	(0.6)	13.1	(0.8)	24.8	(0.8)	29.0	(0.9)	19.1	(0.7)	7.3	(0.5)	1.5	(0.3)	0.1	(0.1)

StatLink http://dx.doi.org/10.1787/888932343285

[Part 1/2]

Table I.2.8

Percentage of students at each proficiency level on the reading subscale *integrate and interpret*, by gender

	Boys – Proficiency levels															
	Below Level 1b (less than 262.04 score points)		Level 1b (from 262.04 to less than 334.75 score points)		Level 1a (from 334.75 to less than 407.47 score points)		Level 2 (from 407.47 to less than 480.18 score points)		Level 3 (from 480.18 to less than 552.89 score points)		Level 4 (from 552.89 to less than 625.61 score points)		Level 5 (from 625.61 to less than 698.32 score points)		Level 6 (above 698.32 score points)	
	%	S.E.	%	S.E.	%	S.E.	%	S.E.	%	S.E.	%	S.E.	%	S.E.	%	S.E.
OECD																
Australia	1.6	(0.2)	5.3	(0.4)	13.9	(0.7)	22.5	(0.8)	26.2	(1.1)	20.0	(0.8)	8.4	(0.6)	2.1	(0.5)
Austria	2.7	(0.5)	9.8	(0.9)	21.5	(1.3)	25.8	(1.5)	23.4	(1.2)	13.6	(1.2)	2.9	(0.6)	0.2	(0.1)
Belgium	1.8	(0.4)	6.3	(0.7)	14.6	(0.8)	21.7	(1.0)	23.7	(1.0)	21.2	(1.1)	9.3	(0.8)	1.3	(0.3)
Canada	0.6	(0.2)	3.3	(0.4)	11.6	(0.6)	23.0	(0.8)	27.9	(0.7)	22.6	(0.7)	9.3	(0.5)	1.5	(0.2)
Chile	1.9	(0.4)	9.5	(1.0)	23.6	(1.3)	31.8	(1.4)	22.8	(1.3)	8.9	(0.9)	1.4	(0.5)	0.1	(0.1)
Czech Republic	1.0	(0.3)	6.4	(0.9)	20.2	(1.4)	29.4	(1.4)	25.3	(1.3)	13.4	(1.1)	3.8	(0.5)	0.4	(0.1)
Denmark	0.8	(0.2)	3.9	(0.5)	14.7	(0.9)	29.4	(1.2)	31.1	(1.2)	16.9	(1.0)	3.1	(0.5)	0.2	(0.1)
Estonia	0.4	(0.2)	3.7	(0.6)	16.2	(1.2)	28.8	(1.4)	31.3	(1.4)	15.7	(0.9)	3.6	(0.6)	0.2	(0.2)
Finland	0.3	(0.1)	2.0	(0.4)	9.7	(0.8)	22.3	(1.0)	31.7	(1.3)	24.2	(1.1)	8.5	(0.7)	1.1	(0.3)
France	3.8	(0.8)	8.1	(0.9)	14.7	(1.1)	22.2	(1.2)	24.0	(1.3)	18.4	(1.1)	7.7	(1.0)	1.2	(0.3)
Germany	1.2	(0.4)	5.8	(0.9)	16.1	(1.1)	25.1	(1.2)	27.3	(1.2)	18.6	(1.4)	5.4	(0.7)	0.5	(0.2)
Greece	1.6	(0.6)	7.4	(1.0)	18.7	(1.5)	28.4	(1.2)	25.7	(1.5)	14.2	(1.1)	3.8	(0.5)	0.3	(0.1)
Hungary	0.8	(0.3)	5.2	(1.0)	16.7	(1.4)	26.5	(1.6)	28.9	(1.6)	17.6	(1.3)	4.1	(0.7)	0.2	(0.1)
Iceland	1.7	(0.3)	6.5	(0.9)	15.5	(1.4)	23.0	(1.1)	27.1	(1.2)	18.8	(1.1)	6.7	(0.6)	0.8	(0.3)
Ireland	2.4	(0.6)	5.9	(0.8)	15.3	(1.2)	25.9	(1.3)	28.2	(1.6)	17.0	(1.2)	4.8	(0.7)	0.5	(0.2)
Israel	5.4	(1.0)	11.1	(0.9)	17.1	(1.1)	23.3	(1.3)	21.8	(1.3)	15.4	(0.9)	5.3	(0.6)	0.7	(0.2)
Italy	1.8	(0.4)	6.9	(0.5)	18.3	(0.7)	26.3	(0.8)	26.1	(0.9)	16.1	(0.6)	4.2	(0.3)	0.3	(0.1)
Japan	1.8	(0.5)	5.0	(0.8)	11.9	(1.1)	21.0	(1.1)	26.0	(1.2)	23.0	(1.2)	10.4	(1.0)	1.8	(0.5)
Korea	0.3	(0.2)	1.5	(0.6)	7.1	(0.8)	18.9	(1.4)	32.4	(1.5)	28.6	(1.7)	10.4	(1.2)	0.9	(0.2)
Luxembourg	3.9	(0.5)	9.8	(0.7)	18.9	(1.0)	23.7	(1.1)	24.1	(1.0)	14.6	(0.8)	4.6	(0.6)	0.5	(0.2)
Mexico	5.5	(0.5)	15.9	(0.8)	28.7	(0.8)	29.1	(0.8)	16.3	(0.7)	4.0	(0.4)	0.4	(0.1)	0.0	(0.0)
Netherlands	0.2	(0.1)	3.6	(0.6)	16.3	(1.9)	25.7	(1.8)	25.8	(1.5)	19.0	(1.6)	8.3	(1.0)	1.1	(0.3)
New Zealand	1.7	(0.4)	5.5	(0.8)	14.0	(0.8)	22.3	(1.1)	24.2	(1.1)	20.2	(1.2)	10.0	(0.9)	2.1	(0.5)
Norway	1.0	(0.3)	5.6	(0.7)	15.5	(1.1)	26.4	(1.3)	28.3	(1.5)	16.8	(1.2)	5.8	(0.9)	0.6	(0.3)
Poland	0.8	(0.3)	5.4	(0.7)	16.2	(1.0)	27.8	(1.4)	27.0	(1.6)	17.2	(1.1)	5.1	(0.6)	0.5	(0.2)
Portugal	0.9	(0.3)	5.7	(0.6)	19.0	(1.3)	28.8	(1.2)	26.8	(1.4)	15.0	(1.3)	3.6	(0.7)	0.2	(0.2)
Slovak Republic	0.8	(0.4)	7.6	(1.1)	22.0	(1.3)	30.6	(1.3)	24.1	(1.3)	12.1	(0.9)	2.6	(0.4)	0.1	(0.1)
Slovenia	0.8	(0.2)	7.4	(0.7)	20.7	(1.2)	27.3	(1.3)	25.6	(1.1)	15.0	(1.0)	3.0	(0.5)	0.2	(0.2)
Spain	1.6	(0.2)	6.0	(0.7)	17.0	(0.8)	28.7	(0.9)	29.6	(0.9)	14.4	(0.7)	2.6	(0.3)	0.1	(0.1)
Sweden	2.8	(0.5)	6.5	(0.8)	16.0	(1.1)	25.1	(1.2)	26.2	(1.5)	16.1	(1.4)	6.2	(0.7)	1.0	(0.3)
Switzerland	1.1	(0.3)	5.9	(0.6)	15.8	(0.9)	24.9	(1.1)	27.1	(1.2)	18.4	(1.1)	6.0	(0.7)	0.9	(0.3)
Turkey	0.6	(0.2)	8.1	(0.9)	27.0	(1.3)	33.6	(1.2)	22.9	(1.4)	7.4	(1.1)	0.5	(0.2)	0.0	c
United Kingdom	1.5	(0.3)	5.9	(0.6)	17.2	(1.0)	25.5	(1.1)	26.0	(1.1)	16.6	(1.0)	6.4	(0.6)	1.0	(0.3)
United States	1.0	(0.4)	6.3	(0.8)	16.3	(1.0)	25.1	(1.2)	24.8	(1.1)	17.9	(1.1)	7.3	(0.8)	1.3	(0.4)
OECD total	1.8	(0.1)	7.0	(0.2)	17.4	(0.4)	25.6	(0.4)	25.0	(0.4)	16.6	(0.4)	5.9	(0.2)	0.9	(0.1)
OECD average	1.7	(0.1)	6.4	(0.1)	17.0	(0.2)	25.9	(0.2)	26.2	(0.2)	16.7	(0.2)	5.4	(0.1)	0.7	(0.0)
Partners																
Albania	15.0	(1.3)	22.9	(1.7)	28.5	(1.9)	21.0	(1.4)	10.2	(1.3)	2.4	(0.4)	0.1	(0.1)	0.0	(0.0)
Argentina	14.5	(1.5)	19.2	(1.5)	25.2	(1.4)	22.9	(1.3)	12.8	(1.2)	4.6	(0.9)	0.8	(0.4)	0.0	(0.1)
Azerbaijan	7.1	(0.9)	27.5	(1.9)	39.7	(1.7)	21.4	(1.7)	4.0	(0.8)	0.3	(0.2)	0.0	(0.0)	0.0	c
Brazil	7.4	(0.6)	21.0	(1.0)	30.6	(1.3)	23.4	(1.1)	12.3	(0.9)	4.4	(0.5)	0.9	(0.2)	0.1	(0.1)
Bulgaria	8.7	(1.3)	16.9	(1.6)	24.0	(1.6)	22.8	(1.5)	18.1	(1.6)	7.9	(1.1)	1.4	(0.4)	0.1	(0.1)
Colombia	5.0	(0.9)	15.0	(1.3)	30.6	(1.6)	29.4	(1.5)	15.5	(1.1)	4.1	(0.7)	0.5	(0.2)	0.0	(0.0)
Croatia	1.1	(0.3)	7.9	(1.0)	22.2	(1.5)	31.1	(1.2)	26.3	(1.4)	10.3	(0.9)	1.0	(0.3)	0.0	(0.0)
Dubai (UAE)	5.8	(0.5)	13.7	(0.8)	22.6	(1.0)	23.2	(1.1)	19.2	(1.2)	11.7	(0.7)	3.4	(0.7)	0.3	(0.2)
Hong Kong-China	0.6	(0.2)	2.8	(0.5)	8.8	(0.9)	19.9	(1.4)	31.6	(1.3)	26.2	(1.5)	8.6	(1.0)	1.4	(0.4)
Indonesia	3.0	(0.6)	21.0	(1.9)	43.4	(1.9)	26.3	(1.8)	5.8	(1.1)	0.4	(0.3)	0.0	(0.0)	0.0	c
Jordan	7.9	(1.2)	18.5	(1.6)	33.4	(1.4)	28.7	(1.6)	9.9	(1.2)	1.5	(0.4)	0.1	(0.1)	0.0	c
Kazakhstan	8.1	(0.7)	25.1	(1.4)	33.0	(1.2)	21.2	(1.2)	10.1	(0.9)	2.4	(0.4)	0.2	(0.1)	0.0	c
Kyrgyzstan	32.3	(1.9)	33.6	(1.6)	22.5	(1.1)	9.0	(1.0)	2.1	(0.5)	0.5	(0.2)	0.0	(0.0)	0.0	c
Latvia	0.7	(0.3)	4.4	(0.9)	20.3	(1.6)	33.2	(1.5)	28.2	(1.7)	11.5	(1.2)	1.6	(0.3)	0.0	(0.0)
Liechtenstein	0.6	(0.7)	6.2	(1.9)	13.6	(3.2)	27.3	(5.0)	29.6	(5.8)	18.0	(3.6)	4.5	(1.7)	0.2	(0.5)
Lithuania	1.5	(0.4)	8.0	(0.8)	25.8	(1.1)	33.8	(1.4)	22.1	(1.1)	7.7	(0.7)	1.1	(0.3)	0.0	c
Macao-China	0.3	(0.1)	3.5	(0.5)	16.3	(0.7)	33.0	(1.0)	31.6	(0.9)	13.1	(0.6)	2.2	(0.4)	0.0	(0.1)
Montenegro	5.8	(0.6)	17.8	(1.0)	32.5	(1.5)	27.4	(1.0)	12.9	(0.8)	3.1	(0.4)	0.4	(0.2)	0.0	c
Panama	13.7	(2.2)	27.0	(2.4)	32.1	(2.5)	19.1	(2.0)	6.4	(1.0)	1.6	(0.5)	0.2	(0.1)	0.0	c
Peru	16.1	(1.4)	24.5	(1.5)	28.6	(1.6)	19.7	(1.1)	8.3	(0.8)	2.3	(0.5)	0.5	(0.2)	0.1	(0.1)
Qatar	17.6	(0.7)	28.0	(0.9)	25.9	(0.8)	14.7	(0.7)	8.5	(0.4)	4.2	(0.4)	0.9	(0.2)	0.1	(0.1)
Romania	5.1	(0.9)	16.9	(1.5)	28.3	(1.5)	29.8	(1.7)	16.0	(1.3)	3.6	(0.7)	0.3	(0.2)	0.0	c
Russian Federation	1.8	(0.4)	8.7	(0.9)	23.0	(1.4)	32.5	(1.5)	22.7	(1.5)	9.0	(1.0)	1.9	(0.4)	0.3	(0.1)
Serbia	2.7	(0.6)	11.8	(1.0)	27.1	(1.3)	31.3	(1.1)	20.2	(1.1)	6.3	(0.7)	0.6	(0.3)	0.0	(0.0)
Shanghai-China	0.1	(0.0)	0.9	(0.3)	5.3	(0.8)	17.5	(1.2)	30.5	(1.7)	30.4	(1.6)	13.5	(1.0)	2.0	(0.4)
Singapore	0.9	(0.2)	4.5	(0.5)	11.6	(0.8)	20.3	(1.0)	26.4	(1.0)	22.6	(1.0)	10.8	(0.8)	2.8	(0.4)
Chinese Taipei	0.8	(0.4)	4.9	(0.7)	14.8	(0.8)	26.4	(1.3)	30.3	(1.4)	18.7	(1.3)	4.0	(0.8)	0.3	(0.2)
Thailand	2.3	(0.4)	17.5	(1.5)	38.5	(1.7)	28.9	(1.4)	10.8	(1.0)	1.8	(0.5)	0.1	(0.1)	0.0	(0.0)
Trinidad and Tobago	12.1	(0.8)	18.5	(0.9)	24.0	(1.2)	23.7	(1.1)	14.8	(0.9)	5.7	(0.8)	1.1	(0.3)	0.1	(0.1)
Tunisia	8.7	(1.0)	21.2	(1.2)	33.2	(1.3)	26.2	(1.6)	9.2	(1.0)	1.5	(0.4)	0.1	(0.1)	0.0	c
Uruguay	7.9	(0.9)	17.3	(1.1)	26.3	(1.4)	26.0	(1.3)	16.1	(1.0)	5.4	(0.7)	1.0	(0.3)	0.1	(0.1)

StatLink http://dx.doi.org/10.1787/888932343285

[Part 2/2]
Percentage of students at each proficiency level on the reading subscale *integrate and interpret*, by gender

Table I.2.8

		Girls – Proficiency levels														
	Below Level 1b (less than 262.04 score points)		Level 1b (from 262.04 to less than 334.75 score points)		Level 1a (from 334.75 to less than 407.47 score points)		Level 2 (from 407.47 to less than 480.18 score points)		Level 3 (from 480.18 to less than 552.89 score points)		Level 4 (from 552.89 to less than 625.61 score points)		Level 5 (from 625.61 to less than 698.32 score points)		Level 6 (above 698.32 score points)	
	%	S.E.	%	S.E.	%	S.E.	%	S.E.	%	S.E.	%	S.E.	%	S.E.	%	S.E.
OECD																
Australia	0.5	(0.1)	2.3	(0.3)	8.0	(0.4)	18.9	(0.7)	28.9	(0.8)	25.7	(0.7)	12.5	(0.6)	3.2	(0.5)
Austria	0.8	(0.3)	5.2	(0.8)	13.8	(1.2)	24.7	(1.8)	28.0	(1.2)	20.6	(1.4)	6.3	(0.7)	0.6	(0.2)
Belgium	1.0	(0.3)	3.9	(0.6)	10.6	(0.8)	19.3	(0.9)	26.0	(1.0)	25.5	(1.1)	11.9	(0.8)	1.8	(0.4)
Canada	0.1	(0.1)	1.2	(0.2)	6.5	(0.4)	18.4	(0.8)	29.7	(0.9)	27.4	(0.7)	13.6	(0.7)	3.0	(0.4)
Chile	0.6	(0.2)	5.4	(0.7)	18.7	(1.5)	33.4	(1.8)	28.3	(1.4)	11.1	(1.1)	2.4	(0.6)	0.1	(0.1)
Czech Republic	0.2	(0.1)	2.4	(0.5)	10.2	(1.1)	22.7	(1.2)	29.6	(1.4)	24.6	(1.6)	9.3	(1.0)	1.1	(0.3)
Denmark	0.3	(0.2)	2.3	(0.4)	10.0	(0.8)	24.2	(1.1)	34.9	(1.3)	22.6	(1.1)	5.6	(0.7)	0.2	(0.1)
Estonia	0.0	(0.0)	0.9	(0.3)	6.7	(0.8)	21.8	(1.3)	35.2	(1.3)	26.5	(1.3)	7.8	(0.8)	1.1	(0.4)
Finland	0.1	(0.1)	0.5	(0.3)	2.9	(0.5)	11.2	(0.9)	27.6	(1.1)	35.7	(1.1)	18.7	(1.0)	3.4	(0.4)
France	1.4	(0.4)	3.6	(0.5)	10.0	(1.0)	18.6	(1.3)	27.4	(1.3)	24.6	(1.7)	11.9	(1.1)	2.3	(0.4)
Germany	0.2	(0.1)	2.5	(0.5)	9.4	(0.9)	19.7	(1.0)	28.6	(1.6)	26.9	(1.4)	11.3	(1.3)	1.3	(0.4)
Greece	0.4	(0.2)	2.7	(0.7)	10.9	(1.0)	24.7	(1.4)	31.3	(1.3)	22.7	(1.5)	6.4	(0.7)	1.0	(0.3)
Hungary	0.1	(0.2)	2.2	(0.7)	8.7	(1.0)	22.2	(1.5)	32.5	(1.8)	25.8	(1.9)	7.9	(1.0)	0.6	(0.2)
Iceland	0.5	(0.2)	1.8	(0.4)	8.3	(0.7)	20.0	(1.2)	31.6	(1.6)	25.6	(1.3)	10.3	(1.0)	1.8	(0.4)
Ireland	0.7	(0.3)	2.2	(0.5)	9.8	(0.8)	22.0	(1.1)	30.4	(1.3)	24.9	(1.2)	9.0	(0.9)	1.0	(0.3)
Israel	1.7	(0.4)	5.4	(0.6)	13.5	(0.8)	22.5	(1.0)	28.8	(1.2)	20.0	(1.2)	7.1	(0.6)	1.0	(0.2)
Italy	0.4	(0.2)	2.1	(0.2)	9.3	(0.4)	22.3	(0.8)	32.5	(0.7)	25.0	(0.7)	7.7	(0.4)	0.9	(0.2)
Japan	0.6	(0.3)	1.6	(0.3)	6.5	(0.8)	16.8	(1.2)	28.3	(1.2)	29.5	(1.6)	13.3	(1.0)	3.4	(0.6)
Korea	0.1	(0.1)	0.3	(0.1)	2.3	(0.5)	12.1	(1.5)	31.0	(1.7)	36.6	(1.6)	15.6	(1.6)	1.9	(0.4)
Luxembourg	1.3	(0.3)	4.5	(0.6)	13.3	(1.1)	23.9	(1.1)	28.0	(1.0)	20.8	(0.9)	7.2	(0.5)	0.9	(0.2)
Mexico	2.6	(0.4)	10.2	(0.6)	25.2	(0.8)	33.4	(0.7)	21.8	(0.8)	6.3	(0.4)	0.6	(0.1)	0.0	(0.0)
Netherlands	0.0	(0.0)	1.8	(0.4)	11.9	(1.4)	23.1	(1.5)	26.5	(1.5)	24.3	(2.0)	10.8	(1.1)	1.5	(0.4)
New Zealand	0.3	(0.2)	1.7	(0.4)	7.7	(0.6)	18.2	(1.0)	26.3	(1.1)	26.5	(1.1)	15.2	(1.3)	4.2	(0.6)
Norway	0.1	(0.1)	1.6	(0.4)	8.0	(0.7)	20.9	(1.4)	31.7	(1.2)	25.1	(1.4)	10.8	(0.9)	1.7	(0.5)
Poland	0.1	(0.1)	0.8	(0.3)	6.9	(0.8)	21.1	(1.4)	32.9	(1.2)	26.7	(1.2)	9.9	(0.8)	1.5	(0.3)
Portugal	0.2	(0.1)	2.2	(0.4)	10.0	(0.9)	25.7	(1.2)	34.2	(1.3)	21.2	(1.0)	6.0	(0.8)	0.5	(0.4)
Slovak Republic	0.3	(0.2)	1.8	(0.4)	10.1	(0.9)	25.6	(1.4)	33.0	(1.8)	22.2	(1.5)	6.4	(0.8)	0.6	(0.3)
Slovenia	0.0	(0.0)	1.5	(0.2)	9.0	(0.7)	23.0	(1.2)	32.9	(1.2)	25.2	(1.3)	7.8	(0.9)	0.5	(0.2)
Spain	0.6	(0.2)	3.0	(0.5)	11.0	(0.8)	26.1	(1.0)	34.8	(1.2)	20.1	(0.9)	4.1	(0.4)	0.3	(0.1)
Sweden	0.9	(0.3)	2.6	(0.6)	9.3	(1.0)	21.6	(1.4)	30.8	(1.5)	22.8	(1.1)	10.0	(0.9)	2.1	(0.4)
Switzerland	0.4	(0.1)	2.6	(0.4)	9.0	(0.7)	19.7	(0.9)	28.9	(1.3)	27.2	(1.3)	10.5	(0.9)	1.6	(0.4)
Turkey	0.2	(0.1)	2.4	(0.5)	13.5	(1.4)	33.9	(1.7)	33.1	(1.7)	14.7	(1.6)	2.0	(0.5)	0.1	(0.1)
United Kingdom	0.6	(0.2)	3.1	(0.5)	12.1	(1.0)	24.5	(1.0)	30.1	(1.0)	20.4	(1.0)	7.9	(0.7)	1.3	(0.3)
United States	0.3	(0.1)	3.1	(0.4)	12.6	(1.1)	24.6	(1.2)	27.3	(1.0)	20.5	(1.2)	9.2	(0.9)	2.3	(0.5)
OECD total	0.7	(0.1)	3.3	(0.1)	11.8	(0.3)	23.6	(0.4)	28.6	(0.4)	21.7	(0.4)	8.6	(0.3)	1.7	(0.2)
OECD average	0.5	(0.0)	2.7	(0.1)	10.2	(0.2)	22.4	(0.2)	30.1	(0.2)	23.7	(0.2)	9.0	(0.2)	1.4	(0.1)
Partners																
Albania	4.0	(0.7)	11.6	(1.0)	24.7	(1.4)	33.5	(1.3)	20.2	(1.5)	5.5	(0.8)	0.5	(0.3)	0.0	c
Argentina	7.7	(1.1)	14.1	(1.1)	24.8	(1.4)	26.8	(1.8)	17.9	(1.3)	7.1	(1.1)	1.6	(0.4)	0.1	(0.1)
Azerbaijan	3.4	(0.8)	19.2	(1.7)	40.4	(1.5)	30.3	(1.6)	6.3	(0.9)	0.4	(0.2)	0.0	(0.0)	0.0	c
Brazil	3.8	(0.4)	14.3	(1.0)	28.1	(1.2)	28.9	(0.9)	16.9	(0.9)	6.5	(0.6)	1.3	(0.3)	0.1	(0.1)
Bulgaria	2.2	(0.5)	8.3	(1.3)	16.7	(1.7)	27.2	(1.9)	25.9	(1.9)	15.2	(1.6)	4.0	(0.7)	0.4	(0.2)
Colombia	4.5	(0.9)	14.5	(1.2)	27.4	(1.5)	30.3	(1.5)	17.3	(1.4)	5.3	(0.8)	0.7	(0.2)	0.0	(0.0)
Croatia	0.1	(0.1)	1.6	(0.4)	11.0	(1.1)	27.4	(1.4)	36.2	(1.5)	20.3	(1.5)	3.4	(0.6)	0.1	(0.1)
Dubai (UAE)	1.0	(0.3)	5.5	(0.7)	15.9	(0.8)	27.9	(1.1)	26.4	(1.1)	16.6	(0.9)	5.8	(0.6)	0.8	(0.3)
Hong Kong-China	0.2	(0.1)	1.1	(0.4)	4.9	(0.7)	15.4	(1.0)	28.6	(1.2)	32.7	(1.5)	14.8	(1.0)	2.3	(0.5)
Indonesia	0.6	(0.2)	9.9	(1.1)	34.7	(2.0)	40.2	(1.7)	13.2	(1.6)	1.3	(0.5)	0.0	c	0.0	c
Jordan	1.7	(0.4)	7.4	(0.9)	22.9	(1.6)	39.1	(1.2)	24.4	(1.5)	4.4	(0.8)	0.2	(0.1)	0.0	(0.0)
Kazakhstan	2.3	(0.5)	13.3	(1.5)	30.5	(1.6)	31.0	(1.3)	17.4	(1.2)	4.9	(0.7)	0.6	(0.2)	0.0	(0.0)
Kyrgyzstan	13.2	(1.2)	30.4	(1.6)	33.3	(1.4)	16.8	(1.1)	5.2	(0.6)	1.0	(0.2)	0.1	(0.1)	0.0	c
Latvia	0.1	(0.1)	1.2	(0.4)	8.3	(1.0)	26.4	(1.5)	37.1	(1.4)	22.5	(1.3)	4.4	(0.6)	0.2	(0.1)
Liechtenstein	0.1	(0.4)	2.3	(1.4)	10.6	(3.7)	19.1	(3.4)	31.5	(4.0)	29.0	(4.4)	6.0	(3.1)	1.3	(1.1)
Lithuania	0.1	(0.1)	1.7	(0.3)	11.1	(1.0)	28.5	(1.7)	33.5	(1.4)	20.1	(1.1)	4.7	(0.7)	0.3	(0.1)
Macao-China	0.0	(0.0)	1.4	(0.3)	8.5	(0.6)	27.7	(1.0)	35.8	(0.9)	21.9	(0.8)	4.5	(0.4)	0.2	(0.1)
Montenegro	1.4	(0.3)	7.5	(1.1)	22.8	(1.1)	33.9	(1.2)	25.0	(1.2)	8.3	(0.7)	1.1	(0.5)	0.0	(0.0)
Panama	9.1	(1.6)	20.6	(2.1)	29.5	(2.3)	23.3	(1.8)	13.3	(2.2)	3.8	(1.0)	0.6	(0.3)	0.0	(0.1)
Peru	11.9	(1.0)	20.3	(1.4)	27.2	(1.4)	24.2	(1.3)	12.0	(1.2)	3.9	(0.8)	0.6	(0.2)	0.1	(0.1)
Qatar	8.1	(0.5)	19.3	(0.7)	26.6	(0.8)	24.7	(0.8)	14.1	(0.5)	5.5	(0.3)	1.5	(0.2)	0.1	(0.1)
Romania	1.7	(0.4)	8.0	(1.0)	22.0	(1.7)	34.5	(1.7)	25.0	(1.7)	7.7	(1.0)	1.2	(0.3)	0.0	(0.0)
Russian Federation	0.5	(0.2)	3.3	(0.4)	12.8	(1.1)	29.6	(1.4)	31.2	(1.5)	16.9	(1.2)	5.1	(0.7)	0.5	(0.2)
Serbia	0.7	(0.2)	4.9	(0.6)	17.4	(1.1)	34.2	(1.2)	30.7	(1.1)	10.5	(0.8)	1.5	(0.3)	0.1	(0.1)
Shanghai-China	0.0	(0.0)	0.2	(0.1)	1.5	(0.3)	9.3	(0.6)	26.2	(1.2)	36.0	(1.1)	22.5	(1.3)	4.2	(0.6)
Singapore	0.2	(0.1)	1.6	(0.3)	8.0	(0.6)	18.0	(0.9)	25.9	(1.0)	27.1	(1.2)	15.1	(0.8)	4.2	(0.6)
Chinese Taipei	0.1	(0.1)	1.5	(0.3)	8.2	(0.8)	22.5	(1.2)	35.2	(1.6)	24.0	(1.3)	7.8	(1.3)	0.7	(0.4)
Thailand	0.6	(0.2)	6.2	(0.7)	29.8	(1.4)	40.7	(1.5)	18.4	(1.1)	4.0	(0.8)	0.3	(0.2)	0.0	(0.0)
Trinidad and Tobago	4.4	(0.7)	10.2	(0.7)	20.0	(1.1)	28.1	(1.4)	22.2	(1.3)	11.4	(0.7)	3.3	(0.5)	0.3	(0.1)
Tunisia	2.9	(0.6)	13.6	(1.2)	32.7	(1.7)	34.0	(1.4)	14.5	(0.9)	2.2	(0.5)	0.1	(0.1)	0.0	(0.0)
Uruguay	2.7	(0.4)	9.4	(0.9)	23.5	(1.0)	31.7	(1.5)	21.8	(1.2)	8.9	(0.7)	1.9	(0.4)	0.1	(0.1)

StatLink ▔▔▔▔ http://dx.doi.org/10.1787/888932343285

[Part 1/1]

Table I.2.9 Mean score, variation and gender differences in student performance on the reading subscale *integrate and interpret*

		All students				Gender differences						Percentiles											
		Mean score		Standard deviation		Boys		Girls		Difference (B – G)		5th		10th		25th		75th		90th		95th	
		Mean	S.E.	S.D.	S.E.	Mean score	S.E.	Mean score	S.E.	Score dif.	S.E.	Score	S.E.	Score	S.E.	Score	S.E.	Score	S.E.	Score	S.E.	Score	S.E.
OECD	Australia	513	(2.4)	102	(1.6)	495	(2.9)	529	(2.8)	**-34**	(3.2)	337	(3.6)	377	(3.1)	444	(2.9)	584	(2.5)	641	(3.6)	673	(4.5)
	Austria	471	(2.9)	99	(2.0)	451	(3.6)	490	(4.0)	**-39**	(5.5)	305	(5.8)	339	(4.4)	402	(4.3)	544	(3.9)	598	(4.1)	626	(4.0)
	Belgium	504	(2.5)	106	(1.8)	492	(3.4)	516	(3.2)	**-24**	(4.4)	320	(5.5)	360	(4.6)	430	(3.5)	584	(2.3)	635	(2.8)	662	(3.4)
	Canada	522	(1.5)	94	(0.9)	507	(1.9)	537	(1.8)	**-30**	(2.2)	363	(3.2)	398	(2.9)	458	(1.9)	590	(1.8)	642	(2.1)	670	(3.0)
	Chile	452	(3.1)	85	(1.7)	442	(3.9)	463	(3.4)	**-21**	(4.0)	310	(5.2)	342	(4.7)	395	(4.0)	510	(3.4)	562	(4.3)	593	(4.8)
	Czech Republic	488	(2.9)	93	(1.5)	465	(3.7)	513	(3.2)	**-48**	(4.4)	334	(4.7)	365	(4.7)	421	(4.0)	555	(3.6)	610	(3.2)	639	(3.3)
	Denmark	492	(2.1)	84	(1.2)	480	(2.5)	504	(2.5)	**-24**	(2.8)	348	(4.9)	381	(3.7)	437	(2.7)	552	(2.3)	597	(3.1)	623	(3.6)
	Estonia	500	(2.8)	84	(1.5)	480	(3.3)	522	(2.9)	**-42**	(2.9)	358	(5.3)	389	(4.0)	444	(3.5)	559	(3.0)	605	(3.9)	634	(4.3)
	Finland	538	(2.3)	88	(1.0)	513	(2.6)	564	(2.6)	**-50**	(2.3)	385	(3.7)	421	(3.6)	482	(2.7)	601	(2.7)	647	(2.9)	674	(3.2)
	France	497	(3.6)	111	(2.8)	477	(4.4)	516	(3.6)	**-39**	(3.9)	300	(8.9)	348	(6.8)	426	(5.2)	577	(4.3)	634	(5.0)	664	(4.7)
	Germany	501	(2.8)	96	(1.9)	481	(3.9)	521	(3.0)	**-40**	(4.3)	335	(5.2)	371	(4.4)	433	(4.3)	572	(3.1)	621	(3.0)	649	(3.7)
	Greece	484	(4.0)	93	(2.0)	464	(4.9)	504	(3.6)	**-40**	(4.0)	328	(6.5)	362	(7.6)	421	(5.4)	551	(3.6)	602	(3.5)	631	(3.6)
	Hungary	496	(3.2)	89	(2.1)	478	(4.0)	514	(3.6)	**-36**	(4.1)	343	(6.7)	376	(5.6)	435	(4.7)	560	(3.9)	609	(3.7)	634	(4.4)
	Iceland	503	(1.5)	98	(1.3)	483	(2.2)	522	(2.2)	**-39**	(3.2)	332	(4.9)	372	(3.1)	438	(3.3)	571	(2.3)	625	(3.0)	654	(2.8)
	Ireland	494	(3.0)	97	(2.1)	476	(4.4)	512	(3.1)	**-37**	(4.8)	328	(7.9)	367	(5.3)	432	(4.3)	562	(2.9)	613	(3.3)	641	(3.9)
	Israel	473	(3.4)	110	(2.4)	454	(5.0)	491	(3.4)	**-37**	(5.3)	281	(7.8)	324	(6.8)	399	(4.9)	552	(3.3)	609	(3.6)	641	(4.1)
	Italy	490	(1.6)	94	(1.3)	469	(2.3)	512	(1.8)	**-43**	(2.7)	328	(3.6)	365	(2.6)	427	(2.1)	558	(1.8)	607	(1.9)	635	(2.1)
	Japan	520	(3.5)	102	(2.6)	502	(5.6)	538	(3.8)	**-36**	(6.8)	340	(9.0)	384	(7.0)	455	(4.8)	591	(3.2)	642	(4.3)	672	(5.1)
	Korea	541	(3.4)	81	(2.1)	526	(4.7)	557	(4.1)	**-31**	(6.0)	398	(8.6)	435	(5.8)	489	(4.3)	598	(3.5)	639	(3.5)	664	(3.7)
	Luxembourg	475	(1.1)	104	(1.1)	457	(1.8)	494	(1.4)	**-37**	(2.4)	294	(4.1)	336	(2.8)	404	(2.2)	551	(1.9)	606	(2.2)	637	(3.3)
	Mexico	418	(2.0)	87	(1.1)	406	(2.2)	431	(2.1)	**-25**	(1.6)	272	(3.5)	305	(2.7)	360	(2.3)	479	(2.1)	529	(2.5)	558	(3.0)
	Netherlands	504	(5.4)	94	(1.8)	494	(5.4)	515	(5.5)	**-22**	(2.5)	353	(5.6)	381	(5.0)	432	(6.2)	575	(6.2)	630	(5.0)	658	(4.9)
	New Zealand	517	(2.4)	105	(1.7)	497	(3.8)	539	(3.0)	**-42**	(4.8)	338	(5.8)	379	(4.7)	445	(3.3)	593	(3.3)	652	(3.6)	681	(5.4)
	Norway	502	(2.7)	94	(1.3)	481	(3.0)	524	(3.2)	**-42**	(3.1)	341	(4.3)	377	(4.3)	440	(3.1)	567	(3.4)	622	(3.6)	652	(4.4)
	Poland	503	(2.8)	91	(1.2)	479	(3.0)	526	(3.0)	**-47**	(2.7)	349	(4.6)	383	(4.1)	442	(3.3)	567	(3.5)	617	(3.3)	648	(3.6)
	Portugal	487	(3.0)	87	(1.5)	469	(3.5)	503	(2.9)	**-34**	(2.3)	340	(4.3)	371	(4.1)	427	(4.1)	548	(3.2)	599	(3.7)	627	(3.5)
	Slovak Republic	481	(2.5)	89	(1.9)	456	(3.4)	505	(2.9)	**-49**	(3.5)	332	(5.4)	366	(4.6)	419	(3.4)	545	(3.0)	596	(3.6)	625	(4.3)
	Slovenia	489	(1.1)	90	(0.9)	464	(1.5)	514	(1.5)	**-50**	(2.3)	335	(3.4)	366	(2.0)	425	(2.3)	555	(2.3)	605	(2.4)	631	(4.8)
	Spain	481	(2.0)	87	(1.0)	468	(2.1)	494	(2.2)	**-27**	(2.1)	329	(4.2)	366	(3.6)	425	(2.8)	541	(1.9)	588	(1.9)	614	(2.3)
	Sweden	494	(3.0)	102	(1.6)	475	(3.4)	514	(3.4)	**-40**	(3.2)	319	(6.0)	362	(4.7)	429	(3.5)	564	(3.5)	624	(3.9)	655	(4.2)
	Switzerland	502	(2.5)	97	(1.5)	484	(2.9)	521	(2.7)	**-37**	(2.6)	334	(4.5)	372	(3.9)	436	(2.8)	572	(2.9)	623	(3.7)	652	(3.9)
	Turkey	459	(3.3)	78	(1.7)	440	(3.5)	480	(3.9)	**-41**	(3.6)	330	(4.5)	358	(3.3)	405	(3.3)	515	(4.3)	562	(5.1)	588	(5.7)
	United Kingdom	491	(2.4)	97	(1.2)	479	(3.6)	501	(3.0)	**-22**	(4.6)	330	(4.0)	364	(3.2)	424	(3.0)	558	(2.8)	615	(3.2)	650	(3.4)
	United States	495	(3.7)	100	(1.7)	484	(4.4)	506	(3.8)	**-22**	(3.7)	331	(3.9)	364	(3.8)	425	(4.1)	565	(4.6)	626	(5.3)	660	(6.0)
	OECD total	490	(1.2)	100	(0.6)	475	(1.5)	505	(1.3)	**-30**	(0.4)	323	(1.6)	359	(1.4)	421	(1.5)	561	(1.4)	617	(1.7)	649	(2.2)
	OECD average	493	(0.5)	94	(0.3)	476	(0.6)	512	(0.5)	**-36**	(0.6)	332	(0.9)	368	(0.8)	430	(0.6)	561	(0.6)	613	(0.6)	642	(0.7)
Partners	Albania	393	(3.8)	98	(2.0)	365	(4.8)	423	(3.9)	**-58**	(4.1)	226	(6.4)	265	(5.9)	329	(4.5)	463	(5.3)	517	(5.1)	547	(4.7)
	Argentina	398	(4.7)	109	(3.4)	379	(5.1)	414	(5.0)	**-34**	(3.8)	210	(10.8)	256	(8.0)	326	(5.4)	473	(5.9)	536	(7.2)	571	(7.1)
	Azerbaijan	373	(2.9)	68	(1.5)	363	(3.3)	384	(3.0)	**-22**	(2.2)	260	(4.5)	285	(4.1)	327	(3.6)	420	(3.1)	460	(4.2)	483	(4.6)
	Brazil	406	(2.7)	94	(1.5)	392	(2.9)	419	(2.8)	**-27**	(1.9)	258	(2.8)	289	(2.9)	341	(2.7)	468	(3.8)	532	(4.3)	568	(5.2)
	Bulgaria	436	(6.4)	107	(2.4)	409	(7.0)	465	(5.7)	**-55**	(4.5)	256	(7.9)	293	(7.8)	360	(8.6)	514	(6.9)	572	(6.5)	604	(6.5)
	Colombia	411	(3.8)	89	(2.0)	407	(4.3)	415	(4.2)	-8	(3.8)	265	(7.4)	299	(5.1)	351	(4.7)	472	(3.7)	525	(4.4)	556	(5.3)
	Croatia	472	(2.9)	83	(1.5)	450	(3.4)	497	(3.5)	**-47**	(4.3)	331	(5.2)	362	(4.0)	415	(4.2)	532	(3.3)	577	(3.0)	602	(3.9)
	Dubai (UAE)	457	(1.3)	106	(1.1)	434	(1.9)	480	(1.7)	**-47**	(2.3)	279	(3.2)	318	(2.4)	383	(2.6)	532	(2.1)	594	(2.9)	627	(3.8)
	Hong Kong-China	530	(2.2)	89	(1.5)	516	(3.6)	546	(3.0)	**-30**	(4.8)	372	(5.1)	412	(4.6)	474	(2.9)	592	(2.9)	639	(3.3)	666	(3.8)
	Indonesia	397	(3.5)	66	(1.8)	380	(3.6)	415	(3.7)	**-35**	(3.1)	291	(4.4)	313	(3.7)	352	(3.7)	442	(4.3)	482	(5.5)	505	(5.2)
	Jordan	410	(3.1)	84	(1.9)	384	(4.5)	437	(4.0)	**-54**	(6.0)	264	(5.9)	300	(5.1)	358	(4.0)	468	(3.5)	513	(3.7)	538	(4.5)
	Kazakhstan	397	(3.0)	87	(1.5)	376	(3.0)	418	(3.6)	**-42**	(2.7)	260	(3.4)	287	(3.0)	336	(3.9)	456	(4.2)	513	(4.9)	544	(5.0)
	Kyrgyzstan	327	(2.9)	88	(1.9)	302	(3.6)	350	(2.9)	**-48**	(2.8)	183	(4.7)	215	(4.6)	269	(3.5)	384	(3.8)	440	(5.1)	475	(5.6)
	Latvia	484	(2.8)	80	(1.5)	462	(3.3)	506	(3.0)	**-44**	(3.0)	352	(5.6)	381	(4.1)	430	(3.6)	541	(3.3)	585	(3.5)	611	(3.4)
	Liechtenstein	498	(4.0)	90	(3.5)	482	(5.3)	515	(6.5)	**-33**	(8.7)	336	(12.2)	373	(10.6)	436	(7.5)	563	(5.9)	610	(7.7)	632	(18.1)
	Lithuania	469	(2.4)	85	(1.5)	440	(2.8)	498	(2.5)	**-58**	(2.6)	331	(4.5)	358	(3.7)	410	(3.4)	528	(2.8)	578	(3.3)	607	(3.4)
	Macao-China	488	(0.8)	77	(0.7)	473	(1.2)	504	(1.0)	**-31**	(1.6)	357	(2.7)	388	(2.2)	436	(1.6)	542	(1.4)	588	(2.1)	613	(2.2)
	Montenegro	420	(1.6)	88	(1.4)	396	(1.5)	446	(2.3)	**-50**	(2.3)	276	(3.7)	308	(3.2)	361	(2.2)	481	(2.5)	533	(2.8)	564	(3.6)
	Panama	372	(5.9)	94	(3.3)	357	(6.3)	387	(6.7)	**-31**	(6.2)	221	(9.6)	254	(8.5)	309	(7.4)	434	(7.3)	496	(9.5)	531	(9.0)
	Peru	371	(4.0)	100	(2.6)	360	(4.2)	382	(5.0)	**-22**	(4.9)	207	(5.8)	243	(4.9)	302	(4.3)	439	(5.4)	500	(7.3)	539	(8.1)
	Qatar	379	(0.9)	105	(0.8)	358	(1.4)	400	(1.0)	**-42**	(1.7)	221	(2.4)	249	(2.1)	303	(1.5)	449	(1.6)	523	(2.7)	565	(3.0)
	Romania	425	(4.0)	87	(2.2)	405	(4.3)	444	(4.4)	**-39**	(4.3)	279	(5.8)	310	(6.0)	366	(5.3)	486	(4.9)	535	(4.6)	563	(5.3)
	Russian Federation	467	(3.1)	90	(1.7)	445	(3.5)	489	(3.3)	**-44**	(2.9)	319	(5.1)	352	(4.4)	408	(3.7)	527	(3.8)	582	(5.0)	616	(5.7)
	Serbia	445	(2.4)	84	(1.5)	426	(3.2)	463	(2.6)	**-37**	(3.1)	304	(4.7)	334	(4.0)	389	(3.1)	504	(2.9)	551	(3.2)	577	(3.1)
	Shanghai-China	558	(2.5)	81	(1.6)	540	(3.2)	576	(2.3)	**-35**	(3.0)	417	(5.7)	449	(4.3)	504	(3.4)	617	(2.8)	659	(3.0)	684	(3.5)
	Singapore	525	(1.2)	101	(1.1)	511	(1.9)	539	(1.7)	**-28**	(2.7)	351	(3.6)	389	(3.3)	455	(1.9)	598	(1.8)	652	(2.2)	683	(2.8)
	Chinese Taipei	499	(2.5)	87	(1.9)	483	(3.7)	515	(3.7)	**-32**	(5.5)	349	(4.4)	383	(3.8)	441	(3.2)	560	(3.3)	607	(5.0)	635	(5.6)
	Thailand	416	(2.6)	72	(1.8)	396	(3.2)	432	(3.0)	**-36**	(3.8)	301	(4.4)	326	(3.8)	367	(2.9)	465	(2.8)	508	(3.8)	537	(6.0)
	Trinidad and Tobago	419	(1.4)	109	(1.2)	392	(2.0)	445	(1.8)	**-53**	(2.6)	232	(3.8)	274	(3.5)	344	(2.2)	494	(2.3)	558	(3.5)	595	(4.3)
	Tunisia	393	(2.7)	81	(1.6)	378	(3.0)	408	(2.9)	**-30**	(2.2)	258	(4.3)	287	(3.5)	341	(3.2)	449	(3.4)	495	(4.2)	523	(5.1)
	Uruguay	423	(2.6)	97	(1.6)	403	(3.1)	440	(2.8)	**-37**	(3.0)	260	(6.5)	297	(3.8)	358	(3.4)	489	(3.0)	547	(3.6)	580	(3.5)

Note: Values that are statistically significant are indicated in bold (see Annex A3).
StatLink http://dx.doi.org/10.1787/888932343285

[Part 1/1]

Table I.2.10 Percentage of students at each proficiency level on the reading subscale *reflect and evaluate*

	Below Level 1b (less than 262.04 score points)		Level 1b (from 262.04 to less than 334.75 score points)		Level 1a (from 334.75 to less than 407.47 score points)		Level 2 (from 407.47 to less than 480.18 score points)		Level 3 (from 480.18 to less than 552.89 score points)		Level 4 (from 552.89 to less than 625.61 score points)		Level 5 (from 625.61 to less than 698.32 score points)		Level 6 (above 698.32 score points)	
	%	S.E.	%	S.E.	%	S.E.	%	S.E.	%	S.E.	%	S.E.	%	S.E.	%	S.E.
OECD																
Australia	1.0	(0.1)	3.2	(0.3)	9.3	(0.5)	18.9	(0.6)	26.8	(0.6)	25.0	(0.6)	12.6	(0.6)	3.2	(0.4)
Austria	4.2	(0.6)	9.0	(0.7)	16.5	(0.8)	22.7	(1.0)	26.2	(1.1)	16.7	(0.8)	4.3	(0.5)	0.4	(0.1)
Belgium	2.2	(0.3)	5.0	(0.4)	11.3	(0.7)	18.8	(0.8)	25.9	(0.8)	24.9	(0.8)	10.7	(0.6)	1.4	(0.3)
Canada	0.3	(0.1)	1.8	(0.1)	6.5	(0.4)	17.6	(0.5)	29.4	(0.6)	28.5	(0.6)	13.2	(0.4)	2.7	(0.3)
Chile	1.3	(0.3)	7.4	(0.7)	20.6	(0.9)	32.4	(1.0)	26.8	(1.0)	10.0	(0.7)	1.4	(0.3)	0.0	(0.0)
Czech Republic	2.6	(0.3)	8.0	(0.7)	18.8	(0.7)	26.7	(1.0)	24.8	(1.0)	14.4	(0.9)	4.2	(0.4)	0.4	(0.1)
Denmark	0.7	(0.2)	3.4	(0.4)	12.6	(0.7)	25.7	(0.8)	31.9	(0.8)	20.0	(1.0)	5.3	(0.5)	0.5	(0.1)
Estonia	0.4	(0.2)	2.7	(0.4)	10.4	(0.7)	25.3	(1.1)	32.4	(1.2)	21.9	(1.1)	6.1	(0.5)	0.7	(0.2)
Finland	0.4	(0.1)	1.3	(0.2)	6.3	(0.6)	16.9	(0.7)	30.5	(0.9)	30.0	(0.9)	12.8	(0.7)	1.8	(0.3)
France	2.4	(0.5)	5.8	(0.6)	12.0	(0.9)	21.0	(1.1)	26.7	(1.0)	21.8	(1.0)	9.1	(0.8)	1.1	(0.3)
Germany	1.5	(0.3)	5.5	(0.6)	12.6	(0.8)	22.6	(0.9)	29.3	(1.1)	22.0	(0.9)	6.0	(0.5)	0.5	(0.2)
Greece	2.2	(0.6)	5.9	(0.9)	13.0	(0.8)	22.7	(1.0)	27.7	(1.0)	20.2	(0.9)	7.0	(0.5)	1.3	(0.2)
Hungary	0.9	(0.3)	4.9	(0.7)	14.1	(1.1)	24.4	(1.3)	29.7	(1.1)	19.7	(1.0)	5.9	(0.5)	0.5	(0.1)
Iceland	1.1	(0.2)	4.5	(0.4)	12.0	(0.7)	22.8	(0.7)	31.4	(0.9)	21.1	(0.8)	6.4	(0.5)	0.7	(0.2)
Ireland	1.3	(0.3)	4.2	(0.6)	11.5	(0.7)	21.5	(0.8)	29.2	(1.0)	22.8	(1.0)	8.5	(0.7)	1.1	(0.3)
Israel	4.0	(0.7)	7.3	(0.4)	13.0	(0.7)	21.4	(0.8)	25.1	(1.0)	19.5	(0.9)	8.0	(0.7)	1.6	(0.3)
Italy	2.6	(0.3)	6.3	(0.3)	14.5	(0.5)	22.8	(0.5)	27.1	(0.6)	19.7	(0.6)	6.2	(0.4)	0.7	(0.1)
Japan	1.9	(0.5)	3.9	(0.5)	9.1	(0.7)	17.8	(0.8)	25.9	(0.9)	25.0	(0.9)	12.7	(0.7)	3.6	(0.4)
Korea	0.3	(0.1)	1.1	(0.4)	5.3	(0.7)	15.5	(1.1)	30.1	(1.4)	31.7	(1.3)	14.0	(1.1)	2.0	(0.4)
Luxembourg	3.5	(0.3)	7.5	(0.5)	15.5	(0.6)	23.9	(0.8)	26.8	(0.7)	16.9	(0.8)	5.3	(0.5)	0.5	(0.1)
Mexico	3.3	(0.3)	10.3	(0.4)	23.8	(0.6)	31.9	(0.6)	23.2	(0.6)	6.8	(0.3)	0.7	(0.1)	0.0	(0.0)
Netherlands	0.1	(0.1)	1.6	(0.3)	11.2	(1.4)	24.8	(1.5)	29.1	(1.3)	23.7	(1.7)	8.8	(0.8)	0.7	(0.2)
New Zealand	0.9	(0.3)	3.4	(0.4)	9.5	(0.6)	17.5	(0.6)	24.0	(0.7)	25.0	(0.7)	14.9	(0.8)	4.7	(0.5)
Norway	0.7	(0.2)	3.6	(0.4)	10.9	(0.6)	22.6	(0.7)	30.7	(0.8)	22.4	(0.9)	8.0	(0.6)	1.1	(0.3)
Poland	0.9	(0.2)	3.6	(0.4)	11.4	(0.8)	24.3	(0.9)	31.3	(0.7)	21.4	(0.9)	6.5	(0.5)	0.6	(0.2)
Portugal	0.7	(0.2)	4.2	(0.5)	12.5	(0.9)	23.7	(0.9)	30.2	(0.9)	20.9	(0.9)	7.0	(0.6)	0.6	(0.2)
Slovak Republic	2.1	(0.4)	7.8	(0.7)	17.5	(0.8)	26.6	(1.2)	26.4	(1.2)	15.4	(0.9)	3.9	(0.4)	0.3	(0.1)
Slovenia	2.3	(0.2)	7.6	(0.4)	16.9	(0.6)	24.2	(0.9)	27.2	(1.2)	17.0	(1.0)	4.4	(0.6)	0.4	(0.2)
Spain	1.9	(0.3)	5.3	(0.4)	13.0	(0.5)	24.9	(0.7)	30.9	(0.7)	19.1	(0.7)	4.5	(0.3)	0.4	(0.1)
Sweden	1.5	(0.3)	4.2	(0.4)	10.8	(0.7)	22.6	(0.8)	29.6	(0.8)	21.2	(0.9)	8.5	(0.7)	1.6	(0.3)
Switzerland	1.0	(0.2)	4.7	(0.5)	12.4	(0.7)	23.0	(0.8)	29.1	(0.9)	21.7	(1.0)	7.1	(0.6)	1.1	(0.3)
Turkey	1.4	(0.3)	6.0	(0.7)	17.3	(1.0)	27.5	(1.2)	27.5	(1.1)	15.8	(1.1)	3.9	(0.5)	0.5	(0.2)
United Kingdom	0.9	(0.2)	3.8	(0.4)	12.2	(0.6)	23.5	(0.8)	28.2	(0.7)	20.9	(1.0)	8.8	(0.6)	1.8	(0.3)
United States	0.5	(0.1)	3.3	(0.5)	11.1	(1.1)	22.2	(1.1)	27.4	(0.9)	23.1	(1.0)	10.2	(0.9)	2.2	(0.4)
OECD total	1.4	(0.1)	4.8	(0.2)	12.9	(0.3)	23.1	(0.3)	27.4	(0.3)	20.7	(0.3)	8.1	(0.3)	1.5	(0.1)
OECD average	1.6	(0.1)	4.9	(0.1)	12.8	(0.1)	23.0	(0.2)	28.2	(0.2)	20.8	(0.2)	7.6	(0.1)	1.2	(0.0)
Partners																
Albania	14.6	(1.2)	18.7	(0.9)	26.2	(1.0)	23.6	(1.0)	13.2	(1.1)	3.3	(0.5)	0.3	(0.1)	0.0	(0.0)
Argentina	10.7	(1.1)	15.6	(1.1)	23.5	(1.2)	25.2	(1.1)	17.0	(1.1)	6.6	(0.8)	1.3	(0.3)	0.1	(0.1)
Azerbaijan	21.5	(1.4)	28.1	(1.0)	28.9	(1.1)	16.2	(0.9)	4.6	(0.6)	0.7	(0.2)	0.1	(0.0)	0.0	c
Brazil	3.8	(0.4)	13.1	(0.6)	26.6	(0.8)	29.6	(0.8)	18.5	(0.9)	7.0	(0.6)	1.4	(0.2)	0.1	(0.1)
Bulgaria	11.3	(1.4)	13.4	(1.1)	19.4	(1.2)	23.0	(1.1)	19.9	(1.4)	10.0	(1.0)	2.6	(0.4)	0.4	(0.2)
Colombia	4.0	(0.7)	13.2	(1.0)	26.3	(1.0)	30.1	(1.3)	19.2	(1.2)	6.3	(0.7)	0.9	(0.2)	0.0	(0.0)
Croatia	2.1	(0.5)	7.4	(0.7)	17.0	(1.0)	25.6	(1.2)	26.4	(1.1)	16.2	(0.9)	4.8	(0.5)	0.5	(0.1)
Dubai (UAE)	3.6	(0.3)	8.4	(0.5)	17.8	(0.7)	23.8	(0.8)	24.2	(0.7)	16.0	(0.6)	5.7	(0.4)	0.7	(0.2)
Hong Kong-China	0.2	(0.1)	1.6	(0.3)	6.2	(0.5)	14.7	(0.7)	29.9	(1.3)	32.0	(1.2)	13.5	(0.9)	1.9	(0.2)
Indonesia	1.9	(0.5)	12.2	(1.1)	35.1	(1.5)	35.8	(1.3)	13.3	(1.3)	1.7	(0.4)	0.0	(0.0)	0.0	c
Jordan	7.6	(0.7)	13.5	(0.9)	26.3	(1.2)	29.8	(0.9)	17.6	(0.9)	4.7	(0.5)	0.5	(0.1)	0.0	(0.0)
Kazakhstan	13.5	(0.9)	23.0	(0.9)	27.5	(1.2)	20.6	(1.0)	11.3	(0.9)	3.6	(0.5)	0.4	(0.1)	0.0	(0.0)
Kyrgyzstan	37.2	(1.6)	26.8	(1.2)	19.2	(0.9)	10.5	(0.7)	4.8	(0.5)	1.3	(0.3)	0.2	(0.1)	0.0	(0.0)
Latvia	0.4	(0.2)	2.9	(0.5)	11.6	(0.9)	27.6	(1.2)	34.1	(1.3)	19.2	(1.3)	4.0	(0.4)	0.2	(0.1)
Liechtenstein	0.2	(0.3)	4.4	(1.3)	12.0	(2.1)	23.0	(3.2)	31.5	(3.1)	22.9	(2.4)	5.7	(1.4)	0.1	(0.3)
Lithuania	1.4	(0.3)	6.9	(0.6)	18.7	(0.8)	29.3	(1.2)	27.3	(1.0)	13.5	(0.7)	2.8	(0.5)	0.2	(0.1)
Macao-China	0.4	(0.1)	3.4	(0.3)	13.9	(0.6)	30.6	(0.8)	33.6	(0.9)	15.6	(0.8)	2.4	(0.3)	0.1	(0.1)
Montenegro	11.7	(0.6)	20.2	(1.0)	26.3	(0.8)	24.8	(0.9)	12.6	(0.8)	3.9	(0.4)	0.5	(0.2)	0.0	(0.0)
Panama	11.9	(1.8)	23.1	(2.0)	27.9	(2.0)	21.5	(1.8)	10.8	(1.4)	4.1	(0.7)	0.7	(0.2)	0.0	(0.0)
Peru	15.2	(1.1)	22.5	(1.2)	26.9	(1.2)	21.4	(0.8)	10.7	(0.9)	2.8	(0.5)	0.4	(0.1)	0.0	(0.0)
Qatar	19.0	(0.5)	20.7	(0.5)	21.6	(0.5)	17.9	(0.5)	12.1	(0.3)	6.1	(0.3)	2.2	(0.2)	0.4	(0.1)
Romania	5.3	(0.8)	12.2	(1.0)	22.7	(1.2)	29.5	(1.4)	21.6	(1.3)	7.4	(0.9)	1.2	(0.3)	0.1	(0.0)
Russian Federation	3.6	(0.6)	10.1	(0.7)	22.1	(1.0)	29.7	(1.1)	22.5	(0.9)	9.5	(0.7)	2.2	(0.4)	0.3	(0.1)
Serbia	3.5	(0.5)	11.4	(0.6)	24.3	(0.9)	30.3	(1.0)	22.3	(1.0)	7.2	(0.6)	1.0	(0.2)	0.0	(0.0)
Shanghai-China	0.2	(0.1)	0.6	(0.2)	4.2	(0.5)	13.2	(0.7)	27.6	(0.9)	32.9	(0.8)	17.9	(0.8)	3.4	(0.4)
Singapore	0.6	(0.1)	2.8	(0.2)	9.0	(0.5)	18.0	(0.8)	27.3	(0.8)	25.3	(0.9)	13.6	(0.7)	3.5	(0.5)
Chinese Taipei	0.9	(0.2)	3.8	(0.4)	11.7	(0.8)	24.8	(1.1)	33.2	(1.2)	20.7	(0.9)	4.5	(0.6)	0.4	(0.2)
Thailand	2.1	(0.4)	12.3	(0.8)	29.3	(0.9)	33.3	(1.1)	18.0	(0.8)	4.3	(0.5)	0.5	(0.2)	0.0	(0.0)
Trinidad and Tobago	11.1	(0.6)	14.6	(0.7)	20.0	(0.8)	24.1	(1.0)	18.9	(1.0)	8.7	(0.5)	2.4	(0.3)	0.3	(0.1)
Tunisia	4.3	(0.5)	11.0	(0.9)	24.0	(1.1)	32.2	(1.1)	21.0	(1.0)	6.5	(0.7)	0.9	(0.3)	0.1	(0.1)
Uruguay	5.2	(0.6)	11.9	(0.7)	21.8	(1.0)	26.9	(0.8)	21.1	(0.7)	10.3	(0.9)	2.6	(0.4)	0.3	(0.1)

StatLink ⏩ http://dx.doi.org/10.1787/888932343285

[Part 1/2]

Percentage of students at each proficiency level on the reading subscale *reflect and evaluate*, by gender

Table I.2.11

	Boys – Proficiency levels																
	Below Level 1b (less than 262.04 score points)		Level 1b (from 262.04 to less than 334.75 score points)		Level 1a (from 334.75 to less than 407.47 score points)		Level 2 (from 407.47 to less than 480.18 score points)		Level 3 (from 480.18 to less than 552.89 score points)		Level 4 (from 552.89 to less than 625.61 score points)		Level 5 (from 625.61 to less than 698.32 score points)		Level 6 (above 698.32 score points)	
	%	S.E.	%	S.E.	%	S.E.	%	S.E.	%	S.E.	%	S.E.	%	S.E.	%	S.E.
Australia	1.6	(0.3)	4.9	(0.4)	12.7	(0.6)	21.3	(0.8)	26.4	(0.9)	21.4	(0.8)	9.4	(0.6)	2.2	(0.4)
Austria	6.0	(0.9)	12.0	(1.0)	20.2	(1.2)	23.7	(1.4)	23.1	(1.2)	12.7	(1.1)	2.3	(0.4)	0.1	(0.1)
Belgium	3.2	(0.6)	6.2	(0.6)	13.1	(0.8)	20.2	(0.9)	25.0	(1.0)	22.2	(1.0)	8.9	(0.7)	1.1	(0.3)
Canada	0.6	(0.1)	2.8	(0.2)	9.0	(0.6)	21.1	(0.8)	30.1	(0.9)	25.2	(0.8)	9.8	(0.5)	1.5	(0.2)
Chile	2.0	(0.6)	9.4	(1.0)	23.3	(1.2)	32.1	(1.3)	23.7	(1.2)	8.5	(0.8)	1.0	(0.3)	0.0	(0.0)
Czech Republic	4.0	(0.5)	10.9	(1.1)	23.8	(1.3)	28.1	(1.3)	21.1	(1.3)	9.8	(0.9)	2.2	(0.3)	0.2	(0.1)
Denmark	1.1	(0.4)	4.8	(0.7)	15.5	(0.9)	29.3	(1.2)	30.7	(1.0)	15.6	(1.1)	2.8	(0.5)	0.2	(0.1)
Estonia	0.7	(0.4)	4.2	(0.7)	14.1	(1.1)	30.5	(1.4)	31.6	(1.8)	15.6	(1.3)	3.1	(0.5)	0.2	(0.2)
Finland	0.6	(0.2)	2.3	(0.4)	10.1	(0.9)	23.7	(1.1)	32.4	(1.2)	23.1	(1.2)	7.1	(0.7)	0.6	(0.2)
France	3.8	(0.7)	8.3	(0.9)	14.7	(1.3)	23.4	(1.5)	24.7	(1.4)	18.0	(1.2)	6.7	(0.7)	0.5	(0.2)
Germany	2.3	(0.4)	7.5	(0.9)	15.8	(1.4)	24.9	(1.4)	28.4	(1.6)	17.3	(1.3)	3.5	(0.5)	0.2	(0.1)
Greece	3.4	(0.9)	9.2	(1.2)	17.5	(1.4)	25.0	(1.3)	25.0	(1.5)	15.1	(1.2)	4.2	(0.6)	0.5	(0.2)
Hungary	1.3	(0.4)	6.8	(1.0)	18.3	(1.4)	26.2	(1.6)	28.6	(1.4)	15.2	(1.3)	3.5	(0.7)	0.2	(0.1)
Iceland	1.9	(0.4)	6.9	(0.7)	16.9	(1.0)	25.7	(1.1)	28.8	(1.3)	15.8	(1.0)	3.8	(0.5)	0.2	(0.1)
Ireland	2.0	(0.6)	5.8	(1.1)	14.0	(1.2)	24.3	(1.1)	27.7	(1.4)	19.8	(1.4)	5.7	(0.8)	0.6	(0.3)
Israel	6.6	(1.1)	10.2	(1.0)	15.4	(1.3)	22.2	(1.2)	22.4	(1.1)	15.8	(1.1)	6.3	(0.9)	1.1	(0.4)
Italy	4.0	(0.5)	9.1	(0.5)	18.7	(0.7)	24.8	(0.7)	24.2	(0.8)	15.0	(0.6)	3.9	(0.3)	0.3	(0.1)
Japan	2.9	(0.8)	5.8	(0.8)	12.1	(1.0)	20.2	(1.2)	25.0	(1.2)	21.4	(1.3)	10.1	(0.9)	2.4	(0.5)
Korea	0.5	(0.2)	1.8	(0.7)	8.0	(1.2)	19.6	(1.6)	32.5	(1.7)	26.8	(1.8)	9.6	(1.2)	1.2	(0.4)
Luxembourg	5.3	(0.6)	10.2	(1.0)	18.0	(1.1)	24.1	(1.2)	24.9	(1.1)	13.8	(1.0)	3.5	(0.6)	0.3	(0.2)
Mexico	4.6	(0.5)	12.8	(0.5)	26.1	(0.8)	31.0	(0.7)	19.7	(0.8)	5.3	(0.3)	0.5	(0.1)	0.0	(0.0)
Netherlands	0.0	(0.0)	2.4	(0.5)	14.3	(1.8)	26.6	(1.7)	29.2	(1.7)	20.5	(1.6)	6.5	(0.8)	0.3	(0.2)
New Zealand	1.6	(0.5)	5.2	(0.7)	13.2	(0.9)	19.9	(1.2)	23.6	(1.3)	22.0	(1.2)	11.3	(0.9)	3.1	(0.5)
Norway	1.2	(0.3)	5.6	(0.7)	15.7	(0.9)	27.5	(1.2)	28.8	(1.0)	16.5	(1.1)	4.5	(0.6)	0.5	(0.1)
Poland	1.7	(0.5)	6.1	(0.7)	16.7	(1.1)	28.3	(1.3)	28.2	(1.2)	15.3	(1.0)	3.6	(0.6)	0.2	(0.1)
Portugal	1.3	(0.3)	6.6	(0.9)	16.9	(1.2)	26.7	(1.1)	27.5	(1.3)	16.2	(1.1)	4.5	(0.5)	0.3	(0.1)
Slovak Republic	3.5	(0.7)	11.7	(1.2)	23.9	(1.2)	27.0	(1.4)	21.1	(1.3)	10.5	(1.0)	2.3	(0.3)	0.1	(0.1)
Slovenia	3.9	(0.4)	12.0	(0.8)	22.7	(1.0)	24.9	(1.0)	23.1	(1.2)	11.3	(1.0)	1.9	(0.4)	0.3	(0.2)
Spain	2.5	(0.4)	6.9	(0.7)	16.1	(1.2)	26.9	(1.1)	29.0	(1.0)	15.2	(0.9)	3.0	(0.4)	0.2	(0.1)
Sweden	2.4	(0.4)	6.5	(0.7)	14.8	(1.0)	25.8	(1.2)	28.3	(1.1)	16.0	(0.9)	5.7	(0.7)	0.6	(0.2)
Switzerland	1.4	(0.3)	6.7	(0.8)	15.8	(1.1)	26.3	(1.3)	27.8	(1.1)	17.1	(1.1)	4.4	(0.6)	0.6	(0.2)
Turkey	2.1	(0.4)	9.2	(1.0)	22.8	(1.3)	29.0	(1.7)	24.2	(1.3)	10.6	(1.1)	1.9	(0.5)	0.1	(0.1)
United Kingdom	1.2	(0.3)	5.2	(0.6)	14.9	(1.0)	24.9	(1.0)	27.0	(1.1)	17.9	(1.1)	7.5	(0.8)	1.4	(0.4)
United States	0.7	(0.2)	4.6	(0.7)	13.5	(1.3)	23.6	(1.5)	26.4	(1.3)	21.6	(1.3)	8.0	(1.0)	1.6	(0.4)
OECD total	2.1	(0.1)	6.6	(0.3)	16.0	(0.5)	24.8	(0.4)	26.0	(0.4)	17.6	(0.4)	6.0	(0.3)	1.0	(0.1)
OECD average	2.4	(0.1)	7.1	(0.1)	16.4	(0.2)	25.3	(0.2)	26.5	(0.2)	16.6	(0.2)	5.1	(0.1)	0.7	(0.0)
Albania	22.6	(1.8)	23.0	(1.7)	26.2	(1.3)	18.4	(1.4)	8.2	(1.3)	1.5	(0.4)	0.1	(0.1)	0.0	c
Argentina	14.8	(1.5)	18.2	(1.5)	24.4	(1.4)	23.6	(1.3)	13.4	(1.1)	4.8	(0.8)	0.8	(0.3)	0.1	(0.1)
Azerbaijan	24.9	(1.8)	29.7	(1.5)	26.9	(1.5)	13.8	(1.0)	4.0	(0.8)	0.6	(0.2)	0.0	(0.1)	0.0	c
Brazil	5.4	(0.6)	16.3	(0.8)	29.1	(1.0)	27.4	(1.0)	15.3	(0.9)	5.3	(0.5)	1.1	(0.2)	0.1	(0.1)
Bulgaria	17.0	(2.0)	17.3	(1.4)	21.2	(1.5)	20.8	(1.7)	15.9	(1.6)	6.6	(0.9)	1.1	(0.4)	0.2	(0.2)
Colombia	4.8	(1.1)	14.4	(1.3)	27.5	(1.3)	30.3	(1.6)	17.1	(1.5)	5.1	(0.8)	0.8	(0.3)	0.0	(0.0)
Croatia	3.4	(0.7)	11.3	(1.1)	21.9	(1.4)	27.4	(1.2)	22.4	(1.2)	11.1	(0.9)	2.3	(0.4)	0.2	(0.1)
Dubai (UAE)	6.4	(0.5)	12.4	(0.8)	21.5	(0.8)	22.6	(1.0)	20.6	(1.2)	12.4	(0.7)	3.6	(0.5)	0.4	(0.3)
Hong Kong-China	0.4	(0.2)	2.5	(0.5)	8.5	(0.8)	17.8	(1.2)	32.7	(1.8)	28.2	(1.7)	8.9	(1.0)	0.8	(0.3)
Indonesia	3.1	(0.8)	17.9	(1.6)	40.7	(1.6)	29.7	(1.8)	8.0	(1.2)	0.6	(0.3)	0.0	c	0.0	c
Jordan	12.2	(1.3)	18.1	(1.2)	30.6	(1.4)	26.2	(1.4)	10.8	(1.1)	1.9	(0.4)	0.2	(0.1)	0.0	(0.0)
Kazakhstan	19.0	(1.2)	27.2	(1.2)	26.0	(1.5)	17.1	(1.2)	8.3	(0.9)	2.2	(0.4)	0.2	(0.1)	0.0	(0.0)
Kyrgyzstan	48.2	(1.8)	24.9	(1.3)	15.3	(1.1)	7.5	(0.8)	3.3	(0.5)	0.8	(0.3)	0.1	(0.1)	0.0	(0.0)
Latvia	0.8	(0.4)	5.0	(0.8)	17.1	(1.6)	31.9	(1.6)	30.3	(1.6)	12.7	(1.6)	2.0	(0.4)	0.1	(0.1)
Liechtenstein	0.2	(0.6)	7.0	(2.5)	15.6	(3.8)	24.5	(4.3)	29.8	(4.3)	18.0	(3.8)	4.9	(2.1)	0.0	c
Lithuania	2.4	(0.5)	10.8	(1.0)	25.5	(1.1)	31.5	(1.3)	21.3	(1.3)	7.5	(0.7)	0.9	(0.3)	0.0	c
Macao-China	0.7	(0.2)	5.2	(0.6)	19.1	(0.9)	33.9	(1.3)	29.2	(1.1)	10.6	(0.9)	1.2	(0.2)	0.0	(0.0)
Montenegro	17.5	(1.0)	25.8	(1.3)	27.1	(1.6)	19.3	(1.5)	8.0	(0.8)	2.0	(0.4)	0.2	(0.2)	0.0	c
Panama	14.5	(2.2)	26.9	(2.3)	28.3	(2.3)	20.0	(2.5)	7.9	(1.2)	2.1	(0.6)	0.3	(0.2)	0.0	c
Peru	18.2	(1.4)	24.9	(1.3)	26.7	(1.2)	19.0	(1.1)	8.6	(0.8)	2.2	(0.5)	0.4	(0.2)	0.0	c
Qatar	26.3	(0.8)	24.4	(0.7)	20.5	(0.7)	13.2	(0.5)	8.7	(0.5)	4.8	(0.3)	1.8	(0.2)	0.3	(0.1)
Romania	8.4	(1.3)	16.3	(1.3)	26.3	(1.5)	27.5	(1.9)	16.2	(1.3)	4.7	(0.8)	0.5	(0.1)	0.0	(0.1)
Russian Federation	5.4	(0.9)	13.8	(1.0)	26.1	(1.3)	29.4	(1.4)	18.1	(1.1)	5.9	(0.6)	1.2	(0.3)	0.1	(0.1)
Serbia	5.9	(0.8)	15.5	(1.0)	27.9	(1.2)	28.3	(1.1)	16.8	(1.2)	5.1	(0.6)	0.5	(0.2)	0.0	(0.0)
Shanghai-China	0.3	(0.1)	1.0	(0.3)	7.1	(0.9)	17.9	(1.0)	31.8	(1.3)	29.3	(1.3)	11.2	(0.9)	1.5	(0.4)
Singapore	0.9	(0.2)	4.4	(0.4)	11.1	(0.7)	20.5	(1.0)	27.3	(1.0)	22.8	(1.2)	10.8	(0.9)	2.2	(0.4)
Chinese Taipei	1.6	(0.5)	5.8	(0.7)	15.2	(1.0)	27.2	(1.5)	31.5	(1.8)	15.7	(1.1)	2.7	(0.7)	0.2	(0.1)
Thailand	4.0	(0.8)	19.3	(1.1)	33.1	(1.2)	28.2	(1.6)	12.5	(1.1)	2.7	(0.6)	0.2	(0.1)	0.0	(0.0)
Trinidad and Tobago	16.5	(1.0)	18.2	(1.2)	22.1	(1.2)	22.3	(1.4)	14.9	(1.4)	5.1	(0.6)	0.8	(0.2)	0.0	(0.1)
Tunisia	7.0	(0.8)	13.9	(1.1)	26.4	(1.5)	30.7	(1.5)	16.7	(1.3)	4.7	(0.8)	0.6	(0.3)	0.0	(0.1)
Uruguay	8.2	(0.9)	16.3	(1.0)	24.6	(1.3)	24.8	(1.1)	17.3	(1.2)	7.2	(1.1)	1.6	(0.4)	0.1	(0.1)

StatLink ⤷ http://dx.doi.org/10.1787/888932343285

[Part 2/2]
Percentage of students at each proficiency level on the reading subscale *reflect and evaluate*, by gender

Table I.2.11

	Girls – Proficiency levels															
	Below Level 1b (less than 262.04 score points)		Level 1b (from 262.04 to less than 334.75 score points)		Level 1a (from 334.75 to less than 407.47 score points)		Level 2 (from 407.47 to less than 480.18 score points)		Level 3 (from 480.18 to less than 552.89 score points)		Level 4 (from 552.89 to less than 625.61 score points)		Level 5 (from 625.61 to less than 698.32 score points)		Level 6 (above 698.32 score points)	
	%	S.E.	%	S.E.	%	S.E.	%	S.E.	%	S.E.	%	S.E.	%	S.E.	%	S.E.
OECD																
Australia	0.3	(0.1)	1.6	(0.2)	6.1	(0.5)	16.6	(0.7)	27.2	(0.9)	28.5	(0.8)	15.6	(0.8)	4.1	(0.5)
Austria	2.6	(0.7)	6.1	(0.9)	12.9	(1.1)	21.7	(1.4)	29.3	(1.6)	20.6	(1.4)	6.2	(0.9)	0.6	(0.2)
Belgium	1.2	(0.3)	3.6	(0.5)	9.4	(0.8)	17.3	(1.0)	26.8	(1.2)	27.6	(1.1)	12.5	(0.9)	1.7	(0.3)
Canada	0.1	(0.0)	0.7	(0.1)	4.1	(0.3)	14.2	(0.6)	28.6	(0.8)	31.8	(0.8)	16.7	(0.6)	3.9	(0.5)
Chile	0.6	(0.2)	5.3	(0.7)	17.9	(1.1)	32.6	(1.5)	30.1	(1.4)	11.6	(1.1)	1.8	(0.4)	0.1	(0.1)
Czech Republic	1.1	(0.3)	4.6	(0.6)	13.3	(1.0)	25.2	(1.2)	29.1	(1.2)	19.7	(1.4)	6.4	(0.6)	0.6	(0.2)
Denmark	0.3	(0.2)	2.1	(0.4)	9.7	(0.9)	22.2	(1.1)	33.0	(1.3)	24.3	(1.3)	7.7	(0.8)	0.7	(0.2)
Estonia	0.1	(0.1)	1.1	(0.3)	6.5	(0.8)	19.8	(1.3)	33.3	(1.5)	28.6	(1.4)	9.4	(0.9)	1.3	(0.3)
Finland	0.1	(0.1)	0.4	(0.2)	2.5	(0.5)	10.0	(0.8)	28.5	(1.6)	36.8	(1.4)	18.6	(1.2)	3.1	(0.5)
France	1.2	(0.4)	3.4	(0.5)	9.5	(0.9)	18.7	(1.3)	28.6	(1.4)	25.5	(1.4)	11.4	(1.2)	1.7	(0.5)
Germany	0.7	(0.2)	3.4	(0.6)	9.2	(1.1)	20.2	(1.2)	30.3	(1.5)	26.9	(1.1)	8.5	(0.9)	0.8	(0.4)
Greece	1.0	(0.4)	2.8	(0.8)	8.7	(1.2)	20.4	(1.1)	30.3	(1.1)	25.2	(1.1)	9.7	(0.8)	2.0	(0.4)
Hungary	0.5	(0.3)	3.0	(0.8)	9.7	(1.2)	22.6	(1.6)	30.8	(1.5)	24.4	(1.3)	8.3	(0.8)	0.8	(0.3)
Iceland	0.3	(0.2)	2.0	(0.4)	7.1	(0.7)	19.8	(1.1)	34.0	(1.3)	26.4	(1.0)	9.0	(0.9)	1.3	(0.5)
Ireland	0.6	(0.2)	2.5	(0.6)	8.8	(0.8)	18.6	(1.0)	30.6	(1.3)	25.9	(1.6)	11.4	(1.2)	1.6	(0.4)
Israel	1.6	(0.4)	4.6	(0.6)	10.7	(0.9)	20.7	(1.1)	27.6	(1.5)	23.1	(1.3)	9.6	(1.0)	2.0	(0.4)
Italy	1.1	(0.2)	3.4	(0.4)	10.1	(0.5)	20.7	(0.6)	30.2	(0.7)	24.7	(0.8)	8.6	(0.6)	1.2	(0.2)
Japan	0.9	(0.3)	2.0	(0.4)	5.8	(0.9)	15.2	(1.2)	26.9	(1.1)	28.8	(1.3)	15.5	(1.0)	5.0	(0.7)
Korea	0.1	(0.1)	0.3	(0.2)	2.3	(0.5)	10.9	(1.2)	27.4	(1.6)	37.2	(1.6)	18.9	(1.8)	2.9	(0.6)
Luxembourg	1.8	(0.3)	4.8	(0.6)	13.0	(0.9)	23.7	(1.2)	28.7	(1.1)	20.2	(1.0)	7.1	(0.5)	0.8	(0.2)
Mexico	2.1	(0.3)	7.9	(0.5)	21.5	(0.7)	32.8	(0.7)	26.5	(0.7)	8.3	(0.4)	0.9	(0.2)	0.0	(0.0)
Netherlands	0.1	(0.1)	0.8	(0.3)	8.1	(1.3)	23.0	(1.9)	29.0	(1.5)	26.9	(2.0)	11.0	(1.1)	1.1	(0.4)
New Zealand	0.2	(0.1)	1.5	(0.4)	5.7	(0.6)	14.9	(0.9)	24.4	(1.1)	28.1	(1.4)	18.7	(1.5)	6.5	(0.7)
Norway	0.2	(0.1)	1.5	(0.4)	6.0	(0.6)	17.5	(1.0)	32.7	(1.3)	28.6	(1.1)	11.7	(1.0)	1.8	(0.5)
Poland	0.1	(0.1)	1.1	(0.4)	6.2	(0.7)	20.3	(1.2)	34.3	(1.1)	27.6	(1.1)	9.4	(0.9)	1.0	(0.3)
Portugal	0.2	(0.1)	1.9	(0.3)	8.4	(0.9)	20.9	(1.1)	32.8	(1.1)	25.4	(1.2)	9.5	(0.9)	1.0	(0.3)
Slovak Republic	0.8	(0.3)	3.9	(0.6)	11.2	(0.8)	26.3	(1.5)	31.6	(1.5)	20.2	(1.2)	5.5	(0.7)	0.5	(0.2)
Slovenia	0.7	(0.2)	3.0	(0.4)	10.9	(0.7)	23.4	(1.4)	31.5	(1.7)	22.9	(1.7)	7.0	(1.0)	0.5	(0.3)
Spain	1.2	(0.2)	3.7	(0.4)	9.9	(0.8)	22.8	(1.2)	32.8	(1.3)	23.1	(0.8)	6.1	(0.4)	0.5	(0.1)
Sweden	0.6	(0.4)	1.8	(0.4)	6.8	(0.7)	19.2	(1.1)	30.9	(1.3)	26.6	(1.4)	11.4	(0.9)	2.6	(0.5)
Switzerland	0.6	(0.2)	2.6	(0.3)	8.8	(1.0)	19.6	(0.9)	30.4	(1.3)	26.5	(1.3)	10.0	(0.9)	1.6	(0.4)
Turkey	0.6	(0.2)	2.6	(0.5)	11.4	(1.1)	26.0	(1.5)	31.1	(1.4)	21.2	(1.7)	6.1	(1.0)	1.0	(0.4)
United Kingdom	0.5	(0.1)	2.5	(0.4)	9.7	(0.7)	22.2	(1.1)	29.2	(1.0)	23.8	(1.5)	9.9	(0.8)	2.2	(0.4)
United States	0.2	(0.1)	2.0	(0.5)	8.6	(1.1)	20.7	(1.3)	28.4	(1.2)	24.7	(1.3)	12.7	(1.1)	2.8	(0.6)
OECD total	0.7	(0.1)	2.9	(0.2)	9.8	(0.3)	21.3	(0.4)	28.9	(0.4)	24.0	(0.4)	10.4	(0.3)	2.1	(0.2)
OECD average	0.7	(0.0)	2.8	(0.1)	9.1	(0.1)	20.6	(0.2)	29.9	(0.2)	25.1	(0.2)	10.1	(0.2)	1.7	(0.1)
Partners																
Albania	6.2	(0.9)	14.1	(1.5)	26.2	(1.5)	29.2	(1.5)	18.5	(1.7)	5.3	(0.9)	0.5	(0.3)	0.0	(0.0)
Argentina	7.2	(1.0)	13.4	(1.2)	22.8	(1.7)	26.6	(1.6)	20.0	(1.4)	8.1	(1.1)	1.7	(0.4)	0.1	(0.1)
Azerbaijan	17.8	(1.5)	26.4	(1.4)	30.9	(1.6)	18.7	(1.3)	5.2	(0.8)	0.8	(0.2)	0.1	(0.1)	0.0	c
Brazil	2.4	(0.3)	10.3	(0.7)	24.3	(0.8)	31.5	(0.9)	21.2	(1.1)	8.4	(0.7)	1.7	(0.3)	0.1	(0.1)
Bulgaria	5.3	(0.9)	9.1	(1.1)	17.4	(1.4)	25.5	(1.3)	24.2	(1.6)	13.8	(1.4)	4.2	(0.6)	0.5	(0.2)
Colombia	3.3	(0.7)	12.0	(1.2)	25.2	(1.3)	29.9	(1.7)	21.2	(1.3)	7.4	(0.8)	1.0	(0.3)	0.0	(0.0)
Croatia	0.6	(0.2)	3.1	(0.6)	11.5	(1.2)	23.5	(1.8)	31.0	(1.6)	22.0	(1.6)	7.5	(0.9)	0.9	(0.3)
Dubai (UAE)	0.7	(0.2)	4.1	(0.4)	14.0	(0.9)	24.9	(1.2)	27.9	(1.6)	19.6	(1.2)	7.8	(0.7)	0.9	(0.3)
Hong Kong-China	0.0	(0.0)	0.6	(0.2)	3.5	(0.5)	11.2	(0.9)	26.7	(1.4)	36.4	(1.4)	18.6	(1.3)	3.0	(0.5)
Indonesia	0.6	(0.3)	6.7	(1.0)	29.5	(2.0)	41.7	(1.6)	18.6	(1.8)	2.7	(0.7)	0.1	(0.1)	0.0	c
Jordan	2.8	(0.5)	8.8	(1.1)	22.0	(1.4)	33.5	(1.1)	24.4	(1.3)	7.6	(0.9)	0.8	(0.3)	0.0	(0.0)
Kazakhstan	7.9	(0.8)	18.7	(1.1)	29.1	(1.4)	24.1	(1.2)	14.5	(1.1)	5.0	(0.7)	0.6	(0.2)	0.0	(0.0)
Kyrgyzstan	26.8	(1.8)	28.7	(1.6)	22.9	(1.3)	13.4	(1.0)	6.2	(0.7)	1.8	(0.3)	0.3	(0.1)	0.0	(0.0)
Latvia	0.0	(0.0)	0.9	(0.4)	6.2	(0.8)	23.4	(1.5)	37.7	(1.8)	25.5	(1.6)	5.9	(0.7)	0.4	(0.2)
Liechtenstein	0.3	(0.6)	1.5	(1.2)	8.0	(3.5)	21.4	(4.6)	33.5	(4.8)	28.3	(4.5)	6.7	(2.6)	0.3	(0.6)
Lithuania	0.3	(0.2)	2.8	(0.5)	11.7	(0.9)	27.0	(1.5)	33.5	(1.6)	19.7	(1.1)	4.6	(0.8)	0.4	(0.2)
Macao-China	0.1	(0.1)	1.6	(0.3)	8.5	(0.5)	27.2	(0.9)	38.0	(1.2)	20.7	(1.0)	3.7	(0.4)	0.2	(0.1)
Montenegro	5.5	(0.7)	14.3	(1.0)	25.5	(1.2)	30.6	(1.3)	17.4	(1.4)	5.9	(0.8)	0.7	(0.4)	0.0	(0.0)
Panama	9.4	(1.9)	19.3	(2.4)	27.5	(2.3)	23.0	(1.9)	13.6	(1.8)	6.0	(1.2)	1.1	(0.4)	0.1	(0.1)
Peru	12.2	(1.1)	20.0	(1.4)	27.2	(1.6)	23.8	(1.1)	12.9	(1.4)	3.5	(0.7)	0.4	(0.2)	0.0	(0.0)
Qatar	11.4	(0.4)	16.9	(0.7)	22.7	(0.8)	22.7	(0.9)	15.7	(0.6)	7.4	(0.4)	2.6	(0.3)	0.6	(0.1)
Romania	2.3	(0.5)	8.2	(1.1)	19.3	(1.6)	31.3	(1.4)	26.8	(1.6)	10.1	(1.4)	1.8	(0.4)	0.2	(0.1)
Russian Federation	1.8	(0.4)	6.4	(0.8)	18.1	(1.6)	30.1	(1.5)	26.7	(1.2)	13.1	(1.2)	3.2	(0.6)	0.4	(0.2)
Serbia	1.1	(0.3)	7.3	(0.7)	20.6	(1.2)	32.3	(1.4)	28.0	(1.4)	9.3	(0.8)	1.4	(0.3)	0.0	(0.1)
Shanghai-China	0.1	(0.0)	0.1	(0.1)	1.3	(0.3)	8.7	(0.7)	23.5	(1.0)	36.5	(1.3)	24.5	(1.2)	5.3	(0.6)
Singapore	0.2	(0.1)	1.2	(0.3)	6.8	(0.8)	15.5	(0.9)	27.4	(1.0)	27.8	(1.1)	16.4	(0.9)	4.9	(0.8)
Chinese Taipei	0.2	(0.1)	1.7	(0.3)	8.2	(0.9)	22.3	(1.4)	34.9	(1.5)	25.7	(1.6)	6.4	(0.5)	0.6	(0.3)
Thailand	0.7	(0.2)	7.0	(0.9)	26.4	(1.3)	37.3	(1.3)	22.3	(1.2)	5.5	(0.8)	0.7	(0.3)	0.0	(0.0)
Trinidad and Tobago	5.8	(0.6)	11.1	(0.9)	17.9	(0.9)	25.9	(1.2)	22.7	(1.2)	12.2	(0.7)	4.0	(0.6)	0.5	(0.2)
Tunisia	1.9	(0.4)	8.4	(0.9)	21.9	(1.1)	33.6	(1.3)	24.9	(1.2)	8.1	(0.8)	1.1	(0.4)	0.1	(0.1)
Uruguay	2.5	(0.4)	8.0	(0.8)	19.3	(1.2)	28.7	(1.1)	24.6	(1.0)	13.0	(1.0)	3.5	(0.5)	0.5	(0.2)

StatLink ᴹˢᴾ http://dx.doi.org/10.1787/888932343285

[Part 1/1]

Table I.2.12 **Mean score, variation and gender differences in student performance on the reading subscale *reflect and evaluate***

		All students				Gender differences						Percentiles											
		Mean score		Standard deviation		Boys		Girls		Difference (B – G)		5th		10th		25th		75th		90th		95th	
		Mean	S.E.	S.D.	S.E.	Mean score	S.E.	Mean score	S.E.	Score dif.	S.E.	Score	S.E.	Score	S.E.	Score	S.E.	Score	S.E.	Score	S.E.	Score	S.E.
OECD	Australia	523	(2.5)	103	(1.4)	501	(3.0)	543	(2.7)	**-42**	(3.1)	344	(3.9)	387	(3.2)	455	(2.8)	595	(2.8)	650	(3.7)	681	(4.6)
	Austria	463	(3.4)	107	(2.4)	439	(4.2)	486	(4.6)	**-48**	(6.2)	270	(7.6)	313	(6.7)	389	(5.9)	543	(3.3)	595	(3.9)	623	(4.1)
	Belgium	505	(2.5)	108	(2.0)	491	(3.7)	520	(3.1)	**-29**	(4.9)	312	(6.6)	357	(4.7)	436	(4.1)	584	(2.6)	634	(2.6)	661	(3.5)
	Canada	535	(1.6)	91	(1.0)	516	(1.9)	555	(1.9)	**-38**	(2.0)	377	(3.0)	416	(2.8)	476	(2.3)	598	(1.8)	649	(2.2)	677	(2.3)
	Chile	452	(3.2)	84	(1.8)	441	(3.7)	465	(3.6)	**-24**	(3.8)	310	(5.6)	342	(4.8)	396	(4.4)	512	(3.2)	559	(3.8)	586	(3.9)
	Czech Republic	462	(3.1)	100	(1.8)	436	(3.9)	491	(3.4)	**-55**	(4.6)	294	(5.6)	331	(5.3)	394	(3.9)	533	(3.7)	591	(4.4)	623	(3.7)
	Denmark	493	(2.6)	88	(1.1)	475	(2.9)	511	(2.9)	**-36**	(2.8)	343	(4.8)	377	(3.6)	435	(3.0)	555	(3.2)	603	(3.6)	631	(3.5)
	Estonia	503	(2.6)	86	(1.7)	479	(3.2)	528	(2.7)	**-49**	(3.1)	355	(5.7)	390	(4.7)	447	(3.8)	562	(2.8)	611	(3.5)	637	(4.5)
	Finland	536	(2.2)	87	(1.1)	506	(2.6)	565	(2.3)	**-59**	(2.2)	384	(5.0)	419	(3.4)	480	(3.1)	597	(2.8)	642	(2.4)	668	(3.4)
	France	495	(3.4)	107	(2.6)	472	(4.3)	517	(3.5)	**-44**	(3.8)	301	(8.2)	349	(6.7)	427	(4.9)	573	(4.0)	627	(4.4)	654	(4.3)
	Germany	491	(2.8)	97	(2.1)	470	(3.9)	513	(2.9)	**-42**	(4.1)	316	(7.6)	357	(6.1)	429	(4.6)	562	(2.8)	609	(2.8)	635	(3.4)
	Greece	489	(4.9)	104	(3.1)	460	(6.3)	518	(3.8)	**-57**	(5.0)	306	(11.4)	350	(10.2)	423	(7.1)	563	(3.5)	617	(3.6)	649	(3.9)
	Hungary	489	(3.3)	93	(2.3)	469	(4.1)	509	(3.7)	**-41**	(4.3)	327	(7.6)	363	(6.6)	425	(4.8)	556	(3.7)	607	(3.7)	634	(3.8)
	Iceland	496	(1.4)	94	(1.2)	470	(2.0)	522	(2.0)	**-52**	(2.9)	329	(4.5)	370	(3.8)	437	(2.6)	562	(2.3)	611	(2.8)	638	(3.5)
	Ireland	502	(3.1)	99	(1.9)	484	(4.2)	522	(3.5)	**-38**	(4.7)	330	(7.9)	371	(5.6)	439	(4.0)	572	(3.0)	624	(3.3)	652	(3.2)
	Israel	483	(4.0)	115	(2.9)	458	(5.5)	506	(4.0)	**-48**	(5.6)	275	(9.4)	324	(8.5)	410	(5.5)	566	(3.5)	623	(3.9)	655	(4.3)
	Italy	482	(1.8)	105	(1.7)	456	(2.5)	509	(2.2)	**-53**	(3.2)	298	(4.8)	342	(3.2)	413	(2.4)	558	(1.9)	610	(2.0)	638	(2.2)
	Japan	521	(3.9)	111	(3.3)	498	(6.0)	545	(4.0)	**-47**	(6.9)	323	(11.6)	375	(8.1)	453	(5.7)	598	(3.4)	653	(3.3)	686	(3.9)
	Korea	542	(3.9)	86	(2.5)	521	(5.4)	565	(4.3)	**-44**	(6.4)	392	(8.9)	429	(6.1)	489	(4.9)	602	(4.1)	646	(4.0)	671	(4.3)
	Luxembourg	471	(1.1)	106	(1.0)	450	(1.8)	492	(1.5)	**-41**	(2.6)	283	(4.3)	329	(3.2)	402	(2.2)	546	(1.9)	602	(2.6)	631	(3.1)
	Mexico	432	(1.9)	88	(1.2)	419	(2.1)	445	(2.0)	**-27**	(1.7)	282	(4.2)	318	(2.8)	375	(2.4)	494	(1.9)	541	(1.9)	568	(2.0)
	Netherlands	510	(5.0)	86	(1.8)	496	(5.0)	524	(5.2)	**-28**	(2.3)	370	(5.0)	397	(5.9)	447	(6.5)	575	(4.9)	624	(3.9)	649	(3.9)
	New Zealand	531	(2.5)	108	(2.0)	506	(3.8)	556	(2.8)	**-51**	(4.6)	343	(6.9)	385	(5.4)	458	(3.6)	609	(2.6)	666	(3.0)	696	(3.6)
	Norway	505	(2.7)	93	(1.3)	478	(3.1)	533	(2.9)	**-55**	(2.7)	343	(4.3)	381	(3.9)	445	(3.7)	571	(3.1)	621	(3.5)	650	(3.4)
	Poland	498	(2.8)	91	(1.3)	469	(3.1)	526	(2.9)	**-56**	(2.6)	340	(4.7)	379	(3.8)	440	(3.1)	562	(3.1)	611	(3.5)	639	(3.5)
	Portugal	496	(3.3)	93	(1.5)	473	(3.7)	519	(3.3)	**-45**	(2.7)	335	(4.6)	372	(4.5)	434	(4.5)	562	(3.3)	614	(3.4)	642	(3.7)
	Slovak Republic	466	(2.9)	98	(2.1)	437	(4.1)	494	(3.0)	**-57**	(4.1)	297	(7.3)	335	(6.3)	400	(4.3)	537	(3.0)	590	(3.6)	619	(3.9)
	Slovenia	470	(1.2)	100	(1.0)	439	(1.6)	503	(1.6)	**-64**	(2.3)	296	(3.7)	335	(2.9)	401	(2.0)	544	(2.0)	596	(3.5)	624	(4.0)
	Spain	483	(2.2)	95	(1.2)	467	(2.6)	501	(2.3)	**-34**	(2.2)	312	(5.0)	356	(3.9)	425	(3.1)	550	(2.2)	598	(2.3)	625	(2.5)
	Sweden	502	(3.0)	100	(1.7)	476	(3.2)	529	(3.3)	**-53**	(2.8)	326	(7.0)	372	(5.4)	442	(3.5)	571	(3.5)	626	(4.2)	658	(4.2)
	Switzerland	497	(2.7)	96	(1.7)	476	(3.3)	519	(2.9)	**-44**	(2.7)	327	(6.1)	368	(5.0)	433	(3.7)	566	(3.3)	616	(3.7)	645	(4.8)
	Turkey	473	(4.0)	94	(2.0)	447	(4.4)	500	(4.5)	**-54**	(4.5)	315	(6.1)	349	(4.8)	409	(4.7)	539	(4.9)	591	(4.7)	621	(5.7)
	United Kingdom	503	(2.4)	98	(1.2)	489	(3.8)	516	(3.1)	**-27**	(4.9)	338	(3.7)	375	(3.3)	437	(3.0)	572	(3.2)	628	(3.3)	661	(3.1)
	United States	512	(4.0)	98	(1.7)	498	(4.6)	527	(4.1)	**-29**	(3.6)	347	(5.7)	382	(5.1)	444	(4.2)	583	(4.8)	637	(5.5)	668	(5.8)
	OECD total	496	(1.3)	102	(0.6)	478	(1.5)	516	(1.3)	**-38**	(1.4)	323	(1.9)	362	(1.5)	429	(1.5)	569	(1.4)	624	(1.7)	655	(1.9)
	OECD average	494	(0.5)	97	(0.3)	472	(0.7)	517	(0.6)	**-44**	(0.7)	325	(1.1)	365	(0.9)	431	(0.7)	564	(0.6)	615	(0.6)	644	(0.7)
Partners	Albania	376	(4.6)	108	(2.3)	342	(5.9)	412	(4.4)	**-70**	(4.8)	188	(8.9)	233	(7.6)	308	(5.9)	454	(5.2)	511	(5.9)	541	(4.9)
	Argentina	402	(4.8)	111	(3.4)	381	(5.1)	420	(5.1)	**-39**	(3.8)	209	(9.8)	257	(7.9)	330	(5.1)	480	(5.8)	542	(6.1)	576	(7.8)
	Azerbaijan	335	(3.8)	91	(2.2)	324	(4.1)	346	(4.0)	**-22**	(2.9)	181	(8.6)	217	(7.3)	273	(4.7)	397	(4.1)	452	(5.2)	483	(5.4)
	Brazil	424	(2.7)	92	(1.5)	408	(2.9)	437	(2.8)	**-29**	(1.8)	273	(3.9)	306	(3.5)	360	(3.0)	486	(3.4)	544	(4.2)	577	(4.5)
	Bulgaria	417	(7.1)	121	(2.6)	384	(7.8)	453	(5.9)	**-70**	(4.9)	206	(10.8)	252	(9.9)	336	(10.3)	505	(6.7)	568	(5.3)	602	(5.1)
	Colombia	422	(4.2)	91	(2.2)	414	(4.9)	429	(4.5)	**-15**	(4.0)	273	(7.7)	305	(6.3)	360	(5.6)	484	(4.8)	538	(4.0)	570	(4.9)
	Croatia	471	(3.5)	100	(2.0)	442	(4.1)	503	(4.4)	**-62**	(5.3)	301	(6.4)	337	(5.7)	402	(4.9)	543	(3.5)	598	(3.5)	628	(4.4)
	Dubai (UAE)	466	(1.1)	108	(0.9)	438	(1.7)	495	(1.5)	**-57**	(2.2)	281	(3.3)	323	(2.4)	392	(2.2)	544	(2.2)	605	(2.9)	636	(2.9)
	Hong Kong-China	540	(2.5)	87	(1.9)	520	(3.7)	562	(3.2)	**-42**	(4.8)	381	(6.5)	421	(4.9)	487	(3.8)	600	(2.8)	645	(2.9)	669	(3.1)
	Indonesia	409	(3.8)	69	(1.9)	388	(3.9)	429	(3.9)	**-40**	(3.4)	294	(6.4)	321	(5.0)	363	(3.9)	455	(4.6)	497	(5.2)	521	(5.5)
	Jordan	407	(3.4)	97	(2.2)	376	(4.9)	439	(4.3)	**-63**	(6.5)	236	(7.9)	279	(6.3)	348	(4.2)	474	(3.7)	525	(3.7)	555	(4.4)
	Kazakhstan	373	(3.4)	101	(1.9)	350	(3.7)	396	(3.7)	**-46**	(2.9)	213	(4.6)	245	(3.9)	302	(3.5)	442	(4.5)	508	(5.6)	543	(6.0)
	Kyrgyzstan	300	(4.0)	112	(2.5)	272	(4.6)	327	(4.1)	**-56**	(3.4)	120	(6.2)	161	(5.5)	225	(4.7)	372	(4.9)	448	(7.3)	495	(7.5)
	Latvia	492	(3.0)	82	(1.7)	467	(3.4)	516	(3.2)	**-49**	(3.2)	353	(6.7)	386	(4.6)	439	(3.7)	549	(3.7)	594	(3.5)	619	(3.2)
	Liechtenstein	498	(3.2)	88	(3.3)	481	(4.7)	516	(5.6)	**-35**	(8.1)	336	(12.3)	373	(12.6)	439	(6.8)	562	(8.0)	605	(7.0)	631	(7.9)
	Lithuania	463	(2.5)	90	(1.6)	432	(2.7)	495	(2.8)	**-63**	(2.7)	311	(5.2)	344	(4.1)	402	(3.4)	527	(3.0)	577	(3.9)	607	(4.7)
	Macao-China	481	(0.8)	79	(0.7)	460	(1.2)	502	(1.2)	**-42**	(1.7)	345	(2.6)	377	(2.3)	429	(1.4)	536	(1.5)	580	(1.8)	605	(2.3)
	Montenegro	383	(1.9)	101	(1.1)	353	(2.1)	414	(2.3)	**-60**	(2.5)	216	(3.8)	253	(3.4)	314	(3.4)	453	(2.5)	510	(3.1)	547	(5.0)
	Panama	377	(6.3)	101	(3.7)	359	(6.8)	395	(7.0)	**-36**	(6.8)	218	(11.5)	251	(9.3)	308	(7.4)	444	(7.4)	513	(8.4)	551	(9.7)
	Peru	368	(4.2)	102	(2.5)	355	(4.5)	381	(5.1)	**-27**	(4.9)	197	(7.2)	236	(5.8)	298	(4.4)	439	(5.3)	500	(6.3)	536	(7.4)
	Qatar	376	(1.0)	124	(0.8)	347	(1.5)	405	(1.2)	**-59**	(1.9)	185	(2.2)	221	(1.6)	285	(1.7)	461	(1.9)	543	(2.5)	591	(3.3)
	Romania	426	(4.5)	97	(2.8)	401	(5.1)	451	(4.7)	**-51**	(4.9)	259	(7.9)	298	(6.8)	363	(6.0)	495	(5.2)	547	(5.4)	576	(5.9)
	Russian Federation	441	(3.7)	98	(2.3)	417	(4.1)	464	(3.9)	**-47**	(3.1)	277	(6.6)	316	(6.3)	377	(4.2)	506	(3.7)	563	(4.6)	597	(4.8)
	Serbia	430	(2.6)	90	(1.6)	408	(3.5)	453	(2.7)	**-45**	(3.3)	277	(5.2)	311	(4.2)	369	(3.0)	494	(2.6)	544	(3.4)	572	(3.3)
	Shanghai-China	557	(2.4)	85	(1.6)	531	(2.9)	582	(2.4)	**-50**	(2.8)	408	(5.9)	445	(4.3)	502	(3.3)	616	(2.8)	661	(2.9)	686	(3.4)
	Singapore	529	(1.1)	100	(1.1)	511	(1.8)	548	(1.6)	**-37**	(2.6)	355	(3.7)	394	(2.7)	462	(2.1)	601	(1.6)	654	(2.5)	684	(4.1)
	Chinese Taipei	493	(2.8)	88	(1.8)	472	(3.7)	514	(3.9)	**-41**	(5.2)	338	(5.3)	376	(3.8)	437	(3.5)	554	(3.1)	599	(3.9)	625	(4.7)
	Thailand	420	(2.8)	80	(2.1)	396	(3.5)	439	(3.2)	**-43**	(3.8)	290	(5.4)	318	(4.4)	365	(3.6)	475	(3.0)	522	(3.7)	552	(5.1)
	Trinidad and Tobago	413	(1.3)	117	(1.1)	381	(1.9)	446	(1.7)	**-65**	(2.5)	210	(5.0)	254	(4.5)	332	(2.7)	497	(2.4)	561	(2.9)	596	(3.5)
	Tunisia	427	(3.0)	91	(1.9)	408	(3.3)	444	(3.1)	**-36**	(2.4)	269	(5.4)	307	(4.1)	370	(3.9)	489	(3.5)	540	(4.5)	569	(5.3)
	Uruguay	436	(2.9)	104	(1.7)	410	(3.5)	458	(3.1)	**-48**	(3.5)	260	(5.7)	299	(5.3)	366	(3.8)	508	(2.9)	569	(4.0)	603	(5.0)

Note: Values that are statistically significant are indicated in bold (see Annex A3).
StatLink http://dx.doi.org/10.1787/888932343285

[Part 1/1]

Gender differences in student performance on the reading scale after taking student programmes into account

Table I.2.13

	Gender differences in reading performance (boys – girls)					
	Observed		Within school		After accounting for the programme level and programme destination in which students are enrolled[1]	
	Score dif.	S.E.	Score dif.	S.E.	Score dif.	S.E.
OECD						
Australia	-37	(3.1)	-37	(2.5)	-35	(2.4)
Austria	-41	(5.5)	-20	(3.4)	-20	(3.4)
Belgium	-27	(4.4)	-17	(2.3)	-16	(2.0)
Canada	-34	(1.9)	-34	(2.1)	-33	(2.1)
Chile	-22	(4.1)	-18	(3.1)	-17	(3.1)
Czech Republic	-48	(4.1)	-33	(2.8)	-32	(2.7)
Denmark	-29	(2.9)	-28	(3.2)	-28	(3.2)
Estonia	-44	(2.5)	-42	(2.9)	-41	(2.9)
Finland	-55	(2.3)	-57	(2.7)	-56	(2.7)
France	-40	(3.7)	-30	(3.5)	-28	(3.5)
Germany	-40	(3.9)	-29	(2.5)	-29	(2.5)
Greece	-47	(4.3)	-34	(3.2)	-34	(3.2)
Hungary	-38	(4.0)	-22	(2.6)	-22	(2.5)
Iceland	-44	(2.8)	-44	(3.4)	-44	(3.4)
Ireland	-39	(4.7)	-35	(4.7)	-34	(4.8)
Israel	-42	(5.2)	-29	(3.8)	-28	(3.8)
Italy	-46	(2.8)	-26	(1.7)	-26	(1.7)
Japan	-39	(6.8)	-28	(2.8)	-28	(2.8)
Korea	-35	(5.9)	-44	(5.9)	-43	(5.8)
Luxembourg	-39	(2.3)	-35	(3.1)	-32	(2.7)
Mexico	-25	(1.6)	-21	(1.9)	-21	(1.9)
Netherlands	-24	(2.4)	-19	(1.8)	-19	(1.8)
New Zealand	-46	(4.3)	-50	(4.9)	-49	(5.0)
Norway	-47	(2.9)	-47	(3.5)	-47	(3.5)
Poland	-50	(2.5)	-51	(3.5)	-51	(3.5)
Portugal	-38	(2.4)	-32	(2.6)	-23	(2.3)
Slovak Republic	-51	(3.5)	-42	(3.0)	-40	(3.0)
Slovenia	-55	(2.3)	-31	(2.3)	-30	(2.4)
Spain	-29	(2.0)	-29	(1.7)	-29	(1.7)
Sweden	-46	(2.7)	-47	(3.2)	-46	(3.1)
Switzerland	-39	(2.5)	-31	(2.5)	-31	(2.4)
Turkey	-43	(3.7)	-32	(3.0)	-32	(3.0)
United Kingdom	-25	(4.5)	-25	(3.3)	-25	(3.4)
United States	-25	(3.4)	-27	(4.3)	-25	(4.2)
OECD total	-33	(1.2)	-29	(1.0)	-29	(0.7)
OECD average	-39	(0.6)	-33	(0.5)	-32	(0.5)
Partners						
Albania	-62	(4.4)	-58	(4.0)	-57	(4.0)
Argentina	-37	(3.8)	-30	(3.2)	-27	(3.1)
Azerbaijan	-24	(2.4)	-22	(2.5)	-23	(2.4)
Brazil	-29	(1.7)	-27	(2.0)	-25	(2.0)
Bulgaria	-61	(4.7)	-46	(3.9)	-45	(3.9)
Colombia	-9	(3.8)	-9	(3.2)	-6	(2.8)
Croatia	-51	(4.6)	-33	(3.5)	-30	(3.6)
Dubai (UAE)	-51	(2.3)	-28	(5.3)	-26	(5.2)
Hong Kong-China	-33	(4.4)	-26	(2.9)	-24	(2.8)
Indonesia	-37	(3.3)	-28	(1.8)	-28	(1.8)
Jordan	-57	(6.2)	-43	(10.0)	-43	(10.0)
Kazakhstan	-43	(2.7)	-41	(2.6)	-40	(2.6)
Kyrgyzstan	-53	(2.7)	-51	(3.0)	-50	(3.0)
Latvia	-47	(3.2)	-45	(2.9)	-44	(2.9)
Liechtenstein	-32	(7.1)	-21	(5.8)	-23	(5.7)
Lithuania	-59	(2.8)	-52	(2.8)	-52	(2.8)
Macao-China	-34	(1.7)	-21	(2.1)	-17	(1.8)
Montenegro	-53	(2.6)	-40	(3.5)	-36	(2.9)
Panama	-33	(6.7)	-19	(4.9)	-18	(4.8)
Peru	-22	(4.7)	-11	(3.3)	-8	(3.2)
Qatar	-50	(1.8)	-36	(6.7)	-33	(5.9)
Romania	-43	(4.4)	-14	(3.9)	-14	(3.9)
Russian Federation	-45	(2.7)	-41	(2.6)	-38	(2.6)
Serbia	-39	(3.0)	-26	(2.7)	-22	(2.6)
Shanghai-China	-40	(2.9)	-33	(2.4)	-33	(2.4)
Singapore	-31	(2.3)	-26	(2.4)	-27	(2.4)
Chinese Taipei	-37	(5.3)	-48	(4.6)	-48	(4.6)
Thailand	-38	(3.8)	-36	(3.0)	-35	(3.0)
Trinidad and Tobago	-58	(2.5)	-46	(2.4)	-40	(2.3)
Tunisia	-31	(2.2)	-22	(2.4)	-21	(2.3)
Uruguay	-42	(3.1)	-37	(3.0)	-30	(2.8)

1. Programme level indicates whether the student is in the lower (ISCED Level 2) or upper (ISCED Level 3) secondary programme. Programme designation indicates the destination of the study programme: A, B or C (see Annex A1).
StatLink ⌗⌗⌗ http://dx.doi.org/10.1787/888932343285

[Part 1/1]

Table I.2.14 **Percentage of students at each proficiency level on the reading subscale *continuous texts***

	Proficiency levels															
	Below Level 1b (less than 262.04 score points)		Level 1b (from 262.04 to less than 334.75 score points)		Level 1a (from 334.75 to less than 407.47 score points)		Level 2 (from 407.47 to less than 480.18 score points)		Level 3 (from 480.18 to less than 552.89 score points)		Level 4 (from 552.89 to less than 625.61 score points)		Level 5 (from 625.61 to less than 698.32 score points)		Level 6 (above 698.32 score points)	
	%	S.E.	%	S.E.	%	S.E.	%	S.E.	%	S.E.	%	S.E.	%	S.E.	%	S.E.
OECD																
Australia	1.1	(0.1)	3.8	(0.3)	10.4	(0.5)	20.6	(0.6)	27.3	(0.6)	23.4	(0.5)	11.0	(0.5)	2.4	(0.4)
Austria	1.9	(0.4)	7.9	(0.7)	17.9	(0.9)	24.5	(0.9)	25.8	(1.0)	17.1	(0.8)	4.6	(0.6)	0.4	(0.1)
Belgium	1.3	(0.3)	4.7	(0.5)	12.5	(0.6)	20.6	(0.8)	25.4	(0.7)	24.3	(0.7)	10.2	(0.5)	1.1	(0.2)
Canada	0.4	(0.1)	2.4	(0.2)	8.3	(0.4)	20.2	(0.7)	28.9	(0.7)	25.9	(0.7)	11.5	(0.5)	2.4	(0.2)
Chile	1.5	(0.3)	7.4	(0.7)	20.8	(1.0)	31.8	(1.0)	26.3	(1.2)	10.3	(0.9)	1.9	(0.3)	0.1	(0.1)
Czech Republic	0.7	(0.2)	5.4	(0.6)	17.0	(0.9)	27.3	(1.0)	27.4	(1.0)	16.4	(0.9)	5.3	(0.4)	0.6	(0.2)
Denmark	0.5	(0.1)	3.3	(0.4)	11.9	(0.6)	25.4	(0.9)	32.4	(0.8)	20.8	(0.8)	5.4	(0.4)	0.5	(0.1)
Estonia	0.3	(0.2)	2.3	(0.4)	11.5	(0.6)	26.0	(1.3)	34.8	(1.1)	20.0	(0.9)	4.7	(0.5)	0.4	(0.2)
Finland	0.2	(0.1)	1.5	(0.2)	6.4	(0.5)	17.0	(0.9)	30.2	(0.8)	30.2	(0.8)	13.1	(0.7)	1.4	(0.2)
France	2.7	(0.5)	6.2	(0.6)	12.5	(0.9)	21.4	(1.2)	25.9	(1.1)	21.4	(1.0)	8.5	(0.8)	1.4	(0.4)
Germany	0.9	(0.2)	4.7	(0.4)	12.9	(0.8)	22.9	(1.3)	28.4	(1.2)	22.8	(0.9)	6.7	(0.5)	0.6	(0.2)
Greece	1.4	(0.4)	5.6	(0.8)	14.5	(1.0)	24.3	(0.9)	27.8	(1.0)	19.5	(1.0)	6.1	(0.6)	0.9	(0.2)
Hungary	0.8	(0.2)	4.1	(0.7)	12.4	(0.9)	23.5	(1.1)	30.1	(1.1)	21.7	(1.0)	6.7	(0.7)	0.6	(0.2)
Iceland	1.5	(0.3)	4.3	(0.5)	11.6	(0.6)	21.4	(0.7)	30.4	(1.0)	21.6	(1.1)	8.0	(0.6)	1.3	(0.3)
Ireland	1.8	(0.4)	4.2	(0.5)	11.8	(0.7)	22.6	(0.9)	29.8	(0.9)	21.6	(1.0)	7.4	(0.8)	0.8	(0.2)
Israel	3.7	(0.6)	7.5	(0.7)	14.6	(0.8)	22.2	(1.1)	25.7	(0.9)	18.5	(0.8)	6.8	(0.5)	1.1	(0.2)
Italy	1.4	(0.2)	5.2	(0.3)	13.9	(0.4)	23.1	(0.5)	28.8	(0.5)	21.0	(0.5)	6.0	(0.3)	0.5	(0.1)
Japan	1.7	(0.4)	3.5	(0.6)	8.6	(0.7)	17.9	(0.7)	27.1	(0.9)	26.7	(0.9)	12.2	(0.8)	2.4	(0.3)
Korea	0.3	(0.1)	1.0	(0.3)	5.1	(0.7)	15.5	(1.0)	32.5	(1.2)	32.7	(1.2)	11.9	(1.0)	1.0	(0.2)
Luxembourg	3.3	(0.3)	7.8	(0.5)	15.4	(0.9)	23.8	(0.8)	26.5	(0.7)	17.4	(0.9)	5.3	(0.5)	0.5	(0.1)
Mexico	3.7	(0.4)	11.4	(0.5)	24.3	(0.6)	32.7	(0.7)	21.8	(0.6)	5.6	(0.3)	0.4	(0.1)	0.0	(0.0)
Netherlands	0.1	(0.1)	2.0	(0.3)	12.3	(1.3)	25.5	(1.5)	27.7	(1.1)	22.8	(1.7)	8.6	(0.9)	0.8	(0.2)
New Zealand	1.2	(0.2)	3.7	(0.4)	10.7	(0.6)	19.4	(0.8)	25.4	(0.8)	23.8	(0.8)	12.8	(0.7)	3.0	(0.4)
Norway	0.8	(0.2)	3.6	(0.4)	11.2	(0.6)	22.4	(0.7)	29.4	(0.9)	22.8	(1.0)	8.5	(0.6)	1.3	(0.2)
Poland	0.7	(0.2)	3.0	(0.4)	11.1	(0.6)	24.4	(0.9)	30.9	(0.8)	22.0	(1.0)	7.2	(0.6)	0.8	(0.2)
Portugal	0.6	(0.2)	4.2	(0.4)	12.7	(0.9)	26.0	(0.9)	30.6	(1.1)	19.9	(1.0)	5.6	(0.5)	0.4	(0.2)
Slovak Republic	0.9	(0.3)	5.1	(0.6)	16.2	(0.9)	27.3	(0.9)	28.7	(1.2)	17.2	(1.1)	4.2	(0.4)	0.5	(0.2)
Slovenia	0.9	(0.1)	5.6	(0.3)	15.3	(0.6)	24.8	(0.9)	28.2	(0.8)	19.1	(0.8)	5.6	(0.6)	0.4	(0.2)
Spain	1.3	(0.2)	4.8	(0.4)	13.2	(0.6)	25.8	(0.6)	31.7	(0.7)	18.7	(0.6)	4.1	(0.3)	0.3	(0.1)
Sweden	1.7	(0.3)	4.3	(0.4)	11.5	(0.8)	23.1	(1.1)	28.9	(1.1)	20.3	(1.0)	8.6	(0.6)	1.6	(0.3)
Switzerland	0.8	(0.1)	4.5	(0.4)	12.5	(0.7)	23.0	(0.8)	29.0	(1.0)	22.2	(0.9)	7.2	(0.7)	0.9	(0.2)
Turkey	0.9	(0.2)	5.2	(0.6)	18.3	(1.0)	31.3	(1.4)	28.9	(1.2)	13.2	(1.2)	2.1	(0.5)	0.1	(0.1)
United Kingdom	1.1	(0.2)	4.5	(0.4)	14.2	(0.7)	25.0	(0.8)	27.9	(0.7)	18.9	(0.9)	7.2	(0.5)	1.2	(0.2)
United States	0.8	(0.2)	4.3	(0.4)	13.6	(0.8)	23.7	(0.9)	26.5	(0.8)	20.0	(0.9)	9.1	(0.9)	1.9	(0.3)
OECD total	1.3	(0.1)	5.0	(0.2)	13.8	(0.3)	24.1	(0.3)	27.3	(0.3)	19.8	(0.3)	7.4	(0.3)	1.2	(0.1)
OECD average	1.3	(0.0)	4.7	(0.1)	13.1	(0.1)	23.7	(0.2)	28.4	(0.2)	20.6	(0.2)	7.2	(0.1)	1.0	(0.0)
Partners																
Albania	10.8	(1.0)	17.4	(1.1)	25.7	(1.2)	25.7	(1.2)	15.9	(1.1)	4.4	(0.7)	0.3	(0.1)	0.0	(0.0)
Argentina	10.8	(1.1)	15.4	(1.0)	24.4	(1.3)	25.4	(1.0)	16.5	(1.1)	6.3	(0.8)	1.1	(0.3)	0.1	(0.1)
Azerbaijan	10.0	(1.0)	26.2	(1.1)	36.2	(1.2)	21.6	(1.3)	5.4	(0.7)	0.5	(0.2)	0.0	(0.0)	0.0	(0.0)
Brazil	5.5	(0.4)	15.1	(0.7)	27.8	(0.8)	27.1	(0.7)	16.6	(0.7)	6.5	(0.5)	1.4	(0.3)	0.1	c
Bulgaria	8.2	(1.1)	12.4	(1.2)	19.6	(1.4)	22.9	(1.2)	21.5	(1.3)	11.9	(1.3)	3.1	(0.7)	0.4	(0.1)
Colombia	4.1	(0.6)	13.8	(1.1)	27.9	(1.2)	31.0	(1.1)	17.9	(1.1)	4.7	(0.5)	0.6	(0.2)	0.0	(0.0)
Croatia	0.9	(0.2)	5.4	(0.5)	15.7	(1.0)	27.1	(1.1)	29.5	(1.3)	17.3	(0.9)	3.7	(0.4)	0.3	(0.1)
Dubai (UAE)	3.9	(0.3)	9.1	(0.5)	17.7	(0.7)	24.9	(0.7)	23.8	(0.7)	14.7	(0.6)	5.2	(0.4)	0.7	(0.2)
Hong Kong-China	0.3	(0.1)	1.8	(0.3)	6.0	(0.5)	16.0	(0.8)	29.4	(1.3)	31.2	(1.0)	13.4	(0.7)	2.0	(0.3)
Indonesia	1.9	(0.4)	13.3	(1.2)	36.2	(1.7)	34.4	(1.3)	12.7	(1.4)	1.4	(0.4)	0.0	(0.0)	0.0	c
Jordan	6.0	(0.6)	11.9	(0.7)	24.3	(0.9)	32.3	(0.8)	20.3	(1.0)	4.8	(0.5)	0.3	(0.1)	0.0	(0.0)
Kazakhstan	5.9	(0.5)	18.1	(1.1)	30.8	(1.0)	26.5	(1.1)	14.4	(1.1)	4.0	(0.6)	0.3	(0.1)	0.0	(0.0)
Kyrgyzstan	28.2	(1.2)	28.9	(1.0)	24.5	(0.9)	12.7	(0.8)	4.6	(0.5)	1.1	(0.2)	0.1	(0.0)	0.0	(0.0)
Latvia	0.3	(0.2)	3.4	(0.6)	13.8	(1.0)	29.3	(1.3)	33.1	(1.1)	17.3	(1.0)	2.7	(0.4)	0.1	(0.0)
Liechtenstein	0.0	c	3.9	(1.3)	13.9	(2.8)	23.2	(2.9)	32.1	(3.4)	22.1	(3.4)	4.2	(1.7)	0.5	(0.6)
Lithuania	0.9	(0.2)	5.3	(0.6)	17.9	(0.7)	29.4	(0.9)	29.1	(0.9)	14.4	(0.8)	2.9	(0.4)	0.2	(0.1)
Macao-China	0.3	(0.1)	3.1	(0.3)	12.8	(0.4)	28.9	(0.7)	33.8	(0.8)	17.4	(0.8)	3.7	(0.4)	0.2	(0.1)
Montenegro	5.8	(0.4)	15.5	(0.6)	26.4	(0.9)	28.6	(1.0)	17.2	(1.0)	5.7	(0.6)	0.8	(0.2)	0.0	(0.1)
Panama	13.4	(2.0)	22.0	(1.8)	27.8	(1.7)	22.3	(1.6)	10.3	(1.2)	3.5	(0.7)	0.6	(0.2)	0.0	(0.0)
Peru	13.5	(0.9)	21.3	(0.9)	27.8	(1.0)	22.7	(1.0)	11.1	(0.8)	3.0	(0.5)	0.5	(0.2)	0.0	(0.0)
Qatar	18.0	(0.4)	21.0	(0.6)	22.2	(0.5)	18.9	(0.5)	12.2	(0.4)	5.6	(0.4)	1.7	(0.2)	0.3	(0.1)
Romania	4.7	(0.7)	12.7	(1.1)	23.5	(1.2)	31.0	(1.3)	21.2	(1.2)	6.2	(0.7)	0.7	(0.2)	0.0	(0.0)
Russian Federation	1.4	(0.3)	6.5	(0.8)	18.9	(1.1)	31.7	(1.0)	27.1	(0.9)	11.4	(0.7)	2.8	(0.4)	0.3	(0.1)
Serbia	1.8	(0.3)	7.9	(0.7)	22.3	(1.3)	33.7	(1.2)	25.6	(0.9)	7.8	(0.7)	0.9	(0.2)	0.1	(0.0)
Shanghai-China	0.1	(0.1)	0.5	(0.1)	3.1	(0.4)	11.9	(0.7)	26.5	(1.1)	34.2	(1.0)	20.1	(1.0)	3.6	(0.4)
Singapore	0.6	(0.1)	3.3	(0.3)	9.9	(0.5)	18.8	(0.7)	27.2	(0.7)	25.0	(1.0)	12.4	(0.6)	2.8	(0.3)
Chinese Taipei	0.7	(0.2)	3.8	(0.4)	11.3	(0.7)	24.3	(1.0)	33.0	(1.2)	21.2	(0.9)	5.2	(0.7)	0.6	(0.2)
Thailand	1.3	(0.3)	10.2	(0.8)	30.5	(1.1)	36.3	(1.4)	17.9	(1.0)	3.6	(0.6)	0.3	(0.2)	0.0	(0.0)
Trinidad and Tobago	10.0	(0.5)	13.8	(0.8)	20.6	(0.8)	24.4	(0.9)	19.2	(0.6)	9.2	(0.4)	2.5	(0.3)	0.3	(0.1)
Tunisia	5.2	(0.5)	13.9	(0.9)	28.7	(1.1)	32.4	(1.5)	16.5	(1.0)	3.1	(0.5)	0.2	(0.1)	0.0	(0.0)
Uruguay	5.7	(0.6)	12.2	(0.6)	22.9	(0.9)	27.6	(1.2)	20.4	(0.8)	9.0	(0.8)	2.1	(0.3)	0.2	(0.1)

StatLink http://dx.doi.org/10.1787/888932343285

[Part 1/2]

Percentage of students at each proficiency level on the reading subscale *continuous texts*, by gender

Table I.2.15

	Boys – Proficiency levels															
	Below Level 1b (less than 262.04 score points)		Level 1b (from 262.04 to less than 334.75 score points)		Level 1a (from 334.75 to less than 407.47 score points)		Level 2 (from 407.47 to less than 480.18 score points)		Level 3 (from 480.18 to less than 552.89 score points)		Level 4 (from 552.89 to less than 625.61 score points)		Level 5 (from 625.61 to less than 698.32 score points)		Level 6 (above 698.32 score points)	
	%	S.E.	%	S.E.	%	S.E.	%	S.E.	%	S.E.	%	S.E.	%	S.E.	%	S.E.
Australia	1.8	(0.2)	5.5	(0.5)	13.5	(0.7)	22.5	(0.8)	26.4	(0.9)	20.2	(0.9)	8.3	(0.7)	1.8	(0.4)
Austria	2.9	(0.6)	10.6	(1.0)	21.8	(1.2)	25.7	(1.2)	23.4	(1.4)	12.8	(1.0)	2.6	(0.4)	0.1	(0.1)
Belgium	1.8	(0.4)	5.8	(0.6)	14.7	(0.8)	22.0	(1.0)	24.3	(1.0)	21.9	(1.1)	8.6	(0.8)	0.8	(0.3)
Canada	0.7	(0.1)	3.7	(0.3)	11.1	(0.6)	22.9	(0.9)	28.6	(1.1)	22.9	(1.0)	8.6	(0.5)	1.4	(0.2)
Chile	2.1	(0.5)	9.8	(1.0)	23.3	(1.4)	31.8	(1.2)	23.5	(1.4)	8.2	(1.0)	1.3	(0.4)	0.1	(0.1)
Czech Republic	1.2	(0.3)	7.7	(0.8)	22.3	(1.5)	30.0	(1.6)	24.4	(1.5)	11.4	(1.0)	2.6	(0.4)	0.2	(0.1)
Denmark	0.7	(0.3)	4.5	(0.6)	14.8	(0.8)	28.3	(1.1)	30.9	(1.2)	16.9	(1.0)	3.6	(0.5)	0.2	(0.1)
Estonia	0.5	(0.4)	3.7	(0.7)	16.3	(1.4)	30.3	(1.6)	32.6	(1.4)	14.0	(1.1)	2.5	(0.4)	0.2	(0.1)
Finland	0.3	(0.1)	2.5	(0.4)	10.2	(0.9)	23.4	(1.3)	32.2	(1.2)	23.6	(1.1)	7.3	(0.7)	0.5	(0.2)
France	4.0	(0.7)	8.6	(1.0)	15.3	(1.2)	23.2	(1.6)	24.3	(1.5)	17.5	(1.2)	6.4	(0.8)	0.8	(0.2)
Germany	1.5	(0.4)	6.2	(0.7)	16.2	(1.1)	26.0	(1.6)	27.4	(1.4)	18.5	(1.2)	3.9	(0.6)	0.3	(0.1)
Greece	2.4	(0.6)	8.7	(1.2)	18.8	(1.3)	26.8	(1.5)	24.3	(1.7)	14.8	(1.3)	3.8	(0.7)	0.4	(0.2)
Hungary	1.3	(0.4)	6.1	(0.9)	16.4	(1.3)	25.8	(1.5)	28.7	(1.5)	17.3	(1.3)	4.1	(0.7)	0.3	(0.3)
Iceland	2.4	(0.5)	6.7	(1.0)	15.9	(1.0)	23.7	(1.0)	27.7	(1.3)	17.6	(1.4)	5.5	(0.5)	0.6	(0.2)
Ireland	2.9	(0.6)	6.0	(0.8)	14.7	(1.0)	24.4	(1.4)	28.9	(1.1)	17.8	(1.2)	5.0	(0.8)	0.3	(0.2)
Israel	5.9	(1.1)	10.5	(0.9)	17.1	(1.1)	22.6	(1.4)	22.9	(1.2)	14.8	(0.9)	5.5	(0.7)	0.8	(0.3)
Italy	2.3	(0.4)	7.7	(0.5)	18.4	(0.7)	25.4	(0.7)	26.1	(0.7)	16.1	(0.7)	3.8	(0.3)	0.3	(0.1)
Japan	2.5	(0.7)	5.2	(0.9)	11.2	(1.0)	19.9	(1.0)	26.6	(1.2)	23.1	(1.4)	9.7	(0.9)	1.8	(0.4)
Korea	0.5	(0.2)	1.6	(0.5)	7.5	(1.0)	19.4	(1.4)	34.6	(1.6)	27.5	(1.8)	8.3	(1.0)	0.7	(0.2)
Luxembourg	5.1	(0.5)	10.7	(0.9)	18.4	(1.1)	23.6	(1.0)	24.5	(1.0)	13.9	(1.0)	3.6	(0.5)	0.3	(0.1)
Mexico	5.1	(0.5)	14.1	(0.7)	27.1	(0.8)	31.3	(0.8)	18.0	(0.7)	4.2	(0.3)	0.3	(0.1)	0.0	(0.0)
Netherlands	0.1	(0.1)	3.0	(0.6)	14.8	(1.5)	27.9	(1.9)	27.0	(1.7)	19.8	(1.6)	6.9	(0.9)	0.5	(0.3)
New Zealand	2.0	(0.5)	5.8	(0.7)	14.1	(1.1)	21.3	(1.4)	24.7	(1.3)	20.3	(1.1)	9.9	(0.7)	1.9	(0.3)
Norway	1.5	(0.3)	5.7	(0.6)	15.0	(1.0)	26.1	(1.1)	28.4	(1.4)	17.6	(1.3)	5.2	(0.6)	0.5	(0.2)
Poland	1.3	(0.5)	5.0	(0.6)	16.1	(1.1)	28.4	(1.3)	28.2	(1.3)	16.3	(1.0)	4.3	(0.7)	0.3	(0.1)
Portugal	1.1	(0.3)	6.5	(0.7)	16.9	(1.4)	28.7	(1.4)	27.2	(1.4)	15.8	(1.1)	3.6	(0.6)	0.2	(0.1)
Slovak Republic	1.4	(0.4)	8.1	(1.1)	22.6	(1.5)	30.1	(1.3)	23.8	(1.7)	11.9	(1.2)	2.1	(0.4)	0.1	(0.1)
Slovenia	1.7	(0.2)	9.1	(0.6)	21.8	(1.2)	26.4	(1.3)	24.4	(1.0)	13.8	(1.0)	2.5	(0.5)	0.2	(0.2)
Spain	1.8	(0.3)	6.4	(0.6)	15.8	(0.9)	27.9	(0.9)	29.9	(1.0)	15.2	(0.7)	2.8	(0.3)	0.2	(0.1)
Sweden	2.8	(0.4)	6.5	(0.6)	15.2	(1.1)	25.3	(1.3)	27.1	(1.4)	16.5	(1.3)	5.9	(0.7)	0.9	(0.3)
Switzerland	1.3	(0.2)	6.0	(0.7)	16.4	(1.0)	25.9	(1.1)	27.9	(1.2)	17.3	(1.4)	4.8	(0.7)	0.5	(0.2)
Turkey	1.4	(0.3)	8.0	(0.9)	24.5	(1.6)	32.5	(1.7)	24.3	(1.5)	8.6	(1.2)	0.7	(0.3)	0.0	c
United Kingdom	1.6	(0.3)	6.0	(0.7)	16.8	(1.0)	26.1	(1.2)	25.8	(1.1)	16.3	(1.0)	6.4	(0.7)	1.0	(0.2)
United States	1.2	(0.3)	5.8	(0.7)	16.0	(1.2)	24.2	(1.2)	25.3	(1.1)	18.4	(1.2)	7.8	(1.1)	1.4	(0.4)
OECD total	2.0	(0.1)	6.8	(0.2)	16.9	(0.4)	25.5	(0.4)	25.7	(0.3)	16.7	(0.4)	5.6	(0.3)	0.8	(0.1)
OECD average	2.0	(0.1)	6.7	(0.1)	16.8	(0.2)	25.9	(0.2)	26.6	(0.2)	16.5	(0.2)	4.9	(0.1)	0.6	(0.0)
Albania	16.9	(1.5)	23.0	(1.6)	27.5	(2.2)	20.7	(1.5)	9.8	(1.3)	2.0	(0.5)	0.1	(0.2)	0.0	c
Argentina	15.1	(1.4)	18.4	(1.6)	25.2	(1.7)	23.1	(1.3)	13.4	(1.2)	4.2	(0.7)	0.6	(0.2)	0.0	(0.1)
Azerbaijan	13.3	(1.4)	30.1	(1.6)	34.7	(1.7)	17.4	(1.3)	4.1	(0.7)	0.4	(0.2)	0.0	(0.0)	0.0	c
Brazil	7.9	(0.6)	19.0	(1.1)	29.1	(1.1)	24.6	(0.9)	13.3	(0.8)	5.0	(0.6)	1.1	(0.3)	0.1	(0.1)
Bulgaria	12.6	(1.7)	16.5	(1.6)	22.4	(1.8)	21.3	(1.3)	17.6	(1.6)	7.8	(0.9)	1.7	(0.5)	0.2	(0.1)
Colombia	4.9	(0.9)	15.1	(1.5)	29.0	(1.9)	30.8	(1.9)	15.7	(1.3)	3.8	(0.6)	0.5	(0.2)	0.0	(0.0)
Croatia	1.6	(0.3)	8.7	(0.9)	21.3	(1.3)	29.6	(1.3)	25.3	(1.6)	11.8	(1.0)	1.6	(0.3)	0.1	(0.1)
Dubai (UAE)	6.6	(0.5)	13.9	(0.8)	20.9	(1.0)	23.3	(0.9)	20.3	(1.0)	11.2	(0.8)	3.5	(0.4)	0.3	(0.2)
Hong Kong-China	0.5	(0.2)	2.5	(0.5)	8.4	(0.8)	18.8	(1.4)	31.8	(2.0)	27.4	(1.4)	9.5	(1.0)	1.1	(0.3)
Indonesia	3.2	(0.7)	18.4	(1.7)	41.7	(1.9)	28.6	(1.6)	7.4	(1.1)	0.6	(0.3)	0.0	c	0.0	c
Jordan	9.8	(1.2)	16.6	(1.2)	28.8	(1.3)	30.3	(1.3)	12.3	(1.2)	2.0	(0.4)	0.1	(0.1)	0.0	(0.0)
Kazakhstan	8.8	(0.8)	24.1	(1.4)	32.5	(1.5)	22.1	(1.1)	10.1	(1.2)	2.3	(0.5)	0.2	(0.1)	0.0	(0.0)
Kyrgyzstan	39.8	(1.6)	29.4	(1.3)	18.7	(1.1)	8.7	(1.1)	2.9	(0.7)	0.6	(0.3)	0.0	c	0.0	c
Latvia	0.6	(0.3)	5.7	(1.2)	20.0	(1.5)	33.0	(1.9)	28.8	(1.7)	10.5	(1.0)	1.4	(0.4)	0.0	(0.1)
Liechtenstein	0.0	c	4.4	(2.0)	17.8	(3.9)	26.3	(4.4)	31.3	(4.0)	17.4	(4.7)	2.4	(2.0)	0.3	(0.7)
Lithuania	1.6	(0.4)	8.5	(1.0)	25.6	(1.2)	32.4	(1.4)	23.3	(1.2)	7.7	(0.8)	0.9	(0.3)	0.0	(0.0)
Macao-China	0.4	(0.2)	4.7	(0.5)	17.2	(0.9)	31.8	(1.1)	31.2	(1.1)	12.3	(0.9)	2.2	(0.4)	0.1	(0.1)
Montenegro	9.2	(0.6)	20.8	(1.0)	29.8	(1.4)	25.1	(1.3)	11.5	(0.9)	3.1	(0.5)	0.4	(0.3)	0.0	(0.0)
Panama	16.4	(2.5)	25.3	(2.2)	28.5	(2.3)	20.7	(2.0)	7.1	(1.0)	1.8	(0.5)	0.2	(0.2)	0.0	(0.0)
Peru	15.9	(1.2)	23.7	(1.1)	28.3	(1.3)	20.6	(1.2)	8.6	(0.8)	2.3	(0.5)	0.5	(0.2)	0.1	(0.1)
Qatar	24.9	(0.6)	24.3	(0.7)	21.7	(0.8)	14.5	(0.7)	8.8	(0.5)	4.2	(0.4)	1.4	(0.2)	0.2	(0.1)
Romania	7.1	(1.1)	17.8	(1.4)	27.2	(1.4)	28.5	(1.7)	15.7	(1.3)	3.4	(0.6)	0.3	(0.1)	0.0	(0.0)
Russian Federation	2.3	(0.6)	9.5	(1.1)	23.9	(1.6)	33.4	(1.5)	22.1	(1.4)	7.1	(0.7)	1.5	(0.3)	0.1	(0.1)
Serbia	2.9	(0.5)	11.7	(0.9)	28.0	(2.0)	32.4	(1.6)	19.2	(1.1)	5.2	(0.8)	0.5	(0.2)	0.1	(0.1)
Shanghai-China	0.1	(0.1)	0.9	(0.3)	5.0	(0.7)	17.0	(1.3)	30.1	(1.5)	31.6	(1.5)	13.5	(1.0)	1.8	(0.3)
Singapore	1.0	(0.2)	5.0	(0.5)	11.8	(0.8)	20.2	(1.0)	27.3	(0.9)	22.7	(1.6)	10.1	(1.1)	1.9	(0.3)
Chinese Taipei	1.2	(0.3)	5.9	(0.4)	14.7	(1.1)	26.8	(1.3)	30.6	(1.1)	17.3	(1.2)	3.2	(0.7)	0.3	(0.2)
Thailand	2.4	(0.7)	16.7	(1.4)	37.2	(1.4)	30.1	(1.5)	11.8	(1.1)	1.8	(0.5)	0.1	(0.1)	0.0	c
Trinidad and Tobago	15.4	(0.8)	17.5	(1.2)	23.1	(1.2)	21.6	(1.3)	15.8	(0.9)	5.6	(0.7)	1.0	(0.2)	0.0	(0.1)
Tunisia	8.1	(0.8)	17.9	(1.3)	30.2	(1.6)	28.7	(1.6)	12.9	(1.0)	2.1	(0.5)	0.1	(0.1)	0.0	c
Uruguay	9.2	(0.9)	16.0	(1.1)	25.4	(1.4)	25.7	(1.3)	16.1	(0.9)	6.2	(1.0)	1.3	(0.3)	0.1	(0.1)

StatLink ⫘ http://dx.doi.org/10.1787/888932343285

[Part 2/2]

Percentage of students at each proficiency level on the reading subscale *continuous texts*, by gender

Table I.2.15

	Girls – Proficiency levels															
	Below Level 1b (less than 262.04 score points)		Level 1b (from 262.04 to less than 334.75 score points)		Level 1a (from 334.75 to less than 407.47 score points)		Level 2 (from 407.47 to less than 480.18 score points)		Level 3 (from 480.18 to less than 552.89 score points)		Level 4 (from 552.89 to less than 625.61 score points)		Level 5 (from 625.61 to less than 698.32 score points)		Level 6 (above 698.32 score points)	
	%	S.E.	%	S.E.	%	S.E.	%	S.E.	%	S.E.	%	S.E.	%	S.E.	%	S.E.
OECD																
Australia	0.4	(0.1)	2.2	(0.3)	7.5	(0.5)	18.7	(0.8)	28.2	(0.9)	26.5	(0.8)	13.5	(0.7)	3.0	(0.4)
Austria	0.9	(0.4)	5.2	(0.9)	14.0	(1.3)	23.3	(1.3)	28.1	(1.4)	21.3	(1.5)	6.5	(0.9)	0.7	(0.2)
Belgium	0.8	(0.3)	3.5	(0.6)	10.1	(0.6)	19.0	(1.1)	26.6	(1.0)	26.8	(1.1)	11.9	(0.7)	1.4	(0.3)
Canada	0.1	(0.1)	1.1	(0.2)	5.3	(0.4)	17.4	(0.7)	29.3	(0.7)	28.9	(0.9)	14.4	(0.7)	3.3	(0.3)
Chile	0.9	(0.3)	4.9	(0.7)	18.1	(1.3)	31.8	(1.6)	29.3	(1.4)	12.4	(1.1)	2.5	(0.4)	0.1	(0.1)
Czech Republic	0.2	(0.1)	2.7	(0.6)	10.9	(1.1)	24.2	(1.2)	30.7	(1.2)	22.1	(1.1)	8.3	(0.7)	0.9	(0.2)
Denmark	0.3	(0.1)	2.0	(0.4)	9.0	(0.8)	22.5	(1.2)	33.9	(1.3)	24.6	(1.4)	7.1	(0.7)	0.7	(0.3)
Estonia	0.0	(0.0)	0.9	(0.4)	6.3	(1.0)	21.4	(1.5)	37.2	(1.3)	26.5	(1.3)	7.0	(0.8)	0.7	(0.3)
Finland	0.1	(0.1)	0.5	(0.2)	2.5	(0.4)	10.6	(0.9)	28.2	(1.2)	36.9	(1.3)	18.9	(1.1)	2.3	(0.4)
France	1.5	(0.5)	3.9	(0.6)	9.8	(0.9)	19.6	(1.3)	27.5	(1.3)	25.1	(1.3)	10.6	(1.1)	2.0	(0.6)
Germany	0.3	(0.2)	3.2	(0.6)	9.5	(0.9)	19.6	(1.5)	29.4	(1.5)	27.3	(1.3)	9.7	(0.8)	1.0	(0.3)
Greece	0.4	(0.2)	2.6	(0.6)	10.3	(1.0)	21.8	(1.1)	31.1	(1.4)	24.0	(1.5)	8.4	(1.3)	1.4	(0.4)
Hungary	0.4	(0.3)	2.2	(0.7)	8.2	(1.1)	21.3	(1.5)	31.5	(1.5)	26.3	(1.4)	9.3	(1.0)	0.9	(0.3)
Iceland	0.5	(0.2)	1.9	(0.4)	7.4	(0.8)	19.1	(1.1)	33.0	(1.3)	25.6	(1.3)	10.4	(0.9)	2.0	(0.5)
Ireland	0.6	(0.3)	2.4	(0.6)	8.8	(0.9)	20.7	(1.2)	30.7	(1.3)	25.6	(1.5)	9.9	(1.0)	1.3	(0.4)
Israel	1.6	(0.4)	4.7	(0.7)	12.1	(0.9)	21.7	(1.3)	28.4	(1.2)	22.0	(1.1)	8.1	(0.7)	1.4	(0.3)
Italy	0.5	(0.1)	2.6	(0.3)	9.0	(0.5)	20.8	(0.7)	31.8	(0.6)	26.3	(0.7)	8.3	(0.5)	0.8	(0.2)
Japan	0.8	(0.3)	1.8	(0.4)	5.8	(0.7)	15.7	(1.2)	27.7	(1.2)	30.4	(1.2)	14.9	(1.1)	3.0	(0.5)
Korea	0.1	(0.1)	0.2	(0.1)	2.5	(0.6)	11.1	(1.2)	30.1	(1.6)	38.5	(1.6)	16.0	(1.6)	1.5	(0.4)
Luxembourg	1.5	(0.4)	4.9	(0.6)	12.4	(1.2)	23.9	(1.1)	28.5	(1.0)	21.1	(1.2)	6.9	(0.7)	0.7	(0.2)
Mexico	2.4	(0.4)	8.8	(0.5)	21.6	(0.8)	34.0	(0.9)	25.5	(0.7)	7.1	(0.4)	0.5	(0.1)	0.0	(0.0)
Netherlands	0.1	(0.1)	1.0	(0.4)	9.8	(1.3)	23.2	(1.6)	28.5	(1.6)	25.8	(2.0)	10.3	(1.1)	1.1	(0.3)
New Zealand	0.3	(0.1)	1.5	(0.4)	7.1	(0.7)	17.4	(1.0)	26.1	(1.1)	27.4	(1.1)	15.9	(1.2)	4.3	(0.6)
Norway	0.1	(0.1)	1.4	(0.3)	7.1	(0.8)	18.6	(1.0)	30.5	(1.1)	28.2	(1.4)	11.9	(1.1)	2.1	(0.4)
Poland	0.1	(0.1)	1.0	(0.3)	6.1	(0.7)	20.3	(1.1)	33.5	(1.4)	27.6	(1.3)	10.2	(0.8)	1.3	(0.3)
Portugal	0.2	(0.1)	1.9	(0.4)	8.7	(0.8)	23.4	(1.1)	33.9	(1.3)	23.8	(1.2)	7.6	(0.7)	0.6	(0.2)
Slovak Republic	0.4	(0.3)	2.1	(0.5)	9.9	(0.9)	24.5	(1.3)	33.5	(1.5)	22.5	(1.4)	6.1	(0.8)	0.9	(0.3)
Slovenia	0.2	(0.1)	2.0	(0.3)	8.6	(0.8)	23.0	(1.0)	32.2	(1.2)	24.7	(1.5)	8.8	(1.1)	0.5	(0.3)
Spain	0.8	(0.2)	3.1	(0.4)	10.4	(0.7)	23.7	(0.9)	33.6	(0.9)	22.4	(0.9)	5.4	(0.5)	0.5	(0.1)
Sweden	0.7	(0.3)	2.0	(0.5)	7.7	(0.9)	20.9	(1.3)	30.8	(1.3)	24.3	(1.4)	11.3	(1.0)	2.3	(0.4)
Switzerland	0.3	(0.1)	3.0	(0.4)	8.4	(0.7)	20.0	(0.9)	30.2	(1.3)	27.2	(1.1)	9.7	(0.8)	1.2	(0.3)
Turkey	0.3	(0.2)	2.2	(0.5)	11.7	(1.2)	30.2	(1.6)	33.8	(1.6)	18.0	(1.6)	3.5	(0.7)	0.2	(0.1)
United Kingdom	0.6	(0.2)	2.9	(0.4)	11.6	(0.8)	24.0	(1.2)	29.9	(1.0)	21.4	(1.1)	8.0	(0.7)	1.5	(0.3)
United States	0.3	(0.2)	2.8	(0.5)	11.0	(0.9)	23.3	(1.1)	27.7	(1.2)	21.8	(1.2)	10.6	(1.1)	2.4	(0.4)
OECD total	0.7	(0.1)	3.2	(0.2)	10.7	(0.3)	22.7	(0.4)	29.1	(0.4)	22.9	(0.4)	9.2	(0.3)	1.6	(0.1)
OECD average	0.5	(0.0)	2.6	(0.1)	9.4	(0.2)	21.5	(0.2)	30.3	(0.2)	24.7	(0.2)	9.5	(0.2)	1.4	(0.1)
Partners																
Albania	4.3	(0.8)	11.4	(1.2)	23.8	(1.5)	30.9	(1.6)	22.2	(1.5)	6.9	(1.0)	0.5	(0.2)	0.0	(0.0)
Argentina	7.1	(1.0)	12.9	(1.0)	23.6	(1.6)	27.4	(1.5)	19.1	(1.5)	8.0	(1.2)	1.6	(0.4)	0.1	(0.1)
Azerbaijan	6.6	(1.0)	22.1	(1.5)	37.8	(1.6)	26.0	(1.7)	6.8	(0.9)	0.7	(0.2)	0.0	(0.0)	0.0	c
Brazil	3.3	(0.3)	11.7	(0.7)	26.6	(0.9)	29.3	(0.9)	19.5	(0.8)	7.8	(0.6)	1.7	(0.3)	0.2	(0.1)
Bulgaria	3.4	(0.6)	8.0	(1.0)	16.6	(1.5)	24.7	(1.8)	25.7	(1.7)	16.3	(1.8)	4.8	(1.0)	0.6	(0.2)
Colombia	3.3	(0.6)	12.6	(1.1)	26.9	(2.0)	31.2	(1.7)	19.8	(1.4)	5.4	(0.6)	0.7	(0.2)	0.1	(0.1)
Croatia	0.2	(0.1)	1.8	(0.4)	9.4	(1.1)	24.4	(1.7)	34.1	(2.0)	23.5	(1.4)	6.1	(0.8)	0.5	(0.2)
Dubai (UAE)	0.9	(0.2)	4.1	(0.4)	14.4	(0.9)	26.5	(1.1)	27.5	(1.1)	18.5	(1.0)	6.9	(0.7)	1.1	(0.3)
Hong Kong-China	0.0	(0.1)	1.0	(0.3)	3.3	(0.5)	12.9	(1.3)	26.6	(1.2)	35.4	(1.3)	17.9	(1.1)	3.0	(0.4)
Indonesia	0.6	(0.3)	8.3	(1.1)	30.9	(2.0)	40.1	(1.8)	17.9	(1.8)	2.2	(0.5)	0.1	(0.1)	0.0	c
Jordan	2.1	(0.4)	7.2	(0.8)	19.8	(1.3)	34.3	(1.3)	28.5	(1.5)	7.6	(0.9)	0.6	(0.2)	0.0	c
Kazakhstan	2.8	(0.5)	11.9	(1.1)	29.1	(1.4)	31.2	(1.6)	18.8	(1.3)	5.7	(0.9)	0.5	(0.2)	0.0	(0.1)
Kyrgyzstan	17.2	(1.3)	28.5	(1.4)	29.9	(1.4)	16.5	(1.0)	6.2	(0.8)	1.6	(0.3)	0.1	(0.1)	0.0	(0.0)
Latvia	0.0	(0.1)	1.1	(0.4)	7.7	(1.0)	25.7	(1.5)	37.4	(1.4)	23.8	(1.5)	4.1	(0.6)	0.1	(0.1)
Liechtenstein	0.0	c	3.3	(1.5)	9.4	(3.3)	19.8	(3.3)	33.0	(4.3)	27.4	(4.4)	6.3	(3.0)	0.7	(0.9)
Lithuania	0.2	(0.1)	2.0	(0.4)	10.0	(0.9)	26.3	(1.1)	35.0	(1.2)	21.3	(1.1)	5.0	(0.7)	0.3	(0.2)
Macao-China	0.1	(0.1)	1.4	(0.3)	8.4	(0.6)	25.8	(0.9)	36.4	(1.1)	22.5	(1.1)	5.2	(0.5)	0.3	(0.1)
Montenegro	2.1	(0.4)	10.0	(0.7)	22.8	(1.0)	32.3	(1.1)	23.2	(1.4)	8.3	(1.0)	1.3	(0.3)	0.1	(0.1)
Panama	10.3	(1.9)	18.9	(2.3)	27.2	(2.1)	23.9	(1.9)	13.5	(1.7)	5.3	(1.1)	0.9	(0.3)	0.0	(0.1)
Peru	11.2	(1.0)	18.7	(1.1)	27.2	(1.5)	24.8	(1.3)	13.7	(1.3)	3.7	(0.7)	0.6	(0.2)	0.0	(0.0)
Qatar	10.9	(0.5)	17.6	(0.8)	22.8	(0.6)	23.4	(0.7)	15.8	(0.8)	7.0	(0.5)	2.1	(0.3)	0.3	(0.1)
Romania	2.3	(0.6)	7.8	(1.0)	19.9	(1.4)	33.4	(1.8)	26.5	(1.5)	8.8	(1.0)	1.1	(0.3)	0.0	(0.1)
Russian Federation	0.5	(0.2)	3.5	(0.6)	13.9	(1.0)	30.1	(1.2)	32.0	(1.2)	15.6	(1.2)	4.0	(0.6)	0.4	(0.2)
Serbia	0.7	(0.3)	4.1	(0.7)	16.5	(1.1)	35.0	(1.3)	32.0	(1.2)	10.4	(1.0)	1.2	(0.3)	0.1	(0.1)
Shanghai-China	0.0	(0.0)	0.2	(0.1)	1.3	(0.3)	6.8	(0.7)	23.0	(1.1)	36.7	(1.2)	26.7	(1.5)	5.4	(0.7)
Singapore	0.2	(0.1)	1.6	(0.3)	7.9	(0.6)	17.4	(0.9)	27.1	(1.1)	27.3	(1.0)	14.8	(1.0)	3.7	(0.6)
Chinese Taipei	0.1	(0.1)	1.7	(0.3)	7.7	(0.7)	21.6	(1.4)	35.5	(1.7)	25.1	(1.3)	7.3	(1.2)	0.9	(0.4)
Thailand	0.5	(0.2)	5.2	(0.8)	25.3	(1.5)	41.0	(1.7)	22.5	(1.5)	4.9	(0.9)	0.5	(0.2)	0.0	(0.0)
Trinidad and Tobago	4.8	(0.5)	10.1	(0.9)	18.1	(0.9)	27.2	(1.0)	22.6	(0.9)	12.8	(0.8)	3.9	(0.7)	0.5	(0.2)
Tunisia	2.5	(0.5)	10.3	(0.9)	27.4	(1.2)	35.8	(1.7)	19.8	(1.2)	4.0	(0.7)	0.3	(0.2)	0.0	(0.0)
Uruguay	2.6	(0.4)	8.7	(0.8)	20.7	(1.0)	29.3	(1.5)	24.2	(1.1)	11.5	(0.9)	2.7	(0.4)	0.2	(0.1)

StatLink ▔▔ http://dx.doi.org/10.1787/888932343285

[Part 1/1]

Table I.2.16 **Mean score, variation and gender differences in student performance on the reading subscale *continuous texts***

		All students				Gender differences						Percentiles											
		Mean score		Standard deviation		Boys		Girls		Difference (B – G)		5th		10th		25th		75th		90th		95th	
		Mean	S.E.	S.D.	S.E.	Mean score	S.E.	Mean score	S.E.	Score dif.	S.E.	Score	S.E.	Score	S.E.	Score	S.E.	Score	S.E.	Score	S.E.	Score	S.E.
OECD	Australia	513	(2.5)	102	(1.4)	493	(3.0)	532	(2.8)	**-38**	(3.1)	336	(4.0)	377	(3.4)	446	(2.6)	585	(2.8)	641	(3.8)	671	(4.5)
	Austria	470	(2.9)	100	(2.0)	448	(3.8)	492	(4.1)	**-44**	(5.7)	301	(4.7)	336	(5.0)	399	(4.2)	544	(3.1)	596	(3.6)	625	(4.7)
	Belgium	504	(2.4)	103	(1.7)	491	(3.4)	518	(3.0)	**-27**	(4.4)	326	(5.6)	365	(4.4)	433	(3.9)	582	(2.3)	631	(2.4)	657	(2.6)
	Canada	524	(1.5)	94	(0.9)	506	(1.9)	543	(1.7)	**-37**	(2.1)	363	(3.7)	401	(2.7)	462	(2.2)	590	(1.9)	642	(2.2)	671	(2.4)
	Chile	453	(3.1)	86	(1.7)	440	(3.9)	466	(3.5)	**-26**	(3.9)	308	(5.2)	340	(4.6)	395	(4.1)	512	(3.3)	563	(3.9)	592	(4.8)
	Czech Republic	479	(2.9)	93	(1.5)	455	(3.7)	507	(3.1)	**-52**	(4.2)	326	(5.3)	358	(4.9)	413	(3.6)	544	(3.2)	601	(3.5)	632	(3.5)
	Denmark	496	(2.1)	86	(1.0)	480	(2.5)	512	(2.6)	**-32**	(2.9)	348	(4.3)	381	(3.2)	439	(2.8)	557	(2.5)	605	(2.8)	632	(3.4)
	Estonia	497	(2.7)	81	(1.6)	475	(3.0)	521	(2.6)	**-46**	(2.3)	359	(4.9)	391	(4.9)	443	(3.6)	553	(2.8)	599	(3.6)	626	(3.8)
	Finland	535	(2.3)	86	(1.0)	507	(2.6)	563	(2.4)	**-56**	(2.3)	384	(5.2)	419	(3.7)	480	(2.8)	597	(2.3)	641	(2.3)	665	(2.9)
	France	492	(3.5)	109	(2.8)	470	(4.3)	512	(3.6)	**-42**	(3.7)	297	(8.6)	344	(7.0)	422	(5.0)	571	(4.3)	625	(4.2)	654	(4.7)
	Germany	496	(2.7)	95	(1.8)	476	(3.7)	517	(3.0)	**-41**	(4.0)	329	(5.5)	366	(5.1)	431	(4.2)	566	(2.9)	613	(2.9)	641	(3.1)
	Greece	487	(4.3)	99	(2.3)	461	(5.4)	512	(3.6)	**-51**	(4.4)	317	(8.5)	355	(7.6)	420	(6.5)	557	(3.6)	610	(3.5)	639	(3.8)
	Hungary	497	(3.3)	93	(2.5)	476	(4.0)	518	(3.7)	**-42**	(4.0)	335	(6.9)	370	(7.2)	436	(4.8)	563	(3.6)	613	(3.6)	639	(3.6)
	Iceland	501	(1.6)	99	(1.3)	477	(2.4)	524	(2.3)	**-48**	(3.5)	327	(5.0)	367	(3.4)	438	(2.7)	569	(2.2)	623	(3.4)	653	(4.1)
	Ireland	497	(3.3)	98	(2.3)	476	(4.5)	517	(3.6)	**-41**	(4.9)	324	(7.8)	368	(6.2)	435	(4.1)	565	(3.5)	616	(4.0)	645	(3.6)
	Israel	477	(3.6)	111	(2.6)	454	(5.1)	499	(3.5)	**-44**	(5.1)	278	(8.7)	325	(7.6)	405	(4.8)	557	(3.4)	614	(3.6)	646	(4.2)
	Italy	489	(1.6)	97	(1.3)	465	(2.3)	514	(1.9)	**-49**	(2.8)	320	(3.7)	358	(3.1)	424	(2.4)	560	(1.8)	609	(1.7)	636	(2.0)
	Japan	520	(3.6)	104	(2.8)	501	(5.7)	541	(3.8)	**-39**	(6.8)	332	(10.6)	382	(8.2)	457	(5.1)	594	(2.9)	644	(3.5)	672	(3.4)
	Korea	538	(3.5)	80	(2.3)	520	(4.8)	558	(4.0)	**-38**	(6.0)	395	(7.4)	431	(6.1)	489	(3.9)	595	(3.4)	635	(3.5)	658	(3.9)
	Luxembourg	471	(1.2)	105	(1.0)	450	(1.9)	493	(1.3)	**-43**	(2.4)	283	(4.4)	327	(3.4)	402	(2.7)	548	(2.2)	602	(2.7)	631	(3.0)
	Mexico	426	(2.0)	87	(1.3)	411	(2.2)	440	(2.1)	**-28**	(1.8)	276	(4.2)	311	(3.0)	369	(2.7)	487	(1.9)	534	(1.9)	560	(2.3)
	Netherlands	506	(5.0)	89	(1.7)	493	(5.0)	519	(5.2)	**-26**	(2.6)	363	(4.6)	390	(5.0)	440	(6.2)	573	(5.4)	623	(4.8)	650	(5.0)
	New Zealand	518	(2.4)	106	(1.7)	495	(3.6)	542	(3.0)	**-47**	(4.6)	336	(5.9)	377	(4.6)	447	(3.3)	594	(2.6)	650	(3.2)	680	(3.5)
	Norway	505	(2.6)	95	(1.3)	480	(3.0)	532	(2.9)	**-52**	(2.9)	341	(4.7)	378	(4.2)	442	(2.8)	574	(3.2)	625	(3.2)	653	(3.8)
	Poland	502	(2.7)	90	(1.4)	476	(2.9)	528	(2.9)	**-53**	(2.5)	349	(4.6)	384	(3.6)	442	(3.5)	566	(3.0)	615	(3.5)	643	(3.5)
	Portugal	492	(3.2)	90	(1.5)	471	(3.7)	512	(3.0)	**-41**	(2.5)	336	(4.0)	372	(5.0)	432	(4.4)	555	(3.4)	605	(3.4)	632	(3.6)
	Slovak Republic	479	(2.6)	91	(1.9)	452	(3.7)	506	(2.7)	**-54**	(3.6)	326	(5.5)	359	(5.5)	417	(4.0)	544	(2.9)	595	(3.3)	623	(3.7)
	Slovenia	484	(1.1)	95	(0.9)	455	(1.6)	514	(1.5)	**-59**	(2.4)	323	(2.3)	355	(2.5)	418	(2.2)	553	(2.1)	605	(2.8)	631	(2.7)
	Spain	484	(2.1)	91	(1.1)	469	(2.3)	500	(2.3)	**-31**	(2.2)	324	(3.6)	363	(3.5)	428	(3.1)	548	(1.8)	595	(1.9)	622	(2.2)
	Sweden	499	(3.0)	101	(1.5)	476	(3.2)	523	(3.3)	**-47**	(2.8)	323	(6.0)	368	(5.0)	435	(3.8)	569	(3.4)	626	(3.5)	657	(3.9)
	Switzerland	498	(2.5)	95	(1.5)	478	(2.9)	519	(2.7)	**-41**	(2.6)	332	(4.6)	370	(4.3)	434	(3.8)	567	(2.9)	616	(3.6)	644	(4.1)
	Turkey	466	(3.5)	84	(1.6)	443	(3.7)	491	(4.1)	**-48**	(3.6)	326	(5.6)	357	(4.3)	409	(3.7)	525	(4.2)	573	(4.8)	599	(5.4)
	United Kingdom	492	(2.4)	98	(1.2)	478	(3.8)	504	(3.0)	**-26**	(4.8)	329	(4.1)	365	(3.2)	425	(3.4)	560	(3.1)	617	(3.0)	649	(4.1)
	United States	500	(3.7)	100	(1.6)	487	(4.4)	513	(3.8)	**-26**	(3.6)	334	(4.1)	368	(4.8)	430	(4.0)	571	(4.6)	632	(5.8)	664	(5.2)
	OECD total	492	(1.2)	100	(0.6)	475	(1.5)	509	(1.3)	**-35**	(1.3)	322	(1.8)	360	(1.5)	424	(1.3)	563	(1.5)	618	(1.8)	649	(2.0)
	OECD average	494	(0.5)	95	(0.3)	473	(0.6)	515	(0.5)	**-42**	(0.6)	330	(1.0)	367	(0.8)	431	(0.7)	562	(0.5)	613	(0.6)	641	(0.6)
Partners	Albania	392	(4.1)	102	(2.0)	359	(5.1)	427	(4.2)	**-67**	(4.4)	216	(6.5)	257	(6.4)	325	(4.8)	467	(5.0)	520	(4.9)	550	(6.2)
	Argentina	400	(4.6)	111	(3.3)	378	(4.9)	419	(4.9)	**-41**	(3.7)	204	(9.3)	256	(8.6)	330	(5.6)	477	(5.8)	537	(6.7)	571	(6.4)
	Azerbaijan	362	(3.3)	76	(1.8)	349	(3.6)	375	(3.3)	**-26**	(2.3)	235	(4.7)	262	(4.5)	310	(4.0)	413	(3.5)	459	(4.4)	487	(5.2)
	Brazil	414	(2.8)	96	(1.6)	396	(3.0)	430	(2.8)	**-34**	(1.7)	258	(3.6)	292	(3.1)	348	(2.7)	478	(3.9)	541	(4.2)	576	(5.3)
	Bulgaria	433	(6.8)	116	(2.8)	401	(7.4)	466	(5.9)	**-65**	(4.7)	230	(7.9)	276	(9.9)	354	(8.2)	517	(6.7)	578	(6.3)	611	(7.2)
	Colombia	415	(3.7)	87	(2.0)	408	(4.4)	422	(4.1)	**-14**	(4.0)	271	(6.2)	302	(5.8)	356	(4.7)	475	(4.2)	525	(4.5)	556	(5.1)
	Croatia	478	(2.9)	90	(1.7)	452	(3.4)	508	(3.7)	**-56**	(4.5)	324	(4.6)	358	(4.1)	417	(3.9)	543	(3.2)	591	(3.6)	618	(4.2)
	Dubai (UAE)	461	(1.2)	108	(1.1)	433	(1.9)	490	(1.7)	**-58**	(2.7)	277	(3.7)	317	(3.9)	388	(2.2)	537	(2.3)	598	(3.4)	632	(3.4)
	Hong Kong-China	538	(2.3)	88	(1.7)	520	(3.5)	559	(3.0)	**-38**	(4.5)	379	(6.4)	421	(5.0)	483	(3.4)	600	(2.5)	644	(2.7)	671	(2.9)
	Indonesia	405	(3.7)	69	(2.0)	386	(3.8)	425	(3.8)	**-39**	(3.2)	292	(5.4)	317	(5.0)	359	(3.8)	452	(4.6)	493	(5.4)	519	(6.1)
	Jordan	417	(3.2)	92	(2.2)	387	(4.6)	447	(4.0)	**-60**	(6.1)	252	(6.0)	294	(5.4)	361	(4.3)	481	(3.2)	528	(3.6)	554	(3.8)
	Kazakhstan	399	(3.1)	89	(1.5)	376	(3.1)	422	(3.6)	**-46**	(2.9)	255	(3.5)	286	(3.7)	338	(3.5)	459	(4.5)	516	(4.6)	548	(4.6)
	Kyrgyzstan	319	(3.2)	100	(2.0)	289	(3.8)	347	(3.1)	**-58**	(2.7)	154	(5.0)	192	(4.5)	252	(4.1)	384	(4.4)	448	(6.0)	487	(6.4)
	Latvia	484	(3.0)	80	(1.6)	459	(3.5)	508	(3.1)	**-49**	(3.2)	347	(6.6)	378	(4.6)	430	(4.2)	541	(3.8)	584	(3.1)	608	(4.4)
	Liechtenstein	495	(3.0)	86	(3.3)	479	(4.8)	513	(5.6)	**-34**	(8.5)	344	(12.8)	378	(8.7)	431	(7.8)	558	(6.2)	604	(7.8)	626	(10.6)
	Lithuania	470	(2.5)	86	(1.7)	440	(2.8)	502	(2.6)	**-62**	(2.6)	325	(5.5)	357	(4.3)	410	(3.6)	531	(2.8)	580	(3.1)	607	(4.8)
	Macao-China	488	(0.9)	80	(0.7)	469	(1.2)	507	(1.1)	**-37**	(1.5)	351	(2.4)	382	(2.1)	434	(1.5)	543	(1.4)	590	(1.7)	617	(2.5)
	Montenegro	411	(1.8)	95	(1.3)	384	(2.0)	440	(2.2)	**-55**	(2.4)	256	(2.9)	289	(3.3)	347	(2.5)	476	(3.1)	532	(3.1)	566	(4.7)
	Panama	373	(6.7)	101	(3.7)	355	(7.0)	392	(7.3)	**-37**	(6.3)	205	(13.4)	246	(10.2)	307	(7.6)	441	(7.3)	505	(9.1)	543	(9.2)
	Peru	374	(3.9)	100	(2.4)	362	(4.0)	387	(4.8)	**-25**	(4.6)	208	(6.6)	244	(4.9)	306	(4.3)	444	(5.0)	502	(6.2)	536	(7.4)
	Qatar	375	(0.9)	119	(0.8)	348	(1.3)	403	(1.1)	**-55**	(1.8)	192	(2.1)	225	(1.8)	288	(1.7)	458	(1.7)	535	(1.9)	578	(2.4)
	Romania	423	(4.0)	92	(2.4)	399	(4.4)	447	(4.3)	**-48**	(4.6)	265	(6.3)	300	(5.8)	362	(5.4)	488	(4.3)	536	(4.7)	566	(4.7)
	Russian Federation	461	(3.1)	88	(1.7)	437	(3.3)	484	(3.2)	**-47**	(2.7)	312	(5.9)	347	(4.4)	403	(3.7)	520	(3.4)	573	(4.1)	605	(4.8)
	Serbia	444	(2.3)	83	(1.7)	423	(3.2)	465	(2.5)	**-43**	(3.3)	302	(4.8)	336	(3.9)	389	(3.4)	502	(2.6)	547	(3.0)	573	(3.6)
	Shanghai-China	564	(2.5)	82	(1.7)	541	(3.1)	587	(2.4)	**-45**	(3.1)	422	(5.6)	456	(4.7)	511	(3.5)	623	(2.9)	665	(2.8)	689	(3.0)
	Singapore	522	(1.1)	100	(1.2)	506	(1.7)	538	(1.5)	**-32**	(2.4)	347	(4.0)	386	(3.8)	455	(2.1)	594	(1.7)	648	(2.8)	677	(3.2)
	Chinese Taipei	496	(2.6)	88	(1.9)	477	(3.7)	516	(3.6)	**-39**	(5.3)	341	(4.8)	379	(4.3)	440	(3.2)	558	(3.5)	604	(4.9)	631	(5.2)
	Thailand	423	(2.8)	73	(1.9)	399	(3.4)	441	(3.2)	**-43**	(4.0)	304	(4.8)	329	(3.7)	373	(3.4)	472	(3.1)	517	(4.0)	544	(5.4)
	Trinidad and Tobago	418	(1.3)	117	(1.2)	385	(2.1)	450	(1.8)	**-65**	(2.9)	215	(5.4)	262	(3.5)	340	(2.6)	500	(2.1)	563	(3.0)	600	(3.5)
	Tunisia	408	(2.9)	85	(1.7)	389	(3.2)	424	(2.8)	**-35**	(2.2)	260	(4.9)	296	(4.2)	353	(3.5)	467	(3.1)	512	(3.9)	538	(4.3)
	Uruguay	429	(2.7)	102	(1.8)	404	(3.4)	451	(2.9)	**-47**	(3.3)	255	(6.9)	295	(6.0)	361	(3.3)	501	(3.5)	559	(3.8)	592	(4.7)

Note: Values that are statistically significant are indicated in bold (see Annex A3).
StatLink http://dx.doi.org/10.1787/888932343285

[Part 1/1]

Table I.2.17 **Percentage of students at each proficiency level on the reading subscale *non-continuous texts***

	Proficiency levels															
	Below Level 1b (less than 262.04 score points)		Level 1b (from 262.04 to less than 334.75 score points)		Level 1a (from 334.75 to less than 407.47 score points)		Level 2 (from 407.47 to less than 480.18 score points)		Level 3 (from 480.18 to less than 552.89 score points)		Level 4 (from 552.89 to less than 625.61 score points)		Level 5 (from 625.61 to less than 698.32 score points)		Level 6 (above 698.32 score points)	
	%	S.E.	%	S.E.	%	S.E.	%	S.E.	%	S.E.	%	S.E.	%	S.E.	%	S.E.
OECD																
Australia	0.9	(0.1)	2.8	(0.3)	8.6	(0.5)	18.9	(0.6)	28.3	(0.7)	25.6	(0.6)	12.2	(0.6)	2.8	(0.4)
Austria	3.2	(0.5)	8.5	(0.8)	15.3	(0.8)	22.4	(1.1)	26.2	(1.1)	18.5	(0.9)	5.4	(0.6)	0.5	(0.2)
Belgium	1.6	(0.3)	4.6	(0.4)	10.8	(0.5)	18.5	(0.8)	26.0	(0.8)	25.6	(0.8)	11.3	(0.6)	1.5	(0.3)
Canada	0.5	(0.1)	2.1	(0.2)	7.5	(0.4)	19.0	(0.5)	30.2	(0.6)	26.9	(0.6)	11.6	(0.5)	2.3	(0.2)
Chile	2.1	(0.3)	8.2	(0.7)	22.7	(1.0)	32.6	(1.1)	24.7	(1.2)	8.5	(0.8)	1.1	(0.4)	0.1	(0.0)
Czech Republic	2.1	(0.5)	5.7	(0.7)	15.8	(1.1)	27.6	(0.9)	27.1	(1.1)	16.5	(0.9)	4.7	(0.5)	0.4	(0.1)
Denmark	0.5	(0.1)	3.4	(0.4)	12.3	(0.6)	26.5	(0.9)	32.8	(0.8)	19.6	(0.9)	4.6	(0.5)	0.3	(0.1)
Estonia	0.6	(0.2)	2.5	(0.4)	9.6	(0.7)	22.0	(1.1)	31.8	(1.2)	23.9	(1.0)	8.2	(0.6)	1.4	(0.3)
Finland	0.3	(0.1)	1.7	(0.2)	6.5	(0.4)	17.3	(0.6)	29.6	(0.7)	29.6	(0.9)	12.9	(0.8)	2.1	(0.3)
France	2.1	(0.4)	5.0	(0.6)	11.3	(0.8)	21.1	(1.1)	28.4	(1.2)	23.1	(1.2)	8.0	(0.8)	1.1	(0.2)
Germany	1.4	(0.3)	5.0	(0.6)	12.2	(0.8)	21.4	(1.1)	28.6	(0.9)	23.1	(0.9)	7.4	(0.6)	0.8	(0.2)
Greece	2.2	(0.5)	6.5	(0.9)	14.9	(0.9)	27.0	(0.9)	29.3	(1.3)	16.4	(0.8)	3.4	(0.4)	0.3	(0.1)
Hungary	1.2	(0.4)	4.8	(0.8)	13.5	(0.8)	24.5	(1.3)	30.7	(1.2)	20.4	(1.1)	4.6	(0.5)	0.3	(0.1)
Iceland	1.4	(0.2)	4.0	(0.4)	11.3	(0.6)	22.7	(0.7)	31.0	(0.9)	21.7	(0.8)	7.1	(0.6)	0.9	(0.3)
Ireland	1.7	(0.4)	4.1	(0.5)	11.2	(0.7)	22.9	(1.0)	31.0	(1.0)	22.0	(1.0)	6.5	(0.5)	0.6	(0.2)
Israel	5.5	(0.7)	8.9	(0.6)	15.1	(0.9)	21.9	(0.9)	23.6	(0.7)	16.8	(0.7)	6.9	(0.6)	1.3	(0.2)
Italy	2.6	(0.3)	6.4	(0.3)	15.2	(0.4)	24.5	(0.6)	27.6	(0.7)	18.1	(0.5)	5.1	(0.3)	0.5	(0.1)
Japan	1.4	(0.3)	3.3	(0.4)	8.5	(0.7)	19.2	(0.8)	29.0	(1.0)	26.2	(1.0)	10.5	(0.7)	2.0	(0.4)
Korea	0.3	(0.2)	0.9	(0.3)	4.8	(0.7)	15.2	(1.0)	30.8	(1.1)	33.1	(1.3)	13.3	(1.1)	1.6	(0.5)
Luxembourg	3.1	(0.3)	7.1	(0.7)	15.4	(0.6)	24.5	(0.7)	27.2	(0.8)	17.6	(0.7)	4.8	(0.3)	0.4	(0.1)
Mexico	3.5	(0.3)	11.8	(0.5)	25.5	(0.5)	32.2	(0.6)	20.9	(0.6)	5.6	(0.3)	0.6	(0.1)	0.0	(0.0)
Netherlands	0.2	(0.1)	2.1	(0.4)	10.8	(1.1)	23.2	(1.5)	27.6	(1.3)	24.6	(1.5)	10.2	(1.1)	1.4	(0.4)
New Zealand	0.9	(0.2)	2.6	(0.3)	8.9	(0.5)	17.7	(0.7)	25.2	(1.0)	25.7	(0.8)	15.0	(0.7)	4.1	(0.4)
Norway	0.7	(0.2)	3.4	(0.4)	11.7	(0.7)	24.7	(1.1)	32.0	(0.8)	20.9	(1.0)	6.1	(0.5)	0.6	(0.2)
Poland	1.1	(0.2)	4.1	(0.5)	12.2	(0.7)	24.5	(0.8)	30.0	(0.8)	20.4	(0.8)	6.8	(0.7)	1.0	(0.2)
Portugal	0.9	(0.2)	4.4	(0.6)	13.2	(0.9)	26.6	(1.0)	30.9	(1.0)	18.7	(0.9)	4.8	(0.5)	0.5	(0.2)
Slovak Republic	1.5	(0.4)	6.1	(0.6)	16.5	(0.9)	28.0	(1.0)	28.6	(1.0)	15.6	(0.9)	3.4	(0.5)	0.3	(0.2)
Slovenia	1.3	(0.2)	5.4	(0.5)	14.9	(0.7)	27.0	(0.9)	31.5	(0.8)	17.1	(0.8)	2.7	(0.4)	0.1	(0.1)
Spain	2.3	(0.3)	5.9	(0.4)	14.8	(0.6)	26.8	(0.7)	30.7	(0.7)	16.1	(0.7)	3.2	(0.2)	0.2	(0.1)
Sweden	1.5	(0.2)	3.9	(0.4)	11.3	(0.7)	23.5	(0.9)	30.7	(0.8)	20.6	(0.8)	7.4	(0.6)	1.1	(0.3)
Switzerland	0.7	(0.1)	3.8	(0.5)	11.1	(0.7)	21.9	(0.4)	30.1	(1.1)	23.2	(0.8)	8.2	(0.7)	0.9	(0.2)
Turkey	1.4	(0.3)	6.5	(0.6)	18.5	(1.1)	30.8	(1.4)	28.4	(1.2)	12.4	(1.1)	2.0	(0.5)	0.1	(0.0)
United Kingdom	1.1	(0.2)	3.5	(0.4)	11.7	(0.6)	22.5	(0.6)	28.6	(0.8)	21.8	(0.8)	9.0	(0.6)	1.9	(0.3)
United States	0.5	(0.1)	3.7	(0.4)	11.9	(0.6)	24.0	(1.0)	28.6	(0.9)	21.5	(1.0)	8.5	(0.8)	1.2	(0.2)
OECD total	1.4	(0.1)	5.0	(0.2)	13.3	(0.3)	24.0	(0.3)	28.0	(0.3)	20.1	(0.3)	7.2	(0.2)	1.1	(0.1)
OECD average	1.5	(0.1)	4.8	(0.1)	12.8	(0.1)	23.6	(0.2)	28.8	(0.2)	20.5	(0.2)	7.0	(0.1)	1.0	(0.0)
Partners																
Albania	16.7	(1.3)	20.3	(1.1)	25.9	(0.9)	22.6	(1.4)	11.6	(1.2)	2.7	(0.4)	0.3	(0.1)	0.0	(0.0)
Argentina	13.3	(1.2)	17.0	(1.1)	23.7	(1.2)	23.6	(1.1)	14.7	(1.3)	6.5	(0.8)	1.2	(0.3)	0.1	(0.1)
Azerbaijan	17.3	(1.5)	25.3	(1.0)	29.8	(1.0)	19.7	(1.2)	6.7	(0.7)	1.1	(0.2)	0.1	(0.1)	0.0	(0.0)
Brazil	6.1	(0.4)	16.5	(0.6)	27.8	(0.9)	26.8	(0.8)	15.5	(0.8)	6.1	(0.5)	1.2	(0.2)	0.1	(0.0)
Bulgaria	11.0	(1.3)	13.1	(1.2)	19.0	(1.3)	22.7	(1.1)	20.1	(1.4)	10.8	(1.1)	2.8	(0.6)	0.4	(0.2)
Colombia	6.3	(0.9)	14.9	(1.1)	27.7	(1.1)	28.3	(1.1)	16.8	(1.1)	5.1	(0.5)	0.8	(0.2)	0.1	(0.0)
Croatia	1.3	(0.3)	5.7	(0.5)	16.6	(1.0)	28.0	(0.9)	29.8	(1.1)	15.2	(0.9)	3.2	(0.4)	0.2	(0.1)
Dubai (UAE)	4.4	(0.2)	9.8	(0.4)	17.6	(0.5)	23.6	(0.7)	23.3	(0.7)	15.4	(0.7)	5.3	(0.4)	0.7	(0.2)
Hong Kong-China	0.4	(0.1)	1.8	(0.3)	7.5	(0.6)	18.9	(0.9)	33.1	(0.9)	28.3	(0.9)	9.2	(0.7)	0.8	(0.1)
Indonesia	4.6	(0.7)	16.2	(1.3)	33.0	(1.5)	31.0	(1.4)	12.8	(1.3)	2.3	(0.6)	0.1	(0.1)	0.0	(0.0)
Jordan	13.7	(1.0)	16.5	(1.0)	24.4	(0.9)	25.0	(0.8)	14.4	(0.8)	5.0	(0.5)	1.0	(0.3)	0.1	(0.1)
Kazakhstan	16.8	(1.0)	20.8	(1.1)	25.3	(0.9)	20.1	(0.9)	11.3	(0.7)	4.6	(0.6)	1.0	(0.3)	0.1	(0.1)
Kyrgyzstan	39.1	(1.4)	26.6	(1.0)	19.7	(0.9)	9.7	(0.7)	3.8	(0.5)	0.9	(0.2)	0.2	(0.1)	0.0	(0.0)
Latvia	0.7	(0.2)	4.0	(0.5)	13.8	(1.0)	26.5	(1.1)	31.4	(1.1)	18.9	(1.0)	4.4	(0.5)	0.3	(0.1)
Liechtenstein	0.4	(0.4)	2.8	(1.2)	10.6	(1.7)	22.7	(2.5)	29.1	(2.6)	28.8	(2.9)	5.4	(1.6)	0.3	(0.5)
Lithuania	1.5	(0.3)	6.9	(0.5)	18.9	(0.8)	29.3	(1.1)	26.9	(1.1)	13.4	(0.8)	2.8	(0.4)	0.2	(0.1)
Macao-China	0.4	(0.1)	2.8	(0.2)	13.6	(0.5)	31.8	(0.7)	34.2	(0.8)	15.0	(0.8)	2.1	(0.2)	0.1	(0.1)
Montenegro	8.7	(0.6)	16.9	(0.8)	26.9	(1.0)	26.4	(0.9)	16.1	(0.8)	4.4	(0.5)	0.6	(0.1)	0.0	(0.0)
Panama	17.8	(2.0)	24.5	(1.6)	26.3	(1.5)	18.4	(1.5)	9.0	(1.2)	3.5	(0.7)	0.5	(0.2)	0.0	(0.0)
Peru	19.0	(1.1)	23.0	(1.0)	26.4	(1.0)	19.7	(1.0)	8.9	(0.9)	2.5	(0.5)	0.5	(0.2)	0.1	(0.0)
Qatar	22.1	(0.4)	22.0	(0.5)	22.1	(0.5)	16.2	(0.5)	10.0	(0.4)	5.4	(0.3)	1.8	(0.2)	0.4	(0.1)
Romania	5.1	(0.7)	12.9	(1.0)	23.4	(1.2)	29.0	(1.3)	21.6	(1.4)	7.1	(0.8)	1.0	(0.3)	0.0	(0.0)
Russian Federation	2.9	(0.5)	8.4	(0.7)	20.7	(1.0)	28.8	(0.8)	24.3	(1.0)	11.3	(0.7)	3.1	(0.4)	0.6	(0.2)
Serbia	3.8	(0.5)	10.5	(0.6)	21.4	(1.0)	30.2	(1.0)	23.7	(1.0)	8.9	(0.6)	1.4	(0.3)	0.1	(0.1)
Shanghai-China	0.2	(0.1)	1.2	(0.3)	5.2	(0.5)	16.2	(0.7)	31.2	(0.9)	31.4	(1.2)	12.8	(0.7)	1.9	(0.3)
Singapore	0.2	(0.1)	2.0	(0.2)	7.3	(0.5)	16.5	(0.6)	27.8	(0.8)	28.0	(0.9)	14.8	(0.7)	3.5	(0.4)
Chinese Taipei	1.0	(0.2)	3.7	(0.4)	11.1	(0.7)	22.8	(0.9)	31.1	(1.2)	22.4	(1.0)	7.0	(0.7)	0.8	(0.2)
Thailand	1.5	(0.3)	10.1	(0.9)	30.5	(1.0)	36.2	(1.1)	17.3	(0.9)	4.0	(0.5)	0.4	(0.2)	0.0	(0.0)
Trinidad and Tobago	9.7	(0.5)	14.0	(0.8)	21.3	(0.7)	24.4	(0.7)	19.2	(0.7)	9.0	(0.4)	2.2	(0.2)	0.3	(0.1)
Tunisia	8.6	(0.7)	18.0	(0.8)	28.6	(0.9)	27.1	(1.0)	13.9	(0.8)	3.4	(0.5)	0.4	(0.2)	0.0	(0.0)
Uruguay	6.9	(0.7)	13.7	(0.8)	22.8	(0.8)	27.2	(0.7)	19.4	(0.8)	8.0	(0.6)	1.8	(0.3)	0.2	(0.1)

StatLink http://dx.doi.org/10.1787/888932343285

[Part 1/2]
Percentage of students at each proficiency level on the reading subscale *non-continuous texts*, by gender

Table I.2.18

	Below Level 1b (less than 262.04 score points)		Level 1b (from 262.04 to less than 334.75 score points)		Level 1a (from 334.75 to less than 407.47 score points)		Level 2 (from 407.47 to less than 480.18 score points)		Level 3 (from 480.18 to less than 552.89 score points)		Level 4 (from 552.89 to less than 625.61 score points)		Level 5 (from 625.61 to less than 698.32 score points)		Level 6 (above 698.32 score points)	
	%	S.E.	%	S.E.	%	S.E.	%	S.E.	%	S.E.	%	S.E.	%	S.E.	%	S.E.
Australia	1.4	(0.2)	4.1	(0.4)	11.3	(0.6)	21.1	(0.7)	27.8	(0.9)	22.5	(1.0)	9.8	(0.8)	2.0	(0.4)
Austria	4.5	(0.7)	11.1	(1.0)	18.5	(1.1)	22.4	(1.4)	23.9	(1.4)	15.4	(1.3)	3.9	(0.7)	0.3	(0.2)
Belgium	2.5	(0.5)	5.8	(0.7)	13.0	(0.7)	19.7	(1.0)	25.0	(1.2)	23.3	(1.1)	9.4	(0.6)	1.3	(0.3)
Canada	0.8	(0.1)	3.2	(0.3)	10.0	(0.6)	21.8	(0.8)	29.7	(0.8)	23.9	(0.7)	9.1	(0.5)	1.5	(0.2)
Chile	3.0	(0.6)	10.0	(0.9)	23.9	(1.4)	31.4	(1.4)	22.5	(1.5)	8.0	(1.0)	1.1	(0.4)	0.1	(0.1)
Czech Republic	3.1	(0.6)	7.8	(0.9)	19.8	(1.7)	29.5	(1.3)	24.5	(1.6)	12.1	(1.0)	3.0	(0.4)	0.3	(0.2)
Denmark	0.8	(0.2)	4.4	(0.5)	14.9	(0.9)	29.3	(1.2)	31.3	(1.3)	16.0	(1.0)	3.1	(0.5)	0.2	(0.2)
Estonia	1.0	(0.3)	3.5	(0.6)	13.1	(1.2)	25.8	(1.6)	30.9	(1.4)	19.7	(1.1)	5.2	(0.6)	0.7	(0.3)
Finland	0.5	(0.1)	2.8	(0.3)	10.0	(0.8)	23.3	(0.9)	31.1	(1.2)	23.7	(1.2)	7.8	(0.7)	0.8	(0.2)
France	3.2	(0.6)	7.3	(0.9)	14.0	(1.1)	22.7	(1.3)	26.3	(1.4)	19.5	(1.2)	6.2	(0.7)	0.7	(0.3)
Germany	2.2	(0.5)	7.1	(0.8)	14.7	(1.1)	24.1	(1.3)	27.4	(1.5)	19.2	(1.4)	5.0	(0.6)	0.4	(0.1)
Greece	3.6	(0.7)	9.4	(1.3)	18.2	(1.4)	28.5	(1.2)	25.7	(1.7)	12.2	(1.0)	2.2	(0.4)	0.1	(0.1)
Hungary	1.4	(0.4)	6.2	(1.0)	16.8	(1.3)	26.9	(1.6)	28.8	(1.3)	16.6	(1.3)	3.0	(0.6)	0.2	(0.1)
Iceland	2.2	(0.4)	5.9	(0.7)	15.1	(1.0)	24.8	(1.1)	28.2	(1.5)	18.3	(1.1)	5.1	(0.6)	0.4	(0.2)
Ireland	2.7	(0.6)	5.9	(0.8)	13.9	(1.1)	25.1	(1.4)	29.8	(1.5)	17.9	(1.2)	4.5	(0.6)	0.3	(0.2)
Israel	8.4	(1.2)	11.1	(0.9)	16.7	(1.2)	21.9	(1.3)	20.6	(1.0)	14.1	(0.9)	6.1	(0.7)	1.2	(0.3)
Italy	4.0	(0.5)	9.0	(0.5)	18.5	(0.6)	25.5	(0.7)	24.3	(0.8)	14.6	(0.7)	3.7	(0.3)	0.3	(0.1)
Japan	2.0	(0.6)	4.6	(0.7)	11.3	(1.2)	21.7	(1.2)	28.2	(1.5)	22.9	(1.4)	8.0	(0.8)	1.3	(0.5)
Korea	0.6	(0.3)	1.5	(0.6)	6.9	(1.1)	18.5	(1.5)	31.4	(1.6)	29.4	(1.6)	10.5	(1.2)	1.2	(0.4)
Luxembourg	4.6	(0.6)	9.2	(1.1)	17.8	(0.9)	24.7	(1.0)	24.9	(1.0)	14.8	(0.9)	3.7	(0.4)	0.2	(0.1)
Mexico	4.6	(0.4)	14.0	(0.8)	27.1	(0.7)	30.6	(0.7)	18.5	(0.8)	4.7	(0.3)	0.5	(0.1)	0.0	(0.0)
Netherlands	0.3	(0.2)	2.9	(0.4)	13.1	(1.5)	25.4	(1.8)	27.1	(1.5)	22.3	(1.7)	8.1	(1.1)	1.0	(0.4)
New Zealand	1.5	(0.3)	4.0	(0.5)	12.5	(0.8)	20.1	(1.0)	25.3	(1.2)	21.6	(1.1)	12.0	(1.0)	3.0	(0.5)
Norway	1.3	(0.3)	4.9	(0.7)	15.7	(1.0)	27.7	(1.2)	30.3	(1.2)	16.1	(1.0)	3.8	(0.6)	0.2	(0.1)
Poland	1.9	(0.4)	6.5	(0.8)	16.7	(1.0)	26.4	(1.4)	27.3	(1.2)	16.2	(1.0)	4.4	(0.6)	0.6	(0.2)
Portugal	1.4	(0.3)	6.4	(0.6)	16.7	(1.3)	28.5	(1.2)	27.9	(1.4)	15.6	(1.1)	3.4	(0.5)	0.3	(0.2)
Slovak Republic	2.3	(0.5)	9.4	(1.0)	21.7	(1.3)	29.6	(1.5)	23.2	(1.3)	11.3	(1.1)	2.3	(0.5)	0.2	(0.2)
Slovenia	2.3	(0.3)	8.3	(0.7)	19.8	(1.0)	28.3	(1.2)	27.7	(1.3)	12.1	(1.0)	1.3	(0.5)	0.1	(0.1)
Spain	3.2	(0.4)	7.6	(0.6)	17.8	(0.8)	27.4	(1.0)	27.9	(1.1)	13.4	(0.9)	2.5	(0.3)	0.2	(0.1)
Sweden	2.3	(0.4)	5.9	(0.6)	15.0	(1.2)	26.3	(1.2)	28.7	(1.1)	16.4	(0.9)	4.8	(0.6)	0.5	(0.2)
Switzerland	1.0	(0.2)	5.4	(0.7)	14.2	(1.0)	24.8	(1.3)	29.6	(1.4)	19.1	(1.1)	5.5	(0.7)	0.6	(0.2)
Turkey	2.1	(0.4)	9.0	(1.0)	22.8	(1.5)	30.9	(1.5)	24.3	(1.7)	9.9	(1.1)	1.0	(0.4)	0.0	c
United Kingdom	1.5	(0.3)	4.8	(0.6)	13.9	(0.9)	24.2	(1.0)	27.0	(1.4)	19.0	(1.1)	7.9	(0.7)	1.5	(0.4)
United States	0.7	(0.2)	4.8	(0.6)	13.7	(1.0)	24.7	(1.1)	28.3	(1.1)	19.8	(1.2)	7.3	(0.8)	0.6	(0.2)
OECD total	2.3	(0.1)	6.6	(0.1)	15.9	(0.2)	25.4	(0.2)	26.9	(0.2)	17.1	(0.2)	5.2	(0.1)	0.7	(0.0)
OECD average	2.0	(0.1)	6.6	(0.2)	15.8	(0.3)	25.2	(0.3)	26.6	(0.4)	17.5	(0.4)	5.7	(0.2)	0.7	(0.1)
Albania	24.2	(2.0)	23.7	(1.7)	24.6	(1.3)	17.2	(1.6)	8.3	(1.4)	1.8	(0.4)	0.1	(0.1)	0.0	c
Argentina	16.8	(1.5)	18.6	(1.4)	23.7	(1.5)	21.8	(1.3)	12.8	(1.2)	5.2	(0.9)	1.1	(0.4)	0.0	(0.1)
Azerbaijan	20.7	(1.8)	26.4	(1.4)	28.5	(1.6)	17.2	(1.6)	6.0	(0.9)	1.1	(0.3)	0.1	(0.1)	0.0	c
Brazil	8.3	(0.6)	18.3	(0.8)	28.3	(1.1)	24.6	(1.0)	13.5	(1.1)	5.6	(0.5)	1.1	(0.3)	0.1	(0.1)
Bulgaria	15.8	(1.9)	16.4	(1.5)	20.9	(1.5)	20.4	(1.5)	16.2	(1.6)	8.1	(0.9)	2.0	(0.5)	0.3	(0.2)
Colombia	6.7	(1.2)	15.1	(1.4)	28.4	(1.4)	27.7	(1.5)	16.3	(1.5)	5.0	(0.7)	0.8	(0.3)	0.1	(0.1)
Croatia	2.2	(0.5)	8.3	(0.8)	21.0	(1.4)	29.2	(1.2)	26.0	(1.6)	11.4	(0.9)	1.9	(0.5)	0.0	(0.1)
Dubai (UAE)	6.9	(0.4)	13.4	(0.6)	19.4	(0.8)	21.8	(0.9)	20.3	(0.9)	13.0	(0.8)	4.6	(0.6)	0.6	(0.3)
Hong Kong-China	0.8	(0.2)	2.3	(0.5)	9.6	(0.8)	21.2	(1.2)	33.4	(1.2)	25.1	(1.3)	7.1	(0.8)	0.5	(0.2)
Indonesia	6.4	(1.0)	21.2	(1.8)	35.7	(1.8)	26.7	(1.8)	8.7	(1.2)	1.3	(0.5)	0.0	(0.1)	0.0	c
Jordan	19.8	(1.7)	20.0	(1.5)	26.0	(1.5)	21.4	(1.3)	9.6	(1.0)	2.7	(0.6)	0.4	(0.2)	0.0	(0.0)
Kazakhstan	22.8	(1.3)	23.7	(1.6)	24.3	(1.3)	16.8	(1.2)	8.4	(1.0)	3.1	(0.5)	0.8	(0.3)	0.1	(0.1)
Kyrgyzstan	47.7	(1.7)	25.1	(1.3)	16.4	(1.1)	7.4	(0.8)	2.8	(0.5)	0.6	(0.2)	0.1	(0.1)	0.0	c
Latvia	1.2	(0.4)	6.4	(1.0)	19.2	(1.6)	29.4	(1.4)	27.4	(1.4)	13.3	(1.1)	3.0	(0.5)	0.1	(0.1)
Liechtenstein	0.7	(0.8)	3.9	(1.6)	13.4	(2.7)	25.4	(3.1)	28.5	(4.0)	23.6	(3.4)	4.2	(1.7)	0.3	(0.7)
Lithuania	2.6	(0.5)	10.7	(0.9)	24.9	(1.1)	31.4	(1.4)	20.9	(1.2)	8.1	(0.8)	1.4	(0.5)	0.0	(0.1)
Macao-China	0.6	(0.2)	4.1	(0.4)	17.4	(0.7)	34.1	(1.0)	30.2	(1.1)	12.1	(0.8)	1.5	(0.2)	0.0	(0.0)
Montenegro	12.3	(0.8)	21.1	(1.1)	29.4	(1.2)	23.0	(1.1)	11.4	(0.8)	2.6	(0.4)	0.3	(0.2)	0.0	(0.0)
Panama	19.7	(2.3)	27.1	(2.1)	26.6	(1.7)	17.9	(2.1)	6.2	(1.0)	2.1	(0.5)	0.4	(0.2)	0.0	(0.0)
Peru	21.2	(1.4)	23.9	(1.1)	26.5	(1.2)	18.5	(1.1)	7.2	(1.0)	2.0	(0.5)	0.6	(0.3)	0.1	(0.1)
Qatar	30.5	(0.6)	22.7	(0.7)	19.5	(0.6)	12.3	(0.5)	8.0	(0.4)	5.0	(0.4)	1.7	(0.3)	0.4	(0.2)
Romania	7.2	(1.2)	16.7	(1.5)	24.7	(1.4)	27.5	(1.9)	17.9	(1.7)	5.4	(0.8)	0.6	(0.2)	0.0	(0.0)
Russian Federation	4.4	(0.8)	11.7	(1.1)	24.6	(1.3)	29.2	(1.2)	19.5	(1.1)	8.3	(0.8)	1.9	(0.4)	0.4	(0.2)
Serbia	5.9	(0.7)	13.8	(0.9)	24.7	(1.2)	28.4	(1.0)	19.4	(1.3)	6.6	(0.7)	1.1	(0.3)	0.1	(0.1)
Shanghai-China	0.4	(0.1)	1.9	(0.5)	7.2	(0.8)	20.1	(1.2)	33.0	(1.2)	27.1	(1.4)	9.2	(0.9)	1.1	(0.3)
Singapore	0.5	(0.1)	3.0	(0.4)	9.3	(0.8)	18.4	(0.9)	27.8	(1.1)	26.5	(1.3)	12.1	(0.8)	2.4	(0.5)
Chinese Taipei	1.8	(0.4)	5.5	(0.7)	13.9	(0.9)	24.6	(1.2)	29.7	(1.3)	19.1	(1.4)	5.0	(0.8)	0.4	(0.2)
Thailand	2.7	(0.6)	14.9	(1.4)	34.7	(1.6)	31.2	(1.4)	13.3	(1.4)	3.0	(0.6)	0.3	(0.1)	0.0	(0.0)
Trinidad and Tobago	14.2	(1.1)	17.1	(1.4)	22.5	(1.0)	22.1	(0.9)	16.3	(0.9)	6.5	(0.5)	1.2	(0.3)	0.1	(0.1)
Tunisia	11.5	(1.0)	20.2	(1.1)	28.6	(1.4)	24.9	(1.4)	11.5	(1.1)	2.9	(0.7)	0.4	(0.2)	0.0	(0.0)
Uruguay	10.4	(1.1)	16.4	(1.0)	22.9	(1.1)	24.7	(1.1)	16.9	(1.0)	7.0	(0.7)	1.6	(0.4)	0.2	(0.1)

StatLink ⟐⟐ http://dx.doi.org/10.1787/888932343285

[Part 2/2]

Percentage of students at each proficiency level on the reading subscale *non-continuous texts*, by gender

Table I.2.18

Girls – Proficiency levels

	Below Level 1b (less than 262.04 score points)		Level 1b (from 262.04 to less than 334.75 score points)		Level 1a (from 334.75 to less than 407.47 score points)		Level 2 (from 407.47 to less than 480.18 score points)		Level 3 (from 480.18 to less than 552.89 score points)		Level 4 (from 552.89 to less than 625.61 score points)		Level 5 (from 625.61 to less than 698.32 score points)		Level 6 (above 698.32 score points)	
	%	S.E.	%	S.E.	%	S.E.	%	S.E.	%	S.E.	%	S.E.	%	S.E.	%	S.E.
Australia	0.4	(0.1)	1.6	(0.2)	6.0	(0.5)	16.8	(1.0)	28.7	(1.1)	28.6	(0.9)	14.5	(0.7)	3.5	(0.5)
Austria	1.9	(0.6)	6.1	(1.0)	12.1	(1.2)	22.4	(1.5)	28.3	(1.5)	21.6	(1.3)	6.8	(0.9)	0.7	(0.2)
Belgium	0.7	(0.2)	3.3	(0.5)	8.6	(0.6)	17.3	(0.9)	27.0	(1.0)	28.0	(1.0)	13.3	(0.9)	1.9	(0.4)
Canada	0.2	(0.1)	1.1	(0.2)	5.0	(0.3)	16.2	(0.6)	30.7	(0.9)	29.8	(0.9)	14.1	(0.7)	3.0	(0.4)
Chile	1.2	(0.3)	6.4	(0.8)	21.4	(1.1)	33.9	(1.3)	27.0	(1.4)	9.0	(1.0)	1.2	(0.3)	0.0	(0.0)
Czech Republic	1.0	(0.4)	3.4	(0.7)	11.2	(1.1)	25.4	(1.4)	30.1	(1.4)	21.6	(1.2)	6.8	(0.8)	0.6	(0.3)
Denmark	0.2	(0.1)	2.4	(0.4)	9.8	(0.8)	23.7	(1.3)	34.4	(1.1)	23.2	(1.3)	6.0	(0.9)	0.4	(0.2)
Estonia	0.2	(0.2)	1.3	(0.5)	5.8	(0.8)	17.9	(1.4)	32.8	(1.6)	28.5	(1.5)	11.4	(1.0)	2.1	(0.5)
Finland	0.1	(0.1)	0.6	(0.2)	2.9	(0.4)	11.3	(0.9)	28.1	(1.4)	35.6	(1.2)	17.9	(1.1)	3.4	(0.5)
France	1.0	(0.4)	2.8	(0.5)	8.8	(0.9)	19.6	(1.2)	30.3	(1.6)	26.5	(2.0)	9.6	(1.2)	1.4	(0.4)
Germany	0.6	(0.2)	2.9	(0.5)	9.6	(0.9)	18.6	(1.3)	29.9	(1.2)	27.2	(1.2)	9.9	(0.9)	1.2	(0.3)
Greece	0.9	(0.4)	3.6	(0.7)	11.8	(1.1)	25.6	(1.0)	32.7	(1.2)	20.5	(1.1)	4.4	(0.7)	0.5	(0.3)
Hungary	0.9	(0.4)	3.4	(0.9)	10.1	(0.9)	22.1	(1.7)	32.5	(1.7)	24.2	(1.6)	6.2	(0.7)	0.5	(0.2)
Iceland	0.5	(0.2)	2.1	(0.4)	7.6	(0.9)	20.6	(1.4)	33.7	(1.7)	25.2	(1.2)	9.0	(0.9)	1.4	(0.5)
Ireland	0.7	(0.3)	2.2	(0.6)	8.4	(0.8)	20.6	(1.2)	32.3	(1.3)	26.2	(1.4)	8.6	(0.9)	0.9	(0.4)
Israel	2.7	(0.5)	6.8	(0.7)	13.5	(0.9)	21.9	(1.0)	26.5	(0.9)	19.4	(0.9)	7.8	(0.8)	1.4	(0.3)
Italy	1.0	(0.2)	3.7	(0.4)	11.7	(0.5)	23.4	(0.8)	31.1	(0.9)	21.8	(0.6)	6.5	(0.4)	0.8	(0.1)
Japan	0.6	(0.3)	1.8	(0.4)	5.6	(0.7)	16.5	(1.2)	29.9	(1.4)	29.7	(1.4)	13.2	(1.2)	2.7	(0.6)
Korea	0.1	(0.1)	0.2	(0.2)	2.5	(0.5)	11.4	(1.2)	30.2	(1.5)	37.2	(1.8)	16.4	(1.7)	2.1	(0.5)
Luxembourg	1.6	(0.4)	4.9	(0.6)	12.8	(0.9)	24.3	(0.9)	29.5	(1.3)	20.4	(0.9)	5.9	(0.6)	0.5	(0.2)
Mexico	2.5	(0.4)	9.7	(0.6)	23.9	(0.7)	33.7	(0.8)	23.2	(0.6)	6.4	(0.4)	0.6	(0.1)	0.0	(0.0)
Netherlands	0.1	(0.1)	1.3	(0.4)	8.5	(1.1)	21.1	(1.6)	28.0	(1.8)	26.9	(2.0)	12.4	(1.4)	1.7	(0.4)
New Zealand	0.2	(0.1)	1.1	(0.3)	5.2	(0.6)	15.2	(1.0)	25.1	(1.2)	29.9	(1.2)	18.1	(0.9)	5.2	(0.6)
Norway	0.2	(0.1)	1.7	(0.4)	7.4	(0.7)	21.7	(1.3)	33.8	(1.4)	25.8	(1.6)	8.4	(0.8)	0.9	(0.3)
Poland	0.3	(0.2)	1.6	(0.4)	7.8	(0.8)	22.6	(1.1)	32.6	(1.5)	24.6	(1.1)	9.1	(1.0)	1.3	(0.4)
Portugal	0.3	(0.2)	2.5	(0.4)	9.8	(0.9)	24.9	(1.3)	33.9	(1.3)	21.8	(1.0)	6.3	(0.8)	0.6	(0.3)
Slovak Republic	0.7	(0.3)	2.8	(0.6)	11.4	(0.9)	26.3	(1.3)	34.0	(1.4)	19.9	(1.1)	4.4	(0.8)	0.5	(0.3)
Slovenia	0.3	(0.1)	2.3	(0.3)	9.7	(0.8)	25.8	(1.3)	35.5	(1.5)	22.2	(1.4)	4.1	(0.6)	0.1	(0.1)
Spain	1.3	(0.2)	4.2	(0.5)	11.7	(0.7)	26.1	(0.9)	33.7	(1.0)	18.9	(0.8)	4.0	(0.4)	0.2	(0.1)
Sweden	0.7	(0.2)	1.9	(0.5)	7.5	(0.8)	20.6	(1.1)	32.7	(1.2)	25.0	(1.2)	10.0	(0.9)	1.6	(0.4)
Switzerland	0.4	(0.1)	2.1	(0.4)	8.0	(0.7)	18.9	(1.1)	30.7	(1.4)	27.5	(1.0)	11.0	(1.0)	1.4	(0.4)
Turkey	0.6	(0.2)	3.8	(0.7)	13.9	(1.3)	30.8	(1.8)	32.7	(1.6)	15.1	(1.6)	3.0	(0.7)	0.1	(0.1)
United Kingdom	0.6	(0.2)	2.2	(0.4)	9.5	(0.9)	20.9	(0.9)	30.1	(1.1)	24.4	(1.2)	10.1	(0.9)	2.3	(0.4)
United States	0.3	(0.1)	2.5	(0.5)	10.0	(0.8)	23.3	(1.4)	28.9	(1.2)	23.3	(1.1)	9.8	(1.1)	1.8	(0.4)
OECD total	0.7	(0.0)	3.0	(0.1)	9.7	(0.1)	21.8	(0.2)	30.6	(0.2)	24.0	(0.2)	8.8	(0.2)	1.4	(0.1)
OECD average	0.8	(0.1)	3.3	(0.2)	10.8	(0.3)	22.8	(0.4)	29.4	(0.4)	22.8	(0.4)	8.7	(0.3)	1.4	(0.1)
Albania	8.7	(1.0)	16.7	(1.3)	27.2	(1.4)	28.3	(1.7)	15.0	(1.5)	3.6	(0.6)	0.4	(0.3)	0.0	(0.0)
Argentina	10.3	(1.2)	15.6	(1.3)	23.6	(1.5)	25.2	(1.3)	16.3	(1.7)	7.6	(1.1)	1.2	(0.4)	0.1	(0.1)
Azerbaijan	13.7	(1.4)	24.1	(1.5)	31.2	(1.5)	22.3	(1.5)	7.5	(0.8)	1.1	(0.4)	0.1	(0.1)	0.0	(0.0)
Brazil	4.2	(0.4)	14.8	(0.7)	27.3	(1.0)	28.7	(1.0)	17.2	(0.9)	6.5	(0.6)	1.2	(0.2)	0.1	(0.1)
Bulgaria	5.8	(0.9)	9.6	(1.3)	17.0	(1.6)	25.2	(1.5)	24.4	(1.7)	13.8	(1.7)	3.7	(0.8)	0.6	(0.3)
Colombia	5.9	(1.0)	14.7	(1.3)	27.2	(1.3)	28.8	(1.4)	17.4	(1.2)	5.1	(0.6)	0.8	(0.3)	0.1	(0.1)
Croatia	0.4	(0.1)	2.7	(0.5)	11.7	(1.1)	26.6	(1.2)	34.0	(1.5)	19.5	(1.4)	4.7	(0.7)	0.3	(0.2)
Dubai (UAE)	1.7	(0.2)	6.1	(0.6)	15.6	(0.8)	25.4	(1.1)	26.4	(1.1)	17.8	(1.1)	6.2	(0.7)	0.8	(0.2)
Hong Kong-China	0.0	(0.0)	1.3	(0.3)	5.1	(0.6)	16.2	(1.0)	32.9	(1.2)	31.8	(1.3)	11.6	(1.0)	1.0	(0.2)
Indonesia	2.9	(0.7)	11.3	(1.2)	30.3	(1.9)	35.3	(1.6)	16.8	(1.8)	3.2	(0.8)	0.2	(0.1)	0.0	(0.0)
Jordan	7.4	(0.9)	13.0	(1.1)	22.8	(1.3)	28.6	(1.3)	19.2	(1.2)	7.4	(0.8)	1.5	(0.4)	0.1	(0.1)
Kazakhstan	10.7	(1.1)	17.7	(1.0)	26.4	(1.2)	23.5	(1.5)	14.3	(1.1)	6.1	(0.9)	1.2	(0.3)	0.1	(0.1)
Kyrgyzstan	31.0	(1.6)	28.1	(1.3)	22.8	(1.2)	11.9	(1.1)	4.8	(0.7)	1.2	(0.3)	0.2	(0.1)	0.0	(0.0)
Latvia	0.3	(0.3)	1.6	(0.5)	8.6	(1.2)	23.6	(1.5)	35.2	(1.4)	24.3	(1.5)	5.8	(0.7)	0.6	(0.2)
Liechtenstein	0.0	c	1.4	(1.5)	7.4	(2.5)	19.7	(3.7)	29.7	(3.5)	34.7	(5.2)	6.7	(2.9)	0.3	(0.7)
Lithuania	0.4	(0.2)	3.1	(0.5)	12.8	(0.9)	27.2	(1.3)	33.0	(1.4)	18.9	(1.1)	4.2	(0.6)	0.3	(0.2)
Macao-China	0.1	(0.1)	1.6	(0.2)	9.6	(0.6)	29.5	(1.1)	38.4	(1.3)	18.1	(1.3)	2.6	(0.3)	0.1	(0.1)
Montenegro	4.9	(0.7)	12.6	(1.1)	24.4	(1.4)	30.1	(1.2)	20.9	(1.2)	6.2	(0.7)	0.9	(0.3)	0.0	(0.1)
Panama	15.9	(2.2)	21.9	(2.2)	25.9	(2.2)	18.9	(1.5)	11.7	(1.6)	4.9	(1.2)	0.7	(0.3)	0.0	c
Peru	16.7	(1.2)	22.2	(1.4)	26.3	(1.3)	20.8	(1.3)	10.5	(1.2)	2.9	(0.8)	0.4	(0.2)	0.1	(0.1)
Qatar	13.4	(0.5)	21.2	(0.6)	24.9	(0.8)	20.3	(0.7)	12.0	(0.5)	5.9	(0.5)	1.9	(0.3)	0.3	(0.1)
Romania	3.1	(0.7)	9.2	(1.1)	22.1	(1.6)	30.3	(1.6)	25.2	(1.6)	8.7	(1.0)	1.4	(0.4)	0.1	(0.1)
Russian Federation	1.4	(0.3)	5.2	(0.6)	16.8	(1.2)	28.4	(1.3)	28.9	(1.4)	14.1	(1.0)	4.3	(0.6)	0.8	(0.3)
Serbia	1.8	(0.4)	7.2	(0.6)	18.0	(1.1)	32.0	(1.7)	27.9	(1.2)	11.2	(0.8)	1.8	(0.4)	0.1	(0.1)
Shanghai-China	0.1	(0.1)	0.4	(0.2)	3.1	(0.4)	12.4	(0.9)	29.4	(1.4)	35.6	(1.6)	16.3	(1.0)	2.7	(0.5)
Singapore	0.0	(0.0)	0.9	(0.2)	5.3	(0.4)	14.5	(0.8)	27.7	(1.1)	29.5	(1.0)	17.5	(1.1)	4.5	(0.5)
Chinese Taipei	0.2	(0.1)	2.0	(0.4)	8.3	(0.8)	21.0	(1.4)	32.6	(1.7)	25.8	(1.4)	8.9	(1.2)	1.1	(0.3)
Thailand	0.6	(0.2)	6.5	(0.8)	27.3	(1.5)	40.0	(1.4)	20.3	(1.1)	4.8	(0.6)	0.5	(0.3)	0.0	(0.0)
Trinidad and Tobago	5.2	(0.6)	11.0	(0.8)	20.1	(0.9)	26.7	(1.1)	22.0	(1.0)	11.4	(0.6)	3.1	(0.4)	0.5	(0.2)
Tunisia	5.9	(0.7)	16.0	(1.1)	28.6	(1.3)	29.0	(1.3)	16.1	(1.3)	3.9	(0.7)	0.4	(0.2)	0.0	(0.0)
Uruguay	3.8	(0.6)	11.3	(0.9)	22.7	(0.9)	29.4	(1.1)	21.7	(1.0)	8.9	(0.8)	2.0	(0.4)	0.2	(0.1)

StatLink ⟐⟐ http://dx.doi.org/10.1787/888932343285

[Part 1/1]

Table I.2.19 Mean score, variation and gender differences in student performance on the reading subscale *non-continuous texts*

		All students				Gender differences						Percentiles											
		Mean score		Standard deviation		Boys		Girls		Difference (B – G)		5th		10th		25th		75th		90th		95th	
		Mean	S.E.	S.D.	S.E.	Mean score	S.E.	Mean score	S.E.	Score dif.	S.E.	Score	S.E.	Score	S.E.	Score	S.E.	Score	S.E.	Score	S.E.	Score	S.E.
OECD	Australia	524	(2.3)	99	(1.4)	507	(2.9)	541	(2.7)	**-34**	(3.1)	352	(3.5)	394	(3.5)	461	(2.5)	594	(2.7)	647	(3.4)	677	(4.0)
	Austria	472	(3.2)	107	(2.3)	453	(4.1)	491	(4.2)	**-38**	(5.6)	283	(6.5)	324	(6.5)	400	(5.6)	551	(3.4)	604	(3.7)	631	(4.0)
	Belgium	511	(2.2)	105	(1.7)	496	(3.5)	526	(2.8)	**-30**	(4.6)	321	(6.9)	368	(4.2)	443	(3.6)	588	(2.4)	637	(2.7)	663	(3.2)
	Canada	527	(1.6)	92	(0.9)	511	(1.8)	544	(1.9)	**-33**	(2.0)	367	(3.3)	407	(2.9)	468	(2.1)	591	(2.0)	641	(2.2)	671	(2.8)
	Chile	444	(3.2)	85	(1.9)	436	(4.1)	451	(3.4)	**-15**	(4.1)	298	(5.2)	333	(4.7)	387	(4.4)	502	(3.3)	552	(4.0)	580	(5.4)
	Czech Republic	474	(3.4)	97	(2.2)	453	(4.5)	498	(3.4)	**-45**	(4.6)	308	(8.0)	350	(6.4)	412	(4.7)	543	(3.9)	597	(3.9)	627	(4.4)
	Denmark	493	(2.3)	85	(1.1)	479	(2.8)	506	(2.7)	**-27**	(3.1)	347	(5.2)	381	(3.9)	436	(2.8)	552	(2.6)	599	(3.1)	625	(3.6)
	Estonia	512	(2.7)	91	(2.0)	491	(3.2)	534	(2.8)	**-43**	(2.7)	357	(6.9)	394	(4.9)	454	(3.7)	573	(2.8)	624	(3.2)	654	(3.5)
	Finland	535	(2.4)	89	(1.0)	508	(2.6)	562	(2.7)	**-54**	(2.4)	378	(4.4)	417	(3.8)	478	(2.9)	598	(3.0)	645	(2.9)	670	(2.9)
	France	498	(3.4)	103	(2.8)	479	(4.3)	517	(3.4)	**-38**	(3.7)	311	(9.7)	360	(7.3)	435	(5.2)	572	(3.8)	621	(4.0)	649	(5.0)
	Germany	497	(2.8)	99	(1.8)	478	(3.9)	518	(3.0)	**-40**	(3.9)	319	(6.2)	361	(4.7)	432	(4.5)	570	(3.3)	618	(2.6)	643	(3.2)
	Greece	472	(4.3)	95	(2.6)	450	(5.5)	493	(3.5)	**-42**	(4.6)	303	(11.3)	344	(9.2)	412	(6.1)	539	(2.9)	588	(2.7)	615	(3.2)
	Hungary	487	(3.3)	92	(2.6)	471	(4.0)	503	(4.0)	**-32**	(4.3)	326	(9.5)	363	(7.2)	427	(4.6)	554	(3.5)	600	(4.0)	625	(4.4)
	Iceland	499	(1.5)	96	(1.4)	478	(2.3)	519	(2.2)	**-41**	(3.3)	331	(5.4)	371	(4.1)	439	(2.8)	566	(1.7)	616	(3.3)	645	(4.2)
	Ireland	496	(3.0)	96	(2.2)	477	(4.3)	516	(3.1)	**-39**	(4.6)	327	(8.1)	372	(5.9)	438	(4.1)	563	(3.0)	611	(3.6)	638	(4.5)
	Israel	467	(3.9)	120	(2.9)	447	(5.8)	486	(3.7)	**-40**	(5.8)	255	(9.9)	305	(8.0)	388	(5.7)	553	(3.8)	615	(4.1)	649	(4.5)
	Italy	476	(1.7)	102	(1.8)	456	(2.5)	498	(2.0)	**-43**	(3.0)	299	(4.2)	342	(3.3)	410	(2.1)	550	(1.7)	601	(1.9)	630	(2.0)
	Japan	518	(3.5)	99	(3.0)	499	(5.6)	537	(3.9)	**-38**	(6.9)	339	(10.3)	388	(7.1)	457	(4.5)	587	(3.1)	636	(4.2)	665	(5.0)
	Korea	542	(3.6)	82	(2.4)	527	(5.1)	559	(3.7)	**-32**	(5.9)	399	(6.5)	436	(6.2)	491	(4.7)	599	(3.6)	643	(3.6)	666	(3.9)
	Luxembourg	472	(1.2)	103	(1.0)	455	(1.9)	489	(1.3)	**-34**	(2.2)	289	(4.1)	334	(3.6)	405	(2.7)	546	(2.0)	597	(2.2)	626	(2.3)
	Mexico	424	(2.0)	87	(1.2)	415	(2.3)	434	(2.1)	**-20**	(1.9)	278	(3.5)	311	(2.9)	367	(2.4)	485	(2.0)	533	(2.4)	560	(2.4)
	Netherlands	514	(5.1)	91	(1.9)	502	(5.1)	527	(5.3)	**-25**	(2.5)	364	(5.1)	395	(5.5)	449	(6.4)	582	(5.4)	632	(4.9)	659	(5.5)
	New Zealand	532	(2.3)	104	(1.7)	511	(3.6)	555	(2.7)	**-44**	(4.4)	354	(5.6)	394	(4.1)	462	(3.5)	607	(3.0)	662	(3.2)	690	(3.7)
	Norway	498	(2.6)	89	(1.4)	477	(3.0)	519	(2.9)	**-42**	(2.7)	344	(5.4)	381	(4.3)	440	(2.9)	560	(3.3)	608	(3.7)	636	(3.9)
	Poland	496	(2.8)	95	(1.6)	473	(3.0)	518	(2.9)	**-46**	(2.5)	333	(6.7)	372	(4.0)	434	(3.6)	562	(3.2)	614	(3.8)	645	(3.4)
	Portugal	488	(3.2)	90	(1.7)	471	(3.7)	504	(3.2)	**-33**	(2.7)	333	(5.6)	370	(4.7)	430	(4.2)	550	(3.4)	601	(3.6)	628	(4.4)
	Slovak Republic	471	(2.8)	92	(2.4)	448	(3.9)	495	(3.0)	**-47**	(3.8)	314	(6.5)	350	(5.2)	410	(3.9)	537	(3.1)	587	(3.7)	615	(4.0)
	Slovenia	476	(1.1)	88	(0.8)	453	(1.6)	500	(1.5)	**-47**	(2.2)	320	(2.9)	358	(2.6)	418	(2.1)	540	(1.7)	584	(2.4)	609	(2.4)
	Spain	473	(2.1)	94	(1.2)	458	(2.5)	487	(2.2)	**-29**	(2.4)	306	(5.1)	348	(3.6)	414	(2.5)	538	(2.1)	586	(2.4)	614	(2.5)
	Sweden	498	(2.8)	97	(1.7)	475	(3.0)	521	(3.2)	**-46**	(2.7)	330	(5.2)	372	(4.1)	439	(3.5)	564	(3.3)	618	(3.5)	647	(4.3)
	Switzerland	505	(2.5)	94	(1.4)	487	(3.0)	524	(2.8)	**-38**	(3.0)	342	(4.8)	378	(4.3)	443	(3.2)	572	(3.3)	622	(3.9)	650	(4.2)
	Turkey	461	(3.8)	86	(1.9)	444	(4.1)	479	(4.3)	**-35**	(3.9)	313	(6.1)	347	(5.2)	404	(4.1)	522	(4.8)	570	(5.1)	596	(6.4)
	United Kingdom	506	(2.3)	99	(1.4)	492	(3.6)	518	(3.0)	**-26**	(4.6)	339	(3.7)	379	(3.0)	440	(2.9)	574	(3.1)	630	(3.8)	663	(5.0)
	United States	503	(3.5)	94	(1.4)	492	(3.9)	514	(3.9)	**-22**	(3.3)	344	(5.2)	379	(4.2)	438	(4.1)	570	(4.1)	624	(4.2)	654	(4.1)
	OECD total	492	(1.1)	99	(0.5)	477	(1.3)	507	(1.3)	**-30**	(1.2)	322	(1.7)	362	(1.5)	426	(1.3)	562	(1.4)	617	(1.4)	647	(1.7)
	OECD average	493	(0.5)	95	(0.3)	475	(0.6)	511	(0.5)	**-36**	(0.7)	327	(1.1)	367	(0.9)	431	(0.7)	560	(0.5)	611	(0.6)	639	(0.7)
Partners	Albania	366	(4.6)	108	(1.9)	339	(5.8)	396	(4.4)	**-57**	(4.7)	178	(7.2)	223	(6.8)	296	(5.5)	444	(5.2)	501	(5.7)	534	(5.4)
	Argentina	391	(5.2)	115	(3.5)	376	(5.5)	404	(5.5)	**-28**	(4.0)	194	(9.5)	240	(7.9)	316	(5.3)	472	(6.5)	538	(7.0)	574	(7.3)
	Azerbaijan	351	(4.2)	93	(2.1)	341	(4.7)	360	(4.2)	**-19**	(2.9)	193	(7.1)	229	(6.7)	288	(5.4)	414	(4.3)	469	(4.6)	501	(5.2)
	Brazil	408	(2.8)	97	(1.6)	398	(3.0)	418	(2.9)	**-20**	(1.7)	253	(3.6)	287	(2.9)	342	(2.9)	473	(4.1)	536	(4.6)	572	(5.6)
	Bulgaria	421	(7.2)	123	(3.0)	393	(8.0)	451	(6.1)	**-58**	(4.8)	204	(9.2)	255	(10.2)	339	(10.4)	511	(6.6)	573	(6.6)	609	(6.8)
	Colombia	409	(4.1)	95	(2.3)	406	(5.1)	411	(4.1)	-5	(4.4)	252	(8.1)	286	(6.7)	346	(5.4)	474	(4.1)	530	(3.9)	561	(4.7)
	Croatia	472	(3.0)	90	(1.9)	451	(3.7)	495	(3.9)	**-44**	(4.8)	319	(5.0)	354	(4.2)	412	(4.4)	536	(3.4)	584	(3.6)	613	(4.3)
	Dubai (UAE)	460	(1.3)	111	(1.0)	440	(1.9)	480	(1.8)	**-41**	(2.6)	270	(2.9)	311	(2.4)	383	(1.9)	541	(2.5)	602	(2.9)	635	(3.5)
	Hong Kong-China	522	(2.3)	85	(1.5)	510	(3.3)	536	(3.1)	**-26**	(4.4)	372	(4.9)	409	(4.7)	471	(3.3)	583	(2.6)	625	(2.8)	649	(3.3)
	Indonesia	399	(4.5)	80	(2.3)	381	(4.6)	416	(4.8)	**-35**	(4.0)	266	(6.6)	295	(5.7)	346	(4.8)	453	(5.3)	500	(6.1)	529	(6.5)
	Jordan	387	(4.1)	114	(2.3)	356	(6.0)	418	(5.1)	**-63**	(7.7)	185	(7.4)	237	(6.7)	316	(5.0)	465	(4.1)	528	(5.3)	562	(6.0)
	Kazakhstan	371	(3.9)	113	(1.8)	347	(4.1)	395	(4.4)	**-48**	(3.5)	185	(5.1)	227	(4.3)	295	(4.6)	448	(4.7)	520	(6.0)	559	(6.7)
	Kyrgyzstan	293	(3.7)	110	(2.2)	269	(4.3)	315	(3.9)	**-46**	(3.2)	113	(6.1)	154	(5.5)	218	(4.4)	364	(4.3)	434	(6.2)	479	(7.0)
	Latvia	487	(3.4)	88	(1.7)	464	(3.8)	510	(3.7)	**-46**	(3.7)	337	(5.3)	371	(4.8)	428	(4.3)	549	(3.4)	596	(3.9)	624	(4.4)
	Liechtenstein	506	(3.2)	86	(3.8)	491	(5.2)	523	(4.7)	**-32**	(7.6)	354	(13.4)	391	(7.9)	446	(7.3)	573	(6.4)	608	(7.6)	632	(10.8)
	Lithuania	462	(2.6)	91	(1.9)	434	(3.0)	491	(2.6)	**-57**	(2.7)	310	(6.1)	343	(4.2)	401	(3.5)	525	(3.0)	579	(3.4)	607	(4.5)
	Macao-China	481	(1.1)	76	(0.8)	467	(1.3)	495	(1.5)	**-28**	(1.8)	352	(2.5)	381	(2.3)	431	(2.1)	533	(1.4)	576	(2.0)	600	(2.8)
	Montenegro	398	(1.9)	99	(1.3)	374	(2.0)	422	(2.6)	**-48**	(2.7)	230	(4.2)	269	(4.1)	333	(3.0)	468	(2.6)	522	(3.5)	553	(4.4)
	Panama	359	(6.5)	106	(3.3)	345	(6.6)	373	(7.6)	**-27**	(6.6)	189	(10.2)	227	(9.1)	287	(7.2)	429	(8.0)	500	(10.1)	541	(10.0)
	Peru	356	(4.4)	105	(2.4)	348	(4.6)	364	(5.4)	**-16**	(4.9)	184	(4.5)	220	(4.3)	283	(4.6)	428	(5.6)	490	(7.1)	528	(8.3)
	Qatar	361	(0.9)	124	(0.8)	338	(1.4)	386	(1.1)	**-48**	(1.8)	171	(3.3)	208	(1.9)	273	(1.5)	443	(2.0)	532	(2.3)	581	(2.5)
	Romania	424	(4.5)	96	(2.7)	406	(5.3)	442	(4.7)	**-35**	(5.0)	261	(7.2)	298	(7.1)	360	(6.1)	492	(5.1)	544	(4.6)	573	(6.1)
	Russian Federation	452	(3.9)	98	(2.2)	430	(4.3)	474	(4.0)	**-44**	(3.1)	288	(7.2)	327	(6.0)	387	(4.4)	519	(4.0)	577	(4.7)	612	(5.8)
	Serbia	438	(2.9)	95	(1.8)	418	(3.8)	457	(3.0)	**-39**	(3.5)	275	(5.2)	313	(4.6)	375	(4.3)	503	(3.4)	555	(3.5)	585	(5.2)
	Shanghai-China	539	(2.4)	84	(1.7)	522	(3.1)	557	(2.4)	**-35**	(3.0)	394	(6.2)	429	(4.6)	486	(3.0)	598	(2.3)	643	(3.4)	668	(3.6)
	Singapore	539	(1.1)	95	(1.2)	524	(1.6)	553	(1.5)	**-29**	(2.2)	373	(3.1)	410	(3.2)	477	(2.0)	605	(1.9)	656	(2.3)	684	(3.3)
	Chinese Taipei	500	(2.8)	93	(1.9)	483	(4.0)	518	(3.8)	**-36**	(5.6)	337	(6.1)	377	(5.4)	440	(3.9)	566	(3.3)	615	(4.1)	642	(4.7)
	Thailand	423	(2.7)	75	(1.9)	406	(3.6)	436	(3.0)	**-31**	(4.0)	302	(4.3)	328	(4.0)	372	(3.6)	472	(2.9)	519	(4.2)	549	(4.8)
	Trinidad and Tobago	417	(1.4)	114	(1.3)	392	(2.3)	441	(2.1)	**-50**	(3.3)	219	(4.7)	265	(4.3)	341	(3.2)	498	(2.4)	561	(2.6)	597	(4.1)
	Tunisia	393	(3.3)	94	(2.2)	380	(3.6)	404	(3.5)	**-24**	(2.8)	234	(4.8)	271	(4.3)	330	(3.4)	457	(4.0)	511	(6.1)	543	(7.5)
	Uruguay	421	(2.7)	105	(1.9)	404	(3.4)	436	(3.0)	**-31**	(3.3)	244	(6.6)	284	(4.5)	351	(3.3)	494	(3.4)	553	(4.3)	587	(5.0)

Note: Values that are statistically significant are indicated in bold (see Annex A3).
StatLink http://dx.doi.org/10.1787/888932343285

[Part 1/1]

Table I.2.20 **Socio-economic indicators and the relationship with performance in reading**

	Socio-economic indicators							
	Mean performance on the reading scale	GDP per capita (in equivalent USD converted using PPPs)[1]	Cumulative expenditure per student between 6 and 15 years (in equivalent USD converted using PPPs)[1]	Percentage of the population in the age group 35-44 years with tertiary education[1]	Proportion of 15-year-olds with an immigrant background	Share of students in their country whose PISA index of economic, social and cultural status is below -1	15-year-old student population	Average index
Australia	515	37 615	72 386	37.6	19.3	3.4	240 851	0.20
Austria	470	36 839	97 789	19.3	15.2	8.4	87 326	0.05
Belgium	506	34 662	80 145	35.3	14.8	9.0	119 140	0.18
Canada	524	36 397	80 451	54.2	24.4	3.7	360 286	0.42
Chile	449	14 106	23 597	24.4	0.5	37.2	247 270	-0.82
Czech Republic	478	23 995	44 761	14.4	2.3	9.2	113 951	-0.33
Denmark	495	36 326	87 642	37.1	8.6	7.2	60 855	0.45
Estonia	501	20 620	43 037	34.6	8.0	6.7	12 978	-0.12
Finland	536	35 322	71 385	43.8	2.6	3.9	61 463	0.62
France	496	32 495	74 659	31.2	13.1	13.9	677 620	0.00
Germany	497	34 683	63 296	26.7	17.6	8.2	766 993	-0.14
Greece	483	27 793	48 422	26.5	9.0	17.7	93 088	-0.30
Hungary	494	18 763	44 342	19.0	2.1	19.1	105 611	-0.47
Iceland	500	36 325	94 847	36.2	2.4	3.5	4 410	0.68
Ireland	496	44 381	75 924	36.8	8.3	10.4	52 794	0.45
Israel	474	26 444	53 321	45.9	19.7	12.7	103 184	-0.10
Italy	486	31 016	77 310	15.2	5.5	21.4	506 733	-0.23
Japan	520	33 635	77 681	48.4	0.3	7.9	1 113 403	0.71
Korea	539	26 574	61 104	42.5	0.0	15.8	630 030	0.28
Luxembourg	472	82 456	155 624	28.4	40.2	16.1	5 124	0.67
Mexico	425	14 128	21 175	15.7	1.9	58.2	1 305 461	-1.33
Netherlands	508	39 594	80 348	32.5	12.1	6.5	183 546	0.30
New Zealand	521	27 020	48 633	39.9	24.7	8.6	55 129	-0.28
Norway	503	53 672	101 265	38.4	6.8	2.4	57 367	0.94
Poland	500	16 312	39 964	18.8	0.0	20.7	448 866	-0.52
Portugal	489	22 638	56 803	14.5	5.5	33.5	96 820	-0.69
Slovak Republic	477	20 270	32 200	13.9	0.5	10.4	69 274	-0.46
Slovenia	483	26 557	77 898	23.7	7.8	10.2	18 773	-0.03
Spain	481	31 469	74 119	32.6	9.5	29.0	387 054	-0.13
Sweden	497	36 785	82 753	32.7	11.7	5.1	113 054	0.31
Switzerland	501	41 800	104 352	36.4	23.5	11.1	80 839	0.26
Turkey	464	13 362	12 708	10.6	0.5	58.0	757 298	-1.46
United Kingdom	494	34 957	84 899	33.0	10.6	5.6	683 380	0.32
United States	500	46 434	105 752	43.0	19.5	10.4	3 373 264	0.56

	Adjusted performance on the reading scale					
	Reading performance adjusted by GPD per capita	Reading performance adjusted by cumulative expenditure per student between 6 and 15 years	Reading performance adjusted by GDP per capita and the percentage of the age group 35-44 years with tertiary education	Reading performance adjusted by the proportion of 15-year-olds with an immigrant background	Reading performance adjusted by the share of students in their country whose PISA index of economic, social and cultural status is below -1	Reading performance adjusted by the size of the 15-year-old student population
Australia	513	514	506	512	502	515
Austria	468	463	488	469	463	470
Belgium	505	503	500	505	499	505
Canada	522	522	492	520	512	524
Chile	457	460	455	452	475	449
Czech Republic	482	484	499	480	472	478
Denmark	493	490	487	495	486	494
Estonia	506	507	494	502	492	500
Finland	535	535	518	538	523	535
France	495	494	495	495	495	496
Germany	496	499	502	495	490	498
Greece	485	488	487	483	486	482
Hungary	500	500	509	496	499	494
Iceland	499	494	494	502	487	500
Ireland	490	494	488	496	491	495
Israel	476	478	452	471	472	473
Italy	487	484	508	487	493	486
Japan	519	518	496	523	512	521
Korea	542	541	522	542	540	540
Luxembourg	451	451	481	464	474	471
Mexico	433	437	443	428	474	427
Netherlands	505	506	507	508	499	508
New Zealand	523	526	507	517	514	520
Norway	494	495	495	504	489	503
Poland	507	508	515	503	507	501
Portugal	493	492	511	491	510	489
Slovak Republic	483	486	498	480	472	477
Slovenia	485	481	493	484	478	482
Spain	481	480	479	481	497	481
Sweden	496	494	496	497	486	497
Switzerland	496	492	495	497	496	500
Turkey	472	478	488	467	513	465
United Kingdom	493	490	492	494	484	495
United States	494	491	485	497	495	506

1. OECD, *Education at a Glance 2010: OECD Indicators.*
http://dx.doi.org/10.1787/888932343285

[Part 1/1]

Table I.2.21 **Country rankings on preferred questions**

		PISA 2009 reading performance rank	Percent-correct rank based on all PISA 2009 questions	Rank on own preferred new PISA 2009 items and link items from previous assessments	Percent-correct rank based on new PISA 2009 questions	Rank on own preferred new PISA 2009 questions
OECD	Australia	8	8	7	7	8
	Austria	33	35	26	26	36
	Belgium	10	10	16	16	10
	Canada	5	5	5	5	5
	Chile	38	30	25	25	24
	Czech Republic	29	31	30	30	33
	Denmark	m	m	m	m	m
	Estonia	12	14	12	12	16
	Finland	3	3	2	2	3
	France	19	20	17	17	18
	Germany	17	15	10	10	19
	Greece	27	29	32	32	29
	Hungary	22	21	23	23	21
	Iceland	m	m	m	m	m
	Ireland	18	16	19	19	12
	Israel	31	33	31	31	32
	Italy	25	25	27	27	27
	Japan	7	7	6	6	6
	Korea	2	2	3	3	2
	Luxembourg	32	34	35	35	34
	Mexico	41	40	39	39	41
	Netherlands	9	9	11	11	9
	New Zealand	6	6	8	8	7
	Norway	11	12	13	13	11
	Poland	14	11	21	21	13
	Portugal	23	23	20	20	26
	Slovak Republic	m	m	m	m	m
	Slovenia	26	27	28	28	30
	Spain	28	28	34	34	28
	Sweden	16	18	18	18	23
	Switzerland	13	13	14	14	14
	Turkey	35	37	36	36	38
	United Kingdom	21	22	15	15	22
	United States	15	17	9	9	17
Partners	Albania	51	49	48	48	48
	Argentina	m	m	m	m	m
	Azerbaijan	m	m	m	m	m
	Brazil	45	45	44	44	44
	Bulgaria	39	39	42	42	35
	Colombia	44	44	45	45	45
	Croatia	30	32	33	33	31
	Dubai (UAE)	36	26	29	29	15
	Hong Kong-China	4	4	4	4	4
	Indonesia	49	54	50	50	54
	Jordan	47	46	46	46	46
	Kazakhstan	50	48	49	49	49
	Kyrgyzstan	55	55	55	55	55
	Latvia	m	m	m	m	m
	Liechtenstein	m	m	m	m	m
	Lithuania	34	36	38	38	37
	Macao-China	24	24	24	24	25
	Montenegro	46	50	51	51	51
	Panama	53	53	54	54	52
	Peru	54	52	52	52	53
	Qatar	52	51	53	53	50
	Romania	42	42	40	40	39
	Russian Federation	37	38	37	37	43
	Serbia	m	m	m	m	m
	Shanghai-China	1	1	1	1	1
	Singapore	m	m	m	m	m
	Chinese Taipei	20	19	22	22	20
	Thailand	m	m	m	m	m
	Trinidad and Tobago	43	43	43	43	42
	Tunisia	48	47	47	47	47
	Uruguay	40	41	41	41	40

StatLink ▬▬▬ http://dx.doi.org/10.1787/888932343285

[Part 1/1]

Table I.3.1 Percentage of students at each proficiency level on the mathematics scale

	Below Level 1 (below 357.77 score points)		Level 1 (from 357.77 to less than 420.07 score points)		Level 2 (from 420.07 to less than 482.38 score points)		Level 3 (from 482.38 to less than 544.68 score points)		Level 4 (from 544.68 to less than 606.99 score points)		Level 5 (from 606.99 to less than 669.30 score points)		Level 6 (above 669.30 score points)	
	%	S.E.	%	S.E.	%	S.E.	%	S.E.	%	S.E.	%	S.E.	%	S.E.
Australia	5.1	(0.3)	10.8	(0.5)	20.3	(0.6)	25.8	(0.5)	21.7	(0.6)	11.9	(0.5)	4.5	(0.6)
Austria	7.8	(0.7)	15.4	(0.9)	21.2	(0.9)	23.0	(0.9)	19.6	(0.9)	9.9	(0.7)	3.0	(0.3)
Belgium	7.7	(0.6)	11.3	(0.5)	17.5	(0.7)	21.8	(0.7)	21.3	(0.8)	14.6	(0.6)	5.8	(0.4)
Canada	3.1	(0.3)	8.3	(0.4)	18.8	(0.5)	26.5	(0.9)	25.0	(0.7)	13.9	(0.5)	4.4	(0.3)
Chile	21.7	(1.2)	29.4	(1.1)	27.3	(1.0)	14.8	(1.0)	5.6	(0.6)	1.2	(0.3)	0.1	(0.1)
Czech Republic	7.0	(0.8)	15.3	(0.8)	24.2	(1.0)	24.4	(1.1)	17.4	(0.8)	8.5	(0.6)	3.2	(0.4)
Denmark	4.9	(0.5)	12.1	(0.8)	23.0	(0.9)	27.4	(1.1)	21.0	(0.9)	9.1	(0.8)	2.5	(0.5)
Estonia	3.0	(0.4)	9.6	(0.7)	22.7	(0.9)	29.9	(0.9)	22.7	(0.9)	9.8	(0.8)	2.2	(0.4)
Finland	1.7	(0.3)	6.1	(0.5)	15.6	(0.8)	27.1	(1.0)	27.8	(0.9)	16.7	(0.8)	4.9	(0.5)
France	9.5	(0.9)	13.1	(1.1)	19.9	(0.9)	23.8	(1.1)	20.1	(1.0)	10.4	(0.7)	3.3	(0.5)
Germany	6.4	(0.6)	12.2	(0.7)	18.8	(0.9)	23.1	(0.9)	21.7	(0.9)	13.2	(0.9)	4.6	(0.5)
Greece	11.3	(1.2)	19.1	(1.0)	26.4	(1.2)	24.0	(1.1)	13.6	(0.8)	4.9	(0.6)	0.8	(0.2)
Hungary	8.1	(1.0)	14.2	(0.9)	23.2	(1.2)	26.0	(1.2)	18.4	(1.0)	8.1	(0.8)	2.0	(0.5)
Iceland	5.7	(0.4)	11.3	(0.5)	21.3	(0.9)	27.3	(0.9)	20.9	(0.9)	10.5	(0.7)	3.1	(0.4)
Ireland	7.3	(0.6)	13.6	(0.7)	24.5	(1.1)	28.6	(1.2)	19.4	(0.9)	5.8	(0.6)	0.9	(0.2)
Israel	20.5	(1.2)	18.9	(0.9)	22.5	(0.9)	20.1	(0.9)	12.0	(0.7)	4.7	(0.5)	1.2	(0.3)
Italy	9.1	(0.4)	15.9	(0.5)	24.2	(0.6)	24.6	(0.5)	17.3	(0.6)	7.4	(0.4)	1.6	(0.1)
Japan	4.0	(0.6)	8.5	(0.6)	17.4	(0.9)	25.7	(1.1)	23.5	(1.0)	14.7	(0.9)	6.2	(0.6)
Korea	1.9	(0.5)	6.2	(0.7)	15.6	(1.0)	24.4	(1.2)	26.3	(1.3)	17.7	(1.0)	7.8	(1.0)
Luxembourg	9.6	(0.5)	14.4	(0.6)	22.7	(0.7)	23.1	(1.0)	19.0	(0.8)	9.0	(0.6)	2.3	(0.4)
Mexico	21.9	(0.8)	28.9	(0.6)	28.3	(0.6)	15.6	(0.6)	4.7	(0.4)	0.7	(0.1)	0.0	(0.0)
Netherlands	2.8	(0.6)	10.6	(1.3)	19.0	(1.4)	23.9	(1.0)	23.9	(1.2)	15.4	(1.2)	4.4	(0.5)
New Zealand	5.3	(0.5)	10.2	(0.5)	19.1	(0.8)	24.4	(0.9)	22.2	(1.0)	13.6	(0.7)	5.3	(0.5)
Norway	5.5	(0.5)	12.7	(0.8)	24.3	(0.9)	27.5	(1.0)	19.7	(0.9)	8.4	(0.6)	1.8	(0.3)
Poland	6.1	(0.5)	14.4	(0.6)	24.0	(0.9)	26.1	(0.8)	19.0	(0.8)	8.2	(0.6)	2.2	(0.4)
Portugal	8.4	(0.6)	15.3	(0.8)	23.9	(0.9)	25.0	(1.0)	17.7	(0.8)	7.7	(0.6)	1.9	(0.3)
Slovak Republic	7.0	(0.7)	14.0	(0.8)	23.2	(1.1)	25.0	(1.5)	18.1	(1.2)	9.1	(0.7)	3.6	(0.6)
Slovenia	6.5	(0.4)	13.8	(0.6)	22.5	(0.7)	23.9	(0.7)	19.0	(0.8)	10.3	(0.6)	3.9	(0.4)
Spain	9.1	(0.5)	14.6	(0.6)	23.9	(0.6)	26.6	(0.6)	17.7	(0.6)	6.7	(0.4)	1.3	(0.2)
Sweden	7.5	(0.6)	13.6	(0.7)	23.4	(0.8)	25.2	(0.8)	19.0	(0.9)	8.9	(0.6)	2.5	(0.3)
Switzerland	4.5	(0.4)	9.0	(0.6)	15.9	(0.6)	23.0	(0.9)	23.5	(0.8)	16.3	(0.8)	7.8	(0.7)
Turkey	17.7	(1.3)	24.5	(1.1)	25.2	(1.2)	17.4	(1.1)	9.6	(0.9)	4.4	(0.9)	1.3	(0.5)
United Kingdom	6.2	(0.5)	14.0	(0.7)	24.9	(0.9)	27.2	(1.1)	17.9	(1.0)	8.1	(0.6)	1.8	(0.3)
United States	8.1	(0.7)	15.3	(1.0)	24.4	(1.0)	25.2	(1.0)	17.1	(0.9)	8.0	(0.8)	1.9	(0.5)
OECD total	9.3	(0.2)	15.5	(0.3)	22.7	(0.3)	23.5	(0.2)	17.3	(0.3)	8.9	(0.2)	2.8	(0.2)
OECD average	8.0	(0.1)	14.0	(0.1)	22.0	(0.2)	24.3	(0.2)	18.9	(0.2)	9.6	(0.1)	3.1	(0.1)
Albania	40.5	(1.8)	27.2	(1.2)	20.2	(1.3)	9.1	(0.8)	2.6	(0.6)	0.4	(0.2)	0.0	(0.0)
Argentina	37.2	(1.8)	26.4	(1.1)	20.8	(1.1)	10.9	(0.9)	3.9	(0.7)	0.8	(0.3)	0.1	(0.1)
Azerbaijan	11.5	(1.0)	33.8	(1.2)	35.3	(1.3)	14.8	(1.0)	3.6	(0.5)	0.9	(0.3)	0.2	(0.1)
Brazil	38.1	(1.3)	31.0	(0.9)	19.0	(0.7)	8.1	(0.6)	3.0	(0.3)	0.7	(0.2)	0.1	(0.1)
Bulgaria	24.5	(1.9)	22.7	(1.1)	23.4	(1.1)	17.5	(1.4)	8.2	(0.9)	3.0	(0.7)	0.8	(0.4)
Colombia	38.8	(2.0)	31.6	(1.3)	20.3	(1.3)	7.5	(0.7)	1.6	(0.3)	0.1	(0.1)	0.0	(0.0)
Croatia	12.4	(0.8)	20.8	(0.9)	26.7	(0.8)	22.7	(1.0)	12.5	(0.8)	4.3	(0.5)	0.6	(0.2)
Dubai (UAE)	17.6	(0.5)	21.2	(0.6)	23.0	(0.8)	19.6	(0.6)	12.1	(0.6)	5.3	(0.4)	1.2	(0.2)
Hong Kong-China	2.6	(0.4)	6.2	(0.5)	13.2	(0.7)	21.9	(0.8)	25.4	(0.9)	19.9	(0.8)	10.8	(0.8)
Indonesia	43.5	(2.2)	33.1	(1.5)	16.9	(1.1)	5.4	(0.9)	0.9	(0.3)	0.1	(0.0)	0.0	c
Jordan	35.4	(1.7)	29.9	(1.2)	22.9	(1.0)	9.5	(0.9)	2.1	(0.4)	0.3	(0.2)	0.0	(0.0)
Kazakhstan	29.6	(1.3)	29.6	(0.9)	23.5	(0.9)	12.0	(0.8)	4.2	(0.5)	0.9	(0.3)	0.3	(0.2)
Kyrgyzstan	64.8	(1.4)	21.8	(1.0)	9.3	(0.8)	3.3	(0.5)	0.7	(0.2)	0.0	(0.0)	0.0	c
Latvia	5.8	(0.7)	16.7	(1.1)	27.2	(1.0)	28.2	(1.1)	16.4	(1.0)	5.1	(0.5)	0.6	(0.1)
Liechtenstein	3.0	(1.0)	6.5	(1.6)	15.0	(2.2)	26.2	(2.3)	31.2	(3.3)	13.0	(2.4)	5.0	(1.4)
Lithuania	9.0	(0.8)	17.3	(0.8)	26.1	(1.1)	25.3	(1.0)	15.4	(0.8)	5.7	(0.6)	1.3	(0.3)
Macao-China	2.8	(0.3)	8.2	(0.5)	19.6	(0.6)	27.8	(0.9)	24.5	(0.8)	12.8	(0.4)	4.3	(0.3)
Montenegro	29.6	(1.1)	28.8	(1.0)	24.6	(1.0)	12.2	(0.7)	3.8	(0.4)	0.9	(0.2)	0.1	(0.1)
Panama	51.5	(2.9)	27.3	(1.7)	13.9	(1.5)	5.6	(0.9)	1.4	(0.4)	0.4	(0.2)	0.0	(0.0)
Peru	47.6	(1.8)	25.9	(1.2)	16.9	(1.3)	6.8	(0.7)	2.1	(0.4)	0.5	(0.2)	0.1	(0.1)
Qatar	51.1	(0.6)	22.7	(0.6)	13.1	(0.5)	7.2	(0.3)	4.2	(0.3)	1.5	(0.2)	0.3	(0.1)
Romania	19.5	(1.4)	27.5	(1.1)	28.6	(1.4)	17.3	(1.0)	5.9	(0.8)	1.2	(0.3)	0.1	(0.1)
Russian Federation	9.5	(0.9)	19.0	(1.2)	28.5	(1.0)	25.0	(1.0)	12.7	(0.9)	4.3	(0.6)	1.0	(0.3)
Serbia	17.6	(1.0)	22.9	(0.8)	26.5	(1.1)	19.9	(1.0)	9.5	(0.6)	2.9	(0.4)	0.6	(0.2)
Shanghai-China	1.4	(0.3)	3.4	(0.4)	8.7	(0.6)	15.2	(0.8)	20.8	(0.8)	23.8	(0.8)	26.6	(1.2)
Singapore	3.0	(0.3)	6.8	(0.6)	13.1	(0.6)	18.7	(0.8)	22.8	(0.6)	20.0	(0.9)	15.6	(0.6)
Chinese Taipei	4.2	(0.5)	8.6	(0.6)	15.5	(0.7)	20.9	(0.9)	22.2	(0.9)	17.2	(0.9)	11.3	(1.2)
Thailand	22.1	(1.4)	30.4	(0.9)	27.3	(1.1)	14.0	(0.9)	4.9	(0.6)	1.0	(0.3)	0.3	(0.2)
Trinidad and Tobago	30.1	(0.8)	23.1	(1.0)	21.2	(0.9)	15.4	(0.6)	7.7	(0.4)	2.1	(0.2)	0.3	(0.1)
Tunisia	43.4	(1.7)	30.2	(1.5)	18.7	(0.9)	6.1	(0.7)	1.3	(0.4)	0.2	(0.2)	0.0	(0.0)
Uruguay	22.9	(1.2)	24.6	(1.1)	25.1	(1.0)	17.0	(0.7)	7.9	(0.5)	2.1	(0.3)	0.3	(0.1)

OECD (rows Australia–United States); *Partners* (rows Albania–Uruguay)

StatLink ⌨ http://dx.doi.org/10.1787/888932343285

[Part 1/2]

Table I.3.2 **Percentage of students at each proficiency level on the mathematics scale, by gender**

		Below Level 1 (below 357.77 score points)		Level 1 (from 357.77 to less than 420.07 score points)		Level 2 (from 420.07 to less than 482.38 score points)		Level 3 (from 482.38 to less than 544.68 score points)		Level 4 (from 544.68 to less than 606.99 score points)		Level 5 (from 606.99 to less than 669.30 score points)		Level 6 (above 669.30 score points)	
		%	S.E.	%	S.E.	%	S.E.	%	S.E.	%	S.E.	%	S.E.	%	S.E.
OECD	Australia	5.2	(0.4)	10.2	(0.6)	19.1	(0.8)	24.8	(0.8)	22.2	(0.8)	13.2	(0.7)	5.4	(0.7)
	Austria	6.4	(0.9)	14.9	(1.2)	19.9	(1.1)	22.6	(1.1)	20.0	(1.2)	11.8	(1.0)	4.3	(0.5)
	Belgium	6.0	(1.0)	10.8	(0.8)	17.0	(0.9)	20.7	(0.9)	21.1	(1.1)	16.6	(1.0)	7.7	(0.7)
	Canada	3.1	(0.4)	7.8	(0.6)	17.8	(0.7)	25.1	(1.1)	25.1	(1.0)	15.6	(0.7)	5.5	(0.4)
	Chile	18.4	(1.3)	27.4	(1.4)	28.0	(1.4)	17.3	(1.4)	7.1	(1.0)	1.6	(0.5)	0.2	(0.2)
	Czech Republic	6.8	(1.0)	14.9	(1.3)	24.4	(1.2)	24.4	(1.6)	17.2	(1.1)	8.5	(0.9)	3.9	(0.6)
	Denmark	3.9	(0.5)	10.8	(0.8)	21.7	(1.1)	28.1	(1.6)	21.9	(1.2)	10.4	(1.1)	3.1	(0.7)
	Estonia	2.7	(0.5)	9.2	(0.8)	21.6	(1.4)	29.6	(1.6)	23.5	(1.2)	11.0	(0.8)	2.4	(0.6)
	Finland	1.7	(0.3)	6.4	(0.7)	16.1	(1.2)	25.8	(1.3)	26.5	(1.1)	17.5	(1.0)	5.9	(0.7)
	France	9.2	(1.0)	12.4	(1.1)	17.9	(1.1)	22.3	(1.3)	21.0	(1.1)	12.7	(1.1)	4.5	(0.6)
	Germany	5.6	(0.8)	11.6	(0.9)	17.7	(1.2)	22.9	(1.1)	21.4	(1.3)	14.8	(1.0)	6.0	(0.6)
	Greece	10.9	(1.6)	17.5	(1.3)	24.7	(1.7)	23.9	(1.5)	15.2	(1.2)	6.6	(0.8)	1.2	(0.3)
	Hungary	8.0	(1.1)	13.7	(1.3)	22.0	(1.5)	24.7	(1.5)	19.4	(1.4)	9.4	(1.0)	2.8	(0.6)
	Iceland	6.3	(0.7)	11.6	(0.9)	19.7	(1.3)	26.0	(1.5)	21.3	(1.3)	11.6	(1.2)	3.6	(0.7)
	Ireland	7.7	(0.9)	12.9	(1.1)	22.8	(1.4)	27.4	(1.5)	21.1	(1.2)	6.9	(0.8)	1.2	(0.4)
	Israel	21.8	(1.6)	17.6	(1.1)	19.7	(1.2)	19.4	(1.0)	13.7	(0.9)	6.1	(0.8)	1.7	(0.5)
	Italy	8.6	(0.6)	14.9	(0.6)	22.7	(0.7)	23.7	(0.7)	18.6	(0.8)	9.2	(0.6)	2.4	(0.2)
	Japan	4.3	(0.9)	8.6	(1.0)	16.7	(1.3)	23.0	(1.2)	23.3	(1.3)	16.5	(1.2)	7.6	(1.1)
	Korea	2.5	(0.8)	6.6	(1.2)	14.8	(1.4)	23.5	(1.6)	25.1	(1.7)	18.5	(1.4)	9.0	(1.4)
	Luxembourg	9.3	(0.8)	12.9	(1.0)	20.4	(1.4)	22.5	(1.1)	20.2	(1.1)	11.3	(1.0)	3.5	(0.6)
	Mexico	20.1	(0.9)	27.4	(0.8)	28.4	(0.8)	17.1	(0.7)	5.9	(0.5)	0.9	(0.2)	0.1	(0.0)
	Netherlands	2.1	(0.5)	9.1	(1.5)	18.0	(1.6)	24.1	(1.4)	23.8	(1.6)	17.0	(1.4)	5.9	(0.7)
	New Zealand	5.6	(0.8)	10.1	(1.1)	18.2	(1.3)	22.6	(1.2)	22.0	(1.2)	14.8	(1.3)	6.6	(0.6)
	Norway	5.9	(0.6)	12.1	(1.0)	23.6	(1.0)	26.9	(1.2)	19.9	(1.0)	9.4	(0.7)	2.1	(0.5)
	Poland	6.7	(0.7)	14.5	(1.1)	22.7	(1.1)	25.1	(1.2)	19.3	(1.0)	8.9	(0.8)	2.8	(0.5)
	Portugal	8.0	(0.7)	14.6	(1.2)	22.3	(1.3)	24.8	(1.6)	18.9	(1.0)	8.7	(0.8)	2.6	(0.5)
	Slovak Republic	7.0	(0.8)	14.4	(1.1)	23.0	(1.2)	24.3	(2.3)	17.4	(1.8)	9.3	(0.9)	4.5	(0.8)
	Slovenia	7.0	(0.5)	13.9	(0.8)	21.8	(0.9)	23.0	(0.9)	19.2	(1.1)	11.0	(1.0)	4.1	(0.6)
	Spain	7.9	(0.6)	13.5	(0.7)	22.6	(0.8)	26.3	(0.9)	19.5	(0.8)	8.4	(0.5)	1.8	(0.2)
	Sweden	8.5	(0.8)	12.9	(0.9)	23.3	(1.0)	25.2	(1.3)	18.3	(1.2)	9.1	(0.8)	2.8	(0.5)
	Switzerland	3.9	(0.5)	8.4	(0.7)	14.5	(0.7)	21.5	(1.1)	23.6	(1.2)	17.9	(1.0)	10.1	(1.0)
	Turkey	16.6	(1.4)	23.8	(1.4)	24.9	(1.2)	17.8	(1.2)	10.4	(1.1)	5.0	(1.1)	1.5	(0.6)
	United Kingdom	5.3	(0.6)	12.2	(0.9)	22.8	(1.1)	27.0	(1.3)	20.0	(1.4)	10.3	(1.0)	2.5	(0.4)
	United States	6.8	(0.7)	13.8	(1.0)	22.9	(1.1)	25.2	(1.3)	19.5	(1.2)	9.3	(1.0)	2.5	(0.6)
	OECD total	8.4	(0.2)	14.6	(0.4)	21.6	(0.4)	23.2	(0.3)	18.4	(0.4)	10.2	(0.3)	3.6	(0.2)
	OECD average	7.6	(0.1)	13.3	(0.2)	21.0	(0.2)	23.8	(0.2)	19.5	(0.2)	10.9	(0.2)	3.9	(0.1)
Partners	Albania	43.5	(2.2)	25.5	(1.5)	18.8	(1.7)	9.0	(1.0)	2.6	(0.9)	0.5	(0.2)	0.0	(0.0)
	Argentina	34.9	(2.0)	26.3	(1.5)	21.0	(1.2)	11.5	(1.2)	5.2	(1.0)	1.0	(0.4)	0.1	(0.1)
	Azerbaijan	10.5	(1.2)	31.6	(1.5)	36.5	(1.6)	16.6	(1.3)	3.8	(0.6)	0.8	(0.3)	0.2	(0.2)
	Brazil	34.2	(1.5)	31.6	(1.3)	20.4	(1.1)	9.0	(0.7)	3.7	(0.4)	1.0	(0.3)	0.1	(0.1)
	Bulgaria	25.5	(2.1)	22.7	(1.7)	22.6	(1.3)	16.9	(1.5)	8.2	(1.1)	3.3	(0.7)	0.9	(0.5)
	Colombia	30.6	(2.3)	31.8	(1.5)	24.0	(1.7)	10.8	(1.2)	2.5	(0.5)	0.2	(0.1)	0.0	(0.0)
	Croatia	11.6	(0.9)	20.2	(1.2)	25.7	(1.1)	22.7	(1.2)	13.6	(1.1)	5.3	(0.7)	0.8	(0.3)
	Dubai (UAE)	19.3	(0.7)	20.5	(0.9)	20.8	(0.8)	18.2	(0.9)	13.1	(0.7)	6.4	(0.6)	1.6	(0.3)
	Hong Kong-China	2.6	(0.6)	5.7	(0.8)	12.4	(1.2)	20.3	(1.2)	25.0	(1.1)	21.2	(1.2)	12.7	(1.3)
	Indonesia	44.5	(2.6)	32.6	(2.2)	15.8	(1.3)	5.9	(1.0)	1.1	(0.4)	0.1	(0.1)	0.0	c
	Jordan	35.1	(2.4)	29.8	(1.9)	23.2	(1.7)	9.4	(1.1)	2.2	(0.6)	0.3	(0.2)	0.0	(0.0)
	Kazakhstan	30.2	(1.5)	29.1	(1.3)	22.7	(1.1)	12.2	(0.9)	4.6	(0.6)	0.9	(0.3)	0.3	(0.2)
	Kyrgyzstan	65.7	(1.8)	20.7	(1.4)	9.3	(0.8)	3.5	(0.7)	0.8	(0.4)	0.1	(0.1)	0.0	c
	Latvia	*6.5	(0.9)	16.7	(1.5)	26.5	(1.6)	27.0	(1.3)	16.8	(1.2)	5.8	(0.8)	0.8	(0.3)
	Liechtenstein	1.8	(1.4)	5.9	(2.6)	13.2	(3.0)	24.9	(3.8)	32.7	(4.9)	14.8	(4.1)	6.7	(2.0)
	Lithuania	9.9	(1.1)	18.2	(1.1)	25.9	(1.7)	24.2	(1.4)	14.7	(1.0)	5.8	(0.6)	1.3	(0.3)
	Macao-China	2.8	(0.4)	7.8	(0.6)	18.3	(0.9)	26.5	(1.2)	24.9	(0.9)	14.3	(0.7)	5.4	(0.5)
	Montenegro	28.0	(1.3)	27.6	(1.5)	25.3	(1.4)	13.0	(1.2)	4.9	(0.5)	1.3	(0.3)	0.1	(0.1)
	Panama	49.9	(3.0)	29.3	(2.3)	13.9	(1.6)	4.9	(1.0)	1.4	(0.5)	0.5	(0.3)	0.0	(0.1)
	Peru	44.5	(2.1)	26.0	(1.3)	18.2	(1.6)	7.7	(0.9)	2.6	(0.6)	0.8	(0.3)	0.2	(0.1)
	Qatar	52.5	(0.8)	21.0	(0.9)	12.3	(0.7)	7.3	(0.5)	4.6	(0.4)	1.9	(0.3)	0.4	(0.1)
	Romania	20.0	(1.8)	26.9	(1.2)	27.3	(1.7)	17.6	(1.6)	6.6	(1.1)	1.6	(0.5)	0.1	(0.2)
	Russian Federation	10.1	(1.2)	18.2	(1.5)	28.1	(1.3)	25.0	(1.3)	13.0	(0.9)	4.5	(0.6)	1.1	(0.4)
	Serbia	16.8	(1.3)	22.4	(1.4)	25.4	(1.6)	19.6	(1.3)	11.0	(1.0)	3.9	(0.7)	0.9	(0.2)
	Shanghai-China	1.6	(0.4)	3.9	(0.6)	8.9	(0.9)	15.4	(1.1)	19.9	(1.2)	23.2	(1.1)	27.1	(1.4)
	Singapore	3.4	(0.4)	6.8	(0.6)	12.3	(0.8)	18.0	(1.0)	22.6	(0.9)	20.0	(1.2)	16.9	(1.0)
	Chinese Taipei	4.7	(0.7)	8.6	(0.8)	15.1	(1.0)	19.2	(1.0)	21.5	(1.2)	18.4	(1.3)	12.6	(1.6)
	Thailand	22.7	(1.6)	28.7	(1.3)	26.9	(1.6)	14.9	(1.2)	5.6	(0.8)	1.0	(0.3)	0.3	(0.2)
	Trinidad and Tobago	31.8	(1.3)	23.4	(1.8)	20.5	(1.2)	14.7	(1.0)	7.3	(0.6)	2.1	(0.5)	0.2	(0.2)
	Tunisia	41.0	(1.8)	28.3	(1.6)	20.4	(1.3)	8.0	(1.1)	1.8	(0.6)	0.4	(0.3)	0.0	(0.1)
	Uruguay	21.6	(1.3)	23.0	(1.3)	24.9	(1.6)	18.1	(1.0)	9.2	(0.8)	2.6	(0.5)	0.5	(0.2)

StatLink http://dx.doi.org/10.1787/888932343285

[Part 2/2]

Table I.3.2 **Percentage of students at each proficiency level on the mathematics scale, by gender**

	Girls – Proficiency levels												
	Below Level 1 (below 357.77 score points)		Level 1 (from 357.77 to less than 420.07 score points)		Level 2 (from 420.07 to less than 482.38 score points)		Level 3 (from 482.38 to less than 544.68 score points)		Level 4 (from 544.68 to less than 606.99 score points)		Level 5 (from 606.99 to less than 669.30 score points)		Level 6 (above 669.30 score points)	
	%	S.E.	%	S.E.	%	S.E.	%	S.E.	%	S.E.	%	S.E.	%	S.E.
OECD														
Australia	5.0	(0.4)	11.3	(0.7)	21.4	(0.7)	26.7	(0.7)	21.2	(0.7)	10.8	(0.6)	3.6	(0.5)
Austria	9.1	(1.1)	16.0	(1.3)	22.4	(1.4)	23.5	(1.3)	19.2	(1.2)	8.1	(0.9)	1.8	(0.4)
Belgium	9.5	(0.9)	11.9	(0.7)	17.9	(0.9)	22.9	(0.8)	21.5	(1.0)	12.4	(0.7)	3.9	(0.5)
Canada	3.2	(0.4)	8.9	(0.5)	19.8	(0.6)	27.9	(1.1)	24.8	(1.0)	12.2	(0.6)	3.3	(0.3)
Chile	25.1	(1.6)	31.4	(1.4)	26.5	(1.2)	12.1	(1.2)	4.1	(0.7)	0.8	(0.2)	0.0	(0.0)
Czech Republic	7.3	(1.0)	15.8	(1.1)	24.0	(1.2)	24.4	(1.4)	17.7	(1.1)	8.4	(0.6)	2.4	(0.4)
Denmark	6.0	(0.7)	13.4	(1.1)	24.3	(1.3)	26.6	(1.5)	20.1	(1.2)	7.7	(0.8)	1.9	(0.4)
Estonia	3.4	(0.7)	10.1	(1.0)	23.9	(1.7)	30.3	(1.8)	21.8	(1.2)	8.6	(1.1)	2.0	(0.5)
Finland	1.7	(0.3)	5.8	(0.7)	15.0	(0.9)	28.4	(1.2)	29.2	(1.3)	16.0	(1.0)	3.9	(0.6)
France	9.7	(1.0)	13.7	(1.4)	21.7	(1.3)	25.3	(1.6)	19.3	(1.5)	8.2	(1.1)	2.1	(0.5)
Germany	7.3	(0.8)	12.9	(1.0)	19.8	(1.0)	23.3	(1.2)	22.0	(1.1)	11.6	(1.2)	3.2	(0.5)
Greece	11.6	(1.3)	20.5	(1.3)	28.0	(1.4)	24.1	(1.1)	12.0	(0.9)	3.3	(0.6)	0.5	(0.2)
Hungary	8.2	(1.3)	14.7	(1.4)	24.5	(1.5)	27.3	(1.5)	17.3	(1.3)	6.9	(0.8)	1.1	(0.3)
Iceland	5.1	(0.7)	11.0	(0.8)	22.8	(1.0)	28.6	(1.3)	20.5	(1.5)	9.4	(0.8)	2.7	(0.5)
Ireland	6.8	(0.7)	14.2	(1.0)	26.3	(1.3)	29.8	(1.6)	17.7	(1.3)	4.6	(0.6)	0.5	(0.2)
Israel	19.3	(1.2)	20.2	(1.2)	25.3	(1.1)	20.7	(1.2)	10.4	(0.9)	3.3	(0.5)	0.6	(0.3)
Italy	9.5	(0.6)	16.9	(0.7)	25.7	(0.7)	25.6	(0.7)	16.0	(0.7)	5.5	(0.4)	0.8	(0.1)
Japan	3.6	(0.6)	8.4	(1.0)	18.2	(1.3)	28.6	(1.5)	23.7	(1.3)	12.7	(1.1)	4.7	(1.0)
Korea	1.3	(0.4)	5.7	(0.7)	16.5	(1.4)	25.4	(1.5)	27.7	(1.5)	16.9	(1.3)	6.5	(1.0)
Luxembourg	9.8	(1.0)	15.9	(0.9)	25.1	(1.0)	23.7	(1.6)	17.7	(1.1)	6.6	(0.6)	1.2	(0.3)
Mexico	23.7	(0.9)	30.3	(0.7)	28.1	(0.7)	14.0	(0.6)	3.4	(0.3)	0.4	(0.1)	0.0	(0.0)
Netherlands	3.5	(0.9)	12.1	(1.6)	19.9	(1.6)	23.7	(1.5)	24.1	(1.4)	13.9	(1.4)	2.9	(0.5)
New Zealand	4.9	(0.6)	10.2	(1.0)	20.0	(1.2)	26.2	(1.2)	22.5	(1.2)	12.4	(1.1)	3.8	(0.6)
Norway	5.1	(0.6)	13.2	(1.0)	25.1	(1.4)	28.2	(1.3)	19.5	(1.1)	7.4	(0.8)	1.5	(0.4)
Poland	5.6	(0.7)	14.3	(1.1)	25.3	(1.2)	27.1	(1.4)	18.7	(1.3)	7.5	(0.8)	1.5	(0.4)
Portugal	8.7	(0.7)	16.0	(0.9)	25.5	(1.1)	25.2	(1.1)	16.6	(1.0)	6.8	(0.7)	1.2	(0.3)
Slovak Republic	7.0	(0.8)	13.7	(1.2)	23.3	(1.6)	25.7	(1.4)	18.8	(1.2)	8.9	(0.9)	2.7	(0.6)
Slovenia	6.0	(0.7)	13.7	(1.2)	23.1	(1.1)	24.9	(1.1)	18.9	(1.1)	9.7	(0.9)	3.6	(0.6)
Spain	10.4	(0.7)	15.7	(0.8)	25.4	(0.9)	26.9	(0.8)	15.8	(0.8)	5.0	(0.4)	0.8	(0.2)
Sweden	6.5	(1.0)	14.3	(1.0)	23.5	(1.4)	25.3	(1.5)	19.6	(0.9)	8.7	(0.8)	2.2	(0.5)
Switzerland	5.1	(0.5)	9.6	(0.8)	17.4	(0.9)	24.5	(1.2)	23.3	(1.0)	14.6	(1.0)	5.5	(0.7)
Turkey	18.9	(1.9)	25.2	(1.5)	25.5	(1.6)	17.0	(1.4)	8.8	(1.1)	3.8	(0.9)	1.0	(0.4)
United Kingdom	7.2	(0.6)	15.6	(1.1)	26.9	(1.2)	27.4	(1.4)	15.8	(1.2)	6.0	(0.7)	1.1	(0.3)
United States	9.5	(1.0)	16.8	(1.4)	26.0	(1.2)	25.2	(1.3)	14.5	(1.1)	6.7	(0.9)	1.2	(0.5)
OECD total	10.1	(0.3)	16.5	(0.5)	23.9	(0.4)	23.9	(0.4)	16.2	(0.3)	7.5	(0.3)	2.0	(0.2)
OECD average	8.4	(0.2)	14.7	(0.2)	23.1	(0.2)	24.9	(0.2)	18.4	(0.2)	8.4	(0.1)	2.2	(0.1)
Partners														
Albania	37.3	(1.9)	29.0	(1.5)	21.6	(1.5)	9.1	(1.0)	2.7	(0.5)	0.3	(0.2)	0.0	c
Argentina	39.1	(2.1)	26.5	(1.7)	20.6	(1.4)	10.3	(1.1)	2.8	(0.6)	0.6	(0.2)	0.1	(0.1)
Azerbaijan	12.5	(1.1)	36.1	(1.6)	34.1	(1.8)	12.9	(1.4)	3.3	(0.6)	0.9	(0.4)	0.2	(0.1)
Brazil	41.6	(1.5)	30.4	(1.0)	17.7	(0.8)	7.4	(0.8)	2.3	(0.4)	0.5	(0.2)	0.0	(0.0)
Bulgaria	23.3	(2.1)	22.6	(1.3)	24.4	(1.4)	18.1	(1.6)	8.2	(1.0)	2.8	(0.9)	0.6	(0.3)
Colombia	46.3	(2.1)	31.4	(1.6)	16.9	(1.6)	4.5	(0.7)	0.8	(0.3)	0.0	(0.0)	0.0	c
Croatia	13.2	(1.3)	21.4	(1.4)	27.9	(1.2)	22.6	(1.4)	11.2	(1.1)	3.2	(0.6)	0.4	(0.2)
Dubai (UAE)	15.9	(0.8)	22.0	(1.2)	25.3	(1.2)	21.0	(0.9)	11.0	(0.9)	4.0	(0.5)	0.8	(0.3)
Hong Kong-China	2.5	(0.5)	6.7	(0.7)	14.2	(1.0)	23.8	(1.2)	25.8	(1.2)	18.4	(1.1)	8.6	(0.9)
Indonesia	42.6	(2.6)	33.7	(2.2)	18.0	(1.6)	5.0	(1.0)	0.8	(0.3)	0.0	(0.0)	0.0	c
Jordan	35.7	(2.4)	29.9	(1.7)	22.6	(1.4)	9.5	(1.4)	2.0	(0.5)	0.2	(0.2)	0.0	c
Kazakhstan	29.0	(1.7)	30.0	(1.4)	24.3	(1.3)	11.9	(1.1)	3.8	(0.5)	0.9	(0.4)	0.2	(0.2)
Kyrgyzstan	64.1	(1.7)	22.8	(1.3)	9.4	(1.0)	3.1	(0.5)	0.7	(0.2)	0.0	(0.0)	0.0	c
Latvia	5.2	(0.9)	16.8	(1.4)	27.9	(1.6)	29.3	(1.4)	15.9	(1.3)	4.4	(0.6)	0.4	(0.2)
Liechtenstein	4.2	(1.6)	7.3	(2.6)	17.0	(4.1)	27.8	(3.7)	29.6	(4.4)	11.0	(2.8)	3.1	(1.7)
Lithuania	8.1	(0.9)	16.3	(1.2)	26.3	(1.1)	26.4	(1.2)	16.0	(1.0)	5.6	(0.9)	1.3	(0.4)
Macao-China	2.8	(0.3)	8.5	(0.7)	20.9	(0.9)	29.1	(1.1)	24.1	(1.1)	11.4	(0.8)	3.2	(0.4)
Montenegro	31.4	(1.4)	30.0	(1.3)	23.9	(1.2)	11.4	(0.9)	2.6	(0.4)	0.5	(0.2)	0.0	(0.1)
Panama	53.0	(3.6)	25.3	(2.2)	13.8	(1.8)	6.2	(1.3)	1.4	(0.4)	0.2	(0.2)	0.0	(0.1)
Peru	50.9	(2.1)	25.8	(1.5)	15.6	(1.2)	6.0	(0.8)	1.5	(0.4)	0.3	(0.1)	0.0	(0.1)
Qatar	49.6	(0.6)	24.5	(0.7)	13.9	(0.6)	7.1	(0.4)	3.7	(0.3)	1.0	(0.2)	0.2	(0.1)
Romania	19.1	(1.6)	28.1	(1.9)	29.8	(1.5)	16.9	(1.3)	5.2	(1.0)	0.8	(0.4)	0.0	(0.1)
Russian Federation	9.0	(0.9)	19.8	(1.2)	28.9	(1.2)	25.0	(1.2)	12.4	(1.1)	4.0	(0.8)	0.8	(0.3)
Serbia	18.5	(1.3)	23.5	(1.2)	27.6	(1.2)	20.3	(1.1)	8.0	(0.7)	1.9	(0.4)	0.3	(0.2)
Shanghai-China	1.3	(0.3)	3.0	(0.5)	8.5	(0.8)	15.0	(1.2)	21.6	(1.0)	24.4	(1.0)	26.2	(1.5)
Singapore	2.6	(0.4)	6.8	(0.8)	13.9	(0.8)	19.4	(1.1)	23.0	(0.9)	20.0	(1.1)	14.3	(0.9)
Chinese Taipei	3.6	(0.5)	8.7	(0.8)	16.0	(1.1)	22.7	(1.5)	22.9	(1.3)	16.1	(1.3)	10.0	(1.6)
Thailand	21.7	(1.5)	31.7	(1.5)	27.6	(1.8)	13.4	(1.1)	4.4	(0.7)	0.9	(0.3)	0.2	(0.2)
Trinidad and Tobago	28.5	(0.8)	22.8	(1.1)	22.0	(1.6)	16.1	(0.9)	8.1	(0.6)	2.1	(0.3)	0.4	(0.2)
Tunisia	45.6	(2.1)	31.8	(2.0)	17.2	(1.3)	4.5	(0.8)	0.9	(0.5)	0.1	(0.1)	0.0	(0.0)
Uruguay	24.1	(1.4)	26.1	(1.5)	25.4	(1.1)	16.0	(1.1)	6.6	(0.7)	1.6	(0.4)	0.2	(0.1)

StatLink http://dx.doi.org/10.1787/888932343285

[Part 1/1]
Table I.3.3 **Mean score, variation and gender differences in student performance on the mathematics scale**

		All students				Gender differences						Percentiles											
		Mean score		Standard deviation		Boys		Girls		Difference (B – G)		5th		10th		25th		75th		90th		95th	
		Mean	S.E.	S.D.	S.E.	Mean score	S.E.	Mean score	S.E.	Score dif.	S.E.	Score	S.E.	Score	S.E.	Score	S.E.	Score	S.E.	Score	S.E.	Score	S.E.
OECD	Australia	514	(2.5)	94	(1.4)	519	(3.0)	509	(2.8)	**10**	(2.9)	357	(3.3)	392	(2.8)	451	(2.5)	580	(3.1)	634	(3.9)	665	(5.0)
	Austria	496	(2.7)	96	(2.0)	506	(3.4)	486	(4.0)	**19**	(5.1)	338	(6.6)	370	(4.4)	425	(3.5)	566	(3.5)	620	(3.5)	650	(3.5)
	Belgium	515	(2.3)	104	(1.8)	526	(3.3)	504	(3.0)	**22**	(4.3)	335	(5.3)	373	(4.9)	444	(3.1)	593	(2.4)	646	(3.0)	675	(3.2)
	Canada	527	(1.6)	88	(1.0)	533	(2.0)	521	(1.7)	**12**	(1.8)	379	(3.0)	413	(2.7)	468	(2.0)	588	(1.9)	638	(2.2)	665	(2.2)
	Chile	421	(3.1)	80	(1.7)	431	(3.7)	410	(3.6)	**21**	(4.1)	293	(4.6)	322	(3.8)	366	(3.1)	473	(4.2)	527	(5.1)	559	(5.8)
	Czech Republic	493	(2.8)	93	(1.8)	495	(3.9)	490	(3.0)	5	(4.1)	342	(5.6)	374	(4.3)	428	(3.5)	557	(3.8)	615	(4.3)	649	(4.7)
	Denmark	503	(2.6)	87	(1.3)	511	(3.0)	495	(2.9)	**16**	(2.7)	358	(4.4)	390	(4.0)	445	(3.1)	564	(3.3)	614	(3.4)	644	(4.6)
	Estonia	512	(2.6)	81	(1.6)	516	(2.9)	508	(2.9)	**9**	(2.6)	378	(6.0)	409	(3.5)	458	(3.7)	567	(2.7)	616	(3.6)	643	(3.6)
	Finland	541	(2.2)	82	(1.1)	542	(2.5)	539	(2.5)	3	(2.6)	399	(4.4)	431	(3.7)	487	(3.0)	599	(2.5)	644	(2.6)	669	(3.6)
	France	497	(3.1)	101	(2.1)	505	(3.8)	489	(3.4)	**16**	(3.8)	321	(5.9)	361	(6.3)	429	(4.8)	570	(3.7)	622	(3.9)	652	(5.4)
	Germany	513	(2.9)	98	(1.7)	520	(3.6)	505	(3.3)	**16**	(3.9)	347	(5.0)	380	(4.7)	443	(4.4)	585	(3.1)	638	(3.5)	666	(3.7)
	Greece	466	(3.9)	89	(2.0)	473	(5.4)	459	(3.3)	**14**	(4.2)	319	(7.3)	352	(5.9)	406	(4.4)	527	(3.6)	580	(4.1)	613	(4.4)
	Hungary	490	(3.5)	92	(2.8)	496	(4.2)	484	(3.9)	**12**	(4.5)	334	(8.4)	370	(7.1)	428	(4.5)	554	(4.5)	608	(5.6)	637	(5.6)
	Iceland	507	(1.4)	91	(1.2)	508	(2.0)	505	(1.9)	3	(2.8)	352	(4.1)	388	(3.4)	447	(2.0)	569	(2.0)	623	(2.8)	652	(3.3)
	Ireland	487	(2.5)	86	(1.6)	491	(3.4)	483	(3.0)	8	(3.9)	338	(5.7)	376	(4.4)	432	(3.1)	548	(2.8)	591	(3.1)	617	(4.3)
	Israel	447	(3.3)	104	(2.4)	451	(4.7)	443	(3.3)	8	(4.7)	272	(6.7)	310	(6.1)	374	(4.6)	520	(4.2)	581	(5.2)	615	(5.2)
	Italy	483	(1.9)	93	(1.7)	490	(2.3)	475	(2.2)	**15**	(2.7)	330	(3.1)	363	(2.4)	420	(1.9)	548	(2.5)	602	(2.5)	632	(2.8)
	Japan	529	(3.3)	94	(2.2)	534	(5.3)	524	(3.9)	9	(6.5)	370	(6.4)	407	(5.4)	468	(4.4)	595	(3.7)	648	(4.8)	677	(5.4)
	Korea	546	(4.0)	89	(2.5)	548	(6.2)	544	(4.5)	3	(7.4)	397	(8.4)	430	(6.8)	486	(5.3)	609	(4.3)	659	(4.6)	689	(6.5)
	Luxembourg	489	(1.2)	98	(1.2)	499	(2.0)	479	(1.3)	**19**	(2.4)	324	(3.9)	360	(3.1)	423	(1.7)	560	(2.2)	613	(2.5)	643	(2.5)
	Mexico	419	(1.8)	79	(1.1)	425	(2.1)	412	(1.9)	**14**	(1.5)	289	(3.2)	318	(2.6)	366	(2.2)	472	(2.1)	520	(2.8)	547	(3.3)
	Netherlands	526	(4.7)	89	(1.7)	534	(4.8)	517	(5.1)	**17**	(2.4)	378	(5.6)	406	(5.6)	460	(6.8)	593	(4.4)	640	(4.4)	665	(3.9)
	New Zealand	519	(2.3)	96	(1.6)	523	(3.2)	515	(2.9)	8	(4.1)	355	(4.9)	392	(4.4)	454	(2.8)	589	(3.1)	642	(3.9)	671	(3.4)
	Norway	498	(2.4)	85	(1.2)	500	(2.7)	495	(2.8)	5	(2.7)	354	(4.1)	387	(3.6)	441	(3.2)	557	(2.9)	608	(3.4)	636	(4.0)
	Poland	495	(2.8)	88	(1.4)	497	(3.0)	493	(3.2)	3	(2.6)	348	(5.2)	380	(3.8)	434	(3.3)	557	(3.2)	609	(4.1)	638	(4.6)
	Portugal	487	(2.9)	91	(1.5)	493	(3.3)	481	(3.1)	**12**	(2.5)	334	(3.8)	367	(3.5)	424	(3.4)	551	(3.4)	605	(4.4)	635	(5.1)
	Slovak Republic	497	(3.1)	96	(2.4)	498	(3.7)	495	(3.4)	3	(3.6)	342	(6.3)	376	(4.7)	432	(3.7)	561	(3.9)	621	(5.4)	654	(6.4)
	Slovenia	501	(1.2)	95	(0.9)	502	(1.8)	501	(1.7)	1	(2.6)	345	(3.6)	379	(2.4)	435	(2.5)	569	(2.3)	628	(3.5)	659	(3.6)
	Spain	483	(2.1)	91	(1.1)	493	(2.3)	474	(2.5)	**19**	(2.2)	328	(4.0)	364	(2.9)	424	(2.5)	546	(2.3)	597	(2.3)	625	(2.9)
	Sweden	494	(2.9)	94	(1.3)	493	(3.1)	495	(3.3)	-2	(2.7)	339	(4.4)	374	(4.2)	432	(3.1)	560	(3.3)	613	(3.9)	643	(4.1)
	Switzerland	534	(3.3)	99	(1.6)	544	(3.7)	524	(3.4)	**20**	(3.0)	363	(4.8)	401	(3.6)	468	(4.2)	604	(3.9)	658	(4.1)	689	(4.8)
	Turkey	445	(4.4)	93	(3.0)	451	(4.6)	440	(5.6)	**11**	(5.1)	304	(5.2)	331	(3.6)	378	(3.8)	506	(6.3)	574	(9.0)	613	(12.2)
	United Kingdom	492	(2.4)	87	(1.2)	503	(3.2)	482	(3.3)	**20**	(4.4)	348	(3.4)	380	(3.1)	434	(3.0)	552	(3.2)	606	(3.9)	635	(3.2)
	United States	487	(3.6)	91	(1.6)	497	(4.0)	477	(3.8)	**20**	(3.2)	337	(4.3)	368	(4.3)	425	(3.9)	551	(4.9)	607	(4.6)	637	(5.9)
	OECD total	488	(1.2)	97	(0.5)	496	(1.3)	481	(1.3)	**15**	(1.3)	329	(1.5)	362	(1.4)	421	(1.4)	557	(1.5)	615	(1.6)	647	(1.8)
	OECD average	496	(0.5)	92	(0.3)	501	(0.6)	490	(0.6)	**12**	(0.6)	343	(0.9)	376	(0.7)	433	(0.6)	560	(0.6)	613	(0.7)	643	(0.8)
Partners	Albania	377	(4.0)	91	(2.2)	372	(4.7)	383	(4.2)	**-11**	(4.1)	226	(7.0)	261	(5.0)	317	(5.2)	438	(4.8)	493	(5.7)	526	(6.5)
	Argentina	388	(4.1)	93	(2.9)	394	(4.5)	383	(4.4)	**10**	(3.4)	231	(7.9)	271	(6.0)	327	(4.3)	451	(5.0)	509	(7.1)	543	(7.0)
	Azerbaijan	431	(2.8)	64	(2.2)	435	(3.1)	427	(3.0)	**8**	(2.7)	334	(3.0)	354	(2.7)	387	(2.9)	469	(3.2)	512	(5.2)	541	(7.0)
	Brazil	386	(2.4)	81	(1.6)	394	(2.4)	379	(2.6)	**16**	(1.7)	261	(3.0)	287	(2.7)	331	(2.3)	435	(3.3)	493	(4.7)	531	(5.9)
	Bulgaria	428	(5.9)	99	(2.8)	426	(6.2)	430	(6.0)	-4	(3.7)	269	(6.9)	302	(5.8)	359	(6.2)	496	(6.6)	555	(9.0)	593	(12.3)
	Colombia	381	(3.2)	75	(1.7)	398	(4.0)	366	(3.3)	**32**	(3.5)	259	(5.8)	286	(5.1)	330	(4.0)	431	(3.4)	479	(4.2)	509	(4.2)
	Croatia	460	(3.1)	88	(1.8)	465	(3.6)	454	(3.9)	**11**	(4.4)	315	(4.8)	347	(4.1)	399	(3.5)	521	(3.8)	574	(5.4)	606	(5.6)
	Dubai (UAE)	453	(1.1)	99	(0.9)	454	(1.5)	451	(1.6)	2	(2.2)	294	(3.1)	326	(2.6)	381	(2.3)	523	(2.1)	584	(3.3)	619	(3.6)
	Hong Kong-China	555	(2.7)	95	(1.8)	561	(4.2)	547	(3.4)	**14**	(5.6)	390	(5.1)	428	(4.9)	492	(3.5)	622	(3.1)	673	(3.9)	703	(4.7)
	Indonesia	371	(3.7)	70	(2.3)	371	(4.1)	372	(4.0)	-1	(3.2)	260	(4.9)	284	(4.6)	324	(3.7)	416	(4.6)	462	(6.4)	493	(8.6)
	Jordan	387	(3.7)	83	(2.6)	386	(5.1)	387	(5.2)	0	(7.1)	249	(7.8)	281	(4.8)	333	(3.5)	443	(4.4)	490	(5.5)	520	(6.9)
	Kazakhstan	405	(3.0)	83	(2.3)	405	(3.1)	405	(3.3)	-1	(2.3)	276	(4.3)	303	(3.3)	347	(3.5)	458	(4.3)	514	(5.3)	548	(7.0)
	Kyrgyzstan	331	(2.9)	81	(2.1)	328	(3.4)	334	(2.8)	**-6**	(2.3)	204	(4.9)	231	(3.9)	278	(3.2)	382	(3.8)	436	(5.3)	473	(7.0)
	Latvia	482	(3.1)	79	(1.4)	483	(3.5)	481	(3.4)	2	(3.2)	352	(4.9)	379	(4.5)	427	(3.7)	537	(3.8)	584	(3.8)	612	(3.7)
	Liechtenstein	536	(4.1)	88	(4.4)	547	(5.2)	523	(5.9)	**24**	(7.6)	384	(17.8)	421	(8.9)	484	(7.9)	593	(5.4)	637	(11.4)	670	(14.9)
	Lithuania	477	(2.6)	88	(1.8)	474	(3.1)	480	(3.0)	**-6**	(3.0)	332	(5.3)	363	(4.2)	417	(3.0)	537	(3.1)	590	(4.0)	621	(5.4)
	Macao-China	525	(0.9)	85	(0.9)	531	(1.3)	520	(1.4)	**11**	(2.0)	382	(2.6)	415	(2.7)	468	(1.6)	584	(1.3)	634	(1.6)	663	(2.5)
	Montenegro	403	(2.0)	85	(1.5)	408	(2.2)	396	(2.4)	**12**	(2.2)	263	(4.1)	295	(4.4)	346	(2.8)	458	(2.2)	509	(2.7)	543	(3.9)
	Panama	360	(5.2)	81	(3.2)	362	(5.6)	357	(6.1)	5	(5.0)	235	(8.2)	261	(7.0)	306	(5.6)	408	(6.8)	466	(8.6)	503	(8.8)
	Peru	365	(4.0)	90	(2.4)	374	(4.6)	356	(4.4)	**18**	(4.0)	222	(4.5)	252	(4.0)	303	(3.7)	424	(5.2)	480	(6.3)	516	(9.0)
	Qatar	368	(0.7)	98	(0.9)	366	(1.2)	371	(1.0)	**-5**	(1.7)	227	(2.4)	255	(1.5)	300	(1.2)	425	(1.5)	506	(2.4)	557	(3.5)
	Romania	427	(3.4)	79	(2.1)	429	(3.9)	425	(3.8)	3	(3.5)	299	(4.4)	326	(4.1)	372	(4.0)	481	(3.6)	530	(5.4)	560	(6.5)
	Russian Federation	468	(3.3)	85	(2.1)	469	(3.7)	467	(3.5)	2	(2.8)	329	(5.1)	360	(4.5)	411	(4.2)	524	(3.8)	576	(5.3)	609	(7.2)
	Serbia	442	(2.9)	91	(1.9)	448	(3.8)	437	(3.2)	**12**	(4.0)	295	(4.8)	327	(4.3)	380	(3.7)	504	(3.2)	560	(4.3)	592	(5.3)
	Shanghai-China	600	(2.8)	103	(2.1)	599	(3.7)	601	(3.1)	-1	(4.0)	421	(7.1)	462	(5.0)	531	(4.0)	674	(3.3)	726	(4.2)	757	(4.6)
	Singapore	562	(1.4)	104	(1.2)	565	(1.9)	559	(2.0)	**5**	(2.5)	383	(3.0)	422	(4.1)	490	(2.9)	638	(2.0)	693	(2.5)	725	(3.8)
	Chinese Taipei	543	(3.4)	105	(2.3)	546	(4.8)	541	(4.8)	5	(6.8)	366	(5.0)	405	(3.8)	471	(3.6)	618	(4.6)	675	(5.4)	709	(6.6)
	Thailand	419	(3.2)	79	(2.5)	421	(3.9)	417	(3.8)	4	(4.2)	295	(4.5)	321	(4.2)	365	(3.5)	469	(3.7)	522	(5.4)	554	(6.8)
	Trinidad and Tobago	414	(1.3)	99	(1.2)	410	(2.3)	418	(1.5)	**-8**	(2.9)	252	(3.9)	287	(2.7)	342	(2.5)	484	(2.5)	546	(1.8)	580	(2.4)
	Tunisia	371	(3.0)	78	(2.3)	378	(3.3)	366	(3.2)	**12**	(2.3)	247	(4.8)	273	(4.3)	318	(3.7)	423	(3.4)	471	(4.9)	499	(6.6)
	Uruguay	427	(2.6)	91	(1.7)	433	(3.0)	421	(2.9)	**12**	(2.7)	278	(3.9)	310	(4.0)	364	(3.4)	490	(3.1)	546	(4.1)	578	(4.5)

Note: Values that are statistically significant are indicated in bold (see Annex A3).
StatLink http://dx.doi.org/10.1787/888932343285

[Part 1/1]

Table I.3.4 **Percentage of students at each proficiency level on the science scale**

		Proficiency levels												
		Below Level 1 (below 334.94 score points)		Level 1 (from 334.94 to less than 409.54 score points)		Level 2 (from 409.54 to less than 484.14 score points)		Level 3 (from 484.14 to less than 558.73 score points)		Level 4 (from 558.73 to less than 633.33 score points)		Level 5 (from 633.33 to less than 707.93 score points)		Level 6 (above 707.93 score points)	
		%	S.E.	%	S.E.	%	S.E.	%	S.E.	%	S.E.	%	S.E.	%	S.E.
OECD	Australia	3.4	(0.3)	9.2	(0.5)	20.0	(0.6)	28.4	(0.7)	24.5	(0.7)	11.5	(0.6)	3.1	(0.5)
	Austria	6.7	(0.8)	14.3	(1.0)	23.8	(1.0)	26.6	(1.0)	20.6	(1.0)	7.1	(0.6)	1.0	(0.2)
	Belgium	6.4	(0.6)	11.7	(0.6)	20.7	(0.6)	27.2	(0.8)	24.0	(0.8)	9.0	(0.6)	1.1	(0.2)
	Canada	2.0	(0.2)	7.5	(0.4)	20.9	(0.5)	31.2	(0.6)	26.2	(0.6)	10.5	(0.4)	1.6	(0.2)
	Chile	8.4	(0.8)	23.9	(1.1)	35.2	(0.9)	23.6	(1.1)	7.9	(0.7)	1.1	(0.2)	0.0	(0.0)
	Czech Republic	4.7	(0.6)	12.6	(0.9)	25.6	(1.0)	28.8	(1.2)	19.9	(0.9)	7.2	(0.6)	1.2	(0.2)
	Denmark	4.1	(0.4)	12.5	(0.7)	26.0	(0.8)	30.6	(1.1)	20.1	(0.8)	5.9	(0.5)	0.9	(0.2)
	Estonia	1.3	(0.3)	7.0	(0.7)	21.3	(1.1)	34.3	(1.1)	25.7	(1.1)	9.0	(0.6)	1.4	(0.3)
	Finland	1.1	(0.2)	4.9	(0.4)	15.3	(0.7)	28.8	(0.9)	31.2	(1.1)	15.4	(0.7)	3.3	(0.3)
	France	7.1	(0.8)	12.2	(0.8)	22.1	(1.2)	28.8	(1.3)	21.7	(1.0)	7.3	(0.7)	0.8	(0.2)
	Germany	4.1	(0.5)	10.7	(0.8)	20.1	(0.9)	27.3	(1.1)	25.0	(1.2)	10.9	(0.7)	1.9	(0.3)
	Greece	7.2	(1.1)	18.1	(1.0)	29.8	(1.0)	27.9	(1.2)	14.0	(1.0)	2.8	(0.3)	0.3	(0.1)
	Hungary	3.8	(0.9)	10.4	(0.9)	25.5	(1.1)	33.2	(1.3)	21.8	(1.2)	5.1	(0.5)	0.3	(0.1)
	Iceland	5.5	(0.5)	12.5	(0.6)	25.8	(0.8)	30.4	(0.9)	18.8	(0.8)	6.1	(0.4)	0.8	(0.2)
	Ireland	4.4	(0.7)	10.7	(1.0)	23.3	(1.2)	29.9	(1.0)	22.9	(0.9)	7.5	(0.7)	1.2	(0.2)
	Israel	13.9	(1.1)	19.2	(0.7)	26.0	(1.0)	24.1	(0.8)	12.8	(0.7)	3.5	(0.4)	0.5	(0.1)
	Italy	6.1	(0.4)	14.5	(0.5)	25.5	(0.6)	29.5	(0.5)	18.6	(0.5)	5.3	(0.3)	0.5	(0.1)
	Japan	3.2	(0.5)	7.5	(0.7)	16.3	(0.9)	26.6	(0.8)	29.5	(1.0)	14.4	(0.7)	2.6	(0.4)
	Korea	1.1	(0.3)	5.2	(0.7)	18.5	(1.2)	33.1	(1.1)	30.4	(1.1)	10.5	(0.9)	1.1	(0.3)
	Luxembourg	8.4	(0.5)	15.3	(0.9)	24.3	(0.7)	27.1	(0.9)	18.2	(0.9)	6.0	(0.5)	0.7	(0.1)
	Mexico	14.5	(0.6)	32.8	(0.6)	33.6	(0.6)	15.8	(0.6)	3.1	(0.3)	0.2	(0.0)	0.0	(0.0)
	Netherlands	2.6	(0.5)	10.6	(1.3)	21.8	(1.5)	26.9	(1.1)	25.3	(1.7)	11.2	(1.1)	1.5	(0.3)
	New Zealand	4.0	(0.5)	9.4	(0.5)	18.1	(1.0)	25.8	(0.9)	25.1	(0.7)	14.0	(0.7)	3.6	(0.4)
	Norway	3.8	(0.5)	11.9	(0.9)	26.6	(0.9)	31.1	(0.7)	20.1	(0.8)	5.9	(0.6)	0.5	(0.1)
	Poland	2.3	(0.3)	10.9	(0.7)	26.1	(0.8)	32.1	(0.8)	21.2	(1.0)	6.8	(0.5)	0.8	(0.2)
	Portugal	3.0	(0.4)	13.5	(0.9)	28.9	(1.1)	32.3	(1.1)	18.1	(1.0)	3.9	(0.5)	0.3	(0.1)
	Slovak Republic	5.0	(0.6)	14.2	(0.9)	27.6	(1.0)	29.2	(0.9)	17.7	(0.9)	5.6	(0.5)	0.7	(0.2)
	Slovenia	3.1	(0.2)	11.7	(0.5)	23.7	(0.7)	28.7	(1.1)	23.0	(0.7)	8.7	(0.6)	1.2	(0.3)
	Spain	4.6	(0.4)	13.6	(0.7)	27.9	(0.7)	32.3	(0.7)	17.6	(0.6)	3.7	(0.3)	0.2	(0.1)
	Sweden	5.8	(0.5)	13.4	(0.8)	25.6	(0.8)	28.4	(0.8)	18.7	(0.9)	7.1	(0.6)	1.0	(0.2)
	Switzerland	3.5	(0.3)	10.6	(0.6)	21.3	(1.1)	29.8	(1.0)	24.1	(1.0)	9.2	(0.7)	1.5	(0.2)
	Turkey	6.9	(0.8)	23.0	(1.1)	34.5	(1.2)	25.2	(1.2)	9.1	(1.1)	1.1	(0.3)	0.0	(0.0)
	United Kingdom	3.8	(0.3)	11.2	(0.7)	22.7	(0.7)	28.8	(1.0)	22.2	(0.8)	9.5	(0.6)	1.9	(0.2)
	United States	4.2	(0.5)	13.9	(0.9)	25.0	(0.9)	27.5	(0.8)	20.1	(0.9)	7.9	(0.8)	1.3	(0.3)
	OECD total	5.4	(0.2)	14.6	(0.3)	24.8	(0.3)	27.1	(0.3)	19.6	(0.3)	7.3	(0.2)	1.1	(0.1)
	OECD average	5.0	(0.1)	13.0	(0.1)	24.4	(0.2)	28.6	(0.2)	20.6	(0.2)	7.4	(0.1)	1.1	(0.0)
Partners	Albania	26.3	(1.6)	31.0	(1.3)	27.7	(1.2)	12.9	(1.3)	2.0	(0.4)	0.1	(0.1)	0.0	c
	Argentina	25.2	(1.7)	27.2	(1.4)	26.7	(1.2)	15.4	(1.1)	4.8	(0.7)	0.6	(0.2)	0.0	(0.0)
	Azerbaijan	31.5	(1.7)	38.5	(1.1)	22.4	(1.1)	6.7	(0.8)	0.8	(0.2)	0.0	(0.0)	0.0	c
	Brazil	19.7	(0.9)	34.5	(1.0)	28.8	(0.9)	12.6	(0.8)	3.9	(0.4)	0.6	(0.1)	0.0	(0.0)
	Bulgaria	16.5	(1.6)	22.3	(1.5)	26.6	(1.3)	21.0	(1.4)	10.9	(1.0)	2.4	(0.5)	0.2	(0.1)
	Colombia	20.4	(1.8)	33.7	(1.2)	30.2	(1.4)	13.1	(1.0)	2.5	(0.3)	0.1	(0.0)	0.0	(0.0)
	Croatia	3.6	(0.5)	14.9	(1.0)	30.0	(1.1)	31.1	(1.0)	16.7	(1.0)	3.5	(0.6)	0.2	(0.1)
	Dubai (UAE)	11.0	(0.5)	19.5	(0.6)	26.0	(0.8)	22.9	(0.7)	14.9	(0.6)	4.8	(0.3)	0.8	(0.2)
	Hong Kong-China	1.4	(0.3)	5.2	(0.6)	15.1	(0.7)	29.4	(1.0)	32.7	(1.0)	14.2	(0.9)	2.0	(0.3)
	Indonesia	24.6	(1.8)	41.0	(1.5)	27.0	(1.6)	6.9	(1.0)	0.5	(0.2)	0.0	(0.0)	0.0	c
	Jordan	18.0	(1.2)	27.6	(1.1)	32.2	(1.2)	17.6	(1.1)	4.1	(0.5)	0.5	(0.2)	0.0	c
	Kazakhstan	22.4	(1.3)	33.0	(1.1)	27.9	(1.1)	12.8	(0.8)	3.6	(0.6)	0.3	(0.2)	0.0	(0.0)
	Kyrgyzstan	52.9	(1.3)	29.0	(0.9)	13.3	(0.8)	4.0	(0.5)	0.7	(0.2)	0.0	(0.0)	0.0	c
	Latvia	2.3	(0.6)	12.5	(1.0)	29.1	(1.1)	35.5	(1.2)	17.6	(1.1)	3.0	(0.5)	0.1	(0.1)
	Liechtenstein	1.4	(0.7)	9.9	(1.9)	23.8	(3.1)	29.8	(3.7)	25.4	(2.7)	9.0	(1.7)	0.7	(0.7)
	Lithuania	3.5	(0.6)	13.5	(0.8)	28.9	(1.0)	32.4	(1.2)	17.0	(0.8)	4.3	(0.4)	0.4	(0.1)
	Macao-China	1.5	(0.2)	8.1	(0.4)	25.2	(0.8)	37.8	(0.7)	22.7	(1.0)	4.5	(0.5)	0.2	(0.1)
	Montenegro	22.2	(1.0)	31.4	(1.0)	29.4	(1.0)	13.6	(0.8)	3.1	(0.4)	0.2	(0.1)	0.0	c
	Panama	32.8	(2.7)	32.4	(2.0)	23.2	(1.9)	9.3	(1.2)	2.2	(0.5)	0.2	(0.1)	0.0	c
	Peru	35.3	(1.5)	33.0	(1.3)	21.7	(1.2)	8.0	(0.8)	1.8	(0.4)	0.2	(0.1)	0.0	(0.0)
	Qatar	36.4	(0.6)	28.8	(0.5)	18.8	(0.6)	9.8	(0.3)	4.8	(0.2)	1.3	(0.1)	0.1	(0.0)
	Romania	11.9	(1.1)	29.5	(1.6)	34.1	(1.7)	19.7	(1.2)	4.4	(0.6)	0.4	(0.1)	0.0	(0.0)
	Russian Federation	5.5	(0.7)	16.5	(1.1)	30.7	(1.1)	29.0	(1.2)	13.9	(0.9)	3.9	(0.5)	0.4	(0.2)
	Serbia	10.1	(0.8)	24.3	(1.0)	33.9	(1.2)	23.6	(0.7)	7.1	(0.6)	1.0	(0.2)	0.0	(0.0)
	Shanghai-China	0.4	(0.1)	2.8	(0.4)	10.5	(0.7)	26.0	(1.0)	36.1	(1.1)	20.4	(1.0)	3.9	(0.5)
	Singapore	2.8	(0.2)	8.7	(0.5)	17.5	(0.6)	25.4	(0.8)	25.7	(0.7)	15.3	(0.7)	4.6	(0.5)
	Chinese Taipei	2.2	(0.3)	8.9	(0.6)	21.1	(0.9)	33.3	(1.0)	25.8	(1.1)	8.0	(0.7)	0.8	(0.2)
	Thailand	12.2	(1.1)	30.6	(1.0)	34.7	(1.3)	17.5	(0.9)	4.4	(0.5)	0.6	(0.3)	0.0	(0.0)
	Trinidad and Tobago	25.1	(0.9)	24.9	(0.9)	25.2	(0.9)	16.0	(0.8)	7.1	(0.4)	1.8	(0.2)	0.1	(0.1)
	Tunisia	21.3	(1.2)	32.4	(1.1)	30.9	(1.0)	13.0	(0.8)	2.2	(0.4)	0.2	(0.1)	0.0	(0.0)
	Uruguay	17.0	(0.9)	25.6	(0.9)	29.3	(1.0)	19.5	(1.0)	7.1	(0.5)	1.4	(0.2)	0.1	(0.0)

StatLink http://dx.doi.org/10.1787/888932343285

[Part 1/2]

Table I.3.5 Percentage of students at each proficiency level on the science scale, by gender

	Boys – Proficiency levels													
	Below Level 1 (below 334.94 score points)		Level 1 (from 334.94 to less than 409.54 score points)		Level 2 (from 409.54 to less than 484.14 score points)		Level 3 (from 484.14 to less than 558.73 score points)		Level 4 (from 558.73 to less than 633.33 score points)		Level 5 (from 633.33 to less than 707.93 score points)		Level 6 (above 707.93 score points)	
	%	S.E.	%	S.E.	%	S.E.	%	S.E.	%	S.E.	%	S.E.	%	S.E.
OECD														
Australia	4.2	(0.4)	9.9	(0.6)	19.4	(0.8)	26.8	(0.8)	24.1	(0.8)	12.1	(0.7)	3.7	(0.6)
Austria	6.6	(1.0)	15.0	(1.2)	22.3	(1.2)	24.8	(1.3)	21.3	(1.4)	8.6	(1.1)	1.3	(0.3)
Belgium	6.6	(0.9)	11.3	(0.8)	20.1	(0.9)	25.8	(1.0)	24.6	(1.2)	10.3	(0.9)	1.3	(0.3)
Canada	2.2	(0.3)	7.7	(0.5)	20.2	(0.7)	29.8	(1.0)	26.6	(1.1)	11.7	(0.7)	1.8	(0.3)
Chile	7.9	(1.0)	23.2	(1.3)	33.8	(1.4)	25.0	(1.5)	8.8	(1.0)	1.3	(0.3)	0.0	(0.1)
Czech Republic	5.0	(0.7)	12.9	(1.2)	25.8	(1.3)	29.1	(1.6)	19.1	(1.1)	6.8	(0.8)	1.3	(0.3)
Denmark	3.7	(0.5)	11.5	(0.8)	25.4	(1.2)	30.2	(1.3)	20.7	(1.1)	7.2	(0.8)	1.3	(0.4)
Estonia	1.4	(0.4)	7.2	(1.0)	21.8	(1.7)	33.0	(1.6)	26.0	(1.4)	9.3	(0.9)	1.4	(0.3)
Finland	1.3	(0.3)	6.2	(0.7)	17.6	(1.1)	28.6	(1.6)	28.6	(1.6)	14.4	(1.0)	3.2	(0.4)
France	8.0	(1.1)	12.5	(1.1)	20.7	(1.4)	26.7	(1.7)	21.9	(1.3)	9.0	(1.0)	1.2	(0.3)
Germany	4.2	(0.6)	10.8	(1.0)	19.9	(1.1)	26.0	(1.6)	24.6	(1.6)	12.1	(1.0)	2.5	(0.5)
Greece	8.3	(1.4)	19.9	(1.5)	29.0	(1.6)	26.1	(1.5)	13.5	(1.2)	3.0	(0.4)	0.2	(0.2)
Hungary	4.3	(1.0)	11.0	(1.1)	24.4	(1.5)	32.3	(1.9)	22.0	(1.6)	5.6	(0.7)	0.4	(0.2)
Iceland	6.5	(0.6)	12.8	(0.9)	23.9	(1.2)	29.0	(1.2)	19.6	(1.2)	7.0	(0.8)	1.1	(0.3)
Ireland	5.5	(1.0)	10.5	(1.0)	22.9	(1.4)	29.2	(1.2)	22.8	(1.2)	7.6	(0.9)	1.4	(0.3)
Israel	15.8	(1.5)	18.9	(1.2)	24.4	(1.7)	22.8	(1.1)	13.3	(1.0)	4.1	(0.5)	0.7	(0.3)
Italy	6.9	(0.6)	15.4	(0.7)	24.6	(0.7)	27.4	(0.8)	18.7	(0.8)	6.3	(0.4)	0.6	(0.1)
Japan	4.1	(0.8)	9.0	(0.9)	16.8	(1.2)	24.7	(1.2)	28.2	(1.6)	14.5	(1.2)	2.6	(0.6)
Korea	1.5	(0.5)	6.0	(1.0)	19.0	(1.8)	31.4	(2.1)	29.2	(1.5)	11.3	(1.2)	1.5	(0.5)
Luxembourg	9.0	(0.7)	15.0	(1.0)	22.3	(0.9)	26.4	(1.2)	19.3	(1.0)	7.1	(0.7)	0.9	(0.2)
Mexico	14.3	(0.7)	31.7	(0.9)	32.9	(0.8)	17.2	(0.9)	3.7	(0.4)	0.3	(0.1)	0.0	(0.0)
Netherlands	2.7	(0.6)	9.6	(1.4)	22.2	(1.9)	27.0	(1.6)	25.3	(1.9)	11.6	(1.2)	1.6	(0.4)
New Zealand	5.3	(0.8)	10.3	(0.7)	18.0	(1.2)	23.4	(1.1)	24.1	(1.4)	14.4	(1.0)	4.4	(0.5)
Norway	4.4	(0.6)	12.5	(1.0)	26.2	(1.3)	30.3	(1.2)	19.7	(1.1)	6.3	(0.9)	0.5	(0.2)
Poland	3.2	(0.5)	12.3	(1.0)	25.8	(1.2)	29.7	(1.2)	20.5	(1.0)	7.5	(0.8)	1.0	(0.3)
Portugal	3.7	(0.5)	14.7	(1.3)	27.9	(1.3)	31.1	(1.2)	17.8	(1.3)	4.5	(0.6)	0.3	(0.2)
Slovak Republic	5.2	(0.7)	15.2	(1.2)	27.6	(1.5)	27.5	(1.4)	16.9	(1.1)	6.7	(0.7)	0.9	(0.3)
Slovenia	4.0	(0.3)	13.8	(0.7)	24.1	(0.8)	26.9	(1.2)	21.8	(0.9)	8.2	(0.7)	1.3	(0.5)
Spain	4.8	(0.5)	13.5	(0.8)	26.2	(0.9)	31.4	(0.8)	19.1	(0.8)	4.7	(0.4)	0.3	(0.1)
Sweden	6.8	(0.7)	13.5	(1.0)	25.2	(1.4)	27.5	(1.1)	18.2	(1.1)	7.4	(0.8)	1.3	(0.4)
Switzerland	3.2	(0.4)	10.3	(0.7)	21.4	(1.1)	28.7	(1.2)	24.4	(1.3)	10.0	(0.9)	2.1	(0.3)
Turkey	8.1	(0.9)	25.2	(1.3)	33.7	(1.2)	23.4	(1.5)	8.8	(1.3)	0.9	(0.3)	0.0	(0.0)
United Kingdom	4.0	(0.6)	10.6	(0.8)	21.8	(1.1)	27.6	(1.2)	22.9	(1.2)	10.7	(0.9)	2.4	(0.4)
United States	3.8	(0.6)	13.2	(1.0)	23.4	(1.2)	27.1	(1.2)	22.0	(1.1)	9.0	(0.9)	1.5	(0.4)
OECD total	5.6	(0.2)	14.7	(0.4)	24.0	(0.4)	26.2	(0.4)	20.0	(0.4)	8.1	(0.3)	1.4	(0.1)
OECD average	5.5	(0.1)	13.3	(0.2)	23.8	(0.2)	27.5	(0.2)	20.5	(0.2)	8.0	(0.1)	1.4	(0.1)
Partners														
Albania	32.0	(2.1)	32.0	(1.5)	24.0	(1.4)	10.3	(1.4)	1.6	(0.4)	0.1	(0.1)	0.0	c
Argentina	27.3	(1.9)	26.4	(1.7)	25.3	(1.4)	15.0	(1.2)	5.3	(0.9)	0.7	(0.2)	0.0	(0.0)
Azerbaijan	33.7	(1.9)	38.4	(1.5)	20.7	(1.2)	6.3	(0.8)	0.8	(0.3)	0.0	(0.0)	0.0	c
Brazil	19.6	(1.0)	34.0	(1.1)	28.7	(1.0)	12.7	(1.0)	4.3	(0.5)	0.7	(0.2)	0.0	(0.0)
Bulgaria	20.4	(2.1)	22.9	(2.1)	24.7	(1.8)	19.0	(1.5)	10.5	(1.2)	2.4	(0.6)	0.2	(0.2)
Colombia	16.7	(2.0)	31.1	(1.8)	33.1	(1.8)	15.7	(1.5)	3.2	(0.6)	0.2	(0.1)	0.0	(0.0)
Croatia	4.4	(0.7)	16.1	(1.2)	30.3	(1.3)	29.2	(1.3)	16.4	(1.3)	3.4	(0.5)	0.2	(0.2)
Dubai (UAE)	15.2	(0.7)	21.8	(0.9)	23.7	(1.2)	20.1	(1.0)	13.8	(0.9)	4.5	(0.5)	0.8	(0.2)
Hong Kong-China	1.6	(0.4)	5.6	(0.9)	15.0	(1.0)	27.8	(1.2)	32.5	(1.4)	15.1	(1.2)	2.4	(0.4)
Indonesia	26.9	(2.3)	41.6	(1.7)	24.8	(1.7)	6.2	(1.1)	0.6	(0.3)	0.0	(0.0)	0.0	c
Jordan	24.2	(2.0)	29.7	(1.6)	28.8	(1.8)	13.7	(1.4)	3.3	(0.7)	0.3	(0.2)	0.0	(0.0)
Kazakhstan	24.8	(1.4)	33.1	(1.5)	25.9	(1.3)	12.1	(1.0)	3.8	(0.7)	0.4	(0.2)	0.0	(0.0)
Kyrgyzstan	57.9	(1.6)	26.4	(1.1)	11.2	(0.9)	3.8	(0.8)	0.6	(0.2)	0.0	(0.1)	0.0	c
Latvia	2.8	(0.8)	14.0	(1.4)	28.9	(1.8)	34.0	(1.6)	16.6	(1.4)	3.5	(0.7)	0.2	(0.2)
Liechtenstein	1.5	(1.3)	7.7	(2.8)	23.3	(3.8)	28.6	(3.9)	28.0	(3.0)	9.8	(2.5)	1.0	(0.9)
Lithuania	4.1	(0.9)	15.9	(1.1)	30.2	(1.6)	31.0	(1.6)	14.8	(0.9)	3.9	(0.6)	0.2	(0.1)
Macao-China	1.8	(0.3)	8.9	(0.6)	25.2	(1.0)	36.2	(1.0)	22.8	(1.4)	4.8	(0.8)	0.3	(0.1)
Montenegro	24.7	(1.8)	32.1	(1.8)	27.4	(1.3)	12.4	(1.3)	3.3	(0.5)	0.3	(0.2)	0.0	c
Panama	32.0	(3.3)	33.8	(3.0)	24.4	(2.6)	7.9	(1.3)	1.7	(0.5)	0.2	(0.1)	0.0	c
Peru	34.9	(1.6)	33.4	(1.3)	21.3	(1.3)	7.9	(0.8)	2.2	(0.5)	0.3	(0.2)	0.0	(0.1)
Qatar	43.2	(0.9)	26.9	(0.7)	15.0	(0.9)	8.4	(0.5)	4.8	(0.4)	1.5	(0.3)	0.2	(0.1)
Romania	13.8	(1.5)	30.9	(1.8)	32.5	(2.0)	17.9	(1.4)	4.5	(0.9)	0.4	(0.3)	0.0	c
Russian Federation	6.2	(0.9)	16.6	(1.3)	30.5	(1.2)	28.3	(1.2)	13.9	(1.1)	4.0	(0.6)	0.5	(0.2)
Serbia	10.8	(1.0)	24.8	(1.4)	32.7	(1.6)	22.4	(1.2)	8.0	(0.7)	1.2	(0.3)	0.0	(0.1)
Shanghai-China	0.5	(0.2)	3.3	(0.5)	11.4	(1.0)	25.1	(1.5)	34.1	(1.5)	20.8	(1.2)	4.8	(0.7)
Singapore	3.6	(0.4)	8.9	(0.8)	16.9	(1.0)	25.2	(1.1)	24.7	(0.9)	15.5	(0.9)	5.3	(0.7)
Chinese Taipei	2.9	(0.5)	9.4	(0.8)	20.4	(1.3)	31.1	(1.5)	26.7	(1.4)	8.6	(0.9)	0.8	(0.3)
Thailand	14.8	(1.7)	32.2	(1.3)	32.0	(1.7)	16.4	(1.5)	4.0	(0.6)	0.5	(0.2)	0.0	(0.0)
Trinidad and Tobago	29.1	(1.3)	24.2	(1.2)	23.5	(1.5)	14.6	(0.9)	6.7	(0.7)	1.7	(0.4)	0.1	(0.1)
Tunisia	22.5	(1.3)	31.1	(1.4)	29.7	(1.3)	14.0	(1.2)	2.5	(0.5)	0.2	(0.2)	0.0	(0.0)
Uruguay	18.3	(1.2)	24.8	(1.2)	28.0	(1.2)	19.7	(1.2)	7.5	(0.7)	1.7	(0.3)	0.1	(0.1)

StatLink http://dx.doi.org/10.1787/888932343285

[Part 2/2]

Table I.3.5 **Percentage of students at each proficiency level on the science scale, by gender**

Girls – Proficiency levels

	Below Level 1 (below 334.94 score points)		Level 1 (from 334.94 to less than 409.54 score points)		Level 2 (from 409.54 to less than 484.14 score points)		Level 3 (from 484.14 to less than 558.73 score points)		Level 4 (from 558.73 to less than 633.33 score points)		Level 5 (from 633.33 to less than 707.93 score points)		Level 6 (above 707.93 score points)	
	%	S.E.	%	S.E.	%	S.E.	%	S.E.	%	S.E.	%	S.E.	%	S.E.
OECD														
Australia	2.7	(0.3)	8.4	(0.5)	20.6	(0.7)	30.0	(0.8)	24.9	(0.8)	10.8	(0.7)	2.5	(0.5)
Austria	6.8	(1.0)	13.5	(1.2)	25.3	(1.6)	28.3	(1.3)	19.9	(1.3)	5.5	(0.7)	0.6	(0.2)
Belgium	6.1	(0.8)	12.1	(0.8)	21.3	(0.9)	28.7	(1.1)	23.4	(1.1)	7.7	(0.6)	0.8	(0.2)
Canada	1.9	(0.2)	7.3	(0.4)	21.6	(0.6)	32.7	(0.8)	25.8	(0.7)	9.3	(0.5)	1.4	(0.2)
Chile	8.9	(0.9)	24.7	(1.3)	36.5	(1.4)	22.2	(1.2)	6.9	(0.9)	0.8	(0.3)	0.0	(0.0)
Czech Republic	4.2	(0.7)	12.3	(1.1)	25.4	(1.4)	28.6	(1.4)	20.9	(1.2)	7.5	(0.8)	1.1	(0.3)
Denmark	4.5	(0.6)	13.4	(0.9)	26.6	(1.1)	31.1	(1.4)	19.5	(1.1)	4.6	(0.6)	0.5	(0.2)
Estonia	1.2	(0.4)	6.9	(0.9)	20.8	(1.7)	35.7	(1.4)	25.4	(1.4)	8.5	(0.9)	1.5	(0.4)
Finland	0.9	(0.2)	3.6	(0.4)	12.9	(0.9)	29.0	(1.3)	33.9	(1.1)	16.3	(0.9)	3.4	(0.4)
France	6.2	(0.8)	11.8	(1.1)	23.3	(1.7)	30.9	(1.7)	21.5	(1.3)	5.7	(0.7)	0.5	(0.2)
Germany	3.9	(0.6)	10.6	(1.0)	20.4	(1.2)	28.8	(1.5)	25.4	(1.4)	9.6	(1.0)	1.4	(0.3)
Greece	6.0	(1.0)	16.4	(1.0)	30.6	(1.2)	29.5	(1.4)	14.4	(1.1)	2.6	(0.4)	0.3	(0.1)
Hungary	3.3	(1.1)	9.6	(0.9)	26.7	(1.3)	34.1	(1.5)	21.6	(1.5)	4.5	(0.6)	0.2	(0.1)
Iceland	4.4	(0.6)	12.2	(0.9)	27.7	(1.3)	31.9	(1.5)	18.0	(1.3)	5.3	(0.6)	0.5	(0.2)
Ireland	3.3	(0.6)	11.0	(1.6)	23.7	(1.5)	30.7	(1.3)	23.0	(1.3)	7.4	(0.9)	0.9	(0.3)
Israel	12.0	(1.0)	19.5	(1.1)	27.6	(1.2)	25.4	(1.0)	12.4	(0.9)	2.9	(0.4)	0.2	(0.1)
Italy	5.3	(0.4)	13.6	(0.6)	26.3	(0.9)	31.6	(0.7)	18.6	(0.6)	4.3	(0.3)	0.3	(0.1)
Japan	2.2	(0.5)	5.9	(0.8)	15.7	(1.1)	28.6	(1.3)	30.9	(1.4)	14.2	(1.0)	2.5	(0.5)
Korea	0.7	(0.3)	4.3	(0.8)	17.9	(1.5)	35.1	(1.6)	31.7	(1.7)	9.7	(1.2)	0.6	(0.2)
Luxembourg	7.9	(0.6)	15.5	(1.1)	26.4	(1.2)	27.9	(1.1)	17.0	(1.1)	4.9	(0.6)	0.5	(0.1)
Mexico	14.8	(0.7)	34.0	(0.8)	34.2	(0.8)	14.4	(0.6)	2.5	(0.3)	0.1	(0.0)	0.0	(0.0)
Netherlands	2.4	(0.7)	11.6	(1.5)	21.5	(1.5)	26.8	(1.4)	25.3	(1.8)	10.9	(1.2)	1.4	(0.3)
New Zealand	2.6	(0.5)	8.4	(0.8)	18.1	(1.3)	28.4	(1.5)	26.2	(1.2)	13.5	(1.0)	2.8	(0.5)
Norway	3.2	(0.5)	11.3	(1.1)	27.1	(1.1)	32.0	(1.0)	20.4	(1.0)	5.5	(0.8)	0.5	(0.2)
Poland	1.4	(0.3)	9.4	(0.9)	26.4	(1.4)	34.4	(1.1)	21.9	(1.2)	6.1	(0.5)	0.5	(0.2)
Portugal	2.4	(0.4)	12.3	(1.3)	29.9	(1.6)	33.5	(1.3)	18.3	(1.1)	3.3	(0.7)	0.2	(0.2)
Slovak Republic	4.9	(0.8)	13.3	(1.2)	27.6	(1.3)	30.8	(1.1)	18.6	(1.2)	4.4	(0.7)	0.5	(0.2)
Slovenia	2.1	(0.3)	9.5	(0.7)	23.3	(1.1)	30.6	(1.5)	24.2	(1.3)	9.3	(1.1)	1.1	(0.4)
Spain	4.4	(0.5)	13.8	(0.9)	29.7	(0.9)	33.3	(0.8)	15.9	(0.7)	2.8	(0.3)	0.1	(0.1)
Sweden	4.7	(0.7)	13.2	(1.0)	26.1	(1.1)	29.4	(1.4)	19.2	(1.0)	6.8	(0.7)	0.7	(0.2)
Switzerland	3.7	(0.5)	10.9	(0.8)	21.3	(1.4)	30.9	(1.3)	23.8	(1.3)	8.4	(0.9)	1.0	(0.2)
Turkey	5.7	(1.0)	20.8	(1.6)	35.5	(1.6)	27.2	(1.7)	9.5	(1.2)	1.3	(0.4)	0.1	(0.1)
United Kingdom	3.7	(0.4)	11.8	(0.9)	23.5	(0.9)	29.9	(1.2)	21.5	(1.2)	8.4	(0.8)	1.4	(0.3)
United States	4.6	(0.6)	14.7	(1.2)	26.7	(1.4)	28.0	(1.1)	18.2	(1.2)	6.7	(0.8)	1.0	(0.4)
OECD total	5.2	(0.2)	14.6	(0.4)	25.7	(0.4)	28.0	(0.4)	19.1	(0.4)	6.5	(0.3)	0.9	(0.1)
OECD average	4.5	(0.1)	12.6	(0.2)	24.9	(0.2)	29.7	(0.2)	20.6	(0.2)	6.8	(0.1)	0.9	(0.0)
Partners														
Albania	20.3	(1.5)	30.0	(1.7)	31.5	(1.8)	15.7	(1.8)	2.5	(0.5)	0.1	(0.1)	0.0	c
Argentina	23.4	(1.9)	27.9	(1.6)	27.9	(1.6)	15.7	(1.5)	4.4	(0.7)	0.6	(0.3)	0.1	(0.1)
Azerbaijan	29.3	(1.8)	38.6	(1.4)	24.3	(1.4)	7.1	(1.0)	0.8	(0.3)	0.0	(0.0)	0.0	c
Brazil	19.8	(1.0)	34.9	(1.2)	28.9	(1.3)	12.5	(0.9)	3.4	(0.4)	0.4	(0.1)	0.0	(0.0)
Bulgaria	12.4	(1.2)	21.6	(1.5)	28.7	(1.4)	23.2	(1.5)	11.4	(1.3)	2.5	(0.5)	0.2	(0.1)
Colombia	23.7	(1.9)	36.0	(1.4)	27.6	(1.6)	10.7	(1.0)	1.9	(0.4)	0.1	(0.1)	0.0	c
Croatia	2.7	(0.6)	13.6	(1.3)	29.7	(1.3)	33.2	(1.5)	17.1	(1.3)	3.6	(0.7)	0.2	(0.1)
Dubai (UAE)	6.7	(0.5)	17.1	(1.0)	28.4	(1.2)	25.9	(1.1)	16.1	(0.8)	5.0	(0.5)	0.8	(0.3)
Hong Kong-China	1.2	(0.3)	4.8	(0.7)	15.2	(1.0)	31.1	(1.5)	32.9	(1.3)	13.1	(1.4)	1.6	(0.4)
Indonesia	22.3	(1.8)	40.5	(2.0)	29.1	(2.0)	7.6	(1.1)	0.5	(0.3)	0.0	(0.0)	0.0	c
Jordan	11.8	(1.3)	25.5	(1.4)	35.6	(1.4)	21.5	(1.7)	4.9	(0.7)	0.6	(0.2)	0.0	(0.0)
Kazakhstan	20.1	(1.5)	32.9	(1.4)	29.8	(1.8)	13.6	(1.1)	3.4	(0.7)	0.2	(0.1)	0.0	(0.0)
Kyrgyzstan	48.2	(1.6)	31.6	(1.3)	15.2	(1.1)	4.2	(0.5)	0.8	(0.3)	0.0	(0.0)	0.0	c
Latvia	1.7	(0.5)	10.9	(1.2)	29.2	(1.7)	37.1	(1.7)	18.6	(1.4)	2.5	(0.6)	0.0	(0.0)
Liechtenstein	1.3	(1.1)	12.4	(2.7)	24.3	(3.7)	31.2	(5.9)	22.4	(4.9)	8.0	(3.0)	0.4	(0.9)
Lithuania	2.9	(0.6)	11.1	(1.0)	27.6	(1.2)	33.9	(1.3)	19.3	(1.1)	4.7	(0.6)	0.5	(0.2)
Macao-China	1.2	(0.2)	7.3	(0.4)	25.1	(0.9)	39.3	(1.1)	22.5	(1.1)	4.3	(0.4)	0.2	(0.1)
Montenegro	19.6	(1.4)	30.7	(1.4)	31.6	(1.4)	14.9	(1.0)	3.0	(0.6)	0.2	(0.2)	0.0	c
Panama	33.5	(3.0)	30.9	(2.3)	22.0	(2.0)	10.7	(1.6)	2.6	(0.8)	0.2	(0.2)	0.0	c
Peru	35.7	(1.9)	32.7	(2.0)	22.1	(1.5)	8.1	(1.1)	1.3	(0.4)	0.1	(0.1)	0.0	(0.0)
Qatar	29.4	(0.7)	30.8	(0.9)	22.6	(0.7)	11.3	(0.5)	4.8	(0.3)	1.1	(0.2)	0.1	(0.1)
Romania	10.1	(1.2)	28.1	(1.9)	35.7	(2.1)	21.4	(1.6)	4.3	(0.6)	0.3	(0.2)	0.0	(0.0)
Russian Federation	4.8	(0.7)	16.5	(1.2)	30.9	(1.4)	29.8	(1.6)	13.9	(1.1)	3.9	(0.6)	0.4	(0.2)
Serbia	9.4	(1.1)	23.7	(1.1)	35.1	(1.4)	24.8	(1.0)	6.2	(0.8)	0.8	(0.2)	0.0	(0.0)
Shanghai-China	0.3	(0.1)	2.2	(0.3)	9.6	(0.9)	26.8	(1.3)	38.0	(1.5)	20.0	(1.2)	3.0	(0.7)
Singapore	1.9	(0.3)	8.5	(0.6)	18.2	(0.8)	25.6	(1.0)	26.7	(1.0)	15.2	(0.8)	3.9	(0.4)
Chinese Taipei	1.4	(0.3)	8.3	(0.8)	21.8	(1.2)	35.4	(1.4)	24.8	(1.4)	7.5	(1.3)	0.8	(0.3)
Thailand	10.2	(1.1)	29.4	(1.4)	36.7	(1.5)	18.3	(1.0)	4.7	(0.6)	0.7	(0.3)	0.0	(0.0)
Trinidad and Tobago	21.0	(0.8)	25.5	(1.3)	26.8	(1.4)	17.3	(1.4)	7.5	(0.6)	1.8	(0.3)	0.1	(0.1)
Tunisia	20.3	(1.3)	33.6	(1.3)	32.0	(1.7)	12.2	(1.0)	1.9	(0.5)	0.1	(0.1)	0.0	(0.0)
Uruguay	15.8	(1.1)	26.4	(1.2)	30.4	(1.3)	19.4	(1.2)	6.8	(0.6)	1.1	(0.3)	0.1	(0.1)

StatLink http://dx.doi.org/10.1787/888932343285

[Part 1/1]

Table I.3.6 Mean score, variation and gender differences in student performance on the science scale

		All students				Gender differences						Percentiles											
		Mean score		Standard deviation		Boys		Girls		Difference (B – G)		5th		10th		25th		75th		90th		95th	
		Mean	S.E.	S.D.	S.E.	Mean score	S.E.	Mean score	S.E.	Score dif.	S.E.	Score	S.E.	Score	S.E.	Score	S.E.	Score	S.E.	Score	S.E.	Score	S.E.
OECD	Australia	527	(2.5)	101	(1.6)	527	(3.1)	528	(2.8)	-1	(3.2)	355	(4.0)	395	(4.0)	461	(2.8)	597	(2.8)	655	(3.9)	688	(5.0)
	Austria	494	(3.2)	102	(2.2)	498	(4.2)	490	(4.4)	8	(5.7)	321	(6.8)	358	(6.2)	424	(4.8)	569	(3.6)	623	(3.3)	653	(3.4)
	Belgium	507	(2.5)	105	(2.3)	510	(3.6)	503	(3.2)	6	(4.5)	321	(6.2)	364	(4.8)	438	(3.6)	583	(2.8)	634	(3.1)	661	(3.2)
	Canada	529	(1.6)	90	(0.9)	531	(1.9)	526	(1.9)	**5**	(1.9)	377	(2.8)	412	(2.7)	469	(2.0)	593	(1.7)	642	(1.7)	669	(2.6)
	Chile	447	(2.9)	81	(1.5)	452	(3.5)	443	(3.5)	**9**	(3.8)	315	(4.3)	343	(4.1)	392	(3.5)	502	(3.6)	553	(3.8)	583	(5.0)
	Czech Republic	500	(3.0)	97	(1.9)	498	(4.0)	503	(3.2)	-5	(4.2)	338	(6.5)	375	(5.6)	437	(3.9)	568	(3.4)	624	(4.0)	657	(4.4)
	Denmark	499	(2.5)	92	(1.3)	505	(3.0)	494	(2.9)	**12**	(3.2)	343	(4.1)	379	(3.9)	438	(3.1)	564	(2.9)	615	(3.7)	645	(3.8)
	Estonia	528	(2.7)	84	(1.6)	527	(3.1)	528	(3.1)	-1	(3.2)	388	(5.0)	419	(4.7)	472	(3.8)	586	(3.1)	635	(3.5)	665	(4.3)
	Finland	554	(2.3)	89	(1.1)	546	(2.7)	562	(2.6)	**-15**	(2.6)	400	(4.2)	437	(4.2)	496	(3.3)	617	(2.9)	665	(3.0)	694	(3.6)
	France	498	(3.6)	103	(2.8)	500	(4.6)	497	(3.5)	3	(3.9)	314	(8.1)	358	(7.1)	433	(5.6)	572	(3.8)	624	(4.2)	653	(4.6)
	Germany	520	(2.8)	101	(1.9)	523	(3.7)	518	(3.3)	6	(4.2)	345	(7.0)	383	(6.2)	452	(4.1)	594	(3.3)	645	(3.5)	675	(3.8)
	Greece	470	(4.0)	92	(2.1)	465	(5.1)	475	(3.7)	**-10**	(3.8)	318	(7.6)	353	(6.3)	409	(5.3)	535	(3.8)	586	(3.6)	616	(3.4)
	Hungary	503	(3.1)	86	(2.9)	503	(3.8)	503	(3.5)	0	(3.8)	348	(11.4)	388	(7.6)	446	(4.6)	564	(3.7)	609	(3.6)	636	(4.4)
	Iceland	496	(1.4)	95	(1.2)	496	(2.1)	495	(2.0)	2	(2.9)	330	(4.3)	370	(4.3)	435	(2.6)	561	(2.2)	616	(2.8)	647	(4.4)
	Ireland	508	(3.3)	97	(2.1)	507	(4.3)	509	(3.8)	-3	(4.8)	341	(8.3)	382	(4.9)	445	(3.7)	576	(3.3)	627	(4.0)	656	(4.4)
	Israel	455	(3.1)	107	(2.4)	453	(4.4)	456	(3.2)	-3	(4.4)	275	(8.1)	314	(5.5)	382	(4.5)	531	(3.3)	590	(4.0)	623	(4.2)
	Italy	489	(1.8)	97	(1.5)	488	(2.5)	490	(2.0)	-2	(2.9)	325	(3.8)	362	(2.6)	424	(2.3)	557	(2.0)	609	(2.0)	639	(2.3)
	Japan	539	(3.4)	100	(2.5)	534	(5.5)	545	(3.9)	-12	(6.7)	361	(8.7)	405	(7.3)	477	(4.8)	610	(3.2)	659	(3.5)	686	(4.1)
	Korea	538	(3.4)	82	(2.3)	537	(5.0)	539	(4.2)	-2	(6.3)	399	(6.5)	431	(5.2)	485	(4.2)	595	(3.7)	640	(3.7)	665	(4.8)
	Luxembourg	484	(1.2)	104	(1.1)	487	(2.0)	480	(1.6)	**7**	(2.6)	304	(4.6)	345	(3.2)	415	(3.1)	558	(2.3)	615	(2.1)	646	(4.0)
	Mexico	416	(1.8)	77	(0.9)	419	(2.0)	413	(1.9)	**6**	(1.6)	291	(2.8)	318	(2.1)	364	(1.7)	468	(2.1)	517	(2.8)	544	(2.8)
	Netherlands	522	(5.4)	96	(2.1)	524	(5.3)	520	(5.9)	4	(3.0)	362	(6.8)	395	(7.0)	453	(7.6)	594	(5.1)	645	(4.8)	673	(4.9)
	New Zealand	532	(2.6)	107	(2.0)	529	(4.0)	535	(2.9)	-6	(4.6)	348	(5.6)	390	(4.3)	461	(4.1)	608	(3.0)	667	(3.3)	697	(3.6)
	Norway	500	(2.6)	90	(1.0)	498	(3.0)	502	(2.8)	-4	(2.8)	346	(4.4)	382	(3.3)	440	(3.0)	563	(2.9)	615	(3.7)	644	(4.0)
	Poland	508	(2.4)	87	(1.2)	505	(2.7)	511	(2.8)	**-6**	(2.7)	364	(3.9)	396	(3.3)	448	(2.7)	569	(2.7)	621	(2.9)	650	(3.8)
	Portugal	493	(2.9)	83	(1.4)	491	(3.4)	495	(3.0)	-3	(2.8)	354	(4.0)	384	(3.7)	436	(3.7)	551	(3.0)	601	(3.3)	627	(3.8)
	Slovak Republic	490	(3.0)	95	(2.6)	490	(4.0)	491	(3.2)	-1	(4.1)	335	(6.0)	371	(4.9)	427	(3.9)	556	(3.4)	612	(4.1)	643	(4.6)
	Slovenia	512	(1.1)	94	(1.0)	505	(1.7)	519	(1.6)	**-14**	(2.5)	355	(2.9)	387	(2.3)	446	(2.0)	580	(2.4)	633	(3.0)	661	(4.3)
	Spain	488	(2.1)	87	(1.1)	492	(2.5)	485	(2.3)	**7**	(2.3)	338	(3.5)	373	(3.2)	431	(3.0)	549	(2.2)	597	(2.2)	625	(2.3)
	Sweden	495	(2.7)	100	(1.5)	493	(3.0)	497	(3.2)	-4	(3.0)	327	(4.7)	367	(4.6)	429	(3.8)	564	(3.4)	622	(3.9)	654	(4.8)
	Switzerland	517	(2.8)	96	(1.4)	520	(3.2)	512	(3.0)	**8**	(2.7)	352	(4.2)	388	(3.6)	452	(3.5)	585	(3.4)	637	(3.8)	667	(4.3)
	Turkey	454	(3.6)	81	(2.0)	448	(3.8)	460	(4.5)	**-12**	(4.1)	322	(5.0)	350	(4.2)	397	(3.3)	510	(4.6)	560	(5.8)	587	(6.4)
	United Kingdom	514	(2.5)	99	(1.4)	519	(3.6)	509	(3.2)	**9**	(4.5)	348	(4.3)	385	(3.6)	447	(3.7)	583	(3.1)	640	(3.3)	672	(3.9)
	United States	502	(3.6)	98	(1.7)	509	(4.2)	495	(3.7)	**14**	(3.3)	341	(4.8)	374	(4.5)	433	(3.9)	572	(4.7)	629	(5.1)	662	(6.7)
	OECD total	496	(1.2)	100	(0.6)	498	(1.5)	494	(1.3)	**4**	(1.3)	331	(1.7)	366	(1.5)	427	(1.4)	568	(1.5)	625	(1.9)	657	(2.1)
	OECD average	501	(0.5)	94	(0.3)	501	(0.6)	501	(0.6)	0	(0.6)	341	(1.0)	377	(0.8)	438	(0.7)	567	(0.6)	619	(0.6)	649	(0.7)
Partners	Albania	391	(3.9)	89	(1.7)	377	(4.8)	406	(4.0)	**-29**	(4.1)	242	(5.4)	276	(4.7)	331	(4.5)	454	(4.8)	504	(4.9)	532	(4.8)
	Argentina	401	(4.6)	102	(3.7)	397	(5.1)	404	(4.8)	**-8**	(3.8)	228	(10.6)	271	(7.6)	334	(5.5)	471	(5.5)	530	(6.6)	564	(7.9)
	Azerbaijan	373	(3.1)	74	(1.6)	370	(3.4)	377	(3.2)	**-7**	(2.6)	257	(4.9)	281	(4.0)	321	(3.6)	421	(3.7)	471	(5.1)	502	(5.6)
	Brazil	405	(2.4)	84	(1.3)	407	(2.6)	404	(2.6)	3	(1.8)	275	(3.5)	302	(3.1)	348	(2.3)	458	(3.4)	517	(4.0)	554	(4.8)
	Bulgaria	439	(5.9)	106	(2.5)	430	(6.8)	450	(5.3)	**-20**	(4.4)	263	(7.6)	302	(7.0)	367	(7.6)	514	(6.8)	575	(5.7)	607	(7.1)
	Colombia	402	(3.6)	81	(1.8)	413	(4.3)	392	(3.7)	**21**	(3.5)	268	(6.6)	298	(6.2)	348	(4.7)	457	(3.6)	506	(3.6)	536	(4.1)
	Croatia	486	(2.8)	85	(1.8)	482	(3.5)	491	(3.9)	-9	(4.7)	348	(4.7)	377	(4.0)	429	(3.7)	546	(3.5)	595	(4.0)	624	(5.0)
	Dubai (UAE)	466	(1.2)	106	(1.1)	453	(1.8)	480	(1.6)	**-27**	(2.4)	294	(2.5)	330	(2.5)	391	(1.6)	542	(1.9)	606	(3.0)	638	(3.3)
	Hong Kong-China	549	(2.8)	87	(2.0)	550	(3.8)	548	(3.4)	3	(4.7)	393	(7.3)	432	(4.9)	494	(3.9)	610	(2.9)	655	(2.9)	681	(3.3)
	Indonesia	383	(3.8)	69	(2.1)	378	(4.2)	387	(4.0)	**-9**	(3.3)	272	(5.4)	296	(4.0)	336	(3.7)	428	(4.6)	472	(6.2)	499	(5.4)
	Jordan	415	(3.5)	89	(2.1)	398	(5.5)	433	(4.2)	**-35**	(6.9)	264	(6.2)	301	(5.4)	357	(4.4)	477	(3.9)	526	(4.4)	556	(5.0)
	Kazakhstan	400	(3.1)	87	(1.7)	396	(3.4)	405	(3.5)	**-9**	(2.9)	262	(4.9)	293	(4.3)	342	(3.4)	458	(3.8)	515	(5.1)	549	(6.1)
	Kyrgyzstan	330	(2.9)	91	(2.0)	318	(3.7)	340	(2.9)	**-22**	(3.1)	183	(4.9)	215	(4.6)	269	(3.9)	388	(3.4)	444	(5.0)	482	(6.1)
	Latvia	494	(3.1)	78	(1.7)	490	(3.7)	497	(3.2)	**-7**	(3.4)	365	(5.7)	392	(4.5)	440	(4.1)	548	(3.2)	593	(4.0)	619	(3.3)
	Liechtenstein	520	(3.4)	87	(3.4)	527	(5.0)	511	(5.1)	**16**	(7.5)	373	(10.5)	402	(9.3)	457	(7.4)	583	(6.2)	631	(9.3)	659	(7.3)
	Lithuania	491	(2.9)	85	(2.1)	483	(3.5)	500	(2.9)	**-17**	(2.9)	351	(6.1)	382	(4.9)	434	(3.7)	549	(3.2)	600	(3.9)	630	(3.7)
	Macao-China	511	(1.0)	76	(0.8)	510	(1.3)	512	(1.2)	-2	(1.5)	381	(2.5)	411	(1.9)	461	(2.0)	564	(1.7)	608	(2.5)	632	(3.2)
	Montenegro	401	(2.0)	87	(1.4)	395	(2.4)	408	(2.6)	**-13**	(3.0)	257	(4.8)	290	(4.1)	343	(3.0)	461	(1.9)	512	(3.0)	543	(3.9)
	Panama	376	(5.7)	90	(2.9)	375	(6.4)	377	(6.6)	-2	(6.1)	232	(7.5)	260	(7.9)	315	(7.7)	436	(6.7)	495	(8.0)	527	(6.3)
	Peru	369	(3.5)	89	(2.1)	372	(3.7)	367	(4.4)	5	(4.2)	225	(5.3)	256	(4.5)	310	(3.7)	428	(4.2)	484	(6.4)	519	(7.8)
	Qatar	379	(0.9)	104	(0.8)	366	(1.4)	393	(1.0)	**-26**	(1.7)	228	(2.4)	257	(1.7)	306	(1.5)	443	(1.7)	524	(2.5)	572	(2.8)
	Romania	428	(3.4)	79	(1.9)	423	(3.9)	433	(3.7)	**-10**	(3.9)	301	(5.0)	327	(4.2)	373	(4.4)	483	(4.0)	530	(4.2)	558	(4.2)
	Russian Federation	478	(3.3)	90	(2.0)	477	(3.7)	480	(3.5)	-3	(2.9)	331	(5.8)	364	(4.7)	418	(4.0)	539	(3.5)	594	(4.6)	628	(5.2)
	Serbia	443	(2.4)	84	(1.6)	442	(3.1)	443	(2.8)	-1	(3.5)	302	(5.0)	334	(4.4)	387	(3.1)	501	(3.0)	548	(3.3)	579	(3.2)
	Shanghai-China	575	(2.3)	82	(1.7)	574	(3.1)	575	(2.3)	-1	(2.9)	430	(4.9)	467	(4.4)	523	(2.9)	632	(2.8)	674	(3.4)	700	(3.3)
	Singapore	542	(1.4)	104	(1.1)	541	(1.8)	542	(1.8)	-1	(2.4)	362	(3.5)	401	(3.1)	471	(2.0)	617	(2.0)	673	(3.0)	704	(4.1)
	Chinese Taipei	520	(2.6)	87	(1.6)	520	(3.7)	521	(4.0)	-1	(5.6)	370	(4.4)	404	(3.6)	464	(3.1)	581	(3.3)	628	(4.3)	654	(4.4)
	Thailand	425	(3.0)	80	(2.0)	418	(3.8)	431	(3.4)	**-13**	(4.0)	297	(5.6)	326	(4.8)	373	(3.2)	477	(3.3)	527	(4.1)	559	(5.7)
	Trinidad and Tobago	410	(1.2)	108	(1.0)	401	(2.1)	419	(1.4)	**-18**	(2.7)	234	(3.6)	271	(3.2)	335	(3.1)	484	(2.9)	552	(2.6)	592	(3.2)
	Tunisia	401	(2.7)	81	(1.9)	401	(2.9)	400	(2.8)	1	(2.0)	265	(4.1)	296	(3.6)	345	(3.2)	458	(3.3)	504	(4.5)	531	(5.4)
	Uruguay	427	(2.6)	97	(1.7)	427	(3.2)	428	(2.6)	-1	(2.8)	268	(5.2)	303	(3.6)	362	(3.4)	493	(3.5)	551	(3.8)	584	(4.2)

Note: Values that are statistically significant are indicated in bold (see Annex A3).
StatLink http://dx.doi.org/10.1787/888932343285

[Part 1/1]

Table I.3.7 **Overlapping of top performers in reading, mathematics and science**

15-year-old students who are:

	not top performers in any of the three domains		top performers only in reading		top performers only in mathematics		top performers only in science		top performers in reading and mathematics but not in science		top performers in reading and science but not in mathematics		top performers in mathematics and science but not in reading		top performers in all three domains		Percentage of top performers in reading who are top performers also in mathematics and science	
	%	S.E.	%	S.E.	%	S.E.	%	S.E.	%	S.E.	%	S.E.	%	S.E.	%	S.E.	%	S.E.
OECD																		
Australia	78.2	(1.0)	2.0	(0.3)	4.1	(0.3)	1.9	(0.2)	1.1	(0.2)	1.5	(0.2)	3.0	(0.3)	8.1	(0.7)	63.8	(2.5)
Austria	84.7	(0.9)	0.9	(0.2)	5.8	(0.5)	1.0	(0.2)	0.6	(0.2)	0.5	(0.2)	3.6	(0.4)	2.9	(0.4)	59.2	(4.9)
Belgium	76.3	(0.8)	2.0	(0.3)	9.0	(0.5)	0.8	(0.1)	2.6	(0.4)	0.5	(0.1)	2.7	(0.3)	6.1	(0.5)	54.8	(3.3)
Canada	76.4	(0.6)	2.5	(0.2)	6.7	(0.4)	1.5	(0.2)	2.2	(0.2)	1.3	(0.2)	2.6	(0.2)	6.8	(0.4)	52.9	(2.0)
Chile	97.6	(0.4)	0.6	(0.2)	0.6	(0.2)	0.4	(0.1)	0.2	(0.1)	0.1	(0.1)	0.2	(0.1)	0.3	(0.1)	27.2	(9.5)
Czech Republic	85.6	(0.9)	0.8	(0.1)	4.6	(0.5)	1.5	(0.3)	0.7	(0.1)	0.5	(0.1)	3.2	(0.4)	3.2	(0.4)	62.7	(4.3)
Denmark	86.1	(0.8)	0.8	(0.2)	5.5	(0.6)	1.2	(0.2)	0.9	(0.2)	0.4	(0.1)	2.6	(0.4)	2.6	(0.3)	54.8	(4.8)
Estonia	83.8	(1.0)	0.8	(0.2)	4.3	(0.4)	2.7	(0.5)	0.8	(0.2)	0.7	(0.2)	3.1	(0.4)	3.8	(0.5)	63.4	(4.3)
Finland	70.6	(1.2)	2.5	(0.3)	6.8	(0.6)	3.2	(0.4)	1.4	(0.2)	2.1	(0.3)	4.9	(0.4)	8.5	(0.6)	58.8	(3.1)
France	82.2	(1.2)	2.6	(0.4)	5.3	(0.4)	0.7	(0.2)	1.8	(0.3)	0.8	(0.2)	2.2	(0.3)	4.4	(0.6)	46.3	(4.0)
Germany	78.5	(1.0)	1.2	(0.3)	6.5	(0.6)	1.7	(0.3)	1.0	(0.2)	0.7	(0.2)	5.6	(0.4)	4.7	(0.6)	61.5	(4.9)
Greece	90.1	(0.7)	3.1	(0.3)	2.9	(0.4)	0.7	(0.2)	0.9	(0.2)	0.4	(0.1)	0.7	(0.2)	1.2	(0.2)	22.0	(3.0)
Hungary	87.6	(1.1)	1.5	(0.3)	4.3	(0.6)	0.5	(0.2)	1.2	(0.3)	0.3	(0.1)	1.5	(0.2)	3.0	(0.5)	49.9	(5.2)
Iceland	83.4	(0.7)	1.9	(0.3)	5.7	(0.6)	0.7	(0.1)	2.0	(0.4)	0.4	(0.2)	1.7	(0.3)	4.2	(0.5)	48.8	(4.8)
Ireland	87.6	(0.9)	2.0	(0.3)	1.4	(0.4)	2.2	(0.4)	0.3	(0.1)	1.6	(0.3)	1.8	(0.3)	3.2	(0.4)	45.3	(4.2)
Israel	89.6	(0.8)	3.3	(0.4)	1.8	(0.3)	0.6	(0.2)	1.3	(0.3)	0.6	(0.1)	0.5	(0.1)	2.2	(0.3)	29.4	(3.3)
Italy	87.4	(0.5)	2.0	(0.2)	4.0	(0.3)	1.0	(0.1)	0.9	(0.1)	0.7	(0.1)	1.9	(0.2)	2.3	(0.2)	38.9	(2.7)
Japan	73.3	(1.2)	2.2	(0.2)	6.1	(0.8)	2.1	(0.3)	1.4	(0.2)	1.5	(0.2)	5.0	(0.5)	8.4	(0.8)	62.3	(2.9)
Korea	71.5	(1.7)	1.7	(0.3)	11.6	(0.8)	0.8	(0.2)	3.6	(0.5)	0.4	(0.2)	3.2	(0.5)	7.2	(0.8)	56.1	(3.3)
Luxembourg	85.5	(0.7)	1.4	(0.2)	5.5	(0.5)	1.1	(0.2)	0.9	(0.1)	0.7	(0.2)	2.2	(0.3)	2.8	(0.4)	48.4	(4.8)
Mexico	99.0	(0.1)	0.2	(0.1)	0.5	(0.1)	0.1	(0.0)	0.1	(0.0)	0.0	(0.0)	0.1	(0.0)	0.1	(0.0)	16.2	(4.5)
Netherlands	77.2	(1.8)	0.8	(0.2)	8.0	(0.7)	1.3	(0.3)	1.3	(0.3)	0.9	(0.3)	3.7	(0.5)	6.8	(0.8)	69.6	(3.5)
New Zealand	74.2	(0.9)	2.3	(0.3)	4.4	(0.4)	2.5	(0.5)	1.5	(0.3)	2.1	(0.3)	3.1	(0.4)	9.9	(0.7)	63.0	(2.3)
Norway	85.5	(1.0)	2.6	(0.4)	3.7	(0.4)	0.9	(0.2)	1.7	(0.3)	0.7	(0.2)	1.4	(0.2)	3.4	(0.4)	40.2	(3.6)
Poland	85.7	(0.8)	2.0	(0.3)	3.7	(0.5)	1.3	(0.3)	1.1	(0.2)	0.7	(0.2)	2.1	(0.3)	3.5	(0.4)	48.2	(3.9)
Portugal	88.2	(0.9)	1.4	(0.2)	5.0	(0.5)	0.5	(0.1)	1.3	(0.3)	0.3	(0.1)	1.5	(0.2)	1.9	(0.3)	39.1	(4.5)
Slovak Republic	85.5	(1.0)	0.7	(0.3)	6.5	(0.7)	0.9	(0.2)	1.1	(0.2)	0.2	(0.1)	2.7	(0.3)	2.4	(0.4)	54.0	(5.0)
Slovenia	83.4	(0.7)	0.4	(0.2)	5.6	(0.5)	1.7	(0.2)	0.6	(0.2)	0.2	(0.2)	4.6	(0.4)	3.3	(0.4)	72.5	(6.6)
Spain	89.7	(0.5)	0.8	(0.1)	4.6	(0.3)	1.0	(0.1)	0.9	(0.1)	0.3	(0.1)	1.3	(0.2)	1.3	(0.2)	38.7	(3.2)
Sweden	84.1	(1.1)	2.6	(0.4)	3.8	(0.5)	1.0	(0.3)	1.3	(0.3)	0.9	(0.2)	1.9	(0.3)	4.3	(0.5)	47.2	(4.1)
Switzerland	73.5	(1.4)	1.2	(0.2)	12.8	(0.8)	0.9	(0.2)	1.8	(0.3)	0.3	(0.1)	4.7	(0.5)	4.8	(0.6)	58.9	(3.9)
Turkey	93.6	(1.2)	0.6	(0.2)	4.1	(0.9)	0.1	(0.1)	0.6	(0.2)	0.1	(0.0)	0.4	(0.1)	0.6	(0.2)	31.0	(7.5)
United Kingdom	84.5	(0.8)	1.3	(0.2)	2.2	(0.3)	2.7	(0.4)	0.6	(0.2)	1.6	(0.2)	2.4	(0.3)	4.6	(0.4)	57.3	(3.7)
United States	85.2	(1.1)	2.1	(0.4)	2.5	(0.4)	1.2	(0.2)	1.0	(0.2)	1.5	(0.3)	1.2	(0.3)	4.6	(0.4)	57.3	(3.7)
OECD total	84.6	(0.4)	1.6	(0.1)	4.1	(0.1)	1.2	(0.1)	1.1	(0.1)	0.9	(0.1)	2.1	(0.1)	5.2	(0.8)	52.8	(4.6)
OECD average	83.7	(0.2)	1.6	(0.0)	5.0	(0.1)	1.2	(0.0)	1.2	(0.0)	0.8	(0.0)	2.5	(0.1)	4.3	(0.2)	53.9	(1.7)
Partners																		
Albania	99.4	(0.2)	0.1	(0.1)	0.3	(0.1)	0.1	(0.0)	0.0	c	0.0	c	0.0	c	0.0	c	0.0	c
Argentina	98.2	(0.4)	0.6	(0.2)	0.4	(0.2)	0.2	(0.1)	0.1	(0.1)	0.1	(0.1)	0.1	(0.1)	0.2	(0.1)	17.3	(11.5)
Azerbaijan	98.9	(0.4)	0.0	(0.0)	1.1	(0.4)	0.0	(0.0)	0.0	c	0.0	c	0.0	c	0.0	c	0.0	c
Brazil	98.2	(0.3)	0.8	(0.1)	0.3	(0.1)	0.1	(0.0)	0.2	(0.1)	0.1	(0.1)	0.1	(0.0)	0.3	(0.1)	19.4	(5.2)
Bulgaria	94.1	(1.1)	1.0	(0.3)	1.8	(0.5)	0.8	(0.2)	0.5	(0.2)	0.4	(0.1)	0.6	(0.2)	0.9	(0.3)	31.8	(5.4)
Colombia	99.3	(0.2)	0.4	(0.1)	0.1	(0.0)	0.1	(0.0)	0.0	(0.0)	0.1	(0.0)	0.0	c	0.0	(0.0)	3.9	(3.0)
Croatia	92.7	(0.8)	1.2	(0.2)	2.1	(0.4)	0.7	(0.2)	0.3	(0.2)	0.4	(0.1)	1.3	(0.3)	1.2	(0.3)	37.8	(7.5)
Dubai (UAE)	90.1	(0.4)	1.4	(0.2)	2.3	(0.3)	1.1	(0.2)	0.7	(0.2)	0.9	(0.2)	1.2	(0.3)	2.3	(0.3)	43.0	(5.2)
Hong Kong-China	66.8	(1.2)	1.2	(0.2)	13.3	(0.8)	1.0	(0.2)	2.5	(0.3)	0.4	(0.2)	6.5	(0.6)	8.4	(0.7)	67.3	(3.2)
Indonesia	99.9	(0.1)	0.0	c	0.1	(0.1)	0.0	c	0.0	c	0.0	c	0.0	c	0.0	c	0.0	c
Jordan	99.2	(0.3)	0.1	(0.1)	0.1	(0.1)	0.3	(0.1)	0.0	(0.0)	0.1	(0.1)	0.1	(0.1)	0.0	c	0.0	c
Kazakhstan	98.5	(0.5)	0.2	(0.1)	0.9	(0.4)	0.1	(0.1)	0.1	(0.1)	0.0	c	0.1	(0.1)	0.1	(0.0)	19.3	(10.5)
Kyrgyzstan	99.8	(0.1)	0.1	(0.1)	0.0	(0.0)	0.0	c	0.0	c	0.0	c	0.0	c	0.0	c	0.0	c
Latvia	92.2	(0.7)	1.1	(0.2)	3.0	(0.4)	0.8	(0.3)	0.6	(0.2)	0.2	(0.1)	1.1	(0.2)	1.0	(0.2)	33.6	(5.4)
Liechtenstein	79.9	(2.3)	0.0	c	9.4	(2.0)	1.7	(1.3)	0.9	(0.7)	0.0	c	4.3	(1.4)	3.5	(1.3)	75.3	(19.1)
Lithuania	91.2	(0.7)	0.5	(0.2)	3.2	(0.5)	1.0	(0.2)	0.5	(0.2)	0.3	(0.1)	1.6	(0.3)	1.6	(0.3)	55.6	(7.3)
Macao-China	81.6	(0.4)	0.5	(0.1)	12.3	(0.6)	0.7	(0.2)	0.9	(0.2)	0.1	(0.1)	2.5	(0.4)	1.4	(0.2)	49.6	(5.0)
Montenegro	98.6	(0.2)	0.3	(0.1)	0.7	(0.2)	0.1	(0.1)	0.1	(0.1)	0.0	(0.0)	0.1	(0.1)	0.1	(0.1)	14.6	(8.9)
Panama	99.2	(0.3)	0.4	(0.2)	0.2	(0.1)	0.1	(0.0)	0.1	(0.1)	0.0	c	0.0	c	0.1	(0.1)	15.9	(15.3)
Peru	99.1	(0.3)	0.3	(0.1)	0.4	(0.2)	0.0	c	0.1	(0.1)	0.0	c	0.0	c	0.1	(0.1)	21.9	(13.1)
Qatar	97.0	(0.2)	0.6	(0.1)	0.7	(0.1)	0.4	(0.1)	0.3	(0.1)	0.3	(0.1)	0.2	(0.1)	0.6	(0.1)	33.3	(4.6)
Romania	98.2	(0.4)	0.4	(0.1)	0.9	(0.3)	0.1	(0.1)	0.1	(0.1)	0.1	(0.0)	0.1	(0.1)	0.1	(0.1)	19.2	(10.1)
Russian Federation	92.1	(0.8)	0.8	(0.2)	2.3	(0.4)	1.4	(0.3)	0.5	(0.1)	0.5	(0.2)	1.1	(0.3)	1.4	(0.3)	44.5	(6.1)
Serbia	95.9	(0.5)	0.3	(0.1)	2.5	(0.5)	0.2	(0.1)	0.2	(0.1)	0.0	c	0.5	(0.1)	0.3	(0.1)	32.7	(8.7)
Shanghai-China	48.3	(1.2)	0.5	(0.1)	22.8	(0.9)	0.6	(0.2)	4.1	(0.5)	0.2	(0.1)	8.8	(0.6)	14.6	(0.9)	75.2	(2.3)
Singapore	62.4	(0.8)	0.6	(0.2)	14.5	(0.7)	1.0	(0.2)	2.5	(0.2)	0.3	(0.1)	6.3	(0.4)	12.3	(0.5)	78.1	(2.0)
Chinese Taipei	71.0	(1.5)	0.1	(0.1)	18.9	(1.1)	0.3	(0.1)	1.1	(0.2)	0.1	(0.0)	4.6	(0.4)	3.9	(0.7)	74.3	(4.0)
Thailand	98.5	(0.5)	0.0	(0.0)	0.8	(0.2)	0.1	(0.1)	0.1	(0.0)	0.0	(0.1)	0.3	(0.1)	0.2	(0.1)	62.6	(17.0)
Trinidad and Tobago	95.5	(0.3)	1.1	(0.2)	1.2	(0.2)	0.6	(0.1)	0.4	(0.1)	0.4	(0.1)	0.5	(0.2)	0.5	(0.2)	20.5	(6.3)
Tunisia	99.5	(0.2)	0.1	(0.1)	0.2	(0.1)	0.1	(0.1)	0.0	c	0.0	c	0.0	(0.0)	0.0	c	0.0	c
Uruguay	96.1	(0.4)	0.8	(0.2)	1.3	(0.2)	0.5	(0.1)	0.3	(0.1)	0.2	(0.1)	0.4	(0.1)	0.4	(0.1)	24.4	(6.3)

StatLink http://dx.doi.org/10.1787/888932343285

[Part 1/2]
Table I.3.8 **Overlapping of top performers in reading, mathematics and science, by gender**

	Boys who are:																	Percentage of boy top performers in reading who are top performers also in mathematics and science	
	not top performers in any of the three domains		top performers only in reading		top performers only in mathematics		top performers only in science		top performers in reading and mathematics but not in science		top performers in reading and science but not in mathematics		top performers in mathematics and science but not in reading		top performers in all three domains			
	%	S.E.	%	S.E.	%	S.E.	%	S.E.	%	S.E.	%	S.E.	%	S.E.	%	S.E.	%	S.E.
OECD																		
Australia	77.8	(1.1)	0.5	(0.2)	5.4	(0.4)	2.4	(0.3)	0.6	(0.1)	0.8	(0.2)	4.7	(0.4)	7.9	(0.8)	80.9	(3.2)
Austria	82.1	(1.2)	0.1	(0.1)	7.7	(0.7)	1.4	(0.4)	0.1	(0.1)	0.3	(0.1)	6.0	(0.8)	2.3	(0.4)	82.2	(6.1)
Belgium	73.7	(1.2)	0.9	(0.3)	12.0	(0.9)	0.8	(0.2)	1.8	(0.3)	0.3	(0.1)	4.0	(0.6)	6.5	(0.7)	69.3	(3.7)
Canada	75.4	(0.8)	0.8	(0.2)	9.1	(0.6)	2.0	(0.3)	1.3	(0.2)	0.7	(0.2)	4.1	(0.3)	6.5	(0.7)	69.8	(3.2)
Chile	97.4	(0.6)	0.3	(0.2)	0.8	(0.3)	0.5	(0.2)	0.2	(0.2)	0.1	(0.1)	0.3	(0.1)	0.5	(0.3)	46.3	(21.5)
Czech Republic	85.9	(1.2)	0.1	(0.1)	5.6	(0.7)	1.4	(0.3)	0.3	(0.2)	0.1	(0.1)	4.3	(0.7)	2.3	(0.4)	81.8	(4.8)
Denmark	84.3	(1.0)	0.2	(0.1)	6.7	(0.9)	1.7	(0.4)	0.3	(0.1)	0.2	(0.2)	4.1	(0.5)	2.4	(0.4)	75.9	(6.8)
Estonia	83.2	(1.1)	0.1	(0.1)	5.7	(0.6)	3.1	(0.5)	0.3	(0.2)	0.2	(0.1)	4.6	(0.7)	2.9	(0.5)	84.7	(6.0)
Finland	72.3	(1.2)	0.4	(0.3)	9.2	(0.8)	3.2	(0.5)	0.6	(0.2)	0.8	(0.3)	7.2	(0.6)	6.4	(0.6)	79.4	(4.7)
France	80.7	(1.4)	0.6	(0.2)	7.6	(0.7)	1.0	(0.3)	1.0	(0.4)	0.5	(0.2)	3.8	(0.6)	4.9	(0.8)	70.2	(5.6)
Germany	76.9	(1.2)	0.1	(0.1)	8.2	(0.7)	2.0	(0.4)	0.3	(0.1)	0.3	(0.3)	8.6	(0.7)	3.7	(0.5)	84.3	(3.5)
Greece	90.0	(1.0)	1.3	(0.3)	4.7	(0.8)	0.8	(0.2)	0.8	(0.3)	0.1	(0.1)	1.1	(0.3)	1.2	(0.3)	34.7	(7.3)
Hungary	86.8	(1.4)	0.2	(0.1)	6.2	(1.0)	0.7	(0.2)	0.7	(0.3)	0.1	(0.1)	2.4	(0.4)	2.9	(0.5)	74.4	(6.3)
Iceland	83.1	(1.1)	0.5	(0.2)	7.4	(0.9)	1.0	(0.2)	0.8	(0.3)	0.3	(0.2)	2.8	(0.5)	4.1	(0.5)	72.4	(7.2)
Ireland	87.9	(1.2)	0.7	(0.3)	2.2	(0.6)	2.5	(0.5)	0.2	(0.1)	0.8	(0.3)	2.9	(0.6)	2.8	(0.4)	62.8	(8.5)
Israel	89.1	(1.2)	1.8	(0.4)	2.9	(0.6)	0.8	(0.2)	1.3	(0.4)	0.4	(0.3)	0.9	(0.3)	2.7	(0.5)	43.3	(4.9)
Italy	86.4	(0.7)	0.5	(0.1)	5.5	(0.4)	1.2	(0.2)	0.6	(0.2)	0.3	(0.1)	3.0	(0.2)	2.4	(0.3)	61.6	(5.0)
Japan	72.4	(1.8)	0.8	(0.2)	8.4	(0.9)	2.1	(0.4)	1.2	(0.3)	0.5	(0.2)	6.9	(0.7)	7.6	(1.0)	74.9	(3.4)
Korea	71.1	(2.3)	0.3	(0.1)	13.9	(1.3)	0.9	(0.2)	2.0	(0.4)	0.2	(0.1)	4.8	(0.7)	6.8	(1.1)	73.3	(4.0)
Luxembourg	83.5	(1.0)	0.0	c	7.9	(0.9)	1.4	(0.3)	0.5	(0.3)	0.2	(0.1)	3.6	(0.5)	2.8	(0.6)	75.7	(11.2)
Mexico	98.8	(0.2)	0.1	(0.0)	0.7	(0.2)	0.1	(0.1)	0.1	(0.0)	0.0	(0.0)	0.1	(0.1)	0.1	(0.0)	28.4	(9.9)
Netherlands	75.4	(1.9)	0.2	(0.1)	10.6	(1.0)	1.1	(0.3)	0.7	(0.2)	0.3	(0.3)	5.2	(0.7)	6.5	(0.9)	83.6	(3.9)
New Zealand	74.0	(1.3)	0.5	(0.2)	5.7	(0.6)	3.2	(0.8)	0.9	(0.3)	0.8	(0.2)	5.2	(0.6)	9.7	(0.9)	81.5	(2.8)
Norway	86.4	(1.0)	0.6	(0.3)	5.2	(0.6)	1.1	(0.3)	1.0	(0.2)	0.3	(0.1)	2.3	(0.4)	3.1	(0.5)	62.0	(4.9)
Poland	85.9	(1.1)	0.4	(0.2)	4.8	(0.7)	1.7	(0.4)	0.5	(0.1)	0.3	(0.2)	3.3	(0.5)	3.2	(0.5)	73.6	(6.0)
Portugal	87.4	(1.1)	0.4	(0.2)	6.5	(0.7)	0.6	(0.2)	0.8	(0.3)	0.1	(0.2)	2.2	(0.4)	1.9	(0.4)	58.1	(8.7)
Slovak Republic	84.8	(1.2)	0.0	c	7.2	(0.8)	1.1	(0.4)	0.4	(0.1)	0.1	(0.1)	4.4	(0.5)	2.0	(0.4)	79.0	(7.1)
Slovenia	83.3	(1.0)	0.0	c	7.0	(0.7)	1.5	(0.3)	0.2	(0.2)	0.0	c	6.2	(0.6)	1.7	(0.5)	85.9	(8.8)
Spain	87.9	(0.7)	0.3	(0.1)	6.2	(0.5)	1.3	(0.2)	0.6	(0.1)	0.2	(0.1)	2.1	(0.3)	1.3	(0.2)	55.4	(5.7)
Sweden	85.3	(1.3)	0.8	(0.3)	4.5	(0.7)	1.4	(0.4)	0.6	(0.3)	0.6	(0.3)	2.8	(0.4)	3.9	(0.6)	65.6	(6.4)
Switzerland	70.7	(1.6)	0.2	(0.1)	16.3	(1.4)	0.9	(0.3)	0.7	(0.2)	0.1	(0.1)	6.9	(0.8)	4.1	(0.5)	79.7	(5.5)
Turkey	93.3	(1.4)	0.1	(0.1)	5.3	(1.2)	0.0	c	0.4	(0.2)	0.0	c	0.5	(0.2)	0.3	(0.1)	41.4	(13.1)
United Kingdom	82.9	(1.3)	0.4	(0.2)	3.2	(0.6)	3.1	(0.5)	0.4	(0.2)	0.9	(0.3)	3.8	(0.5)	5.3	(0.6)	75.7	(4.3)
United States	84.4	(1.3)	0.8	(0.3)	3.6	(0.7)	1.7	(0.4)	0.6	(0.3)	1.2	(0.3)	2.1	(0.4)	5.5	(0.9)	67.6	(5.4)
OECD total	83.8	(0.4)	0.5	(0.1)	5.6	(0.2)	1.4	(0.1)	0.7	(0.1)	0.6	(0.1)	3.3	(0.2)	4.2	(0.3)	70.7	(2.2)
OECD average	83.0	(0.2)	0.5	(0.0)	6.6	(0.1)	1.5	(0.1)	0.7	(0.0)	0.4	(0.0)	3.7	(0.1)	3.8	(0.1)	68.7	(1.3)
Partners																		
Albania	99.4	(0.2)	0.0	c	0.5	(0.2)	0.0	c	0.0	c	0.0	c	0.0	c	0.1	c	0.0	c
Argentina	98.2	(0.4)	0.3	(0.2)	0.7	(0.3)	0.3	(0.2)	0.1	(0.1)	0.1	(0.1)	0.2	(0.2)	0.1	(0.1)	18.0	(13.6)
Azerbaijan	98.9	(0.4)	0.0	c	1.0	(0.4)	0.0	(0.0)	0.0	c	0.0	c	0.0	c	0.0	c	0.0	c
Brazil	98.3	(0.4)	0.4	(0.1)	0.5	(0.2)	0.1	(0.1)	0.2	(0.1)	0.1	(0.1)	0.1	(0.1)	0.3	(0.1)	32.0	(8.5)
Bulgaria	94.6	(1.0)	0.2	(0.1)	2.2	(0.5)	0.9	(0.4)	0.4	(0.3)	0.2	(0.2)	0.8	(0.3)	0.7	(0.3)	49.4	(11.4)
Colombia	99.3	(0.3)	0.3	(0.2)	0.1	(0.1)	0.1	(0.1)	0.1	(0.1)	0.0	c	0.0	c	0.0	(0.0)	7.8	(7.3)
Croatia	92.9	(0.8)	0.3	(0.1)	3.0	(0.5)	0.6	(0.3)	0.2	(0.1)	0.1	(0.1)	2.0	(0.5)	0.9	(0.3)	61.7	(13.9)
Dubai (UAE)	90.0	(0.6)	0.6	(0.2)	3.3	(0.5)	1.0	(0.3)	0.7	(0.3)	0.4	(0.2)	1.7	(0.4)	2.3	(0.4)	57.8	(7.1)
Hong Kong-China	64.6	(1.7)	0.2	(0.1)	16.3	(1.0)	1.1	(0.3)	1.3	(0.3)	0.2	(0.1)	9.1	(1.0)	7.2	(0.9)	80.5	(2.8)
Indonesia	99.9	(0.1)	0.0	c	0.1	(0.1)	0.0	c	0.0	c	0.0	c	0.0	c	0.0	c	0.0	c
Jordan	99.5	(0.3)	0.0	c	0.1	(0.1)	0.2	(0.1)	0.0	c	0.0	c	0.1	(0.1)	0.0	c	0.0	c
Kazakhstan	98.5	(0.5)	0.1	(0.1)	0.9	(0.4)	0.1	(0.1)	0.1	(0.1)	0.0	c	0.2	(0.2)	0.0	c	0.0	c
Kyrgyzstan	99.9	(0.1)	0.0	c	0.1	(0.1)	0.0	c	0.0	c	0.0	c	0.0	c	0.0	c	0.0	c
Latvia	92.0	(0.9)	0.2	(0.2)	3.7	(0.5)	1.0	(0.4)	0.3	(0.2)	0.0	c	1.7	(0.4)	0.9	(0.3)	58.6	(13.2)
Liechtenstein	76.4	(3.8)	0.0	c	12.5	(3.4)	2.0	(1.4)	0.0	c	0.0	c	5.9	(2.3)	2.8	(1.6)	91.4	(18.0)
Lithuania	92.0	(0.8)	0.0	c	3.8	(0.6)	0.8	(0.2)	0.0	c	0.0	c	2.4	(0.5)	0.8	(0.2)	89.1	(11.6)
Macao-China	79.6	(0.7)	0.0	c	14.8	(1.0)	0.6	(0.3)	0.5	(0.2)	0.0	c	3.3	(0.6)	1.2	(0.2)	68.5	(8.4)
Montenegro	98.5	(0.4)	0.0	c	1.1	(0.3)	0.0	c	0.0	c	0.0	c	0.0	c	0.1	(0.1)	38.1	(29.5)
Panama	99.3	(0.4)	0.0	c	0.3	(0.2)	0.1	(0.1)	0.1	(0.1)	0.0	c	0.0	c	0.0	c	0.0	c
Peru	98.7	(0.4)	0.2	(0.1)	0.5	(0.3)	0.0	c	0.1	(0.1)	0.0	c	0.0	c	0.2	(0.1)	29.8	(15.5)
Qatar	96.8	(0.3)	0.3	(0.1)	1.0	(0.2)	0.4	(0.1)	0.3	(0.1)	0.2	(0.1)	0.4	(0.1)	0.7	(0.1)	48.1	(9.6)
Romania	98.1	(0.5)	0.0	c	1.3	(0.5)	0.1	(0.1)	0.1	(0.1)	0.0	c	0.2	(0.2)	0.1	(0.1)	29.0	(22.6)
Russian Federation	92.4	(0.9)	0.2	(0.1)	2.7	(0.5)	1.6	(0.5)	0.2	(0.1)	0.2	(0.1)	1.5	(0.4)	1.2	(0.3)	70.1	(10.3)
Serbia	94.9	(0.7)	0.0	c	3.6	(0.7)	0.2	(0.1)	0.2	(0.1)	0.0	c	0.8	(0.3)	0.3	(0.1)	50.5	(18.7)
Shanghai-China	49.0	(1.7)	0.0	c	24.2	(1.4)	0.7	(0.3)	1.2	(0.3)	0.1	(0.1)	13.0	(0.8)	11.9	(0.9)	90.2	(1.9)
Singapore	61.7	(1.0)	0.1	(0.1)	16.4	(1.1)	1.0	(0.2)	1.1	(0.3)	0.2	(0.1)	8.7	(0.7)	10.8	(0.7)	88.6	(2.9)
Chinese Taipei	68.7	(1.9)	0.0	c	21.5	(1.4)	0.3	(0.1)	0.3	(0.2)	0.0	c	6.3	(0.8)	2.9	(0.7)	88.6	(4.5)
Thailand	98.5	(0.5)	0.0	c	0.9	(0.3)	0.1	(0.1)	0.0	c	0.0	c	0.3	(0.2)	0.1	(0.1)	77.2	(31.2)
Trinidad and Tobago	96.6	(0.5)	0.2	(0.2)	1.3	(0.3)	0.7	(0.2)	0.1	(0.1)	0.2	(0.1)	0.7	(0.3)	0.3	(0.1)	38.3	(12.7)
Tunisia	99.3	(0.3)	0.0	c	0.3	(0.2)	0.1	(0.1)	0.0	c	0.0	c	0.1	(0.1)	0.0	c	0.0	c
Uruguay	95.8	(0.6)	0.3	(0.1)	1.8	(0.4)	0.6	(0.2)	0.2	(0.1)	0.1	(0.1)	0.6	(0.2)	0.5	(0.2)	40.9	(9.8)

StatLink ᵫᵫᵫ http://dx.doi.org/10.1787/888932343285

[Part 2/2]

Table I.3.8 **Overlapping of top performers in reading, mathematics and science, by gender**

		Girls who are:															Percentage of girls top performers in reading who are top performers also in mathematics and science	
		not top performers in any of the three domains		top performers only in reading		top performers only in mathematics		top performers only in science		top performers in reading and mathematics but not in science		top performers in reading and science but not in mathematics		top performers in mathematics and science but not in reading		top performers in all three domains			
		%	S.E.	%	S.E.	%	S.E.	%	S.E.	%	S.E.	%	S.E.	%	S.E.	%	S.E.	%	S.E.
OECD	Australia	78.7	(1.1)	3.3	(0.4)	2.9	(0.4)	1.4	(0.2)	1.7	(0.3)	2.2	(0.3)	1.4	(0.2)	8.3	(0.7)	53.6	(2.8)
	Austria	87.1	(1.2)	1.7	(0.4)	4.0	(0.6)	0.6	(0.2)	1.0	(0.3)	0.7	(0.3)	1.4	(0.4)	3.4	(0.6)	50.1	(6.1)
	Belgium	79.1	(1.0)	3.1	(0.4)	5.9	(0.5)	0.8	(0.2)	3.4	(0.6)	0.7	(0.2)	1.3	(0.3)	5.7	(0.6)	43.7	(4.0)
	Canada	77.5	(0.7)	4.3	(0.3)	4.3	(0.3)	1.0	(0.2)	3.1	(0.4)	1.8	(0.3)	1.0	(0.2)	7.0	(0.5)	43.0	(2.4)
	Chile	97.7	(0.5)	0.9	(0.3)	0.3	(0.2)	0.3	(0.2)	0.2	(0.2)	0.2	(0.1)	0.1	(0.1)	0.2	(0.1)	14.8	(4.6)
	Czech Republic	85.3	(0.9)	1.5	(0.3)	3.4	(0.4)	1.6	(0.4)	1.1	(0.3)	0.8	(0.2)	1.9	(0.4)	4.3	(0.6)	55.0	(5.1)
	Denmark	87.8	(1.0)	1.4	(0.4)	4.3	(0.7)	0.6	(0.2)	1.5	(0.4)	0.6	(0.2)	1.1	(0.4)	2.7	(0.4)	44.3	(5.6)
	Estonia	84.3	(1.4)	1.5	(0.4)	2.9	(0.6)	2.3	(0.6)	1.3	(0.4)	1.3	(0.4)	1.5	(0.4)	4.9	(0.7)	54.9	(5.6)
	Finland	68.9	(1.2)	4.6	(0.5)	4.5	(0.7)	3.1	(0.5)	2.2	(0.4)	3.5	(0.6)	2.6	(0.5)	10.6	(0.9)	50.8	(3.4)
	France	83.7	(1.6)	4.4	(0.7)	3.1	(0.7)	0.5	(0.2)	2.6	(0.5)	1.0	(0.3)	0.7	(0.3)	4.0	(0.6)	33.2	(4.0)
	Germany	80.2	(1.3)	2.3	(0.3)	4.8	(0.7)	1.4	(0.3)	1.7	(0.4)	1.2	(0.3)	2.6	(0.4)	5.7	(0.9)	52.0	(5.4)
	Greece	90.1	(0.9)	4.7	(0.6)	1.2	(0.4)	0.7	(0.3)	1.0	(0.3)	0.7	(0.2)	0.3	(0.1)	1.3	(0.3)	16.6	(3.5)
	Hungary	88.3	(1.3)	2.8	(0.6)	2.4	(0.5)	0.4	(0.2)	1.8	(0.5)	0.5	(0.3)	0.6	(0.2)	3.2	(0.5)	38.4	(4.9)
	Iceland	83.6	(1.0)	3.4	(0.5)	4.0	(0.5)	0.4	(0.2)	3.2	(0.6)	0.5	(0.2)	0.7	(0.3)	4.2	(0.8)	37.2	(5.8)
	Ireland	87.3	(1.1)	3.3	(0.7)	0.6	(0.3)	1.9	(0.5)	0.3	(0.1)	2.3	(0.4)	0.7	(0.3)	3.5	(0.6)	36.9	(5.2)
	Israel	90.0	(0.9)	4.7	(0.6)	0.7	(0.2)	0.5	(0.2)	1.4	(0.3)	0.7	(0.2)	0.2	(0.1)	1.7	(0.4)	19.4	(3.7)
	Italy	88.4	(0.6)	3.5	(0.3)	2.3	(0.3)	0.7	(0.1)	1.1	(0.2)	1.1	(0.1)	0.7	(0.1)	2.1	(0.2)	27.1	(2.3)
	Japan	74.3	(1.7)	3.7	(0.5)	3.7	(0.5)	2.1	(0.4)	1.6	(0.4)	2.5	(0.4)	2.9	(0.6)	9.2	(1.2)	54.2	(3.8)
	Korea	72.1	(2.1)	3.2	(0.6)	9.1	(0.9)	0.6	(0.2)	5.3	(0.9)	0.7	(0.3)	1.3	(0.3)	7.7	(0.9)	45.5	(3.4)
	Luxembourg	87.7	(0.6)	2.6	(0.5)	3.1	(0.4)	0.7	(0.2)	1.2	(0.4)	1.1	(0.4)	0.8	(0.2)	2.7	(0.3)	35.1	(3.6)
	Mexico	99.2	(0.2)	0.3	(0.1)	0.2	(0.1)	0.0	(0.0)	0.1	(0.1)	0.0	(0.0)	0.0	(0.0)	0.0	(0.0)	8.6	(5.4)
	Netherlands	78.9	(1.9)	1.4	(0.3)	5.6	(0.8)	1.4	(0.4)	1.8	(0.6)	1.5	(0.5)	2.3	(0.5)	7.1	(0.9)	60.5	(5.1)
	New Zealand	74.5	(1.2)	4.1	(0.6)	3.0	(0.5)	1.8	(0.4)	2.1	(0.5)	3.4	(0.5)	1.0	(0.3)	10.1	(0.9)	51.3	(3.1)
	Norway	84.7	(1.2)	4.6	(0.7)	2.2	(0.4)	0.7	(0.3)	2.5	(0.5)	1.2	(0.4)	0.5	(0.2)	3.6	(0.5)	30.6	(4.3)
	Poland	85.4	(1.1)	3.6	(0.5)	2.6	(0.5)	0.9	(0.3)	1.7	(0.3)	1.0	(0.2)	0.9	(0.3)	3.8	(0.6)	37.4	(4.0)
	Portugal	88.9	(1.1)	2.3	(0.3)	3.5	(0.5)	0.5	(0.2)	1.7	(0.4)	0.4	(0.3)	0.9	(0.2)	1.8	(0.5)	29.6	(5.2)
	Slovak Republic	86.1	(1.2)	1.3	(0.5)	5.8	(0.8)	0.7	(0.3)	1.9	(0.4)	0.4	(0.2)	1.0	(0.4)	2.8	(0.5)	44.2	(4.9)
	Slovenia	83.5	(0.9)	0.8	(0.3)	4.2	(0.7)	2.0	(0.4)	1.1	(0.4)	0.4	(0.3)	3.0	(0.7)	5.0	(0.7)	68.6	(7.4)
	Spain	91.6	(0.5)	1.4	(0.2)	2.9	(0.3)	0.7	(0.1)	1.2	(0.2)	0.5	(0.1)	0.5	(0.1)	1.2	(0.2)	28.9	(3.9)
	Sweden	82.9	(1.3)	4.4	(0.7)	3.1	(0.6)	0.7	(0.2)	2.1	(0.4)	1.1	(0.3)	1.0	(0.4)	4.6	(0.7)	37.9	(4.7)
	Switzerland	76.3	(1.6)	2.2	(0.5)	9.1	(0.9)	0.8	(0.3)	3.0	(0.6)	0.6	(0.2)	2.5	(0.5)	5.5	(0.9)	49.2	(5.8)
	Turkey	93.8	(1.2)	1.2	(0.4)	2.8	(0.7)	0.2	(0.1)	0.9	(0.4)	0.1	(0.1)	0.2	(0.1)	0.8	(0.3)	27.9	(8.6)
	United Kingdom	86.2	(1.0)	2.1	(0.3)	1.3	(0.3)	2.4	(0.4)	0.7	(0.2)	2.3	(0.4)	1.1	(0.3)	4.0	(0.6)	43.8	(4.7)
	United States	86.0	(1.3)	3.5	(0.7)	1.4	(0.4)	0.6	(0.2)	1.3	(0.4)	1.9	(0.5)	0.3	(0.2)	4.9	(0.9)	41.8	(5.5)
	OECD total	85.5	(0.4)	2.8	(0.2)	2.7	(0.2)	0.9	(0.1)	1.5	(0.1)	1.3	(0.1)	0.9	(0.1)	4.3	(0.3)	43.4	(1.9)
	OECD average	84.4	(0.2)	2.8	(0.1)	3.4	(0.1)	1.0	(0.1)	1.7	0.1	1.1	(0.1)	1.1	(0.1)	4.4	(0.2)	40.2	(0.8)
Partners	Albania	99.4	(0.3)	0.3	(0.2)	0.2	(0.2)	0.0	c	0.0	(0.0)	0.0	c	0.0	c	0.0	c	0.0	c
	Argentina	98.3	(0.4)	0.8	(0.2)	0.2	(0.1)	0.2	(0.1)	0.1	(0.1)	0.0	c	0.1	(0.1)	0.2	(0.2)	17.2	(15.9)
	Azerbaijan	98.8	(0.4)	0.0	c	1.1	(0.4)	0.0	c	0.0	c	0.0	c	0.0	c	0.0	c	0.0	c
	Brazil	98.2	(0.3)	1.1	(0.2)	0.1	(0.1)	0.1	(0.1)	0.1	(0.1)	0.1	(0.1)	0.0	(0.0)	0.2	(0.1)	12.5	(5.5)
	Bulgaria	93.5	(1.3)	1.9	(0.5)	1.3	(0.6)	0.7	(0.2)	0.7	(0.3)	0.6	(0.2)	0.4	(0.2)	1.1	(0.3)	25.3	(6.4)
	Colombia	99.4	(0.2)	0.5	(0.2)	0.0	c	0.0	c	0.0	c	0.1	(0.1)	0.0	c	0.0	c	0.0	c
	Croatia	92.4	(1.0)	2.3	(0.5)	1.0	(0.3)	0.8	(0.3)	0.5	(0.3)	0.8	(0.3)	0.6	(0.3)	1.5	(0.4)	30.0	(6.5)
	Dubai (UAE)	90.1	(0.6)	2.2	(0.4)	1.2	(0.4)	1.3	(0.3)	0.7	(0.3)	1.5	(0.4)	0.7	(0.3)	2.3	(0.4)	33.9	(7.3)
	Hong Kong-China	69.2	(1.6)	2.2	(0.4)	10.0	(1.0)	0.9	(0.3)	3.9	(0.6)	0.6	(0.2)	3.5	(0.6)	9.7	(0.9)	59.2	(4.3)
	Indonesia	99.9	(0.1)	0.0	c	0.0	c	0.0	c	0.0	c	0.0	c	0.0	c	0.0	c	0.0	c
	Jordan	99.0	(0.4)	0.2	(0.2)	0.1	(0.1)	0.4	(0.2)	0.0	c	0.1	(0.1)	0.1	(0.1)	0.0	c	0.0	c
	Kazakhstan	98.6	(0.5)	0.2	(0.1)	0.8	(0.4)	0.1	(0.1)	0.1	(0.1)	0.0	c	0.0	c	0.1	(0.1)	22.3	(13.5)
	Kyrgyzstan	99.8	(0.1)	0.2	(0.1)	0.0	c	0.0	c	0.0	c	0.0	c	0.0	c	0.0	c	0.0	c
	Latvia	92.3	(0.9)	1.9	(0.4)	2.3	(0.5)	0.6	(0.4)	1.0	(0.3)	0.4	(0.1)	0.5	(0.2)	1.1	(0.3)	24.8	(6.2)
	Liechtenstein	83.9	(3.3)	0.0	c	5.9	(2.1)	0.0	c	1.6	(1.4)	0.0	c	2.5	(1.5)	4.2	(1.9)	66.4	(22.9)
	Lithuania	90.3	(1.0)	1.0	(0.3)	2.6	(0.6)	1.3	(0.3)	0.9	(0.4)	0.6	(0.2)	0.9	(0.3)	2.5	(0.5)	49.4	(7.3)
	Macao-China	83.6	(0.8)	0.9	(0.2)	9.8	(0.7)	0.8	(0.2)	1.3	(0.4)	0.2	(0.1)	1.8	(0.3)	1.7	(0.3)	41.5	(6.8)
	Montenegro	98.7	(0.3)	0.6	(0.2)	0.3	(0.2)	0.0	c	0.2	(0.1)	0.0	c	0.1	(0.1)	0.0	c	9.6	(8.8)
	Panama	99.0	(0.4)	0.7	(0.3)	0.0	c	0.0	(0.0)	0.0	c	0.0	c	0.0	c	0.1	(0.1)	11.8	(13.0)
	Peru	99.4	(0.2)	0.3	(0.2)	0.2	(0.1)	0.0	c	0.1	(0.1)	0.0	c	0.0	c	0.0	c	0.0	c
	Qatar	97.3	(0.3)	0.8	(0.2)	0.3	(0.1)	0.2	(0.1)	0.4	(0.1)	0.4	(0.1)	0.0	c	0.5	(0.1)	23.0	(5.1)
	Romania	98.3	(0.5)	0.7	(0.3)	0.5	(0.4)	0.0	c	0.2	(0.1)	0.1	(0.1)	0.0	c	0.2	(0.1)	17.1	(9.8)
	Russian Federation	91.7	(1.0)	1.4	(0.4)	1.8	(0.5)	1.2	(0.3)	0.8	(0.3)	0.7	(0.3)	0.7	(0.3)	1.6	(0.4)	35.3	(6.7)
	Serbia	97.0	(0.6)	0.5	(0.2)	1.4	(0.5)	0.2	(0.1)	0.3	(0.1)	0.0	c	0.3	(0.1)	0.3	(0.1)	24.8	(8.4)
	Shanghai-China	47.6	(1.5)	1.0	(0.2)	21.4	(1.2)	0.5	(0.2)	7.0	(0.9)	0.3	(0.1)	4.8	(0.8)	17.4	(1.2)	67.6	(3.2)
	Singapore	63.2	(0.9)	1.2	(0.3)	12.6	(0.8)	1.0	(0.2)	4.0	(0.5)	0.4	(0.1)	3.9	(0.4)	13.8	(0.7)	71.3	(2.3)
	Chinese Taipei	73.2	(2.1)	0.3	(0.3)	16.3	(1.4)	0.3	(0.1)	1.9	(0.4)	0.1	(0.1)	3.0	(0.6)	4.9	(1.2)	67.7	(5.9)
	Thailand	98.5	(0.5)	0.0	(0.0)	0.6	(0.3)	0.2	(0.1)	0.1	(0.1)	0.1	(0.1)	0.2	(0.2)	0.2	(0.2)	60.9	(20.8)
	Trinidad and Tobago	94.5	(0.5)	1.9	(0.4)	1.1	(0.2)	0.5	(0.2)	0.6	(0.2)	0.5	(0.2)	0.3	(0.1)	0.6	(0.3)	16.8	(6.6)
	Tunisia	99.6	(0.2)	0.2	(0.1)	0.0	c	0.0	c	0.0	c	0.0	c	0.0	c	0.0	c	0.0	c
	Uruguay	96.4	(0.5)	1.2	(0.3)	0.8	(0.2)	0.4	(0.2)	0.4	(0.2)	0.3	(0.1)	0.2	(0.1)	0.4	(0.2)	16.9	(6.4)

StatLink ᴍᴍᴘ http://dx.doi.org/10.1787/888932343285

ANNEX B2
RESULTS FOR REGIONS WITHIN COUNTRIES

[Part 1/1]

Table S.I.a **Percentage of students at each proficiency level on the reading scale**

	Proficiency levels															
	Below Level 1b (less than 262.04 score points)		Level 1b (from 262.04 to less than 334.75 score points)		Level 1a (from 334.75 to less than 407.47 score points)		Level 2 (from 407.47 to less than 480.18 score points)		Level 3 (from 480.18 to less than 552.89 score points)		Level 4 (from 552.89 to less than 625.61 score points)		Level 5 (from 625.61 to less than 698.32 score points)		Level 6 (above 698.32 score points)	
	%	S.E.	%	S.E.	%	S.E.	%	S.E.	%	S.E.	%	S.E.	%	S.E.	%	S.E.
Adjudicated																
Belgium (Flemish Community)	0.4	(0.1)	2.7	(0.4)	10.3	(0.8)	20.1	(0.8)	27.2	(1.1)	26.9	(1.0)	11.3	(0.7)	1.2	(0.3)
Spain (Andalusia)	2.3	(0.7)	6.8	(1.1)	16.9	(1.6)	29.1	(2.5)	31.1	(2.4)	12.1	(1.4)	1.7	(0.5)	0.0	c
Spain (Aragon)	0.7	(0.3)	3.4	(0.6)	11.1	(1.3)	24.8	(1.6)	33.9	(1.6)	21.3	(1.3)	4.5	(0.8)	0.3	(0.2)
Spain (Asturias)	1.3	(0.4)	5.0	(0.9)	11.9	(1.2)	24.4	(1.8)	30.6	(1.3)	21.1	(1.9)	5.4	(0.9)	0.3	(0.2)
Spain (Balearic Islands)	2.6	(0.6)	7.3	(1.0)	17.8	(1.9)	29.8	(1.8)	27.6	(1.7)	13.1	(1.8)	1.7	(0.7)	0.0	c
Spain (Basque Country)	0.7	(0.2)	3.4	(0.5)	11.1	(0.8)	25.5	(0.9)	34.6	(0.8)	20.4	(0.9)	4.2	(0.5)	0.3	(0.1)
Spain (Canary Islands)	2.4	(0.6)	8.8	(1.2)	22.0	(1.7)	28.3	(1.7)	26.1	(1.5)	10.7	(0.9)	1.8	(0.5)	0.0	c
Spain (Cantabria)	0.7	(0.3)	4.7	(0.7)	12.5	(1.2)	25.9	(1.5)	32.3	(2.0)	19.2	(1.8)	4.4	(0.8)	0.3	(0.2)
Spain (Castile and Leon)	0.6	(0.3)	3.2	(0.9)	9.4	(1.4)	22.9	(1.5)	35.2	(1.8)	22.6	(1.6)	5.9	(1.1)	0.2	(0.2)
Spain (Catalonia)	0.7	(0.3)	3.4	(0.8)	9.4	(1.3)	24.5	(1.8)	35.3	(1.8)	23.0	(2.0)	3.6	(0.7)	0.0	c
Spain (Ceuta and Melilla)	7.3	(0.8)	17.3	(1.6)	23.4	(1.8)	24.1	(1.5)	19.0	(1.5)	7.7	(0.8)	1.2	(0.4)	0.0	c
Spain (Galicia)	1.1	(0.3)	4.5	(0.7)	12.8	(1.4)	25.7	(1.3)	32.8	(1.5)	19.5	(1.4)	3.4	(0.8)	0.0	c
Spain (La Rioja)	0.9	(0.4)	4.1	(1.1)	12.1	(1.1)	21.9	(1.7)	31.4	(1.6)	23.5	(1.4)	5.6	(0.9)	0.4	(0.2)
Spain (Madrid)	0.6	(0.3)	2.4	(0.8)	10.1	(1.3)	23.1	(1.7)	34.6	(1.7)	23.3	(1.7)	5.6	(1.1)	0.3	(0.3)
Spain (Murcia)	0.5	(0.3)	3.3	(0.7)	15.2	(1.9)	28.7	(1.8)	33.8	(2.3)	15.9	(1.6)	2.4	(0.6)	0.0	c
Spain (Navarre)	0.5	(0.2)	2.9	(0.6)	11.5	(1.1)	24.9	(1.5)	33.4	(1.9)	21.9	(1.4)	4.6	(0.9)	0.4	(0.2)
United Kingdom (Scotland)	0.8	(0.3)	3.4	(0.6)	12.0	(0.9)	24.9	(1.0)	29.2	(0.9)	20.4	(1.1)	8.0	(0.9)	1.2	(0.3)
Non-adjudicated																
Belgium (French Community)	2.2	(0.5)	7.2	(0.9)	13.9	(1.0)	20.5	(1.0)	24.1	(1.4)	22.5	(1.1)	8.6	(0.8)	1.0	(0.2)
Belgium (German-Speaking Community)	0.7	(0.3)	3.2	(0.8)	13.0	(1.0)	23.7	(1.7)	29.2	(2.1)	23.6	(1.7)	6.0	(1.0)	0.5	(0.3)
Finland (Finnish Speaking)	0.2	(0.1)	1.5	(0.2)	6.1	(0.5)	16.3	(0.7)	30.1	(0.9)	30.9	(0.9)	13.2	(0.8)	1.7	(0.3)
Finland (Swedish Speaking)	0.4	(0.2)	1.9	(0.5)	10.1	(0.9)	23.3	(1.3)	30.4	(1.7)	25.6	(1.6)	7.6	(0.8)	0.7	(0.4)
Italy (Provincia Abruzzo)	1.2	(0.7)	5.0	(0.8)	14.7	(1.4)	26.9	(1.9)	29.5	(1.7)	19.2	(1.7)	3.4	(0.8)	0.1	(0.1)
Italy (Provincia Autonoma di Bolzano)	1.3	(0.7)	4.7	(1.1)	12.0	(1.2)	25.3	(1.3)	30.8	(1.8)	20.2	(1.3)	5.3	(0.6)	0.4	(0.3)
Italy (Provincia Basilicata)	0.5	(0.3)	5.3	(1.2)	18.3	(1.5)	27.7	(1.8)	29.4	(1.6)	15.6	(1.3)	3.0	(0.5)	0.0	c
Italy (Provincia Calabria)	1.8	(0.6)	9.8	(1.8)	21.4	(1.4)	29.2	(2.2)	25.3	(1.7)	11.1	(1.4)	1.4	(0.4)	0.0	c
Italy (Provincia Campania)	2.7	(1.3)	7.7	(1.2)	21.1	(1.7)	29.0	(2.2)	25.8	(2.1)	11.7	(1.9)	1.7	(0.5)	0.2	(0.1)
Italy (Provincia Emilia Romagna)	1.3	(0.6)	4.6	(1.0)	11.7	(1.1)	21.1	(1.7)	26.8	(2.2)	25.5	(2.0)	8.3	(0.9)	0.7	(0.3)
Italy (Provincia Friuli Venezia Giulia)	1.0	(0.5)	2.9	(0.7)	9.5	(1.3)	19.7	(1.6)	30.5	(1.9)	26.4	(1.9)	9.2	(1.2)	0.8	(0.4)
Italy (Provincia Lazio)	0.7	(0.3)	5.5	(1.0)	15.6	(1.5)	26.3	(1.6)	28.1	(1.1)	19.3	(1.2)	4.4	(0.9)	0.1	(0.1)
Italy (Provincia Liguria)	1.5	(1.1)	4.8	(1.7)	12.0	(1.9)	22.9	(1.8)	31.8	(2.4)	20.8	(2.0)	5.9	(1.0)	0.3	(0.2)
Italy (Provincia Lombardia)	0.4	(0.2)	2.7	(0.8)	8.5	(1.3)	17.9	(1.7)	31.5	(2.1)	28.1	(2.0)	9.8	(1.5)	1.1	(0.4)
Italy (Provincia Marche)	0.6	(0.5)	4.5	(1.4)	12.4	(2.2)	22.5	(1.8)	29.4	(2.4)	23.3	(1.8)	6.9	(1.0)	0.5	(0.3)
Italy (Provincia Molise)	0.9	(0.4)	5.7	(0.7)	16.2	(1.4)	28.7	(2.0)	31.3	(1.5)	15.3	(1.3)	1.9	(0.7)	0.0	c
Italy (Provincia Piemonte)	0.8	(0.4)	4.3	(1.2)	13.6	(2.4)	22.2	(1.8)	29.1	(1.9)	22.4	(1.7)	7.0	(1.1)	0.5	(0.2)
Italy (Provincia Puglia)	0.7	(0.5)	3.9	(0.9)	12.9	(1.4)	26.0	(1.9)	31.8	(1.8)	20.5	(1.7)	3.9	(0.8)	0.3	(0.2)
Italy (Provincia Sardegna)	1.9	(0.6)	5.9	(0.9)	16.8	(1.5)	29.4	(1.7)	26.5	(1.7)	16.4	(1.4)	3.1	(0.8)	0.2	(0.1)
Italy (Provincia Sicilia)	3.9	(1.6)	8.1	(1.6)	19.4	(2.6)	26.4	(2.3)	26.1	(2.6)	13.4	(1.6)	2.6	(0.7)	0.1	(0.1)
Italy (Provincia Toscana)	1.2	(0.4)	4.9	(1.0)	13.5	(1.6)	22.3	(1.5)	28.3	(1.9)	23.4	(1.4)	5.9	(0.8)	0.4	(0.3)
Italy (Provincia Trento)	0.7	(0.4)	3.3	(0.7)	10.6	(1.2)	21.8	(1.5)	29.6	(1.8)	24.6	(1.7)	8.7	(1.2)	0.7	(0.3)
Italy (Provincia Umbria)	1.6	(0.6)	5.4	(1.1)	13.4	(1.5)	22.1	(1.7)	28.6	(1.8)	22.0	(1.6)	6.5	(0.9)	0.3	(0.3)
Italy (Provincia Valle d'Aosta)	0.3	(0.2)	2.3	(0.5)	8.8	(0.9)	22.0	(1.4)	31.4	(1.8)	25.9	(1.8)	8.5	(0.9)	0.8	(0.4)
Italy (Provincia Veneto)	0.7	(0.3)	3.5	(1.0)	10.3	(1.5)	21.5	(1.7)	32.3	(1.9)	24.2	(1.8)	6.7	(1.0)	0.7	(0.3)
United Kingdom (England)	1.0	(0.2)	4.1	(0.4)	13.3	(0.8)	24.7	(0.9)	28.9	(1.0)	19.9	(0.9)	7.1	(0.6)	1.0	(0.2)
United Kingdom (Northern Ireland)	0.9	(0.5)	3.9	(0.9)	12.7	(1.1)	23.8	(1.3)	27.8	(1.5)	21.6	(1.2)	7.9	(0.7)	1.4	(0.3)
United Kingdom (Wales)	1.4	(0.3)	5.4	(0.6)	16.3	(0.9)	28.0	(1.2)	28.2	(1.3)	15.8	(1.0)	4.4	(0.5)	0.6	(0.2)

Note: See Table I.2.1 for national data.
StatLink ᐧᐧᐧᐧ http://dx.doi.org/10.1787/888932343304

[Part 1/2]

Table S.I.b **Percentage of students at each proficiency level on the reading scale, by gender**

	Boys – Proficiency levels														
	Below Level 1b (less than 262.04 score points)		Level 1b (from 262.04 to less than 334.75 score points)		Level 1a (from 334.75 to less than 407.47 score points)		Level 2 (from 407.47 to less than 480.18 score points)		Level 3 (from 480.18 to less than 552.89 score points)		Level 4 (from 552.89 to less than 625.61 score points)		Level 5 (from 625.61 to less than 698.32 score points)		Level 6 (above 698.32 score points)	
	%	S.E.	%	S.E.	%	S.E.	%	S.E.	%	S.E.	%	S.E.	%	S.E.	%	S.E.
Adjudicated																
Belgium (Flemish Community)	0.5	(0.2)	3.8	(0.5)	12.6	(1.0)	22.6	(1.2)	26.4	(1.2)	24.0	(1.2)	9.3	(0.9)	0.8	(0.4)
Spain (Andalusia)	2.9	(1.0)	8.1	(1.4)	20.2	(2.1)	28.0	(2.9)	28.6	(2.7)	10.7	(1.5)	1.6	(0.6)	0.0	c
Spain (Aragon)	1.1	(0.5)	5.6	(1.0)	13.3	(1.9)	27.4	(2.0)	32.4	(2.3)	16.9	(1.8)	3.1	(0.8)	0.0	c
Spain (Asturias)	2.0	(0.7)	6.1	(1.3)	15.1	(1.6)	24.9	(2.1)	29.6	(1.9)	17.8	(2.5)	4.4	(1.1)	0.0	c
Spain (Balearic Islands)	3.8	(1.0)	10.1	(1.5)	19.3	(2.1)	32.1	(2.4)	24.0	(2.4)	9.6	(1.5)	1.0	(0.4)	0.0	c
Spain (Basque Country)	1.1	(0.4)	5.2	(0.9)	15.1	(1.0)	27.8	(1.3)	30.9	(1.3)	16.9	(1.1)	2.9	(0.5)	0.2	(0.1)
Spain (Canary Islands)	3.0	(0.9)	10.9	(1.7)	24.7	(2.3)	28.0	(2.2)	22.7	(2.1)	9.1	(1.2)	1.6	(0.5)	0.0	c
Spain (Cantabria)	1.2	(0.5)	7.0	(1.3)	16.0	(2.1)	27.4	(1.8)	29.9	(2.5)	15.4	(1.9)	2.8	(0.7)	0.3	(0.3)
Spain (Castile and Leon)	0.7	(0.4)	5.0	(1.4)	12.4	(1.9)	25.7	(2.1)	33.0	(2.8)	18.4	(2.3)	4.6	(1.2)	0.0	c
Spain (Catalonia)	1.0	(0.4)	5.1	(1.1)	11.4	(1.6)	27.0	(2.1)	34.2	(2.6)	18.7	(2.3)	2.5	(0.9)	0.0	c
Spain (Ceuta and Melilla)	9.9	(1.2)	20.6	(2.1)	21.9	(2.7)	23.3	(1.9)	16.6	(1.4)	6.4	(1.1)	1.1	(0.6)	0.0	c
Spain (Galicia)	1.9	(0.6)	6.7	(1.2)	16.9	(2.0)	26.0	(2.0)	30.1	(2.5)	15.8	(1.5)	2.6	(0.9)	0.0	c
Spain (La Rioja)	1.5	(0.8)	5.6	(1.1)	15.2	(1.9)	24.8	(2.7)	29.0	(2.7)	19.8	(2.0)	4.0	(0.9)	0.0	c
Spain (Madrid)	1.0	(0.6)	3.4	(1.3)	14.2	(1.7)	26.5	(2.6)	31.8	(3.4)	18.9	(2.2)	4.0	(1.1)	0.0	c
Spain (Murcia)	0.6	(0.4)	4.0	(0.9)	17.4	(2.5)	30.5	(2.5)	32.6	(2.7)	13.5	(1.7)	1.5	(0.6)	0.0	c
Spain (Navarre)	0.6	(0.3)	4.2	(1.1)	16.1	(1.6)	26.3	(2.0)	32.2	(2.1)	17.6	(1.9)	2.8	(0.9)	0.0	c
United Kingdom (Scotland)	1.2	(0.4)	4.7	(0.8)	14.9	(1.3)	26.1	(1.6)	27.1	(1.7)	17.7	(1.7)	7.2	(1.3)	1.1	(0.4)
Non-adjudicated																
Belgium (French Community)	3.1	(0.7)	9.2	(1.4)	15.0	(1.4)	21.2	(1.5)	22.5	(1.9)	20.4	(1.8)	7.9	(1.4)	0.8	(0.4)
Belgium (German-Speaking Community)	1.0	(0.5)	5.0	(1.4)	18.4	(1.9)	24.8	(2.2)	27.7	(2.9)	19.0	(2.8)	4.1	(1.2)	0.0	c
Finland (Finnish Speaking)	0.3	(0.1)	2.5	(0.4)	9.8	(0.8)	22.2	(1.1)	32.6	(1.4)	24.2	(1.3)	7.8	(0.9)	0.6	(0.2)
Finland (Swedish Speaking)	0.8	(0.4)	3.3	(0.9)	15.5	(2.0)	29.1	(2.2)	27.9	(2.4)	19.3	(2.3)	3.9	(0.9)	0.0	c
Italy (Provincia Abruzzo)	1.4	(0.9)	7.4	(1.4)	19.9	(2.2)	29.6	(2.2)	26.8	(2.1)	12.9	(1.9)	1.9	(0.8)	0.1	(0.1)
Italy (Provincia Autonoma di Bolzano)	1.9	(1.1)	6.5	(1.6)	17.0	(2.0)	28.3	(2.4)	26.5	(2.5)	16.1	(1.2)	3.6	(0.8)	0.0	c
Italy (Provincia Basilicata)	0.9	(0.6)	7.9	(1.9)	23.6	(1.9)	29.9	(2.6)	24.9	(2.0)	10.6	(1.6)	2.0	(0.7)	0.0	c
Italy (Provincia Calabria)	3.1	(1.0)	15.5	(2.9)	27.1	(2.1)	27.0	(2.6)	19.1	(2.2)	7.2	(1.4)	1.0	(0.6)	0.0	c
Italy (Provincia Campania)	4.3	(1.8)	10.7	(1.7)	27.0	(2.5)	28.8	(2.4)	19.4	(2.4)	8.4	(2.0)	1.3	(0.7)	0.0	c
Italy (Provincia Emilia Romagna)	1.8	(0.8)	5.0	(1.3)	13.9	(1.6)	24.0	(2.3)	26.6	(2.4)	22.6	(2.0)	5.8	(1.0)	0.4	(0.2)
Italy (Provincia Friuli Venezia Giulia)	1.5	(0.8)	5.3	(1.5)	14.2	(1.7)	23.8	(2.5)	28.5	(2.2)	20.2	(2.4)	6.4	(1.1)	0.2	(0.2)
Italy (Provincia Lazio)	1.1	(0.5)	7.9	(1.6)	20.7	(2.3)	28.6	(2.4)	23.9	(2.4)	14.7	(1.9)	3.1	(0.9)	0.0	c
Italy (Provincia Liguria)	2.7	(2.1)	7.0	(2.7)	16.5	(2.8)	26.1	(3.1)	27.4	(3.4)	15.9	(2.8)	4.1	(1.3)	0.0	c
Italy (Provincia Lombardia)	0.7	(0.3)	3.9	(1.4)	11.5	(1.9)	22.2	(2.4)	31.2	(2.4)	23.5	(2.5)	6.4	(1.5)	0.6	(0.3)
Italy (Provincia Marche)	0.8	(0.7)	5.8	(2.2)	15.8	(3.8)	27.7	(2.5)	27.5	(3.7)	17.9	(2.5)	4.3	(1.0)	0.0	c
Italy (Provincia Molise)	1.4	(0.6)	8.9	(1.2)	21.8	(2.0)	30.9	(2.7)	23.4	(2.7)	11.7	(1.8)	1.9	(0.8)	0.0	c
Italy (Provincia Piemonte)	1.2	(0.7)	6.1	(1.9)	16.6	(3.2)	23.3	(2.5)	27.6	(2.3)	19.8	(2.1)	5.0	(1.1)	0.4	(0.3)
Italy (Provincia Puglia)	1.4	(0.9)	6.5	(1.4)	18.1	(2.4)	28.9	(2.5)	27.0	(2.5)	15.6	(2.3)	2.3	(0.7)	0.0	c
Italy (Provincia Sardegna)	3.7	(1.2)	9.0	(1.6)	21.6	(2.1)	32.2	(3.1)	19.6	(2.6)	12.0	(1.5)	1.8	(0.7)	0.0	c
Italy (Provincia Sicilia)	6.3	(2.4)	12.1	(2.5)	24.4	(3.2)	23.7	(3.0)	20.6	(3.0)	10.3	(1.6)	2.4	(0.8)	0.0	c
Italy (Provincia Toscana)	1.8	(0.6)	7.1	(1.5)	18.1	(2.2)	24.9	(2.3)	26.3	(2.0)	17.2	(2.2)	4.3	(1.1)	0.0	c
Italy (Provincia Trento)	1.2	(0.7)	4.9	(1.3)	14.3	(1.9)	25.5	(1.8)	28.0	(2.1)	18.5	(2.4)	6.9	(1.3)	0.7	(0.4)
Italy (Provincia Umbria)	2.8	(1.1)	8.4	(2.0)	17.2	(2.0)	23.5	(2.4)	25.6	(2.5)	18.1	(2.2)	4.1	(1.0)	0.0	c
Italy (Provincia Valle d'Aosta)	0.3	(0.4)	4.0	(1.0)	9.7	(1.6)	23.2	(2.0)	31.3	(2.3)	22.9	(2.5)	8.0	(1.3)	0.6	(0.5)
Italy (Provincia Veneto)	1.3	(0.7)	6.4	(1.8)	15.2	(2.8)	24.6	(2.6)	29.9	(3.0)	18.8	(2.4)	3.6	(0.9)	0.0	c
United Kingdom (England)	1.4	(0.4)	5.6	(0.6)	15.9	(1.2)	25.7	(1.4)	27.2	(1.4)	17.3	(1.4)	6.0	(0.8)	0.9	(0.3)
United Kingdom (Northern Ireland)	1.5	(1.1)	5.6	(1.3)	16.1	(1.8)	24.7	(1.8)	24.7	(2.2)	19.2	(2.0)	7.1	(0.9)	1.1	(0.4)
United Kingdom (Wales)	2.2	(0.5)	7.4	(0.9)	18.9	(1.3)	27.8	(1.6)	25.7	(1.5)	13.6	(1.1)	3.8	(0.6)	0.5	(0.3)

Note: See Table I.2.2 for national data.
StatLink http://dx.doi.org/10.1787/888932343304

[Part 2/2]

Table S.I.b **Percentage of students at each proficiency level on the reading scale, by gender**

	Girls – Proficiency levels															
	Below Level 1b (less than 262.04 score points)		Level 1b (from 262.04 to less than 334.75 score points)		Level 1a (from 334.75 to less than 407.47 score points)		Level 2 (from 407.47 to less than 480.18 score points)		Level 3 (from 480.18 to less than 552.89 score points)		Level 4 (from 552.89 to less than 625.61 score points)		Level 5 (from 625.61 to less than 698.32 score points)		Level 6 (above 698.32 score points)	
	%	S.E.	%	S.E.	%	S.E.	%	S.E.	%	S.E.	%	S.E.	%	S.E.	%	S.E.
Adjudicated																
Belgium (Flemish Community)	0.1	(0.1)	1.6	(0.5)	7.9	(1.0)	17.5	(1.2)	28.1	(1.4)	29.8	(1.4)	13.5	(1.1)	1.5	(0.4)
Spain (Andalusia)	1.5	(0.7)	5.5	(1.3)	13.2	(1.7)	30.3	(2.9)	34.0	(2.9)	13.7	(1.9)	1.8	(0.7)	0.0	c
Spain (Aragon)	0.0	c	1.1	(0.6)	8.9	(1.7)	22.2	(1.9)	35.5	(2.9)	25.9	(2.3)	6.0	(1.1)	0.3	(0.3)
Spain (Asturias)	0.6	(0.5)	3.8	(1.0)	8.5	(1.2)	23.8	(2.6)	31.7	(2.0)	24.8	(2.2)	6.5	(1.4)	0.3	(0.3)
Spain (Balearic Islands)	1.4	(0.6)	4.6	(1.1)	16.3	(2.7)	27.5	(2.7)	31.3	(2.2)	16.6	(3.1)	2.3	(1.3)	0.0	c
Spain (Basque Country)	0.2	(0.1)	1.5	(0.4)	6.8	(0.9)	23.0	(1.4)	38.5	(1.3)	24.0	(1.2)	5.5	(0.7)	0.4	(0.2)
Spain (Canary Islands)	1.7	(0.6)	6.5	(1.7)	18.9	(2.0)	28.6	(2.0)	29.9	(2.4)	12.5	(1.3)	2.0	(0.8)	0.0	c
Spain (Cantabria)	0.3	(0.2)	2.3	(0.6)	8.9	(1.5)	24.3	(2.2)	34.8	(2.2)	23.0	(2.6)	6.0	(1.3)	0.4	(0.2)
Spain (Castile and Leon)	0.4	(0.3)	1.3	(0.7)	6.5	(1.7)	20.1	(2.0)	37.3	(2.0)	26.7	(2.3)	7.2	(1.6)	0.0	c
Spain (Catalonia)	0.4	(0.3)	1.6	(0.8)	7.3	(1.4)	21.9	(2.4)	36.4	(2.0)	27.5	(2.9)	4.7	(1.0)	0.0	c
Spain (Ceuta and Melilla)	4.7	(0.9)	14.1	(1.8)	24.9	(1.9)	24.8	(2.2)	21.2	(2.2)	8.9	(1.3)	1.2	(0.7)	0.0	c
Spain (Galicia)	0.4	(0.3)	2.3	(0.7)	8.7	(1.4)	25.3	(1.9)	35.5	(1.6)	23.4	(1.9)	4.3	(1.1)	0.0	c
Spain (La Rioja)	0.4	(0.2)	2.5	(0.9)	8.9	(1.4)	18.8	(2.2)	34.0	(2.3)	27.4	(2.3)	7.3	(1.5)	0.7	(0.4)
Spain (Madrid)	0.2	(0.2)	1.3	(0.8)	6.0	(1.4)	19.7	(2.0)	37.4	(2.6)	27.7	(3.0)	7.2	(1.5)	0.0	c
Spain (Murcia)	0.5	(0.4)	2.7	(1.0)	13.1	(2.1)	27.0	(2.0)	35.1	(2.6)	18.2	(2.0)	3.3	(1.0)	0.0	c
Spain (Navarre)	0.3	(0.3)	1.4	(0.6)	6.4	(1.2)	23.4	(2.3)	34.7	(2.8)	26.7	(2.2)	6.5	(1.4)	0.6	(0.4)
United Kingdom (Scotland)	0.4	(0.2)	2.2	(0.6)	9.2	(1.0)	23.6	(1.3)	31.4	(1.4)	23.2	(1.5)	8.8	(1.0)	1.2	(0.4)
Non-adjudicated																
Belgium (French Community)	1.2	(0.5)	5.2	(1.1)	12.7	(1.3)	19.8	(1.3)	25.8	(1.7)	24.7	(1.5)	9.3	(0.9)	1.3	(0.4)
Belgium (German-Speaking Community)	0.3	(0.3)	1.3	(0.7)	7.5	(1.3)	22.7	(2.4)	30.8	(2.6)	28.4	(2.4)	8.0	(1.6)	0.9	(0.6)
Finland (Finnish Speaking)	0.1	(0.1)	0.5	(0.2)	2.5	(0.4)	10.2	(0.8)	27.5	(1.2)	37.7	(1.2)	18.7	(1.1)	2.8	(0.5)
Finland (Swedish Speaking)	0.0	c	0.5	(0.4)	4.9	(1.2)	17.7	(1.8)	32.9	(2.3)	31.7	(2.1)	11.1	(1.3)	1.2	(0.7)
Italy (Provincia Abruzzo)	1.0	(0.7)	2.3	(1.0)	9.0	(1.3)	23.9	(2.6)	32.5	(2.4)	26.1	(2.9)	5.1	(1.1)	0.0	c
Italy (Provincia Autonoma di Bolzano)	0.7	(0.5)	2.9	(1.1)	6.9	(1.7)	22.3	(1.6)	35.1	(2.2)	24.3	(1.9)	7.1	(0.9)	0.7	(0.4)
Italy (Provincia Basilicata)	0.0	c	2.5	(0.9)	12.6	(1.7)	25.3	(2.3)	34.4	(2.2)	21.0	(2.0)	4.2	(0.9)	0.0	c
Italy (Provincia Calabria)	0.6	(0.5)	3.9	(1.1)	15.6	(1.5)	31.4	(2.9)	31.7	(2.3)	15.0	(2.4)	1.8	(0.7)	0.0	c
Italy (Provincia Campania)	0.8	(0.7)	3.8	(1.2)	13.4	(2.0)	29.2	(2.9)	34.2	(3.1)	16.1	(2.9)	2.3	(0.7)	0.2	(0.2)
Italy (Provincia Emilia Romagna)	0.9	(0.5)	4.2	(1.0)	9.7	(1.9)	18.4	(2.2)	27.0	(2.9)	28.3	(3.2)	10.6	(1.7)	1.0	(0.5)
Italy (Provincia Friuli Venezia Giulia)	0.4	(0.4)	0.4	(0.5)	4.6	(1.5)	15.3	(1.9)	32.6	(3.0)	33.1	(2.9)	12.3	(2.0)	1.3	(0.7)
Italy (Provincia Lazio)	0.0	c	2.7	(1.6)	9.6	(2.2)	23.6	(2.5)	33.0	(2.4)	24.8	(2.2)	6.0	(1.6)	0.0	c
Italy (Provincia Liguria)	0.0	c	2.2	(1.0)	6.9	(1.4)	19.1	(2.3)	36.9	(2.8)	26.4	(2.1)	8.0	(1.5)	0.5	(0.3)
Italy (Provincia Lombardia)	0.0	c	1.4	(0.8)	5.2	(1.2)	13.1	(2.5)	31.9	(3.0)	33.1	(3.3)	13.6	(2.2)	1.6	(0.8)
Italy (Provincia Marche)	0.0	c	3.0	(1.1)	8.2	(1.6)	16.1	(2.2)	31.6	(2.4)	29.8	(2.4)	9.9	(1.7)	0.9	(0.6)
Italy (Provincia Molise)	0.3	(0.3)	2.3	(0.7)	10.3	(1.6)	26.4	(3.1)	39.7	(3.4)	19.0	(2.2)	2.0	(1.2)	0.0	c
Italy (Provincia Piemonte)	0.4	(0.4)	2.7	(1.2)	10.9	(2.4)	21.1	(2.4)	30.6	(2.8)	24.9	(2.1)	8.9	(1.4)	0.6	(0.3)
Italy (Provincia Puglia)	0.0	c	1.5	(0.6)	7.9	(1.4)	23.3	(2.3)	36.5	(2.1)	25.1	(2.1)	5.4	(1.3)	0.4	(0.4)
Italy (Provincia Sardegna)	0.0	c	2.9	(0.9)	12.3	(2.0)	26.7	(2.6)	32.9	(2.8)	20.4	(2.6)	4.3	(1.2)	0.3	(0.2)
Italy (Provincia Sicilia)	1.5	(1.0)	4.2	(1.6)	14.6	(3.5)	29.0	(2.7)	31.4	(3.4)	16.3	(2.6)	2.8	(1.0)	0.0	c
Italy (Provincia Toscana)	0.5	(0.4)	2.6	(1.2)	8.3	(1.9)	19.5	(1.9)	30.5	(2.8)	30.2	(2.6)	7.8	(1.5)	0.6	(0.4)
Italy (Provincia Trento)	0.0	c	1.5	(0.8)	6.5	(1.3)	17.7	(2.5)	31.4	(2.7)	31.3	(2.5)	10.7	(1.9)	0.7	(0.4)
Italy (Provincia Umbria)	0.5	(0.3)	2.6	(0.9)	9.7	(1.6)	20.8	(2.3)	31.6	(2.5)	25.6	(2.1)	8.9	(1.5)	0.4	(0.3)
Italy (Provincia Valle d'Aosta)	0.0	c	0.7	(0.6)	8.0	(1.5)	20.9	(2.0)	31.4	(2.5)	28.8	(2.1)	9.1	(1.6)	0.9	(0.6)
Italy (Provincia Veneto)	0.0	c	0.8	(0.7)	5.6	(1.5)	18.5	(2.1)	34.6	(2.1)	29.5	(2.6)	9.7	(1.8)	1.2	(0.5)
United Kingdom (England)	0.5	(0.3)	2.7	(0.5)	10.8	(0.9)	23.8	(1.1)	30.5	(1.2)	22.5	(1.3)	8.1	(0.9)	1.1	(0.3)
United Kingdom (Northern Ireland)	0.3	(0.3)	2.3	(0.9)	9.6	(1.2)	23.0	(1.8)	30.7	(1.7)	23.8	(1.6)	8.6	(1.1)	1.7	(0.6)
United Kingdom (Wales)	0.5	(0.2)	3.4	(0.7)	13.7	(1.0)	28.1	(1.3)	30.7	(1.7)	18.0	(1.4)	5.0	(0.7)	0.7	(0.3)

Note: See Table I.2.2 for national data.
StatLink ⧉ http://dx.doi.org/10.1787/888932343304

[Part 1/1]

Table S.I.c **Mean score, variation and gender differences in student performance on the reading scale**

	All students				Gender differences						Percentiles											
	Mean score		Standard deviation		Boys		Girls		Difference (B - G)		5th		10th		25th		75th		90th		95th	
	Mean	S.E.	S.D.	S.E.	Mean score	S.E.	Mean score	S.E.	Score dif.	S.E.	Score	S.E.	Score	S.E.	Score	S.E.	Score	S.E.	Score	S.E.	Score	S.E.
Adjudicated																						
Belgium (Flemish Community)	519	(2.3)	94	(1.8)	505	(3.0)	533	(3.3)	**-28**	(4.1)	357	(5.8)	390	(4.3)	453	(3.1)	589	(2.8)	636	(3.7)	660	(4.1)
Spain (Andalusia)	461	(5.5)	89	(3.0)	451	(5.7)	471	(6.1)	**-21**	(4.8)	299	(10.3)	342	(10.3)	405	(7.5)	523	(4.2)	567	(5.4)	594	(5.9)
Spain (Aragon)	495	(4.1)	85	(2.3)	479	(5.8)	512	(4.1)	**-34**	(5.8)	345	(9.9)	382	(8.2)	441	(5.8)	556	(4.1)	598	(3.9)	624	(5.5)
Spain (Asturias)	490	(4.8)	94	(2.5)	477	(6.0)	505	(5.2)	**-28**	(6.2)	322	(9.7)	363	(7.9)	432	(5.9)	558	(5.5)	604	(5.4)	629	(5.5)
Spain (Balearic Islands)	457	(5.6)	92	(2.7)	440	(6.0)	474	(6.2)	**-34**	(4.7)	294	(9.1)	334	(8.0)	399	(8.1)	521	(6.7)	570	(7.1)	597	(5.1)
Spain (Basque Country)	494	(2.9)	84	(1.8)	477	(3.8)	513	(2.7)	**-35**	(3.4)	345	(7.3)	382	(6.3)	442	(4.0)	553	(2.5)	598	(3.0)	622	(3.3)
Spain (Canary Islands)	448	(4.3)	92	(2.3)	436	(4.7)	461	(4.8)	**-25**	(4.8)	294	(9.2)	329	(7.4)	385	(5.5)	516	(3.9)	562	(3.8)	588	(5.6)
Spain (Cantabria)	488	(4.1)	88	(2.3)	470	(5.2)	506	(4.7)	**-36**	(5.4)	331	(7.8)	368	(6.3)	431	(5.1)	550	(5.5)	597	(6.0)	624	(5.5)
Spain (Castile and Leon)	503	(4.9)	85	(2.1)	487	(6.2)	518	(4.7)	**-31**	(5.8)	349	(10.4)	390	(9.4)	452	(7.3)	562	(4.8)	607	(5.3)	632	(6.7)
Spain (Catalonia)	498	(5.2)	82	(2.4)	484	(5.9)	513	(5.3)	**-29**	(4.4)	345	(11.2)	388	(10.6)	448	(7.2)	557	(4.8)	597	(4.8)	618	(3.9)
Spain (Ceuta and Melilla)	412	(2.5)	104	(1.8)	398	(3.7)	425	(2.9)	**-27**	(4.4)	242	(7.3)	279	(5.0)	336	(5.2)	490	(4.0)	547	(4.9)	577	(5.6)
Spain (Galicia)	486	(4.4)	87	(1.7)	468	(5.2)	503	(4.9)	**-35**	(4.4)	329	(7.8)	368	(7.2)	430	(6.4)	548	(4.7)	593	(5.2)	616	(5.3)
Spain (La Rioja)	498	(2.4)	91	(2.2)	480	(3.1)	516	(3.5)	**-36**	(4.5)	334	(8.6)	372	(5.3)	438	(5.6)	565	(3.7)	608	(4.7)	632	(5.1)
Spain (Madrid)	503	(4.4)	85	(3.2)	486	(5.4)	521	(5.0)	**-36**	(5.9)	355	(8.1)	391	(7.4)	450	(6.4)	562	(4.5)	607	(6.6)	631	(6.9)
Spain (Murcia)	480	(5.1)	80	(2.0)	471	(5.2)	489	(6.1)	**-17**	(5.5)	346	(8.5)	375	(7.0)	425	(8.2)	535	(5.6)	582	(6.3)	606	(6.3)
Spain (Navarre)	497	(3.1)	84	(2.1)	480	(4.2)	516	(3.8)	**-36**	(5.2)	352	(6.6)	385	(5.7)	442	(4.3)	557	(3.5)	600	(5.7)	625	(6.4)
United Kingdom (Scotland)	500	(3.2)	94	(1.5)	488	(4.5)	512	(3.0)	**-24**	(4.1)	341	(6.2)	379	(4.9)	439	(3.6)	567	(3.5)	621	(4.9)	650	(5.2)
Non-adjudicated																						
Belgium (French Community)	490	(4.2)	109	(2.9)	478	(6.2)	503	(4.5)	**-26**	(7.1)	299	(8.0)	338	(8.8)	415	(6.7)	574	(4.1)	624	(3.8)	650	(4.5)
Belgium (German-Speaking Community)	499	(2.8)	90	(2.2)	479	(3.9)	519	(4.2)	**-41**	(5.8)	346	(9.5)	379	(6.8)	437	(4.0)	564	(4.0)	609	(5.3)	637	(9.4)
Finland (Finnish Speaking)	538	(2.4)	86	(1.0)	510	(2.8)	565	(2.5)	**-55**	(2.5)	384	(4.0)	422	(3.8)	483	(3.0)	599	(2.4)	643	(2.7)	667	(2.7)
Finland (Swedish Speaking)	511	(2.6)	87	(2.0)	484	(3.9)	538	(3.0)	**-54**	(4.6)	365	(5.1)	396	(5.2)	453	(3.7)	574	(3.3)	618	(4.5)	648	(5.9)
Italy (Provincia Abruzzo)	480	(4.8)	91	(4.3)	458	(5.8)	504	(5.6)	**-45**	(5.9)	326	(8.4)	362	(7.1)	420	(5.5)	547	(6.6)	592	(6.0)	615	(5.3)
Italy (Provincia Autonoma di Bolzano)	490	(3.2)	93	(2.8)	468	(3.7)	511	(3.1)	**-43**	(3.5)	325	(10.4)	364	(9.3)	433	(5.3)	556	(3.3)	605	(3.8)	630	(4.2)
Italy (Provincia Basilicata)	473	(4.5)	86	(3.0)	452	(6.1)	496	(4.2)	**-43**	(6.2)	330	(9.6)	359	(8.9)	410	(6.4)	536	(4.3)	584	(5.2)	610	(7.4)
Italy (Provincia Calabria)	448	(5.2)	90	(3.7)	421	(7.2)	475	(4.9)	**-54**	(7.3)	297	(10.9)	327	(11.3)	385	(7.5)	512	(5.7)	565	(7.2)	591	(5.4)
Italy (Provincia Campania)	451	(6.6)	93	(5.0)	428	(8.6)	481	(6.3)	**-53**	(8.0)	294	(15.3)	332	(10.8)	389	(7.7)	517	(7.5)	568	(7.6)	595	(7.8)
Italy (Provincia Emilia Romagna)	502	(4.0)	99	(3.9)	489	(4.4)	515	(7.0)	**-27**	(8.5)	326	(11.6)	370	(12.1)	437	(6.3)	577	(4.5)	622	(4.2)	646	(6.1)
Italy (Provincia Friuli Venezia Giulia)	513	(4.7)	92	(3.6)	487	(5.8)	541	(5.4)	**-54**	(6.7)	349	(11.7)	387	(11.4)	456	(7.6)	578	(4.9)	625	(5.3)	650	(6.3)
Italy (Provincia Lazio)	481	(3.9)	91	(2.4)	460	(6.0)	506	(6.7)	**-45**	(9.2)	325	(7.1)	359	(6.7)	417	(6.1)	550	(5.2)	597	(6.7)	622	(7.8)
Italy (Provincia Liguria)	491	(9.3)	94	(7.5)	467	(15.5)	519	(5.2)	**-52**	(15.2)	322	(27.5)	361	(21.9)	433	(14.1)	558	(5.8)	605	(6.2)	633	(6.3)
Italy (Provincia Lombardia)	522	(5.5)	90	(3.1)	501	(6.7)	544	(7.0)	**-43**	(9.0)	360	(12.3)	398	(10.2)	467	(7.7)	585	(6.1)	630	(7.4)	656	(7.8)
Italy (Provincia Marche)	499	(7.3)	92	(5.0)	478	(11.2)	523	(4.2)	**-45**	(12.0)	334	(14.6)	372	(14.6)	436	(12.1)	566	(4.3)	613	(5.3)	639	(5.5)
Italy (Provincia Molise)	471	(2.8)	84	(2.1)	449	(3.7)	493	(3.2)	**-44**	(4.2)	320	(8.1)	359	(7.4)	414	(4.4)	533	(5.5)	576	(5.8)	602	(6.7)
Italy (Provincia Piemonte)	496	(5.9)	95	(3.2)	481	(7.9)	511	(6.0)	**-30**	(8.0)	335	(9.9)	369	(8.9)	429	(10.7)	566	(5.5)	613	(6.0)	639	(6.3)
Italy (Provincia Puglia)	489	(5.0)	86	(3.4)	466	(6.4)	512	(5.3)	**-45**	(6.4)	339	(11.2)	374	(7.5)	434	(6.7)	552	(5.1)	594	(5.8)	620	(6.2)
Italy (Provincia Sardegna)	469	(4.3)	93	(3.4)	442	(5.9)	494	(6.1)	**-53**	(8.0)	310	(8.3)	350	(7.5)	409	(5.6)	537	(5.4)	586	(5.2)	613	(6.8)
Italy (Provincia Sicilia)	453	(8.3)	100	(6.3)	428	(10.7)	477	(9.3)	**-49**	(9.7)	276	(22.5)	322	(14.6)	387	(11.3)	527	(7.3)	576	(6.6)	605	(7.3)
Italy (Provincia Toscana)	493	(4.5)	96	(3.0)	470	(7.0)	518	(6.1)	**-48**	(9.6)	326	(10.3)	359	(9.5)	428	(7.7)	565	(4.0)	608	(4.2)	633	(4.0)
Italy (Provincia Trento)	508	(2.7)	93	(2.3)	488	(4.9)	530	(6.5)	**-42**	(9.9)	343	(6.9)	381	(6.5)	446	(5.2)	575	(3.4)	624	(6.7)	651	(5.6)
Italy (Provincia Umbria)	490	(5.3)	99	(3.7)	467	(7.0)	512	(5.4)	**-45**	(7.6)	314	(13.8)	355	(11.6)	425	(8.8)	563	(4.8)	610	(5.9)	637	(5.5)
Italy (Provincia Valle d'Aosta)	514	(2.2)	86	(2.1)	504	(3.0)	523	(3.3)	**-19**	(4.5)	362	(9.9)	398	(7.0)	459	(3.9)	576	(3.9)	623	(4.3)	649	(6.1)
Italy (Provincia Veneto)	505	(5.2)	90	(4.1)	478	(9.1)	532	(6.4)	**-53**	(12.4)	344	(13.0)	384	(13.0)	448	(8.1)	569	(5.7)	615	(6.1)	640	(7.5)
United Kingdom (England)	495	(2.8)	95	(1.4)	482	(4.3)	507	(3.5)	**-25**	(5.4)	334	(4.9)	370	(3.6)	430	(3.4)	561	(3.9)	616	(3.1)	646	(4.1)
United Kingdom (Northern Ireland)	499	(4.1)	97	(3.5)	485	(7.9)	513	(3.8)	**-29**	(9.4)	336	(13.2)	373	(9.0)	432	(5.5)	569	(3.8)	622	(3.8)	651	(5.4)
United Kingdom (Wales)	476	(3.4)	93	(1.6)	462	(3.9)	490	(3.6)	**-27**	(3.2)	319	(6.2)	356	(5.2)	414	(4.4)	541	(3.6)	595	(4.2)	626	(5.0)

Note: See Table I.2.3 for national data.
Values that are statistically significant are indicated in bold (see Annex A3).
StatLink ᫄᪢᫄ http://dx.doi.org/10.1787/888932343304

[Part 1/1]

Table S.I.d **Percentage of students at each proficiency level on the reading subscale *access and retrieve***

	Below Level 1b (less than 262.04 score points)		Level 1b (from 262.04 to less than 334.75 score points)		Level 1a (from 334.75 to less than 407.47 score points)		Level 2 (from 407.47 to less than 480.18 score points)		Level 3 (from 480.18 to less than 552.89 score points)		Level 4 (from 552.89 to less than 625.61 score points)		Level 5 (from 625.61 to less than 698.32 score points)		Level 6 (above 698.32 score points)	
	%	S.E.	%	S.E.	%	S.E.	%	S.E.	%	S.E.	%	S.E.	%	S.E.	%	S.E.
Adjudicated																
Belgium (Flemish Community)	0.4	(0.1)	2.3	(0.3)	8.0	(0.7)	17.2	(0.8)	25.3	(0.9)	27.1	(1.0)	15.7	(1.0)	3.9	(0.5)
Spain (Andalusia)	4.4	(1.0)	7.1	(1.0)	15.6	(1.4)	28.5	(1.9)	28.1	(1.9)	13.1	(1.3)	3.2	(0.6)	0.1	(0.1)
Spain (Aragon)	2.1	(0.6)	3.9	(0.9)	12.7	(1.1)	24.1	(1.4)	29.3	(1.5)	20.3	(1.7)	6.5	(1.2)	1.1	(0.4)
Spain (Asturias)	2.5	(0.6)	5.7	(0.8)	11.5	(1.2)	21.8	(1.4)	29.1	(1.5)	20.9	(1.7)	7.4	(1.3)	1.1	(0.3)
Spain (Balearic Islands)	5.0	(1.1)	9.0	(1.4)	15.4	(1.2)	25.4	(1.8)	24.2	(1.9)	15.0	(1.6)	5.3	(0.9)	0.8	(0.2)
Spain (Basque Country)	1.4	(0.3)	4.1	(0.5)	11.3	(0.7)	24.1	(0.8)	30.9	(0.8)	20.9	(0.9)	6.4	(0.6)	0.9	(0.2)
Spain (Canary Islands)	4.5	(0.7)	9.9	(1.5)	21.0	(1.4)	25.8	(1.7)	24.3	(1.9)	11.9	(1.1)	2.4	(0.5)	0.2	(0.1)
Spain (Cantabria)	2.1	(0.6)	5.1	(0.7)	13.0	(1.2)	23.3	(1.4)	29.8	(1.4)	19.4	(1.8)	6.6	(1.3)	0.8	(0.3)
Spain (Castile and Leon)	1.3	(0.4)	3.8	(0.8)	10.6	(1.2)	20.1	(1.4)	31.2	(1.4)	22.9	(1.4)	8.8	(1.3)	1.3	(0.4)
Spain (Catalonia)	1.5	(0.4)	4.3	(0.8)	10.8	(1.4)	22.1	(1.8)	31.0	(1.8)	22.7	(1.9)	6.6	(0.9)	0.9	(0.3)
Spain (Ceuta and Melilla)	13.0	(1.1)	16.1	(1.4)	20.7	(1.3)	21.6	(1.5)	17.2	(1.6)	9.3	(0.9)	1.8	(0.4)	0.3	(0.2)
Spain (Galicia)	2.3	(0.5)	5.8	(0.8)	13.1	(1.3)	24.1	(1.5)	29.9	(1.3)	18.8	(1.5)	5.3	(0.9)	0.7	(0.3)
Spain (La Rioja)	2.5	(0.6)	5.0	(0.6)	12.6	(1.3)	22.9	(1.4)	29.8	(1.8)	20.6	(1.4)	5.9	(0.9)	0.8	(0.4)
Spain (Madrid)	1.3	(0.4)	3.8	(0.8)	11.2	(1.2)	23.5	(1.6)	30.3	(1.7)	22.0	(2.0)	7.0	(1.4)	0.9	(0.4)
Spain (Murcia)	1.2	(0.4)	4.7	(0.8)	14.5	(1.4)	25.7	(1.4)	31.1	(1.9)	17.7	(1.6)	4.5	(0.6)	0.7	(0.3)
Spain (Navarre)	1.3	(0.4)	3.9	(0.7)	11.8	(1.1)	24.5	(1.3)	30.9	(2.0)	20.8	(1.4)	6.2	(1.0)	0.6	(0.3)
United Kingdom (Scotland)	1.5	(0.3)	4.4	(0.6)	12.3	(0.9)	21.5	(1.1)	27.3	(1.1)	21.0	(1.4)	9.5	(1.0)	2.5	(0.5)
Non-adjudicated																
Belgium (French Community)	3.3	(0.5)	6.8	(0.9)	14.4	(1.0)	20.2	(1.1)	25.6	(1.3)	21.7	(1.0)	7.2	(0.7)	0.8	(0.2)
Belgium (German-Speaking Community)	1.1	(0.4)	3.9	(1.0)	11.0	(1.1)	21.1	(2.0)	29.9	(2.5)	24.2	(1.9)	7.8	(1.2)	1.0	(0.5)
Finland (Finnish Speaking)	0.8	(0.2)	2.5	(0.3)	7.6	(0.6)	16.9	(1.0)	27.0	(0.9)	27.6	(0.8)	14.4	(0.8)	3.2	(0.4)
Finland (Swedish Speaking)	0.7	(0.3)	3.3	(0.6)	10.3	(1.2)	20.9	(1.4)	27.2	(1.4)	25.1	(1.6)	10.3	(1.2)	2.2	(0.4)
Italy (Provincia Abruzzo)	2.1	(0.6)	5.3	(0.8)	14.5	(1.8)	24.9	(2.2)	28.5	(1.8)	19.2	(1.6)	4.9	(1.0)	0.6	(0.5)
Italy (Provincia Autonoma di Bolzano)	2.0	(0.5)	5.7	(1.1)	11.6	(1.1)	21.5	(1.4)	27.9	(1.7)	21.3	(1.0)	8.4	(0.8)	1.6	(0.3)
Italy (Provincia Basilicata)	2.0	(0.6)	6.4	(1.3)	16.7	(1.2)	25.9	(2.0)	27.0	(1.9)	16.9	(1.8)	4.5	(0.7)	0.5	(0.3)
Italy (Provincia Calabria)	3.9	(1.2)	9.5	(1.8)	18.7	(1.3)	28.2	(2.0)	25.4	(2.6)	11.9	(1.8)	2.3	(0.5)	0.0	c
Italy (Provincia Campania)	4.0	(1.2)	9.0	(1.3)	19.4	(1.7)	25.8	(1.7)	24.9	(1.9)	14.0	(1.8)	2.7	(0.8)	0.2	(0.2)
Italy (Provincia Emilia Romagna)	2.8	(0.8)	5.6	(1.0)	11.8	(1.1)	19.2	(1.5)	26.9	(1.4)	24.4	(1.3)	8.1	(1.1)	1.1	(0.5)
Italy (Provincia Friuli Venezia Giulia)	1.2	(0.5)	4.1	(0.8)	10.2	(1.7)	20.5	(1.5)	29.8	(1.9)	24.3	(2.0)	8.8	(1.2)	1.0	(0.3)
Italy (Provincia Lazio)	2.6	(0.6)	6.2	(1.1)	16.0	(1.9)	25.6	(2.1)	27.4	(1.5)	17.0	(1.3)	4.9	(1.0)	0.4	(0.2)
Italy (Provincia Liguria)	3.1	(1.7)	5.9	(1.7)	12.7	(1.6)	24.2	(1.6)	29.5	(2.4)	18.4	(2.1)	5.7	(0.9)	0.5	(0.2)
Italy (Provincia Lombardia)	1.1	(0.5)	3.8	(0.9)	8.1	(1.4)	18.7	(1.5)	32.1	(1.8)	26.3	(1.9)	8.8	(0.9)	1.1	(0.5)
Italy (Provincia Marche)	2.1	(0.9)	5.4	(1.5)	12.1	(1.7)	22.6	(1.5)	28.3	(2.3)	21.5	(1.6)	7.2	(1.1)	0.9	(0.4)
Italy (Provincia Molise)	2.5	(0.5)	6.5	(0.8)	16.4	(1.0)	27.8	(1.6)	29.5	(1.8)	14.6	(1.6)	2.5	(0.7)	0.0	c
Italy (Provincia Piemonte)	2.4	(1.0)	6.7	(1.5)	13.2	(2.0)	22.9	(2.0)	26.1	(2.1)	20.3	(1.7)	7.3	(1.2)	1.2	(0.4)
Italy (Provincia Puglia)	1.8	(0.8)	5.1	(1.0)	13.7	(1.7)	24.0	(1.9)	28.7	(2.4)	20.0	(1.8)	6.1	(1.0)	0.7	(0.3)
Italy (Provincia Sardegna)	3.5	(0.7)	6.9	(1.1)	16.8	(1.2)	26.0	(1.7)	24.7	(1.6)	16.4	(1.5)	5.1	(1.0)	0.7	(0.3)
Italy (Provincia Sicilia)	5.7	(1.8)	10.1	(2.2)	18.3	(2.1)	23.0	(2.1)	23.7	(2.4)	14.3	(1.7)	4.3	(1.0)	0.5	(0.3)
Italy (Provincia Toscana)	2.8	(0.7)	5.9	(1.0)	12.2	(1.2)	21.9	(1.5)	28.3	(1.7)	22.4	(1.5)	6.0	(1.1)	0.5	(0.3)
Italy (Provincia Trento)	2.0	(0.5)	4.9	(0.7)	11.9	(1.1)	20.4	(1.3)	28.0	(1.9)	23.0	(1.3)	8.4	(1.5)	1.4	(0.5)
Italy (Provincia Umbria)	3.3	(1.0)	6.3	(1.1)	12.9	(1.3)	21.5	(1.4)	28.7	(1.9)	20.2	(1.8)	6.2	(0.8)	0.9	(0.3)
Italy (Provincia Valle d'Aosta)	1.0	(0.4)	4.0	(0.9)	11.1	(1.3)	20.1	(2.0)	30.2	(2.4)	24.8	(1.7)	8.1	(1.6)	0.9	(0.4)
Italy (Provincia Veneto)	1.7	(0.6)	4.0	(1.0)	10.2	(1.3)	21.2	(1.4)	29.2	(1.7)	23.5	(1.5)	8.9	(0.9)	1.2	(0.4)
United Kingdom (England)	1.7	(0.3)	4.8	(0.5)	13.7	(0.7)	23.5	(1.1)	28.3	(1.1)	19.9	(1.1)	7.0	(0.7)	1.1	(0.3)
United Kingdom (Northern Ireland)	1.2	(0.6)	4.4	(0.8)	12.3	(1.1)	22.5	(1.2)	29.4	(1.6)	21.2	(1.3)	7.6	(0.9)	1.5	(0.4)
United Kingdom (Wales)	2.1	(0.4)	5.6	(0.6)	15.2	(0.9)	26.3	(1.2)	29.0	(1.1)	16.0	(1.0)	5.0	(0.5)	0.8	(0.2)

Note: See Table I.2.4 for national data.
StatLink ᴍᴙˢᴾ http://dx.doi.org/10.1787/888932343304

[Part 1/2]

Table S.I.e

Percentage of students at each proficiency level on the reading subscale *access and retrieve*, by gender

	Boys – Proficiency levels															
	Below Level 1b (less than 262.04 score points)		Level 1b (from 262.04 to less than 334.75 score points)		Level 1a (from 334.75 to less than 407.47 score points)		Level 2 (from 407.47 to less than 480.18 score points)		Level 3 (from 480.18 to less than 552.89 score points)		Level 4 (from 552.89 to less than 625.61 score points)		Level 5 (from 625.61 to less than 698.32 score points)		Level 6 (above 698.32 score points)	
	%	S.E.	%	S.E.	%	S.E.	%	S.E.	%	S.E.	%	S.E.	%	S.E.	%	S.E.
Adjudicated																
Belgium (Flemish Community)	0.7	(0.3)	3.3	(0.5)	10.3	(0.9)	19.9	(1.1)	25.9	(1.3)	24.8	(1.0)	12.2	(1.1)	3.0	(0.6)
Spain (Andalusia)	5.6	(1.1)	8.6	(1.2)	18.2	(1.6)	27.1	(1.8)	25.6	(2.1)	11.9	(1.4)	2.8	(0.8)	0.0	c
Spain (Aragon)	3.7	(1.1)	5.5	(1.2)	15.2	(2.0)	25.8	(2.1)	27.4	(2.4)	16.6	(2.4)	5.0	(1.5)	0.8	(0.5)
Spain (Asturias)	3.6	(0.9)	6.9	(1.0)	13.6	(1.9)	22.9	(2.1)	28.2	(2.1)	18.6	(2.1)	5.6	(1.3)	0.6	(0.4)
Spain (Balearic Islands)	7.1	(1.7)	11.5	(2.0)	17.6	(1.8)	25.9	(2.4)	21.3	(2.2)	11.7	(2.0)	4.6	(1.4)	0.3	(0.3)
Spain (Basque Country)	2.3	(0.6)	5.8	(0.7)	14.5	(1.1)	26.5	(1.3)	28.0	(1.4)	17.4	(1.4)	4.9	(0.8)	0.5	(0.2)
Spain (Canary Islands)	5.5	(1.1)	12.7	(2.6)	22.7	(1.8)	25.0	(2.2)	23.0	(2.6)	9.5	(1.8)	1.5	(0.6)	0.0	c
Spain (Cantabria)	3.2	(1.0)	6.7	(1.2)	15.7	(1.9)	24.7	(2.1)	27.4	(1.9)	16.5	(1.9)	4.7	(1.1)	1.0	(0.5)
Spain (Castile and Leon)	1.8	(0.8)	5.4	(1.3)	13.7	(1.9)	22.0	(2.4)	29.2	(1.8)	18.8	(2.1)	8.3	(1.8)	0.7	(0.4)
Spain (Catalonia)	2.0	(0.6)	5.9	(1.4)	12.7	(1.9)	23.3	(2.0)	30.1	(2.6)	20.2	(1.9)	5.3	(0.9)	0.6	(0.4)
Spain (Ceuta and Melilla)	17.3	(1.6)	17.3	(2.0)	19.5	(2.1)	20.3	(2.4)	15.0	(2.1)	8.6	(1.4)	1.6	(0.6)	0.0	c
Spain (Galicia)	3.8	(1.0)	8.3	(1.3)	16.4	(1.9)	23.8	(2.3)	27.3	(2.5)	16.5	(1.7)	3.5	(0.9)	0.5	(0.4)
Spain (La Rioja)	3.6	(0.9)	5.9	(1.0)	15.9	(1.8)	24.7	(2.7)	27.5	(2.9)	17.7	(2.0)	4.4	(0.9)	0.0	c
Spain (Madrid)	1.7	(0.7)	5.6	(1.3)	14.5	(1.9)	26.0	(2.0)	28.9	(2.3)	17.6	(2.1)	5.1	(1.2)	0.6	(0.4)
Spain (Murcia)	1.4	(0.6)	4.6	(1.0)	15.7	(1.8)	28.5	(2.2)	30.0	(2.6)	16.3	(2.4)	3.0	(0.7)	0.6	(0.3)
Spain (Navarre)	1.8	(0.6)	5.7	(1.1)	14.1	(1.6)	26.9	(1.8)	30.2	(2.6)	16.7	(1.6)	4.4	(1.1)	0.0	c
United Kingdom (Scotland)	2.3	(0.6)	6.5	(0.9)	15.3	(1.4)	23.3	(1.4)	24.5	(1.6)	18.1	(1.5)	8.1	(1.1)	2.0	(0.5)
Non-adjudicated																
Belgium (French Community)	4.9	(0.9)	8.3	(1.3)	16.1	(1.4)	20.4	(1.4)	23.3	(1.5)	19.8	(1.5)	6.6	(1.0)	0.6	(0.3)
Belgium (German-Speaking Community)	1.6	(0.7)	6.2	(1.7)	15.5	(1.9)	22.6	(2.5)	28.4	(2.9)	19.3	(2.4)	5.8	(1.5)	0.5	(0.4)
Finland (Finnish Speaking)	1.2	(0.2)	4.0	(0.5)	11.5	(1.2)	22.4	(1.7)	28.1	(1.3)	22.1	(1.3)	9.0	(0.9)	1.7	(0.4)
Finland (Swedish Speaking)	1.5	(0.6)	5.4	(1.2)	13.9	(1.7)	26.1	(2.6)	26.8	(1.9)	18.6	(2.8)	6.8	(1.5)	0.9	(0.4)
Italy (Provincia Abruzzo)	2.3	(0.9)	7.9	(1.3)	18.5	(3.1)	27.1	(2.7)	26.6	(2.4)	14.1	(1.7)	3.0	(0.8)	0.4	(0.4)
Italy (Provincia Autonoma di Bolzano)	2.9	(0.9)	7.8	(1.3)	16.1	(1.7)	23.3	(2.1)	24.3	(2.4)	17.3	(1.4)	7.1	(0.9)	1.1	(0.5)
Italy (Provincia Basilicata)	3.3	(0.9)	9.1	(2.2)	19.9	(1.7)	25.9	(2.2)	24.7	(2.4)	13.7	(1.9)	3.2	(0.8)	0.0	c
Italy (Provincia Calabria)	6.8	(2.0)	14.4	(3.1)	23.2	(2.3)	27.0	(2.5)	19.0	(2.6)	8.0	(1.6)	1.6	(0.7)	0.0	c
Italy (Provincia Campania)	6.1	(1.6)	12.1	(2.2)	23.6	(2.4)	24.7	(1.9)	20.1	(2.2)	10.8	(2.1)	2.4	(0.9)	0.0	c
Italy (Provincia Emilia Romagna)	3.5	(1.3)	6.0	(1.0)	13.4	(1.4)	20.3	(1.8)	26.5	(1.7)	21.6	(2.2)	7.8	(1.4)	0.9	(0.4)
Italy (Provincia Friuli Venezia Giulia)	1.8	(0.8)	6.7	(1.3)	14.5	(2.8)	23.1	(2.5)	28.5	(2.4)	18.9	(2.3)	6.1	(1.2)	0.4	(0.3)
Italy (Provincia Lazio)	3.6	(0.8)	8.7	(2.1)	19.3	(2.9)	27.3	(2.9)	24.2	(2.5)	13.2	(1.7)	3.2	(0.8)	0.3	(0.2)
Italy (Provincia Liguria)	5.0	(3.2)	8.6	(2.7)	15.9	(2.4)	24.9	(2.1)	25.8	(3.6)	15.1	(3.0)	4.7	(1.2)	0.0	c
Italy (Provincia Lombardia)	1.7	(0.9)	5.3	(1.4)	10.2	(1.7)	21.6	(2.1)	31.4	(3.0)	22.3	(2.8)	6.7	(1.2)	0.8	(0.4)
Italy (Provincia Marche)	2.6	(1.4)	6.8	(2.3)	15.3	(2.4)	27.5	(1.9)	25.9	(3.4)	16.7	(2.3)	4.8	(1.2)	0.3	(0.3)
Italy (Provincia Molise)	4.1	(1.0)	10.3	(1.4)	21.7	(1.8)	28.2	(2.4)	22.1	(2.5)	11.6	(2.0)	2.0	(0.9)	0.0	c
Italy (Provincia Piemonte)	3.2	(1.7)	7.7	(2.1)	15.3	(2.4)	23.5	(2.4)	25.0	(2.6)	19.3	(2.2)	5.4	(1.1)	0.7	(0.4)
Italy (Provincia Puglia)	3.1	(1.6)	8.1	(1.6)	17.0	(2.5)	25.8	(2.8)	25.7	(2.9)	15.7	(2.1)	4.3	(0.9)	0.3	(0.3)
Italy (Provincia Sardegna)	6.5	(1.5)	9.8	(1.7)	20.4	(2.1)	28.7	(2.2)	20.1	(2.2)	10.9	(1.3)	3.3	(0.8)	0.4	(0.3)
Italy (Provincia Sicilia)	9.0	(2.8)	13.7	(2.6)	20.9	(2.7)	22.9	(3.5)	18.3	(2.4)	11.0	(1.9)	3.6	(1.0)	0.5	(0.4)
Italy (Provincia Toscana)	4.2	(0.9)	8.3	(1.4)	15.9	(1.9)	24.1	(2.1)	26.4	(2.3)	16.8	(2.4)	4.0	(1.1)	0.3	(0.3)
Italy (Provincia Trento)	3.5	(1.0)	6.8	(1.4)	15.0	(1.9)	23.7	(2.2)	24.6	(3.3)	18.9	(2.5)	6.3	(1.5)	1.1	(0.8)
Italy (Provincia Umbria)	5.6	(1.6)	8.8	(1.7)	15.9	(1.7)	22.3	(1.8)	25.9	(2.3)	16.2	(2.1)	4.6	(0.9)	0.7	(0.4)
Italy (Provincia Valle d'Aosta)	1.7	(0.7)	5.7	(1.6)	11.2	(2.0)	21.9	(2.9)	29.5	(3.2)	22.1	(2.4)	7.5	(2.0)	0.4	(0.4)
Italy (Provincia Veneto)	3.2	(1.3)	6.7	(2.2)	13.8	(2.2)	23.6	(2.2)	27.2	(2.7)	19.1	(2.5)	5.7	(1.1)	0.6	(0.5)
United Kingdom (England)	2.7	(0.5)	6.5	(0.7)	16.4	(1.1)	24.2	(1.4)	26.7	(1.5)	16.8	(1.3)	5.8	(0.9)	0.9	(0.3)
United Kingdom (Northern Ireland)	1.9	(1.1)	6.8	(1.5)	15.8	(1.8)	23.4	(1.8)	26.7	(1.9)	18.0	(1.9)	6.1	(1.0)	1.1	(0.7)
United Kingdom (Wales)	3.4	(0.6)	7.6	(0.9)	18.0	(1.1)	26.4	(1.8)	26.6	(1.8)	13.5	(1.2)	3.8	(0.6)	0.5	(0.2)

Note: See Table I.2.5 for national data.
StatLink http://dx.doi.org/10.1787/888932343304

[Part 2/2]

Percentage of students at each proficiency level on the reading subscale *access and retrieve*, by gender

Table S.I.e

	Girls – Proficiency levels														
	Below Level 1b (less than 262.04 score points)		Level 1b (from 262.04 to less than 334.75 score points)		Level 1a (from 334.75 to less than 407.47 score points)		Level 2 (from 407.47 to less than 480.18 score points)		Level 3 (from 480.18 to less than 552.89 score points)		Level 4 (from 552.89 to less than 625.61 score points)		Level 5 (from 625.61 to less than 698.32 score points)		Level 6 (above 698.32 score points)	
	%	S.E.	%	S.E.	%	S.E.	%	S.E.	%	S.E.	%	S.E.	%	S.E.	%	S.E.
Adjudicated																
Belgium (Flemish Community)	0.2	(0.1)	1.4	(0.4)	5.6	(0.8)	14.5	(1.0)	24.7	(1.4)	29.5	(1.5)	19.4	(1.4)	4.8	(0.7)
Spain (Andalusia)	3.0	(1.1)	5.4	(1.4)	12.6	(2.0)	30.0	(3.0)	31.0	(2.6)	14.4	(1.9)	3.5	(0.9)	0.0	c
Spain (Aragon)	0.5	(0.3)	2.3	(0.9)	10.1	(1.2)	22.4	(1.9)	31.3	(1.9)	24.1	(1.9)	8.0	(1.5)	1.4	(0.6)
Spain (Asturias)	1.4	(0.6)	4.3	(1.0)	9.1	(1.5)	20.5	(2.0)	30.2	(2.1)	23.5	(2.1)	9.4	(1.6)	1.7	(0.6)
Spain (Balearic Islands)	2.8	(0.9)	6.5	(1.4)	13.2	(1.5)	24.8	(2.4)	27.2	(2.4)	18.3	(2.0)	5.9	(1.1)	1.2	(0.5)
Spain (Basque Country)	0.4	(0.2)	2.3	(0.4)	7.9	(0.8)	21.5	(1.1)	34.0	(1.4)	24.6	(1.1)	8.0	(1.0)	1.3	(0.3)
Spain (Canary Islands)	3.5	(0.8)	6.9	(1.4)	19.1	(2.2)	26.6	(2.1)	25.6	(2.2)	14.5	(1.6)	3.5	(0.7)	0.3	(0.3)
Spain (Cantabria)	0.9	(0.5)	3.4	(0.9)	10.2	(1.2)	21.9	(1.9)	32.2	(2.0)	22.4	(2.7)	8.5	(1.9)	0.5	(0.3)
Spain (Castile and Leon)	0.8	(0.4)	2.2	(0.6)	7.5	(1.1)	18.2	(1.7)	33.1	(2.0)	27.0	(2.1)	9.3	(1.2)	1.9	(0.6)
Spain (Catalonia)	1.0	(0.5)	2.7	(0.9)	8.8	(1.5)	20.9	(2.6)	32.0	(2.2)	25.3	(2.7)	8.0	(1.5)	1.3	(0.5)
Spain (Ceuta and Melilla)	8.8	(1.2)	15.0	(1.5)	21.9	(1.6)	22.7	(2.2)	19.3	(2.2)	10.0	(1.4)	1.9	(0.5)	0.4	(0.3)
Spain (Galicia)	0.7	(0.3)	3.3	(1.0)	9.7	(1.4)	24.5	(2.0)	32.6	(1.7)	21.1	(1.9)	7.1	(1.3)	1.0	(0.4)
Spain (La Rioja)	1.4	(0.6)	4.0	(0.9)	9.1	(1.6)	21.0	(2.6)	32.2	(2.5)	23.5	(2.0)	7.6	(1.4)	1.1	(0.5)
Spain (Madrid)	0.8	(0.4)	2.1	(0.8)	8.0	(1.3)	21.0	(2.3)	31.8	(2.4)	26.3	(3.2)	8.9	(1.9)	1.1	(0.6)
Spain (Murcia)	1.1	(0.5)	4.7	(1.3)	13.3	(1.8)	22.9	(1.7)	32.1	(2.6)	19.1	(2.0)	5.9	(1.0)	0.9	(0.5)
Spain (Navarre)	0.7	(0.4)	1.9	(0.8)	9.2	(1.5)	21.7	(1.9)	31.7	(2.1)	25.3	(2.3)	8.2	(1.9)	1.2	(0.8)
United Kingdom (Scotland)	0.7	(0.3)	2.3	(0.6)	9.3	(0.9)	19.8	(1.5)	30.1	(1.5)	23.9	(1.7)	10.9	(1.2)	3.0	(0.6)
Non-adjudicated																
Belgium (French Community)	1.5	(0.4)	5.2	(0.9)	12.7	(1.3)	20.1	(1.5)	28.1	(1.9)	23.7	(1.5)	7.8	(1.0)	0.9	(0.3)
Belgium (German-Speaking Community)	0.6	(0.4)	1.5	(0.8)	6.3	(1.4)	19.4	(2.5)	31.4	(3.3)	29.2	(3.0)	9.9	(1.5)	1.6	(1.0)
Finland (Finnish Speaking)	0.3	(0.2)	1.0	(0.2)	3.7	(0.7)	11.4	(0.9)	25.8	(1.1)	33.2	(1.3)	19.9	(1.1)	4.7	(0.6)
Finland (Swedish Speaking)	0.0	c	1.2	(0.5)	6.8	(1.2)	15.8	(1.5)	27.6	(1.9)	31.4	(2.2)	13.7	(1.7)	3.5	(0.8)
Italy (Provincia Abruzzo)	1.8	(0.4)	2.5	(0.9)	10.1	(2.0)	22.5	(3.4)	30.6	(3.2)	24.9	(2.6)	6.9	(1.7)	0.8	(0.7)
Italy (Provincia Autonoma di Bolzano)	1.0	(0.6)	3.6	(1.2)	7.1	(1.4)	19.7	(1.9)	31.5	(2.0)	25.3	(1.6)	9.7	(1.2)	2.1	(0.4)
Italy (Provincia Basilicata)	0.7	(0.6)	3.6	(0.9)	13.1	(1.9)	25.9	(2.5)	29.5	(2.3)	20.4	(2.7)	5.9	(1.2)	0.8	(0.5)
Italy (Provincia Calabria)	0.9	(0.4)	4.5	(1.5)	14.2	(1.7)	29.5	(2.3)	31.8	(2.9)	15.9	(2.4)	3.0	(0.8)	0.0	c
Italy (Provincia Campania)	1.4	(1.0)	4.9	(1.4)	13.9	(2.2)	27.3	(2.9)	31.1	(2.5)	18.2	(2.5)	3.1	(1.2)	0.0	c
Italy (Provincia Emilia Romagna)	2.2	(0.9)	5.2	(1.6)	10.4	(1.9)	18.2	(2.6)	27.2	(2.7)	27.1	(2.4)	8.5	(1.6)	1.3	(0.6)
Italy (Provincia Friuli Venezia Giulia)	0.6	(0.5)	1.4	(0.8)	5.5	(1.7)	17.8	(1.9)	31.3	(3.1)	30.1	(2.9)	11.8	(1.8)	1.7	(0.7)
Italy (Provincia Lazio)	1.3	(0.5)	3.2	(0.9)	12.2	(2.1)	23.6	(2.3)	31.0	(2.2)	21.4	(2.0)	6.8	(1.6)	0.5	(0.5)
Italy (Provincia Liguria)	0.9	(0.5)	2.8	(1.2)	9.0	(1.8)	23.5	(2.3)	33.7	(2.6)	22.3	(2.1)	6.9	(1.3)	0.9	(0.4)
Italy (Provincia Lombardia)	0.5	(0.3)	2.2	(1.1)	5.7	(1.6)	15.6	(2.3)	32.8	(2.3)	30.6	(2.5)	11.0	(1.3)	1.5	(0.8)
Italy (Provincia Marche)	1.5	(0.9)	3.7	(0.9)	8.2	(1.6)	16.7	(2.1)	31.2	(2.2)	27.2	(2.1)	9.9	(1.7)	1.5	(0.6)
Italy (Provincia Molise)	0.7	(0.4)	2.5	(0.7)	10.8	(1.6)	27.4	(2.5)	37.4	(3.2)	17.8	(2.5)	3.0	(0.9)	0.0	c
Italy (Provincia Piemonte)	1.6	(0.7)	5.7	(1.7)	11.2	(2.3)	22.3	(2.3)	27.2	(2.7)	21.2	(2.3)	9.0	(1.8)	1.7	(0.6)
Italy (Provincia Puglia)	0.4	(0.2)	2.3	(0.8)	10.5	(1.7)	22.3	(2.4)	31.6	(2.7)	24.1	(2.7)	7.9	(1.6)	1.0	(0.6)
Italy (Provincia Sardegna)	0.6	(0.4)	4.2	(1.5)	13.4	(1.9)	23.4	(2.1)	29.1	(2.2)	21.4	(2.4)	6.8	(1.5)	1.0	(0.5)
Italy (Provincia Sicilia)	2.5	(1.4)	6.6	(3.2)	15.7	(2.8)	23.1	(2.2)	29.0	(3.0)	17.4	(2.7)	4.9	(1.4)	0.6	(0.5)
Italy (Provincia Toscana)	1.3	(0.8)	3.2	(1.3)	8.1	(1.7)	19.5	(2.0)	30.5	(2.7)	28.5	(2.1)	8.2	(2.1)	0.7	(0.4)
Italy (Provincia Trento)	0.0	c	2.7	(1.2)	8.5	(1.9)	16.7	(1.7)	31.7	(2.7)	27.6	(2.5)	10.7	(2.1)	1.7	(0.7)
Italy (Provincia Umbria)	1.0	(0.6)	3.9	(1.0)	10.1	(1.4)	20.8	(2.4)	31.3	(2.8)	24.1	(2.4)	7.8	(1.3)	1.1	(0.5)
Italy (Provincia Valle d'Aosta)	0.0	c	2.3	(1.1)	10.9	(1.7)	18.2	(2.6)	30.9	(3.0)	27.4	(2.5)	8.7	(2.0)	1.3	(0.6)
Italy (Provincia Veneto)	0.3	(0.3)	1.3	(0.7)	6.7	(1.6)	19.0	(1.8)	31.2	(2.1)	27.7	(2.5)	11.9	(1.6)	1.8	(0.6)
United Kingdom (England)	0.8	(0.3)	3.1	(0.6)	11.0	(0.9)	22.8	(1.3)	30.0	(1.5)	22.9	(1.7)	8.1	(0.9)	1.3	(0.4)
United Kingdom (Northern Ireland)	0.5	(0.3)	2.1	(0.7)	9.0	(1.2)	21.6	(1.8)	31.9	(2.4)	24.2	(1.7)	8.9	(1.3)	1.8	(0.5)
United Kingdom (Wales)	0.8	(0.3)	3.5	(0.6)	12.5	(1.1)	26.3	(1.4)	31.5	(1.5)	18.4	(1.3)	6.1	(0.8)	1.0	(0.3)

Note: See Table I.2.5 for national data.

StatLink http://dx.doi.org/10.1787/888932343304

[Part 1/1]

Table S.I.f **Mean score, variation and gender differences in student performance on the reading subscale *access and retrieve***

	All students				Gender differences						Percentiles											
	Mean score		Standard deviation		Boys		Girls		Difference (B – G)		5th		10th		25th		75th		90th		95th	
	Mean	S.E.	S.D.	S.E.	Mean score	S.E.	Mean score	S.E.	Score dif.	S.E.	Score	S.E.	Score	S.E.	Score	S.E.	Score	S.E.	Score	S.E.	Score	S.E.
Adjudicated																						
Belgium (Flemish Community)	537	(2.7)	100	(1.8)	520	(3.3)	555	(3.7)	**-35**	(4.5)	362	(5.8)	403	(4.7)	470	(3.6)	609	(3.6)	660	(3.7)	689	(5.0)
Spain (Andalusia)	458	(5.7)	101	(3.7)	447	(5.7)	470	(6.6)	**-24**	(4.9)	271	(14.7)	323	(12.1)	400	(8.2)	527	(4.6)	578	(5.7)	608	(6.6)
Spain (Aragon)	492	(5.3)	99	(3.2)	473	(8.1)	511	(4.7)	**-38**	(7.8)	325	(11.3)	364	(10.7)	432	(7.8)	560	(5.5)	612	(7.3)	643	(7.3)
Spain (Asturias)	492	(5.4)	105	(3.0)	477	(6.3)	508	(6.1)	**-31**	(6.6)	304	(13.0)	349	(11.7)	428	(6.7)	564	(5.2)	618	(6.5)	646	(5.8)
Spain (Balearic Islands)	461	(6.2)	113	(2.9)	441	(6.9)	481	(6.8)	**-40**	(5.4)	262	(14.4)	309	(10.2)	392	(8.2)	539	(6.4)	600	(6.2)	634	(7.5)
Spain (Basque Country)	496	(3.2)	95	(2.1)	477	(4.3)	516	(3.0)	**-39**	(3.9)	329	(8.8)	373	(6.4)	437	(3.9)	561	(3.0)	612	(3.5)	641	(3.9)
Spain (Canary Islands)	444	(4.9)	103	(2.5)	429	(6.1)	460	(5.2)	**-31**	(6.6)	266	(8.6)	307	(9.4)	375	(7.0)	518	(5.3)	571	(4.9)	601	(5.8)
Spain (Cantabria)	488	(5.4)	100	(2.7)	472	(6.6)	505	(5.3)	**-33**	(5.1)	311	(9.6)	358	(8.9)	425	(7.3)	558	(6.1)	611	(6.6)	642	(8.0)
Spain (Castile and Leon)	507	(5.5)	98	(2.7)	491	(7.2)	523	(5.3)	**-32**	(6.6)	334	(12.2)	374	(9.6)	446	(6.6)	575	(5.9)	627	(6.2)	654	(6.8)
Spain (Catalonia)	499	(5.6)	97	(2.5)	486	(6.4)	513	(6.0)	**-27**	(5.4)	325	(10.7)	370	(8.1)	442	(8.5)	565	(5.2)	614	(4.8)	643	(7.4)
Spain (Ceuta and Melilla)	403	(3.3)	123	(2.2)	387	(5.3)	419	(3.5)	**-33**	(6.0)	190	(10.4)	241	(8.4)	320	(5.0)	493	(5.1)	561	(5.2)	596	(7.5)
Spain (Galicia)	483	(5.4)	100	(2.3)	464	(6.3)	503	(5.6)	**-39**	(5.0)	304	(9.1)	350	(9.1)	421	(7.1)	552	(5.7)	604	(6.8)	632	(7.1)
Spain (La Rioja)	488	(2.8)	102	(2.9)	471	(3.8)	505	(4.2)	**-34**	(5.7)	309	(10.4)	354	(7.9)	426	(5.8)	559	(4.6)	607	(6.3)	636	(6.6)
Spain (Madrid)	499	(5.0)	96	(3.3)	481	(6.0)	517	(6.2)	**-36**	(7.5)	332	(9.9)	373	(8.5)	439	(6.1)	565	(5.7)	615	(7.2)	643	(9.3)
Spain (Murcia)	484	(5.4)	93	(3.0)	476	(5.8)	492	(6.4)	**-16**	(6.0)	326	(10.9)	365	(7.8)	422	(7.4)	548	(5.2)	599	(5.6)	626	(5.6)
Spain (Navarre)	495	(3.7)	93	(2.3)	478	(4.9)	514	(4.4)	**-37**	(5.6)	331	(11.7)	373	(7.3)	437	(5.2)	560	(5.4)	610	(4.9)	638	(6.1)
United Kingdom (Scotland)	504	(3.8)	105	(2.1)	486	(5.0)	522	(3.8)	**-36**	(4.5)	327	(8.0)	368	(5.2)	435	(5.1)	576	(4.7)	636	(5.1)	669	(5.8)
Non-adjudicated																						
Belgium (French Community)	484	(4.0)	110	(2.8)	470	(5.9)	498	(4.2)	**-29**	(6.8)	288	(9.4)	335	(8.2)	410	(6.4)	566	(3.6)	617	(3.7)	643	(4.6)
Belgium (German-Speaking Community)	505	(2.9)	96	(2.2)	483	(4.5)	527	(4.0)	**-44**	(6.3)	334	(10.0)	376	(8.1)	442	(4.9)	573	(5.4)	621	(6.8)	649	(7.9)
Finland (Finnish Speaking)	533	(2.9)	99	(1.3)	504	(3.3)	563	(3.0)	**-59**	(2.7)	358	(5.9)	402	(4.4)	471	(4.0)	603	(3.2)	654	(3.3)	683	(3.7)
Finland (Swedish Speaking)	516	(3.1)	99	(2.4)	487	(4.5)	543	(3.7)	**-56**	(5.4)	347	(7.4)	384	(6.8)	450	(4.6)	586	(4.5)	639	(6.4)	670	(5.3)
Italy (Provincia Abruzzo)	481	(5.7)	100	(4.5)	461	(6.4)	503	(7.0)	**-42**	(6.6)	311	(10.2)	352	(8.3)	417	(7.1)	552	(6.7)	603	(6.8)	629	(8.0)
Italy (Provincia Autonoma di Bolzano)	497	(3.5)	105	(2.5)	476	(4.6)	518	(3.2)	**-42**	(4.3)	309	(11.8)	353	(9.8)	430	(6.3)	571	(3.9)	626	(4.2)	656	(5.8)
Italy (Provincia Basilicata)	473	(4.4)	97	(3.1)	454	(6.0)	494	(5.1)	**-40**	(7.0)	309	(11.2)	344	(8.8)	407	(7.0)	544	(4.4)	596	(4.6)	626	(5.9)
Italy (Provincia Calabria)	449	(5.7)	98	(4.1)	420	(8.2)	479	(4.8)	**-58**	(8.2)	274	(14.3)	314	(12.9)	385	(8.3)	518	(5.7)	572	(7.2)	602	(6.4)
Italy (Provincia Campania)	451	(9.4)	103	(4.8)	429	(9.6)	479	(6.9)	**-50**	(8.2)	274	(14.8)	316	(12.7)	385	(8.9)	525	(8.5)	578	(6.8)	606	(8.4)
Italy (Provincia Emilia Romagna)	496	(4.8)	109	(4.4)	487	(5.3)	505	(7.9)	**-19**	(9.4)	300	(14.6)	346	(12.0)	427	(7.9)	575	(4.0)	623	(3.8)	650	(6.2)
Italy (Provincia Friuli Venezia Giulia)	507	(5.4)	99	(4.4)	482	(6.7)	533	(6.1)	**-51**	(7.7)	330	(12.8)	377	(10.7)	447	(7.4)	576	(6.0)	625	(6.1)	652	(6.7)
Italy (Provincia Lazio)	474	(4.0)	100	(2.4)	454	(6.1)	497	(6.6)	**-44**	(9.2)	299	(8.1)	341	(7.8)	408	(6.3)	545	(4.9)	599	(6.7)	628	(6.8)
Italy (Provincia Liguria)	480	(11.2)	102	(7.9)	459	(18.6)	506	(5.6)	**-47**	(17.9)	292	(32.5)	343	(26.5)	420	(16.6)	552	(7.5)	602	(6.4)	634	(7.0)
Italy (Provincia Lombardia)	514	(4.8)	95	(3.9)	497	(7.4)	532	(5.7)	**-35**	(9.7)	335	(16.3)	385	(12.2)	460	(7.5)	578	(4.4)	625	(4.6)	654	(6.7)
Italy (Provincia Marche)	492	(7.8)	102	(5.6)	471	(11.3)	517	(5.4)	**-46**	(12.0)	307	(20.1)	356	(18.0)	427	(11.3)	564	(5.5)	617	(5.3)	645	(4.9)
Italy (Provincia Molise)	465	(3.1)	94	(2.2)	440	(4.2)	491	(3.5)	**-51**	(4.8)	293	(11.8)	340	(6.0)	406	(4.0)	533	(4.2)	581	(5.4)	605	(6.2)
Italy (Provincia Piemonte)	487	(8.1)	107	(5.2)	473	(10.1)	499	(8.1)	**-26**	(9.2)	303	(17.4)	341	(14.3)	418	(12.3)	564	(7.6)	618	(8.6)	649	(9.5)
Italy (Provincia Puglia)	488	(7.0)	99	(5.3)	464	(8.7)	510	(7.5)	**-46**	(8.7)	317	(15.4)	357	(10.3)	423	(9.8)	558	(7.0)	610	(6.0)	639	(8.6)
Italy (Provincia Sardegna)	469	(5.0)	107	(3.7)	439	(6.4)	497	(7.0)	**-58**	(8.6)	284	(12.6)	333	(9.8)	401	(5.8)	544	(6.1)	602	(6.8)	632	(8.4)
Italy (Provincia Sicilia)	451	(10.3)	116	(6.9)	424	(11.9)	476	(13.2)	**-51**	(12.6)	252	(24.2)	300	(16.7)	375	(13.9)	533	(8.0)	593	(7.9)	624	(9.8)
Italy (Provincia Toscana)	487	(5.4)	103	(3.8)	464	(8.0)	513	(6.7)	**-49**	(10.0)	294	(14.5)	347	(11.6)	423	(8.5)	563	(5.4)	608	(5.6)	634	(6.0)
Italy (Provincia Trento)	500	(2.7)	104	(2.7)	477	(4.9)	525	(6.5)	**-47**	(9.9)	314	(13.3)	358	(7.4)	433	(5.0)	574	(5.3)	626	(7.5)	654	(6.3)
Italy (Provincia Umbria)	484	(5.9)	108	(4.6)	460	(7.6)	507	(6.3)	**-47**	(8.2)	288	(18.2)	338	(13.5)	418	(8.9)	559	(5.5)	610	(5.3)	640	(5.9)
Italy (Provincia Valle d'Aosta)	506	(3.0)	96	(2.2)	495	(4.2)	517	(4.0)	**-22**	(5.6)	336	(12.0)	373	(8.0)	445	(5.8)	574	(4.0)	621	(6.3)	650	(5.3)
Italy (Provincia Veneto)	505	(5.0)	100	(4.5)	478	(9.4)	531	(6.1)	**-52**	(12.8)	325	(19.0)	374	(13.3)	445	(7.4)	575	(4.8)	626	(4.6)	658	(7.0)
United Kingdom (England)	491	(3.1)	101	(1.9)	475	(4.7)	506	(3.5)	**-30**	(5.7)	321	(5.6)	360	(5.2)	426	(3.8)	561	(3.3)	616	(4.4)	649	(5.0)
United Kingdom (Northern Ireland)	499	(4.7)	98	(4.0)	481	(8.3)	516	(4.0)	**-35**	(9.3)	330	(13.9)	371	(10.5)	435	(6.6)	567	(3.8)	621	(4.6)	652	(4.7)
United Kingdom (Wales)	477	(3.6)	98	(1.8)	460	(4.3)	494	(3.7)	**-33**	(3.4)	309	(8.1)	351	(5.6)	414	(4.0)	544	(3.9)	598	(4.9)	632	(5.2)

Note: See Table I.2.6 for national data.
Values that are statistically significant are indicated in bold (see Annex A3).
StatLink ᔞᓮᔐᓬ http://dx.doi.org/10.1787/888932343304

[Part 1/1]

Percentage of students at each proficiency level on the reading subscale

Table S.I.g *integrate and interpret*

	Proficiency levels															
	Below Level 1b (less than 262.04 score points)		Level 1b (from 262.04 to less than 334.75 score points)		Level 1a (from 334.75 to less than 407.47 score points)		Level 2 (from 407.47 to less than 480.18 score points)		Level 3 (from 480.18 to less than 552.89 score points)		Level 4 (from 552.89 to less than 625.61 score points)		Level 5 (from 625.61 to less than 698.32 score points)		Level 6 (above 698.32 score points)	
	%	S.E.	%	S.E.	%	S.E.	%	S.E.	%	S.E.	%	S.E.	%	S.E.	%	S.E.
Adjudicated																
Belgium (Flemish Community)	0.5	(0.2)	3.3	(0.6)	11.3	(0.6)	21.0	(0.9)	25.6	(0.9)	25.2	(1.2)	11.6	(1.1)	1.6	(0.4)
Spain (Andalusia)	1.7	(0.6)	6.9	(1.1)	17.0	(1.7)	29.8	(1.6)	30.8	(1.8)	12.1	(1.3)	1.7	(0.5)	0.0	c
Spain (Aragon)	0.5	(0.2)	3.0	(0.7)	11.0	(1.1)	25.6	(1.6)	34.2	(1.6)	20.8	(1.5)	4.6	(0.6)	0.2	(0.1)
Spain (Asturias)	1.2	(0.5)	4.4	(0.8)	12.4	(1.2)	24.6	(1.7)	31.0	(1.4)	20.6	(1.8)	5.3	(0.8)	0.6	(0.3)
Spain (Balearic Islands)	2.1	(0.7)	6.9	(1.0)	19.4	(1.3)	31.3	(1.6)	27.1	(1.7)	11.6	(1.7)	1.5	(0.5)	0.0	c
Spain (Basque Country)	0.5	(0.1)	3.2	(0.5)	11.2	(0.7)	25.4	(1.0)	34.2	(1.0)	20.5	(0.9)	4.6	(0.4)	0.4	(0.1)
Spain (Canary Islands)	2.9	(0.7)	8.7	(1.1)	21.6	(1.4)	28.9	(2.0)	25.8	(2.2)	10.7	(1.0)	1.4	(0.3)	0.0	c
Spain (Cantabria)	0.6	(0.3)	4.7	(0.8)	12.8	(1.2)	25.8	(1.6)	32.2	(1.8)	19.4	(1.6)	4.2	(0.7)	0.3	(0.2)
Spain (Castile and Leon)	0.6	(0.3)	3.1	(0.7)	9.5	(1.3)	24.8	(1.5)	34.7	(1.4)	22.0	(1.5)	5.0	(0.8)	0.2	(0.2)
Spain (Catalonia)	0.5	(0.2)	2.9	(0.7)	10.7	(1.3)	26.0	(1.8)	35.3	(1.7)	20.9	(1.9)	3.6	(0.7)	0.1	(0.1)
Spain (Ceuta and Melilla)	6.3	(0.8)	15.7	(1.1)	25.7	(1.3)	25.0	(1.6)	18.8	(1.3)	7.1	(0.8)	1.2	(0.4)	0.0	c
Spain (Galicia)	1.0	(0.3)	4.5	(0.8)	13.6	(1.5)	26.6	(1.7)	32.9	(1.6)	17.6	(1.3)	3.7	(0.9)	0.0	c
Spain (La Rioja)	0.7	(0.3)	4.1	(0.7)	13.4	(1.2)	21.4	(1.6)	31.1	(1.8)	22.5	(1.6)	6.2	(1.0)	0.6	(0.3)
Spain (Madrid)	0.7	(0.4)	2.7	(0.7)	9.6	(1.1)	22.8	(1.6)	33.4	(1.8)	23.9	(1.7)	6.4	(1.1)	0.5	(0.3)
Spain (Murcia)	0.6	(0.5)	3.5	(0.8)	15.6	(1.8)	28.9	(1.9)	32.7	(2.0)	15.6	(1.8)	3.0	(0.8)	0.0	c
Spain (Navarre)	0.4	(0.2)	3.3	(0.7)	12.2	(1.3)	23.7	(1.4)	34.2	(1.5)	20.4	(1.4)	5.3	(0.8)	0.4	(0.2)
United Kingdom (Scotland)	0.7	(0.3)	3.6	(0.5)	12.3	(0.9)	25.2	(1.1)	28.4	(1.0)	20.3	(1.3)	8.2	(1.0)	1.3	(0.3)
Non-adjudicated																
Belgium (French Community)	2.6	(0.6)	7.4	(0.8)	14.3	(1.0)	20.0	(1.1)	23.9	(1.3)	21.0	(1.0)	9.4	(0.8)	1.5	(0.3)
Belgium (German-Speaking Community)	0.5	(0.3)	3.7	(0.9)	13.8	(1.2)	23.1	(1.1)	26.8	(2.2)	23.4	(2.3)	7.8	(1.1)	0.9	(0.5)
Finland (Finnish Speaking)	0.2	(0.1)	1.2	(0.2)	6.1	(0.4)	16.2	(0.7)	29.7	(0.9)	30.3	(0.9)	14.0	(0.8)	2.3	(0.3)
Finland (Swedish Speaking)	0.4	(0.2)	2.3	(0.4)	9.8	(1.1)	24.6	(1.6)	30.1	(1.5)	24.0	(1.6)	7.9	(0.9)	0.9	(0.4)
Italy (Provincia Abruzzo)	0.8	(0.6)	4.4	(0.7)	14.4	(1.4)	27.1	(2.1)	29.6	(1.7)	19.2	(1.7)	4.3	(1.0)	0.0	c
Italy (Provincia Autonoma di Bolzano)	1.0	(0.6)	4.6	(0.9)	12.4	(1.2)	25.5	(1.8)	31.0	(1.7)	19.9	(1.0)	5.1	(0.8)	0.5	(0.2)
Italy (Provincia Basilicata)	0.4	(0.3)	4.8	(1.2)	16.8	(1.6)	28.6	(2.1)	30.3	(2.0)	16.1	(1.5)	2.9	(0.6)	0.0	c
Italy (Provincia Calabria)	1.7	(1.0)	7.9	(1.7)	21.5	(1.8)	29.8	(2.4)	25.9	(1.5)	11.3	(1.4)	1.8	(0.5)	0.0	c
Italy (Provincia Campania)	2.2	(1.2)	7.0	(1.3)	19.8	(1.8)	29.3	(2.5)	26.5	(1.8)	13.1	(2.0)	2.0	(0.7)	0.1	(0.1)
Italy (Provincia Emilia Romagna)	0.8	(0.3)	3.8	(0.8)	11.3	(1.1)	21.4	(1.8)	27.3	(1.7)	25.5	(1.6)	8.9	(1.2)	0.9	(0.4)
Italy (Provincia Friuli Venezia Giulia)	0.8	(0.6)	3.1	(0.8)	9.3	(1.3)	20.0	(1.5)	30.7	(1.8)	25.7	(1.6)	9.4	(1.2)	1.0	(0.3)
Italy (Provincia Lazio)	0.6	(0.3)	4.1	(0.6)	15.0	(1.4)	26.8	(1.7)	28.8	(1.6)	19.1	(1.6)	5.3	(1.2)	0.2	(0.2)
Italy (Provincia Liguria)	1.5	(1.0)	4.9	(1.9)	11.2	(1.6)	22.9	(1.9)	30.1	(2.6)	21.7	(1.7)	7.0	(1.2)	0.7	(0.3)
Italy (Provincia Lombardia)	0.3	(0.2)	3.1	(1.0)	8.2	(1.0)	17.4	(1.7)	30.7	(2.0)	27.9	(1.8)	10.8	(1.6)	1.5	(0.6)
Italy (Provincia Marche)	0.3	(0.3)	3.3	(1.2)	12.1	(2.6)	23.0	(2.0)	30.3	(2.3)	23.0	(1.9)	7.2	(1.3)	0.8	(0.5)
Italy (Provincia Molise)	0.6	(0.3)	3.9	(0.8)	14.8	(1.4)	31.0	(2.3)	32.6	(2.1)	15.3	(1.7)	1.7	(0.6)	0.0	c
Italy (Provincia Piemonte)	0.7	(0.4)	3.4	(0.9)	12.6	(1.6)	23.8	(1.7)	28.9	(1.8)	22.5	(1.6)	7.4	(1.4)	0.7	(0.3)
Italy (Provincia Puglia)	0.5	(0.3)	3.5	(0.7)	12.8	(1.7)	25.6	(2.3)	33.2	(2.1)	20.4	(1.9)	3.6	(0.7)	0.3	(0.3)
Italy (Provincia Sardegna)	1.4	(0.6)	4.7	(0.9)	18.5	(1.6)	28.4	(1.6)	27.3	(1.6)	16.2	(1.4)	3.2	(0.7)	0.3	(0.2)
Italy (Provincia Sicilia)	3.3	(1.5)	6.6	(1.5)	18.4	(2.3)	27.8	(2.4)	27.2	(2.5)	13.6	(1.8)	2.8	(0.6)	0.2	(0.1)
Italy (Provincia Toscana)	0.8	(0.4)	4.8	(1.0)	12.7	(1.3)	22.3	(1.5)	28.4	(1.7)	24.1	(1.7)	6.5	(1.0)	0.4	(0.3)
Italy (Provincia Trento)	0.6	(0.3)	2.8	(0.7)	10.3	(1.4)	20.9	(1.2)	29.9	(1.6)	24.6	(1.5)	9.8	(1.2)	1.0	(0.3)
Italy (Provincia Umbria)	1.1	(0.4)	5.0	(1.0)	13.6	(1.7)	22.5	(1.7)	28.9	(2.1)	22.0	(1.3)	6.1	(1.1)	0.8	(0.3)
Italy (Provincia Valle d'Aosta)	0.3	(0.2)	2.4	(0.6)	8.2	(1.0)	21.4	(2.1)	32.5	(2.4)	25.6	(1.6)	8.7	(1.3)	0.9	(0.4)
Italy (Provincia Veneto)	0.6	(0.5)	3.1	(1.1)	10.3	(1.5)	21.7	(1.8)	32.3	(2.1)	23.8	(1.8)	7.5	(1.1)	0.7	(0.3)
United Kingdom (England)	1.0	(0.4)	4.4	(0.5)	14.7	(0.9)	24.8	(0.9)	28.2	(1.0)	18.5	(0.9)	7.1	(0.6)	1.2	(0.2)
United Kingdom (Northern Ireland)	1.0	(0.4)	4.3	(0.6)	13.4	(1.2)	24.0	(1.5)	27.0	(1.3)	20.4	(1.3)	8.2	(0.9)	1.6	(0.4)
United Kingdom (Wales)	1.5	(0.3)	6.1	(0.7)	17.8	(1.2)	27.6	(1.1)	26.7	(1.0)	14.9	(1.1)	4.7	(0.6)	0.6	(0.2)

Note: See Table I.2.7 for national data.

StatLink ᐧᐧᐧ http://dx.doi.org/10.1787/888932343304

[Part 1/2]

Table S.I.h **Percentage of students at each proficiency level on the reading subscale** *integrate and interpret,* **by gender**

	Boys – Proficiency levels															
	Below Level 1b (less than 262.04 score points)		Level 1b (from 262.04 to less than 334.75 score points)		Level 1a (from 334.75 to less than 407.47 score points)		Level 2 (from 407.47 to less than 480.18 score points)		Level 3 (from 480.18 to less than 552.89 score points)		Level 4 (from 552.89 to less than 625.61 score points)		Level 5 (from 625.61 to less than 698.32 score points)		Level 6 (above 698.32 score points)	
	%	S.E.	%	S.E.	%	S.E.	%	S.E.	%	S.E.	%	S.E.	%	S.E.	%	S.E.
Adjudicated																
Belgium (Flemish Community)	0.6	(0.2)	4.4	(0.7)	13.5	(0.9)	22.8	(1.2)	24.7	(1.3)	22.7	(1.5)	9.9	(1.1)	1.4	(0.5)
Spain (Andalusia)	1.9	(0.7)	8.5	(1.5)	20.1	(2.0)	29.0	(2.2)	28.3	(2.2)	10.2	(1.4)	1.8	(0.5)	0.0	c
Spain (Aragon)	0.9	(0.4)	5.0	(1.1)	13.1	(2.2)	27.9	(2.4)	32.0	(2.1)	17.8	(2.1)	3.2	(0.7)	0.0	c
Spain (Asturias)	1.9	(0.8)	5.8	(1.2)	14.9	(1.9)	25.4	(1.9)	29.6	(2.0)	17.5	(2.4)	4.4	(1.0)	0.5	(0.3)
Spain (Balearic Islands)	3.0	(0.9)	9.3	(1.5)	22.2	(2.1)	32.2	(2.5)	23.3	(2.3)	8.9	(1.8)	1.1	(0.6)	0.0	c
Spain (Basque Country)	0.8	(0.3)	4.7	(0.7)	15.5	(1.0)	26.9	(1.2)	30.5	(1.4)	17.5	(1.1)	3.6	(0.5)	0.3	(0.2)
Spain (Canary Islands)	3.9	(0.9)	10.3	(1.5)	23.8	(1.7)	28.5	(2.1)	22.7	(2.2)	9.4	(1.2)	1.4	(0.6)	0.0	c
Spain (Cantabria)	1.0	(0.6)	6.7	(1.5)	17.0	(1.8)	26.9	(2.0)	29.6	(2.5)	15.7	(1.9)	2.8	(0.7)	0.3	(0.3)
Spain (Castile and Leon)	0.9	(0.5)	4.8	(1.2)	11.7	(2.0)	27.5	(2.4)	32.3	(2.4)	18.7	(2.0)	4.0	(1.0)	0.0	c
Spain (Catalonia)	0.8	(0.4)	4.3	(1.0)	13.3	(1.8)	27.5	(2.1)	33.3	(2.9)	17.8	(2.1)	2.9	(0.8)	0.0	c
Spain (Ceuta and Melilla)	8.8	(1.4)	18.0	(1.7)	25.6	(1.8)	23.7	(2.6)	16.5	(2.1)	6.3	(1.3)	1.0	(0.6)	0.0	c
Spain (Galicia)	1.8	(0.6)	6.2	(1.4)	17.3	(2.3)	27.2	(2.7)	30.4	(2.6)	14.3	(1.4)	2.7	(0.6)	0.0	c
Spain (La Rioja)	1.1	(0.5)	5.7	(1.1)	16.9	(2.0)	23.8	(2.6)	27.7	(2.2)	19.3	(1.8)	5.3	(1.1)	0.0	c
Spain (Madrid)	1.2	(0.7)	4.1	(1.2)	12.8	(1.8)	25.7	(2.3)	31.2	(2.4)	20.3	(2.5)	4.4	(1.1)	0.3	(0.3)
Spain (Murcia)	0.7	(0.7)	4.3	(1.0)	17.5	(2.3)	29.8	(2.4)	30.3	(2.4)	14.8	(2.0)	2.5	(0.9)	0.0	c
Spain (Navarre)	0.6	(0.3)	5.2	(1.2)	16.3	(1.8)	24.5	(2.2)	33.0	(1.9)	16.7	(1.9)	3.4	(1.0)	0.3	(0.2)
United Kingdom (Scotland)	1.1	(0.4)	4.8	(0.8)	14.6	(1.2)	25.9	(1.4)	26.7	(1.4)	18.1	(1.3)	7.5	(1.2)	1.3	(0.4)
Non-adjudicated																
Belgium (French Community)	3.4	(0.8)	8.7	(1.3)	15.8	(1.5)	20.3	(1.6)	22.5	(1.5)	19.3	(1.4)	8.7	(1.1)	1.2	(0.4)
Belgium (German-Speaking Community)	0.7	(0.5)	5.3	(1.6)	18.7	(2.0)	24.9	(2.5)	24.9	(2.7)	19.6	(2.8)	5.7	(1.4)	0.0	c
Finland (Finnish Speaking)	0.3	(0.2)	1.9	(0.4)	9.4	(0.8)	21.8	(1.0)	32.0	(1.3)	24.6	(1.2)	8.8	(0.7)	1.1	(0.3)
Finland (Swedish Speaking)	0.8	(0.5)	3.9	(0.9)	14.2	(1.6)	29.8	(2.5)	27.9	(2.1)	18.7	(1.9)	4.3	(1.1)	0.4	(0.4)
Italy (Provincia Abruzzo)	0.8	(0.6)	6.5	(1.2)	19.0	(2.3)	30.0	(2.6)	27.1	(2.2)	13.8	(1.8)	2.8	(1.1)	0.0	c
Italy (Provincia Autonoma di Bolzano)	1.7	(1.0)	6.4	(1.5)	17.2	(2.3)	29.4	(3.2)	25.6	(2.5)	16.0	(1.3)	3.5	(1.1)	0.0	c
Italy (Provincia Basilicata)	0.7	(0.5)	7.5	(1.9)	21.8	(1.9)	30.9	(2.4)	26.3	(2.3)	10.9	(1.5)	1.8	(0.6)	0.0	c
Italy (Provincia Calabria)	2.7	(1.7)	12.5	(2.5)	27.4	(2.4)	28.8	(2.6)	19.7	(1.9)	7.4	(1.3)	1.4	(0.7)	0.0	c
Italy (Provincia Campania)	3.3	(1.5)	9.9	(1.9)	25.6	(2.9)	30.0	(2.8)	20.1	(2.5)	9.1	(2.2)	1.8	(0.9)	0.0	c
Italy (Provincia Emilia Romagna)	1.1	(0.6)	4.5	(1.2)	12.8	(1.4)	23.8	(2.4)	28.4	(2.0)	22.1	(1.7)	7.0	(0.9)	0.3	(0.3)
Italy (Provincia Friuli Venezia Giulia)	1.5	(1.0)	5.2	(1.3)	14.5	(1.8)	24.7	(2.0)	27.8	(2.1)	19.5	(2.4)	6.5	(1.5)	0.4	(0.3)
Italy (Provincia Lazio)	1.0	(0.5)	5.8	(1.0)	20.3	(2.2)	28.7	(2.7)	25.7	(2.4)	14.6	(1.8)	3.7	(1.0)	0.3	(0.2)
Italy (Provincia Liguria)	2.7	(1.8)	7.3	(3.2)	15.5	(2.4)	26.1	(2.8)	26.9	(3.8)	15.9	(2.3)	5.2	(1.4)	0.2	(0.3)
Italy (Provincia Lombardia)	0.4	(0.3)	4.8	(1.5)	10.6	(1.6)	21.5	(2.5)	31.1	(2.5)	22.9	(2.5)	7.8	(1.9)	0.8	(0.4)
Italy (Provincia Marche)	0.5	(0.4)	4.3	(2.1)	15.9	(4.6)	27.8	(2.7)	28.6	(3.6)	17.7	(2.8)	5.1	(1.4)	0.0	c
Italy (Provincia Molise)	1.0	(0.6)	6.3	(1.4)	20.9	(2.1)	33.7	(3.2)	24.5	(2.7)	12.0	(2.0)	1.6	(1.1)	0.0	c
Italy (Provincia Piemonte)	1.2	(0.8)	5.0	(1.5)	15.2	(2.2)	24.8	(2.4)	27.1	(2.3)	21.2	(2.2)	5.1	(1.0)	0.4	(0.4)
Italy (Provincia Puglia)	1.0	(0.7)	5.7	(1.2)	18.5	(2.7)	27.9	(2.8)	29.1	(2.7)	15.2	(2.2)	2.4	(0.7)	0.0	c
Italy (Provincia Sardegna)	2.8	(1.2)	7.4	(1.4)	23.7	(2.4)	30.7	(2.3)	21.4	(2.3)	11.3	(1.7)	2.5	(0.8)	0.0	c
Italy (Provincia Sicilia)	5.5	(2.4)	10.9	(2.3)	23.5	(3.6)	24.7	(2.9)	21.5	(3.0)	11.4	(1.6)	2.4	(0.8)	0.0	c
Italy (Provincia Toscana)	1.2	(0.5)	7.0	(1.3)	16.9	(2.0)	25.9	(2.4)	26.2	(2.4)	17.9	(2.6)	4.6	(1.1)	0.2	(0.3)
Italy (Provincia Trento)	1.0	(0.5)	4.0	(1.1)	13.3	(1.8)	25.0	(2.2)	27.6	(2.2)	19.6	(2.1)	8.6	(1.7)	0.8	(0.4)
Italy (Provincia Umbria)	1.8	(0.6)	7.8	(1.7)	17.6	(2.4)	24.2	(2.4)	26.5	(2.6)	17.3	(1.5)	4.2	(1.1)	0.6	(0.4)
Italy (Provincia Valle d'Aosta)	0.4	(0.5)	3.6	(1.1)	8.7	(1.4)	23.0	(2.5)	32.2	(2.7)	24.0	(2.7)	7.6	(1.9)	0.5	(0.4)
Italy (Provincia Veneto)	1.0	(0.9)	5.6	(2.0)	15.2	(3.0)	25.0	(2.5)	29.8	(3.5)	18.8	(2.6)	4.1	(1.0)	0.3	(0.3)
United Kingdom (England)	1.4	(0.3)	5.8	(0.7)	17.4	(1.3)	25.3	(1.3)	26.1	(1.3)	16.6	(1.3)	6.3	(0.7)	1.0	(0.3)
United Kingdom (Northern Ireland)	1.5	(0.8)	6.0	(1.5)	16.0	(1.8)	24.2	(1.7)	24.1	(1.9)	19.2	(2.1)	7.4	(1.2)	1.6	(0.6)
United Kingdom (Wales)	2.4	(0.5)	8.1	(1.0)	19.9	(1.5)	27.3	(1.3)	24.7	(1.3)	13.0	(1.2)	4.1	(0.7)	0.6	(0.3)

Note: See Table I.2.8 for national data.
StatLink ⌐╦═┐ http://dx.doi.org/10.1787/888932343304

[Part 2/2]

Percentage of students at each proficiency level on the reading subscale integrate and interpret, by gender

Table S.I.h

	Girls – Proficiency levels															
	Below Level 1b (less than 262.04 score points)		Level 1b (from 262.04 to less than 334.75 score points)		Level 1a (from 334.75 to less than 407.47 score points)		Level 2 (from 407.47 to less than 480.18 score points)		Level 3 (from 480.18 to less than 552.89 score points)		Level 4 (from 552.89 to less than 625.61 score points)		Level 5 (from 625.61 to less than 698.32 score points)		Level 6 (above 698.32 score points)	
	%	S.E.	%	S.E.	%	S.E.	%	S.E.	%	S.E.	%	S.E.	%	S.E.	%	S.E.
Adjudicated																
Belgium (Flemish Community)	0.3	(0.2)	2.2	(0.6)	8.9	(0.9)	19.0	(1.3)	26.6	(1.2)	27.7	(1.8)	13.4	(1.4)	1.9	(0.5)
Spain (Andalusia)	1.5	(0.7)	5.1	(1.3)	13.5	(2.2)	30.6	(2.4)	33.5	(3.2)	14.3	(1.9)	1.5	(0.8)	0.0	c
Spain (Aragon)	0.0	c	1.0	(0.5)	8.9	(1.4)	23.3	(2.1)	36.5	(3.1)	23.8	(2.2)	6.1	(1.1)	0.2	(0.3)
Spain (Asturias)	0.4	(0.3)	2.9	(0.8)	9.6	(1.2)	23.7	(2.6)	32.5	(1.7)	24.0	(2.3)	6.2	(1.1)	0.8	(0.4)
Spain (Balearic Islands)	1.3	(0.8)	4.6	(1.2)	16.6	(1.6)	30.5	(1.9)	30.9	(2.2)	14.3	(2.2)	1.9	(0.7)	0.0	c
Spain (Basque Country)	0.1	(0.1)	1.5	(0.4)	6.5	(0.8)	23.8	(1.4)	38.0	(1.2)	23.8	(1.1)	5.7	(0.6)	0.6	(0.2)
Spain (Canary Islands)	1.7	(0.8)	6.9	(1.5)	19.2	(1.9)	29.4	(3.2)	29.2	(3.2)	12.2	(1.8)	1.4	(0.8)	0.0	c
Spain (Cantabria)	0.0	c	2.7	(0.6)	8.4	(1.5)	24.6	(2.1)	34.9	(1.9)	23.2	(2.2)	5.6	(1.3)	0.3	(0.2)
Spain (Castile and Leon)	0.3	(0.3)	1.5	(0.6)	7.3	(1.4)	22.3	(2.0)	37.1	(1.7)	25.3	(2.0)	6.0	(1.1)	0.3	(0.2)
Spain (Catalonia)	0.2	(0.2)	1.3	(0.6)	8.0	(1.5)	24.5	(2.9)	37.4	(2.5)	24.0	(2.5)	4.3	(0.9)	0.2	(0.2)
Spain (Ceuta and Melilla)	3.9	(0.7)	13.5	(1.5)	25.9	(1.6)	26.3	(1.8)	21.1	(1.7)	7.8	(1.2)	1.4	(0.5)	0.0	c
Spain (Galicia)	0.0	c	2.7	(0.7)	9.8	(1.4)	25.9	(2.1)	35.3	(1.8)	21.1	(2.3)	4.7	(1.4)	0.0	c
Spain (La Rioja)	0.3	(0.3)	2.4	(0.8)	9.8	(1.7)	18.8	(1.9)	34.6	(2.5)	25.8	(2.4)	7.2	(1.8)	1.1	(0.5)
Spain (Madrid)	0.2	(0.1)	1.2	(0.6)	6.5	(1.3)	19.9	(1.9)	35.6	(2.1)	27.6	(1.9)	8.3	(1.9)	0.8	(0.5)
Spain (Murcia)	0.5	(0.4)	2.6	(1.0)	13.8	(2.3)	27.9	(2.5)	35.1	(2.4)	16.3	(2.2)	3.6	(1.1)	0.0	c
Spain (Navarre)	0.3	(0.3)	1.2	(0.7)	7.7	(1.2)	22.8	(2.1)	35.6	(2.2)	24.5	(2.1)	7.4	(1.6)	0.6	(0.4)
United Kingdom (Scotland)	0.4	(0.3)	2.4	(0.5)	10.1	(1.2)	24.4	(1.7)	30.0	(1.6)	22.5	(1.8)	8.8	(1.2)	1.4	(0.4)
Non-adjudicated																
Belgium (French Community)	1.8	(0.6)	6.0	(1.1)	12.7	(1.5)	19.7	(1.4)	25.2	(1.7)	22.7	(1.4)	10.1	(1.1)	1.8	(0.4)
Belgium (German-Speaking Community)	0.0	c	2.0	(0.8)	8.6	(1.5)	21.3	(2.3)	28.8	(3.2)	27.3	(3.6)	10.0	(1.8)	1.7	(0.9)
Finland (Finnish Speaking)	0.0	c	0.5	(0.2)	2.7	(0.5)	10.6	(0.9)	27.3	(1.2)	36.1	(1.2)	19.1	(1.1)	3.5	(0.5)
Finland (Swedish Speaking)	0.0	c	0.7	(0.5)	5.4	(1.2)	19.5	(1.8)	32.2	(2.1)	29.2	(2.2)	11.5	(1.7)	1.5	(0.7)
Italy (Provincia Abruzzo)	0.8	(0.7)	2.2	(1.0)	9.4	(1.4)	23.9	(2.7)	32.5	(2.7)	25.1	(2.7)	5.9	(1.3)	0.0	c
Italy (Provincia Autonoma di Bolzano)	0.0	c	2.9	(0.9)	7.6	(1.1)	21.5	(1.7)	36.4	(1.7)	23.8	(1.4)	6.8	(1.0)	0.7	(0.4)
Italy (Provincia Basilicata)	0.0	c	2.0	(0.9)	11.4	(1.9)	26.1	(2.5)	34.6	(2.6)	21.7	(2.4)	4.0	(1.1)	0.0	c
Italy (Provincia Calabria)	0.8	(0.6)	3.2	(1.2)	15.5	(2.0)	30.7	(3.5)	32.2	(2.2)	15.3	(2.3)	2.3	(0.7)	0.0	c
Italy (Provincia Campania)	0.7	(0.7)	3.2	(1.0)	12.3	(1.9)	28.2	(3.3)	34.9	(2.6)	18.2	(2.9)	2.3	(0.9)	0.0	c
Italy (Provincia Emilia Romagna)	0.6	(0.3)	3.1	(0.9)	9.9	(1.8)	19.2	(2.5)	26.2	(2.2)	28.7	(2.5)	10.7	(1.8)	1.6	(0.7)
Italy (Provincia Friuli Venezia Giulia)	0.0	c	0.8	(0.5)	3.9	(1.3)	15.0	(1.6)	33.8	(2.4)	32.3	(2.1)	12.5	(2.0)	1.6	(0.6)
Italy (Provincia Lazio)	0.0	c	2.2	(1.1)	9.0	(2.1)	24.6	(2.3)	32.5	(2.4)	24.3	(2.3)	7.1	(2.0)	0.0	c
Italy (Provincia Liguria)	0.0	c	2.1	(1.0)	6.3	(1.3)	19.3	(2.4)	33.8	(2.6)	28.3	(2.4)	9.0	(1.5)	1.2	(0.5)
Italy (Provincia Lombardia)	0.0	c	1.3	(0.8)	5.6	(1.1)	12.8	(2.6)	30.1	(3.2)	33.5	(2.8)	14.2	(2.3)	2.3	(0.9)
Italy (Provincia Marche)	0.0	c	2.2	(0.7)	7.6	(1.8)	17.2	(3.0)	32.2	(2.8)	29.3	(2.3)	9.7	(1.8)	1.6	(0.9)
Italy (Provincia Molise)	0.0	c	1.3	(0.4)	8.4	(1.2)	28.1	(2.6)	41.2	(4.5)	18.8	(3.0)	1.9	(0.7)	0.0	c
Italy (Provincia Piemonte)	0.0	c	2.0	(0.9)	10.1	(1.9)	22.9	(2.4)	30.5	(2.5)	23.7	(2.2)	9.7	(1.3)	1.0	(0.4)
Italy (Provincia Puglia)	0.0	c	1.4	(0.5)	7.3	(1.4)	23.4	(2.8)	37.1	(2.3)	25.5	(2.6)	4.8	(1.1)	0.5	(0.4)
Italy (Provincia Sardegna)	0.0	c	2.2	(1.0)	13.5	(2.1)	26.3	(2.4)	32.9	(2.9)	20.7	(2.6)	3.9	(1.1)	0.4	(0.4)
Italy (Provincia Sicilia)	1.3	(1.0)	2.4	(1.2)	13.5	(2.6)	30.8	(3.5)	32.7	(3.3)	15.8	(2.7)	3.3	(0.9)	0.2	(0.2)
Italy (Provincia Toscana)	0.4	(0.3)	2.4	(1.0)	8.1	(1.4)	18.3	(2.0)	30.8	(2.6)	30.8	(2.4)	8.5	(1.7)	0.6	(0.4)
Italy (Provincia Trento)	0.0	c	1.4	(1.1)	6.9	(1.8)	16.4	(2.6)	32.4	(2.5)	30.2	(2.6)	11.2	(1.8)	1.3	(0.6)
Italy (Provincia Umbria)	0.4	(0.3)	2.3	(0.7)	9.8	(1.6)	20.9	(2.2)	31.2	(2.8)	26.6	(2.1)	7.9	(1.9)	0.9	(0.5)
Italy (Provincia Valle d'Aosta)	0.0	c	1.2	(0.8)	7.8	(1.4)	19.8	(2.7)	32.8	(3.1)	27.2	(3.0)	9.8	(1.6)	1.2	(0.7)
Italy (Provincia Veneto)	0.0	c	0.7	(0.6)	5.5	(1.5)	18.6	(2.7)	34.7	(2.4)	28.6	(2.5)	10.8	(1.9)	1.0	(0.5)
United Kingdom (England)	0.7	(0.2)	3.1	(0.6)	12.1	(1.1)	24.3	(1.1)	30.2	(1.2)	20.4	(1.2)	7.9	(0.8)	1.3	(0.3)
United Kingdom (Northern Ireland)	0.6	(0.4)	2.7	(0.8)	11.0	(1.6)	23.8	(2.0)	29.7	(1.5)	21.5	(1.8)	9.0	(1.5)	1.7	(0.5)
United Kingdom (Wales)	0.7	(0.3)	4.2	(0.7)	15.7	(1.4)	27.9	(1.9)	28.8	(1.6)	16.8	(1.5)	5.3	(0.8)	0.6	(0.3)

Note: See Table I.2.8 for national data.
StatLink ᔕᓂ᠍ᔕ᠍ http://dx.doi.org/10.1787/888932343304

[Part 1/1]

Mean score, variation and gender differences in student performance on the reading subscale *integrate and interpret*

Table S.I.i

	All students				Gender differences						Percentiles											
	Mean score		Standard deviation		Boys		Girls		Difference (B – G)		5th		10th		25th		75th		90th		95th	
	Mean	S.E.	S.D.	S.E.	Mean score	S.E.	Mean score	S.E.	Score dif.	S.E.	Score	S.E.	Score	S.E.	Score	S.E.	Score	S.E.	Score	S.E.	Score	S.E.
Adjudicated																						
Belgium (Flemish Community)	515	(2.5)	98	(2.0)	503	(3.2)	528	(3.6)	**-25**	(4.6)	347	(6.3)	384	(4.9)	444	(3.8)	589	(2.7)	638	(3.6)	664	(4.5)
Spain (Andalusia)	461	(5.2)	87	(2.8)	452	(5.3)	471	(6.1)	**-19**	(4.8)	307	(10.6)	344	(9.9)	406	(7.2)	521	(4.7)	569	(5.3)	595	(5.8)
Spain (Aragon)	496	(3.7)	83	(1.6)	481	(5.0)	511	(4.3)	**-30**	(5.7)	352	(7.4)	387	(5.4)	442	(4.2)	554	(4.1)	599	(4.7)	625	(5.2)
Spain (Asturias)	491	(4.8)	93	(2.7)	478	(6.1)	506	(5.0)	**-28**	(5.9)	329	(10.6)	368	(7.3)	431	(6.2)	557	(5.4)	604	(5.6)	632	(6.1)
Spain (Balearic Islands)	455	(5.3)	88	(2.5)	440	(5.8)	470	(5.9)	**-30**	(4.8)	306	(9.5)	340	(7.6)	397	(7.2)	516	(6.3)	567	(7.7)	588	(6.5)
Spain (Basque Country)	496	(2.9)	84	(1.6)	480	(3.8)	513	(2.6)	**-33**	(3.3)	349	(7.0)	384	(5.6)	442	(3.8)	554	(2.5)	601	(3.1)	626	(2.9)
Spain (Canary Islands)	446	(4.1)	92	(2.5)	435	(4.7)	459	(4.7)	**-23**	(5.3)	289	(9.4)	327	(7.2)	385	(5.8)	514	(3.7)	562	(5.1)	589	(5.4)
Spain (Cantabria)	488	(4.2)	88	(2.1)	472	(5.0)	505	(5.0)	**-33**	(5.5)	332	(7.9)	370	(8.2)	431	(5.9)	550	(5.2)	597	(5.9)	622	(5.5)
Spain (Castile and Leon)	500	(4.9)	83	(2.1)	486	(6.2)	513	(4.8)	**-27**	(6.0)	349	(11.0)	391	(8.2)	448	(6.3)	558	(4.5)	602	(5.4)	627	(5.0)
Spain (Catalonia)	495	(4.8)	81	(2.3)	482	(5.5)	507	(5.0)	**-25**	(4.3)	353	(10.2)	390	(9.3)	443	(5.8)	552	(4.9)	594	(4.7)	615	(6.1)
Spain (Ceuta and Melilla)	415	(2.5)	100	(1.8)	403	(3.8)	426	(3.2)	**-23**	(5.0)	252	(6.4)	289	(5.3)	344	(4.0)	487	(3.9)	545	(4.3)	577	(6.0)
Spain (Galicia)	483	(4.3)	87	(1.6)	467	(4.8)	500	(5.1)	**-33**	(4.4)	331	(6.8)	369	(6.4)	426	(6.5)	544	(4.4)	590	(5.5)	617	(7.3)
Spain (La Rioja)	497	(2.3)	93	(2.0)	481	(3.0)	514	(3.3)	**-33**	(4.2)	337	(7.1)	370	(5.9)	434	(6.1)	565	(4.1)	611	(4.6)	635	(5.1)
Spain (Madrid)	506	(4.5)	86	(3.4)	488	(5.9)	523	(5.2)	**-35**	(7.0)	354	(9.8)	392	(7.7)	452	(5.4)	566	(4.8)	611	(5.8)	636	(6.6)
Spain (Murcia)	479	(5.1)	82	(1.7)	472	(5.2)	486	(6.0)	**-14**	(5.2)	344	(6.0)	375	(6.6)	423	(7.4)	537	(5.9)	582	(5.7)	608	(7.1)
Spain (Navarre)	497	(3.4)	86	(1.9)	480	(4.3)	515	(3.7)	**-35**	(4.7)	348	(8.8)	382	(5.5)	438	(5.1)	556	(4.6)	605	(4.8)	630	(4.8)
United Kingdom (Scotland)	500	(3.0)	95	(1.6)	490	(4.1)	510	(3.4)	**-20**	(4.5)	342	(5.5)	378	(3.8)	435	(3.8)	567	(3.5)	623	(5.0)	656	(6.3)
Non-adjudicated																						
Belgium (French Community)	489	(4.5)	113	(3.0)	479	(6.3)	500	(5.0)	**-22**	(7.1)	295	(8.3)	335	(7.6)	411	(7.2)	575	(4.8)	630	(4.7)	660	(6.6)
Belgium (German-Speaking Community)	501	(3.0)	95	(2.2)	480	(4.6)	522	(4.2)	**-42**	(6.5)	340	(7.2)	371	(6.2)	433	(4.8)	573	(5.0)	620	(6.5)	649	(7.0)
Finland (Finnish Speaking)	540	(2.5)	87	(1.0)	515	(2.8)	566	(2.7)	**-51**	(2.4)	387	(3.8)	423	(4.3)	484	(3.1)	602	(2.8)	648	(3.1)	675	(3.3)
Finland (Swedish Speaking)	509	(2.7)	88	(1.7)	484	(3.7)	534	(3.0)	**-50**	(4.3)	362	(6.9)	395	(4.4)	449	(4.1)	571	(3.2)	621	(4.3)	648	(5.2)
Italy (Provincia Abruzzo)	484	(4.8)	89	(3.9)	465	(5.6)	505	(5.9)	**-41**	(6.0)	331	(8.8)	369	(6.8)	424	(5.3)	550	(5.6)	598	(6.6)	622	(7.4)
Italy (Provincia Autonoma di Bolzano)	490	(3.4)	91	(2.7)	468	(4.0)	511	(3.2)	**-43**	(3.5)	327	(12.9)	365	(7.6)	431	(4.6)	554	(3.3)	604	(4.1)	629	(4.8)
Italy (Provincia Basilicata)	476	(4.4)	84	(2.9)	455	(5.9)	498	(4.2)	**-43**	(6.2)	332	(10.5)	364	(9.4)	416	(6.6)	536	(4.7)	582	(4.4)	610	(5.3)
Italy (Provincia Calabria)	452	(5.4)	88	(4.3)	429	(7.6)	476	(5.2)	**-48**	(7.5)	307	(15.8)	336	(10.5)	390	(7.9)	515	(6.3)	567	(6.9)	596	(6.6)
Italy (Provincia Campania)	458	(6.9)	91	(5.0)	436	(9.0)	486	(6.4)	**-50**	(8.1)	306	(16.1)	339	(10.4)	396	(7.5)	522	(8.0)	573	(8.5)	600	(8.4)
Italy (Provincia Emilia Romagna)	507	(4.0)	96	(3.6)	495	(4.4)	520	(6.7)	**-25**	(8.0)	340	(11.9)	377	(9.1)	442	(6.0)	579	(4.3)	625	(5.0)	648	(6.1)
Italy (Provincia Friuli Venezia Giulia)	513	(4.8)	93	(3.4)	486	(5.8)	543	(5.4)	**-57**	(6.4)	348	(12.4)	386	(10.5)	457	(6.6)	579	(4.8)	627	(5.3)	652	(5.9)
Italy (Provincia Lazio)	487	(3.9)	90	(2.4)	467	(5.7)	509	(6.7)	**-41**	(8.9)	337	(4.9)	368	(6.1)	424	(5.7)	552	(6.0)	603	(6.9)	629	(9.5)
Italy (Provincia Liguria)	496	(8.9)	96	(7.4)	471	(14.6)	525	(5.4)	**-54**	(14.4)	321	(28.1)	365	(23.4)	436	(14.7)	564	(5.3)	612	(7.2)	642	(8.2)
Italy (Provincia Lombardia)	524	(5.6)	91	(2.6)	504	(6.8)	546	(7.1)	**-42**	(8.8)	354	(11.5)	397	(7.7)	468	(7.0)	589	(6.7)	635	(7.1)	663	(7.1)
Italy (Provincia Marche)	503	(7.2)	90	(4.7)	484	(11.2)	527	(4.2)	**-43**	(12.1)	347	(14.2)	380	(15.8)	441	(13.2)	568	(4.8)	618	(4.8)	644	(5.3)
Italy (Provincia Molise)	476	(2.7)	80	(2.0)	455	(3.7)	497	(3.1)	**-42**	(4.2)	339	(6.6)	372	(5.3)	422	(3.6)	535	(4.6)	576	(6.3)	599	(6.4)
Italy (Provincia Piemonte)	500	(5.0)	93	(2.7)	485	(7.2)	514	(5.3)	**-29**	(7.9)	345	(10.2)	377	(5.4)	436	(7.7)	567	(5.6)	615	(5.1)	642	(5.2)
Italy (Provincia Puglia)	491	(4.9)	84	(2.9)	469	(6.3)	511	(5.0)	**-43**	(6.2)	345	(7.0)	376	(8.8)	435	(7.1)	551	(5.4)	592	(5.5)	617	(7.1)
Italy (Provincia Sardegna)	471	(4.5)	91	(3.2)	448	(5.9)	494	(6.4)	**-46**	(7.7)	325	(7.9)	358	(7.7)	409	(6.0)	536	(5.7)	587	(6.6)	614	(6.4)
Italy (Provincia Sicilia)	460	(7.7)	97	(6.2)	436	(10.8)	483	(7.9)	**-47**	(9.6)	292	(26.3)	336	(14.7)	397	(9.8)	529	(7.9)	579	(8.1)	609	(7.3)
Italy (Provincia Toscana)	496	(4.9)	94	(3.1)	475	(7.0)	520	(6.6)	**-46**	(9.5)	329	(10.6)	365	(8.9)	433	(7.3)	567	(5.0)	612	(5.6)	636	(4.8)
Italy (Provincia Trento)	513	(2.7)	92	(2.6)	496	(5.1)	532	(6.3)	**-36**	(9.8)	353	(10.1)	389	(6.8)	451	(5.0)	578	(3.0)	629	(5.8)	656	(5.3)
Italy (Provincia Umbria)	493	(5.3)	96	(3.5)	471	(6.5)	514	(5.6)	**-43**	(6.7)	327	(10.7)	363	(9.6)	429	(9.5)	563	(5.1)	611	(6.7)	639	(7.3)
Italy (Provincia Valle d'Aosta)	516	(2.6)	86	(2.1)	508	(3.5)	525	(3.4)	**-17**	(4.6)	365	(8.4)	403	(5.4)	460	(6.3)	578	(3.8)	624	(5.8)	650	(5.3)
Italy (Provincia Veneto)	507	(5.4)	89	(4.3)	482	(9.1)	532	(6.1)	**-50**	(11.9)	351	(16.0)	387	(12.3)	450	(8.6)	569	(5.6)	616	(5.8)	644	(7.0)
United Kingdom (England)	491	(2.9)	97	(1.4)	479	(4.4)	501	(3.6)	**-22**	(5.6)	330	(4.9)	363	(3.7)	424	(3.6)	558	(3.4)	615	(3.8)	650	(4.0)
United Kingdom (Northern Ireland)	497	(4.2)	99	(3.3)	486	(7.8)	508	(4.4)	**-23**	(9.6)	331	(11.5)	369	(9.1)	429	(5.7)	568	(4.7)	625	(5.0)	657	(5.9)
United Kingdom (Wales)	472	(3.6)	96	(1.7)	460	(4.1)	484	(3.7)	**-24**	(3.1)	313	(6.2)	349	(5.1)	406	(4.3)	539	(4.1)	594	(5.0)	629	(5.5)

Note: See Table I.2.9 for national data.
Values that are statistically significant are indicated in bold (see Annex A3).
StatLink ᴍ⬛ http://dx.doi.org/10.1787/888932343304

[Part 1/1]

Table S.I.j Percentage of students at each proficiency level on the reading subscale *reflect and evaluate*

	Proficiency levels															
	Below Level 1b (less than 262.04 score points)		Level 1b (from 262.04 to less than 334.75 score points)		Level 1a (from 334.75 to less than 407.47 score points)		Level 2 (from 407.47 to less than 480.18 score points)		Level 3 (from 480.18 to less than 552.89 score points)		Level 4 (from 552.89 to less than 625.61 score points)		Level 5 (from 625.61 to less than 698.32 score points)		Level 6 (above 698.32 score points)	
	%	S.E.	%	S.E.	%	S.E.	%	S.E.	%	S.E.	%	S.E.	%	S.E.	%	S.E.
Adjudicated																
Belgium (Flemish Community)	1.1	(0.1)	3.4	(0.3)	9.7	(0.8)	18.7	(0.9)	27.7	(1.0)	26.7	(0.9)	11.1	(0.7)	1.5	(0.4)
Spain (Andalusia)	3.3	(0.8)	7.3	(1.1)	16.0	(1.4)	28.1	(1.5)	29.2	(1.9)	13.5	(1.5)	2.5	(0.6)	0.2	(0.2)
Spain (Aragon)	1.4	(0.5)	3.8	(0.8)	12.3	(1.3)	24.0	(1.7)	32.0	(1.5)	20.5	(1.4)	5.6	(0.7)	0.4	(0.2)
Spain (Asturias)	2.0	(0.8)	5.9	(0.9)	11.9	(1.6)	22.4	(1.9)	29.1	(1.7)	21.6	(1.7)	6.4	(1.1)	0.8	(0.4)
Spain (Balearic Islands)	3.6	(0.8)	8.7	(1.8)	16.2	(2.1)	27.1	(1.7)	27.4	(1.9)	13.9	(2.0)	3.0	(0.8)	0.0	c
Spain (Basque Country)	0.8	(0.3)	3.6	(0.6)	11.5	(0.8)	24.4	(0.9)	34.1	(1.0)	20.5	(1.1)	4.8	(0.4)	0.3	(0.1)
Spain (Canary Islands)	3.7	(0.6)	8.8	(1.3)	19.4	(1.9)	26.4	(1.7)	25.9	(1.7)	12.4	(1.4)	3.1	(0.7)	0.4	(0.2)
Spain (Cantabria)	1.3	(0.4)	4.0	(0.9)	13.4	(1.3)	26.8	(1.7)	30.5	(2.0)	18.8	(1.6)	4.9	(1.0)	0.4	(0.2)
Spain (Castile and Leon)	1.2	(0.4)	3.4	(0.8)	8.7	(1.2)	21.6	(1.4)	33.3	(1.6)	23.8	(1.7)	7.3	(1.1)	0.7	(0.3)
Spain (Catalonia)	0.6	(0.3)	3.5	(1.0)	9.1	(1.4)	20.8	(1.7)	33.9	(1.6)	24.5	(2.0)	7.2	(1.0)	0.4	(0.3)
Spain (Ceuta and Melilla)	9.2	(0.8)	15.9	(1.2)	21.9	(1.2)	23.8	(1.8)	18.5	(1.7)	8.7	(0.8)	1.7	(0.4)	0.2	(0.2)
Spain (Galicia)	1.5	(0.4)	4.6	(0.7)	12.2	(1.3)	23.6	(1.3)	30.4	(1.4)	21.8	(1.5)	5.4	(1.1)	0.4	(0.2)
Spain (La Rioja)	1.3	(0.4)	3.3	(0.7)	12.1	(1.2)	19.8	(1.5)	29.4	(1.6)	25.3	(1.8)	7.9	(1.3)	1.1	(0.5)
Spain (Madrid)	0.9	(0.4)	3.5	(0.8)	9.8	(1.3)	22.7	(1.5)	32.1	(1.7)	24.1	(1.5)	6.5	(1.1)	0.6	(0.3)
Spain (Murcia)	1.1	(0.4)	4.7	(1.1)	15.9	(2.2)	28.2	(1.7)	31.8	(2.1)	15.2	(2.0)	2.9	(0.6)	0.2	(0.1)
Spain (Navarre)	0.8	(0.3)	3.7	(0.6)	10.6	(1.2)	23.8	(1.6)	31.3	(1.6)	22.5	(1.5)	6.7	(1.2)	0.6	(0.3)
United Kingdom (Scotland)	1.1	(0.2)	3.8	(0.5)	12.0	(1.1)	23.9	(1.3)	28.0	(1.2)	20.9	(1.1)	8.7	(0.7)	1.6	(0.4)
Non-adjudicated																
Belgium (French Community)	3.6	(0.7)	6.9	(0.8)	13.1	(1.0)	18.8	(1.1)	23.5	(1.3)	22.6	(1.3)	10.2	(1.0)	1.3	(0.4)
Belgium (German-Speaking Community)	1.5	(0.3)	4.1	(1.1)	14.1	(1.2)	23.3	(2.1)	30.9	(2.1)	21.8	(1.6)	4.2	(0.8)	0.0	c
Finland (Finnish Speaking)	0.3	(0.1)	1.3	(0.3)	6.1	(0.6)	16.6	(0.8)	30.4	(1.0)	30.3	(0.9)	13.1	(0.8)	1.9	(0.3)
Finland (Swedish Speaking)	0.6	(0.3)	2.0	(0.5)	10.0	(1.0)	22.0	(1.7)	31.6	(1.7)	25.0	(1.3)	7.9	(0.9)	0.9	(0.4)
Italy (Provincia Abruzzo)	1.7	(1.0)	6.4	(1.1)	15.0	(1.6)	25.9	(1.7)	27.7	(1.8)	18.3	(1.5)	4.6	(0.9)	0.4	(0.3)
Italy (Provincia Autonoma di Bolzano)	1.6	(0.7)	5.7	(1.0)	12.7	(1.4)	24.3	(1.4)	29.3	(1.3)	19.5	(1.1)	6.2	(0.9)	0.7	(0.2)
Italy (Provincia Basilicata)	1.3	(0.5)	7.5	(1.7)	18.3	(1.6)	26.3	(1.8)	26.5	(1.8)	15.8	(1.6)	4.0	(0.8)	0.3	(0.3)
Italy (Provincia Calabria)	3.7	(1.1)	12.9	(1.9)	21.4	(1.5)	26.8	(2.0)	22.8	(1.8)	10.7	(1.5)	1.7	(0.5)	0.0	c
Italy (Provincia Campania)	4.9	(1.4)	10.0	(1.3)	20.7	(1.7)	26.2	(1.9)	24.9	(1.9)	11.1	(1.6)	2.1	(0.6)	0.2	(0.1)
Italy (Provincia Emilia Romagna)	2.8	(0.9)	4.9	(0.8)	11.7	(1.3)	20.8	(1.8)	25.4	(1.8)	24.1	(1.4)	9.0	(1.1)	1.3	(0.4)
Italy (Provincia Friuli Venezia Giulia)	0.8	(0.3)	3.7	(0.8)	10.4	(1.5)	18.1	(1.3)	28.7	(1.7)	27.0	(1.8)	9.9	(1.2)	1.3	(0.4)
Italy (Provincia Lazio)	1.7	(0.6)	6.7	(1.4)	16.5	(1.6)	24.5	(1.8)	25.5	(1.8)	19.2	(1.5)	5.4	(1.1)	0.4	(0.2)
Italy (Provincia Liguria)	1.6	(1.1)	5.3	(1.7)	13.8	(1.7)	23.2	(1.8)	28.1	(2.1)	21.1	(1.8)	6.2	(1.0)	0.8	(0.3)
Italy (Provincia Lombardia)	0.7	(0.4)	2.7	(0.7)	9.3	(1.3)	18.2	(1.5)	29.6	(1.9)	27.1	(1.9)	10.7	(1.7)	1.8	(0.5)
Italy (Provincia Marche)	1.4	(0.7)	5.4	(1.3)	11.9	(2.1)	22.8	(1.9)	27.7	(2.1)	22.7	(1.8)	7.4	(1.1)	0.8	(0.4)
Italy (Provincia Molise)	2.3	(0.8)	6.7	(0.8)	16.3	(1.2)	26.8	(1.8)	28.6	(1.7)	16.5	(1.4)	3.0	(0.8)	0.0	c
Italy (Provincia Piemonte)	1.6	(0.9)	5.0	(1.0)	13.4	(1.9)	22.2	(1.7)	27.3	(1.6)	22.5	(1.8)	7.2	(1.2)	0.8	(0.3)
Italy (Provincia Puglia)	2.0	(0.8)	5.4	(1.2)	13.0	(1.7)	23.7	(1.7)	29.7	(1.7)	19.9	(1.6)	5.7	(0.9)	0.6	(0.3)
Italy (Provincia Sardegna)	2.8	(0.9)	6.9	(0.9)	16.9	(1.5)	27.7	(2.1)	25.8	(1.7)	15.7	(1.2)	3.8	(0.9)	0.5	(0.3)
Italy (Provincia Sicilia)	7.2	(2.1)	10.8	(2.0)	17.8	(2.1)	24.1	(1.8)	23.9	(2.1)	12.6	(1.6)	3.4	(1.0)	0.3	(0.2)
Italy (Provincia Toscana)	1.8	(0.5)	5.3	(0.9)	13.4	(1.5)	21.7	(1.5)	26.9	(2.2)	23.3	(1.7)	6.9	(1.2)	0.5	(0.3)
Italy (Provincia Trento)	1.1	(0.3)	3.8	(0.7)	12.0	(1.3)	20.6	(1.6)	27.6	(2.0)	23.5	(1.6)	10.3	(1.5)	1.1	(0.4)
Italy (Provincia Umbria)	2.3	(0.5)	6.0	(1.0)	12.7	(1.4)	21.1	(1.4)	28.2	(1.7)	21.7	(1.4)	7.4	(1.4)	0.6	(0.3)
Italy (Provincia Valle d'Aosta)	0.3	(0.2)	2.1	(0.7)	9.4	(1.1)	21.6	(1.5)	31.5	(2.0)	24.3	(1.5)	9.1	(1.0)	1.7	(0.6)
Italy (Provincia Veneto)	0.9	(0.5)	3.4	(0.9)	11.3	(1.7)	20.2	(2.1)	31.4	(1.8)	23.9	(1.9)	8.1	(1.3)	0.7	(0.3)
United Kingdom (England)	0.8	(0.2)	3.7	(0.5)	12.0	(0.7)	23.4	(0.9)	28.2	(0.9)	21.1	(1.2)	8.9	(0.8)	1.8	(0.3)
United Kingdom (Northern Ireland)	1.2	(0.6)	4.2	(0.9)	12.0	(1.0)	21.9	(1.4)	27.6	(1.4)	21.6	(1.1)	9.5	(0.8)	2.0	(0.4)
United Kingdom (Wales)	1.4	(0.4)	5.4	(0.7)	15.1	(1.2)	26.1	(1.2)	28.0	(1.1)	17.2	(1.1)	5.7	(0.6)	1.1	(0.2)

Note: See Table I.2.10 for national data.

StatLink http://dx.doi.org/10.1787/888932343304

[Part 1/2]

Percentage of students at each proficiency level on the reading subscale *reflect and evaluate*, by gender

Table S.I.k

	Below Level 1b (less than 262.04 score points)		Level 1b (from 262.04 to less than 334.75 score points)		Level 1a (from 334.75 to less than 407.47 score points)		Level 2 (from 407.47 to less than 480.18 score points)		Level 3 (from 480.18 to less than 552.89 score points)		Level 4 (from 552.89 to less than 625.61 score points)		Level 5 (from 625.61 to less than 698.32 score points)		Level 6 (above 698.32 score points)	
	%	S.E.	%	S.E.	%	S.E.	%	S.E.	%	S.E.	%	S.E.	%	S.E.	%	S.E.
Adjudicated																
Belgium (Flemish Community)	1.7	(0.3)	4.4	(0.5)	12.0	(1.1)	20.9	(1.2)	27.2	(1.2)	23.7	(1.2)	8.8	(1.0)	1.2	(0.5)
Spain (Andalusia)	3.7	(1.1)	8.6	(1.5)	18.8	(2.4)	27.9	(2.1)	27.3	(2.1)	11.7	(1.5)	1.7	(0.8)	0.0	c
Spain (Aragon)	2.5	(0.9)	6.0	(1.3)	14.4	(2.0)	27.3	(2.0)	29.9	(2.1)	16.1	(1.9)	3.4	(0.8)	0.3	(0.3)
Spain (Asturias)	2.9	(1.0)	7.4	(1.4)	13.6	(2.1)	23.7	(2.1)	28.5	(2.0)	18.4	(2.0)	4.7	(1.1)	0.8	(0.4)
Spain (Balearic Islands)	5.2	(1.2)	11.1	(2.3)	18.4	(2.5)	28.8	(2.2)	25.3	(2.1)	9.4	(1.8)	1.7	(0.8)	0.0	c
Spain (Basque Country)	1.3	(0.5)	5.4	(1.0)	15.7	(1.0)	26.4	(1.3)	31.2	(1.2)	16.4	(1.1)	3.3	(0.4)	0.2	(0.2)
Spain (Canary Islands)	4.9	(1.0)	10.0	(1.5)	21.9	(2.3)	27.0	(2.3)	23.6	(2.1)	10.1	(1.6)	2.2	(0.9)	0.4	(0.3)
Spain (Cantabria)	2.1	(0.7)	5.7	(1.7)	17.0	(2.0)	29.1	(2.8)	27.6	(3.2)	15.4	(2.0)	2.9	(0.9)	0.3	(0.3)
Spain (Castile and Leon)	2.1	(0.8)	5.1	(1.5)	11.1	(1.6)	25.3	(2.0)	31.4	(1.8)	18.2	(2.3)	6.2	(1.3)	0.6	(0.4)
Spain (Catalonia)	1.0	(0.4)	4.8	(1.3)	12.4	(2.1)	23.2	(2.6)	34.3	(2.6)	19.5	(2.6)	4.5	(1.0)	0.0	c
Spain (Ceuta and Melilla)	13.3	(1.3)	18.4	(1.6)	21.1	(1.7)	21.8	(2.5)	16.9	(2.1)	7.2	(1.2)	1.3	(0.5)	0.0	c
Spain (Galicia)	2.3	(0.8)	6.5	(1.3)	15.3	(2.0)	25.4	(1.7)	27.4	(2.4)	18.5	(2.2)	4.3	(0.9)	0.2	(0.2)
Spain (La Rioja)	1.9	(0.7)	4.7	(1.5)	14.3	(1.9)	23.1	(2.4)	28.6	(2.2)	21.7	(1.9)	5.4	(1.3)	0.3	(0.3)
Spain (Madrid)	1.2	(0.7)	5.7	(1.5)	13.9	(2.4)	26.1	(2.0)	29.6	(2.2)	19.4	(2.1)	4.0	(1.3)	0.0	c
Spain (Murcia)	1.2	(0.6)	5.6	(1.3)	18.3	(2.7)	28.2	(2.3)	30.5	(2.4)	13.9	(1.7)	2.1	(0.6)	0.0	c
Spain (Navarre)	1.1	(0.5)	5.3	(1.1)	14.6	(1.6)	26.3	(2.2)	29.5	(1.9)	18.2	(1.9)	4.4	(1.4)	0.6	(0.4)
United Kingdom (Scotland)	1.4	(0.4)	5.5	(0.8)	14.4	(1.5)	25.5	(1.4)	26.3	(1.4)	18.0	(1.5)	7.3	(1.0)	1.5	(0.6)
Non-adjudicated																
Belgium (French Community)	5.0	(1.3)	8.5	(1.2)	14.3	(1.4)	19.1	(1.4)	22.2	(1.5)	20.5	(1.5)	9.2	(1.1)	1.0	(0.5)
Belgium (German-Speaking Community)	2.1	(0.6)	6.3	(1.9)	17.3	(1.9)	25.9	(3.4)	28.9	(2.4)	17.0	(1.9)	2.5	(0.8)	0.0	c
Finland (Finnish Speaking)	0.6	(0.2)	2.2	(0.5)	9.8	(1.0)	23.4	(1.3)	32.6	(1.3)	23.5	(1.4)	7.3	(0.8)	0.6	(0.3)
Finland (Swedish Speaking)	1.2	(0.7)	3.6	(0.9)	15.7	(1.8)	28.2	(2.5)	29.4	(2.6)	17.9	(2.2)	3.6	(1.3)	0.0	c
Italy (Provincia Abruzzo)	2.5	(1.3)	9.3	(1.5)	20.3	(2.4)	28.9	(2.1)	24.2	(2.0)	12.1	(1.9)	2.7	(0.9)	0.1	(0.1)
Italy (Provincia Autonoma di Bolzano)	2.5	(1.1)	7.9	(1.6)	17.6	(2.2)	27.3	(2.3)	25.1	(2.2)	14.8	(1.5)	4.5	(1.2)	0.2	(0.1)
Italy (Provincia Basilicata)	2.1	(0.8)	11.1	(2.4)	22.5	(2.3)	28.0	(2.5)	23.4	(2.2)	9.9	(1.8)	2.5	(0.7)	0.4	(0.3)
Italy (Provincia Calabria)	5.3	(1.5)	20.2	(2.9)	26.9	(2.3)	23.5	(2.5)	16.9	(1.8)	6.3	(1.3)	0.9	(0.5)	0.0	c
Italy (Provincia Campania)	6.8	(1.9)	14.1	(1.9)	25.5	(2.5)	25.7	(2.2)	18.8	(2.3)	7.6	(1.8)	1.4	(0.6)	0.0	c
Italy (Provincia Emilia Romagna)	3.6	(1.5)	5.2	(0.7)	14.0	(2.0)	23.3	(3.1)	26.2	(2.4)	20.6	(1.7)	6.6	(1.2)	0.5	(0.3)
Italy (Provincia Friuli Venezia Giulia)	1.4	(0.6)	5.9	(1.1)	15.8	(2.1)	22.0	(2.2)	27.5	(2.2)	21.6	(2.2)	5.7	(1.2)	0.0	c
Italy (Provincia Lazio)	3.0	(1.2)	9.5	(1.6)	21.4	(2.5)	27.2	(3.0)	20.9	(2.2)	14.4	(2.2)	3.4	(1.0)	0.3	(0.2)
Italy (Provincia Liguria)	2.9	(2.0)	8.0	(2.9)	19.7	(2.6)	25.8	(3.1)	23.9	(3.4)	15.3	(2.7)	4.3	(1.3)	0.0	c
Italy (Provincia Lombardia)	1.2	(0.6)	4.1	(1.0)	12.5	(2.0)	23.2	(1.9)	30.5	(2.8)	21.7	(2.4)	6.4	(1.4)	0.4	(0.2)
Italy (Provincia Marche)	1.7	(0.9)	6.6	(2.0)	15.7	(3.7)	27.7	(2.4)	26.1	(3.4)	17.1	(2.2)	4.8	(1.2)	0.3	(0.3)
Italy (Provincia Molise)	3.6	(1.2)	9.6	(1.3)	20.7	(2.0)	28.2	(3.1)	22.4	(2.6)	12.6	(1.8)	2.9	(1.1)	0.0	c
Italy (Provincia Piemonte)	2.2	(1.1)	7.1	(2.0)	16.4	(2.3)	23.8	(2.6)	26.3	(2.1)	19.5	(2.2)	4.5	(1.0)	0.0	c
Italy (Provincia Puglia)	3.6	(1.6)	8.2	(1.9)	16.8	(2.8)	26.0	(2.2)	27.3	(2.1)	14.4	(2.1)	3.5	(0.9)	0.0	c
Italy (Provincia Sardegna)	5.0	(1.5)	10.5	(1.6)	21.6	(2.7)	29.1	(2.9)	20.8	(2.1)	10.8	(1.5)	2.1	(0.8)	0.0	c
Italy (Provincia Sicilia)	11.7	(3.5)	14.1	(2.3)	21.1	(2.9)	22.2	(2.3)	18.4	(2.0)	9.5	(1.3)	2.7	(0.7)	0.2	(0.2)
Italy (Provincia Toscana)	2.7	(0.7)	7.6	(1.3)	17.9	(2.0)	25.0	(2.0)	24.3	(2.5)	17.5	(2.2)	4.6	(1.0)	0.3	(0.3)
Italy (Provincia Trento)	1.5	(0.6)	6.0	(1.3)	15.6	(2.3)	24.8	(2.7)	26.1	(2.2)	17.3	(1.8)	7.7	(1.8)	1.0	(0.6)
Italy (Provincia Umbria)	3.7	(0.9)	9.2	(1.7)	15.7	(2.0)	23.0	(2.1)	25.0	(2.0)	18.2	(1.7)	4.8	(1.0)	0.3	(0.3)
Italy (Provincia Valle d'Aosta)	0.5	(0.4)	3.5	(1.3)	10.9	(1.6)	25.1	(2.7)	29.7	(3.5)	21.3	(2.3)	7.7	(1.9)	1.4	(0.6)
Italy (Provincia Veneto)	1.5	(0.8)	5.8	(1.7)	17.1	(3.2)	23.4	(2.8)	29.0	(3.0)	18.1	(2.4)	4.7	(1.0)	0.3	(0.3)
United Kingdom (England)	1.1	(0.3)	5.0	(0.7)	14.7	(1.2)	24.8	(1.2)	27.2	(1.3)	18.0	(1.3)	7.8	(1.0)	1.4	(0.4)
United Kingdom (Northern Ireland)	1.9	(1.1)	6.2	(1.5)	14.8	(1.3)	23.4	(2.0)	25.4	(1.9)	19.2	(1.7)	7.7	(1.4)	1.4	(0.6)
United Kingdom (Wales)	2.3	(0.6)	7.4	(0.9)	18.0	(1.8)	25.8	(2.1)	26.5	(1.3)	14.9	(1.3)	4.3	(0.7)	0.8	(0.3)

Note: See Table I.2.11 for national data.

StatLink http://dx.doi.org/10.1787/888932343304

[Part 2/2]

Percentage of students at each proficiency level on the reading subscale *reflect and evaluate*, by gender

Table S.I.k

	Girls – Proficiency levels															
	Below Level 1b (less than 262.04 score points)		Level 1b (from 262.04 to less than 334.75 score points)		Level 1a (from 334.75 to less than 407.47 score points)		Level 2 (from 407.47 to less than 480.18 score points)		Level 3 (from 480.18 to less than 552.89 score points)		Level 4 (from 552.89 to less than 625.61 score points)		Level 5 (from 625.61 to less than 698.32 score points)		Level 6 (above 698.32 score points)	
	%	S.E.	%	S.E.	%	S.E.	%	S.E.	%	S.E.	%	S.E.	%	S.E.	%	S.E.
Adjudicated																
Belgium (Flemish Community)	0.5	(0.2)	2.4	(0.4)	7.4	(1.0)	16.3	(1.3)	28.3	(1.6)	29.8	(1.4)	13.6	(1.0)	1.8	(0.4)
Spain (Andalusia)	2.8	(0.9)	5.8	(1.3)	12.9	(2.2)	28.3	(2.3)	31.4	(3.0)	15.4	(2.4)	3.3	(0.8)	0.0	c
Spain (Aragon)	0.3	(0.3)	1.6	(0.6)	10.1	(1.8)	20.6	(2.1)	34.1	(2.1)	24.9	(2.0)	7.8	(1.1)	0.6	(0.3)
Spain (Asturias)	1.1	(0.7)	4.2	(0.9)	9.9	(1.6)	20.8	(2.3)	29.8	(2.3)	25.1	(2.2)	8.3	(1.5)	0.8	(0.6)
Spain (Balearic Islands)	2.0	(0.8)	6.4	(1.7)	13.9	(2.7)	25.4	(2.5)	29.5	(2.9)	18.4	(2.7)	4.2	(1.2)	0.0	c
Spain (Basque Country)	0.2	(0.1)	1.7	(0.4)	7.0	(0.8)	22.3	(1.2)	37.2	(1.6)	24.9	(1.6)	6.4	(0.7)	0.4	(0.2)
Spain (Canary Islands)	2.5	(0.6)	7.4	(1.6)	16.6	(2.1)	25.8	(2.3)	28.4	(1.9)	14.9	(2.1)	4.0	(1.4)	0.4	(0.3)
Spain (Cantabria)	0.6	(0.4)	2.2	(0.8)	9.7	(1.4)	24.5	(2.4)	33.4	(2.5)	22.3	(2.3)	6.9	(1.4)	0.4	(0.4)
Spain (Castile and Leon)	0.5	(0.3)	1.7	(0.7)	6.4	(1.3)	18.0	(1.8)	35.1	(2.3)	29.2	(1.8)	8.3	(1.4)	0.8	(0.4)
Spain (Catalonia)	0.2	(0.3)	2.1	(1.0)	5.7	(1.3)	18.3	(2.7)	33.4	(2.0)	29.7	(2.3)	9.9	(1.4)	0.6	(0.5)
Spain (Ceuta and Melilla)	5.3	(0.8)	13.4	(1.5)	22.7	(1.6)	25.9	(2.3)	20.1	(2.0)	10.3	(1.7)	2.2	(0.8)	0.2	(0.2)
Spain (Galicia)	0.7	(0.3)	2.8	(0.6)	9.1	(1.3)	21.9	(1.8)	33.4	(2.4)	25.1	(2.4)	6.6	(1.6)	0.6	(0.3)
Spain (La Rioja)	0.6	(0.4)	1.7	(0.8)	9.7	(1.5)	16.4	(1.7)	30.1	(2.6)	29.1	(2.8)	10.5	(1.8)	1.8	(0.7)
Spain (Madrid)	0.6	(0.4)	1.2	(0.6)	5.7	(1.1)	19.4	(2.3)	34.5	(2.3)	28.7	(2.0)	8.9	(1.4)	1.0	(0.6)
Spain (Murcia)	1.0	(0.6)	3.7	(1.4)	13.5	(2.2)	28.2	(2.2)	33.2	(2.8)	16.5	(2.6)	3.7	(1.0)	0.2	(0.2)
Spain (Navarre)	0.5	(0.4)	1.9	(0.9)	6.2	(1.3)	21.0	(2.3)	33.4	(2.5)	27.2	(2.3)	9.2	(1.6)	0.6	(0.5)
United Kingdom (Scotland)	0.7	(0.3)	2.1	(0.5)	9.7	(1.2)	22.2	(1.8)	29.7	(1.8)	23.7	(1.5)	10.0	(1.1)	1.8	(0.5)
Non-adjudicated																
Belgium (French Community)	2.2	(0.7)	5.1	(1.0)	11.9	(1.1)	18.5	(1.4)	24.8	(1.5)	24.7	(2.0)	11.2	(1.6)	1.6	(0.5)
Belgium (German-Speaking Community)	0.8	(0.4)	1.8	(0.7)	10.7	(1.9)	20.6	(3.0)	33.1	(3.7)	26.7	(2.8)	5.9	(1.4)	0.0	c
Finland (Finnish Speaking)	0.1	(0.1)	0.4	(0.2)	2.4	(0.5)	9.6	(0.8)	28.1	(1.7)	37.1	(1.5)	19.0	(1.3)	3.2	(0.5)
Finland (Swedish Speaking)	0.0	c	0.5	(0.4)	4.4	(0.9)	15.9	(1.6)	33.8	(2.6)	31.8	(2.5)	12.1	(1.7)	1.5	(0.9)
Italy (Provincia Abruzzo)	0.9	(0.7)	3.1	(1.4)	9.3	(1.5)	22.5	(3.1)	31.6	(2.6)	25.3	(2.8)	6.7	(1.8)	0.8	(0.5)
Italy (Provincia Autonoma di Bolzano)	0.7	(0.5)	3.4	(1.0)	7.8	(1.3)	21.2	(1.8)	33.4	(1.8)	24.3	(1.4)	7.8	(1.0)	1.2	(0.4)
Italy (Provincia Basilicata)	0.5	(0.4)	3.5	(1.1)	13.7	(1.7)	24.5	(2.1)	29.8	(2.4)	22.2	(2.6)	5.6	(1.6)	0.0	c
Italy (Provincia Calabria)	2.0	(0.9)	5.5	(1.2)	15.7	(1.9)	30.1	(3.0)	28.9	(2.6)	15.2	(2.4)	2.5	(0.8)	0.0	c
Italy (Provincia Campania)	2.4	(1.1)	4.7	(1.5)	14.5	(2.6)	27.0	(2.9)	32.7	(2.9)	15.5	(2.4)	3.0	(1.2)	0.3	(0.2)
Italy (Provincia Emilia Romagna)	2.1	(0.8)	4.7	(1.3)	9.5	(1.8)	18.5	(2.1)	24.6	(2.4)	27.4	(2.6)	11.3	(1.7)	2.0	(0.8)
Italy (Provincia Friuli Venezia Giulia)	0.0	c	1.4	(0.9)	4.7	(1.5)	13.9	(2.1)	30.0	(2.2)	32.9	(2.8)	14.5	(2.1)	2.4	(0.8)
Italy (Provincia Lazio)	0.2	(0.3)	3.4	(1.7)	10.8	(2.4)	21.4	(2.0)	30.9	(2.7)	24.9	(2.3)	7.7	(1.8)	0.5	(0.4)
Italy (Provincia Liguria)	0.0	c	2.1	(0.8)	6.9	(1.4)	20.2	(2.3)	33.0	(2.2)	27.8	(2.6)	8.5	(1.6)	1.3	(0.7)
Italy (Provincia Lombardia)	0.2	(0.2)	1.1	(0.7)	5.9	(1.6)	12.6	(2.1)	28.5	(2.4)	33.1	(2.8)	15.4	(2.8)	3.3	(1.1)
Italy (Provincia Marche)	1.1	(0.6)	3.8	(1.0)	7.4	(1.2)	17.0	(2.2)	29.6	(2.4)	29.3	(2.6)	10.5	(1.8)	1.4	(0.8)
Italy (Provincia Molise)	0.8	(0.4)	3.5	(0.8)	11.6	(1.5)	25.3	(2.1)	35.1	(3.1)	20.6	(2.3)	3.0	(1.1)	0.0	c
Italy (Provincia Piemonte)	1.0	(0.9)	3.0	(1.1)	10.6	(2.2)	20.7	(2.1)	28.3	(2.5)	25.2	(2.7)	9.8	(1.9)	1.3	(0.6)
Italy (Provincia Puglia)	0.6	(0.3)	2.7	(0.9)	9.4	(1.6)	21.4	(2.3)	32.1	(2.2)	25.1	(2.4)	7.8	(1.7)	0.9	(0.5)
Italy (Provincia Sardegna)	0.7	(0.5)	3.4	(1.2)	12.5	(2.1)	26.3	(2.7)	30.4	(2.5)	20.4	(2.2)	5.5	(1.4)	0.8	(0.4)
Italy (Provincia Sicilia)	2.9	(1.4)	7.5	(2.8)	14.6	(2.6)	26.0	(2.5)	29.2	(3.2)	15.5	(2.8)	4.1	(1.5)	0.3	(0.3)
Italy (Provincia Toscana)	0.9	(0.5)	2.8	(1.3)	8.4	(1.7)	18.1	(2.1)	29.8	(2.1)	29.7	(2.6)	9.5	(2.0)	0.8	(0.5)
Italy (Provincia Trento)	0.6	(0.4)	1.4	(0.7)	8.0	(1.5)	16.0	(2.1)	29.2	(2.6)	30.4	(3.0)	13.0	(2.6)	1.3	(0.6)
Italy (Provincia Umbria)	0.8	(0.4)	3.0	(0.9)	9.8	(1.4)	19.3	(2.3)	31.3	(2.6)	25.0	(2.1)	9.8	(2.3)	1.0	(0.6)
Italy (Provincia Valle d'Aosta)	0.0	c	0.8	(0.5)	7.9	(1.5)	18.1	(2.1)	33.2	(2.4)	27.3	(2.2)	10.6	(1.4)	1.9	(0.9)
Italy (Provincia Veneto)	0.0	c	1.0	(0.6)	5.8	(1.5)	17.2	(2.2)	33.7	(2.3)	29.4	(2.7)	11.5	(2.1)	1.1	(0.6)
United Kingdom (England)	0.5	(0.2)	2.5	(0.5)	9.5	(0.9)	22.0	(1.4)	29.2	(1.2)	24.1	(1.7)	10.0	(1.0)	2.3	(0.5)
United Kingdom (Northern Ireland)	0.5	(0.3)	2.3	(0.6)	9.5	(1.4)	20.5	(1.8)	29.7	(1.8)	23.8	(1.6)	11.2	(1.1)	2.6	(0.7)
United Kingdom (Wales)	0.5	(0.3)	3.4	(0.8)	12.2	(1.0)	26.3	(1.4)	29.5	(1.4)	19.6	(1.7)	7.1	(0.9)	1.4	(0.4)

Note: See Table I.2.11 for national data.
StatLink http://dx.doi.org/10.1787/888932343304

[Part 1/1]

Table S.I.I

Mean score, variation and gender differences in student performance on the reading subscale *reflect and evaluate*

	All students				Gender differences						Percentiles											
	Mean score		Standard deviation		Boys		Girls		Difference (B – G)		5th		10th		25th		75th		90th		95th	
	Mean	S.E.	S.D.	S.E.	Mean score	S.E.	Mean score	S.E.	Score dif.	S.E.	Score	S.E.	Score	S.E.	Score	S.E.	Score	S.E.	Score	S.E.	Score	S.E.
Adjudicated																						
Belgium (Flemish Community)	517	(2.5)	99	(1.5)	502	(3.3)	533	(3.3)	**-31**	(4.3)	339	(4.7)	382	(4.0)	454	(3.8)	588	(3.3)	635	(3.3)	662	(4.6)
Spain (Andalusia)	461	(6.3)	96	(3.1)	450	(6.5)	472	(6.9)	**-22**	(5.1)	285	(12.0)	330	(11.1)	403	(7.9)	527	(6.5)	574	(6.1)	602	(7.1)
Spain (Aragon)	493	(4.7)	92	(2.8)	473	(6.7)	514	(4.2)	**-41**	(6.2)	331	(13.5)	371	(7.7)	434	(7.0)	558	(4.9)	605	(5.0)	632	(4.1)
Spain (Asturias)	491	(5.2)	101	(2.4)	476	(6.6)	507	(5.7)	**-31**	(6.8)	310	(10.1)	352	(7.4)	427	(6.0)	563	(6.3)	612	(6.5)	639	(6.5)
Spain (Balearic Islands)	458	(7.3)	101	(4.0)	439	(7.6)	478	(8.0)	**-39**	(5.6)	278	(9.7)	319	(11.5)	395	(9.6)	530	(6.5)	581	(6.6)	609	(6.6)
Spain (Basque Country)	495	(3.0)	86	(2.0)	476	(4.0)	514	(2.8)	**-38**	(3.6)	340	(7.7)	379	(5.9)	441	(4.1)	554	(2.8)	600	(2.4)	626	(3.8)
Spain (Canary Islands)	453	(4.9)	100	(2.5)	439	(5.2)	468	(5.6)	**-29**	(4.9)	278	(9.7)	320	(6.7)	387	(6.0)	523	(5.8)	577	(7.3)	610	(11.2)
Spain (Cantabria)	487	(4.2)	91	(2.8)	469	(4.9)	506	(4.9)	**-37**	(5.1)	332	(9.6)	367	(6.3)	429	(5.3)	550	(6.2)	601	(6.2)	628	(7.5)
Spain (Castile and Leon)	507	(5.2)	92	(2.5)	488	(7.0)	525	(5.0)	**-36**	(6.9)	339	(13.3)	388	(9.3)	453	(6.3)	569	(5.5)	617	(5.7)	645	(6.3)
Spain (Catalonia)	508	(6.0)	89	(2.9)	489	(6.6)	527	(5.8)	**-38**	(4.1)	344	(12.6)	390	(11.1)	453	(9.1)	570	(6.3)	614	(6.1)	641	(6.1)
Spain (Ceuta and Melilla)	412	(2.6)	113	(2.1)	395	(4.2)	429	(3.5)	**-35**	(5.6)	224	(9.7)	268	(6.3)	334	(4.1)	495	(4.1)	556	(5.0)	590	(6.6)
Spain (Galicia)	491	(4.7)	95	(2.4)	474	(5.6)	509	(4.8)	**-34**	(4.6)	321	(9.8)	363	(7.8)	434	(6.6)	560	(4.9)	607	(4.9)	631	(6.5)
Spain (La Rioja)	506	(2.5)	96	(2.4)	487	(3.4)	525	(4.0)	**-38**	(5.4)	339	(7.5)	375	(6.1)	443	(5.0)	574	(3.7)	622	(5.9)	649	(5.6)
Spain (Madrid)	504	(4.6)	89	(3.1)	482	(5.9)	526	(4.9)	**-44**	(6.2)	344	(13.8)	384	(7.8)	450	(5.1)	566	(5.2)	611	(6.8)	637	(5.8)
Spain (Murcia)	475	(5.7)	87	(2.8)	466	(5.6)	483	(6.8)	**-17**	(5.5)	327	(11.5)	359	(8.5)	418	(8.2)	536	(5.1)	582	(5.4)	610	(6.4)
Spain (Navarre)	501	(3.5)	90	(2.1)	482	(4.6)	521	(4.3)	**-39**	(5.9)	342	(9.8)	380	(5.9)	443	(4.2)	565	(5.1)	613	(5.3)	639	(5.9)
United Kingdom (Scotland)	501	(3.4)	98	(1.6)	488	(4.9)	515	(3.3)	**-28**	(4.6)	335	(6.2)	374	(5.0)	436	(4.0)	571	(4.6)	627	(5.0)	661	(6.9)
Non-adjudicated																						
Belgium (French Community)	491	(4.7)	117	(3.4)	478	(7.2)	505	(5.1)	**-27**	(8.6)	281	(11.6)	331	(9.2)	414	(8.0)	579	(4.4)	632	(4.9)	660	(5.2)
Belgium (German-Speaking Community)	487	(3.0)	97	(2.5)	466	(4.9)	508	(3.9)	**-42**	(6.5)	331	(7.6)	365	(6.3)	428	(5.2)	556	(3.8)	600	(6.0)	622	(5.2)
Finland (Finnish Speaking)	537	(2.4)	87	(1.2)	508	(2.8)	567	(2.5)	**-59**	(2.4)	386	(5.2)	421	(3.9)	483	(3.3)	599	(2.8)	643	(2.3)	669	(3.2)
Finland (Swedish Speaking)	512	(2.8)	88	(1.9)	481	(4.1)	542	(3.2)	**-61**	(4.8)	363	(6.8)	394	(4.8)	455	(3.6)	574	(3.0)	621	(4.5)	650	(5.0)
Italy (Provincia Abruzzo)	478	(5.0)	99	(5.0)	451	(6.1)	506	(5.7)	**-55**	(6.2)	307	(11.6)	347	(8.9)	414	(7.0)	549	(4.4)	601	(6.4)	626	(6.4)
Italy (Provincia Autonoma di Bolzano)	488	(3.3)	98	(2.8)	464	(4.1)	512	(3.1)	**-48**	(3.8)	316	(10.2)	355	(7.7)	425	(5.3)	557	(3.5)	611	(4.1)	640	(5.1)
Italy (Provincia Basilicata)	468	(5.4)	96	(3.8)	444	(7.0)	495	(5.3)	**-50**	(7.2)	307	(15.3)	341	(10.7)	402	(7.5)	538	(4.8)	592	(5.6)	621	(6.4)
Italy (Provincia Calabria)	438	(5.6)	98	(3.9)	407	(7.6)	469	(5.5)	**-62**	(7.6)	276	(12.0)	306	(9.5)	367	(9.7)	510	(6.5)	564	(7.6)	594	(7.7)
Italy (Provincia Campania)	442	(7.0)	102	(5.2)	416	(9.4)	474	(6.4)	**-58**	(9.1)	263	(18.0)	306	(12.8)	376	(9.2)	515	(7.5)	568	(7.6)	598	(8.6)
Italy (Provincia Emilia Romagna)	498	(5.2)	109	(5.3)	482	(5.2)	514	(8.3)	**-32**	(9.1)	303	(19.9)	354	(12.2)	429	(7.3)	580	(4.7)	627	(7.8)	656	(5.9)
Italy (Provincia Friuli Venezia Giulia)	514	(5.0)	97	(3.2)	485	(5.6)	546	(6.0)	**-61**	(6.2)	339	(10.9)	380	(10.6)	453	(7.4)	583	(4.7)	630	(4.7)	658	(7.2)
Italy (Provincia Lazio)	478	(4.2)	99	(2.7)	452	(6.6)	508	(7.2)	**-56**	(10.0)	305	(14.2)	344	(8.8)	408	(5.8)	553	(5.7)	604	(6.2)	631	(6.9)
Italy (Provincia Liguria)	490	(9.0)	98	(6.2)	462	(14.6)	522	(5.4)	**-61**	(14.0)	318	(23.9)	356	(20.1)	425	(12.9)	562	(6.8)	611	(6.0)	639	(7.4)
Italy (Provincia Lombardia)	521	(6.1)	95	(3.4)	495	(6.8)	549	(7.9)	**-54**	(9.9)	353	(11.1)	392	(8.9)	463	(8.6)	588	(7.5)	635	(7.5)	664	(9.3)
Italy (Provincia Marche)	496	(7.3)	99	(4.6)	474	(11.0)	522	(4.9)	**-48**	(12.0)	322	(14.0)	359	(15.2)	431	(12.7)	569	(6.2)	618	(6.0)	645	(6.8)
Italy (Provincia Molise)	468	(3.7)	95	(3.5)	447	(4.8)	491	(3.7)	**-44**	(4.6)	300	(12.4)	342	(8.1)	407	(4.7)	537	(4.8)	585	(6.3)	607	(7.2)
Italy (Provincia Piemonte)	494	(6.2)	100	(4.2)	475	(8.2)	512	(6.3)	**-37**	(8.4)	322	(12.7)	360	(11.3)	426	(9.2)	567	(5.3)	617	(6.2)	644	(8.8)
Italy (Provincia Puglia)	487	(5.4)	98	(4.4)	461	(7.3)	512	(5.8)	**-51**	(7.6)	314	(15.9)	356	(13.2)	424	(6.8)	556	(5.8)	606	(5.8)	634	(6.6)
Italy (Provincia Sardegna)	466	(4.6)	100	(3.7)	436	(6.4)	494	(6.4)	**-58**	(8.8)	294	(13.0)	337	(11.1)	403	(6.2)	537	(5.6)	590	(6.3)	620	(7.3)
Italy (Provincia Sicilia)	441	(9.1)	115	(7.2)	412	(11.3)	468	(10.6)	**-57**	(11.1)	238	(25.2)	286	(19.2)	364	(13.5)	524	(8.4)	581	(6.8)	610	(9.3)
Italy (Provincia Toscana)	492	(4.8)	101	(3.4)	467	(7.3)	519	(6.3)	**-52**	(9.7)	314	(12.1)	355	(11.1)	424	(9.0)	567	(5.0)	614	(5.2)	639	(4.7)
Italy (Provincia Trento)	508	(2.9)	99	(2.4)	485	(5.5)	533	(6.8)	**-48**	(10.6)	336	(8.8)	374	(6.3)	440	(6.5)	581	(4.8)	632	(5.5)	658	(6.4)
Italy (Provincia Umbria)	490	(5.4)	105	(4.3)	465	(7.2)	514	(5.6)	**-49**	(8.2)	303	(12.9)	346	(11.1)	424	(9.6)	566	(4.6)	617	(6.9)	645	(7.0)
Italy (Provincia Valle d'Aosta)	517	(3.0)	89	(2.1)	504	(4.0)	529	(3.9)	**-25**	(5.2)	369	(6.3)	399	(5.3)	456	(6.6)	578	(4.2)	630	(5.9)	658	(6.6)
Italy (Provincia Veneto)	506	(5.7)	93	(4.2)	478	(9.3)	533	(7.3)	**-55**	(12.3)	342	(10.1)	377	(11.6)	445	(8.3)	572	(6.2)	620	(7.4)	647	(6.5)
United Kingdom (England)	504	(3.0)	98	(1.5)	491	(4.6)	517	(3.7)	**-26**	(5.9)	339	(4.6)	376	(4.3)	438	(3.7)	573	(4.3)	629	(4.0)	661	(3.9)
United Kingdom (Northern Ireland)	504	(4.5)	102	(3.8)	487	(8.4)	521	(4.3)	**-34**	(10.1)	332	(12.7)	370	(9.7)	436	(6.5)	576	(3.7)	633	(4.2)	665	(5.5)
United Kingdom (Wales)	483	(3.8)	97	(1.8)	468	(4.4)	498	(3.8)	**-31**	(3.4)	319	(7.9)	356	(5.2)	418	(4.9)	550	(4.7)	607	(4.8)	640	(4.9)

Note: See Table I.2.12 for national data.
Values that are statistically significant are indicated in bold (see Annex A3).
StatLink ᵃᵐˢᵖ http://dx.doi.org/10.1787/888932343304

[Part 1/1]

Table S.I.m **Percentage of students at each proficiency level on the reading subscale *continuous texts***

	Below Level 1b (less than 262.04 score points)		Level 1b (from 262.04 to less than 334.75 score points)		Level 1a (from 334.75 to less than 407.47 score points)		Level 2 (from 407.47 to less than 480.18 score points)		Level 3 (from 480.18 to less than 552.89 score points)		Level 4 (from 552.89 to less than 625.61 score points)		Level 5 (from 625.61 to less than 698.32 score points)		Level 6 (above 698.32 score points)	
	%	S.E.	%	S.E.	%	S.E.	%	S.E.	%	S.E.	%	S.E.	%	S.E.	%	S.E.
Adjudicated																
Belgium (Flemish Community)	0.4	(0.1)	2.6	(0.4)	10.7	(0.6)	20.9	(1.1)	26.5	(0.9)	26.3	(0.8)	11.5	(0.8)	1.2	(0.3)
Spain (Andalusia)	2.5	(0.8)	7.2	(1.1)	15.8	(1.3)	28.2	(1.3)	30.7	(1.9)	13.2	(1.2)	2.3	(0.6)	0.0	c
Spain (Aragon)	0.9	(0.4)	3.4	(0.6)	10.4	(1.3)	24.3	(1.7)	33.1	(1.9)	22.4	(1.8)	5.0	(0.7)	0.4	(0.2)
Spain (Asturias)	1.5	(0.5)	5.0	(0.8)	11.5	(1.1)	23.4	(2.2)	29.4	(1.5)	21.4	(1.6)	7.2	(1.1)	0.6	(0.3)
Spain (Balearic Islands)	3.0	(0.7)	7.3	(0.9)	16.8	(1.5)	27.7	(1.6)	28.5	(2.0)	13.9	(1.8)	2.7	(0.8)	0.1	(0.1)
Spain (Basque Country)	0.6	(0.2)	3.6	(0.6)	10.7	(0.8)	24.2	(0.9)	34.4	(1.1)	21.2	(0.9)	4.8	(0.5)	0.4	(0.1)
Spain (Canary Islands)	3.1	(0.6)	8.5	(1.5)	19.8	(1.8)	26.9	(1.7)	26.2	(1.5)	13.0	(1.4)	2.5	(0.6)	0.1	(0.1)
Spain (Cantabria)	0.9	(0.4)	4.7	(0.6)	12.3	(1.6)	24.5	(1.5)	32.5	(2.0)	19.5	(1.6)	5.2	(0.7)	0.4	(0.2)
Spain (Castile and Leon)	0.8	(0.3)	3.1	(0.6)	8.8	(1.2)	21.7	(1.2)	34.2	(1.5)	24.2	(1.5)	6.7	(1.0)	0.5	(0.3)
Spain (Catalonia)	0.6	(0.2)	3.1	(0.7)	9.4	(1.4)	24.3	(1.8)	33.5	(2.1)	23.2	(1.9)	5.4	(0.9)	0.4	(0.2)
Spain (Ceuta and Melilla)	7.7	(0.8)	15.8	(1.4)	23.9	(1.4)	23.7	(1.2)	18.7	(1.3)	8.4	(0.9)	1.6	(0.4)	0.1	(0.1)
Spain (Galicia)	1.1	(0.2)	4.7	(0.8)	13.3	(1.4)	24.0	(1.5)	31.8	(1.3)	19.9	(1.4)	5.0	(0.8)	0.2	(0.2)
Spain (La Rioja)	1.1	(0.5)	3.8	(1.1)	11.8	(1.2)	21.2	(1.5)	30.2	(2.0)	24.4	(1.6)	6.9	(0.9)	0.6	(0.3)
Spain (Madrid)	0.6	(0.3)	2.7	(0.6)	9.5	(1.0)	22.2	(1.5)	34.1	(1.9)	23.6	(1.5)	6.5	(1.3)	0.8	(0.4)
Spain (Murcia)	0.6	(0.3)	3.3	(0.7)	14.4	(1.6)	27.5	(1.6)	33.6	(1.8)	16.9	(1.6)	3.5	(0.9)	0.3	(0.2)
Spain (Navarre)	0.6	(0.3)	3.0	(0.7)	11.2	(1.1)	24.4	(1.5)	31.8	(1.5)	22.7	(1.4)	5.7	(0.8)	0.5	(0.3)
United Kingdom (Scotland)	1.0	(0.2)	4.0	(0.5)	12.5	(0.8)	25.2	(1.1)	28.4	(0.9)	19.4	(1.1)	8.1	(0.7)	1.3	(0.2)
Non-adjudicated																
Belgium (French Community)	2.5	(0.6)	7.3	(0.8)	14.6	(1.1)	20.2	(1.1)	23.9	(1.2)	21.9	(1.1)	8.7	(0.7)	1.0	(0.3)
Belgium (German-Speaking Community)	0.4	(0.3)	4.1	(1.0)	13.8	(1.1)	22.8	(1.6)	28.6	(1.6)	23.0	(1.7)	6.6	(1.2)	0.6	(0.4)
Finland (Finnish Speaking)	0.2	(0.1)	1.5	(0.2)	6.1	(0.5)	16.6	(1.0)	30.2	(0.8)	30.6	(0.8)	13.4	(0.7)	1.5	(0.2)
Finland (Swedish Speaking)	0.3	(0.2)	2.4	(0.5)	10.5	(1.2)	23.8	(1.5)	30.4	(1.9)	24.4	(1.8)	7.7	(0.8)	0.5	(0.2)
Italy (Provincia Abruzzo)	0.9	(0.6)	5.0	(0.8)	14.3	(1.3)	25.6	(1.8)	29.4	(1.6)	20.2	(1.6)	4.3	(0.8)	0.3	(0.3)
Italy (Provincia Autonoma di Bolzano)	1.5	(0.6)	4.7	(1.0)	12.3	(1.1)	25.1	(1.6)	29.6	(1.8)	20.7	(1.0)	5.7	(0.6)	0.4	(0.2)
Italy (Provincia Basilicata)	0.6	(0.5)	5.2	(1.1)	15.8	(1.7)	28.2	(2.0)	28.8	(2.0)	17.2	(1.3)	3.9	(0.6)	0.3	(0.2)
Italy (Provincia Calabria)	2.1	(0.9)	8.8	(1.5)	20.8	(1.4)	28.1	(2.4)	26.4	(2.2)	11.7	(1.4)	2.1	(0.5)	0.0	c
Italy (Provincia Campania)	2.6	(1.2)	8.3	(1.5)	19.2	(1.8)	27.0	(2.2)	26.6	(1.9)	13.5	(1.9)	2.7	(0.7)	0.2	(0.2)
Italy (Provincia Emilia Romagna)	1.3	(0.4)	4.5	(0.8)	10.7	(1.1)	21.2	(1.5)	25.6	(1.6)	25.8	(1.4)	10.0	(0.9)	0.9	(0.4)
Italy (Provincia Friuli Venezia Giulia)	1.1	(0.6)	2.8	(0.6)	9.6	(1.6)	19.5	(1.4)	29.0	(1.8)	27.0	(1.5)	9.8	(1.3)	1.1	(0.4)
Italy (Provincia Lazio)	0.7	(0.3)	5.6	(1.1)	15.9	(1.9)	24.5	(1.6)	27.8	(1.3)	20.0	(1.3)	5.1	(0.9)	0.3	(0.2)
Italy (Provincia Liguria)	1.3	(1.0)	4.7	(1.5)	11.5	(1.7)	22.6	(1.5)	31.2	(2.4)	21.6	(1.9)	6.6	(1.0)	0.5	(0.3)
Italy (Provincia Lombardia)	0.7	(0.4)	2.4	(0.7)	8.5	(1.0)	17.3	(1.8)	31.1	(1.9)	29.1	(2.0)	9.8	(1.4)	1.0	(0.3)
Italy (Provincia Marche)	0.7	(0.5)	4.1	(1.3)	11.9	(2.3)	22.4	(1.9)	29.6	(2.2)	23.1	(2.0)	7.6	(1.3)	0.6	(0.3)
Italy (Provincia Molise)	1.1	(0.4)	5.4	(0.9)	15.5	(1.2)	27.9	(1.7)	30.1	(2.0)	17.1	(1.8)	2.7	(0.6)	0.0	c
Italy (Provincia Piemonte)	1.0	(0.5)	4.4	(1.0)	12.8	(1.6)	21.7	(1.6)	28.6	(1.9)	22.7	(1.9)	8.0	(1.3)	0.7	(0.3)
Italy (Provincia Puglia)	0.8	(0.4)	3.9	(0.8)	12.8	(1.5)	24.1	(1.9)	32.3	(1.9)	21.6	(2.1)	4.3	(1.1)	0.2	(0.2)
Italy (Provincia Sardegna)	1.6	(0.6)	5.4	(0.9)	16.9	(1.4)	28.1	(1.8)	27.1	(1.8)	16.2	(1.4)	4.4	(1.0)	0.2	(0.2)
Italy (Provincia Sicilia)	3.6	(1.5)	7.5	(1.5)	19.0	(2.7)	25.9	(2.2)	26.7	(2.2)	14.4	(1.8)	2.9	(0.8)	0.0	c
Italy (Provincia Toscana)	1.2	(0.4)	5.4	(1.2)	12.5	(1.3)	22.0	(1.9)	28.4	(2.6)	23.9	(1.9)	6.2	(0.7)	0.4	(0.3)
Italy (Provincia Trento)	0.9	(0.3)	3.5	(0.6)	10.4	(1.1)	20.8	(1.4)	29.2	(1.7)	24.7	(1.9)	9.7	(1.0)	0.8	(0.3)
Italy (Provincia Umbria)	1.4	(0.5)	6.0	(1.3)	12.7	(1.5)	21.0	(1.6)	28.4	(1.9)	23.0	(1.5)	6.9	(1.0)	0.6	(0.3)
Italy (Provincia Valle d'Aosta)	0.2	(0.2)	2.7	(0.6)	7.7	(1.3)	20.7	(1.8)	32.2	(2.0)	26.1	(2.0)	9.5	(1.4)	0.9	(0.5)
Italy (Provincia Veneto)	0.8	(0.4)	3.7	(1.0)	10.3	(1.7)	20.8	(2.0)	32.2	(1.8)	24.3	(1.8)	7.1	(1.0)	0.9	(0.3)
United Kingdom (England)	1.1	(0.3)	4.4	(0.5)	14.3	(0.8)	24.8	(0.9)	27.9	(0.9)	19.0	(1.1)	7.2	(0.6)	1.3	(0.3)
United Kingdom (Northern Ireland)	1.0	(0.5)	4.6	(0.8)	12.6	(1.3)	24.2	(1.1)	26.5	(1.4)	21.0	(1.1)	8.4	(0.8)	1.7	(0.3)
United Kingdom (Wales)	1.5	(0.3)	6.0	(0.6)	16.6	(1.1)	27.8	(1.4)	27.1	(1.2)	15.9	(0.9)	4.5	(0.6)	0.6	(0.2)

Note: See Table I.2.14 for national data.
StatLink ⌂≡⌐ http://dx.doi.org/10.1787/888932343304

[Part 1/2]

Table S.I.n

Percentage of students at each proficiency level on the reading subscale *continuous texts*, by gender

	Boys – Proficiency levels														
	Below Level 1b (less than 262.04 score points)		Level 1b (from 262.04 to less than 334.75 score points)		Level 1a (from 334.75 to less than 407.47 score points)		Level 2 (from 407.47 to less than 480.18 score points)		Level 3 (from 480.18 to less than 552.89 score points)		Level 4 (from 552.89 to less than 625.61 score points)		Level 5 (from 625.61 to less than 698.32 score points)		Level 6 (above 698.32 score points)	
	%	S.E.	%	S.E.	%	S.E.	%	S.E.	%	S.E.	%	S.E.	%	S.E.	%	S.E.
Adjudicated																
Belgium (Flemish Community)	0.6	(0.2)	3.7	(0.6)	13.3	(0.9)	22.9	(1.3)	25.7	(1.3)	23.6	(1.1)	9.4	(1.0)	0.9	(0.4)
Spain (Andalusia)	3.3	(0.9)	8.7	(1.6)	18.1	(2.0)	28.1	(1.9)	29.0	(2.0)	11.0	(1.3)	1.8	(0.6)	0.0	c
Spain (Aragon)	1.6	(0.7)	5.8	(1.0)	12.3	(1.9)	27.6	(2.2)	31.6	(2.3)	17.2	(2.3)	3.6	(0.9)	0.3	(0.3)
Spain (Asturias)	2.0	(0.7)	6.6	(1.1)	13.2	(1.6)	25.0	(2.7)	28.7	(2.1)	18.6	(2.0)	5.5	(1.3)	0.4	(0.3)
Spain (Balearic Islands)	4.3	(1.0)	9.9	(1.3)	18.3	(2.0)	29.7	(1.8)	25.3	(2.2)	10.7	(1.9)	1.7	(0.7)	0.0	c
Spain (Basque Country)	1.0	(0.3)	5.6	(1.0)	14.9	(1.1)	26.6	(1.1)	30.9	(1.5)	17.5	(1.1)	3.3	(0.5)	0.1	(0.1)
Spain (Canary Islands)	4.4	(1.0)	9.8	(2.0)	22.7	(2.3)	27.0	(2.2)	23.2	(1.9)	10.8	(1.3)	1.9	(0.5)	0.0	c
Spain (Cantabria)	1.6	(0.8)	6.8	(1.4)	16.0	(2.3)	26.1	(2.3)	30.0	(2.7)	15.6	(1.8)	3.3	(0.7)	0.5	(0.3)
Spain (Castile and Leon)	1.0	(0.5)	4.9	(1.1)	11.3	(1.8)	25.7	(1.9)	31.9	(2.4)	19.7	(2.0)	5.2	(1.1)	0.0	c
Spain (Catalonia)	0.8	(0.4)	4.9	(1.1)	12.1	(2.1)	26.2	(2.1)	32.9	(3.0)	19.1	(2.0)	3.7	(1.0)	0.3	(0.2)
Spain (Ceuta and Melilla)	10.8	(1.5)	18.1	(2.4)	23.5	(2.0)	22.7	(1.9)	16.9	(1.7)	6.6	(1.3)	1.4	(0.5)	0.0	c
Spain (Galicia)	1.7	(0.5)	7.1	(1.5)	16.9	(2.1)	24.7	(2.4)	29.2	(2.3)	17.0	(1.7)	3.3	(0.7)	0.0	c
Spain (La Rioja)	1.8	(0.8)	5.2	(1.4)	14.8	(1.9)	24.6	(2.1)	28.2	(2.7)	20.2	(1.8)	5.0	(1.1)	0.0	c
Spain (Madrid)	1.0	(0.6)	4.1	(1.1)	13.0	(1.5)	25.7	(2.1)	32.3	(2.6)	19.0	(1.9)	4.6	(1.2)	0.3	(0.3)
Spain (Murcia)	0.6	(0.4)	4.3	(0.8)	16.4	(2.2)	29.4	(2.3)	31.9	(2.7)	14.6	(1.8)	2.6	(0.7)	0.0	c
Spain (Navarre)	0.9	(0.4)	4.5	(1.1)	15.0	(1.7)	26.0	(1.9)	31.1	(2.1)	18.9	(1.7)	3.4	(0.9)	0.0	c
United Kingdom (Scotland)	1.5	(0.4)	5.3	(0.9)	15.2	(1.1)	26.2	(1.3)	26.2	(1.4)	17.4	(1.4)	7.0	(0.9)	1.2	(0.4)
Non-adjudicated																
Belgium (French Community)	3.4	(0.8)	8.4	(1.1)	16.5	(1.7)	20.9	(1.8)	22.5	(1.5)	19.9	(1.6)	7.6	(1.1)	0.8	(0.4)
Belgium (German-Speaking Community)	0.6	(0.5)	6.1	(2.0)	18.2	(2.6)	25.3	(3.1)	27.3	(2.2)	18.5	(2.4)	3.9	(1.5)	0.0	c
Finland (Finnish Speaking)	0.3	(0.1)	2.4	(0.5)	9.8	(0.9)	23.0	(1.4)	32.5	(1.3)	23.9	(1.2)	7.5	(0.7)	0.6	(0.2)
Finland (Swedish Speaking)	0.6	(0.3)	4.2	(0.8)	15.8	(2.1)	29.8	(2.7)	27.6	(2.9)	18.1	(2.3)	3.8	(1.1)	0.0	c
Italy (Provincia Abruzzo)	1.0	(0.6)	7.3	(1.2)	19.5	(1.9)	29.4	(2.4)	25.9	(2.2)	14.1	(1.7)	2.5	(0.9)	0.2	(0.2)
Italy (Provincia Autonoma di Bolzano)	2.0	(1.1)	6.8	(1.6)	17.3	(1.7)	28.5	(2.1)	25.9	(2.3)	16.0	(1.4)	3.4	(0.9)	0.2	(0.2)
Italy (Provincia Basilicata)	1.0	(0.9)	7.9	(1.7)	20.6	(2.2)	30.7	(2.8)	25.5	(2.7)	11.9	(1.6)	2.1	(0.8)	0.0	c
Italy (Provincia Calabria)	3.3	(1.6)	14.3	(2.6)	27.8	(2.5)	25.8	(2.9)	20.2	(2.9)	7.3	(1.3)	1.3	(0.7)	0.0	c
Italy (Provincia Campania)	3.9	(1.7)	11.6	(2.0)	24.5	(2.8)	28.3	(2.7)	20.7	(2.5)	9.0	(2.0)	1.8	(0.7)	0.2	(0.2)
Italy (Provincia Emilia Romagna)	1.8	(0.8)	5.0	(1.0)	12.9	(1.4)	23.4	(2.5)	27.1	(2.2)	22.6	(1.8)	6.9	(1.1)	0.4	(0.3)
Italy (Provincia Friuli Venezia Giulia)	1.8	(0.9)	5.0	(1.3)	14.7	(1.9)	23.9	(2.1)	27.3	(1.9)	21.1	(2.1)	5.8	(1.2)	0.5	(0.3)
Italy (Provincia Lazio)	1.3	(0.5)	8.1	(1.6)	20.8	(2.7)	27.8	(2.4)	23.8	(1.9)	14.8	(1.8)	3.2	(0.9)	0.2	(0.3)
Italy (Provincia Liguria)	2.4	(1.9)	7.0	(2.6)	15.4	(2.8)	26.6	(2.6)	28.4	(3.2)	15.8	(2.5)	4.2	(1.2)	0.0	c
Italy (Provincia Lombardia)	1.2	(0.6)	3.4	(1.1)	11.9	(1.7)	21.4	(2.5)	31.9	(2.9)	23.7	(2.9)	6.1	(1.4)	0.5	(0.3)
Italy (Provincia Marche)	0.8	(0.7)	5.5	(2.1)	15.9	(3.8)	27.3	(2.5)	28.0	(3.4)	17.9	(2.5)	4.6	(1.1)	0.0	c
Italy (Provincia Molise)	1.7	(0.7)	8.4	(1.4)	21.6	(1.9)	30.0	(3.1)	22.8	(2.7)	13.2	(1.8)	2.4	(1.0)	0.0	c
Italy (Provincia Piemonte)	1.5	(0.8)	6.1	(1.6)	15.9	(2.4)	22.8	(2.5)	28.3	(2.5)	19.4	(2.7)	5.5	(1.3)	0.4	(0.3)
Italy (Provincia Puglia)	1.5	(0.8)	6.1	(1.4)	18.3	(2.4)	26.9	(2.4)	29.1	(2.4)	15.5	(2.3)	2.4	(0.7)	0.0	c
Italy (Provincia Sardegna)	3.3	(1.2)	8.5	(1.7)	22.5	(1.9)	30.1	(2.4)	21.7	(2.0)	11.1	(1.7)	2.8	(0.8)	0.0	c
Italy (Provincia Sicilia)	6.1	(2.5)	11.6	(2.5)	23.7	(3.4)	24.2	(2.9)	21.4	(2.7)	10.7	(1.5)	2.2	(0.6)	0.0	c
Italy (Provincia Toscana)	1.7	(0.6)	8.1	(1.8)	16.9	(1.9)	24.9	(2.4)	26.4	(2.5)	17.9	(2.5)	3.9	(1.0)	0.0	c
Italy (Provincia Trento)	1.5	(0.6)	5.2	(1.4)	14.2	(1.7)	24.9	(2.2)	27.6	(1.9)	18.9	(2.7)	7.2	(1.7)	0.0	c
Italy (Provincia Umbria)	2.3	(0.9)	9.0	(2.0)	16.8	(2.3)	23.3	(2.0)	25.4	(2.5)	18.1	(2.1)	4.7	(1.1)	0.4	(0.4)
Italy (Provincia Valle d'Aosta)	0.4	(0.5)	4.4	(1.1)	9.0	(2.1)	21.5	(1.9)	32.5	(2.3)	23.4	(2.3)	8.3	(1.9)	0.0	c
Italy (Provincia Veneto)	1.3	(0.6)	6.6	(2.1)	15.5	(3.0)	24.2	(2.4)	30.0	(2.8)	18.3	(2.2)	3.7	(0.9)	0.0	c
United Kingdom (England)	1.5	(0.4)	5.9	(0.8)	16.9	(1.3)	26.0	(1.4)	25.9	(1.4)	16.3	(1.2)	6.4	(0.9)	1.0	(0.3)
United Kingdom (Northern Ireland)	1.6	(0.9)	6.7	(1.5)	15.7	(2.0)	25.6	(2.0)	23.8	(2.1)	18.0	(1.7)	7.3	(1.1)	1.4	(0.4)
United Kingdom (Wales)	2.4	(0.5)	8.3	(0.9)	19.1	(1.3)	27.2	(1.4)	25.2	(1.5)	13.7	(1.2)	3.7	(0.6)	0.4	(0.2)

Note: See Table I.2.15 for national data.
StatLink http://dx.doi.org/10.1787/888932343304

[Part 2/2]

Percentage of students at each proficiency level on the reading subscale *continuous texts*, by gender

Table S.I.n

	Girls – Proficiency levels															
	Below Level 1b (less than 262.04 score points)		Level 1b (from 262.04 to less than 334.75 score points)		Level 1a (from 334.75 to less than 407.47 score points)		Level 2 (from 407.47 to less than 480.18 score points)		Level 3 (from 480.18 to less than 552.89 score points)		Level 4 (from 552.89 to less than 625.61 score points)		Level 5 (from 625.61 to less than 698.32 score points)		Level 6 (above 698.32 score points)	
	%	S.E.	%	S.E.	%	S.E.	%	S.E.	%	S.E.	%	S.E.	%	S.E.	%	S.E.
Adjudicated																
Belgium (Flemish Community)	0.2	(0.1)	1.4	(0.4)	8.1	(0.9)	18.7	(1.4)	27.5	(1.4)	29.1	(1.2)	13.6	(1.1)	1.5	(0.4)
Spain (Andalusia)	1.7	(0.9)	5.5	(1.3)	13.3	(2.0)	28.3	(2.1)	32.5	(3.0)	15.7	(1.9)	2.9	(1.0)	0.0	c
Spain (Aragon)	0.2	(0.2)	0.9	(0.5)	8.5	(1.7)	20.9	(2.4)	34.7	(2.7)	27.8	(2.2)	6.4	(1.0)	0.5	(0.3)
Spain (Asturias)	1.0	(0.6)	3.3	(1.0)	9.5	(1.4)	21.6	(2.5)	30.3	(2.3)	24.6	(2.1)	9.0	(1.6)	0.8	(0.4)
Spain (Balearic Islands)	1.7	(0.8)	4.6	(1.1)	15.3	(2.2)	25.7	(2.6)	31.7	(2.9)	17.0	(2.5)	3.8	(1.3)	0.0	c
Spain (Basque Country)	0.1	(0.1)	1.4	(0.4)	6.3	(0.7)	21.8	(1.2)	38.0	(1.1)	25.2	(1.2)	6.5	(0.8)	0.6	(0.2)
Spain (Canary Islands)	1.7	(0.9)	7.0	(1.9)	16.6	(1.9)	26.7	(2.3)	29.4	(2.0)	15.4	(2.3)	3.1	(1.2)	0.2	(0.2)
Spain (Cantabria)	0.0	c	2.5	(0.7)	8.4	(1.4)	22.8	(2.1)	35.1	(2.5)	23.5	(2.1)	7.2	(1.3)	0.3	(0.3)
Spain (Castile and Leon)	0.5	(0.4)	1.3	(0.6)	6.4	(1.2)	17.9	(1.6)	36.4	(2.0)	28.5	(2.2)	8.2	(1.4)	0.8	(0.4)
Spain (Catalonia)	0.4	(0.3)	1.3	(0.7)	6.5	(1.2)	22.3	(2.0)	34.1	(2.0)	27.5	(2.4)	7.3	(1.2)	0.6	(0.4)
Spain (Ceuta and Melilla)	4.7	(0.9)	13.7	(1.7)	24.3	(2.2)	24.7	(2.2)	20.6	(2.1)	10.1	(1.7)	1.8	(0.7)	0.0	c
Spain (Galicia)	0.5	(0.3)	2.2	(0.7)	9.6	(1.5)	23.3	(2.0)	34.5	(1.8)	22.8	(1.9)	6.7	(1.3)	0.3	(0.3)
Spain (La Rioja)	0.4	(0.3)	2.3	(0.9)	8.6	(1.4)	17.5	(1.8)	32.4	(3.4)	28.8	(2.7)	8.9	(1.5)	1.1	(0.5)
Spain (Madrid)	0.3	(0.3)	1.2	(0.6)	6.0	(1.1)	18.7	(2.1)	36.0	(2.4)	28.2	(2.2)	8.4	(2.0)	1.2	(0.7)
Spain (Murcia)	0.5	(0.3)	2.4	(1.0)	12.4	(2.1)	25.5	(2.2)	35.3	(2.3)	19.1	(2.2)	4.4	(1.5)	0.3	(0.3)
Spain (Navarre)	0.3	(0.3)	1.4	(0.6)	7.1	(1.1)	22.6	(2.1)	32.6	(2.5)	27.0	(2.1)	8.2	(1.5)	0.9	(0.4)
United Kingdom (Scotland)	0.5	(0.2)	2.6	(0.5)	9.8	(1.1)	24.2	(1.6)	30.7	(1.4)	21.5	(1.4)	9.2	(0.9)	1.5	(0.3)
Non-adjudicated																
Belgium (French Community)	1.5	(0.6)	6.1	(1.2)	12.6	(1.2)	19.4	(1.4)	25.4	(1.5)	24.0	(1.5)	9.8	(1.0)	1.2	(0.4)
Belgium (German-Speaking Community)	0.0	c	2.1	(0.8)	9.3	(2.1)	20.3	(2.1)	30.0	(2.2)	27.7	(2.4)	9.3	(1.5)	1.1	(0.6)
Finland (Finnish Speaking)	0.1	(0.1)	0.5	(0.2)	2.3	(0.4)	10.1	(1.0)	27.8	(1.3)	37.4	(1.3)	19.4	(1.2)	2.4	(0.4)
Finland (Swedish Speaking)	0.0	c	0.6	(0.4)	5.2	(1.0)	18.0	(1.8)	33.2	(2.0)	30.5	(2.5)	11.6	(1.6)	0.9	(0.5)
Italy (Provincia Abruzzo)	0.8	(0.7)	2.4	(1.0)	8.5	(1.3)	21.4	(2.3)	33.2	(2.3)	26.9	(2.6)	6.4	(1.3)	0.4	(0.4)
Italy (Provincia Autonoma di Bolzano)	1.0	(0.7)	2.6	(1.0)	7.2	(1.3)	21.7	(2.1)	33.3	(2.0)	25.5	(1.8)	8.0	(1.3)	0.7	(0.3)
Italy (Provincia Basilicata)	0.0	c	2.3	(0.8)	10.6	(1.7)	25.4	(2.3)	32.3	(2.2)	23.0	(2.0)	5.7	(1.0)	0.4	(0.3)
Italy (Provincia Calabria)	0.9	(0.5)	3.2	(1.1)	13.8	(1.5)	30.4	(3.1)	32.6	(2.4)	16.2	(2.2)	2.9	(0.8)	0.0	c
Italy (Provincia Campania)	0.8	(0.8)	4.2	(1.7)	12.3	(2.0)	25.3	(3.0)	34.2	(2.6)	19.2	(2.7)	3.8	(1.0)	0.0	c
Italy (Provincia Emilia Romagna)	0.8	(0.4)	4.1	(1.2)	8.7	(2.0)	19.2	(2.8)	24.2	(2.5)	28.7	(2.2)	13.0	(1.7)	1.3	(0.6)
Italy (Provincia Friuli Venezia Giulia)	0.5	(0.4)	0.6	(0.5)	4.2	(1.8)	14.7	(1.9)	30.9	(2.1)	33.4	(2.1)	14.1	(2.1)	1.8	(0.7)
Italy (Provincia Lazio)	0.0	c	2.7	(1.3)	10.1	(2.5)	20.7	(2.1)	32.5	(2.5)	26.1	(2.3)	7.3	(1.7)	0.0	c
Italy (Provincia Liguria)	0.0	c	2.0	(0.8)	7.0	(1.1)	18.0	(1.9)	34.4	(2.9)	28.3	(2.3)	9.2	(1.3)	0.9	(0.5)
Italy (Provincia Lombardia)	0.0	c	1.4	(1.0)	4.7	(1.0)	12.7	(2.3)	30.2	(2.5)	35.1	(2.6)	14.0	(2.4)	1.7	(0.7)
Italy (Provincia Marche)	0.5	(0.3)	2.5	(0.7)	7.2	(1.2)	16.6	(2.4)	31.5	(2.6)	29.3	(2.6)	11.2	(1.9)	1.1	(0.6)
Italy (Provincia Molise)	0.4	(0.3)	2.2	(0.7)	9.1	(1.4)	25.8	(2.4)	37.9	(3.0)	21.3	(3.2)	3.1	(1.2)	0.0	c
Italy (Provincia Piemonte)	0.6	(0.4)	2.8	(1.1)	9.9	(2.1)	20.7	(2.3)	28.9	(2.5)	25.7	(2.1)	10.4	(1.8)	1.0	(0.4)
Italy (Provincia Puglia)	0.0	c	1.7	(0.8)	7.6	(1.2)	21.5	(2.5)	35.3	(2.3)	27.5	(2.9)	6.1	(1.9)	0.3	(0.3)
Italy (Provincia Sardegna)	0.0	c	2.5	(0.9)	11.7	(1.9)	26.3	(2.3)	32.2	(2.5)	21.0	(2.4)	6.0	(1.6)	0.3	(0.3)
Italy (Provincia Sicilia)	1.2	(0.8)	3.5	(1.4)	14.4	(3.5)	27.5	(3.1)	31.7	(2.9)	17.9	(2.8)	3.6	(1.3)	0.0	c
Italy (Provincia Toscana)	0.6	(0.4)	2.5	(1.1)	7.6	(2.0)	18.8	(2.2)	30.7	(3.4)	30.6	(2.8)	8.7	(1.4)	0.6	(0.5)
Italy (Provincia Trento)	0.0	c	1.7	(0.8)	6.2	(1.3)	16.2	(2.2)	31.0	(2.7)	31.0	(2.8)	12.5	(1.9)	1.1	(0.5)
Italy (Provincia Umbria)	0.5	(0.4)	3.1	(1.1)	8.9	(1.5)	18.8	(2.2)	31.2	(2.7)	27.7	(2.4)	8.9	(1.5)	0.9	(0.4)
Italy (Provincia Valle d'Aosta)	0.0	c	1.0	(0.7)	6.5	(1.5)	19.8	(2.8)	31.9	(2.8)	28.8	(2.7)	10.7	(1.7)	1.3	(0.8)
Italy (Provincia Veneto)	0.0	c	0.9	(0.6)	5.3	(1.3)	17.5	(2.3)	34.3	(2.2)	30.0	(2.8)	10.3	(1.7)	1.4	(0.5)
United Kingdom (England)	0.7	(0.2)	2.9	(0.5)	11.7	(1.0)	23.7	(1.3)	29.9	(1.1)	21.5	(1.4)	8.0	(0.9)	1.5	(0.4)
United Kingdom (Northern Ireland)	0.5	(0.4)	2.6	(0.7)	9.7	(1.4)	22.9	(1.5)	29.0	(1.5)	23.8	(1.6)	9.5	(1.2)	1.9	(0.5)
United Kingdom (Wales)	0.6	(0.3)	3.7	(0.7)	14.1	(1.4)	28.5	(2.3)	29.0	(1.6)	18.1	(1.3)	5.3	(0.8)	0.8	(0.3)

Note: See Table I.2.15 for national data.
StatLink ㅤ http://dx.doi.org/10.1787/888932343304

[Part 1/1]

Table S.I.o **Mean score, variation and gender differences in student performance on the reading subscale *continuous texts***

	All students				Gender differences						Percentiles											
	Mean score		Standard deviation		Boys		Girls		Difference (B – G)		5th		10th		25th		75th		90th		95th	
	Mean	S.E.	S.D.	S.E.	Mean score	S.E.	Mean score	S.E.	Score dif.	S.E.	Score	S.E.	Score	S.E.	Score	S.E.	Score	S.E.	Score	S.E.	Score	S.E.
Adjudicated																						
Belgium (Flemish Community)	517	(2.4)	94	(1.7)	504	(3.1)	532	(3.3)	**-28**	(4.1)	357	(5.6)	390	(3.7)	451	(3.3)	588	(3.2)	635	(3.5)	660	(3.3)
Spain (Andalusia)	463	(5.6)	93	(3.4)	452	(5.5)	475	(6.7)	**-22**	(5.1)	299	(12.1)	337	(9.6)	406	(7.7)	527	(4.8)	574	(5.4)	603	(7.2)
Spain (Aragon)	498	(4.4)	87	(2.4)	479	(6.0)	517	(4.6)	**-37**	(6.0)	345	(12.0)	383	(8.9)	442	(6.0)	559	(4.3)	604	(4.1)	628	(4.6)
Spain (Asturias)	495	(5.1)	98	(2.6)	481	(6.2)	509	(5.5)	**-28**	(6.2)	322	(9.7)	362	(8.6)	435	(5.7)	565	(6.4)	615	(6.8)	644	(6.6)
Spain (Balearic Islands)	461	(6.1)	96	(2.8)	443	(6.8)	479	(6.7)	**-36**	(5.8)	290	(10.7)	333	(8.0)	401	(8.3)	527	(7.8)	580	(9.3)	608	(8.7)
Spain (Basque Country)	497	(2.9)	85	(1.9)	478	(4.0)	517	(2.6)	**-39**	(3.6)	344	(8.0)	382	(6.2)	443	(4.0)	557	(2.2)	601	(2.9)	627	(3.3)
Spain (Canary Islands)	453	(4.4)	98	(2.3)	439	(4.5)	469	(5.3)	**-29**	(5.1)	288	(6.8)	326	(7.6)	388	(5.7)	524	(3.8)	574	(4.6)	603	(6.2)
Spain (Cantabria)	491	(4.2)	90	(2.3)	473	(4.9)	510	(5.1)	**-37**	(5.3)	329	(10.5)	368	(6.8)	434	(5.6)	553	(5.0)	603	(4.8)	630	(5.5)
Spain (Castile and Leon)	507	(5.4)	87	(2.3)	490	(6.5)	524	(5.3)	**-34**	(5.7)	351	(11.3)	393	(10.0)	454	(6.7)	568	(5.4)	613	(6.0)	639	(6.3)
Spain (Catalonia)	503	(5.2)	85	(2.4)	487	(6.0)	519	(5.1)	**-32**	(4.2)	348	(11.5)	390	(10.1)	450	(6.9)	563	(5.4)	607	(4.9)	629	(5.2)
Spain (Ceuta and Melilla)	415	(2.7)	107	(1.8)	400	(3.9)	429	(3.7)	**-30**	(5.2)	238	(6.1)	276	(5.6)	340	(5.4)	493	(3.9)	553	(5.1)	586	(5.8)
Spain (Galicia)	488	(4.4)	92	(2.0)	471	(5.2)	506	(5.0)	**-36**	(4.6)	327	(7.9)	364	(8.3)	428	(6.6)	553	(4.5)	601	(5.6)	626	(5.4)
Spain (La Rioja)	502	(2.5)	94	(2.2)	483	(3.1)	521	(3.6)	**-38**	(4.6)	337	(9.3)	373	(6.6)	439	(5.1)	571	(4.7)	614	(4.8)	642	(5.5)
Spain (Madrid)	507	(4.7)	87	(3.7)	488	(5.9)	527	(5.2)	**-38**	(6.3)	355	(9.0)	393	(7.1)	454	(5.5)	567	(4.7)	612	(7.5)	640	(8.9)
Spain (Murcia)	485	(5.3)	83	(2.0)	475	(5.2)	494	(6.4)	**-19**	(5.5)	346	(6.7)	375	(6.6)	428	(6.6)	542	(5.7)	589	(5.4)	616	(8.7)
Spain (Navarre)	500	(3.1)	87	(2.1)	483	(4.0)	519	(3.9)	**-36**	(5.2)	349	(9.0)	385	(5.3)	442	(4.6)	562	(4.1)	609	(4.4)	634	(5.2)
United Kingdom (Scotland)	497	(3.1)	97	(1.7)	485	(4.4)	510	(3.1)	**-25**	(4.2)	335	(6.2)	374	(4.5)	433	(3.5)	566	(4.5)	623	(4.1)	653	(4.0)
Non-adjudicated																						
Belgium (French Community)	488	(4.4)	111	(2.9)	476	(6.1)	501	(4.8)	**-25**	(6.9)	296	(9.3)	336	(7.4)	410	(6.8)	573	(4.0)	624	(4.1)	652	(4.3)
Belgium (German-Speaking Community)	497	(2.7)	92	(2.1)	476	(3.6)	518	(4.1)	**-43**	(5.4)	340	(7.7)	371	(6.8)	431	(5.0)	566	(4.0)	612	(6.3)	638	(7.3)
Finland (Finnish Speaking)	537	(2.4)	86	(1.1)	509	(2.8)	565	(2.6)	**-56**	(2.4)	385	(5.5)	422	(4.0)	482	(3.0)	598	(2.3)	642	(2.4)	666	(2.8)
Finland (Swedish Speaking)	508	(2.6)	87	(1.9)	480	(3.8)	535	(2.9)	**-56**	(4.4)	361	(7.8)	393	(4.8)	449	(5.1)	571	(3.3)	618	(4.3)	643	(5.4)
Italy (Provincia Abruzzo)	485	(4.6)	93	(4.4)	462	(5.5)	510	(5.0)	**-48**	(6.3)	326	(8.7)	363	(7.2)	424	(6.6)	552	(5.6)	600	(5.5)	623	(5.2)
Italy (Provincia Autonoma di Bolzano)	490	(3.0)	94	(2.5)	467	(3.7)	514	(3.1)	**-47**	(4.1)	323	(12.9)	363	(9.2)	431	(4.7)	558	(2.7)	607	(3.4)	633	(3.9)
Italy (Provincia Basilicata)	479	(4.5)	88	(3.4)	456	(6.2)	503	(4.4)	**-47**	(6.8)	328	(12.3)	360	(9.2)	417	(6.2)	542	(4.0)	592	(4.8)	620	(5.2)
Italy (Provincia Calabria)	452	(5.4)	92	(4.1)	424	(7.6)	481	(5.0)	**-56**	(7.6)	298	(12.9)	330	(11.5)	388	(7.9)	519	(5.9)	569	(7.1)	598	(7.5)
Italy (Provincia Campania)	457	(7.1)	97	(5.4)	432	(9.1)	488	(6.8)	**-56**	(8.3)	293	(16.8)	330	(11.9)	391	(8.6)	527	(8.4)	577	(7.6)	606	(7.5)
Italy (Provincia Emilia Romagna)	507	(4.1)	100	(3.7)	492	(4.2)	521	(7.1)	**-29**	(8.4)	327	(11.9)	373	(8.9)	440	(7.7)	581	(4.7)	629	(4.5)	653	(5.7)
Italy (Provincia Friuli Venezia Giulia)	515	(5.1)	95	(3.7)	486	(6.1)	546	(5.8)	**-60**	(7.1)	350	(13.2)	386	(8.6)	456	(8.9)	583	(5.1)	630	(6.3)	655	(6.5)
Italy (Provincia Lazio)	484	(3.9)	94	(2.5)	461	(5.9)	511	(6.7)	**-50**	(9.0)	324	(8.3)	357	(8.7)	418	(6.9)	554	(4.9)	603	(6.3)	629	(8.2)
Italy (Provincia Liguria)	495	(8.9)	95	(7.3)	470	(14.9)	525	(5.2)	**-55**	(14.8)	323	(25.3)	368	(20.5)	436	(13.1)	561	(5.8)	613	(5.2)	640	(6.1)
Italy (Provincia Lombardia)	522	(5.3)	91	(3.1)	500	(6.5)	546	(7.1)	**-47**	(9.3)	356	(9.0)	398	(9.2)	466	(7.9)	586	(5.6)	630	(6.3)	656	(7.6)
Italy (Provincia Marche)	501	(7.6)	93	(5.3)	479	(11.5)	527	(4.7)	**-48**	(12.4)	336	(17.5)	374	(16.0)	438	(12.5)	569	(5.3)	618	(5.9)	642	(9.1)
Italy (Provincia Molise)	475	(2.8)	87	(2.4)	452	(3.8)	499	(3.5)	**-47**	(4.8)	320	(9.6)	361	(7.4)	416	(4.2)	540	(5.1)	583	(5.2)	608	(6.2)
Italy (Provincia Piemonte)	499	(6.3)	97	(3.7)	481	(8.4)	516	(6.0)	**-34**	(8.2)	332	(9.5)	368	(8.7)	433	(10.1)	570	(5.8)	620	(7.0)	648	(6.3)
Italy (Provincia Puglia)	492	(5.0)	88	(3.4)	468	(6.3)	515	(5.3)	**-48**	(6.4)	338	(9.7)	372	(9.2)	434	(7.2)	555	(5.0)	599	(5.8)	623	(8.1)
Italy (Provincia Sardegna)	473	(4.3)	94	(3.4)	445	(5.7)	500	(6.1)	**-55**	(7.7)	311	(5.2)	353	(5.2)	411	(5.5)	541	(5.8)	592	(7.3)	623	(7.8)
Italy (Provincia Sicilia)	458	(8.0)	100	(5.9)	432	(10.4)	484	(8.8)	**-52**	(9.3)	284	(24.9)	329	(15.7)	391	(9.6)	531	(7.7)	581	(6.9)	607	(7.6)
Italy (Provincia Toscana)	494	(4.7)	96	(3.4)	470	(7.1)	520	(6.1)	**-50**	(9.5)	321	(11.7)	359	(11.5)	431	(8.4)	566	(4.8)	610	(4.8)	634	(5.0)
Italy (Provincia Trento)	510	(2.8)	95	(2.7)	487	(5.1)	534	(6.8)	**-47**	(10.4)	341	(10.6)	381	(8.7)	447	(5.7)	579	(4.9)	628	(4.9)	653	(4.9)
Italy (Provincia Umbria)	493	(5.6)	101	(3.8)	469	(7.0)	516	(5.8)	**-48**	(7.2)	315	(11.5)	353	(11.1)	427	(9.6)	568	(5.5)	614	(5.7)	641	(8.5)
Italy (Provincia Valle d'Aosta)	518	(2.6)	87	(2.2)	507	(3.3)	530	(3.5)	**-23**	(4.4)	365	(10.6)	403	(9.1)	462	(6.6)	580	(3.1)	627	(5.4)	653	(5.9)
Italy (Provincia Veneto)	506	(5.3)	91	(4.3)	478	(9.1)	533	(6.4)	**-55**	(12.3)	342	(16.0)	381	(12.1)	447	(8.5)	569	(5.0)	615	(5.6)	645	(7.6)
United Kingdom (England)	492	(2.9)	98	(1.4)	479	(4.6)	504	(3.6)	**-26**	(5.8)	329	(5.2)	365	(3.9)	425	(4.1)	560	(3.8)	617	(3.6)	650	(4.7)
United Kingdom (Northern Ireland)	499	(4.3)	100	(3.6)	483	(8.0)	514	(4.2)	**-31**	(9.6)	329	(12.4)	369	(10.0)	431	(6.0)	570	(3.7)	626	(4.9)	657	(5.2)
United Kingdom (Wales)	474	(3.4)	95	(1.5)	460	(4.0)	488	(3.6)	**-28**	(3.4)	315	(6.2)	350	(4.9)	411	(4.8)	540	(4.1)	595	(4.4)	627	(4.6)

Note: See Table I.2.16 for national data.
Values that are statistically significant are indicated in bold (see Annex A3).
StatLink ᵐˢᴸ http://dx.doi.org/10.1787/888932343304

[Part 1/1]

Table S.I.p **Percentage of students at each proficiency level on the reading subscale *non-continuous texts***

	Proficiency levels															
	Below Level 1b (less than 262.04 score points)		Level 1b (from 262.04 to less than 334.75 score points)		Level 1a (from 334.75 to less than 407.47 score points)		Level 2 (from 407.47 to less than 480.18 score points)		Level 3 (from 480.18 to less than 552.89 score points)		Level 4 (from 552.89 to less than 625.61 score points)		Level 5 (from 625.61 to less than 698.32 score points)		Level 6 (above 698.32 score points)	
	%	S.E.	%	S.E.	%	S.E.	%	S.E.	%	S.E.	%	S.E.	%	S.E.	%	S.E.
Adjudicated																
Belgium (Flemish Community)	0.8	(0.2)	2.9	(0.4)	8.9	(0.6)	17.8	(0.9)	26.3	(1.0)	27.9	(1.0)	13.3	(0.9)	2.0	(0.4)
Spain (Andalusia)	3.8	(0.9)	7.3	(1.1)	17.9	(2.0)	28.6	(1.2)	28.9	(1.8)	11.8	(1.4)	1.5	(0.5)	0.1	(0.1)
Spain (Aragon)	1.5	(0.4)	3.8	(0.7)	13.3	(1.1)	25.6	(1.5)	30.6	(1.8)	19.9	(1.6)	5.1	(0.8)	0.2	(0.2)
Spain (Asturias)	2.4	(0.7)	5.4	(0.7)	12.6	(1.2)	24.8	(1.7)	29.6	(1.8)	20.1	(1.5)	4.7	(0.7)	0.2	(0.2)
Spain (Balearic Islands)	4.0	(0.9)	8.8	(1.5)	18.2	(1.5)	29.5	(1.3)	26.5	(1.8)	11.1	(1.6)	1.8	(0.6)	0.0	c
Spain (Basque Country)	1.3	(0.3)	4.0	(0.5)	12.1	(0.7)	25.6	(1.2)	33.2	(1.0)	19.4	(1.0)	4.1	(0.5)	0.4	(0.1)
Spain (Canary Islands)	3.8	(0.7)	10.0	(1.4)	23.3	(1.6)	29.3	(1.4)	24.3	(1.7)	8.5	(1.1)	0.8	(0.4)	0.0	c
Spain (Cantabria)	1.6	(0.5)	5.3	(0.9)	14.0	(1.3)	25.9	(1.4)	31.4	(1.5)	17.1	(1.5)	4.4	(1.0)	0.3	(0.2)
Spain (Castile and Leon)	1.0	(0.3)	3.5	(0.7)	11.0	(1.2)	23.7	(1.5)	34.1	(1.6)	21.7	(1.7)	4.7	(0.9)	0.3	(0.2)
Spain (Catalonia)	1.8	(0.4)	4.2	(0.9)	11.0	(1.3)	23.8	(2.0)	33.3	(1.9)	21.1	(1.9)	4.6	(0.9)	0.2	(0.2)
Spain (Ceuta and Melilla)	11.0	(0.9)	17.3	(1.2)	23.7	(1.6)	22.6	(1.6)	17.9	(1.8)	6.7	(0.7)	0.7	(0.3)	0.0	c
Spain (Galicia)	2.0	(0.4)	5.2	(0.7)	13.5	(1.3)	26.9	(1.4)	32.0	(1.2)	17.5	(1.5)	2.7	(0.5)	0.1	(0.1)
Spain (La Rioja)	2.1	(0.5)	5.2	(0.8)	13.7	(1.2)	22.6	(1.9)	28.7	(2.1)	21.0	(2.8)	6.2	(1.0)	0.5	(0.3)
Spain (Madrid)	1.2	(0.5)	3.9	(0.8)	12.1	(1.4)	23.1	(1.9)	32.5	(1.2)	21.0	(1.6)	5.7	(0.9)	0.4	(0.3)
Spain (Murcia)	1.0	(0.4)	5.3	(1.1)	15.8	(1.6)	29.0	(1.4)	32.3	(2.1)	14.4	(1.6)	2.1	(0.6)	0.2	(0.2)
Spain (Navarre)	1.0	(0.3)	4.5	(0.9)	13.1	(1.3)	26.0	(1.7)	32.3	(1.7)	18.8	(1.4)	4.0	(0.7)	0.3	(0.2)
United Kingdom (Scotland)	0.7	(0.2)	3.0	(0.4)	10.5	(0.8)	22.0	(1.1)	29.1	(1.2)	22.9	(1.1)	9.9	(0.9)	1.8	(0.3)
Non-adjudicated																
Belgium (French Community)	2.6	(0.6)	6.7	(0.8)	13.2	(0.9)	19.4	(1.1)	25.5	(1.2)	22.8	(1.2)	8.9	(0.7)	1.0	(0.2)
Belgium (German-Speaking Community)	1.1	(0.2)	2.2	(0.7)	12.2	(1.4)	23.9	(1.9)	30.7	(1.7)	23.7	(1.8)	5.7	(1.0)	0.4	(0.3)
Finland (Finnish Speaking)	0.3	(0.1)	1.7	(0.3)	6.4	(0.5)	17.0	(0.7)	29.5	(0.8)	29.9	(0.9)	13.0	(0.8)	2.1	(0.3)
Finland (Swedish Speaking)	0.5	(0.2)	2.0	(0.6)	8.1	(1.1)	22.1	(1.3)	30.5	(1.7)	25.4	(1.5)	10.2	(1.0)	1.2	(0.4)
Italy (Provincia Abruzzo)	1.9	(0.5)	6.3	(1.1)	15.9	(1.5)	28.4	(1.9)	27.3	(2.0)	16.5	(1.9)	3.5	(0.9)	0.2	(0.2)
Italy (Provincia Autonoma di Bolzano)	1.8	(0.5)	5.2	(0.8)	12.1	(1.1)	24.0	(1.3)	29.6	(1.5)	19.9	(1.0)	6.5	(0.9)	0.9	(0.3)
Italy (Provincia Basilicata)	2.5	(0.7)	7.9	(1.1)	19.1	(1.7)	27.0	(1.4)	27.2	(1.6)	13.5	(1.4)	2.6	(0.9)	0.0	c
Italy (Provincia Calabria)	3.2	(0.9)	11.7	(1.6)	22.7	(1.7)	29.0	(2.2)	22.7	(1.8)	9.0	(1.2)	1.5	(0.5)	0.1	(0.2)
Italy (Provincia Campania)	4.5	(1.4)	9.7	(1.1)	22.0	(1.7)	29.0	(1.8)	23.6	(2.4)	9.3	(1.7)	1.8	(0.6)	0.0	c
Italy (Provincia Emilia Romagna)	2.9	(0.9)	5.2	(0.8)	12.5	(1.4)	21.6	(1.8)	26.6	(1.4)	23.5	(1.5)	7.0	(0.9)	0.7	(0.3)
Italy (Provincia Friuli Venezia Giulia)	0.8	(0.4)	3.6	(0.9)	9.5	(1.4)	21.9	(2.1)	31.3	(1.8)	24.3	(1.9)	7.8	(1.5)	0.8	(0.4)
Italy (Provincia Lazio)	2.0	(0.5)	7.5	(1.7)	16.2	(1.4)	25.7	(1.7)	27.6	(1.6)	16.9	(1.7)	3.8	(0.9)	0.3	(0.2)
Italy (Provincia Liguria)	2.3	(1.6)	6.1	(1.9)	12.9	(1.7)	24.2	(1.9)	29.1	(2.2)	20.3	(2.2)	4.8	(0.9)	0.3	(0.2)
Italy (Provincia Lombardia)	0.9	(0.5)	2.9	(0.8)	8.8	(1.1)	19.5	(1.7)	31.5	(2.0)	26.4	(2.1)	8.9	(1.2)	1.2	(0.4)
Italy (Provincia Marche)	1.6	(0.8)	5.7	(1.6)	13.2	(1.6)	23.0	(1.6)	27.9	(2.2)	21.9	(1.9)	6.3	(1.0)	0.4	(0.2)
Italy (Provincia Molise)	2.0	(0.5)	6.9	(1.5)	18.7	(1.5)	29.5	(1.9)	28.0	(2.1)	13.1	(1.6)	1.7	(0.7)	0.0	c
Italy (Provincia Piemonte)	1.0	(0.4)	5.2	(1.1)	14.4	(1.7)	23.3	(1.5)	29.1	(2.0)	20.4	(1.7)	6.1	(0.9)	0.5	(0.3)
Italy (Provincia Puglia)	1.4	(0.6)	5.1	(1.1)	14.7	(1.6)	27.3	(2.3)	29.8	(2.0)	17.1	(1.6)	4.1	(1.1)	0.5	(0.2)
Italy (Provincia Sardegna)	3.7	(0.9)	6.6	(1.0)	18.7	(1.7)	29.1	(1.8)	25.7	(1.9)	12.7	(1.6)	3.2	(0.8)	0.3	(0.2)
Italy (Provincia Sicilia)	6.4	(2.1)	10.4	(2.1)	20.3	(2.5)	25.6	(2.5)	23.4	(2.3)	11.5	(1.5)	2.2	(0.7)	0.1	(0.1)
Italy (Provincia Toscana)	2.4	(0.7)	5.5	(1.0)	14.2	(1.9)	22.7	(2.0)	27.6	(1.8)	21.2	(1.5)	5.8	(0.9)	0.5	(0.3)
Italy (Provincia Trento)	1.0	(0.4)	4.4	(0.8)	12.2	(1.6)	22.1	(1.3)	30.5	(1.6)	22.0	(1.4)	7.0	(0.8)	0.8	(0.3)
Italy (Provincia Umbria)	3.3	(1.0)	6.3	(0.9)	13.9	(1.3)	23.5	(1.8)	27.7	(1.7)	19.1	(1.5)	5.6	(0.9)	0.5	(0.2)
Italy (Provincia Valle d'Aosta)	0.7	(0.3)	3.5	(0.7)	11.3	(1.4)	24.8	(1.4)	28.7	(1.6)	22.0	(1.5)	8.2	(0.9)	0.9	(0.4)
Italy (Provincia Veneto)	1.4	(0.6)	3.9	(0.9)	10.6	(1.4)	21.6	(1.9)	30.1	(1.9)	22.8	(1.9)	8.5	(1.1)	1.1	(0.4)
United Kingdom (England)	1.1	(0.2)	3.4	(0.4)	11.6	(0.8)	22.4	(0.8)	28.5	(0.9)	21.8	(0.9)	9.1	(0.7)	2.0	(0.3)
United Kingdom (Northern Ireland)	1.1	(0.4)	3.5	(0.7)	11.3	(1.0)	22.2	(1.2)	28.9	(1.4)	22.6	(1.1)	8.6	(0.5)	1.8	(0.5)
United Kingdom (Wales)	1.4	(0.3)	5.2	(0.8)	13.9	(1.0)	26.0	(1.2)	28.1	(1.2)	18.5	(1.0)	6.0	(0.6)	0.9	(0.2)

Note: See Table I.2.17 for national data.
StatLink http://dx.doi.org/10.1787/888932343304

[Part 1/2]

Percentage of students at each proficiency level on the reading subscale *non-continuous texts*, by gender

Table S.I.q

	Boys – Proficiency levels														
	Below Level 1b (less than 262.04 score points)		Level 1b (from 262.04 to less than 334.75 score points)		Level 1a (from 334.75 to less than 407.47 score points)		Level 2 (from 407.47 to less than 480.18 score points)		Level 3 (from 480.18 to less than 552.89 score points)		Level 4 (from 552.89 to less than 625.61 score points)		Level 5 (from 625.61 to less than 698.32 score points)		Level 6 (above 698.32 score points)	
	%	S.E.	%	S.E.	%	S.E.	%	S.E.	%	S.E.	%	S.E.	%	S.E.	%	S.E.
Adjudicated																
Belgium (Flemish Community)	1.3	(0.3)	3.8	(0.5)	11.0	(0.9)	20.0	(1.3)	26.0	(1.5)	25.4	(1.2)	10.9	(1.0)	1.6	(0.5)
Spain (Andalusia)	5.2	(1.3)	9.2	(1.7)	19.9	(2.3)	27.2	(1.6)	26.0	(2.4)	10.9	(2.0)	1.5	(0.6)	0.0	c
Spain (Aragon)	2.6	(0.7)	5.5	(1.2)	15.8	(1.9)	27.2	(2.1)	28.7	(2.1)	16.0	(1.9)	4.1	(1.0)	0.2	(0.2)
Spain (Asturias)	3.2	(0.8)	7.1	(1.1)	15.4	(2.0)	25.7	(2.0)	26.4	(2.1)	17.6	(2.0)	4.3	(1.0)	0.2	(0.2)
Spain (Balearic Islands)	5.8	(1.3)	10.8	(1.9)	19.4	(1.9)	29.9	(2.2)	23.4	(2.1)	8.9	(1.7)	1.8	(0.8)	0.0	c
Spain (Basque Country)	2.2	(0.5)	5.6	(0.8)	16.0	(1.0)	26.4	(1.5)	29.8	(1.4)	16.6	(1.1)	3.2	(0.5)	0.2	(0.1)
Spain (Canary Islands)	4.4	(0.9)	11.4	(1.4)	24.2	(2.0)	29.9	(2.1)	22.2	(1.6)	7.5	(1.4)	0.5	(0.3)	0.0	c
Spain (Cantabria)	2.5	(0.8)	7.4	(1.4)	17.7	(1.8)	26.6	(1.7)	27.9	(2.2)	14.4	(1.8)	3.2	(0.9)	0.3	(0.3)
Spain (Castile and Leon)	1.3	(0.5)	5.3	(1.2)	14.4	(1.9)	25.2	(2.6)	31.4	(2.3)	17.8	(1.8)	4.3	(1.1)	0.0	c
Spain (Catalonia)	2.6	(0.7)	5.6	(1.5)	13.4	(1.8)	25.7	(2.7)	31.2	(2.8)	18.1	(2.4)	3.3	(1.1)	0.1	(0.1)
Spain (Ceuta and Melilla)	14.4	(1.5)	18.4	(1.8)	23.2	(1.8)	21.8	(2.4)	15.4	(2.6)	5.9	(1.2)	0.8	(0.5)	0.0	c
Spain (Galicia)	3.1	(0.8)	7.5	(1.1)	16.8	(2.0)	26.2	(2.0)	29.6	(2.1)	14.5	(1.5)	2.2	(0.7)	0.0	c
Spain (La Rioja)	3.1	(0.9)	6.9	(1.2)	16.0	(1.8)	24.5	(2.3)	25.9	(2.4)	18.1	(1.9)	5.1	(1.3)	0.3	(0.2)
Spain (Madrid)	1.6	(0.9)	6.0	(1.3)	16.4	(2.0)	24.3	(2.5)	30.4	(2.0)	17.1	(2.5)	3.9	(0.9)	0.0	c
Spain (Murcia)	1.1	(0.7)	5.5	(1.4)	17.6	(2.3)	29.3	(2.3)	31.6	(3.0)	13.2	(1.6)	1.4	(0.7)	0.2	(0.2)
Spain (Navarre)	1.5	(0.5)	6.6	(1.4)	17.1	(1.9)	27.6	(2.3)	28.9	(2.4)	15.8	(2.0)	2.3	(0.8)	0.2	(0.2)
United Kingdom (Scotland)	1.1	(0.3)	4.4	(0.7)	13.2	(1.3)	23.6	(1.4)	26.9	(1.7)	19.8	(1.6)	8.9	(1.1)	1.9	(0.5)
Non-adjudicated																
Belgium (French Community)	4.0	(1.0)	8.3	(1.3)	15.4	(1.3)	19.3	(1.6)	23.7	(1.5)	20.9	(1.7)	7.6	(1.0)	0.9	(0.4)
Belgium (German-Speaking Community)	1.7	(0.4)	3.3	(1.2)	16.1	(2.0)	26.3	(2.5)	29.8	(2.5)	18.8	(2.4)	4.0	(1.0)	0.0	c
Finland (Finnish Speaking)	0.4	(0.1)	2.8	(0.5)	9.9	(0.8)	23.0	(1.0)	31.2	(1.2)	24.0	(1.3)	7.9	(0.7)	0.8	(0.3)
Finland (Swedish Speaking)	1.0	(0.4)	3.4	(1.1)	11.8	(1.6)	28.0	(2.0)	29.5	(2.1)	19.4	(2.2)	6.4	(1.2)	0.3	(0.3)
Italy (Provincia Abruzzo)	2.1	(0.9)	9.6	(1.5)	19.9	(2.3)	29.5	(2.3)	23.7	(2.2)	12.4	(1.8)	2.5	(1.0)	0.2	(0.3)
Italy (Provincia Autonoma di Bolzano)	2.8	(0.7)	7.4	(1.4)	15.7	(1.7)	27.0	(2.3)	25.0	(1.9)	16.0	(1.4)	5.4	(1.0)	0.7	(0.3)
Italy (Provincia Basilicata)	4.1	(1.1)	10.7	(1.6)	22.4	(2.3)	27.3	(2.2)	23.4	(2.4)	10.1	(2.1)	1.9	(1.0)	0.0	c
Italy (Provincia Calabria)	5.2	(1.5)	17.6	(3.1)	26.6	(2.2)	26.5	(2.8)	16.5	(2.0)	6.5	(1.3)	1.0	(0.5)	0.0	c
Italy (Provincia Campania)	6.8	(1.8)	12.9	(1.7)	26.7	(2.2)	27.0	(2.1)	18.4	(2.6)	7.0	(1.9)	1.2	(0.4)	0.0	c
Italy (Provincia Emilia Romagna)	3.6	(1.4)	5.8	(1.1)	13.9	(1.9)	23.4	(2.3)	26.8	(2.2)	20.6	(2.0)	5.6	(1.2)	0.3	(0.3)
Italy (Provincia Friuli Venezia Giulia)	1.3	(0.7)	5.9	(1.6)	14.1	(1.9)	24.4	(2.9)	28.0	(2.2)	20.0	(2.2)	6.1	(1.6)	0.3	(0.3)
Italy (Provincia Lazio)	2.8	(0.9)	10.2	(2.4)	20.3	(2.1)	26.8	(2.4)	23.0	(2.0)	13.6	(2.0)	3.0	(1.0)	0.0	c
Italy (Provincia Liguria)	4.0	(2.9)	9.3	(3.3)	16.4	(2.5)	26.3	(3.2)	24.5	(3.2)	15.7	(2.7)	3.6	(1.0)	0.0	c
Italy (Provincia Lombardia)	1.4	(0.8)	4.4	(1.5)	11.7	(1.6)	22.9	(2.6)	30.5	(3.1)	21.8	(3.0)	6.5	(1.4)	0.7	(0.3)
Italy (Provincia Marche)	2.2	(1.3)	7.3	(2.8)	16.4	(2.4)	27.5	(1.8)	25.0	(3.3)	17.2	(2.3)	4.1	(1.0)	0.2	(0.2)
Italy (Provincia Molise)	3.2	(0.9)	10.0	(1.6)	24.5	(2.6)	29.3	(3.2)	21.2	(2.5)	10.2	(2.1)	1.5	(0.8)	0.0	c
Italy (Provincia Piemonte)	1.6	(0.8)	6.2	(1.8)	15.7	(2.1)	25.0	(3.0)	28.4	(3.0)	18.0	(2.5)	4.7	(0.9)	0.4	(0.3)
Italy (Provincia Puglia)	2.2	(1.0)	8.1	(1.8)	18.2	(2.6)	29.1	(3.0)	25.7	(2.3)	13.7	(2.1)	2.6	(0.9)	0.3	(0.2)
Italy (Provincia Sardegna)	6.8	(1.5)	9.6	(1.7)	22.6	(2.1)	30.3	(3.3)	18.3	(2.5)	9.8	(2.0)	2.3	(0.9)	0.0	c
Italy (Provincia Sicilia)	10.4	(3.3)	14.1	(2.4)	21.9	(3.6)	22.9	(3.3)	19.4	(2.8)	9.3	(1.6)	1.9	(0.9)	0.0	c
Italy (Provincia Toscana)	3.5	(0.9)	8.1	(1.5)	18.4	(2.7)	24.6	(2.6)	24.6	(2.2)	16.1	(2.1)	4.4	(1.2)	0.3	(0.2)
Italy (Provincia Trento)	1.7	(0.8)	6.4	(1.7)	15.3	(2.2)	24.1	(1.8)	28.7	(2.5)	17.7	(2.8)	5.4	(1.1)	0.6	(0.4)
Italy (Provincia Umbria)	5.5	(1.6)	8.6	(1.4)	17.1	(1.7)	23.6	(2.4)	25.0	(2.3)	16.1	(1.9)	3.9	(1.0)	0.0	c
Italy (Provincia Valle d'Aosta)	1.2	(0.5)	5.1	(1.2)	12.4	(2.4)	26.0	(2.2)	28.0	(2.1)	18.4	(2.3)	8.0	(1.5)	1.0	(0.6)
Italy (Provincia Veneto)	2.7	(1.1)	6.4	(1.7)	14.6	(2.8)	24.1	(2.8)	27.4	(3.1)	18.3	(2.4)	6.0	(1.2)	0.5	(0.4)
United Kingdom (England)	1.5	(0.4)	4.7	(0.7)	13.8	(1.1)	24.2	(1.3)	27.1	(1.6)	19.1	(1.3)	8.0	(0.9)	1.5	(0.4)
United Kingdom (Northern Ireland)	1.7	(1.2)	5.3	(1.2)	14.7	(1.6)	23.3	(1.7)	25.8	(2.3)	20.3	(1.9)	7.4	(1.4)	1.6	(0.6)
United Kingdom (Wales)	2.3	(0.5)	7.0	(1.2)	16.4	(1.4)	26.1	(1.4)	26.4	(1.7)	16.0	(1.2)	5.1	(0.7)	0.7	(0.3)

Note: See Table I.2.18 for national data.
StatLink ᴍᔆᴸ http://dx.doi.org/10.1787/888932343304

[Part 2/2]

Percentage of students at each proficiency level on the reading subscale *non-continuous texts,* by gender

Table S.I.q

	Girls – Proficiency levels															
	Below Level 1b (less than 262.04 score points)		Level 1b (from 262.04 to less than 334.75 score points)		Level 1a (from 334.75 to less than 407.47 score points)		Level 2 (from 407.47 to less than 480.18 score points)		Level 3 (from 480.18 to less than 552.89 score points)		Level 4 (from 552.89 to less than 625.61 score points)		Level 5 (from 625.61 to less than 698.32 score points)		Level 6 (above 698.32 score points)	
	%	S.E.	%	S.E.	%	S.E.	%	S.E.	%	S.E.	%	S.E.	%	S.E.	%	S.E.
Adjudicated																
Belgium (Flemish Community)	0.3	(0.2)	2.0	(0.4)	6.8	(0.8)	15.4	(1.2)	26.6	(1.1)	30.5	(1.3)	15.8	(1.2)	2.5	(0.6)
Spain (Andalusia)	2.3	(0.8)	5.3	(1.2)	15.7	(2.3)	30.2	(1.7)	32.2	(3.1)	12.8	(1.9)	1.5	(0.6)	0.0	c
Spain (Aragon)	0.3	(0.2)	2.0	(0.5)	10.8	(1.3)	23.9	(1.9)	32.5	(2.4)	23.9	(2.2)	6.3	(1.5)	0.3	(0.2)
Spain (Asturias)	1.6	(0.7)	3.5	(0.9)	9.5	(1.4)	23.8	(2.8)	33.2	(2.5)	23.0	(1.9)	5.1	(1.3)	0.2	(0.2)
Spain (Balearic Islands)	2.2	(0.9)	6.9	(1.5)	16.9	(2.2)	29.1	(2.2)	29.6	(2.6)	13.3	(2.0)	1.9	(0.6)	0.0	c
Spain (Basque Country)	0.3	(0.2)	2.2	(0.5)	8.0	(0.9)	24.7	(1.5)	36.8	(1.2)	22.4	(1.2)	5.1	(0.7)	0.5	(0.2)
Spain (Canary Islands)	3.3	(1.0)	8.5	(2.0)	22.2	(2.4)	28.6	(2.2)	26.6	(2.7)	9.6	(1.4)	1.1	(0.7)	0.0	c
Spain (Cantabria)	0.7	(0.4)	3.2	(0.8)	10.3	(1.7)	25.1	(2.0)	34.9	(2.1)	19.8	(2.2)	5.6	(1.6)	0.3	(0.2)
Spain (Castile and Leon)	0.7	(0.4)	1.7	(0.7)	7.7	(1.3)	22.3	(2.3)	36.8	(2.2)	25.4	(2.2)	5.0	(1.1)	0.3	(0.3)
Spain (Catalonia)	1.0	(0.5)	2.7	(0.8)	8.4	(1.6)	21.8	(2.6)	35.6	(2.3)	24.2	(2.6)	6.0	(1.4)	0.0	c
Spain (Ceuta and Melilla)	7.7	(1.0)	16.3	(1.7)	24.2	(2.4)	23.4	(2.2)	20.3	(1.8)	7.4	(1.2)	0.7	(0.4)	0.0	c
Spain (Galicia)	0.9	(0.4)	2.9	(0.6)	10.1	(1.5)	27.6	(1.9)	34.4	(1.4)	20.6	(2.4)	3.3	(0.9)	0.2	(0.2)
Spain (La Rioja)	1.0	(0.4)	3.5	(1.0)	11.2	(1.5)	20.5	(2.8)	31.7	(2.7)	24.0	(2.6)	7.4	(1.3)	0.7	(0.5)
Spain (Madrid)	0.8	(0.5)	1.8	(0.6)	7.9	(1.3)	21.9	(2.4)	34.7	(2.0)	25.0	(2.2)	7.5	(1.2)	0.5	(0.4)
Spain (Murcia)	0.8	(0.5)	5.1	(1.6)	13.9	(1.7)	28.6	(1.9)	32.9	(2.4)	15.6	(2.3)	2.8	(0.7)	0.0	c
Spain (Navarre)	0.5	(0.4)	2.3	(0.8)	8.7	(1.5)	24.3	(2.3)	35.9	(2.3)	22.0	(1.9)	5.9	(1.5)	0.4	(0.4)
United Kingdom (Scotland)	0.3	(0.3)	1.6	(0.5)	7.7	(1.2)	20.4	(1.8)	31.3	(1.4)	26.1	(1.5)	10.9	(1.1)	1.7	(0.4)
Non-adjudicated																
Belgium (French Community)	1.2	(0.5)	5.0	(1.0)	10.8	(1.1)	19.5	(1.3)	27.4	(1.7)	24.8	(1.6)	10.3	(1.2)	1.0	(0.4)
Belgium (German-Speaking Community)	0.5	(0.0)	0.0	c	8.2	(1.5)	21.4	(2.5)	31.6	(2.6)	28.8	(2.5)	7.6	(1.6)	0.7	(0.6)
Finland (Finnish Speaking)	0.2	(0.1)	0.6	(0.2)	2.8	(0.4)	11.0	(0.9)	27.9	(1.1)	35.9	(1.3)	18.2	(1.2)	3.5	(0.6)
Finland (Swedish Speaking)	0.0	c	0.5	(0.3)	4.4	(1.0)	16.3	(2.0)	31.5	(2.6)	31.3	(2.3)	14.0	(1.5)	2.0	(0.7)
Italy (Provincia Abruzzo)	1.6	(0.5)	2.6	(1.0)	11.4	(1.6)	27.2	(2.7)	31.3	(3.0)	21.1	(2.8)	4.6	(1.3)	0.3	(0.3)
Italy (Provincia Autonoma di Bolzano)	0.9	(0.6)	3.1	(0.9)	8.4	(1.6)	21.0	(2.2)	34.3	(2.8)	23.8	(1.5)	7.6	(1.3)	1.1	(0.4)
Italy (Provincia Basilicata)	0.8	(0.6)	5.0	(1.1)	15.6	(2.2)	26.5	(1.7)	31.4	(2.3)	17.1	(1.9)	3.3	(1.1)	0.0	c
Italy (Provincia Calabria)	1.2	(0.6)	5.7	(1.1)	18.7	(2.4)	31.5	(2.6)	29.1	(2.4)	11.6	(2.0)	2.0	(0.8)	0.0	c
Italy (Provincia Campania)	1.4	(1.0)	5.7	(1.4)	16.0	(2.3)	31.6	(2.8)	30.3	(3.1)	12.3	(2.1)	2.6	(1.1)	0.0	c
Italy (Provincia Emilia Romagna)	2.3	(1.0)	4.6	(1.3)	11.2	(1.8)	19.8	(2.4)	26.5	(2.4)	26.3	(2.3)	8.3	(1.6)	1.1	(0.5)
Italy (Provincia Friuli Venezia Giulia)	0.0	c	1.1	(0.7)	4.6	(1.4)	19.1	(2.1)	34.9	(2.5)	28.9	(2.6)	9.7	(2.0)	1.4	(0.7)
Italy (Provincia Lazio)	1.0	(0.6)	4.3	(1.8)	11.5	(2.1)	24.4	(2.6)	32.9	(2.4)	20.8	(2.5)	4.8	(1.0)	0.0	c
Italy (Provincia Liguria)	0.2	(0.3)	2.5	(1.0)	8.8	(1.7)	21.8	(2.2)	34.4	(2.5)	25.6	(2.5)	6.2	(1.2)	0.5	(0.3)
Italy (Provincia Lombardia)	0.3	(0.3)	1.3	(0.7)	5.6	(1.2)	15.6	(2.0)	32.5	(2.3)	31.5	(2.5)	11.4	(1.9)	1.7	(0.6)
Italy (Provincia Marche)	0.9	(0.6)	3.7	(0.8)	9.2	(1.5)	17.7	(2.7)	31.3	(3.5)	27.5	(2.8)	8.9	(1.9)	0.7	(0.5)
Italy (Provincia Molise)	0.6	(0.4)	3.6	(0.8)	12.5	(1.7)	29.7	(2.4)	35.2	(3.1)	16.3	(2.5)	2.0	(1.0)	0.0	c
Italy (Provincia Piemonte)	0.4	(0.4)	4.3	(1.3)	13.1	(2.3)	21.6	(2.0)	29.9	(2.5)	22.7	(2.1)	7.5	(1.2)	0.6	(0.3)
Italy (Provincia Puglia)	0.6	(0.4)	2.2	(0.8)	11.5	(1.9)	25.6	(2.8)	33.6	(2.9)	20.2	(2.0)	5.6	(1.7)	0.7	(0.4)
Italy (Provincia Sardegna)	0.9	(0.6)	3.7	(1.2)	15.0	(2.3)	28.0	(2.2)	32.7	(2.8)	15.3	(2.7)	4.0	(1.2)	0.4	(0.3)
Italy (Provincia Sicilia)	2.5	(1.3)	6.9	(3.0)	18.8	(3.0)	28.2	(2.9)	27.2	(3.3)	13.6	(2.2)	2.5	(0.8)	0.2	(0.2)
Italy (Provincia Toscana)	1.2	(0.8)	2.6	(1.1)	9.6	(1.8)	20.7	(2.2)	30.9	(2.7)	26.8	(2.3)	7.4	(1.3)	0.7	(0.5)
Italy (Provincia Trento)	0.3	(0.4)	2.1	(0.8)	8.7	(1.8)	19.9	(2.2)	32.5	(2.8)	26.7	(3.3)	8.7	(1.3)	1.0	(0.5)
Italy (Provincia Umbria)	1.2	(0.6)	4.2	(1.0)	10.7	(1.7)	23.5	(2.4)	30.3	(2.4)	22.0	(2.2)	7.3	(1.4)	0.8	(0.4)
Italy (Provincia Valle d'Aosta)	0.0	c	2.0	(0.8)	10.1	(1.5)	23.6	(2.1)	29.5	(2.5)	25.4	(2.1)	8.4	(1.3)	0.8	(0.4)
Italy (Provincia Veneto)	0.0	c	1.5	(0.8)	6.8	(1.6)	19.3	(2.7)	32.6	(2.3)	27.0	(3.0)	10.8	(2.0)	1.8	(0.7)
United Kingdom (England)	0.6	(0.2)	2.2	(0.4)	9.6	(1.0)	20.6	(1.1)	29.9	(1.3)	24.4	(1.4)	10.2	(1.0)	2.4	(0.5)
United Kingdom (Northern Ireland)	0.5	(0.3)	1.9	(0.7)	8.1	(1.1)	21.2	(1.7)	31.9	(1.9)	24.7	(1.5)	9.7	(1.2)	2.0	(0.6)
United Kingdom (Wales)	0.6	(0.2)	3.4	(0.6)	11.3	(1.1)	25.9	(1.9)	29.8	(1.4)	21.1	(1.1)	6.9	(0.9)	1.0	(0.3)

Note: See Table I.2.18 for national data.
StatLink ⌐⌐⌐▱ http://dx.doi.org/10.1787/888932343304

[Part 1/1]

Mean score, variation and gender differences in student performance on the reading subscale

Table S.I.r *non-continuous texts*

	All students				Gender differences						Percentiles											
	Mean score		Standard deviation		Boys		Girls		Difference (B – G)		5th		10th		25th		75th		90th		95th	
	Mean	S.E.	S.D.	S.E.	Mean score	S.E.	Mean score	S.E.	Score dif.	S.E.	Score	S.E.	Score	S.E.	Score	S.E.	Score	S.E.	Score	S.E.	Score	S.E.
Adjudicated																						
Belgium (Flemish Community)	526	(2.5)	98	(1.7)	512	(3.2)	541	(3.4)	**-29**	(4.3)	351	(5.5)	393	(3.5)	461	(3.4)	598	(2.8)	646	(3.4)	671	(4.5)
Spain (Andalusia)	453	(6.0)	95	(3.0)	442	(6.9)	465	(5.6)	**-23**	(4.5)	283	(14.1)	327	(11.9)	394	(7.4)	519	(5.8)	566	(6.6)	592	(7.1)
Spain (Aragon)	489	(4.3)	91	(2.5)	473	(6.7)	505	(3.5)	**-33**	(6.5)	332	(11.0)	370	(8.3)	429	(5.8)	554	(4.3)	602	(5.2)	628	(5.2)
Spain (Asturias)	482	(4.2)	98	(2.8)	469	(5.6)	497	(4.5)	**-28**	(6.1)	303	(8.1)	351	(8.1)	422	(5.2)	553	(4.9)	600	(5.4)	625	(4.7)
Spain (Balearic Islands)	448	(6.3)	96	(2.6)	435	(6.7)	462	(6.6)	**-27**	(4.7)	275	(12.8)	318	(10.4)	388	(9.2)	517	(6.5)	564	(5.7)	591	(5.2)
Spain (Basque Country)	489	(3.1)	88	(2.0)	473	(3.9)	506	(2.9)	**-33**	(3.4)	332	(8.0)	373	(6.1)	435	(4.0)	550	(2.5)	596	(2.8)	622	(3.5)
Spain (Canary Islands)	435	(4.3)	92	(2.0)	427	(4.4)	444	(5.3)	**-17**	(5.0)	277	(7.9)	316	(8.0)	375	(5.7)	502	(4.3)	550	(5.1)	578	(5.3)
Spain (Cantabria)	481	(4.3)	93	(2.5)	464	(5.4)	498	(4.8)	**-34**	(5.2)	319	(7.0)	357	(8.4)	422	(5.2)	544	(5.0)	594	(5.9)	624	(6.4)
Spain (Castile and Leon)	496	(4.7)	87	(2.2)	482	(6.0)	509	(4.6)	**-27**	(5.5)	340	(8.7)	377	(7.7)	442	(6.9)	557	(4.5)	600	(5.1)	625	(6.2)
Spain (Catalonia)	491	(6.1)	93	(2.6)	476	(6.7)	506	(6.3)	**-30**	(4.9)	321	(14.3)	369	(9.4)	437	(8.0)	555	(5.6)	598	(6.7)	624	(6.6)
Spain (Ceuta and Melilla)	398	(2.7)	111	(2.4)	385	(4.3)	411	(3.2)	**-25**	(5.2)	210	(12.6)	255	(7.5)	323	(5.5)	481	(4.8)	540	(5.0)	570	(6.1)
Spain (Galicia)	476	(4.7)	92	(2.2)	460	(5.8)	492	(5.1)	**-32**	(5.4)	312	(10.6)	355	(7.7)	421	(5.4)	540	(5.0)	586	(4.4)	611	(5.4)
Spain (La Rioja)	487	(3.0)	101	(2.8)	471	(3.8)	504	(3.9)	**-33**	(5.0)	314	(9.6)	353	(7.5)	422	(5.1)	560	(4.1)	610	(5.2)	636	(6.8)
Spain (Madrid)	494	(4.8)	92	(3.3)	476	(5.7)	513	(5.6)	**-37**	(6.4)	333	(10.4)	372	(6.9)	436	(5.7)	558	(5.5)	607	(5.8)	632	(6.6)
Spain (Murcia)	472	(5.0)	85	(2.0)	467	(5.6)	478	(5.9)	**-11**	(6.0)	325	(10.7)	359	(8.2)	418	(6.0)	532	(4.9)	576	(5.7)	603	(4.8)
Spain (Navarre)	486	(3.8)	89	(2.2)	468	(5.1)	505	(4.4)	**-37**	(5.9)	329	(9.0)	368	(6.5)	430	(5.0)	548	(4.1)	594	(4.5)	620	(5.7)
United Kingdom (Scotland)	511	(3.4)	96	(1.8)	498	(4.9)	524	(3.2)	**-26**	(4.3)	348	(6.3)	386	(5.6)	447	(4.5)	579	(4.3)	634	(5.3)	664	(5.1)
Non-adjudicated																						
Belgium (French Community)	492	(3.8)	110	(2.7)	478	(6.1)	507	(4.3)	**-30**	(7.6)	294	(8.6)	340	(7.4)	418	(6.2)	574	(4.3)	625	(4.1)	651	(4.6)
Belgium (German-Speaking Community)	499	(2.8)	91	(2.2)	481	(3.8)	519	(4.0)	**-38**	(5.4)	353	(7.1)	383	(5.8)	440	(5.2)	565	(3.7)	609	(5.0)	634	(6.8)
Finland (Finnish Speaking)	536	(2.6)	89	(1.1)	509	(2.8)	563	(2.9)	**-54**	(2.6)	380	(4.6)	419	(4.5)	479	(3.0)	598	(3.0)	646	(3.0)	671	(3.0)
Finland (Swedish Speaking)	519	(2.8)	89	(2.1)	492	(4.2)	545	(3.0)	**-54**	(4.9)	367	(8.1)	404	(6.6)	459	(4.3)	583	(4.2)	631	(4.4)	657	(4.6)
Italy (Provincia Abruzzo)	471	(5.3)	94	(3.2)	452	(6.4)	492	(6.0)	**-39**	(6.1)	311	(10.9)	349	(8.3)	410	(5.6)	539	(6.7)	589	(8.2)	617	(7.2)
Italy (Provincia Autonoma di Bolzano)	490	(3.3)	100	(2.8)	470	(4.2)	510	(3.4)	**-40**	(4.3)	313	(10.8)	358	(8.1)	431	(4.9)	559	(3.5)	612	(4.7)	642	(6.1)
Italy (Provincia Basilicata)	458	(4.9)	95	(3.0)	439	(6.3)	479	(5.0)	**-40**	(6.3)	297	(10.6)	332	(6.8)	394	(7.4)	527	(5.6)	577	(7.3)	605	(7.8)
Italy (Provincia Calabria)	437	(5.0)	94	(3.4)	411	(7.3)	463	(5.2)	**-52**	(7.7)	278	(9.2)	312	(9.5)	372	(7.6)	504	(5.8)	556	(6.0)	585	(7.1)
Italy (Provincia Campania)	438	(6.7)	99	(4.9)	415	(8.9)	467	(6.6)	**-52**	(9.3)	270	(18.4)	312	(12.6)	375	(7.6)	507	(8.2)	558	(8.6)	591	(9.2)
Italy (Provincia Emilia Romagna)	491	(5.1)	105	(4.5)	479	(5.6)	503	(7.8)	**-24**	(8.7)	298	(18.5)	350	(11.2)	426	(8.2)	569	(4.2)	615	(5.1)	641	(5.9)
Italy (Provincia Friuli Venezia Giulia)	508	(4.4)	92	(3.4)	486	(5.6)	530	(5.6)	**-44**	(7.4)	343	(13.8)	387	(9.0)	450	(5.4)	572	(5.2)	621	(5.5)	645	(6.5)
Italy (Provincia Lazio)	471	(4.4)	97	(2.6)	452	(6.7)	493	(7.0)	**-40**	(9.9)	300	(7.0)	339	(9.4)	406	(5.8)	542	(5.4)	591	(6.5)	619	(7.4)
Italy (Provincia Liguria)	482	(10.4)	99	(8.2)	458	(17.0)	511	(5.8)	**-52**	(16.3)	303	(29.5)	348	(27.5)	422	(14.5)	554	(5.4)	601	(6.2)	626	(6.2)
Italy (Provincia Lombardia)	515	(5.6)	92	(2.9)	496	(7.0)	537	(6.6)	**-40**	(8.8)	350	(12.0)	392	(8.8)	460	(7.2)	580	(5.5)	626	(6.5)	653	(5.3)
Italy (Provincia Marche)	490	(7.4)	99	(4.9)	469	(11.1)	514	(5.1)	**-45**	(12.1)	312	(18.4)	353	(15.3)	425	(12.1)	563	(5.0)	611	(5.1)	638	(6.0)
Italy (Provincia Molise)	459	(2.7)	90	(2.1)	438	(3.8)	481	(3.3)	**-43**	(4.8)	303	(7.4)	341	(5.3)	400	(5.5)	525	(4.5)	572	(4.8)	598	(7.2)
Italy (Provincia Piemonte)	489	(5.8)	96	(3.4)	477	(7.0)	500	(6.7)	**-22**	(7.8)	323	(10.0)	358	(11.8)	424	(8.6)	558	(5.5)	607	(6.7)	637	(5.4)
Italy (Provincia Puglia)	480	(6.3)	92	(4.4)	459	(7.7)	499	(6.8)	**-40**	(7.3)	319	(15.9)	359	(10.3)	420	(8.3)	544	(7.4)	595	(8.9)	622	(9.6)
Italy (Provincia Sardegna)	457	(5.3)	99	(4.3)	430	(7.5)	482	(6.9)	**-52**	(9.2)	283	(14.8)	334	(9.3)	396	(5.9)	524	(6.9)	579	(7.9)	610	(8.1)
Italy (Provincia Sicilia)	436	(9.7)	112	(9.4)	412	(12.5)	459	(10.7)	**-48**	(11.3)	246	(28.1)	297	(18.6)	368	(12.6)	516	(6.8)	568	(7.0)	598	(8.1)
Italy (Provincia Toscana)	485	(4.9)	101	(3.2)	463	(6.8)	509	(6.8)	**-46**	(9.4)	309	(13.6)	348	(8.9)	418	(8.3)	559	(4.7)	608	(5.3)	635	(6.8)
Italy (Provincia Trento)	498	(2.9)	95	(2.6)	480	(5.0)	519	(6.4)	**-39**	(9.7)	331	(8.8)	370	(7.0)	435	(4.9)	565	(4.4)	615	(4.1)	646	(5.8)
Italy (Provincia Umbria)	478	(5.5)	104	(4.2)	456	(7.0)	499	(6.0)	**-43**	(7.7)	290	(13.9)	338	(11.2)	413	(8.5)	554	(6.5)	604	(6.9)	632	(5.4)
Italy (Provincia Valle d'Aosta)	502	(2.4)	93	(1.8)	493	(3.3)	512	(3.6)	**-19**	(5.0)	342	(7.3)	382	(7.0)	441	(5.0)	569	(3.6)	622	(4.4)	650	(6.3)
Italy (Provincia Veneto)	504	(5.4)	97	(4.3)	479	(9.8)	528	(7.2)	**-49**	(13.6)	332	(15.4)	378	(12.7)	444	(7.6)	572	(6.0)	623	(5.6)	652	(6.8)
United Kingdom (England)	506	(2.8)	99	(1.7)	493	(4.4)	519	(3.6)	**-26**	(5.5)	340	(4.3)	380	(3.6)	440	(3.5)	575	(3.8)	631	(4.4)	664	(5.8)
United Kingdom (Northern Ireland)	506	(4.3)	98	(4.2)	491	(8.2)	520	(3.6)	**-29**	(9.5)	339	(14.2)	380	(9.2)	441	(6.7)	573	(3.5)	627	(3.8)	658	(4.6)
United Kingdom (Wales)	486	(3.4)	97	(1.6)	472	(4.0)	500	(3.6)	**-28**	(3.5)	320	(6.3)	359	(5.2)	423	(4.1)	554	(3.5)	609	(4.0)	639	(4.7)

Note: See Table I.2.19 for national data.
Values that are statistically significant are indicated in bold (see Annex A3).

StatLink ⬛🔗 http://dx.doi.org/10.1787/888932343304

[Part 1/1]

Table S.I.s **Percentage of students at each proficiency level on the mathematics scale**

	Proficiency levels													
	Below Level 1 (less than 357.77 score points)		Level 1 (from 357.77 to less than 420.07 score points)		Level 2 (from 420.07 to less than 482.38 score points)		Level 3 (from 482.38 to less than 544.68 score points)		Level 4 (from 544.68 to less than 606.99 score points)		Level 5 (from 606.99 to less than 669.30 score points)		Level 6 (above 669.30 score points)	
	%	S.E.	%	S.E.	%	S.E.	%	S.E.	%	S.E.	%	S.E.	%	S.E.
Adjudicated														
Belgium (Flemish Community)	4.2	(0.6)	9.3	(0.7)	16.3	(0.9)	21.3	(1.1)	22.1	(1.2)	18.2	(0.8)	8.7	(0.8)
Spain (Andalusia)	12.8	(1.6)	17.9	(1.4)	26.7	(1.4)	25.0	(1.8)	13.3	(1.6)	3.9	(0.9)	0.3	(0.3)
Spain (Aragon)	6.8	(1.2)	11.3	(1.3)	20.5	(1.7)	25.1	(1.8)	22.0	(1.5)	10.9	(1.3)	3.4	(0.7)
Spain (Asturias)	8.8	(1.0)	12.0	(1.4)	20.8	(1.9)	27.2	(1.8)	21.1	(1.8)	8.5	(1.3)	1.6	(0.4)
Spain (Balearic Islands)	12.7	(1.3)	17.3	(1.9)	25.3	(1.8)	24.7	(1.9)	15.1	(1.5)	4.4	(0.6)	0.5	(0.2)
Spain (Basque Country)	5.3	(0.7)	9.6	(0.7)	20.5	(0.8)	28.6	(1.2)	23.2	(1.3)	10.5	(0.7)	2.2	(0.3)
Spain (Canary Islands)	18.1	(1.7)	25.2	(1.3)	27.5	(1.9)	20.1	(1.4)	7.7	(0.8)	1.3	(0.5)	0.1	(0.1)
Spain (Cantabria)	8.1	(1.0)	13.6	(1.4)	22.0	(1.6)	25.1	(1.5)	19.2	(1.6)	9.4	(1.2)	2.5	(0.5)
Spain (Castile and Leon)	5.1	(1.0)	10.3	(1.3)	18.6	(1.3)	27.5	(1.5)	23.1	(2.0)	11.9	(1.3)	3.5	(0.8)
Spain (Catalonia)	7.3	(1.2)	11.8	(1.5)	23.4	(1.6)	27.1	(1.6)	20.0	(1.4)	8.6	(1.4)	1.8	(0.5)
Spain (Ceuta and Melilla)	29.1	(1.2)	21.6	(1.4)	21.6	(1.6)	17.0	(1.5)	8.6	(1.0)	1.8	(0.4)	0.4	(0.2)
Spain (Galicia)	6.9	(1.0)	13.4	(1.3)	25.1	(1.9)	27.6	(1.8)	20.0	(1.7)	6.2	(1.0)	0.7	(0.2)
Spain (La Rioja)	8.3	(1.1)	11.1	(1.3)	19.7	(1.8)	25.5	(1.5)	20.3	(1.5)	11.0	(1.2)	4.0	(0.6)
Spain (Madrid)	6.3	(0.9)	12.8	(1.6)	23.4	(1.4)	27.9	(1.3)	19.3	(1.3)	8.5	(1.2)	1.9	(0.6)
Spain (Murcia)	8.0	(1.4)	16.3	(1.7)	26.7	(1.7)	26.4	(1.8)	17.0	(1.6)	5.2	(0.8)	0.4	(0.2)
Spain (Navarre)	5.5	(1.1)	9.6	(1.1)	19.5	(1.1)	27.6	(1.4)	24.3	(2.3)	11.3	(1.5)	2.1	(0.5)
United Kingdom (Scotland)	6.2	(0.7)	13.5	(1.0)	23.5	(1.1)	25.5	(1.4)	18.9	(1.1)	9.1	(0.7)	3.2	(0.5)
Non-adjudicated														
Belgium (French Community)	12.2	(1.3)	13.8	(0.9)	19.0	(1.1)	22.4	(1.2)	20.2	(1.1)	10.0	(0.8)	2.3	(0.4)
Belgium (German-Speaking Community)	4.3	(0.7)	10.8	(1.4)	18.8	(1.9)	23.7	(1.8)	26.9	(1.8)	13.0	(1.4)	2.5	(0.7)
Finland (Finnish Speaking)	1.7	(0.3)	6.0	(0.5)	15.3	(0.9)	27.0	(1.0)	28.0	(0.9)	17.0	(0.8)	5.0	(0.6)
Finland (Swedish Speaking)	1.9	(0.5)	8.0	(1.2)	19.4	(1.6)	28.9	(1.6)	25.4	(2.1)	12.7	(1.5)	3.6	(0.8)
Italy (Provincia Abruzzo)	9.3	(1.4)	16.8	(2.1)	25.2	(2.1)	26.5	(1.6)	16.4	(1.8)	5.1	(1.5)	0.7	(0.4)
Italy (Provincia Autonoma di Bolzano)	5.5	(1.2)	11.2	(1.1)	21.5	(1.4)	27.4	(1.8)	20.6	(1.3)	11.2	(0.9)	2.6	(0.4)
Italy (Provincia Basilicata)	8.0	(1.4)	18.9	(1.6)	27.4	(1.8)	25.2	(1.9)	14.3	(1.3)	5.1	(0.9)	1.1	(0.3)
Italy (Provincia Calabria)	14.4	(2.0)	25.2	(1.9)	30.5	(1.7)	19.7	(1.7)	8.2	(1.5)	1.8	(0.6)	0.0	c
Italy (Provincia Campania)	14.7	(2.2)	23.2	(2.1)	29.0	(2.3)	19.8	(2.1)	9.1	(1.5)	3.4	(1.2)	0.8	(0.6)
Italy (Provincia Emilia Romagna)	8.2	(1.6)	12.6	(1.8)	19.4	(1.5)	24.2	(1.9)	20.3	(1.4)	11.9	(1.2)	3.3	(0.5)
Italy (Provincia Friuli Venezia Giulia)	4.8	(1.2)	10.1	(1.4)	21.8	(1.3)	27.4	(1.6)	22.5	(1.8)	10.6	(1.2)	2.8	(0.5)
Italy (Provincia Lazio)	9.9	(1.3)	18.2	(1.3)	27.1	(2.2)	22.8	(1.6)	15.6	(1.6)	5.4	(1.3)	1.0	(0.5)
Italy (Provincia Liguria)	7.8	(2.2)	13.8	(2.2)	21.9	(2.1)	28.0	(2.1)	19.1	(2.3)	7.7	(1.3)	1.6	(0.6)
Italy (Provincia Lombardia)	4.8	(1.1)	8.9	(1.2)	19.3	(1.9)	28.2	(1.6)	24.8	(1.8)	11.6	(1.4)	2.5	(0.6)
Italy (Provincia Marche)	5.9	(0.9)	12.4	(1.4)	22.2	(2.1)	28.1	(2.0)	21.9	(2.2)	8.0	(1.1)	1.5	(0.4)
Italy (Provincia Molise)	10.5	(1.1)	18.7	(1.3)	26.9	(2.3)	26.5	(1.9)	12.2	(1.9)	4.5	(1.1)	0.6	(0.3)
Italy (Provincia Piemonte)	8.4	(1.4)	13.1	(2.0)	22.2	(1.8)	25.5	(1.5)	20.8	(1.9)	8.2	(1.3)	1.8	(0.4)
Italy (Provincia Puglia)	6.9	(1.3)	15.5	(1.5)	25.7	(2.2)	25.1	(1.7)	17.6	(2.2)	7.4	(1.6)	1.9	(0.6)
Italy (Provincia Sardegna)	12.6	(1.8)	19.9	(1.8)	28.9	(1.7)	23.3	(1.7)	11.8	(1.4)	3.2	(0.6)	0.3	(0.2)
Italy (Provincia Sicilia)	14.8	(2.3)	21.5	(2.4)	26.6	(1.9)	20.5	(1.8)	11.6	(1.9)	4.3	(0.9)	0.5	(0.3)
Italy (Provincia Toscana)	7.0	(1.3)	13.9	(1.4)	22.7	(1.8)	26.9	(1.9)	19.4	(1.8)	8.5	(1.6)	1.7	(0.6)
Italy (Provincia Trento)	4.1	(0.7)	10.3	(1.4)	19.8	(1.4)	28.8	(1.6)	23.1	(1.7)	10.9	(1.3)	3.0	(0.7)
Italy (Provincia Umbria)	9.0	(1.1)	15.4	(1.5)	22.5	(1.6)	25.7	(1.9)	18.3	(1.2)	7.4	(1.1)	1.7	(0.5)
Italy (Provincia Valle d'Aosta)	5.3	(1.0)	11.9	(1.1)	24.6	(1.8)	25.5	(1.7)	21.2	(1.9)	9.1	(1.3)	2.5	(0.5)
Italy (Provincia Veneto)	4.2	(1.1)	11.7	(1.3)	21.2	(1.6)	28.5	(1.6)	21.6	(1.8)	10.4	(1.4)	2.4	(0.6)
United Kingdom (England)	6.1	(0.6)	13.7	(0.9)	24.8	(1.1)	27.5	(1.3)	18.0	(1.2)	8.2	(0.7)	1.7	(0.3)
United Kingdom (Northern Ireland)	6.5	(0.8)	14.9	(1.1)	24.6	(1.2)	24.9	(1.5)	18.9	(1.0)	8.5	(0.9)	1.8	(0.4)
United Kingdom (Wales)	8.4	(0.8)	17.9	(1.1)	28.4	(1.0)	26.1	(1.1)	14.3	(0.9)	4.4	(0.5)	0.6	(0.2)

Note: See Table I.3.1 for national data.
StatLink ⟨⟩ http://dx.doi.org/10.1787/888932343304

[Part 1/2]

Table S.I.t **Percentage of students at each proficiency level on the mathematics scale, by gender**

	Boys - Proficiency levels													
	Below Level 1 (less than 357.77 score points)		Level 1 (from 357.77 to less than 420.07 score points)		Level 2 (from 420.07 to less than 482.38 score points)		Level 3 (from 482.38 to less than 544.68 score points)		Level 4 (from 544.68 to less than 606.99 score points)		Level 5 (from 606.99 to less than 669.30 score points)		Level 6 (above 669.30 score points)	
	%	S.E.	%	S.E.	%	S.E.	%	S.E.	%	S.E.	%	S.E.	%	S.E.
Adjudicated														
Belgium (Flemish Community)	3.0	(0.7)	8.8	(0.9)	15.7	(1.0)	20.7	(1.5)	21.2	(1.6)	19.3	(1.4)	11.2	(1.2)
Spain (Andalusia)	10.9	(1.9)	16.2	(1.6)	24.3	(2.7)	26.6	(2.4)	16.2	(2.2)	5.2	(1.5)	0.5	(0.4)
Spain (Aragon)	6.7	(1.5)	9.4	(1.6)	19.3	(1.9)	24.1	(2.2)	22.3	(2.2)	13.3	(1.8)	4.9	(1.3)
Spain (Asturias)	8.6	(1.1)	11.5	(1.6)	19.3	(2.7)	26.1	(2.6)	22.2	(2.5)	10.1	(1.9)	2.3	(0.6)
Spain (Balearic Islands)	11.5	(1.5)	15.5	(2.1)	23.5	(1.8)	24.5	(2.1)	17.8	(2.3)	6.4	(1.2)	0.7	(0.3)
Spain (Basque Country)	5.8	(1.0)	9.5	(0.9)	19.1	(1.0)	26.8	(1.7)	23.7	(1.6)	12.2	(0.9)	3.0	(0.5)
Spain (Canary Islands)	15.9	(1.6)	23.7	(1.8)	26.8	(2.4)	22.3	(1.7)	9.2	(1.1)	1.9	(0.7)	0.2	(0.2)
Spain (Cantabria)	7.7	(1.2)	12.4	(1.7)	20.4	(1.8)	24.1	(2.2)	21.2	(2.0)	10.9	(1.5)	3.2	(0.7)
Spain (Castile and Leon)	5.4	(1.2)	10.3	(1.9)	16.0	(1.7)	25.5	(1.7)	23.5	(2.5)	14.0	(1.8)	5.2	(1.4)
Spain (Catalonia)	6.3	(1.2)	11.2	(2.0)	21.2	(2.6)	25.2	(2.7)	22.5	(1.8)	10.9	(1.7)	2.8	(0.8)
Spain (Ceuta and Melilla)	28.9	(1.9)	19.4	(2.1)	20.1	(1.9)	17.5	(1.7)	10.5	(1.3)	2.9	(0.9)	0.6	(0.3)
Spain (Galicia)	6.7	(1.1)	11.7	(2.1)	25.2	(2.4)	26.2	(2.1)	21.4	(2.1)	7.8	(1.2)	1.0	(0.4)
Spain (La Rioja)	6.7	(1.1)	11.5	(1.8)	19.2	(2.2)	23.4	(2.2)	20.2	(2.0)	13.3	(1.7)	5.8	(1.0)
Spain (Madrid)	5.8	(1.2)	12.7	(2.4)	22.5	(2.3)	26.5	(1.6)	20.1	(1.6)	10.1	(1.6)	2.3	(0.8)
Spain (Murcia)	7.2	(1.5)	15.3	(2.1)	24.4	(2.1)	25.3	(2.2)	20.9	(2.2)	6.4	(1.2)	0.6	(0.3)
Spain (Navarre)	4.6	(1.4)	9.2	(1.5)	19.9	(1.9)	25.7	(2.7)	24.5	(3.0)	13.2	(2.2)	2.9	(0.8)
United Kingdom (Scotland)	5.9	(0.9)	13.0	(1.2)	21.2	(1.6)	25.2	(1.9)	19.7	(2.0)	10.9	(1.1)	4.2	(0.8)
Non-adjudicated														
Belgium (French Community)	9.9	(2.0)	13.2	(1.3)	18.7	(1.6)	20.7	(1.3)	20.9	(1.6)	13.2	(1.3)	3.3	(0.6)
Belgium (German-Speaking Community)	3.3	(0.9)	11.9	(1.9)	17.9	(2.8)	21.9	(2.8)	25.7	(2.6)	16.1	(2.3)	3.2	(1.0)
Finland (Finnish Speaking)	1.7	(0.4)	6.3	(0.7)	15.9	(1.2)	25.7	(1.4)	26.6	(1.1)	17.7	(1.1)	6.0	(0.7)
Finland (Swedish Speaking)	2.3	(0.8)	8.0	(1.6)	19.5	(2.3)	27.5	(2.4)	24.7	(3.5)	13.6	(1.9)	4.4	(1.1)
Italy (Provincia Abruzzo)	10.1	(1.8)	15.8	(2.2)	22.9	(2.6)	26.7	(2.1)	17.2	(2.6)	6.3	(1.9)	1.0	(0.7)
Italy (Provincia Autonoma di Bolzano)	5.5	(1.7)	10.7	(1.6)	20.1	(2.3)	24.2	(2.5)	21.2	(1.7)	14.4	(1.4)	3.9	(0.8)
Italy (Provincia Basilicata)	6.8	(2.1)	17.8	(2.3)	25.9	(2.6)	24.3	(3.0)	16.1	(1.9)	7.3	(1.7)	1.8	(0.6)
Italy (Provincia Calabria)	14.1	(2.6)	23.6	(2.5)	30.5	(2.5)	19.6	(2.3)	9.4	(1.9)	2.5	(0.8)	0.0	c
Italy (Provincia Campania)	14.3	(2.7)	21.4	(2.1)	28.1	(2.7)	20.8	(2.5)	10.2	(2.0)	4.3	(1.3)	1.0	(0.7)
Italy (Provincia Emilia Romagna)	5.9	(1.6)	10.2	(1.9)	17.9	(2.3)	22.4	(2.5)	21.7	(2.1)	16.3	(1.8)	5.6	(1.0)
Italy (Provincia Friuli Venezia Giulia)	5.7	(1.5)	9.9	(1.6)	20.6	(2.2)	24.6	(2.5)	22.2	(2.4)	13.1	(1.7)	3.8	(0.8)
Italy (Provincia Lazio)	9.8	(1.9)	16.8	(1.7)	25.7	(3.1)	21.7	(1.8)	16.9	(1.7)	7.2	(1.7)	1.8	(0.7)
Italy (Provincia Liguria)	9.0	(3.5)	14.2	(3.3)	18.2	(2.1)	25.2	(2.6)	20.9	(3.2)	10.1	(2.2)	2.4	(0.9)
Italy (Provincia Lombardia)	3.7	(1.0)	9.1	(1.9)	17.6	(2.5)	27.0	(2.4)	25.7	(2.8)	13.2	(2.1)	3.6	(0.9)
Italy (Provincia Marche)	4.4	(1.2)	12.0	(2.4)	21.3	(2.4)	26.7	(2.8)	23.6	(2.7)	10.0	(1.6)	1.9	(0.6)
Italy (Provincia Molise)	11.2	(1.5)	18.7	(1.8)	24.7	(2.7)	23.9	(2.2)	13.2	(1.7)	7.2	(1.9)	1.1	(0.7)
Italy (Provincia Piemonte)	6.5	(1.5)	11.8	(2.2)	20.7	(2.5)	25.0	(2.3)	22.9	(3.2)	10.4	(1.8)	2.7	(0.6)
Italy (Provincia Puglia)	6.0	(1.7)	14.5	(1.8)	24.8	(2.6)	24.4	(2.8)	19.4	(2.7)	8.2	(1.9)	2.7	(1.0)
Italy (Provincia Sardegna)	13.2	(1.8)	19.2	(2.5)	26.8	(2.7)	23.4	(2.7)	12.2	(1.9)	4.7	(0.9)	0.5	(0.3)
Italy (Provincia Sicilia)	16.5	(3.2)	19.8	(2.6)	23.7	(2.7)	19.6	(2.3)	13.6	(2.5)	6.1	(1.1)	0.8	(0.5)
Italy (Provincia Toscana)	6.5	(1.3)	13.6	(1.9)	21.7	(2.6)	23.6	(2.0)	20.3	(2.4)	11.7	(2.4)	2.6	(0.9)
Italy (Provincia Trento)	4.0	(1.1)	9.9	(1.6)	18.4	(1.7)	26.3	(3.0)	23.7	(2.4)	13.2	(2.3)	4.4	(1.2)
Italy (Provincia Umbria)	9.4	(1.8)	13.8	(1.7)	20.5	(1.6)	23.5	(2.9)	20.1	(2.1)	10.2	(1.8)	2.5	(0.9)
Italy (Provincia Valle d'Aosta)	3.8	(1.3)	7.6	(1.3)	21.6	(2.2)	25.7	(3.2)	24.3	(3.6)	13.1	(2.1)	3.9	(0.9)
Italy (Provincia Veneto)	3.4	(0.9)	11.1	(2.2)	20.0	(2.1)	27.4	(2.3)	22.5	(2.3)	12.1	(2.1)	3.4	(0.9)
United Kingdom (England)	5.0	(0.7)	11.9	(1.1)	22.7	(1.4)	27.3	(1.5)	20.3	(1.7)	10.5	(1.2)	2.4	(0.4)
United Kingdom (Northern Ireland)	6.1	(1.2)	13.5	(1.7)	23.7	(1.8)	23.6	(1.9)	19.6	(1.5)	10.8	(1.6)	2.7	(0.7)
United Kingdom (Wales)	7.4	(1.1)	15.4	(1.4)	26.5	(1.3)	27.3	(1.5)	16.8	(1.2)	5.7	(0.8)	0.9	(0.4)

Note: See Table I.3.2 for national data.

StatLink ᴬᴵˢᴾ http://dx.doi.org/10.1787/888932343304

[Part 2/2]

Table S.I.t **Percentage of students at each proficiency level on the mathematics scale, by gender**

	Girls - Proficiency levels													
	Below Level 1 (less than 357.77 score points)		Level 1 (from 357.77 to less than 420.07 score points)		Level 2 (from 420.07 to less than 482.38 score points)		Level 3 (from 482.38 to less than 544.68 score points)		Level 4 (from 544.68 to less than 606.99 score points)		Level 5 (from 606.99 to less than 669.30 score points)		Level 6 (above 669.30 score points)	
	%	S.E.	%	S.E.	%	S.E.	%	S.E.	%	S.E.	%	S.E.	%	S.E.
Adjudicated														
Belgium (Flemish Community)	5.4	(0.9)	9.9	(1.0)	16.9	(1.3)	21.9	(1.2)	23.0	(1.3)	16.9	(1.1)	6.1	(0.9)
Spain (Andalusia)	15.0	(2.1)	19.7	(2.0)	29.4	(2.1)	23.2	(2.3)	10.1	(2.1)	2.4	(0.8)	0.0	c
Spain (Aragon)	6.9	(1.5)	13.2	(1.9)	21.7	(2.4)	26.1	(2.2)	21.8	(2.0)	8.4	(1.2)	1.9	(0.6)
Spain (Asturias)	9.1	(1.4)	12.5	(1.7)	22.6	(2.1)	28.4	(1.8)	19.9	(2.0)	6.7	(1.4)	0.8	(0.5)
Spain (Balearic Islands)	13.9	(1.8)	19.1	(2.5)	27.1	(2.8)	24.9	(2.6)	12.4	(2.2)	2.4	(1.0)	0.3	(0.2)
Spain (Basque Country)	4.7	(0.6)	9.7	(0.8)	22.0	(1.0)	30.6	(1.2)	22.8	(1.4)	8.8	(0.8)	1.4	(0.3)
Spain (Canary Islands)	20.4	(2.4)	26.9	(2.1)	28.3	(2.3)	17.6	(1.9)	6.1	(1.4)	0.7	(0.4)	0.0	c
Spain (Cantabria)	8.6	(1.3)	14.9	(1.8)	23.7	(2.3)	26.1	(1.9)	17.1	(2.1)	7.9	(1.5)	1.7	(0.6)
Spain (Castile and Leon)	4.8	(1.1)	10.3	(1.7)	21.1	(1.9)	29.3	(2.2)	22.7	(2.3)	9.9	(1.5)	1.8	(0.6)
Spain (Catalonia)	8.4	(1.7)	12.4	(1.7)	25.7	(2.3)	29.2	(2.2)	17.3	(2.2)	6.2	(1.6)	0.7	(0.4)
Spain (Ceuta and Melilla)	29.2	(1.7)	23.8	(2.1)	22.9	(2.3)	16.5	(1.9)	6.7	(1.2)	0.8	(0.4)	0.0	c
Spain (Galicia)	7.1	(1.4)	15.0	(2.0)	25.1	(2.7)	29.0	(2.9)	18.7	(2.2)	4.7	(1.2)	0.4	(0.3)
Spain (La Rioja)	10.0	(1.6)	10.8	(1.6)	20.3	(2.4)	27.7	(2.3)	20.5	(1.9)	8.6	(1.4)	2.1	(0.7)
Spain (Madrid)	6.9	(1.3)	12.8	(1.9)	24.2	(2.1)	29.2	(2.0)	18.5	(1.9)	6.9	(1.4)	1.5	(0.8)
Spain (Murcia)	8.8	(2.0)	17.3	(2.1)	29.0	(2.5)	27.5	(2.5)	13.2	(1.6)	4.0	(1.1)	0.0	c
Spain (Navarre)	6.5	(1.4)	10.1	(1.4)	19.1	(2.4)	29.7	(2.8)	24.1	(2.4)	9.2	(1.9)	1.3	(0.5)
United Kingdom (Scotland)	6.5	(0.9)	14.0	(1.7)	25.9	(1.6)	25.7	(1.6)	18.2	(1.5)	7.4	(1.0)	2.2	(0.5)
Non-adjudicated														
Belgium (French Community)	14.7	(1.6)	14.5	(1.3)	19.2	(1.4)	24.2	(1.7)	19.5	(1.7)	6.7	(1.0)	1.2	(0.4)
Belgium (German-Speaking Community)	5.4	(0.9)	9.7	(2.0)	19.7	(2.6)	25.5	(2.4)	28.1	(2.3)	9.8	(1.6)	1.8	(0.9)
Finland (Finnish Speaking)	1.7	(0.4)	5.7	(0.8)	14.7	(1.0)	28.3	(1.2)	29.4	(1.4)	16.2	(1.1)	4.0	(0.6)
Finland (Swedish Speaking)	1.5	(0.8)	8.0	(1.6)	19.3	(2.0)	30.3	(2.4)	26.1	(2.5)	11.9	(1.8)	2.9	(0.9)
Italy (Provincia Abruzzo)	8.5	(1.8)	17.8	(2.5)	27.6	(2.6)	26.2	(2.7)	15.5	(2.5)	3.9	(1.7)	0.4	(0.4)
Italy (Provincia Autonoma di Bolzano)	5.5	(1.1)	11.7	(1.4)	23.0	(1.9)	30.6	(2.2)	20.1	(2.0)	8.0	(1.0)	1.3	(0.4)
Italy (Provincia Basilicata)	9.4	(1.6)	20.1	(2.2)	29.0	(2.4)	26.2	(2.4)	12.4	(1.6)	2.8	(0.7)	0.2	(0.2)
Italy (Provincia Calabria)	14.6	(2.2)	26.8	(2.4)	30.5	(2.3)	19.8	(2.3)	7.0	(1.4)	1.1	(0.6)	0.0	c
Italy (Provincia Campania)	15.4	(2.5)	25.6	(2.5)	30.3	(3.0)	18.4	(2.7)	7.7	(2.0)	2.2	(1.3)	0.5	(0.5)
Italy (Provincia Emilia Romagna)	10.5	(2.1)	14.9	(2.5)	20.8	(1.9)	25.9	(3.2)	19.0	(2.0)	7.7	(1.4)	1.1	(0.6)
Italy (Provincia Friuli Venezia Giulia)	3.8	(1.6)	10.3	(2.4)	23.1	(2.1)	30.4	(2.6)	22.7	(2.3)	7.9	(1.3)	1.7	(0.7)
Italy (Provincia Lazio)	9.9	(2.0)	19.8	(2.1)	28.7	(2.3)	24.1	(2.6)	14.0	(2.6)	3.3	(1.1)	0.2	(0.3)
Italy (Provincia Liguria)	6.4	(1.5)	13.3	(2.2)	26.2	(3.1)	31.3	(3.0)	17.0	(2.9)	5.0	(1.3)	0.8	(0.4)
Italy (Provincia Lombardia)	5.9	(2.0)	8.7	(1.5)	21.1	(2.4)	29.5	(2.4)	23.9	(2.2)	9.7	(1.5)	1.2	(0.6)
Italy (Provincia Marche)	7.7	(1.1)	12.9	(1.6)	23.3	(2.7)	29.8	(2.7)	19.9	(3.0)	5.5	(1.3)	0.9	(0.5)
Italy (Provincia Molise)	9.7	(1.4)	18.8	(2.2)	29.3	(3.1)	29.3	(3.1)	11.1	(2.9)	1.6	(0.8)	0.0	c
Italy (Provincia Piemonte)	10.2	(2.0)	14.3	(2.2)	23.7	(2.3)	25.9	(2.9)	18.8	(2.1)	6.1	(1.1)	1.0	(0.4)
Italy (Provincia Puglia)	7.8	(1.7)	16.4	(2.0)	26.5	(2.7)	25.8	(2.2)	15.8	(2.4)	6.6	(1.8)	1.1	(0.5)
Italy (Provincia Sardegna)	12.0	(2.5)	20.6	(2.8)	30.9	(2.5)	23.1	(2.2)	11.4	(1.8)	1.8	(0.7)	0.0	c
Italy (Provincia Sicilia)	13.2	(2.2)	23.3	(3.5)	29.5	(2.3)	21.4	(2.5)	9.7	(2.3)	2.6	(1.2)	0.3	(0.2)
Italy (Provincia Toscana)	7.6	(1.9)	14.2	(2.3)	23.8	(2.7)	30.5	(2.8)	18.3	(2.3)	5.0	(1.1)	0.8	(0.5)
Italy (Provincia Trento)	4.2	(1.1)	10.7	(1.9)	21.3	(2.4)	31.4	(2.8)	22.5	(2.3)	8.3	(1.3)	1.6	(0.6)
Italy (Provincia Umbria)	8.7	(1.6)	16.9	(2.2)	24.3	(2.5)	27.7	(2.6)	16.6	(1.7)	4.8	(1.0)	0.9	(0.4)
Italy (Provincia Valle d'Aosta)	6.8	(1.6)	16.1	(2.2)	27.5	(2.7)	25.3	(2.3)	18.2	(1.8)	5.1	(1.3)	1.0	(0.5)
Italy (Provincia Veneto)	5.0	(1.8)	12.2	(2.0)	22.4	(2.2)	29.5	(2.2)	20.6	(2.8)	8.8	(1.5)	1.4	(0.7)
United Kingdom (England)	7.1	(0.7)	15.4	(1.3)	26.8	(1.5)	27.8	(1.7)	15.8	(1.4)	6.0	(0.9)	1.0	(0.3)
United Kingdom (Northern Ireland)	6.8	(1.0)	16.3	(1.5)	25.4	(1.9)	26.1	(1.8)	18.2	(1.3)	6.2	(1.2)	1.0	(0.6)
United Kingdom (Wales)	9.3	(1.0)	20.3	(1.4)	30.3	(1.6)	24.9	(1.3)	11.7	(1.2)	3.2	(0.6)	0.3	(0.2)

Note: See Table I.3.2 for national data.
StatLink http://dx.doi.org/10.1787/888932343304

[Part 1/1]

Table S.I.u **Mean score, variation and gender differences in student performance on the mathematics scale**

	All students				Gender differences						Percentiles											
	Mean score		Standard deviation		Boys		Girls		Difference (B – G)		5th		10th		25th		75th		90th		95th	
	Mean	S.E.	S.D.	S.E.	Mean score	S.E.	Mean score	S.E.	Score dif.	S.E.	Score	S.E.	Score	S.E.	Score	S.E.	Score	S.E.	Score	S.E.	Score	S.E.
Adjudicated																						
Belgium (Flemish Community)	537	(3.1)	99	(1.8)	546	(3.6)	527	(3.9)	19	(4.5)	366	(5.4)	402	(4.6)	466	(4.4)	613	(3.6)	663	(3.7)	689	(4.0)
Spain (Andalusia)	462	(5.2)	89	(2.7)	474	(5.5)	448	(6.2)	26	(5.0)	307	(11.7)	344	(9.2)	404	(6.1)	524	(5.9)	575	(6.8)	600	(7.9)
Spain (Aragon)	506	(5.2)	96	(2.9)	515	(7.5)	496	(5.0)	19	(7.3)	340	(10.9)	379	(8.8)	443	(5.8)	573	(5.8)	626	(6.7)	656	(7.4)
Spain (Asturias)	494	(4.6)	94	(2.5)	499	(5.4)	487	(5.2)	12	(5.0)	324	(8.5)	367	(8.1)	435	(6.7)	560	(5.5)	607	(6.8)	633	(6.0)
Spain (Balearic Islands)	464	(4.5)	93	(2.7)	475	(4.8)	454	(5.7)	21	(5.4)	303	(9.5)	342	(6.4)	405	(5.9)	531	(4.7)	580	(5.5)	606	(4.1)
Spain (Basque Country)	510	(2.8)	87	(1.8)	513	(3.8)	506	(2.6)	8	(3.3)	355	(7.3)	396	(5.3)	455	(3.6)	570	(3.1)	618	(2.8)	644	(3.1)
Spain (Canary Islands)	435	(4.1)	82	(1.9)	443	(4.1)	426	(4.9)	17	(3.9)	301	(9.8)	328	(6.1)	378	(5.5)	494	(4.3)	541	(4.9)	568	(5.5)
Spain (Cantabria)	495	(5.0)	95	(2.6)	503	(5.2)	486	(6.4)	17	(6.0)	335	(7.2)	370	(6.2)	431	(5.8)	562	(6.5)	616	(7.1)	645	(7.4)
Spain (Castile and Leon)	514	(5.3)	92	(2.2)	522	(6.8)	507	(5.2)	14	(5.6)	356	(12.2)	392	(7.7)	455	(6.2)	577	(5.6)	629	(7.1)	657	(7.4)
Spain (Catalonia)	496	(6.0)	90	(2.2)	506	(6.4)	485	(6.7)	22	(4.9)	338	(9.2)	377	(8.9)	439	(7.4)	558	(6.5)	609	(7.5)	636	(8.9)
Spain (Ceuta and Melilla)	417	(2.4)	101	(2.3)	422	(3.8)	412	(2.9)	11	(4.6)	255	(6.7)	289	(4.9)	346	(3.8)	490	(4.4)	549	(6.4)	576	(7.5)
Spain (Galicia)	489	(4.3)	84	(1.6)	494	(4.5)	484	(5.2)	11	(4.6)	344	(7.1)	380	(5.9)	435	(5.2)	550	(4.6)	594	(5.0)	617	(5.8)
Spain (La Rioja)	504	(2.7)	101	(2.7)	513	(3.6)	494	(3.6)	19	(4.7)	326	(11.3)	369	(7.8)	440	(5.2)	574	(4.1)	628	(6.2)	660	(6.7)
Spain (Madrid)	496	(4.4)	88	(2.1)	502	(5.0)	491	(5.6)	11	(6.0)	349	(7.7)	380	(6.6)	438	(5.5)	557	(5.1)	608	(6.8)	634	(5.8)
Spain (Murcia)	478	(5.6)	84	(2.5)	486	(5.5)	469	(6.7)	17	(4.4)	334	(9.3)	370	(8.9)	422	(7.4)	538	(6.4)	585	(6.1)	611	(5.1)
Spain (Navarre)	511	(3.6)	88	(2.3)	518	(4.4)	504	(4.4)	14	(5.3)	351	(12.2)	393	(8.5)	456	(5.4)	574	(4.0)	618	(5.8)	643	(6.6)
United Kingdom (Scotland)	499	(3.3)	93	(1.8)	506	(4.5)	492	(3.5)	14	(4.8)	348	(5.1)	381	(5.2)	436	(3.8)	563	(4.9)	619	(5.0)	651	(6.0)
Non-adjudicated																						
Belgium (French Community)	488	(3.9)	104	(2.9)	501	(5.9)	476	(4.4)	25	(6.8)	308	(8.0)	345	(6.9)	416	(5.9)	566	(4.4)	617	(4.4)	644	(4.6)
Belgium (German-Speaking Community)	517	(2.5)	88	(1.8)	523	(3.4)	511	(3.9)	11	(5.4)	365	(7.5)	396	(4.7)	455	(5.8)	582	(3.1)	625	(4.9)	651	(5.7)
Finland (Finnish Speaking)	541	(2.3)	82	(1.2)	543	(2.7)	540	(2.7)	3	(2.7)	400	(4.9)	432	(3.9)	488	(3.1)	600	(2.6)	644	(2.7)	670	(3.7)
Finland (Swedish Speaking)	527	(2.9)	81	(1.7)	528	(4.0)	525	(3.7)	2	(5.1)	392	(6.8)	421	(4.1)	471	(4.1)	582	(5.0)	630	(6.5)	656	(6.7)
Italy (Provincia Abruzzo)	476	(6.7)	88	(4.2)	480	(7.5)	471	(7.3)	8	(6.3)	324	(12.0)	362	(9.4)	417	(6.2)	538	(8.5)	587	(11.3)	612	(11.2)
Italy (Provincia Autonoma di Bolzano)	507	(3.2)	90	(3.1)	515	(4.7)	499	(2.8)	16	(4.1)	354	(12.8)	390	(8.1)	449	(5.0)	570	(3.3)	623	(3.4)	650	(4.0)
Italy (Provincia Basilicata)	474	(4.4)	84	(2.5)	484	(6.0)	464	(4.8)	20	(6.4)	340	(7.5)	367	(7.9)	415	(6.3)	532	(5.0)	584	(6.6)	615	(8.0)
Italy (Provincia Calabria)	442	(5.1)	79	(2.3)	446	(6.1)	438	(5.7)	8	(6.3)	317	(6.3)	341	(6.7)	387	(6.1)	495	(5.4)	546	(7.5)	577	(8.7)
Italy (Provincia Campania)	447	(7.8)	90	(6.5)	452	(8.8)	439	(8.9)	13	(8.4)	304	(18.0)	339	(9.1)	388	(6.1)	504	(9.3)	560	(11.9)	597	(18.8)
Italy (Provincia Emilia Romagna)	503	(4.7)	98	(3.7)	522	(6.2)	484	(5.9)	38	(8.0)	332	(12.5)	370	(11.7)	435	(7.9)	574	(5.4)	627	(5.6)	655	(6.9)
Italy (Provincia Friuli Venezia Giulia)	510	(4.6)	88	(3.7)	514	(5.6)	505	(5.5)	9	(6.0)	360	(11.6)	395	(9.1)	454	(5.4)	571	(4.5)	622	(4.0)	649	(6.3)
Italy (Provincia Lazio)	473	(5.5)	88	(3.4)	480	(6.6)	464	(6.7)	16	(8.1)	330	(8.4)	358	(6.9)	412	(5.4)	535	(8.7)	589	(9.4)	617	(13.0)
Italy (Provincia Liguria)	491	(9.3)	90	(4.0)	497	(14.9)	485	(6.2)	11	(14.2)	335	(16.4)	370	(13.8)	432	(13.2)	554	(8.8)	604	(7.5)	633	(7.5)
Italy (Provincia Lombardia)	516	(5.6)	86	(3.0)	523	(7.1)	508	(7.7)	16	(9.4)	361	(12.4)	399	(12.5)	459	(8.0)	577	(5.5)	623	(6.1)	650	(5.9)
Italy (Provincia Marche)	499	(4.5)	86	(2.3)	507	(7.5)	488	(3.5)	19	(7.9)	349	(10.2)	384	(6.2)	443	(6.3)	559	(5.4)	605	(5.4)	631	(5.8)
Italy (Provincia Molise)	467	(2.7)	85	(2.5)	472	(3.9)	461	(3.0)	11	(4.3)	323	(8.9)	355	(5.4)	410	(3.9)	525	(6.4)	578	(6.7)	608	(10.9)
Italy (Provincia Piemonte)	493	(6.0)	93	(2.7)	505	(7.5)	481	(6.3)	24	(7.1)	335	(12.4)	369	(10.2)	431	(7.4)	559	(6.3)	607	(6.3)	638	(5.5)
Italy (Provincia Puglia)	488	(6.9)	88	(3.8)	495	(7.2)	481	(8.1)	13	(6.9)	344	(9.3)	374	(9.1)	427	(6.3)	550	(11.0)	604	(9.1)	634	(10.3)
Italy (Provincia Sardegna)	456	(5.2)	86	(3.4)	459	(5.8)	454	(6.6)	6	(7.1)	311	(13.9)	347	(7.6)	401	(6.3)	514	(5.5)	566	(4.9)	593	(5.2)
Italy (Provincia Sicilia)	450	(8.8)	98	(8.8)	454	(10.9)	447	(9.6)	6	(10.4)	294	(20.5)	334	(11.8)	392	(8.3)	515	(9.0)	574	(9.8)	605	(9.6)
Italy (Provincia Toscana)	493	(5.4)	90	(3.4)	501	(6.9)	485	(5.9)	16	(7.6)	339	(9.1)	374	(7.6)	434	(7.0)	557	(7.3)	608	(9.2)	639	(8.6)
Italy (Provincia Trento)	514	(2.5)	86	(2.1)	522	(4.0)	506	(5.2)	16	(7.9)	366	(8.0)	400	(5.2)	457	(4.8)	574	(3.3)	623	(3.8)	652	(6.0)
Italy (Provincia Umbria)	486	(4.1)	93	(2.4)	494	(6.2)	478	(4.4)	16	(7.0)	331	(6.6)	364	(7.0)	422	(6.4)	551	(4.4)	603	(5.5)	632	(7.6)
Italy (Provincia Valle d'Aosta)	502	(2.3)	86	(2.2)	522	(3.2)	483	(3.4)	39	(4.6)	357	(5.9)	390	(7.4)	444	(4.1)	565	(3.5)	614	(6.0)	642	(6.3)
Italy (Provincia Veneto)	508	(5.6)	86	(2.9)	515	(7.1)	501	(7.5)	15	(10.0)	364	(9.7)	395	(8.4)	449	(7.5)	568	(7.3)	619	(7.4)	647	(7.8)
United Kingdom (England)	493	(2.9)	87	(1.5)	504	(3.9)	483	(3.9)	21	(5.3)	349	(4.3)	381	(4.1)	435	(3.6)	552	(3.9)	606	(4.5)	634	(3.9)
United Kingdom (Northern Ireland)	492	(3.1)	89	(2.1)	501	(5.9)	484	(4.0)	17	(7.8)	348	(4.2)	378	(4.6)	429	(4.1)	557	(3.6)	608	(5.1)	637	(5.2)
United Kingdom (Wales)	472	(3.0)	82	(1.5)	482	(3.6)	462	(3.2)	20	(3.3)	336	(5.3)	366	(4.6)	417	(3.4)	528	(3.9)	578	(4.1)	607	(4.5)

Note: See Table I.3.3 for national data.
Values that are statistically significant are indicated in bold (see Annex A3).
StatLink ⫶⫶⫶ http://dx.doi.org/10.1787/888932343304

[Part 1/1]

Table S.I.v **Percentage of students at each proficiency level on the science scale**

	Proficiency levels													
	Below Level 1 (less than 334.94 score points)		Level 1 (from 334.94 to less than 409.54 score points)		Level 2 (from 409.54 to less than 484.14 score points)		Level 3 (from 484.14 to less than 558.73 score points)		Level 4 (from 558.73 to less than 633.33 score points)		Level 5 (from 633.33 to less than 707.93 score points)		Level 6 (above 707.93 score points)	
	%	S.E.	%	S.E.	%	S.E.	%	S.E.	%	S.E.	%	S.E.	%	S.E.
Adjudicated														
Belgium (Flemish Community)	3.8	(0.5)	9.1	(0.9)	19.1	(0.8)	27.6	(1.0)	26.9	(1.0)	12.0	(0.9)	1.5	(0.3)
Spain (Andalusia)	7.0	(1.1)	16.9	(1.8)	31.2	(1.6)	29.5	(1.9)	13.2	(1.5)	2.3	(0.6)	0.0	c
Spain (Aragon)	3.5	(0.7)	10.3	(1.3)	23.8	(1.7)	34.5	(1.7)	22.8	(1.6)	4.9	(0.9)	0.4	(0.2)
Spain (Asturias)	4.5	(0.8)	11.9	(1.1)	23.2	(1.5)	32.5	(1.6)	21.7	(1.6)	5.8	(1.1)	0.4	(0.3)
Spain (Balearic Islands)	8.3	(1.2)	18.7	(2.0)	31.9	(2.1)	27.3	(1.9)	12.2	(1.4)	1.5	(0.4)	0.1	(0.1)
Spain (Basque Country)	2.6	(0.5)	11.2	(0.8)	29.4	(1.0)	35.9	(1.0)	17.7	(1.0)	3.1	(0.4)	0.2	(0.1)
Spain (Canary Islands)	9.4	(1.3)	22.3	(1.8)	31.5	(1.9)	25.3	(1.7)	9.6	(1.3)	1.7	(0.4)	0.0	c
Spain (Cantabria)	4.0	(0.7)	12.2	(1.2)	25.3	(1.6)	31.4	(1.5)	20.9	(1.7)	5.6	(0.9)	0.6	(0.3)
Spain (Castile and Leon)	2.5	(0.6)	8.9	(1.1)	22.0	(1.6)	34.6	(1.4)	24.0	(1.5)	7.4	(1.1)	0.6	(0.3)
Spain (Catalonia)	3.9	(1.0)	12.4	(1.4)	25.5	(1.9)	32.5	(2.1)	21.0	(1.9)	4.4	(1.1)	0.3	(0.3)
Spain (Ceuta and Melilla)	24.0	(1.2)	23.5	(1.4)	24.3	(1.6)	18.7	(1.0)	7.8	(0.9)	1.6	(0.5)	0.1	(0.1)
Spain (Galicia)	3.0	(0.6)	10.3	(1.1)	24.0	(1.6)	34.5	(1.6)	22.6	(2.0)	5.3	(1.0)	0.3	(0.2)
Spain (La Rioja)	3.9	(0.7)	10.2	(1.3)	22.1	(1.8)	33.2	(1.9)	23.7	(1.4)	6.5	(0.9)	0.5	(0.3)
Spain (Madrid)	2.6	(0.6)	10.5	(1.2)	24.5	(1.9)	33.7	(1.8)	22.7	(1.8)	5.7	(1.1)	0.4	(0.2)
Spain (Murcia)	4.2	(1.0)	15.5	(1.4)	29.1	(1.8)	31.7	(1.6)	16.8	(1.9)	2.7	(0.6)	0.0	c
Spain (Navarre)	2.6	(0.5)	10.2	(1.2)	25.3	(1.4)	32.4	(1.4)	23.5	(1.4)	5.4	(0.7)	0.6	(0.3)
United Kingdom (Scotland)	3.1	(0.4)	11.0	(0.8)	24.0	(1.2)	28.9	(1.0)	22.0	(1.1)	9.3	(0.9)	1.7	(0.3)
Non-adjudicated														
Belgium (French Community)	9.7	(1.1)	15.0	(1.0)	22.6	(1.2)	26.6	(1.3)	20.4	(1.2)	5.3	(0.7)	0.5	(0.2)
Belgium (German-Speaking Community)	2.3	(0.6)	9.7	(1.2)	22.1	(1.9)	30.2	(1.9)	26.0	(1.8)	8.9	(1.2)	0.7	(0.4)
Finland (Finnish Speaking)	1.1	(0.2)	4.8	(0.4)	14.8	(0.8)	28.6	(1.0)	31.5	(1.2)	15.8	(0.8)	3.4	(0.4)
Finland (Swedish Speaking)	1.6	(0.5)	7.3	(0.9)	21.8	(1.7)	31.4	(1.8)	26.9	(1.6)	9.3	(1.0)	1.6	(0.4)
Italy (Provincia Abruzzo)	5.7	(1.3)	15.6	(1.7)	28.4	(2.3)	30.5	(1.6)	16.2	(1.9)	3.2	(0.9)	0.2	(0.2)
Italy (Provincia Autonoma di Bolzano)	3.1	(0.7)	9.9	(0.8)	22.4	(1.5)	33.4	(1.7)	22.2	(1.2)	8.1	(0.8)	0.8	(0.3)
Italy (Provincia Basilicata)	6.3	(1.0)	20.3	(1.8)	31.0	(1.4)	27.9	(1.8)	12.0	(1.0)	2.4	(0.5)	0.0	c
Italy (Provincia Calabria)	10.8	(1.7)	24.3	(1.7)	33.1	(2.0)	22.4	(1.9)	8.2	(1.1)	1.1	(0.3)	0.0	c
Italy (Provincia Campania)	11.3	(2.1)	22.0	(1.9)	31.4	(1.9)	24.0	(1.9)	9.6	(1.7)	1.6	(0.5)	0.0	c
Italy (Provincia Emilia Romagna)	5.3	(1.2)	10.7	(1.2)	22.4	(1.7)	29.0	(2.1)	23.3	(1.8)	8.5	(1.2)	0.8	(0.3)
Italy (Provincia Friuli Venezia Giulia)	3.2	(1.1)	7.9	(1.2)	20.2	(1.8)	31.8	(2.0)	25.6	(1.5)	10.1	(1.1)	1.2	(0.5)
Italy (Provincia Lazio)	5.4	(1.0)	16.0	(1.7)	27.8	(2.2)	30.3	(1.7)	17.0	(1.5)	3.4	(0.9)	0.0	c
Italy (Provincia Liguria)	5.5	(1.8)	11.9	(2.0)	23.3	(2.1)	33.2	(2.6)	19.5	(2.3)	6.1	(1.2)	0.5	(0.3)
Italy (Provincia Lombardia)	3.3	(1.0)	7.7	(1.5)	18.1	(2.0)	33.2	(1.8)	27.3	(2.0)	9.4	(1.2)	1.1	(0.4)
Italy (Provincia Marche)	3.6	(1.0)	11.8	(2.4)	23.3	(2.1)	32.6	(2.3)	22.4	(1.7)	5.7	(0.9)	0.5	(0.2)
Italy (Provincia Molise)	6.3	(1.0)	16.8	(1.4)	32.3	(2.1)	30.6	(1.7)	11.9	(1.1)	2.1	(0.5)	0.0	c
Italy (Provincia Piemonte)	4.3	(1.0)	12.6	(1.9)	24.4	(1.8)	29.6	(1.8)	22.3	(1.7)	6.1	(0.9)	0.6	(0.3)
Italy (Provincia Puglia)	4.8	(1.1)	14.0	(1.5)	27.6	(2.3)	29.8	(1.7)	18.9	(1.9)	4.5	(1.1)	0.4	(0.3)
Italy (Provincia Sardegna)	6.0	(1.2)	17.3	(1.7)	30.3	(2.0)	29.1	(1.6)	14.1	(1.4)	3.2	(0.7)	0.0	c
Italy (Provincia Sicilia)	11.7	(2.2)	21.0	(2.6)	28.3	(2.1)	26.0	(2.6)	10.8	(1.7)	2.1	(0.7)	0.0	c
Italy (Provincia Toscana)	4.5	(1.3)	12.8	(1.3)	24.7	(1.6)	30.8	(2.0)	20.2	(1.7)	6.4	(1.4)	0.7	(0.4)
Italy (Provincia Trento)	2.8	(0.7)	9.2	(1.2)	20.5	(1.4)	30.9	(2.4)	24.9	(2.0)	10.2	(1.0)	1.4	(0.5)
Italy (Provincia Umbria)	5.2	(1.3)	12.6	(1.3)	24.9	(1.6)	30.2	(1.9)	20.7	(1.5)	5.8	(0.8)	0.6	(0.3)
Italy (Provincia Valle d'Aosta)	2.4	(0.7)	8.4	(1.1)	21.3	(1.7)	33.2	(2.0)	25.5	(1.9)	8.1	(0.9)	1.1	(0.4)
Italy (Provincia Veneto)	2.4	(0.7)	9.3	(1.6)	21.3	(2.3)	33.3	(2.1)	24.7	(1.9)	8.3	(1.2)	0.7	(0.3)
United Kingdom (England)	3.8	(0.4)	11.0	(0.8)	22.3	(0.9)	28.8	(1.2)	22.5	(1.0)	9.7	(0.7)	1.9	(0.3)
United Kingdom (Northern Ireland)	4.4	(1.2)	12.3	(0.9)	21.8	(1.3)	28.2	(1.5)	21.6	(1.1)	9.7	(1.1)	2.1	(0.4)
United Kingdom (Wales)	4.8	(0.6)	13.9	(1.1)	26.3	(1.2)	29.2	(1.1)	18.1	(0.9)	6.8	(0.6)	1.0	(0.2)

Note: See Table I.3.4 for national data.
StatLink ⫶⫶⫶⫶ http://dx.doi.org/10.1787/888932343304

[Part 1/2]

Table S.I.w **Percentage of students at each proficiency level on the science scale, by gender**

	Boys – Proficiency levels													
	Below Level 1 (less than 334.94 score points)		Level 1 (from 334.94 to less than 409.54 score points)		Level 2 (from 409.54 to less than 484.14 score points)		Level 3 (from 484.14 to less than 558.73 score points)		Level 4 (from 558.73 to less than 633.33 score points)		Level 5 (from 633.33 to less than 707.93 score points)		Level 6 (above 707.93 score points)	
	%	S.E.	%	S.E.	%	S.E.	%	S.E.	%	S.E.	%	S.E.	%	S.E.
Adjudicated														
Belgium (Flemish Community)	3.8	(0.6)	9.1	(1.1)	19.0	(1.0)	26.2	(1.2)	26.8	(1.2)	13.1	(1.2)	1.9	(0.5)
Spain (Andalusia)	6.4	(1.4)	15.7	(1.9)	29.0	(2.1)	30.5	(2.1)	15.1	(1.8)	3.3	(1.1)	0.0	c
Spain (Aragon)	3.9	(1.1)	10.4	(1.5)	21.8	(2.1)	33.8	(2.5)	23.5	(2.0)	6.1	(1.2)	0.5	(0.5)
Spain (Asturias)	4.4	(1.1)	12.2	(1.7)	20.6	(2.1)	31.1	(2.2)	23.6	(2.4)	7.6	(1.6)	0.5	(0.5)
Spain (Balearic Islands)	8.9	(1.9)	17.3	(2.2)	29.6	(2.7)	28.0	(2.1)	13.9	(1.8)	2.2	(0.8)	0.1	(0.2)
Spain (Basque Country)	2.7	(0.6)	11.7	(1.2)	27.8	(1.2)	34.0	(1.2)	19.5	(1.3)	4.0	(0.6)	0.3	(0.1)
Spain (Canary Islands)	8.3	(1.3)	22.2	(1.9)	29.5	(1.9)	25.8	(2.2)	11.8	(1.9)	2.3	(0.8)	0.0	c
Spain (Cantabria)	4.0	(1.0)	11.6	(1.6)	23.6	(2.1)	30.3	(2.1)	22.9	(2.1)	6.6	(1.0)	0.9	(0.5)
Spain (Castile and Leon)	2.9	(0.8)	10.0	(1.8)	19.9	(1.7)	32.2	(2.1)	25.4	(1.9)	8.7	(1.4)	0.9	(0.4)
Spain (Catalonia)	3.8	(1.2)	12.1	(1.7)	23.3	(2.3)	32.1	(2.7)	22.9	(2.2)	5.4	(1.5)	0.3	(0.4)
Spain (Ceuta and Melilla)	26.0	(1.8)	21.2	(1.9)	24.4	(2.3)	18.0	(1.6)	8.4	(1.2)	1.8	(0.9)	0.0	c
Spain (Galicia)	3.8	(0.9)	10.3	(1.6)	24.0	(2.3)	32.1	(2.3)	23.4	(2.7)	5.9	(1.2)	0.3	(0.3)
Spain (La Rioja)	4.1	(0.8)	10.9	(1.9)	21.8	(2.7)	31.1	(2.5)	23.5	(2.1)	8.1	(1.2)	0.6	(0.4)
Spain (Madrid)	3.3	(1.0)	11.2	(1.6)	23.5	(2.2)	30.6	(2.2)	24.3	(2.1)	6.6	(1.3)	0.5	(0.3)
Spain (Murcia)	2.7	(0.9)	13.7	(1.7)	27.4	(2.3)	31.8	(2.3)	20.4	(2.7)	3.9	(1.0)	0.0	c
Spain (Navarre)	2.4	(0.7)	10.1	(1.5)	24.0	(2.4)	31.6	(2.2)	24.4	(1.7)	6.6	(1.1)	0.9	(0.5)
United Kingdom (Scotland)	3.3	(0.6)	10.6	(1.2)	22.5	(1.4)	28.5	(1.3)	22.8	(1.7)	10.4	(1.3)	2.0	(0.4)
Non-adjudicated														
Belgium (French Community)	10.3	(1.9)	14.1	(1.3)	21.3	(1.6)	25.2	(1.8)	21.7	(1.9)	6.8	(1.0)	0.6	(0.3)
Belgium (German-Speaking Community)	2.4	(1.1)	11.2	(1.6)	22.3	(2.5)	27.5	(2.5)	25.7	(2.8)	10.7	(1.6)	0.0	c
Finland (Finnish Speaking)	1.3	(0.3)	6.0	(0.7)	17.2	(1.1)	28.5	(1.7)	28.8	(1.7)	14.8	(1.0)	3.3	(0.4)
Finland (Swedish Speaking)	2.2	(0.9)	8.4	(1.5)	23.9	(2.6)	29.4	(2.1)	25.8	(2.7)	8.4	(1.7)	1.8	(0.7)
Italy (Provincia Abruzzo)	5.9	(1.8)	16.9	(2.1)	29.1	(2.7)	28.7	(2.1)	16.0	(2.5)	3.1	(1.1)	0.3	(0.3)
Italy (Provincia Autonoma di Bolzano)	3.4	(1.0)	10.6	(1.5)	22.4	(2.4)	30.9	(2.7)	21.9	(1.8)	9.8	(0.9)	1.1	(0.5)
Italy (Provincia Basilicata)	6.4	(1.7)	21.4	(2.6)	29.7	(1.9)	25.9	(2.6)	13.1	(1.6)	3.3	(0.8)	0.0	c
Italy (Provincia Calabria)	12.5	(2.4)	26.9	(2.0)	31.0	(2.5)	20.8	(2.1)	7.4	(1.5)	1.4	(0.5)	0.0	c
Italy (Provincia Campania)	13.7	(2.7)	24.0	(2.3)	30.0	(2.1)	21.3	(2.4)	9.4	(2.0)	1.5	(0.7)	0.0	c
Italy (Provincia Emilia Romagna)	4.3	(1.2)	9.3	(1.4)	21.3	(2.3)	28.3	(2.7)	24.8	(2.2)	10.8	(1.6)	1.2	(0.5)
Italy (Provincia Friuli Venezia Giulia)	4.4	(1.6)	10.2	(1.6)	19.6	(2.0)	29.4	(2.6)	23.9	(2.1)	11.3	(1.4)	1.3	(0.5)
Italy (Provincia Lazio)	5.0	(1.1)	17.6	(2.6)	28.2	(2.5)	27.9	(2.3)	17.1	(1.8)	4.1	(1.1)	0.0	c
Italy (Provincia Liguria)	6.9	(2.8)	13.9	(2.9)	22.6	(2.2)	29.9	(3.1)	18.7	(3.2)	7.2	(1.9)	0.7	(0.4)
Italy (Provincia Lombardia)	4.1	(1.3)	8.1	(1.8)	16.8	(2.8)	31.7	(2.3)	26.7	(3.2)	11.2	(1.8)	1.4	(0.5)
Italy (Provincia Marche)	3.5	(1.3)	13.0	(4.0)	23.3	(3.0)	31.7	(3.7)	21.8	(2.8)	6.0	(1.1)	0.7	(0.4)
Italy (Provincia Molise)	7.2	(1.3)	16.9	(2.0)	31.1	(2.6)	28.3	(2.5)	13.2	(1.9)	3.3	(1.0)	0.0	c
Italy (Provincia Piemonte)	3.3	(0.8)	11.3	(1.8)	23.7	(2.9)	29.4	(2.9)	23.9	(2.2)	7.6	(1.5)	0.8	(0.4)
Italy (Provincia Puglia)	5.1	(1.9)	14.1	(1.8)	26.6	(2.9)	28.4	(2.3)	19.6	(2.3)	5.6	(1.4)	0.5	(0.4)
Italy (Provincia Sardegna)	7.0	(1.6)	17.2	(2.4)	30.9	(2.2)	27.3	(2.1)	13.5	(1.8)	3.8	(1.1)	0.0	c
Italy (Provincia Sicilia)	14.1	(3.2)	21.8	(3.1)	25.3	(2.5)	23.2	(2.9)	12.6	(1.8)	2.8	(1.0)	0.0	c
Italy (Provincia Toscana)	4.8	(1.8)	13.9	(2.3)	25.2	(2.5)	27.7	(2.7)	19.4	(2.5)	8.0	(1.8)	1.0	(0.6)
Italy (Provincia Trento)	2.6	(0.8)	10.1	(1.4)	20.1	(1.9)	28.9	(2.4)	23.5	(2.3)	12.3	(1.4)	2.4	(0.9)
Italy (Provincia Umbria)	6.7	(1.7)	13.5	(2.0)	23.4	(1.9)	28.1	(2.3)	20.3	(2.3)	7.0	(1.1)	0.9	(0.6)
Italy (Provincia Valle d'Aosta)	2.9	(1.0)	7.4	(1.8)	18.4	(2.5)	30.9	(2.6)	28.0	(3.5)	10.8	(1.5)	1.5	(0.7)
Italy (Provincia Veneto)	2.7	(1.0)	10.6	(2.4)	21.8	(2.4)	30.8	(2.8)	24.4	(3.1)	9.1	(1.6)	0.7	(0.5)
United Kingdom (England)	4.0	(0.7)	10.3	(1.0)	21.6	(1.3)	27.5	(1.5)	23.2	(1.5)	10.8	(1.1)	2.5	(0.4)
United Kingdom (Northern Ireland)	5.2	(1.9)	12.0	(1.7)	21.7	(2.2)	25.6	(1.9)	21.9	(1.9)	10.9	(1.8)	2.8	(0.7)
United Kingdom (Wales)	5.4	(0.8)	13.3	(1.4)	24.3	(1.7)	28.6	(1.4)	19.1	(1.3)	8.1	(1.0)	1.3	(0.4)

Note: See Table I.3.5 for national data.
StatLink http://dx.doi.org/10.1787/888932343304

[Part 2/2]

Table S.I.w **Percentage of students at each proficiency level on the science scale, by gender**

	Girls – Proficiency levels													
	Below Level 1 (less than 334.94 score points)		Level 1 (from 334.94 to less than 409.54 score points)		Level 2 (from 409.54 to less than 484.14 score points)		Level 3 (from 484.14 to less than 558.73 score points)		Level 4 (from 558.73 to less than 633.33 score points)		Level 5 (from 633.33 to less than 707.93 score points)		Level 6 (above 707.93 score points)	
	%	S.E.	%	S.E.	%	S.E.	%	S.E.	%	S.E.	%	S.E.	%	S.E.
Adjudicated														
Belgium (Flemish Community)	3.8	(0.6)	9.0	(1.0)	19.2	(1.2)	29.2	(1.4)	26.9	(1.4)	10.8	(1.0)	1.1	(0.3)
Spain (Andalusia)	7.6	(1.5)	18.3	(2.4)	33.6	(2.5)	28.3	(2.6)	11.0	(2.0)	1.2	(0.5)	0.0	c
Spain (Aragon)	3.0	(0.6)	10.2	(1.5)	25.7	(2.3)	35.2	(2.1)	22.0	(2.2)	3.7	(1.2)	0.0	c
Spain (Asturias)	4.7	(1.0)	11.5	(1.5)	26.1	(2.0)	34.0	(2.2)	19.5	(2.3)	3.8	(0.9)	0.4	(0.4)
Spain (Balearic Islands)	7.6	(1.9)	20.2	(2.6)	34.2	(3.4)	26.6	(3.6)	10.5	(2.0)	0.9	(0.5)	0.0	c
Spain (Basque Country)	2.5	(0.5)	10.7	(0.8)	31.0	(1.4)	37.9	(1.7)	15.7	(1.3)	2.1	(0.5)	0.0	c
Spain (Canary Islands)	10.7	(2.1)	22.5	(2.8)	33.7	(2.7)	24.8	(2.0)	7.3	(1.3)	1.0	(0.4)	0.0	c
Spain (Cantabria)	4.1	(0.9)	12.7	(1.8)	26.9	(2.3)	32.6	(2.3)	18.8	(2.1)	4.5	(1.2)	0.3	(0.2)
Spain (Castile and Leon)	2.1	(0.8)	7.9	(1.3)	24.1	(2.3)	36.9	(2.0)	22.7	(2.2)	6.1	(1.3)	0.3	(0.3)
Spain (Catalonia)	3.9	(1.1)	12.7	(1.9)	27.8	(2.3)	33.0	(2.6)	18.9	(2.3)	3.4	(1.1)	0.3	(0.3)
Spain (Ceuta and Melilla)	22.1	(1.7)	25.8	(2.2)	24.2	(2.3)	19.3	(1.5)	7.2	(1.3)	1.4	(0.5)	0.0	c
Spain (Galicia)	2.2	(0.7)	10.3	(1.5)	23.9	(1.8)	36.8	(1.9)	21.8	(2.0)	4.6	(1.2)	0.0	c
Spain (La Rioja)	3.6	(1.1)	9.4	(1.3)	22.5	(2.3)	35.4	(2.5)	24.0	(2.0)	4.7	(1.2)	0.0	c
Spain (Madrid)	1.8	(0.6)	9.7	(1.6)	25.5	(2.9)	36.7	(2.3)	21.0	(2.3)	4.9	(1.4)	0.3	(0.3)
Spain (Murcia)	5.6	(1.5)	17.2	(1.9)	30.8	(2.2)	31.5	(2.5)	13.2	(2.2)	1.6	(0.5)	0.0	c
Spain (Navarre)	2.7	(0.9)	10.3	(1.5)	26.8	(2.7)	33.2	(2.6)	22.5	(2.1)	4.1	(1.0)	0.4	(0.3)
United Kingdom (Scotland)	2.9	(0.6)	11.5	(1.2)	25.6	(1.7)	29.2	(1.3)	21.2	(1.5)	8.2	(1.3)	1.4	(0.4)
Non-adjudicated														
Belgium (French Community)	9.0	(1.4)	15.9	(1.2)	23.9	(1.5)	28.0	(1.6)	19.0	(1.4)	3.8	(0.7)	0.4	(0.2)
Belgium (German-Speaking Community)	2.1	(0.8)	8.2	(1.7)	22.0	(3.0)	33.1	(2.6)	26.5	(2.0)	7.1	(1.6)	1.1	(0.6)
Finland (Finnish Speaking)	0.9	(0.2)	3.5	(0.5)	12.4	(1.1)	28.7	(1.3)	34.3	(1.2)	16.8	(1.0)	3.5	(0.5)
Finland (Swedish Speaking)	1.0	(0.5)	6.1	(1.1)	19.9	(1.9)	33.4	(2.4)	28.0	(2.5)	10.3	(1.9)	1.3	(0.7)
Italy (Provincia Abruzzo)	5.6	(1.3)	14.2	(2.0)	27.7	(2.9)	32.5	(2.5)	16.5	(2.6)	3.4	(1.0)	0.0	c
Italy (Provincia Autonoma di Bolzano)	2.8	(0.9)	9.3	(1.0)	22.5	(1.6)	35.9	(1.9)	22.6	(1.8)	6.5	(1.1)	0.5	(0.3)
Italy (Provincia Basilicata)	6.3	(1.1)	19.1	(2.1)	32.4	(2.0)	30.1	(2.2)	10.7	(1.4)	1.4	(0.5)	0.0	c
Italy (Provincia Calabria)	9.1	(1.9)	21.7	(2.4)	35.3	(2.5)	24.1	(2.5)	9.1	(1.6)	0.8	(0.4)	0.0	c
Italy (Provincia Campania)	8.1	(1.7)	19.6	(2.6)	33.4	(3.1)	27.6	(2.4)	9.8	(2.2)	1.6	(0.7)	0.0	c
Italy (Provincia Emilia Romagna)	6.2	(1.6)	12.1	(1.7)	23.4	(2.3)	29.7	(2.6)	21.9	(2.2)	6.2	(1.3)	0.5	(0.3)
Italy (Provincia Friuli Venezia Giulia)	1.8	(0.9)	5.5	(1.6)	20.8	(2.5)	34.4	(3.7)	27.5	(2.6)	8.8	(1.6)	1.2	(0.6)
Italy (Provincia Lazio)	5.9	(1.8)	14.2	(1.9)	27.3	(3.0)	33.1	(2.6)	16.8	(2.1)	2.6	(0.9)	0.0	c
Italy (Provincia Liguria)	4.0	(1.3)	9.6	(1.7)	24.1	(3.2)	37.0	(3.3)	20.3	(2.6)	4.8	(1.2)	0.0	c
Italy (Provincia Lombardia)	2.3	(1.0)	7.2	(1.9)	19.5	(3.1)	34.8	(2.4)	27.9	(2.5)	7.4	(1.3)	0.8	(0.5)
Italy (Provincia Marche)	3.8	(1.2)	10.5	(1.8)	23.3	(2.3)	33.8	(1.9)	23.0	(2.1)	5.3	(1.2)	0.3	(0.3)
Italy (Provincia Molise)	5.3	(1.2)	16.8	(2.6)	33.5	(3.9)	33.0	(2.9)	10.5	(1.8)	0.8	(0.6)	0.0	c
Italy (Provincia Piemonte)	5.3	(2.0)	13.8	(2.6)	25.1	(2.3)	29.8	(3.1)	20.8	(2.4)	4.8	(1.2)	0.3	(0.3)
Italy (Provincia Puglia)	4.4	(1.0)	13.8	(2.2)	28.6	(2.9)	31.1	(2.6)	18.2	(2.3)	3.5	(1.2)	0.3	(0.4)
Italy (Provincia Sardegna)	4.9	(1.6)	17.4	(2.3)	29.6	(2.8)	30.7	(2.6)	14.7	(1.7)	2.6	(0.7)	0.0	c
Italy (Provincia Sicilia)	9.3	(2.0)	20.4	(3.4)	31.2	(2.9)	28.6	(3.7)	9.1	(2.1)	1.4	(0.7)	0.0	c
Italy (Provincia Toscana)	4.1	(1.5)	11.5	(1.7)	24.2	(2.4)	34.1	(2.5)	21.1	(2.2)	4.6	(1.4)	0.4	(0.3)
Italy (Provincia Trento)	3.1	(1.3)	8.3	(2.0)	20.8	(2.3)	33.1	(3.4)	26.4	(2.9)	7.9	(1.7)	0.4	(0.4)
Italy (Provincia Umbria)	3.7	(1.5)	11.7	(2.0)	26.3	(2.3)	32.3	(2.2)	21.1	(2.3)	4.6	(1.1)	0.3	(0.3)
Italy (Provincia Valle d'Aosta)	1.9	(0.9)	9.4	(1.6)	24.1	(2.3)	35.5	(3.5)	23.0	(2.3)	5.4	(1.2)	0.6	(0.6)
Italy (Provincia Veneto)	2.1	(0.9)	8.1	(2.1)	20.8	(3.3)	35.8	(3.2)	25.1	(2.6)	7.6	(1.3)	0.7	(0.3)
United Kingdom (England)	3.7	(0.5)	11.6	(1.0)	23.1	(1.1)	29.9	(1.4)	21.8	(1.4)	8.6	(0.9)	1.4	(0.3)
United Kingdom (Northern Ireland)	3.7	(1.1)	12.6	(1.4)	21.9	(1.9)	30.6	(1.9)	21.3	(1.7)	8.5	(1.1)	1.5	(0.6)
United Kingdom (Wales)	4.3	(0.7)	14.4	(1.2)	28.3	(1.6)	29.7	(1.4)	17.1	(1.3)	5.4	(0.8)	0.7	(0.3)

Note: See Table I.3.5 for national data.
StatLink http://dx.doi.org/10.1787/888932343304

[Part 1/1]

Table S.I.x **Mean score, variation and gender differences in student performance on the science scale**

	All students		Standard deviation		Gender differences				Difference (B – G)		Percentiles											
	Mean score				Boys		Girls				5th		10th		25th		75th		90th		95th	
	Mean	S.E.	S.D.	S.E.	Mean score	S.E.	Mean score	S.E.	Score dif.	S.E.	Score	S.E.	Score	S.E.	Score	S.E.	Score	S.E.	Score	S.E.	Score	S.E.
Adjudicated																						
Belgium (Flemish Community)	526	(2.9)	98	(2.0)	529	(3.6)	523	(3.6)	5	(4.3)	350	(6.3)	392	(5.6)	461	(4.4)	598	(3.2)	647	(4.0)	673	(4.5)
Spain (Andalusia)	469	(5.3)	88	(2.9)	477	(5.8)	461	(6.3)	16	(5.5)	318	(9.9)	353	(9.2)	413	(7.1)	531	(5.9)	579	(5.7)	605	(5.8)
Spain (Aragon)	505	(4.3)	86	(1.9)	509	(5.6)	502	(5.0)	6	(6.1)	353	(8.5)	392	(6.7)	451	(5.8)	566	(4.9)	610	(4.3)	635	(6.8)
Spain (Asturias)	502	(4.9)	92	(2.2)	508	(5.8)	495	(5.8)	13	(6.1)	340	(8.7)	376	(7.1)	443	(6.5)	566	(5.8)	613	(6.2)	641	(5.4)
Spain (Balearic Islands)	461	(5.7)	88	(2.2)	466	(6.2)	456	(6.7)	10	(5.8)	310	(9.5)	346	(9.4)	404	(8.4)	523	(6.6)	573	(4.9)	599	(5.7)
Spain (Basque Country)	495	(2.5)	78	(1.3)	498	(3.5)	492	(2.4)	6	(3.2)	361	(5.0)	393	(4.0)	444	(3.3)	548	(2.4)	593	(3.2)	618	(3.9)
Spain (Canary Islands)	452	(4.1)	89	(2.6)	459	(5.1)	444	(4.7)	15	(5.2)	304	(9.0)	338	(7.4)	390	(5.7)	515	(4.8)	565	(5.8)	596	(7.7)
Spain (Cantabria)	500	(4.7)	90	(1.9)	506	(5.1)	494	(5.6)	12	(5.3)	346	(7.8)	381	(6.8)	440	(5.3)	564	(5.8)	614	(5.3)	641	(5.4)
Spain (Castile and Leon)	516	(4.9)	86	(2.5)	519	(6.5)	513	(5.2)	6	(6.2)	367	(9.6)	402	(8.8)	461	(6.5)	575	(4.9)	625	(6.1)	649	(7.7)
Spain (Catalonia)	497	(5.9)	88	(2.4)	502	(6.4)	493	(6.4)	9	(5.0)	345	(8.3)	380	(10.3)	440	(7.3)	561	(6.2)	606	(6.7)	631	(7.0)
Spain (Ceuta and Melilla)	416	(2.6)	109	(2.2)	414	(4.0)	418	(2.9)	-5	(4.6)	240	(7.9)	279	(6.1)	338	(4.6)	494	(3.8)	555	(4.8)	590	(7.0)
Spain (Galicia)	506	(4.9)	86	(1.5)	505	(5.4)	507	(5.3)	-1	(4.3)	357	(9.0)	393	(6.4)	449	(6.7)	566	(5.7)	611	(5.7)	637	(6.6)
Spain (La Rioja)	509	(2.6)	91	(2.4)	510	(3.5)	508	(3.6)	2	(4.9)	349	(8.5)	389	(7.2)	452	(5.0)	573	(4.1)	619	(3.8)	643	(5.3)
Spain (Madrid)	508	(4.2)	86	(2.4)	508	(4.6)	507	(5.8)	1	(6.2)	364	(8.0)	394	(5.5)	450	(6.4)	568	(4.8)	614	(6.7)	640	(6.3)
Spain (Murcia)	484	(5.3)	84	(2.5)	496	(5.4)	472	(6.2)	24	(4.6)	342	(8.7)	372	(7.4)	426	(7.2)	544	(5.8)	590	(6.1)	616	(5.3)
Spain (Navarre)	509	(3.2)	85	(2.0)	513	(3.9)	504	(4.1)	9	(4.6)	363	(7.1)	396	(7.4)	451	(5.4)	570	(3.8)	613	(4.8)	642	(6.3)
United Kingdom (Scotland)	514	(3.5)	96	(1.4)	519	(4.4)	510	(4.0)	9	(4.7)	358	(6.0)	391	(4.4)	449	(4.1)	582	(4.4)	638	(4.6)	669	(5.6)
Non-adjudicated																						
Belgium (French Community)	482	(4.2)	109	(4.0)	486	(6.2)	478	(4.8)	8	(7.2)	293	(11.1)	337	(8.0)	411	(6.1)	562	(4.4)	612	(4.1)	640	(5.1)
Belgium (German-Speaking Community)	519	(2.8)	89	(2.0)	519	(3.8)	520	(4.3)	-1	(6.0)	369	(8.5)	399	(6.1)	455	(5.4)	585	(4.3)	632	(5.0)	657	(6.7)
Finland (Finnish Speaking)	556	(2.5)	89	(1.2)	548	(3.0)	564	(2.7)	-16	(2.8)	402	(4.4)	439	(4.4)	498	(3.6)	618	(2.8)	666	(3.4)	695	(3.3)
Finland (Swedish Speaking)	528	(3.0)	88	(1.9)	522	(4.1)	534	(3.8)	-12	(5.1)	381	(8.3)	415	(3.7)	468	(4.9)	589	(3.8)	638	(5.5)	667	(5.9)
Italy (Provincia Abruzzo)	480	(5.7)	91	(4.9)	478	(6.5)	483	(6.6)	-4	(6.3)	327	(15.5)	364	(7.9)	422	(7.1)	544	(6.9)	591	(7.7)	619	(10.0)
Italy (Provincia Autonoma di Bolzano)	513	(2.5)	90	(2.0)	514	(3.3)	512	(3.0)	2	(3.8)	356	(9.2)	392	(5.4)	456	(4.2)	574	(2.8)	628	(4.2)	656	(3.9)
Italy (Provincia Basilicata)	466	(3.9)	86	(2.2)	468	(5.3)	464	(4.8)	4	(6.7)	325	(6.9)	355	(5.8)	406	(5.7)	526	(4.6)	577	(5.1)	607	(5.6)
Italy (Provincia Calabria)	443	(5.5)	86	(3.2)	437	(6.8)	449	(6.4)	-12	(7.1)	299	(8.3)	331	(8.0)	384	(7.1)	502	(7.3)	555	(7.7)	584	(7.6)
Italy (Provincia Campania)	446	(6.8)	93	(6.0)	439	(8.9)	456	(6.7)	-17	(8.7)	294	(16.7)	327	(11.8)	386	(8.1)	511	(7.9)	565	(8.9)	592	(8.3)
Italy (Provincia Emilia Romagna)	508	(4.8)	99	(4.1)	519	(5.3)	497	(6.7)	22	(7.6)	331	(15.3)	378	(10.5)	443	(6.8)	579	(5.9)	631	(6.2)	657	(7.5)
Italy (Provincia Friuli Venezia Giulia)	524	(4.8)	92	(4.2)	519	(6.6)	529	(5.6)	-10	(7.7)	360	(14.2)	402	(11.8)	466	(7.7)	589	(5.0)	639	(4.2)	663	(3.8)
Italy (Provincia Lazio)	482	(5.0)	89	(3.2)	481	(5.9)	483	(6.9)	-1	(7.8)	332	(8.7)	364	(7.5)	420	(6.7)	546	(6.0)	595	(6.3)	622	(7.8)
Italy (Provincia Liguria)	498	(9.9)	94	(4.6)	494	(15.9)	503	(6.1)	-9	(15.0)	331	(16.2)	371	(17.8)	438	(14.0)	561	(8.0)	615	(8.0)	644	(9.6)
Italy (Provincia Lombardia)	526	(5.8)	92	(4.1)	526	(7.9)	525	(7.0)	0	(9.4)	363	(16.0)	403	(13.0)	472	(7.7)	588	(5.0)	636	(6.2)	663	(7.5)
Italy (Provincia Marche)	504	(6.5)	89	(3.3)	504	(10.6)	504	(4.4)	0	(10.6)	348	(11.1)	382	(11.2)	446	(10.5)	566	(5.0)	615	(6.0)	641	(5.8)
Italy (Provincia Molise)	469	(2.8)	84	(2.5)	471	(4.1)	468	(3.1)	3	(4.7)	325	(7.8)	359	(7.3)	415	(4.6)	526	(4.3)	574	(5.4)	603	(7.8)
Italy (Provincia Piemonte)	501	(5.2)	93	(2.6)	510	(6.3)	493	(6.2)	17	(7.1)	338	(8.1)	375	(7.9)	440	(7.7)	568	(5.1)	617	(5.9)	646	(6.9)
Italy (Provincia Puglia)	490	(6.3)	90	(3.8)	492	(7.3)	489	(7.5)	3	(7.8)	337	(12.1)	373	(10.0)	430	(6.9)	555	(7.9)	605	(7.0)	633	(7.9)
Italy (Provincia Sardegna)	474	(4.5)	89	(2.8)	471	(5.9)	477	(6.0)	-6	(7.6)	327	(11.4)	360	(7.3)	414	(5.2)	536	(5.6)	589	(5.9)	619	(6.7)
Italy (Provincia Sicilia)	451	(8.2)	98	(6.2)	448	(10.8)	454	(8.5)	-6	(10.3)	284	(21.5)	326	(13.2)	387	(9.5)	520	(7.4)	573	(7.9)	605	(9.9)
Italy (Provincia Toscana)	500	(5.7)	94	(4.2)	499	(8.3)	500	(6.2)	-1	(9.3)	340	(13.8)	376	(10.7)	437	(7.9)	565	(7.3)	617	(9.7)	647	(9.9)
Italy (Provincia Trento)	523	(3.6)	94	(3.2)	526	(4.8)	519	(7.4)	8	(10.0)	360	(11.1)	399	(9.5)	460	(6.8)	589	(4.2)	640	(4.9)	669	(7.5)
Italy (Provincia Umbria)	497	(5.0)	96	(4.1)	495	(6.8)	499	(5.7)	-3	(7.0)	334	(16.8)	373	(10.2)	435	(7.9)	564	(5.1)	616	(5.1)	642	(5.2)
Italy (Provincia Valle d'Aosta)	521	(2.6)	88	(2.3)	531	(3.3)	512	(3.9)	19	(5.0)	366	(8.0)	404	(6.4)	465	(4.6)	583	(4.8)	630	(4.5)	658	(6.9)
Italy (Provincia Veneto)	518	(5.1)	88	(3.2)	516	(8.1)	520	(7.0)	-4	(11.2)	364	(10.9)	399	(9.8)	461	(7.5)	580	(6.0)	627	(7.1)	655	(7.5)
United Kingdom (England)	515	(3.0)	99	(1.6)	520	(4.3)	510	(3.7)	10	(5.4)	349	(5.1)	385	(4.5)	448	(4.4)	584	(3.8)	641	(3.8)	673	(4.5)
United Kingdom (Northern Ireland)	511	(4.4)	103	(3.9)	514	(8.7)	509	(4.5)	5	(10.4)	341	(12.1)	378	(9.0)	440	(7.3)	584	(5.0)	642	(5.8)	676	(5.7)
United Kingdom (Wales)	496	(3.5)	95	(1.4)	500	(4.0)	491	(4.0)	9	(3.7)	336	(5.8)	373	(5.2)	430	(4.5)	561	(3.8)	619	(3.8)	655	(5.2)

Note: See Table I.3.6 for national data.
Values that are statistically significant are indicated in bold (see Annex A3).
StatLink ⟲ http://dx.doi.org/10.1787/888932343304

[Part 1/1]

Table S.I.y **Overlapping of top performers in reading, mathematics and science**

	15-year-old students who are:																Percentage of top performers in reading who are top performers also in mathematics and science	
	not top performers in any of the three domains		top performers only in reading		top performers only in mathematics		top performers only in science		top performers in reading and mathematics but not in science		top performers in reading and science but not in mathematics		top performers in mathematics and science but not in reading		top performers in all three domains			
	%	S.E.	%	S.E.	%	S.E.	%	S.E.	%	S.E.	%	S.E.	%	S.E.	%	S.E.	%	S.E.
Adjudicated																		
Belgium (Flemish Community)	70.4	(1.2)	1.0	(0.2)	12.1	(0.8)	1.2	(0.2)	3.0	(0.4)	0.6	(0.2)	3.7	(0.5)	8.0	(0.8)	64.0	(3.5)
Spain (Andalusia)	94.1	(1.1)	0.5	(0.3)	2.7	(0.8)	0.9	(0.3)	0.4	(0.2)	0.3	(0.2)	0.6	(0.4)	0.5	(0.3)	29.3	(11.0)
Spain (Aragon)	83.4	(1.6)	1.0	(0.5)	8.9	(1.3)	1.0	(0.4)	1.4	(0.4)	0.3	(0.2)	1.9	(0.4)	2.0	(0.5)	42.3	(8.6)
Spain (Asturias)	87.0	(1.6)	1.3	(0.4)	4.2	(0.8)	1.2	(0.3)	1.2	(0.3)	0.4	(0.3)	2.0	(0.7)	2.7	(0.6)	47.9	(8.5)
Spain (Balearic Islands)	93.9	(0.9)	0.7	(0.5)	3.4	(0.6)	0.4	(0.2)	0.4	(0.2)	0.2	(0.1)	0.6	(0.3)	0.5	(0.3)	27.6	(15.1)
Spain (Basque Country)	85.7	(0.8)	1.0	(0.3)	8.2	(0.7)	0.4	(0.1)	1.8	(0.3)	0.1	(0.1)	1.2	(0.3)	1.5	(0.3)	34.1	(4.3)
Spain (Canary Islands)	96.2	(0.7)	1.2	(0.4)	0.7	(0.4)	0.9	(0.3)	0.2	(0.2)	0.3	(0.2)	0.4	(0.2)	0.2	(0.2)	9.9	(9.0)
Spain (Cantabria)	85.2	(1.6)	1.1	(0.3)	6.4	(0.9)	1.4	(0.5)	1.1	(0.4)	0.4	(0.2)	2.3	(0.6)	2.1	(0.5)	45.1	(7.8)
Spain (Castile and Leon)	81.8	(1.7)	0.9	(0.3)	8.0	(1.2)	1.3	(0.5)	1.3	(0.5)	0.6	(0.4)	2.7	(0.5)	3.3	(0.7)	53.4	(7.3)
Spain (Catalonia)	87.1	(1.9)	1.0	(0.3)	6.1	(1.2)	1.2	(0.5)	1.1	(0.4)	0.3	(0.2)	1.9	(0.6)	1.3	(0.5)	34.8	(11.8)
Spain (Ceuta and Melilla)	96.3	(0.5)	0.6	(0.2)	1.2	(0.4)	0.8	(0.5)	0.3	(0.2)	0.1	(0.1)	0.4	(0.2)	0.3	(0.2)	21.2	(15.6)
Spain (Galicia)	89.4	(1.3)	1.1	(0.4)	3.4	(0.7)	1.9	(0.5)	0.5	(0.2)	0.7	(0.3)	1.8	(0.5)	1.2	(0.4)	33.8	(8.8)
Spain (La Rioja)	82.8	(1.4)	1.1	(0.5)	7.7	(1.1)	1.0	(0.4)	1.5	(0.6)	0.2	(0.1)	2.5	(0.6)	3.3	(0.6)	54.7	(8.3)
Spain (Madrid)	86.4	(1.4)	1.2	(0.4)	4.9	(0.8)	1.5	(0.4)	1.4	(0.4)	0.6	(0.3)	1.3	(0.3)	2.7	(0.8)	46.2	(7.6)
Spain (Murcia)	92.7	(1.0)	0.7	(0.3)	2.9	(0.7)	0.8	(0.3)	0.9	(0.3)	0.2	(0.2)	1.1	(0.4)	0.7	(0.3)	28.2	(10.9)
Spain (Navarre)	83.8	(1.6)	1.2	(0.5)	7.6	(1.3)	1.3	(0.4)	1.3	(0.6)	0.2	(0.2)	2.4	(0.6)	2.1	(0.5)	43.6	(9.2)
United Kingdom (Scotland)	83.2	(1.2)	1.5	(0.4)	3.2	(0.4)	1.9	(0.4)	1.0	(0.3)	1.0	(0.3)	2.5	(0.5)	5.6	(0.8)	61.0	(4.7)
Non-adjudicated																		
Belgium (French Community)	83.7	(1.2)	3.3	(0.5)	5.1	(0.7)	0.3	(0.1)	2.1	(0.6)	0.4	(0.1)	1.3	(0.4)	3.8	(0.5)	39.6	(4.4)
Belgium (German-Speaking Community)	81.5	(1.6)	1.3	(0.5)	6.9	(1.1)	1.0	(0.4)	0.7	(0.6)	0.7	(0.4)	4.1	(0.8)	3.8	(0.8)	58.5	(10.2)
Finland (Finnish Speaking)	70.0	(1.1)	2.5	(0.3)	6.8	(0.6)	3.2	(0.4)	1.4	(0.2)	2.2	(0.4)	5.0	(0.5)	8.8	(0.7)	58.8	(3.1)
Finland (Swedish Speaking)	79.6	(1.5)	1.6	(0.4)	6.7	(1.0)	1.7	(0.5)	1.1	(0.4)	0.7	(0.2)	3.6	(0.7)	4.9	(0.8)	58.8	(5.6)
Italy (Provincia Abruzzo)	91.2	(1.9)	1.3	(0.5)	3.4	(1.3)	0.9	(0.5)	0.6	(0.3)	0.7	(0.3)	0.9	(0.5)	1.0	(0.4)	27.1	(8.4)
Italy (Provincia Autonoma di Bolzano)	82.5	(0.9)	1.2	(0.3)	6.4	(0.6)	1.9	(0.5)	1.0	(0.3)	0.7	(0.2)	3.5	(0.6)	2.9	(0.6)	51.0	(7.4)
Italy (Provincia Basilicata)	91.7	(1.0)	1.5	(0.4)	3.7	(0.7)	0.5	(0.2)	0.6	(0.3)	0.0	c	0.9	(0.4)	1.0	(0.3)	30.6	(8.4)
Italy (Provincia Calabria)	96.6	(0.8)	0.8	(0.3)	1.3	(0.5)	0.4	(0.2)	0.0	c	0.0	c	0.2	(0.2)	0.3	(0.2)	23.6	(12.0)
Italy (Provincia Campania)	94.4	(1.6)	0.6	(0.4)	3.0	(1.5)	0.5	(0.3)	0.4	(0.2)	0.4	(0.2)	0.2	(0.2)	0.5	(0.2)	27.1	(9.7)
Italy (Provincia Emilia Romagna)	79.6	(1.3)	2.5	(0.6)	7.0	(1.1)	1.5	(0.5)	1.6	(0.4)	1.2	(0.5)	3.0	(0.8)	3.7	(0.7)	40.9	(5.7)
Italy (Provincia Friuli Venezia Giulia)	80.4	(1.6)	3.0	(0.6)	4.1	(0.7)	2.2	(0.6)	1.2	(0.4)	1.0	(0.4)	3.2	(0.7)	4.8	(0.7)	48.5	(4.9)
Italy (Provincia Lazio)	90.2	(1.7)	2.0	(0.5)	3.5	(0.9)	0.7	(0.5)	0.7	(0.3)	0.6	(0.3)	1.0	(0.4)	1.2	(0.4)	26.2	(6.2)
Italy (Provincia Liguria)	86.8	(1.9)	2.1	(0.6)	3.5	(0.8)	1.1	(0.5)	1.0	(0.4)	0.7	(0.3)	2.4	(0.9)	2.4	(0.6)	38.8	(7.1)
Italy (Provincia Lombardia)	80.0	(2.0)	3.3	(0.7)	4.6	(0.8)	1.4	(0.5)	1.5	(0.5)	1.3	(0.4)	3.1	(0.6)	4.8	(1.0)	43.9	(5.4)
Italy (Provincia Marche)	85.8	(1.2)	2.8	(0.6)	4.0	(0.9)	1.2	(0.4)	1.2	(0.4)	0.8	(0.4)	1.7	(0.6)	2.6	(0.5)	34.9	(6.9)
Italy (Provincia Molise)	93.6	(1.2)	0.9	(0.4)	3.0	(0.8)	0.3	(0.3)	0.4	(0.3)	0.0	c	1.2	(0.4)	0.5	(0.4)	26.9	(18.1)
Italy (Provincia Piemonte)	85.6	(1.5)	2.7	(0.7)	3.7	(0.9)	1.0	(0.4)	1.3	(0.5)	0.7	(0.3)	2.2	(0.6)	2.8	(0.6)	37.8	(6.2)
Italy (Provincia Puglia)	87.8	(2.1)	1.7	(0.5)	5.1	(1.3)	0.8	(0.3)	0.6	(0.3)	0.6	(0.3)	2.3	(0.7)	1.3	(0.5)	31.8	(7.3)
Italy (Provincia Sardegna)	93.6	(0.8)	1.6	(0.5)	1.2	(0.4)	0.8	(0.4)	0.4	(0.2)	0.6	(0.3)	1.1	(0.5)	0.8	(0.3)	23.7	(8.7)
Italy (Provincia Sicilia)	93.1	(1.3)	1.3	(0.4)	3.0	(0.9)	0.5	(0.2)	0.4	(0.3)	0.2	(0.2)	0.7	(0.4)	0.8	(0.4)	28.3	(11.4)
Italy (Provincia Toscana)	85.6	(1.9)	2.3	(0.5)	4.3	(1.0)	1.3	(0.5)	0.7	(0.3)	0.5	(0.3)	2.4	(0.8)	2.8	(0.7)	44.1	(8.3)
Italy (Provincia Trento)	80.3	(1.2)	2.6	(0.8)	4.4	(0.7)	2.2	(0.6)	1.0	(0.4)	0.9	(0.5)	3.7	(0.8)	4.8	(0.8)	51.4	(6.1)
Italy (Provincia Umbria)	86.3	(1.2)	2.8	(0.6)	3.7	(0.9)	1.1	(0.3)	0.8	(0.3)	0.7	(0.3)	2.0	(0.5)	2.6	(0.7)	38.2	(7.6)
Italy (Provincia Valle d'Aosta)	83.3	(1.5)	2.7	(0.6)	3.7	(0.9)	1.4	(0.5)	1.2	(0.4)	1.1	(0.4)	2.3	(0.6)	4.4	(0.7)	47.3	(6.9)
Italy (Provincia Veneto)	82.7	(2.1)	2.0	(0.5)	5.3	(1.0)	1.5	(0.4)	1.0	(0.4)	1.0	(0.4)	3.1	(0.8)	3.4	(0.6)	45.5	(6.6)
United Kingdom (England)	84.4	(1.0)	1.3	(0.2)	2.2	(0.3)	2.8	(0.5)	0.5	(0.2)	1.6	(0.3)	2.5	(0.4)	4.6	(0.5)	57.3	(4.5)
United Kingdom (Northern Ireland)	83.8	(1.1)	1.5	(0.4)	2.3	(0.4)	2.4	(0.6)	0.6	(0.2)	2.1	(0.5)	2.2	(0.4)	5.1	(0.7)	55.0	(6.2)
United Kingdom (Wales)	90.1	(0.8)	0.9	(0.3)	1.1	(0.3)	2.5	(0.4)	0.2	(0.1)	1.4	(0.3)	1.3	(0.3)	2.5	(0.4)	49.6	(5.1)

Note: See Table I.3.7 for national data.

StatLink ⫘ http://dx.doi.org/10.1787/888932343304

[Part 1/2]

Table S.I.z **Overlapping of top performers in reading, mathematics and science, by gender**

| | Boys who are: | | | | | | | | | | | | | | | | Percentage of boy top performers in reading who are top performers also in mathematics and science | |
| | not top performers in any of the three domains | | top performers only in reading | | top performers only in mathematics | | top performers only in science | | top performers in reading and mathematics but not in science | | top performers in reading and science but not in mathematics | | top performers in mathematics and science but not in reading | | top performers in all three domains | | | |
	%	S.E.	%	S.E.	%	S.E.	%	S.E.	%	S.E.	%	S.E.	%	S.E.	%	S.E.	%	S.E.
Adjudicated																		
Belgium (Flemish Community)	67.9	(1.5)	0.2	(0.1)	15.3	(1.4)	1.1	(0.3)	1.5	(0.4)	0.3	(0.2)	5.5	(0.7)	8.2	(1.1)	80.4	(4.1)
Spain (Andalusia)	92.4	(1.5)	0.0	c	3.7	(1.3)	1.2	(0.6)	0.3	(0.2)	0.3	(0.3)	1.1	(0.6)	0.7	(0.4)	44.0	(18.5)
Spain (Aragon)	80.3	(2.4)	0.2	(0.2)	12.3	(1.9)	1.1	(0.6)	0.6	(0.5)	0.3	(0.2)	3.0	(0.7)	2.3	(0.6)	67.8	(11.3)
Spain (Asturias)	85.5	(2.1)	0.4	(0.3)	5.2	(1.2)	1.7	(0.6)	0.9	(0.4)	0.0	c	3.1	(1.2)	3.2	(0.9)	70.2	(10.1)
Spain (Balearic Islands)	92.0	(1.2)	0.2	(0.2)	5.2	(1.2)	0.7	(0.4)	0.3	(0.3)	0.0	c	1.0	(0.4)	0.5	(0.3)	47.9	(21.0)
Spain (Basque Country)	83.9	(1.1)	0.3	(0.2)	10.4	(1.0)	0.6	(0.2)	1.1	(0.3)	0.1	(0.1)	2.0	(0.5)	1.6	(0.3)	51.8	(8.0)
Spain (Canary Islands)	95.6	(1.0)	0.7	(0.4)	0.9	(0.5)	1.2	(0.6)	0.3	(0.3)	0.4	(0.2)	0.7	(0.4)	0.0	c	14.6	(18.1)
Spain (Cantabria)	83.9	(1.6)	0.0	c	7.8	(1.3)	1.7	(0.8)	0.6	(0.4)	0.0	c	3.5	(1.1)	2.3	(0.7)	73.6	(12.9)
Spain (Castile and Leon)	79.2	(2.3)	0.0	c	10.4	(1.7)	1.3	(0.5)	0.7	(0.5)	0.0	c	4.3	(1.1)	3.8	(1.1)	78.4	(9.2)
Spain (Catalonia)	84.3	(2.4)	0.3	(0.3)	8.9	(1.6)	1.4	(0.7)	0.8	(0.4)	0.0	c	2.7	(0.9)	1.4	(0.7)	51.4	(16.5)
Spain (Ceuta and Melilla)	95.2	(0.8)	0.3	(0.3)	2.1	(0.7)	0.9	(0.8)	0.0	c	0.0	c	0.6	(0.4)	0.0	c	33.2	(28.3)
Spain (Galicia)	88.3	(1.6)	0.0	c	4.5	(0.9)	2.0	(0.6)	0.4	(0.3)	0.4	(0.3)	2.5	(0.6)	1.3	(0.7)	47.7	(17.9)
Spain (La Rioja)	79.6	(2.1)	0.0	c	11.0	(1.9)	1.1	(0.4)	0.6	(0.5)	0.0	c	4.2	(0.9)	3.3	(0.8)	80.2	(12.0)
Spain (Madrid)	85.0	(1.5)	0.3	(0.2)	6.8	(1.2)	1.9	(0.8)	0.9	(0.4)	0.0	c	2.1	(0.6)	2.5	(0.9)	61.3	(11.4)
Spain (Murcia)	91.6	(1.5)	0.0	c	4.0	(1.0)	1.2	(0.5)	0.0	c	0.0	c	1.7	(0.6)	0.9	(0.5)	59.8	(18.4)
Spain (Navarre)	82.0	(2.1)	0.0	c	9.7	(1.8)	1.7	(0.6)	0.7	(0.4)	0.0	c	3.6	(1.2)	2.0	(0.7)	67.6	(14.4)
United Kingdom (Scotland)	81.8	(1.7)	0.5	(0.3)	4.4	(0.6)	2.1	(0.6)	0.9	(0.4)	0.6	(0.3)	3.4	(0.7)	6.3	(1.1)	76.1	(4.9)
Non-adjudicated																		
Belgium (French Community)	81.0	(1.7)	1.7	(0.6)	7.9	(1.1)	0.5	(0.2)	2.1	(0.6)	0.3	(0.2)	2.0	(0.7)	4.6	(0.7)	53.1	(6.9)
Belgium (German-Speaking Community)	78.8	(2.4)	0.0	c	9.4	(2.0)	1.5	(0.7)	0.0	c	0.0	c	6.1	(1.4)	3.3	(1.1)	78.4	(11.6)
Finland (Finnish Speaking)	71.7	(1.3)	0.4	(0.3)	9.2	(0.8)	3.3	(0.5)	0.6	(0.2)	0.8	(0.3)	7.4	(0.7)	6.6	(0.7)	79.4	(4.7)
Finland (Swedish Speaking)	80.0	(2.0)	0.3	(0.4)	9.1	(1.9)	1.7	(0.6)	0.5	(0.4)	0.0	c	5.1	(1.3)	3.3	(1.0)	78.5	(11.3)
Italy (Provincia Abruzzo)	91.2	(2.3)	0.0	c	4.5	(1.7)	0.9	(0.6)	0.5	(0.4)	0.3	(0.3)	1.4	(0.6)	0.9	(0.5)	44.5	(15.0)
Italy (Provincia Autonoma di Bolzano)	79.2	(1.3)	0.2	(0.2)	9.4	(1.1)	2.2	(0.5)	0.4	(0.3)	0.2	(0.2)	5.6	(0.9)	2.9	(0.6)	78.6	(8.8)
Italy (Provincia Basilicata)	89.9	(1.8)	0.3	(0.3)	5.8	(1.3)	0.6	(0.4)	0.4	(0.3)	0.0	c	1.5	(0.7)	1.3	(0.5)	60.8	(14.1)
Italy (Provincia Calabria)	96.2	(1.1)	0.0	c	1.8	(0.7)	0.5	(0.4)	0.0	c	0.0	c	0.4	(0.4)	0.4	(0.3)	43.4	(30.5)
Italy (Provincia Campania)	93.8	(1.8)	0.0	c	3.9	(1.5)	0.4	(0.3)	0.3	(0.3)	0.2	(0.2)	0.4	(0.4)	0.7	(0.4)	46.4	(20.1)
Italy (Provincia Emilia Romagna)	75.3	(2.0)	0.3	(0.2)	11.2	(1.8)	2.0	(0.8)	1.1	(0.6)	0.4	(0.3)	5.3	(1.4)	4.3	(0.8)	70.1	(9.3)
Italy (Provincia Friuli Venezia Giulia)	79.5	(2.0)	0.8	(0.5)	6.1	(1.1)	2.5	(0.7)	1.0	(0.5)	0.3	(0.3)	5.3	(1.1)	4.5	(0.8)	68.6	(7.9)
Italy (Provincia Lazio)	89.2	(2.3)	0.7	(0.4)	5.3	(1.4)	0.7	(0.4)	0.6	(0.4)	0.5	(0.4)	1.6	(0.6)	1.5	(0.7)	45.0	(11.6)
Italy (Provincia Liguria)	85.3	(2.9)	0.6	(0.4)	5.3	(1.2)	1.2	(0.8)	0.9	(0.4)	0.4	(0.4)	4.0	(1.6)	2.4	(1.0)	55.6	(13.3)
Italy (Provincia Lombardia)	80.0	(2.6)	0.6	(0.3)	6.0	(1.3)	2.0	(0.6)	0.8	(0.4)	0.0	c	5.1	(1.1)	4.9	(1.3)	71.0	(9.8)
Italy (Provincia Marche)	85.7	(1.8)	0.7	(0.5)	6.0	(1.5)	1.1	(0.5)	0.8	(0.4)	0.5	(0.4)	2.7	(1.0)	2.4	(0.6)	54.4	(13.1)
Italy (Provincia Molise)	90.8	(1.7)	0.4	(0.3)	4.9	(1.4)	0.5	(0.4)	0.6	(0.6)	0.0	c	2.0	(0.7)	0.8	(0.9)	43.3	(27.0)
Italy (Provincia Piemonte)	84.1	(2.0)	1.0	(0.7)	5.6	(1.5)	1.4	(0.9)	0.9	(0.5)	0.3	(0.3)	3.5	(1.0)	3.1	(0.8)	58.1	(9.2)
Italy (Provincia Puglia)	87.3	(2.5)	0.6	(0.4)	5.7	(1.6)	1.0	(0.5)	0.3	(0.3)	0.2	(0.3)	3.6	(1.0)	1.3	(0.5)	53.0	(14.9)
Italy (Provincia Sardegna)	93.3	(1.3)	0.4	(0.2)	1.9	(0.6)	1.0	(0.4)	0.5	(0.4)	0.0	c	1.9	(0.8)	0.9	(0.4)	47.5	(16.2)
Italy (Provincia Sicilia)	91.8	(1.4)	0.6	(0.6)	3.9	(1.1)	0.7	(0.5)	0.0	c	0.0	c	1.2	(0.6)	1.1	(0.7)	45.5	(27.5)
Italy (Provincia Toscana)	83.4	(2.8)	0.4	(0.3)	6.7	(1.6)	1.5	(0.6)	0.5	(0.4)	0.4	(0.3)	3.9	(1.4)	3.3	(1.0)	72.1	(9.6)
Italy (Provincia Trento)	78.2	(1.8)	0.7	(0.5)	5.8	(1.1)	2.8	(0.9)	0.6	(0.4)	0.7	(0.6)	5.5	(1.2)	5.7	(1.3)	74.9	(11.2)
Italy (Provincia Umbria)	84.9	(2.0)	0.8	(0.5)	5.8	(1.6)	1.4	(0.6)	0.5	(0.4)	0.0	c	3.6	(0.8)	2.8	(1.0)	63.4	(15.6)
Italy (Provincia Valle d'Aosta)	79.4	(2.0)	1.0	(0.6)	5.9	(1.7)	2.0	(0.8)	1.4	(0.7)	0.6	(0.4)	4.2	(1.1)	5.6	(1.4)	64.8	(10.9)
Italy (Provincia Veneto)	82.0	(2.6)	0.3	(0.3)	7.3	(1.5)	1.9	(0.9)	0.6	(0.4)	0.3	(0.2)	5.0	(1.3)	2.6	(0.7)	68.0	(11.3)
United Kingdom (England)	82.7	(1.5)	0.4	(0.3)	3.2	(0.7)	3.2	(0.6)	0.3	(0.2)	0.9	(0.3)	4.0	(0.6)	5.3	(0.7)	76.1	(5.1)
United Kingdom (Northern Ireland)	81.9	(2.0)	0.5	(0.3)	3.5	(0.6)	2.9	(0.8)	0.5	(0.3)	1.2	(0.6)	3.5	(0.8)	6.0	(1.0)	73.5	(6.6)
United Kingdom (Wales)	88.6	(1.1)	0.3	(0.2)	1.6	(0.6)	3.4	(0.6)	0.1	(0.1)	1.1	(0.3)	2.1	(0.5)	2.8	(0.6)	65.3	(6.5)

Note: See Table I.3.8 for national data.
StatLink ⌸⌁⌸ http://dx.doi.org/10.1787/888932343304

[Part 2/2]

Table S.I.z **Overlapping of top performers in reading, mathematics and science, by gender**

| | Girls who are: | | | | | | | | | | | | | | | | Percentage of girl top performers in reading who are top performers also in mathematics and science | |
	not top performers in any of the three domains		top performers only in reading		top performers only in mathematics		top performers only in science		top performers in reading and mathematics but not in science		top performers in reading and science but not in mathematics		top performers in mathematics and science but not in reading		top performers in all three domains			
	%	S.E.	%	S.E.	%	S.E.	%	S.E.	%	S.E.	%	S.E.	%	S.E.	%	S.E.	%	S.E.
Adjudicated																		
Belgium (Flemish Community)	73.1	(1.5)	1.8	(0.4)	8.8	(0.9)	1.3	(0.3)	4.5	(0.7)	0.9	(0.3)	1.9	(0.5)	7.9	(0.9)	52.4	(4.7)
Spain (Andalusia)	96.0	(1.2)	0.6	(0.6)	1.6	(0.7)	0.5	(0.4)	0.6	(0.4)	0.0	c	0.0	c	0.3	(0.2)	15.4	(12.0)
Spain (Aragon)	86.6	(1.5)	1.8	(0.9)	5.5	(1.1)	0.9	(0.4)	2.3	(0.7)	0.4	(0.3)	0.7	(0.4)	1.8	(0.8)	28.6	(10.8)
Spain (Asturias)	88.8	(1.6)	2.4	(0.8)	3.0	(0.9)	0.6	(0.4)	1.6	(0.5)	0.8	(0.7)	0.8	(0.5)	2.1	(0.9)	30.7	(11.8)
Spain (Balearic Islands)	95.8	(1.7)	1.2	(0.8)	1.6	(0.7)	0.0	c	0.5	(0.4)	0.3	(0.3)	0.2	(0.2)	0.0	c	16.0	(17.0)
Spain (Basque Country)	87.6	(0.8)	1.8	(0.4)	5.9	(0.6)	0.2	(0.1)	2.5	(0.6)	0.2	(0.1)	0.4	(0.2)	1.4	(0.4)	24.2	(6.0)
Spain (Canary Islands)	96.8	(0.8)	1.6	(0.7)	0.5	(0.4)	0.7	(0.4)	0.0	c	0.0	c	0.0	c	0.0	c	5.5	(6.7)
Spain (Cantabria)	86.6	(2.0)	2.0	(0.6)	4.9	(1.1)	1.2	(0.4)	1.8	(0.5)	0.7	(0.4)	1.0	(0.4)	2.0	(0.7)	30.6	(8.6)
Spain (Castile and Leon)	84.3	(1.9)	1.7	(0.6)	5.8	(1.3)	1.2	(0.7)	1.9	(0.8)	1.1	(0.8)	1.2	(0.6)	2.8	(0.8)	37.8	(7.8)
Spain (Catalonia)	89.9	(1.9)	1.8	(0.7)	3.2	(1.1)	0.9	(0.4)	1.4	(0.5)	0.5	(0.3)	1.0	(0.7)	1.3	(0.6)	25.7	(11.0)
Spain (Ceuta and Melilla)	97.3	(0.7)	0.8	(0.4)	0.4	(0.3)	0.8	(0.4)	0.0	c	0.0	c	0.3	(0.2)	0.0	c	15.8	(17.1)
Spain (Galicia)	90.5	(1.7)	1.7	(0.6)	2.3	(0.8)	1.7	(0.6)	0.7	(0.4)	1.0	(0.5)	1.1	(0.5)	1.1	(0.4)	24.9	(8.0)
Spain (La Rioja)	86.1	(1.8)	2.1	(0.9)	4.3	(1.0)	0.8	(0.6)	2.4	(1.1)	0.3	(0.3)	0.8	(0.4)	3.2	(1.0)	40.7	(9.7)
Spain (Madrid)	87.8	(1.9)	2.0	(0.7)	2.9	(0.9)	1.0	(0.5)	1.9	(0.7)	0.8	(0.5)	0.6	(0.4)	2.9	(1.1)	38.2	(10.9)
Spain (Murcia)	93.9	(1.3)	1.2	(0.6)	1.8	(0.8)	0.4	(0.3)	1.5	(0.5)	0.2	(0.2)	0.5	(0.4)	0.5	(0.4)	14.3	(11.0)
Spain (Navarre)	85.8	(2.0)	2.4	(0.9)	5.4	(1.5)	0.8	(0.7)	1.9	(1.0)	0.4	(0.5)	0.9	(0.4)	2.2	(0.7)	32.2	(8.7)
United Kingdom (Scotland)	84.7	(1.7)	2.5	(0.6)	2.0	(0.7)	1.7	(0.6)	1.2	(0.4)	1.5	(0.6)	1.5	(0.5)	4.9	(0.7)	48.5	(6.0)
Non-adjudicated																		
Belgium (French Community)	86.5	(1.3)	4.9	(0.8)	2.3	(0.5)	0.2	(0.1)	2.1	(0.7)	0.6	(0.2)	0.5	(0.2)	3.0	(0.6)	28.1	(5.0)
Belgium (German-Speaking Community)	84.2	(2.0)	2.3	(0.9)	4.3	(1.4)	0.6	(0.5)	0.0	c	1.3	(0.7)	2.0	(0.8)	4.4	(1.4)	48.7	(13.3)
Finland (Finnish Speaking)	68.2	(1.3)	4.7	(0.6)	4.5	(0.8)	3.2	(0.5)	2.2	(0.4)	3.6	(0.6)	2.6	(0.5)	10.9	(0.9)	50.7	(3.6)
Finland (Swedish Speaking)	79.3	(2.0)	2.9	(0.7)	4.4	(1.0)	1.8	(0.7)	1.7	(0.6)	1.2	(0.5)	2.2	(0.8)	6.4	(1.3)	52.1	(6.8)
Italy (Provincia Abruzzo)	91.2	(2.1)	2.5	(1.0)	2.1	(1.2)	0.9	(0.6)	0.7	(0.5)	1.0	(0.4)	0.0	c	1.0	(0.5)	19.6	(8.4)
Italy (Provincia Autonoma di Bolzano)	85.9	(1.3)	2.1	(0.7)	3.4	(0.8)	1.6	(0.7)	1.6	(0.6)	1.1	(0.4)	1.3	(0.5)	3.0	(1.0)	38.1	(11.0)
Italy (Provincia Basilicata)	93.7	(1.1)	2.7	(0.8)	1.3	(0.5)	0.3	(0.3)	0.8	(0.5)	0.0	c	0.3	(0.3)	0.6	(0.5)	13.8	(10.9)
Italy (Provincia Calabria)	97.0	(1.0)	1.3	(0.7)	0.7	(0.5)	0.3	(0.3)	0.0	c	0.0	c	0.0	c	0.3	(0.2)	15.6	(13.2)
Italy (Provincia Campania)	95.0	(1.8)	1.0	(0.6)	1.9	(1.5)	0.6	(0.4)	0.5	(0.4)	0.7	(0.4)	0.0	c	0.3	(0.3)	13.1	(10.0)
Italy (Provincia Emilia Romagna)	83.7	(1.7)	4.6	(1.1)	3.0	(0.8)	1.0	(0.6)	2.1	(0.7)	1.9	(0.8)	0.8	(0.4)	3.0	(0.9)	26.2	(6.3)
Italy (Provincia Friuli Venezia Giulia)	81.4	(2.3)	5.3	(1.3)	2.0	(0.8)	1.9	(0.8)	1.4	(0.6)	1.8	(0.7)	1.1	(0.7)	5.2	(1.1)	38.1	(6.4)
Italy (Provincia Lazio)	91.5	(1.9)	3.6	(1.1)	1.4	(0.8)	0.7	(0.6)	0.8	(0.5)	0.8	(0.5)	0.4	(0.4)	0.9	(0.5)	14.4	(7.8)
Italy (Provincia Liguria)	88.5	(2.0)	3.8	(1.2)	1.5	(0.7)	0.9	(0.5)	1.2	(0.8)	1.0	(0.4)	0.6	(0.5)	2.5	(0.6)	29.1	(6.5)
Italy (Provincia Lombardia)	80.0	(2.5)	6.3	(1.2)	3.1	(0.9)	0.8	(0.5)	2.3	(0.9)	2.0	(0.7)	0.9	(0.5)	4.6	(1.1)	30.2	(4.6)
Italy (Provincia Marche)	86.0	(1.8)	5.2	(1.3)	1.5	(0.9)	1.4	(0.7)	1.7	(0.7)	1.2	(0.7)	0.5	(0.3)	2.7	(0.7)	25.4	(6.9)
Italy (Provincia Molise)	96.6	(1.2)	1.4	(0.8)	1.0	(0.6)	0.0	c	0.0	c	0.0	c	0.0	c	0.0	c	7.9	(10.9)
Italy (Provincia Piemonte)	87.0	(1.9)	4.3	(1.0)	2.0	(0.6)	0.5	(0.3)	1.6	(0.7)	1.0	(0.4)	1.0	(0.5)	2.6	(0.8)	27.2	(7.3)
Italy (Provincia Puglia)	88.2	(2.4)	2.7	(0.7)	4.5	(1.5)	0.5	(0.4)	0.8	(0.4)	0.9	(0.6)	1.0	(0.5)	1.4	(0.7)	23.4	(9.2)
Italy (Provincia Sardegna)	93.8	(1.2)	2.7	(0.8)	0.5	(0.4)	0.7	(0.6)	0.3	(0.3)	0.9	(0.5)	0.4	(0.4)	0.7	(0.5)	14.7	(10.1)
Italy (Provincia Sicilia)	94.4	(1.7)	1.9	(0.8)	2.1	(1.1)	0.3	(0.2)	0.0	c	0.4	(0.4)	0.3	(0.3)	0.5	(0.3)	15.6	(9.2)
Italy (Provincia Toscana)	88.1	(1.8)	4.3	(1.1)	1.6	(0.7)	1.1	(0.7)	1.0	(0.5)	0.7	(0.5)	0.8	(0.5)	2.3	(0.7)	27.6	(7.1)
Italy (Provincia Trento)	82.7	(2.0)	4.8	(1.4)	2.8	(0.8)	1.5	(0.7)	1.5	(0.7)	1.2	(0.7)	1.7	(0.8)	3.9	(1.0)	34.5	(7.3)
Italy (Provincia Umbria)	87.7	(1.8)	4.7	(1.1)	1.7	(0.7)	0.8	(0.4)	1.0	(0.5)	1.1	(0.5)	0.5	(0.4)	2.5	(0.7)	27.1	(5.8)
Italy (Provincia Valle d'Aosta)	87.1	(1.7)	4.3	(1.1)	1.5	(0.6)	0.9	(0.8)	1.0	(0.8)	1.5	(0.6)	0.4	(0.3)	3.2	(1.0)	32.4	(8.5)
Italy (Provincia Veneto)	83.4	(2.5)	3.7	(0.9)	3.4	(1.0)	1.0	(0.5)	1.3	(0.6)	1.3	(0.5)	1.3	(0.5)	4.1	(0.9)	38.0	(6.8)
United Kingdom (England)	86.0	(1.2)	2.1	(0.4)	1.2	(0.4)	2.5	(0.5)	0.7	(0.3)	2.4	(0.4)	1.1	(0.4)	4.0	(0.5)	43.7	(5.6)
United Kingdom (Northern Ireland)	85.6	(1.3)	2.5	(0.7)	1.2	(0.5)	1.9	(0.6)	0.7	(0.4)	2.8	(0.6)	1.0	(0.4)	4.2	(1.0)	41.1	(8.2)
United Kingdom (Wales)	91.7	(1.0)	1.5	(0.6)	0.5	(0.3)	1.6	(0.5)	0.3	(0.2)	1.8	(0.5)	0.6	(0.2)	2.2	(0.5)	37.7	(6.2)

Note: See Table I.3.8 for national data.
StatLink ⟶ http://dx.doi.org/10.1787/888932343304

Annex C

THE DEVELOPMENT AND IMPLEMENTATION OF PISA –
A COLLABORATIVE EFFORT

INTRODUCTION

PISA is a collaborative effort, bringing together scientific expertise from the participating countries, steered jointly by their governments on the basis of shared, policy-driven interests.

A PISA Governing Board on which each country is represented determines, in the context of OECD objectives, the policy priorities for PISA and oversees adherence to these priorities during the implementation of the programme. This includes the setting of priorities for the development of indicators, for the establishment of the assessment instruments and for the reporting of the results.

Experts from participating countries also serve on working groups that are charged with linking policy objectives with the best internationally available technical expertise. By participating in these expert groups, countries ensure that the instruments are internationally valid and take into account the cultural and educational contexts in OECD Member countries, the assessment materials have strong measurement properties, and the instruments place an emphasis on authenticity and educational validity.

Through National Project Managers, participating countries implement PISA at the national level subject to the agreed administration procedures. National Project Managers play a vital role in ensuring that the implementation of the survey is of high quality, and verify and evaluate the survey results, analyses, reports and publications.

The design and implementation of the surveys, within the framework established by the PISA Governing Board, is the responsibility of external contractors. For PISA 2009, the questionnaire development was carried out by a consortium led by Cito International in partnership with the University of Twente. The development and implementation of the cognitive assessment and of the international options was carried out by a consortium led by the Australian Council for Educational Research (ACER). Other partners in this consortium include cApStAn Linguistic Quality Control in Belgium, the *Deutsches Institut für Internationale Pädagogische Forschung* (DIPF) in Germany, the National Institute for Educational Policy Research in Japan (NIER), the *Unité d'analyse des systèmes et des pratiques d'enseignement* (aSPe) in Belgium and WESTAT in the United States.

The OECD Secretariat has overall managerial responsibility for the programme, monitors its implementation on a day-to-day basis, acts as the secretariat for the PISA Governing Board, builds consensus among countries and serves as the interlocutor between the PISA Governing Board and the international consortium charged with the implementation of the activities. The OECD Secretariat also produces the indicators and analyses and prepares the international reports and publications in co-operation with the PISA consortium and in close consultation with Member countries both at the policy level (PISA Governing Board) and at the level of implementation (National Project Managers).

The following lists the members of the various PISA bodies and the individual experts and consultants who have contributed to PISA.

Chair of the PISA Governing Board: Lorna Bertrand

OECD countries

Australia: Tony Zanderigo

Austria: Mark Német

Belgium: Christiane Blondin, Isabelle Erauw and Micheline Scheys

Canada: Pierre Brochu, Patrick Bussière and Tomasz Gluszynski

Chile: Leonor Cariola

Czech Republic: Jana Strakova

Denmark: Tine Bak

Estonia: Maie Kitsing

Finland: Jari Rajanen

France: Bruno Trosseille

Germany: Annemarie Klemm, Maximilian Müller-Härlin and Elfriede Ohrnberger

Greece: Panagiotis Kazantzis (1/7/05 – 31/03/10) Vassilia Hatzinikita (from 31/03/10)

Hungary: Benő Csapó

Iceland: Júlíus K. Björnsson

Ireland: Jude Cosgrove

Israel: Michal Beller

Italy: Piero Cipollone

Japan: Ryo Watanabe

Korea: Whan Sik Kim

Luxembourg: Michel Lanners

Mexico: Francisco Ciscomani

Netherlands: Paul van Oijen

New Zealand: Lynne Whitney

Norway: Anne-Berit Kavli

Poland: Stanislaw Drzazdzewski

Portugal: Carlos Pinto Ferreira

Slovak Republic: Julius Hauser, Romana Kanovska and Paulina Korsnakova

Slovenia: Andreja Barle Lakota

Spain: Carme Amorós Basté and Enrique Roca Cobo

Sweden: Anita Wester

Switzerland: Ariane Baechler Söderström and Heinz Rhyn

Turkey: Meral Alkan

United Kingdom: Lorna Bertrand and Mal Cooke

United States: Daniel McGrath and Eugene Owen

Observers

Albania: Ndricim Mehmeti

Argentina: Liliana Pascual

Azerbaijan: Talib Sharifov

Brazil: Joaquim José Soares Neto

Bulgaria: Neda Kristanova

Colombia: Margarita Peña

Croatia: Michelle Braš-Roth

Dubai (United Arab Emirates): Mariam Al Ali

Hong Kong-China: Esther Sui-chu Ho

Indonesia: Mansyur Ramli

Jordan: Khattab Mohammad Abulibdeh

Kazakhstan: Yermekov Nurmukhammed Turlynovich

Kyrgyz Republic: Inna Valkova

Latvia: Andris Kangro

Liechtenstein: Christian Nidegger

Lithuania: Rita Dukynaitė

Macao-China: Kwok-cheung Cheung

Montengegro: Zeljko Jacimovic

Panama: Arturo Rivera

Peru: Liliana Miranda Molina

Qatar: Adel Sayed

Romania: Roxana Mihail

Russian Federation: Galina Kovalyova

Serbia: Dragica Pavlovic Babic

Shanghai-China: Minxuan Zhang

Singapore: Low Khah Gek

Chinese Taipei: Chih-Wei Hue and Fou-Lai Lin

Thailand: Precharn Dechsri

Trinidad and Tobago: Harrilal Seecharan

Tunisia: Kameleddine Gaha

Uruguay: Andrés Peri

PISA 2009 National Project Managers

Albania: Alfonso Harizaj

Argentina: Antonio Gutiérrez

Australia: Sue Thomson

Austria: Ursula Schwantner

Azerbaijan: Emin Meherremov

Belgium: Ariane Baye and Inge De Meyer

Brazil: Sheyla Carvalho Lira

Bulgaria: Svetla Petrova

Canada: Pierre Brochu and Tamara Knighton

Chile: Ema Lagos

Chinese Taipei: Pi-Hsia Hung

Colombia: Francisco Ernesto Reyes

Croatia: Michelle Braš Roth

Czech Republic: Jana Paleckova

Denmark: Niels Egelund

Dubai (United Arab Emirates): Mariam Al Ali

Estonia: Gunda Tire

Finland: Jouni Välijärvi

France: Sylvie Fumel

Germany: Nina Jude and Eckhard Klieme

Greece: Panagiotis Kazantzis (from 1/7/05 to 18/11/08)
Chryssa Sofianopoulou (from 18/11/08)

Hong Kong-China: Esther Sui-chu Ho

Hungary: Ildikó Balázsi

Iceland: Almar Midvik Halldorsson

Indonesia: Burhanuddin Tola

Ireland: Rachel Perkins

Israel: Inbal Ron Kaplan and Joel Rapp

Italy: Laura Palmerio

Japan: Ryo Watanabe

Jordan: Khattab Mohammad Abulibdeh

Kazakhstan: Damitov Bazar Kabdoshevich

Korea: Kyung-Hee Kim

Kyrgyz Republic: Inna Valkova

Latvia: Andris Kangro

Liechtenstein: Christian Nidegger

Lithuania: Jolita Dudaitė

Luxembourg: Bettina Boehm

Macao-China: Kwok-cheung Cheung

Mexico: María-Antonieta Díaz-Gutiérrez

Montenegro: Verica Ivanovic

Netherlands: Erna Gille

New Zealand: Maree Telford

Norway: Marit Kjaernsli

Panama: Zoila Castillo

Peru: Liliana Miranda Molina

Poland: Michal Federowicz

Portugal: Anabela Serrão

Qatar: Asaad Tounakti

Romania: Silviu Cristian Mirescu

Russian Federation: Galina Kovalyova

Serbia: Dragica Pavlovic Babic

Shanghai-China: Jing Lu and MinXuan Zhang

Singapore: Chia Siang Hwa and Poon Chew Leng

Slovak Republic: Paulina Korsnakova

Slovenia: Mojca Straus

Spain: Lis Cercadillo

Sweden: Karl-Göran Karlsson

Switzerland: Christian Nidegger

Thailand: Sunee Klainin

Trinidad and Tobago: Harrilal Seecharan

Tunisia: Kameleddine Gaha

Turkey: Müfide Çaliskan

United Kingdom: Jenny Bradshaw and Mal Cooke

United States: Dana Kelly and Holly Xie

Uruguay: María Sánchez

OECD Secretariat

Andreas Schleicher (Overall co-ordination of PISA and partner country/economy relations)

Marilyn Achiron (Editorial support)

Marika Boiron (Editorial support)

Simone Bloem (Analytic services)

Francesca Borgonovi (Analytic services)

Niccolina Clements (Editorial support)

Michael Davidson (Project management and analytic services)

Juliet Evans (Administration and partner country/economy relations)

Miyako Ikeda (Analytic services)

Maciej Jakubowski (Analytic services)

Guillermo Montt (Analytic services)

Diana Morales (Administrative support)

Soojin Park (Analytic services)

Mebrak Tareke (Editorial support)

Sophie Vayssettes (Analytic services)

Elisabeth Villoutreix (Editorial support)

Karin Zimmer (Project management)

Pablo Zoido (Analytic services)

PISA Expert Groups for PISA 2009

Reading Expert Group

Irwin Kirsch (Education Testing Service, New Jersey, USA)

Sachiko Adachi (Nigata University, Japan)

Charles Alderson (Lancaster University, UK)

John de Jong (Language Testing Services, Netherlands)

John Guthrie (University of Maryland, USA)

Dominique Lafontaine (University of Liège, Belgium)

Minwoo Nam (Korea Institute of Curriculum and Evaluation)

Jean-François Rouet (University of Poitiers, France)

Wolfgang Schnotz (University of Koblenz-Landau, Germany)

Eduardo Vidal-Abarca (University of Valencia, Spain

Mathematics Expert Group

Jan de Lange (Chair) (Utrecht University, Netherlands)

Werner Blum (University of Kassel, Germany)

John Dossey (Illinois State University, USA)

Zbigniew Marciniak (University of Warsaw, Poland)

Mogens Niss (University of Roskilde, Denmark)

Yoshinori Shimizu (University of Tsukuba, Japan)

Science Expert Group

Rodger Bybee (Chair) (BSCS, Colorado Springs, USA)

Peter Fensham (Queensland University of Technology, Australia)

Svein Lie (University of Oslo, Norway)

Yasushi Ogura (National Institute for Educational Policy Research, Japan)

Manfred Prenzel (University of Kiel, Germany)

Andrée Tiberghien (University of Lyon, France)

Questionnaire Expert Group

Jaap Scheerens (Chair) (University of Twente, Netherlands)

Pascal Bressoux (Pierre Mendès University, France)

Yin Cheong Cheng (Hong Kong Institute of Education, Hong Kong-China)

David Kaplan (University of Wisconsin – Madison, USA)

Eckhard Klieme (DIPF, Germany)

Henry Levin (Columbia University, USA)

Pirjo Linnakylä (University of Jyväskylä, Finland)

Ludger Wößmann (University of Munich, Germany)

PISA Technical Advisory Group

Keith Rust (Chair) (Westat, USA)

Ray Adams (ACER)

John de Jong (Language Testing Services, Netherlands)

Cees Glas (University of Twente, Netherlands)

Aletta Grisay (Consultant, Saint-Maurice, France)

David Kaplan (University of Wisconsin – Madison, USA)

Christian Monseur (University of Liège, Belgium)

Sophia Rabe-Hesketh (University of California – Berkeley, USA)

Thierry Rocher (Ministry of Education, France)

Norman Verhelst (CITO, Netherlands)

Kentaro Yamamoto (ETS, New Jersey, USA)

Rebecca Zwick (University of California – Santa Barbara, USA)

PISA 2009 Consortium for questionnaire development

Cito International

Johanna Kordes

Hans Kuhlemeier

Astrid Mols

Henk Moelands

José Noijons

University of Twente

Cees Glas

Khurrem Jehangir

Jaap Scheerens

PISA 2009 Consortium for the development and implementation of the cognitive assessment and international options

Australian Council for Educational Research

Ray Adams (Director of the PISA 2009 Consortium)

Susan Bates (Project administration)

Alla Berezner (Data management and analysis)

Yan Bibby (Data processing and analysis)

Esther Brakey (Administrative support)

Wei Buttress (Project administration and quality monitoring)

Renee Chow (Data processing and analysis)

Judith Cosgrove (Data processing and analysis and national centre support)

John Cresswell (Reporting and dissemination)

Alex Daraganov (Data processing and analysis)

Daniel Duckworth (Reading instruments and test development)

Kate Fitzgerald (Data processing and sampling)

Daniel Fullarton (IT services)

Eveline Gebhardt (Data processing and analysis)

Mee-Young Handayani (Data processing and analysis)

Elizabeth Hersbach (Quality assurance)

Sam Haldane (IT services and computer-based assessment)

Karin Hohlfield (Reading instruments and test development)

Jennifer Hong (Data processing and sampling)

Tony Huang (Project administration and IT services)

Madelaine Imber (Reading instruments and administrative support)

Nora Kovarcikova (Survey operations)

Winson Lam (IT services)

Tom Lumley (Print and electronic reading instruments and test development)

Greg Macaskill (Data management and processing and sampling)

Ron Martin (Science instruments and test development)

Barry McCrae (Electronic Reading Assessment manager, science instruments and test development)

Juliette Mendelovits (Print and electronic reading instruments and test development)

Martin Murphy (Field operations and sampling)

Thoa Nguyen (Data processing and analysis)

Penny Pearson (Administrative support)

Anna Plotka (Graphic design)

Alla Routitsky (Data management and processing)

Wolfram Schulz (Management and data analysis)

Dara Searle (Print and electronic reading instruments and test development)

Naoko Tabata (Survey operations)

Ross Turner (Management, mathematics instruments and test development)

Daniel Urbach (Data processing and analysis)

Eva Van de gaer (Data analysis)

Charlotte Waters (Project administration, data processing and analysis)

Maurice Walker (Electronic Reading Assessment and sampling)

Wahyu Wardono (Project administration and IT services)

Louise Wenn (Data processing and analysis)

Yan Wiwecka (IT services)

Westat

Eugene Brown (Weighting)

Fran Cohen (Weighting)

Susan Fuss (Sampling and weighting)

Amita Gopinath (Weighting)

Sheila Krawchuk (Sampling, weighting and quality monitoring)

Thanh Le (Sampling, weighting, and quality monitoring)

Jane Li (Sampling and weighting)

John Lopdell (Sampling and weighting)

Shawn Lu (Weighting)

Keith Rust (Director of the PISA Consortium for sampling and weighting)

William Wall (Weighting)

Erin Wilson (Sampling and weighting)

Marianne Winglee (Weighting)

Sergey Yagodin (Weighting)

The National Institute for Educational Research in Japan

Hidefumi Arimoto (Reading instruments and test development)

Hisashi Kawai (Reading instruments and test development)

cApStAn Linguistic Quality Control

Steve Dept (Translation and verification operations)

Andrea Ferrari (Translation and verification methodology)

Laura Wäyrynen (Verification management)

Unité d'analyse des systèmes et des pratiques d'enseignement (aSPe)

Ariane Baye (Print reading and electronic reading instruments and test development)

Casto Grana-Monteirin (Translation and verification)

Dominique Lafontaine (Member of the Reading Expert Group)

Christian Monseur (Data analysis and member of the TAG)

Anne Matoul (Translation and verification)

Patricia Schillings (Print reading and electronic reading instruments and test development)

Deutsches Institut für Internationale Pädagogische Forschung (DIPF)

Cordula Artelt (University of Bamberg) (Reading instruments and framework development)

Michel Dorochevsky (Softcon) (Software Development)

Frank Goldhammer (Electronic reading instruments and test development)

Dieter Heyer (Softcon) (Software Development)

Nina Jude (Electronic reading instruments and test development)

Eckhard Klieme (Project Co-Director at DIPF)

Holger Martin (Softcon) (Software Development)

Johannes Naumann (Electronic reading instruments and test development)

Jean-Paul Reeff (International Consultant)

Heiko Roelke (Project Co-Director at DIPF)

Wolfgang Schneider (University of Würzburg) (Reading instruments and framework development)

Petra Stanat (Humboldt University, Berlin) (Reading instruments and test development)

Britta Upsing (Electronic reading instruments and test development)

Other experts

Tobias Dörfler, (University of Bamberg) (Reading instrument development)

Tove Stjern Frønes (ILS, University of Oslo) (Reading instrument development)

Béatrice Halleux (Consultant, HallStat SPRL) (Translation/verification referee and French source development)

Øystein Jetne (ILS, University of Oslo) (Print reading and electronic reading instruments and test development)

Kees Lagerwaard (Institute for Educational Measurement of Netherlands) (Math instrument development)

Pirjo Linnakylä (University of Jyväskylä) (Reading instrument development)

Anne-Laure Monnier (Consultant, France) (French source development)

Jan Mejding (Danish Schoool of Education, University of Aarhus) (Print reading and electronic reading development)

Eva Kristin Narvhus (ILS, University of Oslo) (Print reading and electronic reading instruments, test instruments and test development)

Rolf V. Olsen (ILS, University of Oslo) (Science instrument development)

Robert Laurie (New Brunswick Department of Education, Canada) (Science instrument development)

Astrid Roe (ILS, University of Oslo) (Print reading and electronic reading instruments and test development)

Hanako Senuma (University of Tamagawa, Japan) (Math instrument development)

Other contributors to this publication

Fung-Kwan Tam (Layout)

ORGANISATION FOR ECONOMIC CO-OPERATION AND DEVELOPMENT

The OECD is a unique forum where governments work together to address the economic, social and environmental challenges of globalisation. The OECD is also at the forefront of efforts to understand and to help governments respond to new developments and concerns, such as corporate governance, the information economy and the challenges of an ageing population. The Organisation provides a setting where governments can compare policy experiences, seek answers to common problems, identify good practice and work to co-ordinate domestic and international policies.

The OECD member countries are: Australia, Austria, Belgium, Canada, Chile, the Czech Republic, Denmark, Finland, France, Germany, Greece, Hungary, Iceland, Ireland, Israel, Italy, Japan, Korea, Luxembourg, Mexico, the Netherlands, New Zealand, Norway, Poland, Portugal, the Slovak Republic, Slovenia, Spain, Sweden, Switzerland, Turkey, the United Kingdom and the United States. The European Commission takes part in the work of the OECD.

OECD Publishing disseminates widely the results of the Organisation's statistics gathering and research on economic, social and environmental issues, as well as the conventions, guidelines and standards agreed by its members.

OECD PUBLISHING, 2, rue André-Pascal, 75775 PARIS CEDEX 16
(98 2010 07 1 P) ISBN 978-92-64-09144-3 – No. 57725 2010